Winner's Electoral College Vote %	Winner's Popular Vote %	Congress	House Majority Party	House Minority Party	Senate Majority Party	Senate Minority Party
**	No popular vote	1st	38 Admin †	26 Opp	17 Admin	9 Opp
		2nd	37 Fed ††	33 Dem-R	16 Fed	13 Dem-R
**	No popular vote	3rd	57 Dem-R	48 Fed	17 Fed	13 Dem-R
		4th	54 Fed	52 Dem-R	19 Fed	13 Dem-R
**	No popular vote	5th	58 Fed	48 Dem-R	20 Fed	12 Dem-R
		6th	64 Fed	42 Dem-R	19 Fed	13 Dem-R
HR**	No popular vote	7th	69 Dem-R	36 Fed	18 Dem-R	13 Fed
		8th	102 Dem-R	39 Fed	25 Dem-R	9 Fed
92.0	No popular vote	9th	116 Dem-R	25 Fed	27 Dem-R	7 Fed
		10th	118 Dem-R	24 Fed	28 Dem-R	6 Fed
69.7	No popular vote	11th	94 Dem-R	48 Fed	28 Dem-R	6 Fed
		12th	108 Dem-R	36 Fed	30 Dem-R	6 Fed
59.0	No popular vote	13th	112 Dem-R	68 Fed	27 Dem-R	9 Fed
		14th	117 Dem-R	65 Fed	25 Dem-R	11 Fed
84.3	No popular vote	15th	141 Dem-R	42 Fed	34 Dem-R	10 Fed
		16th	156 Dem-R	27 Fed	35 Dem-R	7 Fed
99.5	No popular vote	17th	158 Dem-R	25 Fed	44 Dem-R	4 Fed
		18th	187 Dem-R	26 Fed	44 Dem-R	4 Fed
HR	39.1 †††	19th	105 Admin	97 Dem-J	26 Admin	20 Dem-J
		20th	119 Dem-J	94 Admin	28 Dem-J	20 Admin
68.2	56.0	21st	139 Dem	74 Nat R	26 Dem	22 Nat R
		22nd	141 Dem	58 Nat R	25 Dem	21 Nat R
76.6	54.5	23rd	147 Dem	53 AntiMas	20 Dem	20 Nat R
		24th	145 Dem	98 Whig	27 Dem	25 Whig
57.8	50.9	25th	108 Dem	107 Whig	30 Dem	18 Whig
		26th	124 Dem	118 Whig	28 Dem	22 Whig
79.6	52.9					
–	52.9	27th	133 Whig	102 Dem	28 Whig	22 Dem
		28th	142 Dem	79 Whig	28 Whig	25 Dem
61.8	49.6	29th	143 Dem	77 Whig	31 Dem	25 Whig
		30th	115 Whig	108 Dem	36 Dem	21 Whig
56.2	47.3	31st	112 Dem	109 Whig	35 Dem	25 Whig
–	–	32nd	140 Dem	88 Whig	35 Dem	24 Whig
85.8	50.9	33rd	159 Dem	71 Whig	38 Dem	22 Whig
		34th	108 Rep	83 Dem	40 Dem	15 Rep
58.8	45.6	35th	118 Dem	92 Rep	36 Dem	20 Rep
		36th	114 Rep	92 Dem	36 Dem	26 Rep
59.4	39.8	37th	105 Rep	43 Dem	31 Rep	10 Dem
		38th	102 Rep	75 Dem	36 Rep	9 Dem
91.0	55.2					
–	–	39th	149 Union	42 Dem	42 Union	10 Dem
		40th	143 Rep	49 Dem	42 Rep	11 Dem
72.8	52.7	41st	149 Rep	63 Dem	56 Rep	11 Dem
		42nd	134 Rep	104 Dem	52 Rep	17 Dem
81.9	55.6	43rd	194 Rep	92 Dem	49 Rep	19 Dem
		44th	169 Rep	109 Dem	45 Rep	29 Dem
50.1	47.9 †††	45th	153 Dem	140 Rep	39 Rep	36 Dem
		46th	149 Dem	130 Rep	42 Dem	33 Rep
58.0	48.3	47th	147 Rep	135 Dem	37 Rep	37 Dem
–	–	48th	197 Dem	118 Rep	38 Rep	36 Dem

Source for election data: Svend Peterson. *A Statistical History of American Presidential Elections*. New York: Frederick Ungar Publishing, 1963. Updates: Richard Scammon, *America Votes 15*. Washington D.C.: Congressional Quarterly, 1983.

Abbreviations:
Admin = Administration supporters
AntiMas = Anti-Masonic
Dem = Democratic
Dem-R = Democratic-Republican
Fed = Federalist
Dem-J = Jacksonian Democrats
Nat R = National Republican
Opp = Opponents of administration
Rep = Republican
Union = Unionist

FOURTH EDITION

American Government

FOURTH EDITION

American Government

Susan Welch
∎
The Pennsylvania
State University

John Gruhl

Michael Steinman

John Comer
∎
University of Nebraska—Lincoln

West Publishing Company

St. Paul   New York   Los Angeles   San Francisco

Production Credits

Copyeditor: Laura Beaudoin
Composition: Carlisle Communications, Inc.
Artwork: Michael Thomas Associates/Century Design
Cover Image: "Stars and Stripes West Coast Style" by
John McConnell
Cover Design: Roslyn M. Stendahl, Dapper Design
Index: E. Virginia Hobbs
Dummy Artist: John Edeen

Student Study Guide

A study guide has been developed to assist students in mastering the concepts presented in this text. It reinforces chapter material presenting it in a concise format with review questions. An examination copy is available to instructors by contacting West Publishing Company. Students can purchase the study guide from the local bookstore under the title *Study Guide to Accompany American Government,* Fourth Edition, prepared by Susan M. Rigdon.

Copyright © 1986, 1988,
1990 By WEST PUBLISHING COMPANY
Copyright © 1992 By WEST PUBLISHING COMPANY
50 W. Kellogg Boulevard
P. O. Box 64526
St. Paul, MN 55164-0526

Printed in the United States of America

99 98 97 96 95 94 93 92   8 7 6 5 4 3 2 1 0

Library of Congress Cataloging-in-Publication Data

American government / Susan Welch . . . [et. al.].—4th ed.
       p.   cm.
    Includes bibliographical references and index.
    ISBN 0-314-92915-0
    1. United States—Politics and government.   I. Welch,
Susan.
    JK274.A54754   1992   91–28178
    320.973—dc20   CIP ∞

To Our Families

Brief Contents

Contents

ix

Preface

American politics is exciting, important, and controversial, yet sometimes texts convey just the opposite to students. They try to cover everything, and in the process leave students stuffed with facts but bewildered as to their meaning. The excitement of American politics is lost.

As in previous editions, this fourth edition of our text, *American Government,* tries to interest students in learning about many important and controversial issues. We believe an introductory course succeeds if most students develop an understanding of major ideas, an interest in learning more about American government, and an ability to begin to understand and evaluate the news they hear about American political issues. Although a firm grounding in the essential "nuts and bolts" of American government is crucial, other approaches should be used for motivating students' interest in government.

We offer the essential "nuts and bolts" of American government, but we also want the student to understand why (and sometimes how) these important features have evolved, their impact on government and individuals, and why they are controversial (if they are) and worth learning. For example, we prefer students to leave the course remembering why campaign finance laws were created and why they have the impact they do than to memorize specific dollar limitations on giving for different types of candidates from different types of organizations. The latter will change or will soon be forgotten, but understanding the "whys" will help the student understand the campaign finance issue long after the course is over.

We have also tried to interest students by describing and discussing the impact of various features of government. For example, students who do not understand why learning about voter registration laws is important may "see the light" when they understand the link between such laws and low voter turnout.

Therefore, a particular emphasis throughout the book is on the *impact* of government: how individual features of government affect its responsiveness to different groups (in Lasswell's terms, "Who gets what and why?"). We realize that nothing in American politics is simple; rarely does one feature of government produce, by itself, a clear outcome. Nevertheless, we think that students will be more willing to learn about government if they see some relationships between how government operates and the impact it has on them as citizens of America.

Changes in the Fourth Edition

After the third edition, we wrote a smaller version of this book, entitled Understanding American Government. We used that opportunity to rewrite and reduce in size each of the first fifteen chapters of the text. We have taken advantage of that rewriting in preparing this fourth edition. Though this edition contains the complete set of chapters, they are slightly shorter and we believe even more readable than those in the third edition.

We have made other significant changes. We have added a "Comparative Perspectives" feature in many chapters. We believe that as students learn about their own government, it is useful for them to see the differences and similarities in ways we organize our political life contrasted with other societies. The idea that we are increasingly linked to other societies around the world and that students need to better understand other societies is a cliche, but no less true even so. In order to promote such understanding, most chapters contain a short box examining an important issue or institution in comparative perspective, such as why federalism does not work well in Yugoslavia (chapter 3), ways other democracies control campaign costs (chapter 9), and the pros and cons of a parliamentary system (chapter 11).

We have of course taken this opportunity to update the text. There is significant new material in every chapter. The Persian Gulf War, its politics, media coverage, and aftermath are thoroughly covered. Events in the Soviet Union continue to surprise us, and chapter 19 (basically written before the August 1991 coup attempt but updated after) contains a new discussion of the post-Cold War era. We now have a better perspective than in 1989 to reflect on the consequences of the Reagan administration policies and to better gauge the politics of the Bush administration. Other important events that have unfolded in the past two years—the Keating Five conflict of interest case, the savings and loan scandal, the new conservatism of the U.S. Supreme Court, the recession and its impact—are extensively discussed.

Writing a fourth edition gives us a chance to improve coverage in ways suggested by our students and readers. We have been extremely pleased by the reaction of instructors and students to our first three editions. We were especially pleased to win the American Government Textbook Award from the Women's Caucus for Political Science of the American Political Science Association. But we are also glad to respond to suggestions for improvement. We enlarged our treatment of the fundamentals of democracy in Chapter 1 with the intention of giving students a better understanding of what such concepts of equality, sovereignty, majority rule, and minority rights really mean. The media chapter has been extensively revised to take into account the substantial new research on media and politics. Susan Rigdon of the University of Illinois is largely responsible for the fourth edition revisions in chapters 17 through 20. She has extensively revised and reorganized the chapters on foreign and military policy in order to reflect the changed nature of international relations and tools of international relations.

Features of Each Chapter

Student interest and analytic abilities grow when confronted with a clash of views about important issues. Today there is much discussion about how to stimulate the critical thinking abilities of students. Beginning with the first edition, our text has provided features especially designed to do this by involving students in the controversies—and excitement—of American politics.

You Are There.   Each chapter opens with a scenario called "You Are There." In a page or two the student reads about a real-life political dilemma faced by a public official or a private citizen involved in a controversial issue. Students are asked to put themselves in that individual's shoes, to weigh the pros and cons, and to decide what should be done. The instructor may want to poll the entire class and use the "You Are There" as a basis for class discussion. In the "Epilogue" at the end of the chapter, we reveal the actual decision and discuss it in light of the ideas presented in the chapter.

About one-third of the "You Are There" features are new to this edition and include scenarios relating to George Bush's decision to invade Iraq (chapter 4), actions of the Keating 5 (chapter 9), and Senator Newt Gingrich's role in dealing with the federal budget crisis (chapter 17).

Focus on an Issue.   A second feature designed to stimulate students' critical abilities is the "Focus on an Issue," found in each chapter. Each focus describes an important current issue or controversy—such as affirmative action or who should decide where to bury nuclear waste—and raises a number of key questions to help students think systematically about its pros and cons. Class discussion or written assignments can be based on this feature.

Boxes.   In each chapter several boxes highlighting interesting aspects of American politics draw the students into the material. Many illustrate how government and politics really work in a particular situation—how a corporation lobbies for government benefits, how a seemingly powerless group is able to organize for political action, how interest groups solicit money by mail, and how political polls are done—while others highlight features of government that may be of particular interest to students—what standard of risk should government use in regulating acne medication, how ethnicity shapes voting behavior, and the impact of federal programs on students.

Several other features help students organize their study:

Outline.   Each chapter begins with an outline of its contents.

Key Terms. Key terms are boldfaced within the text and listed at the end of each chapter.

Further Reading. A brief, annotated list of further readings contains works that might be useful to a student doing research or looking for further reading.

Glossary. A glossary at the end of the book defines terms that may be unfamiliar to students.

The Organization and Contents of the Book

While the basic organization of American government books is fairly standard, our text has a unique chapter on money and politics and a half chapter on environmental politics. Other features include a civil rights chapter that integrates a thorough treatment of constitutional issues concerning minorities and women; a discussion of the civil rights and women's rights movements, and contemporary research on the political status of these groups. We include in this chapter the special legal problems of Hispanics and Indians.

Substantive policy chapters reinforce the emphasis on the impact of government action. Our social welfare policy chapter is unique in its treatment of social welfare programs for the middle income and wealthy as well as the poor. A chapter on economic policymaking complements the section on budgeting found in the chapter on Congress. The treatment of economic policy highlights the relationship between politics and the economy, and should help the student better understand issues such as the deficit, inflation, and unemployment. The chapter on regulation and the environment emphasizes the underlying rationale for regulation and its problems and benefits. A chapter on military spending highlights many current and recurrent political issues in military preparedness and the leadership of our military forces. The chapter on foreign policy places current foreign policy issues in the context of the history of our foreign policy aims, especially since World War II.

Some instructors will prefer not to use any of the policy chapters. The book stands as a whole without them, as many policy examples are integrated into the rest of the text. Different combinations of the policy chapters may also be used, as each chapter is independent.

The organization of the book is straightforward. After material on democracy, the Constitution, and federalism, the book covers linkages, including money and politics, then institutions, and finally policy. Civil liberties and rights are treated after the chapter on the judiciary. But the book is flexible enough that instructors can modify the order of the chapters. Some instructors will prefer to cover institutions before process. Others may prefer to discuss civil liberties and rights when discussing the Constitution. Still others may wish to integrate some of the policy chapters into the treatment of institutions. For example, the economic policy chapter could be used in conjunction with the section in the Congress chapter on the budget. The military spending chapter illustrates several points made in the chapter on Congress and could be used with it. The foreign policy chapter fits nicely with the treatment of the presidency. The chapter on regulation and environmental policy could serve as a case study following the chapter on bureaucracy.

Supplementary Materials

The supplementary materials complement the book.

Instructor's Manual. Written by the authors of the text, the instructor's manual provides lectures, lecture suggestions, and in-class exercises for each chapter. Suggestions for out-of-class papers and projects are also provided. A student questionnaire is included to allow instructors to collect student data that can be used in class throughout the semester as a comparison with national poll data presented in the book.

Instructional Materials on Diskettes. The lectures and other material in the instructor's manual are provided on computer diskettes. So is the student questionnaire, which will spare instructors the trouble of having it retyped or re-entered on computer disks.

Student Study Guide. An excellent Student Guide, written by Susan Rigdon of the University of Illinois, provides students with exercises emphasizing the major points of each chapter. Chapter objectives and key terms are reviewed. Practice multiple choice questions are provided. Unlike many such guides, this one also helps the students learn to write essays, thus emphasizing the improvement of analytic skills. Essay writing tips are given, then illustrated in each chapter.

Videodisc. Developed to support concepts in the book, our disk combines use of video clips, charts, and graphs. It is approximately 50 minutes long and is comprised of 4 to 6 minute segments that can be used to enhance lectures.

Videotapes. Qualified adopters are entitled to choose from West's Political Science Video Library. A list of tapes is available upon request. In addition, the *Government by Consent* video collection and *Equal Justice Under the Law* series, are available.

Transparency Acetates and Masters. Fifty full-color acetates of important maps and illustrations from the text are offered to adopters, as well as over 100 transparency masters of charts, graphs, and maps.

Acknowledgments

We would like to thank the many people who have aided and sustained us during the lengthy course of this project. Our current and former University of Nebraska colleagues have been most tolerant and helpful. We thank them all. In particular, we appreciate the assistance of John Hibbing, Philip Dyer, Robert Miewald, Beth Theiss-Morse, Louis Picard, John Peters, David Rapkin, Peter Maslowski, David Forsythe, W. Randy Newell, and Steven Daniels who provided us with data, bibliographic information, and other insights that we have used here. We are especially grateful to Philip Dyer, Alan Booth, Louis Picard, Robert Miewald, and John Hibbing who read one or more chapters and saved us from a variety of errors.

We are also grateful to the many other readers of our draft manuscript. Without their assistance the book would have been less accurate, complete, and lively.

Reviewers include:

ALAN ABRAMOWITZ, State University of New York at Stony Brook.
LARRY ADAMS, Baruch College-City University of New York
DANNY M. ADKISON, Oklahoma State University
JAMES ALT, Harvard University
KEVIN BAILEY, North Harris Community College
KENNETTE M. BENEDICT, Northwestern University
TIMOTHY BLEDSOE, Wayne State University
JON BOND, Texas A&M University

PAUL R. BRACE, New York University
JAMES R. BROWN, JR., Central Washington University
RICHARD A. CHAMPAGNE, University of Wisconsin, Madison
MICHAEL CONNELLY, Southwestern Oklahoma State University
GARY COPELAND, University of Oklahoma
GEORGE H. COX, JR., Georgia Southern College
PAIGE CUBBISON, Miami-Dade University
LANDON CURRY, Southwest Texas State University
JACK DESARIO, Case Western Reserve University
ROBERT E. DICLERICO, West Virginia University
ERNEST A. DOVER, JR., Midwestern State University
GEORGIA DUERST-LAHTI, Beloit College
ANN H. ELDER, Illinois State University
GHASSAN E. EL-EID, Butler University
C. LAWRENCE EVANS, College of William and Mary
MURRAY FISCHEL, Kent State University
BOBBE FITZHUGH, Eastern Wyoming College
MARIANNE FRASER, University of Utah
JARVIS GAMBLE, Owens Technical College
PHILLIP L. GIANOS, California State University—Fullerton
DORIS A. GRABER, University of Illinois—Chicago
RUTH M. GRUBEL, University of Wisconsin—Whitewater
STEFAN D. HAAG, Austin Community College
EDWARD HARPHAM, University of Texas—Dallas
PETER O. HASLUND, Santa Barbara City College
RICHARD P. HEIL, Fort Hays State University
PEGGY HEILIG, University of Illinois at Urbana
CRAIG HENDRICKS, Long Beach City College
MARJORIE HERSHEY, Indiana University
SAMUEL B. HOFF, Delaware State College
ROBERT D. HOLSWORTH, Virginia Commonwealth University
JESSE C. HORTON, San Antonio College
GERALD HOUSEMAN, Indiana University
JERALD JOHNSON, University of Vermont
LOCH JOHNSON, University of Georgia
EVAN M. JONES, St. Cloud State University
HENRY C. KENSKI, University of Arizona
MARSHALL R. KING, Maryville College
ORMA LINDFORD, Kansas State University
PETER J. LONGO, Kearney State College
ROGER C. LOWERY, University of North Carolina—Wilmington
JAROL B. MANHEIM, The George Washington University

MARGERY MARZAHN AMBROSIUS, Kansas State University

MATTHEW MOEN, University of Maine

MICHAEL NELSON, Vanderbilt University

WALTER NOELKE, Angelo State University

THOMAS PAYETTE, Henry Ford Community College

THEODORE B. PEDELISKI, University of North Dakota

JERRY PERKINS, Texas Tech University

TONI PHILLIPS, University of Arkansas

C. HERMAN PRITCHETT, University of California—Santa Barbara

CHARLES PRYSBY, University of North Carolina—Greensboro

SANDRA L. QUINN-MUSGROVE, Our Lady of the Lake University

DONALD R. RANISH, Antelope Valley Community College

LINDA RICHTER, Kansas State University

JERRY SANDVICK, North Hennepin Community College

ELEANOR A. SCHWAB, South Dakota State University

EARL SHERIDAN, University of North Carolina—Wilmington

EDWARD SIDLOW, Northwestern University

CYNTHIA SLAUGHTER, Angelo State University

JOHN SQUIBB, Lincolnland Community College

M.H. TAJALLI-TEHRANI, Southwest Texas State University

R. MARK TILLER, Austin Community College

GORDON J. TOLLE, South Dakota State University

RICHARD UNRUH, Fresno Pacific College

JAY VAN BRUGGEN, Clarion University of Pennsylvania

KENNY WHITBY, University of South Carolina

ANN WYNIA, North Hennepin Community College

We are also grateful to those instructors who have used the book and relayed their comments and suggestions to us. Our students at the University of Nebraska have also provided invaluable reactions to the previous editions.

Others too have been of great assistance to us. Susan M. Rigdon spent innumerable hours reviewing the manuscript and providing many substantive and editorial suggestions. Margery M. Ambrosius generously helped gather information for several tables. Angie Bowman and Michael Moore provided essential service and help in producing the ancillary materials for the book.

Several people at West Publishing also deserve our thanks. Clark Baxter has been a continual source of encouragement and optimism from the beginning of the first edition through the last decision on the fourth. We are greatly in debt to David Farr, who designed and produced the first edition of the book, and to Emily Autumn who was a model of efficiency and patience in producing the fourth.

Finally, the contribution of our spouses—Nancy Comer, Linda Steinman, and Alan Booth—can hardly be summarized in a sentence or two. But we are very appreciative that they were supportive all the time and patient most of the time.

About the Authors

Susan Welch received her A.B. and Ph.D. degrees from the University of Illinois at Urbana-Champaign. She is currently Dean of the College of Liberal Arts and Professor of Political Science at Pennsylvania State University. Her teaching and research areas include legislatures, state and urban politics, and women and minorities in politics. She is co-editor of the *American Politics Quarterly*.

John Gruhl, a Professor of Political Science, received his A.B. from DePauw University in Greencastle, Indiana and his Ph.D. from the University of California at Santa Barbara. Since joining the University of Nebraska faculty in 1976, he has taught and done research in the areas of judicial process, criminal justice, and civil rights and liberties. He won University of Nebraska campus wide distinguished teaching awards in 1979 and 1986 for excellence in undergraduate teaching.

Michael Steinman graduated from George Washington University with a B.A. in 1964. His M.A. and Ph.D. degrees are from the University of Chicago. A professor of Political Science at the University of Nebraska-Lincoln, he teaches courses in public administration and does research in policing and domestic violence. In 1984 he won a campus wide distinguished teaching award for his development and implementation of a Keller Plan Introduction to American Government course.

John Comer is a Professor of Political Science at the University of Nebraska. He received his A.B. in political science from Miami University of Ohio in 1965, and his Ph.D. from the Ohio State University in 1971. His teaching and research focus on interest groups, public opinion, voting behavior, and political parties.

PART ONE

The American System

Italian immigrants arrive at Ellis Island, New York, in 1910.

1 American Democracy

Elementary students in Brentwood, California, where the multicultural present looks like America's future.

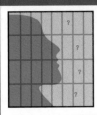

Politics, Pollution, and the Public Interest

It is 1990. You are Terry Bruce, a Democratic member of the House of Representatives since 1984 from Illinois' 19th District. Your district consists of farmers and small-town residents, who are typically Republican, and the more Democratic communities of Champaign and Urbana, home of the University of Illinois. You are faced with a dilemma about how to vote on an important piece of environmental legislation.

You could not have won your first House election without the support of environmentalists around the university campus. Because of this and your own commitment to environmental goals, you tried to get a seat on the powerful Energy and Commerce Committee, which handles all environmental legislation. Although you did not succeed in your first term, since new members rarely get important committee assignments, you did win a seat in your second term by persuading its chair, John Dingell, that you would be a loyal member. And a loyal member you were. You voted for bills he supported and against those he opposed. He became your mentor. You hoped that cooperating with Dingell would eventually increase your influence.

Your choice of mentor was a good one. Dingell is well known for building coalitions by exchanging favors with House members and interest groups to achieve his goals. He is also well known for denying members and groups that do not cooperate with him the legislation they want.

George Bush made a campaign promise to give environmental goals a high priority. Seven months after his inauguration, he introduced a clean air bill. Throughout the 1980s, attempts to strengthen existing clean air legislation were killed by opposition from industry interests, such as the automakers, who worried that stronger antipollution laws would increase their costs of operation. The goals of Bush's proposal are to reduce levels of carbon monoxide and urban smog, acid rain, and toxic industrial emissions. You support these goals but wonder if the powerful coalition opposing more environmental legislation can be overcome. Tackling carbon monoxide is a case in point.

Carbon monoxide, widely defined as a major health threat, is produced mostly by car and truck emissions. Elected officials and interest groups disagree about how to reduce these emissions. Bush wants to require the use of cleaner fuels in nine cities with particularly serious air pollution problems. He also wants automakers to build 1 million new cars a year that use methanol, a clean-burning natural gas product that his state of Texas produces in abundance. Farmers, however, want Congress to require more use of ethanol, which is made from corn and blended with gasoline to make gasohol.

Your mentor, John Dingell, does not like alternate fuel proposals. He represents the automakers in his Detroit district who oppose these proposals. They say the requirement for cleaner fuels would force a redesign of their products and production processes. They argue that this would raise their costs at a time when sales are falling and foreign competition is rising. They also warn that they cannot easily sell cars that use cleaner fuel and they may need to lay off workers.

These conflicting pressures affect your constituency. General Motors and Marathon Petroleum are major employers there. Executives from the latter say requiring more methanol or ethanol use will mean lower sales, lower profits, and increased unemployment. No one in Congress "wants to come back to his district and hear industry say 'Hey, we're shutting down or laying off because of some new clean air law.' "[1] Moreover, your constituency does not have a big air pollution problem.

On the other hand, you also have over 10,000 farm families in your district who would benefit from legislation mandating a wider use of gasohol. And environmentalists back home are demanding that you give the environment top priority. Is promoting clean air legislation to benefit other parts of the country worth risking increased unemployment at home?

Your committee is considering whether to recommend Bush's proposals or its own version of them to the House. What positions should you take in the committee? The proposals pit farmers and environmentalists who want Congress to require use of cleaner fuels against the auto and oil industries who oppose this. Each group defines the public interest in its own way. You believe the country needs a new clean air act but are unsure how much to compromise in order to get it. You will make many people unhappy whatever you do. Moreover, what you do will affect your relationship with Dingell. He sides with the automakers and expects you to do the same. He will try to erase your influence in the committee and in the House if you do not help him.

What should you do? Your choices include the following:

- Side with farmers and environmentalists by making the reduction of carbon monoxide levels your top priority, and ignore the complaints and warnings from big oil companies and the automakers.
- Side with Dingell, the automakers, and the oil companies because you do not want to push lower national carbon monoxide levels if it means increased unemployment in your district and because you want to stay in Dingell's good graces.

Inconsistencies dominate American politics. We take pride in our government but look down on our politicians.[2] We visit Washington to marvel at the Washington Monument, the Jefferson and Lincoln Memorials, the Capitol, and the White House. We show these symbols of our democracy to our children, hoping they will revere them. We cherish the Declaration of Independence and the Constitution.

At the same time, we do not trust our government officials and often describe politics as "dirty." Bob Dylan used strong words to express this view: "I think politics is an instrument of the Devil. Politics is what kills; it doesn't bring anything alive. It's corrupt. Anybody knows that."[3] Few parents want their children to be "politicians." Even the word sounds nasty, raising images of Watergate, payoffs, and "smoke-filled rooms."

America has a split political personality in other ways too. Most people have a low opinion of Congress, yet we reelect almost all of its members. We love democracy, yet half of us do not vote, even in presidential elections. We criticize big government while complaining that it does not do very much.

How have these inconsistencies developed? Is government an unresponsive, alien force or does government work for some people? If it does, for whom does it work, and why? We will begin to answer these questions by discussing American diversity and how it affects what we want government to do.

American Diversity

"Here is not merely a nation but a teeming Nation of nations."[4] Poet Walt Whitman's statement tells us a lot about our country and its politics. America is a diverse nation, peopled by individuals from all over the world. We are a conglomeration of different religions, races, ethnic groups, cultural traditions, and socioeconomic groups.

Ethnic and Economic Diversity

Diversity exists because all of us are immigrants or descendents of immigrants. Even those we call native Americans crossed a land bridge from Asia about 50,000 years ago. The next major wave of immigration occurred in the early 1600s with people from Britain, Holland, France, and Spain. These first European colonists came for a variety of reasons, some to find a place to practice their religion, others to escape political tyranny, and still others to make their fortunes. British culture and the English language soon became dominant. Although all immigrants have had to adapt to this culture, succeeding generations have helped modify it into a unique, American culture.

The immigration of Africans began in 1619 and continued through the early 1800s. Unlike other immigrant groups, most blacks did not come freely. They were brought in chains as slaves. This fact has had a profound impact on American culture and politics.

A fourth major wave of immigration occurred in the mid-1800s. It included millions of people from Ireland fleeing the potato famine and Germans escaping political turmoil. Most immigrants since then also came for economic, religious, and political reasons. Starting in the late 1800s and continuing until World War I, another influx included many Chinese and Japanese laborers and millions of Italians, Poles, and Jews.

Beginning in the 1970s, the latest major wave has included Vietnamese, Cambodians, Russian Jews, and Latin Americans. Most are Asians and Mexicans. The entry of 6 million legal and at least 2 million illegal immigrants in the 1980s accounted for over one-third of the nation's growth in that decade. Immigration has fueled the growth of Sunbelt states like California, Texas, and Florida and has ensured that industrial states such as New York and Illinois would not lose population. Many demographers expect as much or more immigration in the 1990s.[5]

These 1910 immigrants from Bohemia and Bulgaria illustrate the European character of most early twentieth century immigration. Meals served at Ellis Island around this time featured beef stew, boiled potatoes, and rye bread with herring for Jews, and crackers and milk for women and children.

The Statue of Liberty welcomes newcomers by proclaiming, "Give me your tired, your poor, your huddled masses yearning to breathe free. . . ." Nevertheless, "old Americans," worried about threats to what they regard as the American "character," do not always share this sentiment. Native Americans resisted the first European immigrants and with good reason. The "Know-Nothings" won popularity in the 1840s by spreading fear of a Catholic takeover. Patriotic fervor during World War I produced hostility toward Americans of German birth or descent. For example, in 1918, Iowa's governor required all groups of two or more people to speak only English, even when using the telephone.[6] From 1924 to 1965, federal law limited immigration from most areas outside western Europe. As indicated in the Focus on an Issue box, the debate continues about whether today's immigrants are an asset or a problem for our society.

Though each generation of immigrants has faced resentment from preceding generations, each has contributed to the building of America. Early European immigrants settled the eastern seaboard and pushed west to open the frontier. African immigrants helped build the South's economy with their slave labor. Germans helped develop the Midwest into an agricultural heartland, while Irish, Italian, Polish, and Russian

newcomers provided labor for America's industrial revolution and turned many cities into huge metropolises. In 1910, 40% of New York City's population was foreign born, and another 40% had foreign-born parents. In many other major cities, including Chicago, Cleveland, and Boston, at least half of the population was foreign born or had parents who were.[7] Chinese immigrants helped build the transcontinental railroad linking East and West, and Japanese and Hispanics helped California become our top food producer. All immigrant groups have gone on from their initial roles to play a fuller part in American life.

There is evidence that America is a melting pot for millions. Among white, non-Jewish ethnic groups, so much intermarriage has occurred that many people cannot identify their ancestry. In the 1980 census, nearly 40 million Americans could name no specific ancestry, and almost 70 million more reported multiple ancestries.[8] This blending continues. For example, although more than 90% of Italian-Americans age 65 and over have two parents of Italian ancestry, only 18% of Italian children under 5 have.[9]

America is not a melting pot for others, however. These include new immigrants as well as at least 20% of native-born Americans whose skin color, language, or religion mark them as different. For example, comprising 12% of the population, blacks were Americans long before the ancestors of most whites. Yet they have experienced the most consistent and severe discrimination.

Hispanics (including several diverse groups of Spanish origin, primarily Mexican-Americans, Cuban-Americans, and Puerto Ricans) comprise about 9% of the population. Like blacks, Hispanics tend to be less educated and have lower incomes than other white Americans. Although they also face discrimination, Hispanics are integrating into the larger society faster than blacks.

Asian-Americans, the fastest growing minority, are less than 3% of the population. They have achieved considerable economic success despite harsh discrimination in the past and more subtle forms today. For example, although Asian-Americans are represented far beyond their population share at most top universities, many suspect that some universities have set informal admissions quotas to limit their numbers.

Like Asian-Americans, Jews have faced discrimination and have tried to achieve success through education. Until about 30 years ago, many universities and colleges imposed ceilings on the enrollment of

WHERE THE IMMIGRANTS LIVE
IN NEW YORK CITY
By country of origin

**European &
Middle Eastern**
En — England
F — France
Gr — Germany
G — Greece
Ir — Iran
Is — Israel
It — Italy
P — Poland
Po — Portugal
R — Rumania
U — U.S.S.R.
Y — Yugoslavia

Hispanic
A — Argentina
C — Columbia
Cu — Cuba
D — Dominican Republic
E — Ecuador
Pa — Panama
Pe — Peru

Caribbean
B — Barbados
Gn — Grenada
Gu — Guyana
H — Haiti
J — Jamaica
T — Trinidad

Asian & Pacific
Ch — China
In — India
Ja — Japan
K — Korea
Ph — Philippines

BRONX

MANHATTAN

QUEENS

Harlem

Jackson Heights

Elmhurst

Flushing

Astoria

Greenpoint

Chinatown

Sunset Park

BROOKLYN

STATEN ISLAND

Brighton Beach

Size depicts concentration of aliens in
the area based on registration with U.S.
Dept. of Immigration & Naturalization

Jewish students and hiring of Jewish faculty. This discrimination, which also occurred in banks, other corporations, and private clubs, is much reduced now.

Over the years, immigrants have brought skills and energy, new ideas, and old traditions to America. Although some immigrant ways eventually become part of the American experience, others do not. The resulting diversity means that religious, racial, and ethnic differences as well as economic and regional ones shape opinions about public issues. For example,

many Catholics are against abortion, while many mainline Protestants are pro-choice. Asians fear that university admission targets for Hispanics and blacks will reduce their opportunities, while most blacks and Hispanics support these recruitment goals.

Economic differences also divide our nation. Though we think of ourselves as a land of opportunity, most people who are born poor stay poor. Opportunities knock harder and more often for those who are born into the upper and middle classes. And,

FOCUS ON AN ISSUE

Is Immigration in the Public Interest?

In many chapters, we will "focus" on an issue related to the chapter's topic. This "Focus" examines the controversy over whether immigration is in the public interest.

Several years ago Americans enthusiastically celebrated the birthday of the Statue of Liberty, America's symbolic welcome to immigrants. Yet despite the honor most Americans accord our immigrant tradition, they disagree about the consequences of welcoming more of the world's "huddled masses" to our shores.[1]

Many people wrongly think that immigration is something that happened mainly in the past. The second largest wave of immigration in any decade occurred between 1981 and 1990 and promises to continue into the 1990s. It would also be wrong to think that America is the only nation affected by immigration. The fall of the Iron Curtain in Europe has allowed many eastern Europeans to move west. New Soviet emigration policies may result in 2 million Soviets leaving that country, many to Israel.

Current immigration is noteworthy for something other than its scale. Historically, most immigrants to the United States were Europeans. Today, however, 85% are Asians or Latin Americans; Europeans account for only 11%.[2] This trend is producing major changes in the ethnic and cultural mix of areas where newcomers concentrate, particularly California, Florida, Texas, New York, Illinois, and New Jersey. The mix has changed in part because of conditions over which we have limited control. Most immigrants come from countries that are poor or where civil wars or other violence make life dangerous, such as parts of Asia and Latin America. Many newcomers are poor Mexicans lured by the American dream and our long, porous border over which they can escape the shambles of their native economy.

The government decides who legally can enter the country. For about 100 years, it imposed very few limitations on immigration. In the late 1800s, however, it began to reflect the white, Anglo-Saxon, Protestant majority's view that immigration threatens the American "character." Until 1965 the government allowed little immigration from outside the western hemisphere. A 1965 law reversed this trend by allowing up to 20,000 people a year to immigrate from any one country. It also let newcomers send for members of their families after establishing residence here. In 1980, Congress let foreigners with a "well-founded fear of persecution" apply for sanctuary here too.

Not all recent immigrants are Hispanic or Asian; Soviet Jews comprise a significant proportion.

Under these laws, legal immigration averaged about 600,000 people a year. Much larger numbers of illegal immigrants, mostly from Mexico, led Congress to reform immigration laws again in 1986.

To reduce illegal immigration, the 1986 act called for more guards to patrol our borders and sought to lower the employment opportunities of illegal aliens by creating penalties for employers who hired them. The act did not accomplish its goals. While illegal immigration initially fell, it rose again in 1990 and is still increasing. The Border Patrol has not gotten the money to hire enough guards to stop more than a fraction of the illegal immigrants trying to enter the United States. In addition, the act did little to stop illegal aliens from buying forged social security cards and other papers cheaply to establish their legal status and produced few penalties for those who hired these individuals. Indeed, the act led to more discrimination when some employers, fearful of its penalties, refused to hire anyone, including citizens and legal aliens, who "looked" like an immigrant.

Congress passed a new immigration act in 1990 authorizing stronger measures to end job discrimination. It also nearly tripled the number of skilled workers and their families who can move here every year, and it allowed in 10,000 millionaires annually, who must set up a new business or invest substantially in existing businesses in poor parts of the country.

That so many millions of people want to settle here indicates the continuing attractiveness of America to the rest of the world. But it also can cause problems. Thinking about the following questions will help you reflect on whether immigration is in the public interest.

Do Immigrants Take Jobs and Income Away from Citizens?

Immigration critics charge that newcomers take jobs away from people who are already here. They also charge that immigrant labor lowers wages because immigrants will work for less. In contrast, others argue that newcomers have little effect because immigrants take jobs that others do not want. Still others point out that immigrants might actually increase employment by making it possible for some industries to hire low-wage workers rather than move their operations to Third World nations to stay competitive.

The evidence for these contrasting arguments is not entirely clear. The fairest summary is that the continuing supply of immigrants, especially illegal immigrants, keeps wages low for unskilled jobs in restaurants, food processing plants, and other traditionally low-wage industries.[3] This supply also keeps wages paid by fruit and vegetable growers low. However, the effect of immigration on wages is small because most legal immigrants, many of whom are highly educated and skilled, do not work in these low-wage industries. The effect of immigration on wages also hits newer residents more; a 10% increase in immigration lowers the average wages of native-born Americans by just .2% compared to 2% for foreign-born residents.[4]

Fifty yards from the border, the Immigration & Naturalization agents stopped this car, opened the trunk, and found three illegal immigrants, all with jobs waiting for them in the U.S.

Moreover, immigration increases total employment. Some native workers are displaced, but more benefit from the increased economic activity that immigrants bring.

Do Immigrants Cause Increased Taxes?

Some people argue that immigrants cost taxpayers money by using government services and not paying taxes. In fact, each *illegal* alien may cost all levels of government about $1,300 a year after subtracting the taxes that each one pays (everyone pays sales taxes and many illegal immigrants also pay income taxes through payroll deductions). However, *legal* immigrants do not cost government anything. They pay as much or more in taxes as they receive in government services.[5]

The costs of immigration, therefore, fall mainly on communities with large numbers of illegal aliens. Although illegal aliens do not receive much government assistance for the poor, they do make heavy demands on health and education facilities. For example, in a recent year Los Angeles County spent $15 million for obstetrical care for illegal aliens.[6]

Do Immigrants Worsen Race Relations?

Some people worry that new immigrants will worsen our already troubled race relations. In some areas, considerable enmity exists between black citizens and newcomers who often compete for the same jobs. Such is the case with African-Americans and Hispanic immigrants in Miami. Moreover, tension between native-born Americans and immigrants is not confined to people of different races. In Florida many black citizens who are conscious of their long struggle to overcome racism resent having to compete with black Haitian immigrants.

On the other hand, it is possible that demographic changes brought about by immigration might make race relations better. For example, experts predict that within two decades California will have no racial or ethnic majority. Hispanics, blacks, and Asians together will comprise a majority. Under these multi-ethnic conditions, traditional black-white hostility might dwindle as ethnic distinctions become more complex. Intermarriage rates among different groups might increase as they have done among European ethnic groups, further blurring ethnic distinctions.[7]

Do Immigrants Endanger or Enhance Our Way of Life?

Some native-born Americans are worried that immigration will threaten their way of life. They fear non-English languages, different cultural traditions and religious practices, nonwhite skin colors, and nondemocratic political traditions.

continued on next page

There is no question that America has changed as newcomers have introduced new ways. Many of us now eat tacos, Chinese stir-fry, and gyros sandwiches and dance to reggae music. Religious and ethnic diversity has increased dramatically. America is no longer the white, steak and potatoes, Anglo-Saxon, Protestant nation it was 200 years ago even though many of the political, economic, and cultural values of the Founders still dominate. But how much change do we want and how fast can we accommodate it?

Some, but not all, of those who fear that immigrants will change America in undesirable ways are racist or bigoted. As one veteran said, "We didn't go to war to bring the foreign people here."[8]

There have always been people who stereotype newcomers as criminals or parasites. Italians and Jews bore this stigma in earlier times. A man in Brownsville, Texas, wondered if Hispanic immigrants "could be terrorists, or bandits, or typhoid carriers."[9] Critics now point to the many Cubans and Latin Americans who live in south Florida and charge that they are making it an illegal drug center and a hotbed of right-wing political intrigue complete with political assassinations. They fail to mention that most immigrants are not involved in the drug trade and that it prospers because millions of native-born Americans buy illegal drugs.

Others just dislike change. One need not be a racist or a bigot to think that the American way of life should stay as it is regardless of the excellence of other cultures. We can admire other traditions without wanting to adopt them.

In addition, some people see illegal immigration as a threat to our sovereignty. Former President Reagan said, "The simple truth is that we've lost control of our borders . . . and no nation can do that and survive."[10]

Finally, some people oppose immigration because they believe that continued population growth will strain our country's resources and contribute to the deterioration of its environment. On the other hand, some people argue that concerns about high levels of immigration are unfounded. The foreign-born proportion of our population fell from over 14% in the early 1900s to just 6% in 1987.[11] Our population would shrink without immigration because our birth rates are at less than replacement levels.[12]

In addition, newcomers can bring cultural enrichment and energy. In recent years, for example, Asian immigrants have revitalized core areas of many American cities with new shops and businesses. Many Asian children outperform native-born children in school. One-quarter of the valedictorians and salutatorians in San Diego high schools recently were foreign born, as were thirteen of seventeen valedictorians in Boston in 1989.

America's political culture has always been open to change. The "American character" has never been fixed because immigrants have always influenced it even as they were adapting to it. For 300 years, this openness has helped make America a prosperous, democratic society. Whether it will continue to do so depends on how well we can adapt to increasing diversity.

1. The term "huddled masses" is from the poem by Emma Lazarus inscribed on the Statue of Liberty.

2. Rita Arocha, "A Wave of Immigration to Match the Turn of the Century's," *Washington Post National Weekly Edition*, August 1–7, 1988, p. 31.

3. "Illegal Aliens Depress Wages for Some in US," *New York Times*, March 20, 1988, p. 16; Thomas Muller and Thomas Espenshade, *The Fourth Wave: California's Newest Immigrants* (Washington, D.C.: Urban Institute Press, 1985), pp. 101–22; Philip Martin, "Labor Intensive Agriculture," *Scientific American* 249 (October 1983): 57; Leon Bouvier and Robert Gardner, "Immigration to the U.S.: The Unfinished Story," *Population Bulletin* 41 (November, 1986): 28–31; Peter Passell, "So Much for Assumptions about Immigration and Jobs," *New York Times*, April 15, 1990, p. 4E; K. F. McCarthy and R. B. Valdez, *Current and Future Effects of Mexican Immigration in California* (Santa Monica, Calif.: The Rand Corporation, 1986).

4. George J. Borjas, *Friends or Strangers: The Impact of Immigrants on the U.S. Economy* (New York: Basic Books, 1990).

5. Immigration and Naturalization Service study cited in Bouvier and Gardner, "Immigration to the U.S.," p. 31; Julian Simon, "Immigrants, Taxes, and Welfare in the United States," *Population and Development Review* 10 (March, 1984): 55–69.

6. "Illegal Baby Boom in Los Angeles," FAIR Immigration Report, August 1986, cited in Bouvier and Gardner, "Immigration to the U.S.," p. 31.

7. An examination of intergroup marriage rates is found in Stanley Lieberson and Mary Waters *Many Strands* (New York: Russell Sage Foundation, 1988), p. 173.

8. Eric Schmitt, "As the Suburbs Speak More Spanish, English Becomes a Cause," *New York Times*, February 26, 1989, p. 6E.

9. Jacob V. Lamar, "The Immigration Mess," *Time*, February 27, 1989, p. 15.

10. See Dick Kirschten, "Mix-Up at the INS," January 5, 1991, pp. 21–23, and Maya Weber, "Circling Wagons at INS," February 23, 1991, p. 461. Both articles are in the *National Journal*.

11. Borjas, *Friends or Strangers*.

12. Bouvier and Gardner, "Immigration to the U.S.," p. 26; Thomas Espenshade, Leon Bouvier, and W. Brian Arthur, "Immigration and the Stable Population Model," *Demography* 19 (February 1982): 125–33.

although our society is not as class conscious as many others, our personal economic situations play an important part in shaping our views toward politics and our role in it. In 1988, for example, most poor Americans did not vote and most who did voted for Michael Dukakis. Most well-off Americans voted and voted overwhelmingly for George Bush.

Despite a sometimes overwhelming diversity, most Americans share some common goals and values. Indeed, these goals and values are often what attracts new immigrants. We idealize our nation's Founders and the reasons why they fought a revolution. Most support our form of government: one survey showed that only 5% think it needs fundamental change.[10]

And most of us believe that America is a land of opportunity for those willing to work hard.

Shared values reduce the strains produced by our differences. They also allow us to compete intensely on some issues but cooperate on others. For example, Protestant fundamentalists and Catholic leaders disagree strongly about aid to parochial schools but agree on opposing abortion. Rich and poor differ over the role government should play in reducing unemployment but largely agree about how we should deal with the Soviet Union. Jews and blacks sometimes disagree over the use of quotas, but both favor more public spending for social programs. Majorities of Americans of all ancestries who have been in the United States a generation want to tighten immigration laws but disagree how to do it. Thus, although most Americans share some basic beliefs, our "nation of nations" is crosscut with cleavages. These divisions affect how responsive government can be and to whom it is responsive.

Diversity and the Public Interest

Diversity produces different perceptions of the world. As a result, people tend to define society's problems differently and have conflicting views about what government should do about them. This means that, although government officials typically justify their actions in terms of the "public interest," that interest is usually impossible to define to everyone's satisfaction.

Thus, whether a policy will further the public interest is almost always a matter for political debate. People disagree about what government should do and whether government is responsive because they have different views of their own interests and those of society.

The existence of disagreement leads to **politics,** the competition to shape government's impact on society's problems and goals. Government can coerce us to do things because it is supposed to represent the public interest.[11] Politics, though, entails not only conflict but cooperation. It brings people together when they realize that cooperation is the only way to address problems. For some issues, they discover that their shared values are more important than their differences.

While the conflict in politics gives us reason to be skeptical about individuals' and groups' claims that they seek the public interest, cooperation in politics gives us reason to accept the possibility that the public interest can be achieved. Thus, the Greek philosopher Aristotle wrote 2,000 years ago that politics was the most noble thing in which people could engage, partly because it helped them to know themselves and partly because it forced them to relate to others. Individuals had their own needs, but they had to consider other citizens' needs too.

The conflict and cooperation in politics are channeled through government. We call our form of government a "democracy."

"We can't come to an agreement about how to fix your car, Mr. Simons. Sometimes that's the way things happen in a democracy."

Source: Drawing by Handelsman; © 1987 The New Yorker Magazine, Inc.

Characteristics of Democracy

Democracy was invented by ancient Greek city-states (the term democracy, meaning authority of the people, is a Greek term). The principles that shape our democracy are also rooted in the Judeo-Christian tradition and in British history.

Value of the Individual

Democracy emphasizes the value of the individual.[12] This principle has roots in the Judeo-Christian belief that every individual is equal and has worth before God. It also shaped the works of the British philosophers Thomas Hobbes and John Locke. Briefly, they wrote that individuals give some of their rights to government so it can protect them from each other. Individuals then use their remaining liberties to pursue their individually defined visions of the good life. These ideas are part of social contract theory, which we discuss in chapter 2.

Influenced by these ideas, early Americans emphasized liberty over other goals of government. This is reflected in the Declaration of Independence and the Constitution and Bill of Rights. James Madison, for example, justified the Constitution by writing that government's job is to protect the "diversity" of interests and abilities that exists among individuals. Liberty is also reflected in our long tradition of rights, deriving from Britain's. Usually these are rights against the government—for example, government shall not deny freedom of assembly, and government shall not engage in unreasonable searches and seizures. Essentially, this means the overall right to be left alone by the government. Such individualistic values have molded popular expectations. Immigrants often came and still come to America to be their own bosses: to farm their own farms, manufacture or sell their own products, and worship their own way. Although the opportunities for many individuals to get ahead in America are limited by prejudice and poverty, living in a society with an explicit commitment to individual worth can be exciting and liberating.

Political Equality

Although the Judeo-Christian belief that all people are equal in the eyes of God reflects one type of equality, it led logically to other types, such as political equality. The ancient Greek emphasis on the opportunity and responsibility of all citizens to participate in ruling their city-states also contributed to our notion of political equality. Thus, the Declaration of Independence proclaimed that "all men are created equal." This did not mean that all people are born with equal virtues or abilities. It meant that all (excluding male slaves and all women) are born with equal standing before government and entitled to equal rights.

Inevitably, some people use their virtues or abilities to amass more wealth and power than others and have more influence over government. The ancient Greeks feared that democracy could not tolerate extremes of wealth and poverty. They thought that a wealthy minority, out of smugness, and an impoverished minority, out of desperation, would try to act independently of the rest of the people and consequently disregard the public interest. Early Americans worried less about this. They thought that they could create a government that would protect individual diversity and still survive (as we will discuss more fully in chapter 2).

Americans have always considered themselves relatively equal politically and socially if not economically. Alexis de Tocqueville, a perceptive Frenchman who traveled through the United States in the 1830s, observed that Americans felt more equal than Europeans did. De Tocqueville attributed this feeling to the absence of a hereditary monarchy and aristocracy in this country. There was no tradition in America of looking up to kings and queens and aristocrats as one's "betters."

A belief in political equality leads to **popular sovereignty,** or rule by the people. Abraham Lincoln expressed this concept when he spoke of "government of the people, by the people and for the people." If individuals are equal, no one person or small group has the right to rule others. Instead, the people collectively rule themselves. Of course, not all the people can be a president, a member of Congress, or a judge. But these officials are not the rulers; they are the representatives of the people, who together have authority as the rulers.

Majority Rule

Commitments to the principles of individual worth and political equality lead to majority rule. That is, when there are disagreements over policies, majorities rather than minorities decide. If individuals are equal, then policies should be determined according to the desires of the greater number. Otherwise, some individuals would be bestowed with more authority than others.

Majority rule helps provide the support necessary to control the governed. Those in the minority go along because they accept this principle and expect to be in the majority on other issues. At a minimum, the minority expects those in the majority to respect their basic rights. If these expectations are not fulfilled, the minority is less likely to accept majority rule and tolerate majority decisions. Thus, majority rule necessarily entails minority rights.

Minority Rights

While majority rule is important, it sometimes conflicts with minority rights. Majorities make decisions *for* "the people" but in doing so do not *become* "the people." "The people" includes members of the majority *and* members of the minority. As a result, majorities that harm minority rights diminish everyone's rights. Sadly, as James Madison and other writers of the Constitution feared, majorities in the United States have sometimes forgotten this and denied minorities their rights. For example, the government put Americans of Japanese descent into special camps during World War II. At other times, blacks were slaves; religious minorities could not practice their beliefs; those with unpopular opinions lost basic rights; and women could not vote.

Thus, democratic principles sometimes contradict each other. These principles are goals more than depictions of reality. Americans have struggled for two centuries to reconcile practice with democratic aims and to perfect a system of government that was revolutionary for its time and remains the envy of many around the world.

Direct and Indirect Democracy

Our description of democracy must include one additional refinement. Democracies may be either direct or indirect. A **direct democracy** permits citizens to vote on most issues. The best example of a direct democracy is the town meeting, which has been the traditional government of almost all New England towns for 350 years. Although town meetings today are often attended by relatively small numbers of citizens, they still offer one of the few opportunities people have to rule themselves directly. Citizens attending them make their own laws (e.g., whether to put parking meters on the main street) and elect officers to enforce them (such as the police chief and city clerk).

Our national government is an **indirect democracy,** or a **republic.** Citizens have an indirect impact on government because they select policymakers to make decisions for them. Thus, members of Congress, not rank-and-file citizens, vote bills into law.

Classical Democracy

Democratic principles come alive when individuals participate in government. The ancient Greek philosopher Aristotle concluded that there were three types of government in the city-states of his day: democracies, societies ruled by the many; monarchies, societies ruled by one person—kings, queens, or emperors; and aristocracies, societies ruled by a few elites. Aristotle's definition of democracy emphasized the importance of citizen participation in government through debating, voting, and holding office. We call this description **classical democracy**. In a classical democracy, citizens are committed to learning about and participating in government. They are well informed, discuss public affairs regularly, tell public officials what they think, and vote. Political scientists initially accepted this as a fairly accurate view of American politics.

Political scientists discovered by the 1940s, however, using information from surveys and voter turnout records, that many fewer citizens take advantage of their democratic rights than classical democratic theory predicts. For example, voting is a routine political activity. It is the easiest way to participate in politics and the least costly in terms of time and energy. Yet only one-half of Americans vote in presidential elections and only one-third have voted in recent congressional elections. Even fewer vote in purely local elections. Instead of being motivated to participate in politics as in a classical democracy, most citizens are little involved. In fact, one-fifth of the electorate does nothing at all political, not even discussing politics.[13]

Only about one-tenth of the population takes full advantage of opportunities to participate. These activists, the "gladiators" of politics, give money to candidates, make phone calls, distribute leaflets, write letters to legislators, attend meetings, or join neighbors

Why Not Direct Democracy?

The writers of the Constitution could not have created a direct democracy allowing every citizen to vote on every issue even if they had wanted to. In the eighteenth century, people did not have telephones, automobiles, television, fax machines, or computers. Everyone could not gather together in one place or communicate instantaneously. Thus, indirect democracy was the only feasible kind of democracy for a population distributed widely over a huge territory.

In the late nineteenth and early twentieth centuries, many states adopted forms of direct democracy that allowed voters to vote on proposed legislation. Since 1898, through mechanisms called the referendum and initiative, more than 17,000 proposals have been voted upon, with one-third becoming law.[1] In 1988, Americans voted on 238 statewide proposals (and hundreds of local ones) in 41 states from banning smoking on the job in Oregon to closing nuclear power plants in Massachusetts. In 1990, there were 45 initiatives in 24 states on education issues alone.

Despite this experience, support for direct democracy at the national level is mixed.[2] On the face of it, this may seem strange in that today cable television and computers permit instantaneous communication. We can see and hear live events and respond to them from wherever we are. Experimental systems in several communities let individuals discuss and express their views on many public issues via cable.

Nevertheless, direct democracy still presents some problems. Many homes and public places lack cable hookups and computers. Allowing people to vote at home would encourage more participation, but how could we make sure individuals did not vote more than once or interfere with someone else's vote?

A more compelling argument against direct democracy is that most people are not interested in politics or well informed about public issues.[3] Even interested people may lack the time to inform themselves enough to cast well-considered votes on hard-to-understand policy questions. Thus, at the state level single-interest lobbies tend to control what is voted upon by citizens. Voter turnout is unrepresentative of the public, particularly the poor and those with little education. Because of the way ballot proposals are worded and a general lack of public information, more than one-third of the voters cast referendum ballots contrary to their expressed preferences on the issues.[4]

Furthermore, direct democracy sometimes threatens minority rights. Initiatives have proposed quarantining AIDS victims and establishing English as an official language. Some courts have overturned popular votes when they think they endanger minority rights. Judicial protection is not always certain, however, and takes time to put into effect.

In addition, our public problems are often too complex to allow government to consider and adopt policies

to work for a common end (such as neighborhood preservation).

Moreover, political participation is class based; people who participate tend to have more money and education. One explanation for this is that the American working class and lower class, unlike their counterparts in many European countries, lack strong trade unions and political parties to represent them. American trade unions involve mostly the middle and better-off working classes. American political parties appeal more to middle-class than working-class interests too. Thus, the poor do not have strong organizations to promote their political participation.

The poor also tend to belong to fewer organizations of any kind (civic groups, labor unions, or issue-oriented groups such as the Sierra Club) than the middle or upper classes. As a result, they have fewer opportunities to be drawn into political action through such associations.

In addition, political participation requires both time and money. Many poor adults are single heads of families with little spare time for political activity or resources for transportation and babysitters.

Race and ethnicity explain political participation too, but not as well. Blacks and Hispanics participate less than others, but this is due primarily to their average lower education and income levels. Those with education and income levels equal to average non-Hispanic whites participate at equal or higher levels.

Age also explains participation in politics. Young people participate much less than their elders. The middle-aged—the highest participators—are more apt to be established in a career and family life and have more time and money to devote to political activities. They are also less apt to be infirm than older people.

Thus, American government is not a classical democracy. Only a small minority of citizens fully participates in politics. Majorities cannot rule when most

Source: Cathy Guisewite; © 1988 Universal Press Syndicate. Reprinted with permission.

quickly. A long process of writing, rewriting, and amending often contributes to a law's effectiveness. Even an informed electorate would find it difficult to vote on final drafts of legislation that are sometimes hundreds of pages long with many complex provisions.

The demise of the New England town meeting, the bastion of direct democracy, illustrates these problems. Local issues, like national ones, have grown much more complex. As a result, planners, budget officers, and engineers dominate town meetings because they have more expertise than most citizens.[5] Coalitions, such as those including land developers and unions, have a lot of influence because they have more at stake than most people, who find many issues complex and unrelated to their interests. As a result, attendance rarely exceeds 5% of the citizenry, and meetings are often canceled for lack of a quorum. Thus, the politics of town meetings have become a microcosm of national politics. Direct democracy cannot work in the governance of big cities, states, and the nation when it does not thrive in small towns.

1. David B. Magleby, *Direct Legislation: Voting on Ballot Propositions in the United States* (Baltimore: Johns Hopkins University Press, 1985).
2. Thomas E. Cronin, "Public Opinion and Direct Democracy," *PS: Political Science and Politics* 31 (Summer 1988): 612–19.
3. F. Christopher Arterton, "Political Participation and 'Teledemocracy,'" *PS: Political Science and Politics* 31 (Summer 1988): 620–27. See also Thomas Cronin, *Direct Democracy: The Politics of Initiative, Referendum and Recall* (Cambridge, Mass.: Harvard University Press, 1989).
4. Magleby, *Direct Legislation.*
5. Robert Preer, "Who Took the Town out of the Town Meeting," *Washington Post National Weekly Edition,* August 4, 1986, p. 22. See also F. Christopher Arterton, *Teledemocracy: Can Technology Protect Democracy?* (Beverly Hills, Calif.: Sage Library of Social Research, 1987).

people do not take advantage of their rights by voting or trying to influence government or each other.[14] Furthermore, those who do participate are not representative of the whole population in class and other social characteristics. This can have an important impact on the kind of public policy we have. Elected officials chosen by people with more money and education are unlikely to have the same perspectives as those chosen by people with less money and education.

Contemporary Theories of American Democracy

Revelations of low levels of participation prompted political scientists to find other ways to explain the workings of American democracy.

Pluralism

In the 1950s, many political scientists thought they knew how American democracy operated. In a theory called **pluralism,** they sought to reconcile democratic principles with the evidence that most people do not participate actively in politics.

Pluralists maintain that government is responsive to groups of citizens working together to promote their common interests.[15] Individuals join others with like beliefs to influence government.

The pluralist view maintains that enough people belong to enough interest groups that government ultimately hears everyone. This produces, according to pluralist theory, a kind of balance in which no group loses so often that it stops competing. As a result, no group or small number of groups can dominate government. This encourages people to continue to "play the game" by finding ways to compromise with each

How Political Scientists Study Government

The facts, concepts, and perspectives in this book are largely the product of decades of work by hundreds of political scientists. We want our readers to know how political scientists study government. This knowledge may help explain why political scientists and citizens develop different interpretations of government and its actions. Knowing about how we study government also shows how our methods shape our understanding of politics and how they compare to those of other fields such as English, accounting, or psychology.

Political scientists have always studied "normative" questions, questions about how people *should* behave with regard to political matters. Normative students of government ask such questions as: What is justice? How can we achieve it? Or, putting it differently, what should the individual's relationship be to others in society and to government? Aristotle and Plato asked such questions. So did the ancient Roman Cicero, church thinkers St. Augustine and St. Thomas Aquinas, as well as John Locke, Jean-Jacques Rosseau, and Karl Marx. Although they lived and wrote in different times and places, their thoughts are still relevant because they asked basic questions about a subject—human nature—that has not changed much over time.

Everyone asks normative questions because we all want society, acting through government, to resolve its

(our) problems and make life better. To know what "better" is, we have to think in a normative way.

Niccolo Machiavelli's work represents a major qualitative change in the history of political science. Writing in the late 1400s and early 1500s, Machiavelli was much less concerned with the normative issues of perfect justice and government. As a diplomat for the city of Florence, he was a participant in government and interested in more practical matters. The Italy of his time was divided into many parts. The disagreements and wars between them invited France and other European powers to interfere in Italian affairs. He worried about this and devoted himself to thinking of ways to remedy the situation.

Machiavelli asked "empirical" questions. That is, he wanted to know about the world as it was and not as it should be. He thought he knew what it should be. Although Aristotle and others had also asked empirical questions, their goals were essentially normative. Machiavelli and other Renaissance thinkers opened new doors because they wanted to study the world as it is.

The goals of empirical political science are to describe politics and government accurately and to explain why things happen the way they do. Over time, political scientists have developed different ways to do this. A century ago, scholars asked mostly legal questions, such as what do

other. It also leads government to avoid major policy changes to maintain the balance and the popular support that comes with it.

Pluralist theory is attractive because it says democracy can "work" without everyone participating in politics. Actual participation is by group leaders and paid staff who represent rank-and-file members to government. There is some validity to this theory. There are thousands of interest groups in Washington employing experts to represent them in congressional corridors, bureaucratic agencies, and courtrooms.

As chapter 5 shows, however, many people and issues fall through the cracks of interest group representation. The poor are especially unlikely to be organized and to have many resources to fight political battles. Groups do not represent them well or at all. In addition, intense competitions between well-organized groups on some issues—such as abortion—do not always make compromise possible.

Groups may not always even represent the interests of their members. In 1915, Robert Michels for-

mulated the "iron law of oligarchy."[16] This "law" says that effective power in a group, no matter what its size, usually goes to a few, an oligarchy or an elite. In fact, groups create elites by electing officers and hiring staffs. As they spend more time on group affairs and develop ties to public officials, group leaders may come to see group interests differently than do many members.

Source: Drawing by Mankoff; © 1981 The New Yorker Magazine, Inc.

the Constitution and laws say about how government works? That most political scientists were trained in law schools then helps explain why they took this approach.

Political scientists soon became aware that the law is not the only influence on people. They began asking other questions. One of the first concerned institutions: Do the institutions people work in and the jobs they hold affect their behavior? Do people doing the same job in government do it the same way? What is the impact of organizing government a certain way, such as hiring civil servants because of their expertise instead of their political loyalties?

After World War I, some political scientists began to wonder if focusing on institutions was enough. People are not always motivated by rules and procedures. Scholars wanted to know what people were actually doing, not just what the law or institutional procedures said they were supposed to do. They consequently developed what became known as a behavioral approach: see what people are really doing and *then* try to explain their behavior by using whatever perspective is relevant. Are group memberships or psychological variables important? How does a person's self-interest affect behavior? Do people behave differently with respect to different kinds of issues or when problems seem more or less important?

The behavioral approach became increasingly popular after World War II. By the 1970s, many political scientists began giving it a policy focus by studying specific issues to discover how politics and government work. By examining public opinion, interest groups, and parts of government, they try to explain why government does or does not do certain things in response to public problems.

Some scholars today use another approach called social choice. They think costs and benefits shape political behavior as well as economic behavior. For example, they maintain that individuals will not vote unless they expect the benefits from voting to outweigh expected costs. They try to explain why people vote by comparing predicted and actual rates of voting after theoretically identifying the costs and benefits of this behavior.

Political scientists try to know why government works as it does, to find cause and effect relationships: What causes certain attitudes and behaviors? What predicts government's actions? For example, why do people with more education tend to be more involved in politics than those with less? Is it time spent in school, what people learn, or something different? We appreciate the complexity of such questions and do not expect to find final answers soon. However, we think pursuing them is important. In this book, we have used a variety of approaches to describe and explain American politics and government.

Elitism

Problems with pluralist theory, especially its failure to acknowledge the limited power of citizens with average or below-average incomes, led some political scientists to search for another explanation of how American democracy works. A second school of thought gained considerable support in the 1960s. This theory, called **elitism,** stated that American democracy was much less democratic than pluralists believed.

Elite theory maintains that the holders of a few top jobs in key parts of society rule. They are the leaders of major corporations (such as IBM, Exxon, General Motors, and AT&T), major universities (such as Harvard, Chicago, and Stanford), major foundations (Ford, Rockefeller, and Johnson), and major media outlets (the *New York Times, Washington Post,* CBS, NBC, and ABC). Elite jobs are also found in important parts of government, such as the Defense Department.

One political scientist identified 7,314 key jobs in major organizations such as these.[17] Some especially important jobs led to memberships on the boards of directors of other organizations. In addition, he found that about 4,300 elite business leaders controlled well over 50% of America's corporate wealth and that almost 40% of them had once held a government post. If this is right, relatively few people share the most powerful jobs and make some of the most important decisions in America.

Shared backgrounds help tie many elite members together. This was a major conclusion of one of the most famous elite theorists, the sociologist C. Wright Mills.[18] He noted that many elite members had gone to the same prep schools and universities and belonged to the same church denominations. Having like backgrounds and heading key organizations, they developed similar views about how government should work.

Elite theory does not limit elite membership to those with elite backgrounds, however. One does not have to attend a prep school like Choate, graduate from Princeton, and be an Episcopalian. Anyone committed to elite views who rises to the top of a major organization can belong. Elite theory includes important labor leaders among the chosen few even if their backgrounds do not include silver spoons.

Elite theorists acknowledge that elite members compete with each other. However, they see intra-elite competition as jockeying for more benefits rather than as a major threat to elite cohesion. Thus, some elite members want to cut military spending to lower the budget deficit, which they think hurts the economy; others in defense industries disagree. Although the two sides may not agree on this issue, they agree about most things and deal with their differences in a non-combative way.

Most elite members agree about equating the public interest with protecting the status quo. From an elite perspective, this is not selfish. Like many people, elite members define the nation's well-being in terms of their own. President Eisenhower's defense secretary, Charles Wilson, a former executive at General Motors, replied to charges that his corporate background might bias his public performance by saying, "What is good for the country is good for General Motors, and what's good for General Motors is good for the country."

Elite theory is believable. A 1988 survey reported that 73% of a large sample believed that government is run by "a few big interests."[19] Many of us get confused and frustrated about politics. It is often hard to know what is *really* going on in Washington. Elite theory offers an easy explanation: "they" have met in posh, smoked-filled rooms to cut a deal. Anyone who knows anything about tax law has probably had such thoughts.

It is misleading, however, to think that a few powerful people determine everything. America's diversity produces too many different interests and opinions to permit this. Elite members do not always get what they want. Environmentalists have won big victories over major oil and utility companies. In the face of industry opposition, consumer groups and conservationists have gotten government to require automobile safety and fuel efficiency standards. In 1988, voters in California passed an initiative proposal to cut auto insurance rates by 20%. The insurance industry spent $43 million opposing the proposal while supporters spent only $300,000. Nevertheless, elite theory is still useful. It reminds us that tremendous inequalities of resources exist, enabling some parts of society to influence government more than others.

Current Views

Political scientists have had spirited debates about whether pluralism or elitism is the best explanation of American politics. Gradually, most have come to see that neither explains everything. Interest groups do not represent everyone, especially the poor, the working class, and the apathetic. Elites do not decide everything and sometimes lose important battles. Sometimes policy reveals a mix of influences. For example, President Bush's energy program of drilling for more oil, fighting to preserve access to Persian Gulf oil, and promoting nuclear power reflects elite views in the energy business. But it is also likely that most Americans prefer this approach to changing their lifestyles to lower energy consumption and dependence on foreign resources. Thus, both elite and pluralist theory can be used to explain Bush's energy program.

Current perspectives on how government works stress the "veto" many interest groups have in issues affecting them. Their close ties with congressional committees and subcommittees considering legislation allow them to stop policy ideas they dislike. This happened with provisions of President Carter's energy plan and with many of President Reagan's budget cut recommendations. So many powerful groups have this clout that attempts to alter the status quo often fail. Efforts to bring about major changes in national domestic priorities are extremely difficult.

The difficulties created by interest group vetoes often contribute to what one observer calls the "blame game."[20] Politicians representing different interests, seeing no chance of getting what they want, try to make themselves look good by blaming others for inaction. For example, although they agreed privately that cuts were needed, Democrats in Congress have accused Republicans of hurting the elderly by supporting Social Security cuts to lower the budget deficit; and Presidents Reagan and Bush often blamed Congress for deficits although they never proposed a balanced budget. The blame game reinforces problems created by interest group vetoes by encouraging elected officials to distrust each other and by furthering public cynicism about government's responsiveness.

Given the presence of many strong groups and their veto opportunities, passing a law often means fashioning compromises out of competing group views.[21] This often leads to vaguely worded laws giving actual policymaking authority to bureaucrats who work less visibly with interest group help. In effect, agencies and interest groups, not Congress, often legislate. Thus, chemical industry lobbyists help write regulations on hazardous waste, and military contractors help the Pentagon write weapons contracts.

The growth of bureaucratic policymaking makes our democracy more indirect than the writers of the Constitution intended. Most citizens cannot monitor and influence the actions of a president, 535 members of Congress organized into over 300 committees and subcommittees, *and* bureaucratic agencies. The leaders of major interest groups can, and this gives them considerable power. The possibility that these leaders may be relatively independent of their rank-and-file memberships makes them even more important.

These views challenge both pluralism and elitism by concluding that government responds to many but not all groups. This and the importance of group leaders suggest a hybrid explanation of American government stressing the clout of more powerful groups, whose leaders may belong to a larger, more diversified elite.

Conclusion: Is Government Responsive?

Who gets what, and why? To whom is government responsive? Democracy assumes that majorities control government. Indirect democracy assumes that people control their representatives. However, political scientists find that most people do not try to control government and the organizations and leaders who say they represent them. Novelist Kurt Vonnegut's depiction of the "Money River" seconds this conclusion.[22] The river symbolizes America's rich flow of wealth and opportunity. The winners in America, he writes, are successful "slurpers" from this river: those with more money, education, and the chance to give their children an inside track to the future. Some are so good at slurping that they can afford "slurping lessons" from specialists like lawyers and tax consultants to make them even better slurpers. Their major worry is that other people might hear them slurping and want to get close to the river too.

Democracy requires government's river of benefits to be open to all. Yet most people do not approach the riverbank. The average individual has little power. This is the fundamental conclusion of both pluralism and elitism. Those who succeed in influencing government, the people with political power, have strong interest groups to represent them—a pluralist conclusion—or have elite positions. Either way, government benefits usually flow to those who are already getting them.

The Elusive Public Interest

Terry Bruce faced conflicting demands when he made his decision. He wanted a new clean air law but he also wanted to please business interests and to stay on the good side of John Dingell, his powerful mentor.

Bruce's first response was to try to make everyone happy. He voted for most of Dingell's pro-industry positions on acid rain and toxic industrial emissions and asked him, in return, to support the use of ethanol in 44 cities. This would raise ethanol sales substantially and let Bruce satisfy the environmentalists and farmers in his district.

Sensing that a House majority wanted to do something about carbon monoxide levels, Dingell offered a compromise 21-city requirement. This weak response disappointed Bruce, who concluded that "we weren't going to be good soldiers and not get anything out of it."[23] To get the votes he needed to pass the 44-city requirement, Bruce built a coalition of farmers, environmentalists, and other groups concerned about parts of the bill related to acid rain and toxic industrial emissions. These included labor unions that wanted to protect coal miners' jobs from acid rain controls and conservative Republicans who wanted to protect small businesses from smog controls. Each coalition member knew it could not get everything it wanted in the bill and supported the

Los Angeles and its smog.

others to get something it could accept. Thus, Bruce and the environmentalists had to vote for weaker measures to fight acid rain and smog to get enough votes to require more use of alternate fuels.

Getting these disparate forces to collaborate was a challenge. For example, farmers and environmentalists had a history of opposing each other over issues such as pesticide use, agricultural runoff, and land use. One observer described the initial efforts of these groups to work together as "a prickly dance." Yet the coalition held together and got so many votes that Dingell had to accept the 44-city requirement.

While he eventually won and Congress passed a historic clean air act, Bruce took his lumps from Dingell. Dingell scolded him during a committee meeting by reminding him how he got on the committee, how Dingell had invited him to go on

expense-paid trips to Europe and Central America, and how his chances to advance were in the chairman's hands.

To underscore his unhappiness, Dingell did not put Bruce on the committee of House members and senators that wrote the final draft of the bill before Congress sent it to Bush for his signature. Dingell noted that loyalty is "one of the important tests" when he makes such appointments.[24] Not getting on the committee was a setback for Bruce because the committee could drop, add, or change key parts of the bill and because Dingell chaired it. Bruce had to spend all summer and fall working anxiously through allies on the committee to protect what he had won in the House.

The debate over the Clean Air Act reflected the existence of different private interests and definitions of the public interest. This diversity requires members of Congress to build coalitions to pass bills by voting for each others' proposals. Is a list of the interests combined in a winning coalition a statement of the public interest? Probably not. It is more often evidence of the bargaining skills of coalition builders and of how interests sometimes overlap. Thus, Bruce's coalition included environmentalists as well as those who wanted weaker anti-smog measures to protect small businesses.

Bruce's efforts alienated his mentor. Time will tell whether this lowers his influence or whether the new coalition will survive to win more victories. To the extent that the coalition continues to include environmentalists, we might expect it to have more success since public opinion polls show that since the 1970s Americans have consistently given the environment a high priority. However, the interests the coalition defeated suggest a difficult future for the clean air coalition. Elite interests such as the automobile and oil companies do not lose many battles. While most Americans are concerned about the environment, relatively few get involved in politics or belong to groups that fight pollution. Moreover, elite members have more resources to lobby the agencies that develop regulations to implement legislation. An attorney for environmental groups observed that his clients "are really not staffed up to follow the administrative process."[25] As a result, the coalition's victory in Congress could be diluted by industry lobbying in the bureaucracy. Congress's view of the public interest may not be the same as the bureaucracy's.

KEY TERMS

politics	republic
popular sovereignty	classical democracy
direct democracy	pluralism
indirect democracy	elitism

FURTHER READING

F. Chris Arterton, *Teledemocracy* (Beverly Hills, Calif.: Sage, 1987). *After investigating 13 local projects using interactive communications, Arterton concluded that technology can improve citizen access but cannot achieve direct democracy.*

John E. Chubb and Paul E. Peterson, *Can the Government Govern?* (Washington, D.C.: Brookings Institution, 1989). *A collection of case studies showing how the public interest often suffers when elected officials and bureaucrats avoid hard policy choices by playing the blame game with each other and "special interests."*

Ted Conover, *Coyotes* (New York: Vintage, 1988). *A report of a year lived among illegal Mexican immigrants to the United States and the smugglers ("coyotes") whom immigrants pay dearly to bring them across the border.*

Harold Lasswell, *Politics: Who Gets What, When, How* (New York: New World Publishing, 1958). *A classic treatment of some very practical political problems.*

Dave Moore, *Dark Sky, Dark Land: Stories of Hmong Boy Scouts of Troop 100* (Eden Prairie, Minn.: Tessera Publishing, 1989). *Harrowing stories of escape from a war-torn land to a new life in America.*

Michael Pertschuk, *Giant Killers* (New York: W. W. Norton, 1986). *A public interest lobbyist describes several major congressional battles in the 1980s showing that the side with money and status does not always win.*

Hedrick Smith, *The Power Game: How Washington Works* (New York: Random House, 1988). *A Pulitzer Prize–winning journalist's account of the colorful personalities and complex alliances that shape national policymaking. Loaded with good anecdotes.*

NOTES

1. Michael Weisskopf, "Between a Rock and a Bunch of Lobbies," *Washington Post National Weekly Edition*, February 12–18, 1990, p. 31.
2. Gabriel A. Almond and Sidney Verba, *The Civic Culture* (Boston: Little, Brown, 1965), p. 64.
3. Kurt Loder, "Bob Dylan: The Rolling Stone Interview," *Rolling Stone Magazine*, June 21, 1984, p. 18.
4. Walt Whitman, *Leaves of Grass and Selected Prose*, Lawrence Buell, ed. (New York: Random House, 1981), p. 449.
5. The data in this paragraph are from Barbara Vobejda, "The Land of the Immigrant and the Home of Diversity," *Washington Post National Weekly Edition*, March 18–24, 1991, p. 34.
6. Robert Reinhold, "Resentment Against New Immigrants," *New York Times*, October 26, 1986, p. 6E.
7. Susan Welch and Timothy Bledsoe, *Urban Reform and Its Consequences* (Chicago: University of Chicago Press, 1988), p. 2.
8. Bureau of the Census, *General Social and Economy Characteristics: U.S. Summary* (Washington, D.C.: U.S. Government Printing Office, 1980), Section 2, Table 76.
9. Richard D. Alba, "The Twilight of Ethnicity Among Americans of European Ancestry: The Case of Italians," in Richard Alba, ed., *Ethnicity and Race in the U.S.A.: Toward the Twenty-First Century* (London: Routledge & Kegan Paul, 1985), pp. 134–58. Discussed in David Brinkerhoff and Lynn White, *Sociology*, 2nd ed. (St. Paul, Minn.: West Publishing, 1988), p. 259.
10. Ronald Inglehart, "The Renaissance of Political Culture," *American Political Science Review* 82 (December 1988): 1213.
11. H. H. Gerth and C. Wright Mills, trans. and eds., *From Max Weber: Essays in Sociology* (New York: Oxford University Press, 1958), p. 78.
12. Louis Hartz, *The Liberal Tradition in America* (New York: Harcourt, Brace, 1955).
13. This discussion draws on Sidney Verba and Norman Nie, *Participation in America* (New York: Harper & Row, 1972); and Stephen Earl Bennett and Linda L. M. Bennett, "Political Participation," in Samuel Long, ed., *Annual Review of Political Science* (Norwood, N.J.: Ablex Publishing Group, 1986).
14. Robert A. Dahl, *A Preface to Democratic Theory* (Chicago: University of Chicago Press, 1956), p. 142.
15. See Arthur F. Bentley, *The Process of Government* (Chicago: University of Chicago Press, 1908); and David Truman, *The Governmental Process* (New York: A. A. Knopf, 1951).
16. Robert Michels, *Political Parties* (New York: Collier Books, 1915).
17. Thomas R. Dye, *Who's Running America? The Bush Era* (Englewood Cliffs, N.J.: Prentice-Hall, 1990), p. 12.
18. C. Wright Mills, *The Power Elite* (New York: Oxford University Press, 1956).
19. "Opinion Outlook," *National Journal*, September 17, 1988, p. 2344.
20. Hedrick Smith, *The Power Game: How Washington Works* (New York: Random House, 1988), chapter 17.
21. For example, see Theodore J. Lowi, *The End of Liberalism*, 2nd ed. (New York: W. W. Norton, 1979).
22. Kurt Vonnegut, Jr., *God Bless You, Mr. Rosewater, or Pearls Before Swine* (New York: Delacorte Press, 1965), p. 104.
23. Michael Weisskopf, "Cutting Off the Power at the Source," *Washington Post National Weekly Edition*, October 22–28, 1990, p. 33.
24. Ibid., p. 34. Other sources on Bruce and the passage of the Clean Air Act are Margaret E. Kriz, "Switching to Gas," *National Journal*, October 27, 1990, pp. 2589–91 and Michael Weisskopf, "Divide and Conquer: The Clean Air Act's Story," *Washington Post National Weekly Edition*, December 31, 1990–January 6, 1991, p. 34.
25. Carol Matlack, "It's Round Two in Clean Air Fight," *National Journal*, January 26, 1991, pp. 226–27.

The Constitution

The Constitution is on view at the National Archives. At night it is lowered into its vault 20 feet below the floor.

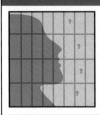

The Case
of the Confidential Tapes

When five burglars were arrested in the Watergate building in Washington, D.C., in June 1972, no one expected this apparently routine break-in to lead to the White House. However, the *Washington Post* assigned two ambitious young reporters, Bob Woodward and Carl Bernstein, to the story, and the duo uncovered a series of bizarre connections. The burglars, who had been caught installing wiretaps on the phones of the Democratic National Committee, had links with President Richard Nixon's Committee to Reelect the President (CREEP).

The administration dismissed the break-in as the work of overzealous underlings. Indeed, it was hard to imagine that high officials in the administration could be responsible. In public opinion polls, Nixon enjoyed an enormous lead, almost 20%, over the various Democrats vying for their party's nomination to challenge him in the fall election. Risky tactics seemed unnecessary. But Woodward and Bernstein discovered that White House staff members had engaged in other criminal and unethical actions to sabotage the Democrats' campaign.

Nixon won reelection handily, but the Watergate revelations forced his two top aides to resign and prompted the Senate to establish a special committee to investigate what was being called the **Watergate scandal.** During the committee's televised hearings, one presidential staff member revealed what had been unknown to all but a handful of presidential aides, that Nixon secretly tape-recorded conversations in the Oval Office.

The tapes could confirm or refute charges of White House complicity in the break-in and cover-up.

Nixon refused to release the tapes, prompting Special Prosecutor Archibald Cox to file suit to force him to do so. Judge John Sirica ordered Nixon to release the tapes, but when Sirica's order was upheld by a federal appeals court, Nixon demanded that his

Washington Post reporters Carl Bernstein (left) and Bob Woodward uncovered the Watergate scandal.

new attorney general fire Cox. The attorney general and his deputy both refused and resigned in protest. Then the third-ranking official in the Justice Department, Robert Bork, fired the special prosecutor.

The public furor over this "Saturday Night Massacre" was so intense that Nixon finally did release some tapes. But one crucial tape contained a mysterious eighteen-minute gap that a presidential aide speculated was caused by "some sinister force."

To mollify critics Nixon appointed a new special prosecutor, Leon Jaworski. After his investigation, Jaworski presented evidence to a grand jury that indicted seven of the president's aides for the cover-up, specifically for obstruction of justice, and even named the president as an "unindicted coconspirator."

The House Judiciary Committee considered impeaching the president, and Jaworski subpoenaed more tapes. Nixon issued edited transcripts of the conversations but not the tapes themselves. Dissatisfied, Jaworski went to court, where Judge Sirica

continued on next page

ordered Nixon to release the tapes. When Nixon refused, Jaworski appealed directly to the Supreme Court.

You are Chief Justice Warren Burger, appointed to the Court by President Nixon in 1969 partly because of your calls for more law and order. Three of your brethren also were appointed by Nixon. In the case of *United States v. Nixon,* you are faced with a question that could lead to a grave constitutional showdown with the president. Special Prosecutor Jaworski claims he needs the tapes because they contain evidence pertaining to the upcoming trial of the president's aides indicted for the coverup. Without all relevant evidence, which possibly could vindicate the aides, the trial court might not convict them.

President Nixon claims he has **executive privilege**—authority to withhold information from the courts and Congress. Although the Constitution does not mention such a privilege, Nixon claims the privilege is implicit in the powers of the presidency. Without it presidents could not guarantee confidentiality in conversations with other officials or even foreign leaders. This could make it difficult for them to govern.

There are few precedents to guide you. Many past presidents exercised executive privilege when pressed for information by Congress. In these instances, Congress would ordinarily acquiesce rather than sue for the information, so the courts did not rule on the existence of the privilege. Once, in 1953, the Eisenhower administration invoked the privilege, and the Supreme Court upheld the claim. However, this case involved national security.[1]

In addition to considering the merits of the opposing sides, you also need to consider the extent of the Court's power. The Court lacks strong means to enforce its rulings. It has to rely on its authority as the highest interpreter of the law in the country. Therefore, if the Court orders Nixon to relinquish the tapes and Nixon refuses, there would be little the Court could do. The refusal would show future officials that they could disregard your orders with impunity.

In this high-stakes contest, do you and your brethren on the Court order Nixon to turn over the tapes, or do you accept his claim of executive privilege?

Senate Watergate Committee Chair Sam Ervin (D-N.C.) questions presidential advisor John Dean (center, with glasses) about his conversations with the president concerning the scandal.

OUTLINE

Early settlers came to America for many reasons. Some came to escape religious persecution, others to establish their own religious orthodoxy. Some came to get rich, others to avoid debtors' prison. Some came to enrich their families or companies in the Old World, others to flee the closed society of that world. Some came as free persons, others as indentured servants or slaves. Few came to practice self-government. Yet the desire for self-government was evident from the beginning. The settlers who arrived in Jamestown in 1607 established the first representative assembly in America. The pilgrims who reached Plymouth in 1620 drew up the Mayflower Compact in which they vowed to "solemnly & mutually in the presence of God, and one of another, covenant and combine our selves together into a civill body politick." They pledged to establish laws for "the generall good of the colonie" and in return promised "all due submission and obedience."

During the next century and a half, the colonies adopted constitutions and elected representative assemblies. Of course, the colonies lived under British rule; they had to accept the appointment of royal governors and the presence of British troops. But a vast ocean separated the two continents. At such a distance, Britain could not wield the control it might at closer reach. Consequently, it granted the colonies a measure of autonomy, with which they practiced a degree of self-government.

These early efforts toward self-government led to conflict with the mother government. In 1774 the colonies established the Continental Congress to coordinate their action. Within months the conflict reached flashpoint, and the Congress urged the colonies to form their own governments. In 1776 the Congress adopted the Declaration of Independence.

After six years of war, the Americans accepted the British surrender. At the time it seemed they had met their biggest test. Yet they would find fomenting a revolution easier than fashioning a government and drafting a declaration of independence easier than crafting a constitution.

The Articles of Confederation

Even before the war ended, the Continental Congress passed a constitution, and in 1781 the states ratified it. This first constitution, the **Articles of Confederation,** formed a "league of friendship" among the states. As a confederation, it allowed each state to retain its "sovereignty" and "independence." That is, it made the states supreme over the national government.

The Articles established a Congress, with one house in which each state had one vote. But the Articles strictly limited the powers that Congress could exercise, and they provided no executive or judicial branch.

The Articles reflected the colonial experience under the British government. The leaders feared a powerful central government with a powerful executive like a king. They thought that such a government would be too strong and too distant to guarantee individual liberty. Additionally, the Articles reflected a lack of national identity among the people. Most did not view themselves as Americans yet. As Edmund Randolph remarked, "I am not really an American, I am a Virginian."[2] Consequently, the leaders established a very decentralized government that left most authority to the states.

The government satisfied many people. Most people were small farmers, and most of them were content. Although economic recovery after the war lagged and many farmers sank into debt and faced foreclosure, they felt they could influence the state governments to help them. They pressured some legislatures to cancel or postpone their debts or at least to issue cheap paper money so they could pay their debts with cheaper money than they had borrowed. These small farmers realized they could not as readily influence a distant central government.

On the other hand, bankers, merchants, and manufacturers, and those who were in the upper classes, were frustrated by the government under the Articles.

AMERICAN DIVERSITY

Founding Mothers

Charles Francis Adams, a grandson of President John Adams and Abigail Adams, declared in 1840, "The heroism of the females of the Revolution has gone from memory with the generation that witnessed it, and nothing, absolutely nothing remains upon the ear of the young of the present day."[1] That statement is still true today; in the volumes written about the revolutionary and Constitution-making eras, much is said of the "founding fathers" and very little about the "founding mothers." Although no women were at the Constitutional Convention, in many other ways women contributed significantly to the political ferment of the time. The political role of women during the Constitution-making era was probably greater than it would be again for a century.

Before the revolutionary war, women were active in encouraging opposition to the British. Groups of women, some called the "daughters of liberty," led boycotts of British goods as part of the protest campaign against taxation without representation. A few women were political pamphleteers, helping to increase public sentiment for independence. One of those pamphlet writers, Mercy Otis Warren, of Massachusetts, was thought to be the first person to urge the Massachusetts delegates to the Continental Congress to vote for separation from England.[2] Throughout the period before and after the Revolution, Warren shared her political ideas in personal correspondence with leading statesmen of the time, such as John Adams and Thomas Jefferson. Later she wrote a three-volume history of the American Revolution.

Many women were part of the American army during the battles for independence. Most filled traditional woman's roles as cooks, sewers, and nurses, but some disguised themselves as men (this was before a military bureaucracy mandated preenlistment physical exams) and fought in battle. One such woman, wounded in action in 1776, is the only revolutionary war veteran buried at West Point. Still other women fought to defend their homes using hatchets, farm implements, and pots of boiling lye in addition to muskets.

Following independence, some women continued an active political role. Mercy Warren, for example, campaigned against the proposed Constitution because she felt it was not democratic enough.

A SOCIETY of PATRIOTIC LADIES,
AT
EDENTON in NORTH CAROLINA.

Plate V.

This English political cartoon satirizes a gathering of leading women in North Carolina who drew up a resolution to boycott taxed English goods and tea.

Independence did not bring any improvement in the political rights of women. In fact, after the Constitution was adopted, some rights that women had held before were gradually lost, such as the right of some women to vote. It was to be another century before the rights of women became a full-fledged part of our national political agenda.

1. Quoted in Linda Grant DePauw and Conover Hunt, *Remember the Ladies* (New York: Viking Press, 1976), p. 9.
2. Alice Felt Tyler, *Freedom's Ferment* (New York: Harper & Row, 1962).

They envisioned a great commercial empire rather than the agricultural society the country had. More than local trade, they wanted national and even international trade. For this they needed uniform laws, stable money, sound credit, and enforceable debt collection. They needed a strong central government that could protect them against debtors and against state governments sympathetic to debtors. The Articles provided neither the foreign security nor the domestic climate necessary to nourish these requisites of a commercial empire.

After the war the army disbanded, leaving the country vulnerable to hostile forces surrounding it. Britain maintained outposts with troops in the Northwest Territory (now the Midwest), in violation of the peace treaty, and an army in Canada. Spain, which had occupied Florida and California for a long time and had claimed the Mississippi River Valley as a result of a treaty before the war, posed a threat. Barbary pirates from northern Africa seized American ships and sailors.

Congress could not raise an army, because it could not draft individuals directly, or finance an army, because it could not tax individuals directly. Instead, it had to ask the states for soldiers and money. The states, however, were not always sympathetic to the problems of the distant government. And although Congress could make treaties with foreign countries, the states made, or broke, treaties independently of Congress. Without the ability to establish a credible army or negotiate a binding treaty, the government could not get the British troops out of the country. Neither could it get the British government to ease restrictions on shipping or the Spanish government to permit navigation on the Mississippi River.

In addition to an inability to confront foreign threats, the Articles demonstrated an inability to cope with domestic crises. The country bore a heavy war debt that brought the government close to bankruptcy. Since Congress could not tax individuals directly, it could not shore up the shaky government.

In short, the government under the Articles seemed too decentralized to ensure either peace or prosperity. The Articles, one leader concluded, gave Congress the privilege of asking for everything, while reserving to each state the prerogative of granting nothing.[3] A similar situation exists today in the United Nations, which must rely on member countries to furnish troops for its peacekeeping forces and dues for its operating expenses.

Thus, the debate over the Articles reflected a conflict between two competing visions of the future American political economy—agricultural or commercial.[4] Most American leaders espoused the latter, and they prevailed.

The Constitution

The Constitutional Convention

The shortcomings of the Articles worried the leaders, and **Shays' Rebellion** scared them. In western Massachusetts in 1786 and early 1787, farmers protested the state legislature's decision not to issue cheap paper money and courts' decisions to foreclose mortgages on farms and throw debtors in jails. Bands of farmers blocked the entrances to courthouses. Led by a man named Daniel Shays, some marched to the Springfield arsenal to seize weapons. Although they were defeated by the militia, their revolt frightened the wealthy, who were the creditors. To them it raised the specter of

Massachusetts militiamen fire into the ranks of Shays' rebels.

"mob rule." Just months after the revolt, the Continental Congress approved a convention for "the sole and express purpose of revising the Articles of Confederation."

The Setting.   The **Constitutional Convention** convened in Philadelphia, then the country's largest city, in 1787. Of 74 delegates chosen by the state legislatures, 55 attended the convention. They met at the Pennsylvania State House—now Independence Hall—in the same room where some of them had signed the Declaration of Independence 11 years before.

Delegates came from every state except Rhode Island. That state was controlled by farmers and debtors who feared that the convention would weaken states' powers to relieve debtors of their debts.

The delegates were distinguished by their education, experience, and enlightenment. Benjamin Franklin, of Pennsylvania, was the best-known American in the world. He had been a printer, scientist, and diplomat. At 81 he was the oldest delegate. George Washington, of Virginia, was the most respected American

in the country. As the commander of the revolutionary army, he was a national hero. He was chosen to preside over the convention. The presence of men like Franklin and Washington gave the convention legitimacy.

The delegates quickly determined that the Articles were hopeless. Rather than revise them, as instructed by Congress, the delegates decided to start over and draft a new constitution. But what would they substitute for the Articles?

The Predicament.   The delegates came to the convention because they suffered under a government that was too weak. Yet previously Americans had fought a revolution because they chafed under a government that was too strong. "The nation lived in a nearly constant alternation of fears that it would cease being a nation altogether or become too much of one."[5] People feared both anarchy and tyranny.

This predicament was made clear by the diversity of opinions among the leaders. At one extreme was Patrick Henry, of Virginia, who had been a firebrand of the Revolution. He felt the country would become

George Washington presides over the signing of the Constitution at the Constitutional Convention.

too strong, perhaps even become a monarchy, in re-action to the current problems with the Articles. Al-though chosen as a delegate to the convention, he said he "smelt a rat" and did not attend. At the other ex-treme was Alexander Hamilton, of New York, who had been an aide to General Washington during the war and had seen the government's inability to supply and pay its own troops. Since then he had called for a stronger national government. He wanted one that could veto the laws of the state governments. And he wanted one person to serve as chief executive for life and others to serve as senators for life. He did attend the convention but, finding little agreement with his proposals, participated infrequently.

In between were those like James Madison, of Virginia, who was a nationalist but less extreme than Hamilton. Small and frail, timid and self-conscious as a speaker, he was nonetheless intelligent, savvy, and audacious. He had been instrumental behind the scenes in convening the convention and securing George Washington's attendance. (He publicized that Washington would attend without asking Washington first. Washington, who was in retirement, was not amused but did reluctantly attend because of the ex-pectation that he would.[6]) Drawing upon his study of governments in history to learn why many had failed, Madison had secretly drafted a plan for a new govern-ment that was a total departure from the Articles. Madison's ideas set the agenda for the convention. In the end, his views, more than anyone else's, would prevail, and he would be called the Father of the Con-stitution.

Consensus.   Despite disagreements, the delegates did see eye to eye on the most fundamental issues. They agreed that the government should be a republic—an indirect democracy—in which people could vote for at least some of the officials who would represent them. This was the only form of government they seriously considered. They also agreed that the national government should be supreme over the state governments. At the same time, they thought that the government should be limited, with checks to prevent it from exercising too much power.

They agreed that the national government should have three separate branches—legislative, executive, and judicial—to exercise separate powers. They thought that both the legislative and executive branches should be strong.

Conflict.   Although there was considerable agree-ment over the fundamental principles and elemental structure of the new government, the delegates quar-reled about the specific provisions concerning repre-sentation, slavery, and trade.

Representation.   There was sharp conflict between delegates from large states and small states. Large states sought a strong central government that they could control; small states feared a government that would control them.

When the convention began, Edmund Randolph introduced the Virginia Plan drafted by Madison. Ac-cording to this plan, the central government would be strong. The legislature would have more power than under the Articles, and a national executive and na-tional judiciary also would have considerable power. The legislature would be divided into two houses, with representation based on population in each.

But delegates from the small states calculated that the three largest states—Pennsylvania, Virginia, and Massachusetts—would have a majority of the repre-sentatives and could control the legislature. These del-egates countered with the New Jersey Plan, intro-duced by William Paterson. According to this plan, the central government would be relatively strong, al-though not as strong as under the Virginia Plan. But the primary difference was that the legislature would be one house, with representation by states, which would have one vote each. This was exactly the same as the structure of Congress under the Articles, also designed to prevent the large states from controlling the legislature.

The convention deadlocked. George Washington wrote that he almost despaired of reaching agreement. To ease tensions Benjamin Franklin suggested that the delegates begin each day with a prayer, but they could not agree on this either; Alexander Hamilton insisted they did not need "foreign aid."

Faced with the possibility that the convention would disband without a constitution, the delegates compromised. Delegates from Connecticut and other states proposed a plan in which the legislature would have two houses. In one, representation would be based on population, and members would be elected by voters. In the other, representation would be by states, and members would be selected by state legis-latures. Presumably the large states would dominate the former, the small states the latter. The delegates narrowly approved this **Great Compromise,** or Connecticut Compromise. Delegates from the large states still objected, but those from the small states made it clear that such a compromise was necessary for their agreement and, in turn, their states' ratification. The large states, though, did extract a concession that all taxing and spending bills must originate in the house in which representation was based on population. This provision would allow the large states to take the initiative on these important measures.

The compromise was "great" in that it not only resolved this critical issue but paved the way for resolution of other issues.

Slavery.   In addition to conflict between large states and small states over representation, there was conflict between northern states and southern states over slavery and economic trade.

With representation in one house based on population, the delegates had to decide how to apportion the seats. They did not consider Indians part of the population, but delegates from the South, where slaves numbered one-third of the population, wanted to count slaves as part of the population in order to boost the number of their representatives. Delegates from the North, where most states had halted slavery or at least the slave trade in the years after the Revolution, did not want to count slaves at all. They pointed out that slaves were not considered persons when it came to rights such as voting. In the **Three-fifths Compromise,** the delegates agreed to count three-fifths of the slaves in apportioning the seats.

Although this compromise tacitly accepted the institution of slavery, southerners worried that northerners might try to restrict the slave trade. Southerners pushed through one provision forbidding Congress to ban the importation of slaves before 1808 and another provision requiring free states to return any escaped slaves to their owners in slave states. In these provisions southerners won most of what they wanted; even the provision permitting Congress to ban the slave trade in 1808 was only a small concession to northerners because planters would have enough slaves by then to fulfill their need for slaves by "breeding" rather than importing them.

Yet the framers were embarrassed by the hypocrisy of claiming to have been enslaved by the British while allowing enslavement of blacks. The Framers' embarrassment is reflected in their language. The three provisions reinforcing slavery never mention "slavery" or "slaves"; one gingerly refers to "free persons" and "other persons."

The unwillingness to tackle the slavery issue more directly has been called the "Greatest Compromise" by one political scientist.[7] But an attempt to abolish slavery would have led the five southern states to refuse to ratify the Constitution.

Trade.   Other compromises followed, including one on trade restrictions of manufactured and agricultural goods. With a manufacturing economy in the North and an agricultural economy in the South, the North sought protection for its businesses, whereas the South wanted free trade for its plantations. Specifically, northerners wanted a tax on British manufactured goods imported into this country. Without a tax, these goods were cheaper than northern goods; therefore a tax would make northern goods more competitive—and prices for southern consumers more expensive. Southerners wanted a guarantee that there

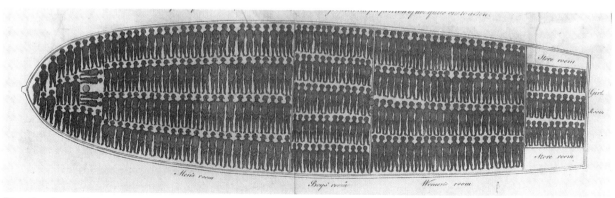

Plan of a slave ship.

The Pennsylvania Packet, and Daily Advertiser.

[Price Four-Pence.] WEDNESDAY, September 19, 1787. [No. 2690.]

WE, the People of the United States, in order to form a more perfect Union, establish Justice, insure domestic Tranquility, provide for the common Defence, promote the General Welfare, and secure the Blessings of Liberty to Ourselves and our Posterity, do ordain and establish this Constitution for the United States of America.

ARTICLE I.

Sect. 1. ALL legislative powers herein granted shall be vested in a Congress of the United States, which shall consist of a Senate and House of Representatives.

Sect. 2. The House of Representatives shall be composed of members chosen every second year by the people of the several states, and the electors in each state shall have the qualifications requisite for electors of the most numerous branch of the state legislature.

No person shall be a representative who shall not have attained to the age of twenty-five years, and been seven years a citizen of the United States, and who shall not, when elected, be an inhabitant of that state in which he shall be chosen.

Representatives and direct taxes shall be apportioned among the several states which may be included within this Union, according to their respective numbers, which shall be determined by adding to the whole number of free persons, including those bound to service for a term of years, and excluding Indians not taxed, three-fifths of all other persons. The actual enumeration shall

would be no tax on exported goods that would make their agricultural products less competitive in England. The delegates compromised by allowing Congress to tax imported goods but not exported goods. Tariffs on imported goods would prove to be a major controversy between the North and South in the years leading up to the Civil War.

With all issues resolved, a committee was appointed to write the final draft. Gouverneur Morris, of Pennsylvania, was the member of the committee most responsible for the polished style of the document. He was also largely responsible for the stirring preamble. In earlier drafts the preamble had not referred to "the people" but had listed the states. Morris's change signaled a shift in emphasis from the states to the people directly.

After 17 weeks of debate, the Constitution was ready. On September 17, 1787, 39 of the original 55 delegates signed it. Some delegates had left when they saw the direction the convention was taking, and 3 others refused to sign, feeling that the Constitution gave too much authority to the national government. Most of the rest were not entirely happy with the result—even Madison, who was most responsible for the content of the document, was despondent that his plan for a national legislature was compromised by having one house with representation by states—but they thought it was the best they could do. Benjamin Franklin had some qualms, but he was more optimistic. Referring to the sun painted on the back of George Washington's chair, he remarked that throughout the proceedings he had wondered whether it was a rising or setting sun. "But now . . . I have the happiness to know that it is a rising and not a setting sun."

Features of the Constitution

William Gladstone, a British prime minister in the nineteenth century, said the American Constitution was "the most wonderful work ever struck off at a given time by the brain and purpose of man."[8] To see why it was unique, it is necessary to examine its major features.

A Written Constitution. The Founders established the idea of a written constitution, first in the Articles of Confederation and then more prominently in the Constitution itself. Other Western countries had constitutions that served as their supreme law, but these constitutions were not written or, if written, not as a single document. For example, the British constitution, which consisted of various customs, declarations, acts of Parliament, and precedents of courts, was partly unwritten and partly written. To Americans this was no constitution at all. They felt that a constitution should be a fundamental law above all other laws—not a mixture of customs and laws.

This belief is reflected in Americans' use of social contract theory. A **social contract,** not a literal contract like a business contract, is an implied agreement between the people and their government. The people give up part of their liberty to the government, which in exchange protects the remainder of their liberty. The Mayflower Compact was a very general form of social contract, whereas the written Constitution, stipulating the powers and limits of government, was a more specific form of social contract.

A Republic. As explained in chapter 1, the Founders distinguished between a **republic** and a **democracy.** They created a republic. Also called an "indirect democracy," this form of government is one in which people vote for representatives who make decisions for them.

The Founders opposed a "direct democracy" in which the will of the people becomes law. Some city-states of ancient Greece and medieval Europe had direct democracies but could not sustain them. The Founders thought that a large country would have even less ability to do so because people could not be brought together in one place in order to act. The Founders also believed that human nature was such that people could not withstand the passions of the moment and would be swayed by a demagogue to take unwise action. Eventually, democracy would collapse into tyranny. "Remember," John Adams wrote, "democracy never lasts long. It soon wastes, exhausts, and murders itself. There never was a democracy yet that did not commit suicide."[9]

The Founders and the People

Democracy is "the worst of all political evils."

—Elbridge Gerry

"[T]he people have ever been and ever will be unfit to retain the exercise of power in their own hands."

—William Livingston

"[T]he people [should] have as little to do as may be about the government."

—Roger Sherman

"Notwithstanding the oppression and injustice experienced among us from democracy, the genius of the people is in favor of it, and the genius of the people must be consulted."

—George Mason

"It seems indispensable that the mass of citizens should not be without a voice in making the laws which they are to obey, in choosing the magistrates who are to administer them."

—James Madison

In part these statements reflect the Founders' support for republicanism and opposition to democracy, as they defined the terms. But in a more general sense, these statements reflect the Founders' ambivalence about "the people." Rationally they believed in popular sovereignty, but emotionally they feared it. Perhaps no statement illustrates this ambivalence more than the one by New England clergyman Jeremy Belknap: "Let it stand as a principle that government originates from the people; but let the people be taught . . . that they are not able to govern themselves."

Source: Richard Hofstadter, *The American Political Tradition and the Men Who Made It* (New York: Vintage, 1948), pp. 3–17.

The Founders favored a republic because they firmly believed that the people should have some voice in government in order for it to be based on the consent of the governed. So the Founders provided that the people could elect representatives to the House and that the state legislators, themselves elected by the people, could select senators and members of the Electoral College, who would choose the president. In this way the people would have a voice but one filtered through their presumably wiser representatives.

The Founders considered a democracy radical and a republic only slightly less radical. Because they believed that the country could not maintain a democracy, they worried that it might not be able to maintain a republic either. When the Constitutional Convention closed, Benjamin Franklin was approached by a woman who asked, "Well, Doctor, what have we got, a republic or a monarchy?" Franklin responded, "A republic, madam, if you can keep it."

Fragmentation of Power.   Other countries assumed that government must have a concentration of power in order to be strong enough to govern. However, when the Founders made our national government more powerful than it had been under the Articles, they feared that they also had made it more capable of oppression, and therefore they fragmented its power.

The Founders believed that people were selfish, coveting more and more property, and that leaders lusted after more and more power. They assumed such human nature was unchangeable. Madison speculated, "If men were angels, no government would be necessary." But, alas, Madison said, men are not angels. Therefore, "In framing a government which is to be administered by men over men, the great difficulty lies in this: you must first enable the government to control the governed; and in the next place oblige it to control itself."[10] The Founders decided that the way to oblige government to control itself was to structure it to prevent any one leader, group of leaders, or factions of people from exercising power over more than a small part of it. Thus, the Founders fragmented government's power. This is reflected in three concepts they built into the structure of government—federalism, separation of powers, and checks and balances.

Federalism.   The first division of power was between the national government and the state governments. This division of power is called **federalism.** Foreign governments had been "unitary"; that is, the central government wielded all authority. At the other extreme, the U.S. government under the Articles had been "confederal," which meant that although there was some division of power, the state governments wielded almost all authority. The Founders wanted a strong national government, but they also wanted, or at least realized they would have to accept, reasonably strong state governments as well. They invented a federal system as a compromise between the unitary and confederal systems.

Separation of Powers.   The second division of power was within the national government. The power to make, administer, and judge the laws was split into three branches—legislative, executive, and judicial (see table 1). In the legislative branch, the power was split further into two houses. This **separation of powers** contrasts with the British parliamentary system in which its legislature, Parliament, is supreme. Both executive and judicial officials are drawn from it and responsible to it. Madison expressed the American view of such an arrangement when he said that "the accumulation of all powers, legislative, executive, and judiciary, in the same hands . . . may justly be pronounced the very definition of tyranny."[11]

To reinforce the separation of powers, officials of the three branches were chosen by different means. Representatives were elected by the people (at that time mostly white men who owned property), senators were selected by the state legislatures, and the president was selected by the Electoral College, whose members were selected by the states. Only federal judges were chosen by officials in the other branches. They were nominated by the president and confirmed by the Senate. Once appointed, however, they were allowed to serve for "good behavior"—essentially life—so they had much independence. (Since the Constitution was written, the Seventeenth Amendment has provided for election of senators by the people, and the state legislatures have provided for election of members of the Electoral College by the people.)

Officials of the branches were also chosen at different times. Representatives were given a two-year term, senators a six-year term (with one-third of them up for reelection every two years), and the president a four-year term. These staggered terms would make it less likely that temporary passions in society would bring about a massive switch of officials or policies.

The Senate was designed to act as a conservative brake on the House, due to senators' selection by state legislatures and their longer terms. After returning from France, Thomas Jefferson met with George Washington over breakfast. Jefferson protested the establishment of a legislature with two houses. Washington supposedly asked, "Why did you pour that coffee into your saucer?" "To cool it," Jefferson replied. Similarly, Washington explained, "We pour legislation into the senatorial saucer to cool it."[12]

Table 1 ■ Federalism and Separation of Powers

		Separation of Powers: Division of Power by Function		
		Legislative	*Executive*	*Judicial*
Federalism: Division of Power by Level	*National*	Congress	President	Federal courts
	State	Legislature	Governor	State courts
	Local	County commission, city council, and other local legislative bodies	Mayor and other local chief executives	Local courts

Figure 1 ■ Checks and Balances

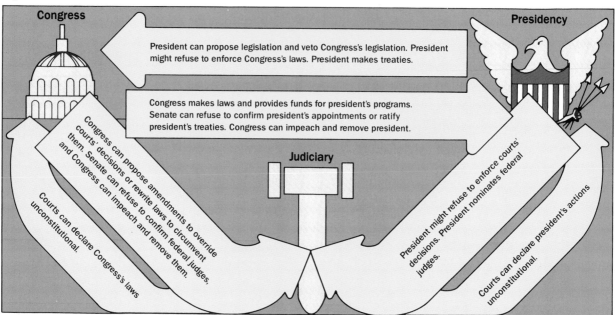

Most of the major checks and balances between the three branches are explicit in the Constitution, though some are not. For example, the courts' power to declare congressional laws or presidential actions unconstitutional—their power of "judicial review"—is not mentioned. And the president's power to refuse to enforce congressional laws or judicial decisions is not mentioned or even implied. In fact, it contradicts the Constitution, but sometimes it is asserted by the president nonetheless.

Checks and Balances. To guarantee separation of powers, the Founders built in overlapping powers called **checks and balances** (see figure 1). Madison suggested that "the great security against a gradual concentration of the several powers in the same department consists in giving those who administer each department the necessary constitutional means and personal motives to resist encroachments by the others. . . . *Ambition must be made to counteract ambition.*"[13] Thus, each branch was given some authority over the others. If one branch abused its power, the others could use their checks to thwart it.

Thus, rather than a simple system of separation of powers, ours is a complex, even contradictory, system of both separation of powers and checks and balances. The principle of separation of powers gives each branch its own sphere of authority, but the system of checks and balances allows each branch to intrude into the other branches' spheres. For example, because of separation of powers, Congress makes the laws, but due to checks and balances, the president can veto

them and the courts can rule them unconstitutional. In these ways all three branches are involved in legislating. Thus, one political scientist calls ours "a government of separated institutions sharing powers."[14]

With federalism, separation of powers, and checks and balances, the Founders expected conflict. They invited the parts of government to struggle against each other in order to limit each other's ability to dominate all. At the same time, the Founders hoped for "balanced government." The national and state governments would represent different interests, and the branches within the national government would represent different interests. The House would represent the "common" people and the large states, the Senate the wealthy people and the small states, the president all the people, and the Supreme Court the Constitution. The parts of government would have to compromise in order to get anything accomplished. Although each part would struggle for more power, it could not accumulate enough to dominate the others. Eventually its leaders would have to compromise and adopt policies in the interest of all of the parts and their constituencies. Paradoxically, then, the Founders expected narrow conflict to produce broader harmony.

Motives of the Founders

To understand the Constitution better, it is useful to consider the motives of the Founders. Were they selfless patriots, sharing their wisdom and experience? Or were they selfish property owners, protecting their interests? To answer these questions it is necessary to look at the philosophical ideas, political experience, and economic interests that influenced these men.

Philosophical Ideas. The Founders were exceptionally well-educated intellectuals who incorporated philosophical ideas into the Constitution. At a time when the average person did not dream of going to college, a majority of the Founders graduated from college. As learned men, they shared a common library of writers and philosophers.

The framers of the Constitution reflected the ideals of the Enlightenment, a pattern of thought emphasizing the use of reason, rather than tradition or religion, to solve problems; they studied past governments to determine why they had failed in the hope that they could apply these lessons to the present.

From all accounts they engaged in a level of debate at the convention that was rare in politics, citing philosophers ranging from the ancient Greeks to the modern British and French. Even when they did not mention them explicitly, their comments seemed to reflect the writings of particular philosophers.

The views of John Locke, a seventeenth-century English philosopher, underlay many of the ideas of the Founders. In fact, his views permeate the Declaration of Independence and Constitution more than those of any other single person.

Locke, like some previous philosophers, believed that people had **natural rights.** These rights were inherent; they existed from the moment people were born. And they were inalienable; they were given by God so could not be taken away. One of the most important was the right to property. When people worked the land, clearing it and planting it, they mixed their labor with it. This act, according to Locke, made the land their property. Some people, due to more work or luck, would accumulate more property than others. Thus, the right to property would result in inequality of wealth. Yet he thought it would lead

to greater productivity for society. This view of property appealed to Americans who saw an abundance of land in the new country.

Locke wrote that people came together to form government through a social contract that established a **limited government,** strong enough to protect their rights but not too strong to threaten these rights. This government should not act without the consent of the governed. To make its decisions, this government should follow majority rule. (Locke never resolved the conflict between majority rule and natural rights—that is, between majority rule and minority rights for those who disagree with the majority.)

The views of Charles de Montesquieu, an eighteenth-century French philosopher, also influenced the debate at the convention and the provisions of the Constitution itself. Others had suggested separation of powers before, but Montesquieu refined the concept and added that of checks and balances. The Founders, referring to him as "the celebrated Montesquieu," cited him more than any other thinker.[15] (Presumably they cited him more than Locke because by this time Locke's views had so permeated American society that the Founders considered them just "common sense."[16])

The principles of the system of mechanics formulated by Isaac Newton, an eighteenth-century British mathematician, also pervaded the provisions of the Constitution. As Newton viewed nature as a machine, so the Founders saw the constitutional structure as a machine, with different parts having different functions and balancing each other. Newton's principle of action and reaction is manifested in the Founders' system of checks and balances. The natural environment and the constitutional structure both were viewed as self-regulating systems.[17]

Political Experience. Although the Founders were intellectuals, they were also practical politicians. According to one interpretation, they were "first and foremost superb democratic politicians" and the convention was "a nationalist reform caucus which had to operate with great delicacy and skill in a political cosmos full of enemies."[18]

The Founders brought extensive political experience to the convention: 8 had signed the Declaration of Independence; 39 had served in Congress; 7 had been governors; many had held other state offices; some had helped write their state constitutions. The framers drew upon this experience. For example, while they cited Montesquieu in discussing separation of powers, they also referred to the experience of colonial and state governments that already had some separation of powers.

As practical politicians, "no matter what their private dreams might be, they had to take home an acceptable package and defend it—and their own political futures—against predictable attack."[19] So they compromised the difficult issues and ducked the stickiest ones. Ultimately, they pieced together a Constitution that allowed each delegate to go home and announce that his state won something.

Economic Interests.   Historian Charles Beard sparked a lively debate when he published *An Economic Interpretation of the Constitution* in 1913.[20] Beard argued that those with money and investments in manufacturing and shipping dominated the Constitutional Convention and state ratification conventions and that they produced a document that would increase their wealth. However, later scholars questioned Beard's facts and interpretations, pointing out that support for the Constitution was not based strictly on wealth; Elbridge Gerry, one of the richest men in the country, opposed the Constitution, whereas Hamilton and Madison, both of more modest means, supported it.[21]

Although some of Beard's specific points do not hold up, his underlying position that the Founders represented an elite that sought to protect its property from the masses seems more valid. The delegates to the Constitutional Convention were an elite. They included prosperous planters, manufacturers, shippers, and lawyers. About one-third were slaveowners. Most came from families of prominence and married into other families of prominence. Not all were wealthy, but most were at least well-to-do. Only one, a delegate from Georgia, was a yeoman farmer like most men in the country. In short, "this was a convention of the well-bred, the well-fed, the well-read, and the well-wed."[22]

The Founders supported the right to property. The promise of land and perhaps riches enticed most immigrants to come to America.[23] A desire for freedom from arbitrary taxes and trade restrictions spurred some colonists to fight in the Revolution. And the inability of the government under the Articles to provide a healthy economy prompted the Founders to convene the Constitutional Convention. They probably agreed with Madison that "the first object of government" is to protect property.[24]

The Founders' emphasis on property was not as elitist as it might seem, however. Land was plentiful and, with westward expansion, even more would be available. Already most men were middle-class farmers who owned some property. Many who owned no property could foresee the day when they would, so most Americans wanted to protect property.

The Founders diverged from the farmers in their desire to protect other property in addition to land, such as wealth and credit. So they included provisions to protect commerce, including imports and exports, contracts, and debts, and provisions to regulate currency, bankruptcy, and taxes.

Political scientists and historians disagree about which of these three influences on the Founders—philosophical, political, and economic—was most important. Actually the influences are difficult to separate because they reinforce each other; the framers' ideas point to the same sort of constitution that their political experience and economic interests do.[25]

"Religious freedom is my immediate goal, but my long range plan is to go into real estate."

Constitutional Provisions Protecting Property

"The Times, Places and Manner of holding Elections for Senators and Representatives, shall be prescribed in each State by the Legislature thereof."	Allows state to set property qualifications to vote.
"The Congress shall have Power . . . To coin Money."	Centralizes currency.
"No State shall . . . emit bills of credit."	Prevents states from printing paper money.
"Congress shall have Power . . . To establish uniform Laws on the subject of Bankruptcies."	Allows Congress to prevent states from relieving debtors of obligation to pay.
"No State shall . . . pass any . . . Law impairing the Obligation of Contracts."	Prevents states from relieving debtors of obligation to pay.
"The United States shall guarantee to every State [protection] against domestic Violence."	Protects states from debtor uprisings.
"Congress shall have Power . . . To provide for calling forth the Militia to execute the Laws of the Union, suppress Insurrections."	Protects creditors from debtor uprisings.

Ratification of the Constitution

The Constitution specified that ratification would occur through conventions in the states and that the document would take effect with approval of conventions in 9 of the 13 states. The framers purposely did not provide for approval by the state legislatures because they feared that some legislatures would reject it because it reduced their power. Too, the framers wanted the broader base of support for the new government that ratification conventions would provide.

Technically the procedures for ratification were illegal. According to the Articles of Confederation, which were still in effect, any changes had to be approved by all 13 states. However, the framers suspected that they would not find support in all states.

Indeed, ratification was uncertain. Many people opposed the Constitution, and there was a lively campaign against it in newspapers, pamphlets, and mass meetings. And although the procedures required ratification by only 9 states, the framers realized that they needed support from all of the largest states and much of the public to lend legitimacy to the new government.

Knowing opponents would charge them with setting up a national government to dominate the state governments, those who supported the Constitution ingeniously adopted the name **Federalists** to emphasize a real division of power between the national and state governments. They dubbed their opponents **Antifederalists** to imply that they did not want a division of power between the governments.

The Antifederalists faulted the Constitution for lacking a bill of rights. The Constitution did contain some protection for individual rights, such as the provision that the writ of habeas corpus, which protects against arbitrary arrest and detention, cannot be suspended except during rebellion or invasion, and the provision that a criminal defendant has a right to a jury trial. But the framers made no effort to include most of the rights people believed they had, because most states already had a bill of rights in their own constitutions. They also thought that by fragmenting power no branch could become strong enough to deny individual rights. Yet critics demanded provisions protecting various rights of criminal defendants and freedom of the press. In response, the Federalists promised to propose amendments guaranteeing these rights as soon as the government began.

The Antifederalists criticized the Constitution for other reasons. Localists at heart, they were wary of entrusting power to officials far away; they correctly claimed that republics historically worked only in small geographical areas where the population was

The Federalist Papers

Out of the great debate over ratification came a series of essays considered the premier example of American political philosophy. Titled the *Federalist Papers,* these essays were written by Alexander Hamilton *(left),* James Madison *(center),* and John Jay. At the urging of Hamilton, the authors wrote 85 essays that appeared in New York newspapers during the ratification debates there. The authors tried to convince delegates to the convention to vote for ratification.

In the fashion of the time, the papers were published anonymously—by "Publius" (Latin for "Public Man"). They were so unified in approach that few of the authors' contemporaries could discern their pens at work. Given the arguments and compromises at the Constitutional Convention, one political scientist speculated that the framers who read the essays "must have discovered with some surprise what a coherent and well-thought-out document they had prepared."[1]

Despite the unity of the papers, political scientists have identified the authors of individual ones. Hamilton wrote most of those describing the defects of the Articles, Madison most of those explaining the structure of the new government, including the famous #10 and #51 (reprinted at the back of this book). Before he became sick, Jay, who was secretary of foreign affairs, wrote a few concerning foreign policy.

Actually there is little evidence that the essays swayed any of the delegates. Yet they have endured because readers see them as an original source of political thinking and as one of the best guides to the intentions of the Framers.

1. John P. Roche, ed., *Origins of American Political Thought* (New York: Harper & Row, 1967), p. 163.

more homogeneous and the officials were closer to the people. They worried that the central government, to function effectively, would accumulate too much power and the presidency would become a monarchy or Congress an aristocracy. One delegate to the Massachusetts convention blasted the Federalists:

> These lawyers, and men of learning and moneyed men, that talk so finely, and gloss over matters so smoothly, to make us poor illiterate people swallow down the pill, expect to get into Congress themselves; they expect to . . . get all the power and all the money into their own hands, and then they will swallow up all us little folks . . . just as the whale swallowed up Jonah![26]

But the Antifederalists had no alternative plan. They were divided; some wanted to amend the Articles and others wanted to reject both the Articles and the Constitution in favor of some yet undetermined form of government. Their lack of unity on an alternative was instrumental in their inability to win support.[27]

Ratification was quick in some states, a bitter struggle in others. Within three months after the Constitutional Convention, Delaware became the first state to ratify, and six months later New Hampshire became the necessary ninth. Virginia and New York followed, but they ratified only by narrow margins. Indeed, New York ratified by only three votes after New York City threatened to secede from the state if it did not ratify. So the Constitution took effect and the new government began in 1788, with George Washington becoming president. Within one year, North Carolina and Rhode Island, both of which initially rejected the Constitution, became the last states to approve it.

Changing the Constitution

The framers expected their document to last; Madison wrote, "We have framed a constitution that will probably be still around when there are 196 million people."[28] Yet because the framers realized it would need some changes, they drafted a Constitution that can be changed either formally by constitutional amendment or informally by judicial interpretation or political practice. In doing so, they left a legacy for later governments. "The example of changing a Constitution, by assembling the wise men of the state, instead of assembling armies," Jefferson noted, "will be worth as much to the world as the former examples we had given them."[29]

By Constitutional Amendment.   That the Articles of Confederation could be amended only by a unanimous vote of the states posed an almost insurmountable barrier to any amendment at all. The framers of the Constitution made sure this experience would not repeat itself. On the other hand, they did not make amendment easy; although the procedures do not require unanimity, they do require widespread agreement.

Procedures.   The procedures for amendment entail action by both the national government and the state governments. Amendments can be proposed in either of two ways—by a two-thirds vote of both houses of Congress or by a national convention called by Congress at the request of two-thirds of the state legislatures. Congress then specifies which way amendments must be ratified—either by three-fourths of the state legislatures or by ratifying conventions in three-fourths of the states. Among these avenues, the usual route has been proposal by Congress and ratification by state legislatures (see figure 2).

Figure 2 ■ Avenues for Constitutional Amendment

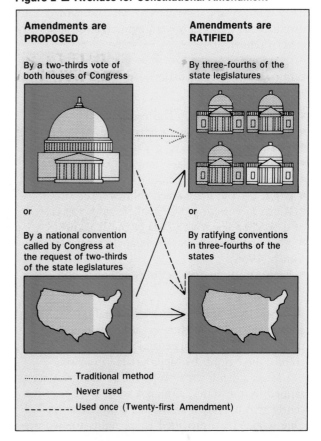

Amendments are PROPOSED

By a two-thirds vote of both houses of Congress

or

By a national convention called by Congress at the request of two-thirds of the state legislatures

Amendments are RATIFIED

By three-fourths of the state legislatures

or

By ratifying conventions in three-fourths of the states

.... Traditional method

———— Never used

-------- Used once (Twenty-first Amendment)

Amendments.   In the first Congress under the Constitution, the Federalists fulfilled their promise to support a bill of rights. Madison drafted the amendments, Congress proposed them, and the states ratified 10 of them in 1791. This **Bill of Rights** includes freedom of expression—speech, press, assembly, and religion (First Amendment). It also includes numerous rights for those accused of crimes—protection against unreasonable searches and seizures (Fourth), protection against compulsory self-incrimination (Fifth), guarantee of due process of law (Fifth), the right to counsel and a jury trial in criminal cases (Sixth), and protection against excessive bail and fines, and cruel and unusual punishment (Eighth). It also includes a jury trial in civil cases (Seventh).

In addition to these major rights, the Bill of Rights includes two amendments that grew out of the colonial experience with Great Britain—the right to bear arms for a militia (Second) and the right not to have soldiers quartered in homes during peacetime (Third). The Bill of Rights also includes two general amendments—a statement that the listing of these rights does not mean these are the only ones people have (Ninth) and a statement that the powers not given to the national government are reserved to the states (Tenth).

Among the other 16 amendments to the Constitution, the strongest theme is the expansion of citizenship rights:

- Abolition of slavery (Thirteenth, 1865)
- Equal protection, due process of law (Fourteenth, 1868)
- Right to vote for black men (Fifteenth, 1870)
- Direct election of senators (Seventeenth, 1913)
- Right to vote for women (Nineteenth, 1920)
- Right to vote in presidential elections for District of Columbia residents (Twenty-third, 1960)
- Abolition of poll tax in federal elections (Twenty-fourth, 1964)
- Right to vote for persons eighteen and older (Twenty-sixth, 1971).

Another theme is the increase of federal power. Many amendments, notably those regarding voting, take authority away from the states and authorize Congress to enforce these rights by "appropriate legislation."

Most amendments proposed by Congress were ratified by the states, although some were not. Recently, two proposed amendments were not ratified. One would have provided equal rights for women (this amendment will be discussed in chapter 15), and the other would have given congressional representation to the District of Columbia, as though it were a state.

Although the Constitution expressly provides for change by amendment, its ambiguity about some subjects and silence about others virtually guarantee change by interpretation and practice as well.

By Judicial Interpretation.   If there is disagreement about what the Constitution means, who is to interpret it? Although the Constitution does not say, the judicial branch has taken on this role. To decide disputes brought to them, the courts must determine what the relevant provisions of the Constitution mean. By saying the provisions mean one thing rather than another, the courts can, in effect, change the Constitution. Woodrow Wilson called the Supreme Court "a constitutional convention in continuous session." The Court has acted as a safety valve, diffusing pressure for new amendments by interpreting the Constitution in such a way as to bring about the same results as new amendments.

By Political Practice. Political practice has accounted for some very important changes. These include the rise of political parties and the demise of the Electoral College as an independent body. They also include the development of the cabinet to advise the president and the development of the committee system to operate the two houses of Congress.

The Founders would be surprised to learn that only 16 amendments, aside from the Bill of Rights, have been adopted in about 200 years. In part this is due to their wisdom, but in part it is due to changes in judicial interpretation and political practice, which have combined to create a "living Constitution."

Conclusion: Is the Constitution Responsive?

Soon after ratification, the Constitution became accepted by the people. It took on the aura of a secular Bible. People embraced it, consulted it for guidance, cited it for support, and debated the meaning of its provisions.

The Constitution has proven to be so popular that many countries have copied aspects of it. Almost all of

FOCUS ON AN ISSUE

Should We Have a Constitutional Amendment Making English the Official National Language?

The influx of immigrants in recent decades means that many Americans cannot speak English. This concern has prompted calls to make English the official national language. Groups like U.S.English and English First have sounded the alarm: "If this continues, the next American president could well be elected by people who can't read or speak English!"

Although the Constitution does not provide for an official language, 17 states, 13 of them in the last half of the 1980s, have passed laws making English their official language. Some laws have had as much effect as proclaiming a state bird, but others have had more impact. In California, some cities with large Asian populations have restricted foreign-language signs. One city council ousted librarians for buying foreign-language books and magazines. In other communities, teachers have forbidden students from speaking Spanish, even among themselves, and numerous hospitals have forbidden employees from speaking any language but English. One official reprimanded a worker who spoke Spanish to a co-worker in the hallway, while another fined workers who spoke Filipino even to patients who spoke that language.[1]

A constitutional amendment making English the official national language has been introduced in Congress. It is not clear exactly what effect the amendment would have, but election ballots and other government forms now printed in various languages probably would be printed only in English. Bilingual education programs in the schools probably would be scaled back. The amendment is not intended to restrict private use of foreign languages or their religious or ceremonial use.

Is There a Problem?

Although some immigrant communities are so large that individuals can survive without learning English, most immigrants need to learn English to function more efficiently and make themselves more employable. Moreover, society needs them to learn English because a common language allows people to settle their differences through communication and persuasion. Thus, immigrants who refuse to learn English surround themselves with "a cocoon of language from which [they] cannot escape and which others cannot penetrate."[2]

A six-year-old immigrant ponders the mysteries of English.

The problem is not a new one. In 1751 Benjamin Franklin complained,

Why should the Palatine [region in Germany] boors be suffered to swarm into our settlements, and, by herding together, establish their language and manners, to the exclusion of ours? Why should Pennsylvania, founded by the English, become a colony of aliens, who will shortly be so numerous as to Germanize us, instead of our Anglifying them?[3]

Yet we survived this and later waves of immigrants without an amendment making English the national language. In 1906, however, Congress did make the ability to speak English a requirement for naturalization.

Today's immigrants are more diverse in their origins and languages than past immigrants. Los Angeles offers election ballots in Spanish, Japanese, Chinese, Vietnamese, Korean, and Tagalog. Its county courts provide interpreters for about 80 languages. Even so, confusion occurs. A police officer testified that he had read a suspect his Miranda rights in the Tai-shan dialect of Chinese, but because

continued on next page

the judge discovered that the suspect understood only the Cantonese dialect, he had to disregard the suspect's confession.[4]

Bilingual education, which provides instruction in their native language for students who do not speak English, was proposed in the 1960s. In 1968 Congress encouraged bilingual education by providing federal funding, and in 1974 the Supreme Court, in a case brought by Chinese parents, held that schools must teach students in a language they can understand.[5] The Court said that this can be their native language or it can be English if they have been taught English. These federal actions prompted about half the states to offer bilingual programs in a total of about 80 languages, from Spanish to Yapese.

These programs are controversial, and the debate revolves around politics as much as education. Some proponents of bilingual education, especially Hispanic groups, see it as a way to preserve the students' native language and heritage. So they want it not as a temporary bridge until students learn English but as a permanent fixture for them through high school. These proponents consider it a necessary component of multiculturalism. They say that students with another native language tend to fail in school not solely or primarily because they cannot speak English but because they feel shame for not being part of the dominant group in society. Bilingual education, then, becomes a symbol of rebellion against the dominance of Anglo-Americans.[6]

Many opponents of bilingual education dismiss the need for multiculturalism and resent challenges to the dominance of traditional values. Other opponents acknowledge the benefit of maintaining students' native language and culture but say this is not as important as helping them succeed in the broader society. Yet, in all the debate, it remains unclear whether bilingual education helps or hinders students in their efforts to learn English.

Is an Amendment Necessary to Solve the Problem?

Immigrants face strong pressures to learn English. For most it is a practical necessity even without an amendment. As immigrants stay in this country longer, they are more likely to learn English. Their children and grandchildren are even more likely to do so. Contrary to some common misperceptions, this is as true for Hispanics as for past immigrants. According to one survey in south Florida, 98% of Hispanics thought it was important for their children to read and write "perfect English."[7] Cuban Americans, for example, are learning English as fast or faster than any other group of immigrants in history.[8]

Would an Amendment Be Useful For Symbolic Purposes?

Proponents of the amendment think it would be a symbol of national unity at a time when there is more diversity than ever before. They see English as one of the threads that bind Americans together. Opponents say the amendment is a reflection of xenophobia—a fear of foreigners—and would be a symbol of intolerance of diversity.

Thus, the debate is not simply over the wisest policy to encourage immigrants to learn English. In part, the debate is over the idea of assimilation itself. Proponents speak of "the melting pot," with different groups blending together, whereas opponents sometimes speak of "a stew," with different groups retaining some distinctiveness.

Although proponents of the amendment worry that the dominance of English is declining in the United States, ironically it is increasing in the rest of the world. It is in fact becoming a global language. People who do not speak each other's language increasingly use English to communicate with each other. Most countries use English in their air-traffic-control systems, and most use it to store their computer data. The European Economic Community uses English as its administrative language.[9]

Would An Amendment Create New Problems?

Although supporters believe the amendment will solve problems by encouraging immigrants to learn English, opponents believe it will create new problems. The amendment might be a poor way to say "Welcome." If the amendment breeds intolerance and divisiveness rather than unity, it could impede assimilation rather than accelerate it.

The amendment could result in more discrimination against immigrants. Abolition of bilingual ballots might disfranchise some, and abolition of bilingual government forms might make it difficult for some to receive government services for which they are eligible. The amendment also would restrict freedom of speech. A federal court in fact struck down Arizona's law as a violation of the First Amendment.

With these considerations in mind, do you think the amendment would be beneficial or not?

1. Eloise Salholz, "Say It in English," *Newsweek,* February 20, 1989, p. 23; Margaret Carlson, "Only English Spoken Here," *Time,* December 5, 1988, p. 29; Elaine Elinson, "On the Job, English Only Rules Are on the Rise," *Civil Liberties,* Fall, 1990, p. 5.
2. Rita Toften, "Letters," *Time,* September 15, 1986, p. 10.
3. Lance Morrow, "Immigrants," *Time,* July 8, 1985, p. 25.
4. Otto Friedrich, "The Changing Face of America," *Time,* July 8, 1985, p. 29.
5. *Lau v. Nichols,* 414 U.S. 563 (1974).
6. Richard Bernstein, "In U.S. Schools a War of Words," *New York Times Magazine,* October 14, 1990, p. 34; Paul Taylor, "Is Bilingual Better?" *Washington Post National Weekly Edition,* April 30, 1984.

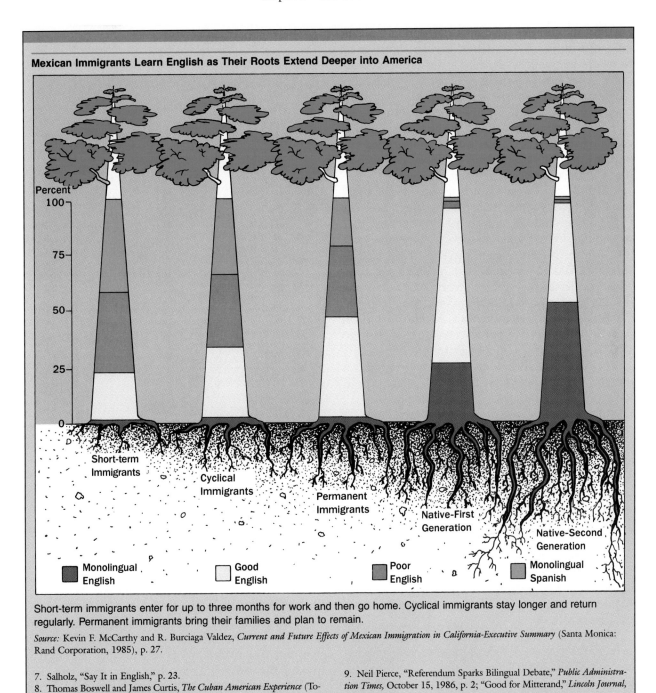

Mexican Immigrants Learn English as Their Roots Extend Deeper into America

Short-term immigrants enter for up to three months for work and then go home. Cyclical immigrants stay longer and return regularly. Permanent immigrants bring their families and plan to remain.

Source: Kevin F. McCarthy and R. Burciaga Valdez, *Current and Future Effects of Mexican Immigration in California-Executive Summary* (Santa Monica: Rand Corporation, 1985), p. 27.

7. Salholz, "Say It in English," p. 23.
8. Thomas Boswell and James Curtis, *The Cuban American Experience* (Totowa, N.J.: Rowman & Allanheld, 1983), p. 191.

9. Neil Pierce, "Referendum Sparks Bilingual Debate," *Public Administration Times,* October 15, 1986, p. 2; "Good for Mitterand," *Lincoln Journal,* June 19, 1990.

the 170-plus nations in the world today have a constitution written as a single document. Many have provisions similar to those in our Constitution. The Kenyan constitution speaks of "freedom of expression," the Costa Rican gives the "right to petition," and the West German says that "all persons shall be equal before the law." And officials and groups in, of all unlikely places, South Africa and the Soviet Union are considering provisions in our Constitution as they change theirs.[30]

But the brevity of our Constitution remains unique; with just 89 sentences, it is far shorter than those of other nations. Because it is short, it is necessarily general; because it is general, it is necessarily ambiguous; because it is ambiguous, it is necessarily open to interpretation. This provides succeeding generations the opportunity to adapt the Constitution to changing times. The longer, more detailed, and less flexible constitutions of other nations become outdated and periodically need complete revision.

In 1987 our Constitution celebrated its bicentennial as the oldest written constitution in the world. The Constitution and its governing institutions have proven responsive enough to survive. During the same 200 years, France, for example, has had 10 distinct constitutional orders, including five republics, two empires, one monarchy, one plebiscitary dictatorship, and one puppet dictatorship during World War II.

Although the Constitution is responsive enough to have survived, is it responsive enough to allow us to solve our problems? Can a constitution written by a small circle of men whose fastest mode of travel was horseback continue to serve masses of diverse people, some of whom have traveled by spaceship?

Intended to construct a government responsive to the masses of people to a limited extent, the Constitution set up a republic, which allowed the people to elect some representatives who would make their laws. This gave the people more say in government than people in other countries enjoyed at the time.

But the Constitution was intended to construct a government unresponsive to the masses of people to a large extent. It was expected to filter the public's passions and purify their selfish desires. Consequently, the Founders limited participation in government, allowing people to vote only for members of the House of Representatives—not for members of the Senate or the president.

Moreover, the Founders structured government to fragment its powers; federalism, separation of powers, and checks and balances combine to make it difficult for any one group to capture all of government. Instead, one faction might control one branch, another faction another branch, and so on, with the result a standoff. Any group that attempts to promote policies that benefit only its own members will meet resistance. It must compromise and adopt policies that benefit others too.

Since the time of the founding, changes in the Constitution, whether by amendment, interpretation,

Soon after their deaths, the Founders became venerated by the people. Here George Washington is pictured ascending to heaven.

or practice, have expanded opportunities for participation in government. But the changes have done little to modify the structure of fragmented powers, which remains the primary legacy of the Founders.

This structure has prevented many abuses of power, though it has not always worked. During the Vietnam War, for example, one branch—the presidency—exercised vast power while the others acquiesced. This structure also has provided the opportunity for one branch to pick up the slack when the others became sluggish. The overlapping of powers ensured by checks and balances allows every branch to act on virtually every issue it chooses to. In the 1950s President Eisenhower and Congress were reluctant to push for civil rights for blacks, but the Supreme Court did so by declaring segregation unconstitutional in a series of cases.

But the system's very advantage has become its primary disadvantage. In their efforts to fragment power so that no branch could accumulate too much,

Comparative Perspective: The Limits of Federalism

Federalism can help a nation deal with diversity by providing at least two levels of government, allowing groups rebuffed at one level to gain access at another. It also allows subnational units (like states and localities) to compete for power, which, as Madison argued, may deter any one group from dominating others. However, federalism is not a cure-all for problems created by diversity. Yugoslavia is a good example.

To try to grasp Yugoslavia's problems, imagine a United States where blacks live mostly in a few states that they govern, Chinese Americans in other states that they control, and whites in yet another set of states where they rule. Then imagine all blacks were Protestant, Chinese were Muslim, and whites Catholic, and that, as in fact is true today, white income was much higher than that of blacks with that of the Chinese in between. To complete this scenario, imagine that bordering on the black states was a nation of blacks and bordering on the Chinese states a country peopled by people of Chinese descent. How likely would it be that individuals in this imaginary United States would want to remain Americans? How would one design a federal system providing enough autonomy to the individual states to keep them together but not so much autonomy that the nation fragmented?

This scenario is imaginary, but Yugoslavia's problems are quite real and even more complex. Yugoslavia, formed after World War I largely out of part of the defeated Austro-Hungarian Empire, has one of the most heterogeneous populations in the world; its major population groups include Serbians, Croats, Muslims, Slovenes, Albanians, and several smaller groups, from Bulgarians to Ukrainians. The largest ethnic group, the Serbs, comprises less than 40% of the population, the next largest group, the Croats, about 20%. These ethnic groups tend to live together in territorial units. Consequently, the country of Yugoslavia is organized into six republics and two autonomous regions, each having a different major population group: most of those living in Serbia are Serbs, those in Croatia are Croats, and so on. However, ethnic conflict is exacerbated because minority ethnic groups live within some republics. For example, within Serbia and Macedonia are large groups of Albanians, many of whom speak only Albanian and whose territory lies adjacent to the country of Albania.

Ethnic conflict is also increased because religious, linguistic, economic, and political differences largely coincide with ethnic ones. Serbs are mostly members of the Eastern

continued on next page

The Constitutional Bases of Federalism

Major Features of the System

As we saw in chapter 2, the Founders were unsure how to solve the problem of national versus state powers. All wanted limited government. Although they saw federalism as one way to limit government power by dividing it, there was little debate over the concept of federalism, and the main outlines emerged only as the Founders dealt with other issues. The major features of nation-state relationships outlined by the Constitution include a strong national government, prohibition of certain powers to the states, and some limitations on national powers.

Strong National Government. Although the Founders did not all agree on how strong the national government should be, all did agree that they wanted a national government stronger than that of the Articles of Confederation. They wanted a national government able to tax without the permission of the states, and one able to carry out foreign and domestic policies without the states' consent. Thus, the Constitution grants many specific powers to Congress, including taxation and regulation of commerce, which gives tremendous power to the national government and allows it to be independent of the will of the state governments. Congress's power to make all laws **"necessary and proper,"** sometimes called the **implied powers clause,** for carrying out its specific powers also strengthened the national government. This grant

Orthodox religion, while Croats are Roman Catholic. Members of different groups also speak different languages, so Yugoslavia has four official languages—and two alphabets. Wealth is very unequally distributed among the different ethnic groups, with the northerners, including the Slovenians and Croatians, having substantially more income that the Serbs, Macedonians, and Albanians farther south. Partly as a consequence of these economic differences, the poorer Serbs cling to a Communist government in their republic, while their northern neighbors adopted non-Communist governments.

The national government's constitutional powers are weak. It is probably the most decentralized government in the world. Its major constitutional powers focus on foreign affairs, though each republic has its own foreign minister. The chief executive of the nation is actually a committee of the heads of each republic. The legislative body is composed of representatives of the legislatures in the republics. In fact, all national institutions except the army are comprised of individuals nominated or elected by the republics.

From the end of World War II the 1980s, however, the constitutionally weak national government was held together by a strong single-party system, the Communist party, and its leader, Josip Broz Tito. Loyalty to Tito and to the party tended to moderate ethnic conflict. After Tito's death in 1980, ethnic conflict worsened. With the weakening of the Communist party in Yugoslavia, as

throughout most of the rest of Eastern Europe in 1990, long-standing ethnic conflicts were further exacerbated. By 1990, violent conflict between ethnic groups increased, especially between the Serbs and Albanians and the Serbs and Croatians.

The Yugoslav federal structure has had great difficulty dealing with these rivalries. The republics are not paying their taxes to the federal government, and Serbia has imposed heavy taxes on goods "imported" from Croatia and Slovenia. The Croats, in turn, have imposed taxes on Serbs owning property in parts of Croatia. By 1991, the country appeared on the verge of civil war, and army leaders threatened to act to protect lives and property if the civilian government did not move to settle the crisis. In 1991, both Croatia and Slovenia declared their independence from Yugoslavia. Military government or civil war appear likely if independence is not acceptable to the other republics or if negotiations fail. Without a strong national party as a tie, it is difficult for Yugoslavs to find a common bond.

Sources: Bogdan Denitch, *Limits and Possibilities* (Minneapolis: University of Minnesota Press, 1990); Pedro Ramet, *Nationalism and Federalism in Yugoslavia, 1963–1983* (Bloomington: Indiana University Press, 1984); Fred Singleton, *A Short History of the Yugoslav Peoples* (Cambridge: Cambridge University Press, 1985); Stephen Engelberg, "Feuds Crippling Yugoslav Economy," *New York Times,* April 22, 1991; Steven Burg and Michael Berbaum, "Community, Integration, and Stability in Multinational Yugoslavia," *American Political Science Review* 83 (June, 1989), pp. 535–556.

of power soon was interpreted to mean that Congress could legislate in almost any area it wished.

In addition, the **supremacy clause,** which says treaties, the Constitution, and "laws made in pursuance thereof" are to be the supreme law of the land, contributed to a strong national government.

Although it was a compromise decision, a president independent of Congress and the state legislatures also strengthened the national government. The president's power to be commander in chief and to execute the laws of the United States further enlarged national powers.

Prohibition of Certain Powers to the States.   The Constitution forbids states to undertake actions that might conflict with the power of the national government; they cannot enter into treaties, keep troops or navies, make war, print or coin money or levy import or export taxes on goods. These prohibitions reaf-

firmed that the national government was to be supreme in making foreign policy and regulating interstate commerce. Under the Articles, the national government was limited in both these areas. The new Constitution also forbade states to infringe on certain rights of individuals. For example, states could not pass a law making an action a crime and then punish citizens who committed the "crime" before it was made illegal (called an *ex post facto* law).

Some Limitations on National Powers.   The Constitution prohibits the creation of new states within existing states, the combination of two states, or the change of existing state boundaries without the approval of the legislatures of the affected states.

The Tenth Amendment granted to the states and to the people those powers not granted by the Constitution to the national government. At the time, this was considered a significant limit on national powers.

Federalism and the "Mischiefs of Faction"

Probably the most influential work of American political theory was written by James Madison in Federalist Paper #10 (reprinted in the appendix to this book). This work helps explain the attraction of a federalist system for Madison and many of the other Founders.

In Federalist #10, Madison asserted that it is inevitable that factions—groups of citizens seeking some goal contrary to the rights of other citizens or to the well-being of the whole country—will threaten the stability of nations. To cure the **"mischiefs of faction"** Madison said that government had either to remove the causes of faction or control its effects.

Madison believed that the government could never remove the causes of faction because this would require changing selfish human nature, which he thought impossible. It also would require taking away freedom by outlawing opinions and strictly regulating behavior. People would inevitably have different ideas and beliefs, and government, he thought, should not try to prevent this.

Because one could not remove the causes of faction without too greatly inhibiting freedom, Madison recommended that a properly constructed government should controls its effects. If a faction were less than a majority, Madison believed that it could be controlled through majority rule, the majority defeating the minority faction. However, if the faction were a majority, then a greater problem arose, but one for which Madison had an answer.

To control a majority faction, one had only to limit the ability of a majority to carry out its wishes. Madison believed that this was impossible in a small democracy, where there is little check on a majority determined to do something. But in a large federalist system, there are many checks on a majority faction—more interests competing with each other and large distances to separate those who might scheme to deprive others of liberty. As Madison noted, "The influence of factious leaders may kindle a flame within their particular States, but will be unable to spread a general conflagration through the other States." Having many states and having them spread over a large territory were, in Madison's view, major checks against majority tyranny.

Since then, the broad construction of Congress's "necessary and proper" powers has made the Tenth Amendment inconsequential. There are periodic attempts to breathe life into this amendment, but they have thus far been largely without success.[3]

These three features—a strong national government, prohibition of certain powers to the states, and some limitations on national powers—ensured a strong national government as well as a significant role for the states. The Founders believed that this arrangement would limit the ability of any one government to tyrannize its citizens and that the diversity of interests in the system would prevent the formation of a national majority that could trample minority rights. Similarly, a central government would ensure that states could protect the rights of their citizens against arbitrary local majorities. Many believed that the primary virtue of a federal system was that the authority of government was limited because it was divided between two levels.

Interpretations of Federalism

The Founders left the exact details of the nation-state relationship vague because they could not agree on specifics. It is not surprising that different views of federalism emerged.[4]

Nation-Centered Federalism. In *The Federalist Papers,* Alexander Hamilton clearly articulated the view that national power was to be supreme. This nation-centered view of federalism rests on the assumption that the Constitution is a document ratified by the people. The states have many powers, but the national government has the ultimate responsibility for preserving the nation and the viability of the states as well. Nation-centered federalism was the view held by northerners in justifying a war to prevent the southern states from seceding in 1861.

State-Centered Federalism. Another view, later used by southerners to justify their defiance of the central government before the Civil War, held that the Constitution is a product of state action. In this view, the states created the union. State-centered federalists argue that the grant of powers to Congress is limited to those items specifically mentioned in Article I. Madison said, "The powers delegated . . . to the federal government are few and defined. Those which are to remain in the state governments are numerous and indefinite."[5] In this view, any attempt by Congress to go beyond these explicitly listed powers violates state authority.

Dual Federalism.   **Dual federalism** is the idea that the Constitution created a system in which nation and state each have separate grants of power, with each supreme in its own sphere. In this view, the two levels of government are essentially equal. Their differences derive from their different jurisdictions, not from any inequality.

Cooperative Federalism.   The term **cooperative federalism** refers to the continuing cooperation among federal, state, and local officials in carrying out the business of government. The term encompasses the relationship of federal and state officials when distributing payments to farmers, providing welfare services, planning highways, organizing centers for the elderly, and carrying out all the functions that the national and state governments jointly fund and organize. It also refers to informal cooperation in locating criminals, tracking down mysterious diseases, and many other activities. A person speaking of cooperative federalism is not evaluating the legalistic relationship of national and state governments but rather referring to day-to-day joint activities.

Changes in Federalism and the Growth of Government

In 200 years, our national government has grown from a few hundred people with relatively limited impact on the residents of 13 small states to a government employing millions, affecting the daily lives of most of the population of more than 240 million people. This transformation is closely related to the changing way in which Americans understand the federal system.

Over the years, the dominant interpretations of federalism have shifted among the nation-centered, state-centered, and dual views. Changing interpretations have reflected court opinions, pressing economic needs, the philosophies of those in the executive and legislative branches, and changing public demands.

The most general trend has been away from state-centered and toward nation-centered federalism, but there have been significant shorter-term trends in the opposite direction. Moreover, the term cooperative federalism has come into use, since World War II, to describe everyday relations between national and state officials.

Early Nationalist Period

Very soon after the Constitution was ratified, the federal courts became the arbiters of the Constitution. (Note that we are using "federal" to mean "national," a confusing but common usage. "Federal government" normally means "national government.") John Marshall, chief justice of the United States from 1801 to 1835, was a firm nationalist, and the decisions of his court emphasized the need for a strong national government. The Marshall-led Supreme Court not only held that decisions of the state courts could be overturned by the federal courts, it also, in the case of *McCulloch v. Maryland,* gave approval to the broad interpretation of Congress's implied powers in the Constitution.

McCulloch v. Maryland.   The broad interpretation of the clause giving Congress the right to make all laws "necessary and proper" to carry out the powers that the Constitution gives it grew out of a case involving the establishment of a national bank.

Ironically, it was John Calhoun, later to become the leading states' rights advocate, who introduced a bill to charter a Bank of the United States (B.U.S.). The bill passed, and in 1817 the bank went into business, setting up branches in cities across the country. However, it was immediately unpopular because it competed with smaller banks operating under state laws and because some of its branches engaged in reckless and even fraudulent practices.

In an attempt to diminish the competition from the B.U.S., the government of Maryland levied a tax on the notes issued by the Baltimore branch of the bank. The B.U.S. refused to pay, but the Maryland state courts upheld the right of Maryland to tax the bank. The case then went to the Supreme Court.

In *McCulloch v. Maryland,* John Marshall wrote one of his most influential decisions.[6] Pronouncing the tax unconstitutional, Marshall wrote that "the power to tax involves the power to destroy." The states

In a spirit of optimism amidst the turmoil of the Civil War, Congress in 1862 established federal support for the land grant colleges, a striking example of intergovernmental cooperation in the nineteenth century. Today many of these institutions are among our finest universities. Here, students plow on the campus of Pennsylvania State University, one of the first land grant colleges.

should not have the power to destroy the bank, he stated, because the bank was "necessary and proper" to carry out Congress's powers to collect the taxes, borrow money, regulate commerce, and raise an army. Marshall argued that if the goal of the legislation is legitimate and constitutional, "all means which are appropriate, which are plainly adapted to that end, which are not prohibited, but consistent with the letter and spirit of the Constitution, are constitutional."

Thus, Marshall interpreted "necessary" quite loosely. The bank was probably not necessary, but it was "useful." This interpretation of the implied powers clause allowed Congress to wield much more authority than the Constitution gave it explicitly.

Although there was some negative reaction—"a deadly blow has been struck at the sovereignty of the states," said one Baltimore newspaper—the Court maintained its strongly nationalistic position as long as Marshall was chief justice.

Early Growth of Government.   At the same time the courts were interpreting national powers broadly, the national government was exercising its powers on a rather small scale. The federal government had only 1,000 employees in the administration of George Washington, and this number increased to 33,000 during the presidency of James Buchanan 70 years later. It raised relatively little revenue. But state governments were also small and had limited functions. There were only a few federal-state cooperative activities. For example, the federal government gave land to the states to support education and participated in joint federal-state-private ventures, such as canal-building projects initiated by the states.

Thus, the early nationalist period was characterized by the growth of nation-centered federalism in legal doctrine, by small-scale state and national government, and by a few intergovernmental cooperative activities responding to the needs of an expanding nation.

Pre–Civil War Period

In 1836, the Court began to interpret the Tenth Amendment as a strict limitation on federal powers, holding that powers to provide for public health, safety, and order were *exclusively* powers of the state government, not of the national government. This dual federalism interpretation eroded some of the nation-centered federal interpretations of the Marshall Court while continuing to uphold the rights of the federal courts to interpret the Constitution.

At the same time, champions of the state-centered view of federalism were gaining ascendance in the South. Southern leaders feared that the federal government, dominated by the increasingly populous North, would regulate or even abolish slavery. John Calhoun, one of the leading proponents for the state-centered view, even went so far as to say that a state could nullify laws of Congress (the doctrine of nullification). According to Calhoun, a state could withdraw from the Union if it wished. When the South did secede from the Union in 1861, it called itself the Confederate States of America, emphasizing the supremacy of the states embedded in a confederal system.

After the Civil War, the vision of state-centered federalism largely lost its credibility. Some southern segregationists tried to revive the idea in the 1950s and 1960s as a protest against federal laws and actions to further the civil rights of blacks; the Alabama legislature even passed a nullification resolution in 1950. However, the idea had lost its legitimacy for most people.

The Civil War to the New Deal

After the Civil War, vast urbanization and industrialization took place throughout the United States. Living and working conditions for many city dwellers were appalling. Adults as well as children who moved into the cities often took jobs in sweatshops—factories where they worked long hours in unsafe conditions for low pay.

Spurred by revelations of these unsafe and degrading conditions, states and sometimes Congress tried to regulate working conditions, working hours, and pay through such means as child labor and industrial safety laws. Beginning in the 1880s, a conservative Supreme Court used the dual federalism doctrine to rule unconstitutional many of these attempts. It often decided that Congress and the states had overstepped their powers. From 1874 to 1937, the Supreme Court found 50 federal and 400 state laws unconstitutional.[7] Before the Civil War, in contrast, the Court overturned only 2 congressional and 60 state laws.

At the same time that the Court was limiting both state and national action in regulating business and industry, both levels of government were slowly expanding. The revenues of both grew—the United States through an income tax finally ratified in 1913, the states and localities through gasoline and cigarette taxes, higher property taxes, and some state income taxes. Federal support for state programs also grew through land and case grants given by the federal government to the states.[8] By the late 1920s, however, most governmental functions still rested primarily in state and local hands. The states were clearly the dominant partner in providing most services, from health and sanitation to police and fire protection. The federal government provided few direct services to individuals, nor did it regulate their behavior. The Great Depression signaled a dramatic shift in this arrangement.

The New Deal

To grasp the scope of the changes that have taken place in our federal structure between 1930 and today, consider the report of a sociologist who studied community life in Muncie, Indiana.[9] In 1924 the federal government in Muncie was symbolized by little more than

The schools, roads, airports, and post offices in many towns were built in the 1930s by civilians put to work in the Works Progress Administration (WPA). Though the term "boondoggle" was coined in reference to some WPA projects, the agency was successful in putting millions to work and improving the nation's public buildings, roads, and bridges.

President Roosevelt's confidence, along with the hopes people had in his New Deal programs, led to public support for the expansion of the role of the federal government.

the post office and the American flag. Today, two-thirds of the households in Muncie depend in part on federal funds—federal employment, Social Security, welfare payments, food stamps, veterans benefits, student scholarships and loans, Medicare and Medicaid, and many other smaller programs.

In large part, the Great Depression brought about these changes. During the stock market crash of 1929, wealthy people became poor overnight. In the depths of the Depression one-fourth of the workforce was unemployed, and banks failed daily.

Unlike today, there was no systematic national program of relief for the unemployed then—no unemployment compensation, no food stamps, no welfare, nothing to help put food on the table and pay the rent. Millions were hungry, homeless, and hopeless. States and localities, which had the responsibility for providing relief to the poor, were overwhelmed; they did not have the funds or organizational resources to cope with the millions needing help. And private charities did not have enough resources to even begin to assume the burden.

The magnitude of the economic crisis led to the election of a Democrat, Franklin Delano Roosevelt, in 1932. He formulated, and Congress passed, a program called the **New Deal.** Its purpose was to stimulate economic recovery and aid the victims of the depression who were unemployed, hungry, and often in ill health. New Deal legislation regulated many ac-

Pioneers, Cowboys, and Federal Aid

When we think of "winning the West," we imagine hardy pioneers fighting brave Indians and being rescued by the dashing cavalry. We rarely think of the role of the federal government. President Reagan, for example, liked to recall the pioneers "settling the prairies and crossing the mountains without the help of the federal government. . . . They didn't need an urban renewal program or community development grant."[1]

The reality, however, is quite different. The federal government financed much of the exploration and settling of the West. The Lewis and Clark expedition, for example, was commissioned and financed by the Jefferson administration. The federal government also funded later explorers, from Zebulon Pike (memorialized at Pike's Peak) to John Frémont.

Once the West was explored, the government helped pay for its settlement. Settlers demanded federal troops, and later road builders, doctors, and mail service—all provided by the federal government. In a huge giveaway in 1862, the federal government offered 160 acres of free land to any settler willing to live on it for five years. This land had previously been surveyed and mapped, courtesy of the federal government. Washington later gave away more land, this time to railroads building a continental railway system to link settlers in the West with the rest of the United States.

Although many hardy pioneers deserve recognition for their endurance and bravery, the story of winning the West would be incomplete without acknowledging the federal government's role. The U.S. Cavalry was not the only federal agency that came to the pioneer's assistance!

1. Cited in Jon Margolis, "The Wild West Took Government Handouts Too," *Chicago Tribune*, July 25, 1980.

tivities of business and labor, set up a welfare system for the first time, and began on a large scale federal-state cooperation in funding and administering programs through federal **grants-in-aid.** These grants-in-aid provided federal money to states (and occasionally to local governments) to set up programs to help people—for example, the aged poor or the unemployed.

These measures had strong political support, although they were opposed by many business and conservative groups and initially by the Supreme Court, which was still following the dual federalism doctrine.

But after the reelection of Roosevelt in 1936, the Court became more favorable toward New Deal legislation, and later resignations of two conservative judges ensured that the Court would be sympathetic to the New Deal (see chapter 13 for more on the Court and the New Deal).

The Court decisions approving New Deal legislation were, in a sense, a return to the nation-centered federalism of John Marshall's day. But although the Supreme Court ratified much of the New Deal, it also approved more sweeping *state* regulations of business and labor than had the more conservative pre–New Deal Court. Thus, the change in court philosophy did not enlarge the federal role at the expense of the powers of the state. *It enlarged the powers of both state and federal government.* In doing so, it responded to preferences on the part of taxpayers for a more active government to cope with the tragedy of the depression. The limited government desired by the Founders became less limited as both state and national government grew.

Changes in patterns of taxing and spending soon reflected the green light given to federal involvement with the states and localities. As figure 2 indicates, the federal share of spending for domestic needs (omitting spending for the military) nearly tripled from 17% in 1929, before the New Deal, to 47% in 1939, a decade later. The state share stayed constant while the local share dropped dramatically. Local governments did not spend less, but the state and federal governments spent more. Likewise state spending increased, but not as much as federal spending. The federal government raised more revenue and in turn gave much of it to the states and localities in the form of grants-in-aid to carry out programs such as unemployment compensation, free school lunches, emergency welfare relief, farm surpluses to the needy, and other programs.

The New Deal brought a dramatic change in the relationship of the national government to its citizens. Before this, when the national government directly touched the lives of citizens, it usually was to give or sell them something, such as land for settlers or subsidies for businesses helping develop the frontier.[10] With New Deal programs the federal government directly affected the lives of its citizens through its regulations (of banks and working conditions, for example) and its policies designed to protect the poor (such as Social Security and Aid to Dependent Children).

After the New Deal

During the years that followed the initiation of the New Deal, federal aid to states increased steadily but not dramatically. But federal support to the states carried conditions. For example, local administrators of Aid to Dependent Children programs had to be hired through a merit system, not because of political or personal connections. Construction funds for highways could be spent only on highways whose designs met professional standards. Thus, federal "strings" accompanied federal money.

By the 1950s, some public officials became uneasy about the growing federal involvement in so many state and local programs. Yet under President Eisenhower, a Republican concerned about the growth of federal involvement, many new federal grants-in-aid to the states were added, ranging from the massively expensive interstate highway program to collegiate programs in science, engineering, and languages. Federal grants-in-aid spending nearly tripled during his administration (1952–1960).

The 1960s witnessed an explosion in federal programs. Mostly a consequence of President Lyndon Johnson's Great Society, new programs of federal aid

Figure 2 ■ Government Spending
Before and After the New Deal

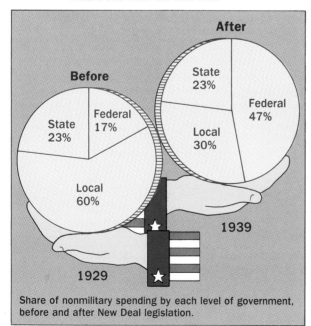

Share of nonmilitary spending by each level of government, before and after New Deal legislation.

Source: "Significant Features of Fiscal Federalism," *Advisory Commission on Intergovernmental Relations* (Washington, D.C.: U.S. Government Printing Office, 1979), p. 7.

The siting of nuclear waste dumps raises many issues. We will deal with those involving low-level waste, that is, items with relatively low levels of radioactivity such as clothing and tools used in the production or use of nuclear power. (High-level waste mainly consists of spent fuel from nuclear power and weapons plants.) Some low-level waste controversies have to do with the potential hazards of such dumps, a hotly contested issue. But the primary issues we examine here deal not with health and safety but with federalism.

Should the Federal Government or the State Governments Choose the Sites?

Those in favor of letting the federal government decide where to place the sites argue that the potential health hazards, should nuclear waste contaminate soil, water, or air, are interstate in nature. Radiation contamination in the air or water would not respect state boundaries. No one state could cope with contamination alone. Moreover, the benefits from the use of nuclear materials (such as the electricity generated by nuclear power plants) are not confined to the states where nuclear waste occurs.

Leaving the decision to the states could lead to delay and may lead to unacceptable risk. Some states, especially those that are highly urbanized, have no appropriate sites for hazardous waste. Other states have appropriate sites, but state officials delay making decisions that will be unpopular to localities near where the sites are to be located. States may try to enter into agreements with other states for access to their facilities, but there is no incentive for a state to take another's wastes. The ultimate result of a state-by-state approach may be too many sites (because each state eventually would have to have one), each meeting different safety standards.

Defenders of a state role in nuclear waste dump decisions point out that state action might be as fast as federal.

It took years for the federal government to develop dump sites for high-level radioactive wastes, largely because the same NIMBY sentiments permeating negotiations among states also affect negotiations within Congress.

Supporters of a strong state role also argue that sites for low-level nuclear waste should be acceptable to state and local communities. State decision makers are closer to the local communities that will be affected.

Should Both the States and the Federal Government Be Involved?

In response to these points of view, Congress developed a compromise requiring states to have an acceptable disposal site by 1993. States could choose a site within their borders, or they could form interstate compacts to pool their resources to build waste sites. Forty-two states have formed compacts. A few, such as Texas, New York, and Massachusetts, have decided to go it alone, while others have not decided what to do.

The federal mandate to the states is a middle ground between letting each state decide for itself what to do and having the federal government make all the decisions. The compromise allows states to have some say in where the sites in their region will be located while forcing them to do something about a problem that can no longer be avoided.

Defenders of the federal plan believe it is a good compromise. The federal government itself did not have to locate these dumps, thus saving federal officials the agony of deciding what communities would be the unlucky recipients. Some state officials were attracted to the compact idea, figuring that in a multistate compact, there would be a good chance that their state would be able to ship its waste elsewhere. And most citizens were not opposed to the compacts because they did not know at the time where the sites would be. *continued on next page*

---

each state decides whether to enforce the standard itself or let the federal government do it. For example, Congress established surface mining regulations that outline detailed standards that coal mining operators must meet. States that wish to regulate these mines themselves submit plans that meet federal standards. If a state decides not to regulate, if its plan does not meet federal standards, or if the state does not carry out the plan satisfactorily, the federal agency in charge does the regulating itself.[16] This joint activity is found in

several areas, including occupational safety and environmental regulation.

Federal Mandates. Sometimes the federal government will direct states to do something. This is called a mandate. For example, in 1984 Congress passed legislation requiring states to deal with the problem of divorced parents who are not paying child support. Most children of divorce do not receive their court-ordered child support. Some receive nothing, others

The plan's opponents are largely those who believe the country will not need as many dumps as the plan is leading to and those who do not want the dumps in their states or localities. NIMBY sentiments were aroused as soon as the compacts began to decide where to put their dumps. In several compacts no state has agreed to be the dump site for an entire region, and the process of site selection has fallen behind the federal schedules. In states designated as dump sites, such as Illinois, Michigan, Nebraska, and North Carolina, counties and communities have mobilized to fight against location in their areas. For that reason, sites have been chosen only in two states and no licenses to construct and operate the sites have been approved.[1]

Should Citizens Have the Right to Keep Radioactive Waste Dumps from Their Communities?

If both the federal and state governments are involved, where does that leave people in communities who do not want to live near radioactive waste, no matter how "low level"?

Most of us value our democratic system and believe in majority rule. Presumably, then, if a majority of citizens do not want a particular enterprise near their community, they should be able to exclude it. As one citizen protesting a waste site near her community put it, "The risk would be ours. The choice should be ours."[2]

Indeed, local citizens are acting to preserve their communities from unwanted activities of all sorts: "Developers of everything from hotel and airport extensions to soup kitchens and McDonald's restaurants have met the NIMBY squads. . . . NIMBY's organize, march, sue and petition to block [those] they think are threatening them." And NIMBYs often block housing for the poor, halfway homes for the mentally retarded, and other social service facilities that communities or neighborhoods believe will bring in "undesirable people."[3]

In all of these cases, the concept of majority rule is ambiguous. There is not one majority, but many—local, state, regional, and national. Which one, or ones, should rule? Normally local majorities do not have veto power over decisions made at the state, regional, and national levels. But when local residents believe that their quality of life will be harmed by the possibility of contamination from hazardous waste, it is difficult not to be sympathetic.

As with many other kinds of political decisions, those with the least political clout are most likely to get stuck with undesirable outcomes. Rural communities in the South and Midwest and communities with older, poorer, and less-educated populations tend to resist undesirable projects less than others, sometimes because they are desperate for any kind of economic development, and sometimes because they have less political clout to veto projects. This means that siting of waste dumps and other undesirable facilities is likely to occur near people who have little political power.[4]

1. William Robbins, "Most Governors Stalled, Keep Dumps Out," *Nebraska Observer*, November 2, 1990, p. 3 (from *New York Times*).
2. A. J. Laukaitis, "Compacts Face New Challenge," *Lincoln Star*, February 12, 1989, p. 1.
3. William Glaberson, "Coping in the Age of 'Nimby,'" *New York Times*, June 19, 1988, Section 3, p. 1.
4. Ibid., p. 25.

less than ordered. To remedy this, and reduce the proportion of children living in poverty, the federal government required the states to deduct child support from the wages of parents who fall behind on payments. The state is also to deduct payments automatically from paychecks of fathers of children whose mothers are on welfare.[17] This federal legislation also required the states to develop nonbinding minimum guidelines for child support to help judges and lawyers in divorce cases determine what is reasonable. States that fail to carry out these mandates risk losing the federal contributions to their welfare funds.

In a sense, of course, this legislation is part of the grant-in-aid system, and grants are the "carrot" that will propel states to comply with the wishes of Congress. But the major rationale for the legislation was not to provide new grants to the states, although some money will be made available to them. Rather, the legislation was designed to force the states to deal with a pressing public problem that they were not adequately addressing—the increasing number of children living in poverty—by requiring more support from their fathers (or, in a few cases, mothers).

Some mandates can be a huge burden on state finances. Since the 1980s the federal government has reduced aid to states but saddled them with new fiscal responsibilities, such as increased coverage of Medicaid benefits. States have responded by cutting benefit levels or throwing many formerly eligible people out of programs such as Medicaid and unemployment insurance.

A little-known example of federal-state-local cooperation is firefighting in wilderness areas. In 1988, more than 15,000 firefighters converged to fight summer fires in Yellowstone and surrounding areas. Led by members of the U.S. Forest Service and other federal agencies, the firefighters were sent by state and local governments of every state.

Interstate Relations

Constitutional Mandates.   The Constitution established rules governing states' relationships with each other. One important provision is the **full faith and credit clause,** which requires states to recognize each other's contracts. If you marry in Ohio, Pennsylvania must recognize your marriage. The Constitution also provides that if a fugitive from justice flees from one state to another, he or she is supposed to be extradited, that is, sent back to the state with jurisdiction. Usually this is routine, but occasionally people fleeing from the law will arouse some sympathy (perhaps the decision to arrest was racially motivated, for example) and put the governor of the state in which they took refuge in the embarrassing position of challenging the motives or procedures of officials in another state.

Voluntary Cooperation.   Most state-to-state interaction is informal and voluntary, with state officials consulting with officials in other states about common problems and states borrowing ideas from one another. A justice of the Supreme Court, Oliver Wendell Holmes, indicated that states are "laboratories for . . . novel social and economic experiments without risk to the rest of the country." States can innovate, and other states can try out these ideas without having a national policy.

Most regions of the nation have their own formal and informal networks. For example, governors meet regularly to talk about problems common to their region. New ideas and policies developed in one state are likely to spread to neighboring states with similar problems. Sometimes cooperative groups of state officials are set up for very specific purposes. For example, the Western Governors' International Market Development Project was designed to open steam coal markets in Asia.[18] Sometimes states enter into formal agreements, called interstate compacts, to deal with a common problem—operating a port or allocating water from a river basin, for example.

Interstate Competition.   In recent years, states from the Sunbelt (the West and the South) have joined to promote policies of special interest to their growing regions. Faced with economic decline, the Frostbelt states (the East and industrial Midwest) also have organized a lobby to direct more federal aid to their part of the country and to increase awareness of their regional needs.

Critics of the federal grant system have argued that federal grants have stimulated the decline of the East and industrial Midwest at the expense of the West and South. In general, this is not true. Although some states in the Sunbelt have received more federal grant money than their residents paid in taxes, this is also true of about the same proportion of Frostbelt states.[19] In fact, federal grants are largely determined by population, which explains more than 95% of the variation in the amounts of federal grants that each state receives.[20]

The Sunbelt states receive more federal money not from federal grants but primarily from military spending (and in the Southwest, spending for projects bringing water to residents and businesses). In one recent year, the Defense Department alone spent in California more than three times as much as produced by California's large agricultural industry and one and a half times as much as its tourism business.[21]

Changing economic patterns and an overall loss of economic competitiveness by the United States in the world market have stimulated vigorous competition among the states to attract new businesses and jobs. They advertise the advantages of their states to prospective new businesses: low taxes, good climate, a skilled workforce, low wages, and little government regulation. This growing competition prompts states to give tax advantages and other financial incentives to businesses willing to relocate there.

Critics believe that these offers serve mostly to erode a state's tax base and have little impact on most business relocation decisions. Evidence indicates that low taxes are not the primary reason for business relocation.[22] Nevertheless, without some special break for business, states now feel at a competitive disadvantage in recruiting them.

Interest groups, business magazines, and individual researchers contribute to state competitiveness by ranking the states on indicators purporting to measure business climate and quality of life (see table 2). These rankings, often widely publicized by the media, intensify competition among states who are trying to "look good" for business relocation and tourism. Business interests use rankings to pressure states to adopt legislation more favorable to business. Liberal organizations tend to rank states highly that have extensive public services; conservatives give high marks to those with low taxes. The relative weight of taxes and public services against business decisions to relocate or expand is unclear.

Table 2 ■ Some State Rankings

	State Ranked	
	Highest	**Lowest**
Violent and property crimes	Florida	North Dakota
Alcohol consumption	Nevada	Utah
Business climate	Massachusetts	Alabama
Library book circulation	Iowa	Oklahoma
Percent of people of English descent	Utah	North Dakota

Source: Jerry Hagstrom and Robert Guskind, "Playing the State Ranking Game—A New Pastime Catches On," *National Journal* June 30, 1984, pp. 1270–72; Deborah Kasouf, "State Economic Index Adds Fuel to Debate," *Public Administration Times,* April 15, 1987, p. 12.

Wyoming served as an "experimental laboratory" by allowing women to vote long before the Nineteenth Amendment granted all women that right. Here Wyoming women are pictured voting in the 1888 presidential election.

Conclusion: Is Federalism Responsive?

Across the United States, our beliefs in democracy, freedom, and equality bind us together. In many ways we are becoming more alike, as rapid transportation, television and other forms of instant communication, fast-food franchises, hotel chains, and other nationwide businesses bring about an increasing similarity in what we think about, our tastes in culture and food, and even political activities. But to say that Alabama is more like New York that is used to be is certainly not to say they are alike. Our federal system helps us accommodate this diversity by allowing both state and federal governments a role in making policy.

Our Founders probably did not foresee a federal system like the one we have now; the federal government has surpassed the states in power and scope of action. Yet one of the paradoxes of our system is that as the national government has gained extraordinary power, so have the states and localities. All levels of government are stronger than in the eighteenth century. Federal power *and* state power have grown hand in hand.

It is probably foolish to pretend to know how the Founders might deal with our complex federal system. However, many of them were quite astute politicians who would undoubtedly recognize that our system evolved because various groups over time demanded national action. Yet we continue to believe in local control and grass-roots government. Our system is a logical outcome of our contradictory impulses for national solutions and local control.

Is such a complex system responsive? It is very responsive in that groups and individuals making a demand that is rejected at one level of government can go to another level. The federal system creates multiple points of access, each with power to satisfy political demands. Yet the system is less responsive in that the same multiple levels and points of access also block demands. Civil rights groups, for example, were able to win voting rights for blacks in most states before the 1960s. But they were still blocked in several states until the national government acted. Thus federalism creates opportunities for influence, but it also creates possibilities for roadblocks to achieving national political action. This, of course, is what Madison foresaw.

EPILOGUE

A Conservative Votes to Expand Federal Influence on Drinking Ages

Jesse Helms joined 80 other senators in passing the bill. Only 16 senators dissented.[23] Although the expansion of federal power to regulate drinking ages would seem to contradict the principles of Helms and other conservatives in the Republican-controlled Senate, support for the bill was overwhelming in both parties. The bill was passed by a voice vote in the House and signed into law by another leading Republican conservative, Ronald Reagan.

Those who might otherwise resist the expansion of federal power voted for this bill because they believed it offered a way to reduce highway deaths. By raising the legal drinking age, the number of teenaged drunk drivers would be reduced, they hoped. They may also have voted for the bill because of the overwhelming public support for raising the drinking age (79%, including 61% of 18–24-year-olds favored such a move).[24]

Although the funds spent in this bill are minimal, the decision to fund the program in a time of budgetary scarcity illustrates why and how federal programs have grown over the years. Conservatives as well as liberals often see the federal government as the appropriate agent to carry out what they believe are worthy policies. Resistance to a bigger federal government takes second place to a desired policy objective. In this light, big government is bad only when it wants to do something you do not want it to do.

KEY TERMS

federalism
unitary system
confederal system
political culture
"necessary and proper"
implied powers clause
supremacy clause
dual federalism
cooperative federalism

"mischiefs of faction"
McCulloch v. Maryland
New Deal
grants-in-aid
new federalism
general revenue sharing
block grants
full faith and credit clause

FURTHER READING

Thomas Anton, *American Federalism and Public Policy* (Philadelphia: Temple University Press, 1989). *An overview of our current federal system and how it shapes public policy.*

Kenneth Davis, *The New Deal Years* (New York: Random House, 1986). *A voluminous account of how Roosevelt shaped the New Deal, and how it changed the nature of government.*

Daniel Elazar, *American Federalism: A View from the States,* 3rd ed. (New York: Harper & Row, 1984). *Explores the development of intergovernmental relations and examines American political cultures.*

Paul Peterson, Barry Rabe, and Kenneth Wong, *When Federalism Works* (Washington, D.C.: Brookings, 1986). *Challenges prevailing wisdom to argue that most federal grant programs work.*

Jeffrey Pressman and Aaron Wildavsky, *Implementation* (Berkeley, Calif.: University of California Press, 1973). *The difficulties of translating federal laws into working programs when dealing with a multiplicity of state and local governments.*

John Steinbeck, *The Grapes of Wrath* (New York: Viking, 1939). *A novel portraying the conditions facing the country that set the stage for the New Deal.*

NOTES

1. Daniel Elazar, *American Federalism: A View from the States,* 3rd ed. (New York: Harper & Row, 1984).

2. Paul Taylor, "End of the Louisiana Hayride," *Washington Post National Weekley Edition,* March 18, 1985, p. 13.

3. A 1976 Supreme Court decision used the Tenth Amendment as a reason to forbid the federal government to extend minimum wage and hour laws to state and local government employees. See *National League of Cities v. Usery,* 426 U.S. 833 (1976). This decision was partially overruled in 1985. See *Garcia v. San Antonio Metropolitan Transit Authority,* 83 L.Ed. 2d 1016 (1985).

4. The following discussion is drawn from Richard Leach, *American Federalism* (New York: W. W. Norton, 1970), chapter 1.

5. James Madison, Alexander Hamilton, and John Jay, *The Federalist Papers,* #45. Several editions.

6. *McCulloch v. Maryland,* 4 Wheat. 316 (1819).

7. Alfred Kelly and Winfred Harbeson, *The American Constitution: Its Origins and Development* (New York: W. W. Norton, 1976).

8. Daniel Elazar, *The American Partnership* (Chicago: University of Chicago Press, 1962).

9. Perhaps because he is a sociologist (!), Theodore Caplan did not fully appreciate the extent of federal involvement in Muncie, even in 1924 — the support of veterans, schools, roads, and hospitals by federal land grants. Nevertheless, his major point is valid: the federal presence there was nothing compared to now. Caplan is quoted in Daniel Walker, *Toward a Functioning Federalism* (Cambridge, Mass.: Winthrop, 1981), pp. 3–4.

10. Theodore Lowi, *The Personal President* (Ithaca, N.Y.: Cornell University Press, 1985).

11. See, for example, Julie Rovner, "Deep Schisms Still Imperil Welfare Overhaul," *Congressional Quarterly Weekly Report 46* (June 18, 1988): 1647–50. See also Timothy G. O'Rourke and Rickey Vallier, "Resurgent Governors in the Federal System," *The Political Science Teacher* 1 (Fall 1988): 5–7.

12. W. John Moore, "Stopping the States," *National Journal,* July 21, 1990, p. 1758.

13. Paul Peterson, Barry Rabe, and Kenneth Wong, *When Federalism Works* (Washington, D.C.: Brookings, 1986). See also John Schwartz, *America's Hidden Success,* 2nd ed. (New York: W. W. Norton, 1988).

14. Martha Derthick, "American Federalism: Madison's Middle Ground in the 1980's," *Public Administration Review* 47 (January/February, 1987): 66–74.

15. Neil Berch, "Why Do Some States Play the Federal Aid Game Better than Others?" *American Politics Quarterly,* forthcoming, 1992.

16. Frank Thompson and Michael Scicchitano, "State Implementation Effort and Federal Regulatory Policy: The Case of Occupational Safety and Health," *Journal of Politics* 47 (1985): 686–703.

17. See Mary Ann Glendon, *Abortion and Divorce in Western Law* (Cambridge, Mass.: Harvard University Press, 1987), pp. 87–88.

18. John Kincaid, "The American Governors in International Affairs," *Publius* 14 (July 1984): 107.

19. Tax Foundation, Inc., reported in *National Journal,* June 11, 1983.

20. Gary Copeland and Kenneth J. Meier, "Pass the Biscuits Pappy: Congressional Decision Making and Federal Grants," *American Politics Quarterly* 12 (January 1984): 3–21.

21. Neal Peirce, "The Last Great Pork Barrel," *Lincoln Sunday Journal-Star,* June 8, 1986.

22. Enid F. Beaumont and Harold Hovey, "State, Local and Federal Development Policies: New Federalism Patterns, Chaos, or What?" *Public Administration Review* 45 (March/April 1985): 327–32; Barry Rubin and C. Kurt Zarn, "Sensible State and Local Development," *Public Administration Review* 45 (March/April 1985): 333–39.

23. *Congressional Quarterly Weekly Report,* June 30, 1984, pp. 1557–58 and 1580.

24. George Gallup, "79% Back Higher Drinking Age," *Lincoln Sunday Journal-Star,* July 1, 1984, p. 3A.

PART TWO

Links Between
People and Government

Public Opinion

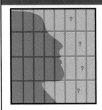
Should the President Launch a Military Strike?

You are George Bush. It is January 16, 1991, and you are faced with the decision whether to authorize military action against Iraq. The previous August, Iraq invaded its small neighboring nation of Kuwait and incorporated it as a new province. In the following weeks, you dispatched over 200,000 American troops to Saudi Arabia, which borders Iraq. And, you proposed economic sanctions against Iraq (not allowing goods to go in or out of the country), hoping that Iraq would eventually withdraw from Kuwait.

Initially, your publicly stated goal, and that of the other nations sending troops to the area, was to insure that Iraq did not invade Saudi Arabia and other oil-producing states in the region. But privately, with U.S. military leaders, you began preparations for military action. Your goal was not only to force Iraq to withdraw from Kuwait but to topple the government of Saddam Hussein, its leader, and weaken its military forces so the country could not be a threat in the region for years. Thus, after the November congressional elections, you doubled American troop strength to over 400,000.

Part of the preparation for war was to convince the American public that war was the right thing. Thus, between August and January, you worked hard at influencing public opinion. At first, this was rather difficult because we had supported Iraq in its earlier war with Iran. We, and other Western nations, sold Iraq weapons and overlooked its use of chemical weapons against Iran and some of its own people. But Iraq was not a salient issue for most Americans, and so you felt you could have a big influence on how the public thinks about Iraq.

As a way of shaping U.S. public opinion, as well as legitimizing military force to the rest of the world, you asked the United Nations to authorize the use of force against Iraq. After intense lobbying by you and Secretary of State James Baker, the United Nations

Security Council set a deadline of January 15 for an Iraqi withdrawal. The U.N. resolutions also approved the use of military force after the 15th if Iraq refused to withdraw. The public supported the U.N. resolutions. Many hoped that economic sanctions would succeed and eliminate the necessity of war. Indeed, public opinion polls have shown that a majority want to give sanctions time to work.

Protesters question the president's motives.

To convince the public that war is necessary, you warned that the continued availability of cheap oil was in jeopardy. If Iraq were to take over another oil-producing country, such as Saudi Arabia, it might dominate the world's oil market. Higher prices would be detrimental to our economy as well as to those of other developed countries. But this argument seemed remote to the public. Moreover, it gave rise to protestors' insistence that there be "no blood for oil." The goal did not seem to justify the price. Because of traditional American views on foreign policy, it is hard to convince the public to embark on a major war purely for national economic policies. It is easier if leaders can cite moral reasons. Then the war becomes a crusade, a "good war."

You did argue that we had an obligation to protect small countries from being taken over by neighboring dictatorships. But few Americans came from Kuwait and few others knew much about the country. Indeed, some commentators who did know more about it questioned whether it was truly a nation—or merely "an oil corporation with a flag." It is a country ruled by a large family and many lifelong residents are not even allowed citizenship. In any event, many Americans expressed doubts about whether we should be the world's police force, coming to the aid of every small country unable to defend itself.

To evoke a moral justification, you also spoke of establishing a "new world order." Perhaps the time had finally arrived when many nations would come together to punish a bully in their midst, signaling others that such actions would not be tolerated. Perhaps, this could even lead ultimately to peace in the strife-torn Middle East. This vision inspired some Americans, but you did not articulate it clearly, so it was lost on many others.

You also said that we needed to protect our troops who were already in the Middle East near the Iraqi border. But many Americans remembered this justification for escalating the Vietnam War, and the idea that you would send more troops in order to protect the troops you had already sent rang hollow.

Finally, in casting about for a justification that would resonate with the public, you mentioned Iraq's potential nuclear capability. Iraqi scientists were trying to produce nuclear weapons. American officials predicted that they might be able to produce one bomb in six months or in one year, or maybe not for five years, but certainly sometime in the not-too-distant future. (Officials also predicted that they might be able to produce a quantity of bombs in 10 years.) Although we had learned to live with other unfriendly countries who had the bomb, living with one run by Hussein was another matter for many Americans. In Hussein, said one analyst, "Central casting had sent us the perfect Arab villain." You publicly compared him with Adolph Hitler. Hussein's use of poison gas on a rebellious ethnic minority in his own country, his threat to use chemical and biological weapons, and now the possibility that he might use nuclear weapons were enough to convince a majority of the public that there were moral reasons for going to war. Iraq's potential nuclear capability was the only one of these reasons that a majority of the public cited as a sufficient justification. Once you learned this from your pollsters, you cited this justification more and more.

Your efforts yielded results. By December, 54% of the public favored going to war and only 34% were opposed. As the January deadline approached, that support increased. Members of Congress were divided, with many favoring continued sanctions. Still, in January, a small majority of members in both houses voted to authorize your use of troops.

When a last-minute meeting between Baker and the Iraqi foreign minister does not produce an Iraqi commitment to withdraw, you believe the moment has come to launch a military strike. One concern you have, however, is whether or not Americans will continue to support military action. If support wanes, it is unlikely that military force will be successful if it is drawn out over months or years. Right now the public and press are supportive. There is little questioning of your assumptions about the nature of the struggle, though some people want to wait a little longer to see if economic sanctions will work. Others, however, have less patience and want to "get it over with." But you recall the Vietnam War. Popular and elite support for the war was high in the beginning, but it eroded over time to a point where the nation was riven with conflict about the wisdom of, and reasons for, the war. You have promised the nation that if we go to war, Iraq will not be another Vietnam. War, however, is seldom predictable.

You know that when you send troops support will be initially high. There is always a "rally 'round the flag" effect when troops come under fire. But how firm will this support be? Even now, polls show less than majority support for war if "only" 1,000 troops die. It seems unlikely that a land war could have that few deaths. And, even though the public seems to support going to war, some polls indicate that an equal number want to apply the economic sanctions longer.

Your military advisors assure you that the United States and its allies can win a war and in a short time. Opponents of the war, however, point to the possibility of thousands of American casualties as well as the possible greater instability of the region after a war. What do you do? Do you proceed with your plans for war and assume a confused and ambivalent public will support your decision? Or do you wait?

Sources: Henry Allen, "The Good, the Bad and the Ugly," *Washington Post National Weekly Edition,* January 14–20, 1991, p. 11; Ann Devroy and Dan Balz, "George Bush: Unwavering, Unbending From the Start," *Washington Post National Weekly Edition,* January 21–27, 1991, p. 8; Notes and Comment, *The New Yorker,* January 14, 1991, p. 22; Donald Kaul, "OK, Now Let's Go Sanctions Route," *Lincoln Journal-Star,* January 20, 1991, p. 18; "All Things Considered," National Public Radio, November 26, 1990.

OUTLINE

Our feelings about public opinion are contradictory. On the one hand, in a democracy we want leaders to be responsive to public opinion. Yet often we complain that our elected officials do not lead but simply follow the latest trends in public opinion polls. In this chapter, we will explore public opinion to better understand this contradiction. We will describe how public opinion is formed and measured and discuss the pattern of public opinion on some important issues. Finally, we will assess the extent to which government is responsive to public opinion. Because political science is primarily interested in opinions that affect government, the focus of this chapter is public opinion about political issues, personalities, institutions, and events.

Nature of Public Opinion

We can define **public opinion** as the collection of individual opinions toward issues or objects of general interest, that is, those that concern a significant number of people.[1] Public opinion can be described in terms of direction, intensity, and stability. Direction refers to liking or disliking. Public opinion is usually mixed: some individuals have a positive opinion, others negative. Intensity refers to the degree of liking or disliking. Intense opinions are more likely to be the basis for behavior. Gun enthusiasts strongly opposed to gun control are likely to act on their opinions and vote against members of Congress who support gun registration.

Most public issues are not of interest to most people. Individuals may feel intensely about one or two issues that directly affect them, but not everyone, or even a majority, is intense about the same issues. The relative absence of severe economic and social divisions in the United States explains the lack of intense opinions. With the possible exception of the racial and states' rights issues that almost destroyed the nation in the 1860s, there has been nothing like the long-standing, divisive class and religious conflicts of many European nations.

Opinions also differ in stability. An opinion is more likely to change when an individual lacks intensity or information about an issue or object. Thus, an opinion of one's country is more stable than an opinion of a presidential candidate. For example, polls show that support for each party's candidate goes up during the party's convention. According to the polling director for the *Washington Post,* the swings in 1988 were among independents and weak Democrats and Republicans. "They watch the Republican convention and feel Republican, and they watch the Democratic convention and feel Democratic."[2]

Formation of Public Opinion

People have opinions about issues and objects because they learn them in a process called **political socialization.**

As with other types of learning, individuals learn about politics by being exposed to new information from parents, peers, schools, the media, political leaders, and the community. These are referred to as **agents of political socialization.** Individuals also can learn about politics through direct personal experience.

Political learning begins at an early age and continues through life. Reasoning capacity as well as the demands placed upon an individual influence what is learned.[3] Very young children are unable to distinguish the political from the nonpolitical world. In fact, young children have difficulty separating political figures from cartoon characters. Some confuse the political with the religious. Twenty-five percent of a sample of five- and six-year-olds reported that the president takes his orders directly from God.[4] By first grade, however, children begin to see government as distinct and unique.[5]

The inability to understand abstract concepts or complex institutions means the child's conception of government is limited. Most identify government with the president.[6] Children can recognize the president—they see him on television—and understand that he is a leader of the nation much as the parent is a leader of the family. In general, experiences with parents and other adult figures provide children with a basis for understanding remote authority figures such as the president.[7] Positive feelings toward

parents are also responsible for positive feelings toward the president. Children describe the president as good and helpful[8] and view him as more powerful than he really is.[9]

With age, children develop greater capacity to learn, and greater demands are placed upon them. They are introduced to political ideas and institutions by parents, teachers, and peers. Thus, their conception of government broadens to include Congress and such things as voting, freedom, and democracy. The idealization of the president gives way to a more complex and realistic image. The process can be accelerated by events and parental and community reaction to them. Research in the early 1970s showed that children were much less positive toward the president and government than they had been in the 1960s. The 1970s were a period when support for government among adults was declining. The Watergate scandal in 1973 lowered both adults' and childrens' evaluations of the president (see figure 1).[10]

These effects did not last, however. Although children socialized in the late 1960s and early 1970s were more cynical toward government than others, as they matured, their opinions changed and became less cynical.[11]

In adolescence, political understanding expands still further. Children discuss politics with family and friends. Political activity, however limited, is underway. By their middle teens, individuals begin to develop coherent positions on issues and show some ability to think in liberal-conservative terms.[12] (Definitions of liberal and conservative are discussed later in this chapter.) Fifteen- and sixteen-year-olds have political opinions similar to many adults. They begin to recognize faults in the system but still believe that the United States is better than other countries. They rate the country low in limiting violence and fostering political morality, but they rate it high in providing educational opportunities, a good standard of living, and science and technology.[13] For most, the positive feelings toward American government learned earlier are reinforced.

In adulthood, opinions toward specific policies and personalities develop, and political activity becomes more serious. Most Americans have not developed a critical perspective, and few are asked or pushed to criticism by the schools, press, political parties, or political institutions. Although disillusionment with government in general rises, it is basically passive

Figure 1 ■ Watergate Affected Children's Attitudes Toward the President

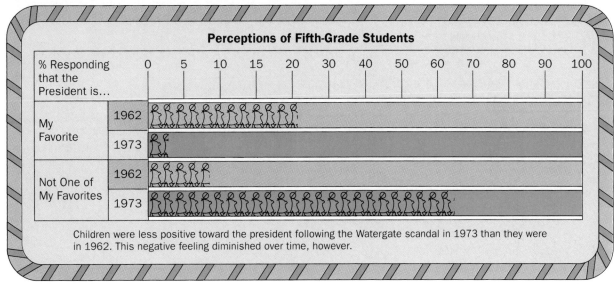

Children were less positive toward the president following the Watergate scandal in 1973 than they were in 1962. This negative feeling diminished over time, however.

Source: F. Chris Arterton, "The Impact of Children's Attitudes toward Political Authority," *Political Science Quarterly* 89 (June 1984): 269–88.

and directed toward political leaders rather than institutions.[14] In the absence of a major upheaval, depression, or war, for most, the positive feelings developed toward government early in life are likely to remain and perhaps even cushion the impact of such events if they occur.[15]

Agents of Political Socialization

Family.   Children are not born little Republicans and Democrats. Most learn these allegiances from the family. Individuals are influenced by the family throughout life. Families are particularly important in shaping the opinions of children, however, because of the strong emotional ties among members and because of parents' near exclusive control of their childrens' early lives.

The family influences opinions in several ways. First, parents share their opinions directly with children, who may adopt them.

Second, parents say or do things that children imitate. They may overhear parents' comments about the Republican or Democratic party, for example, and repeat what they hear. Many initially learn a party identification in this way.

Third, children may transfer or generalize opinions from parents to other objects. When children are less positive toward parents, they are also less positive toward the president and other authority figures.[16]

Fourth, the family shapes the personality of the child. This may affect the child's political opinions. For example, the family contributes to self-image. Individuals who are self-confident are more likely to participate in politics than others.

Fifth, the family places children in a network of social and economic relationships that influences how they view the world and how the world views them. White children who live in a middle-class suburb are quite likely to view themselves and the world around them differently than black children who live in a large city ghetto.

The influence of the family is strongest when children clearly perceive what the parents' opinion is and that the matter is important to the parents. In the case of party identification, cues are frequent and unambiguous. In one study, 72% of a sample of high school seniors could identify their parents' party identification, whereas no more than 36% could identify their parents' opinion on any other issue.[17]

Today, however, the family has less opportunity to influence the child. Parents no longer have exclusive control during a child's preschool years, and the number of households with both parents working or with a single parent who works means that children have

In every society, children are socialized to revere the symbols of their nation. Soviet school children dance in front of a picture of V. I. Lenin, leader of the Russian Revolution; American children pledge allegiance to the flag. With the dramatic changes taking place in the Soviet Union, symbols like Lenin are sources of divisiveness rather than unity.

fewer daily contact hours with parents. Consequently, other agents of socialization are becoming more influential. For example, we turn more often to the schools to deal with problems the family dealt with in the past.

School. A child of our acquaintance came to the United States at the age of five and could not speak English and did not know the name of his new country. After a few months of kindergarten, he knew that George Washington and Abraham Lincoln were good presidents, he was able to recount stories of the Pilgrims, he could draw the flag, and he felt strongly that the United States was the best country in the world. This child illustrates strikingly the importance of the school in political socialization and how values and symbols of government are explicitly taught in American schools, as they are in schools in every nation.[18]

Schools promote patriotic rituals, such as beginning each day with the Pledge of Allegiance, and include patriotic songs and programs in many activities.

In the lower grades, children celebrate national holidays such as Washington's birthday and Thanksgiving and learn the history and symbols associated with them. Such exercises foster awe and respect for government.

In the upper grades, mock conventions, elections, Girls' and Boys' State, and student government introduce students to the operation of government. School clubs often operate with democratic procedures and reinforce the concepts of voting and majority rule. The state of Illinois even let the state's elementary school children vote to select the official state animal, fish, and tree, thus conveying the message that voting is the way we decide things.

Curricula and textbooks also foster commitment to government; civics or government courses are offered in most schools and in many places are required of all students. Textbooks, particularly those used in elementary grades, emphasize compliance with authority and the need to be "good" citizens. Even text-

Opinions on Abortion

Issues that involve moral questions have the greatest potential to be divisive. Slavery was a moral issue that almost destroyed the nation. In the first decades of this century, prohibition banning the sale of alcoholic beverages was a divisive moral issue. In the 1970s, abortion emerged as a moral issue. Although not everyone feels strongly about it, many are sharply divided over some important aspects of this issue.

There are two dimensions to the abortion issue. One involves the health and safety of the mother or the child. The vast majority of Americans endorse legal abortion in cases in which the mother's health may be endangered, the child is likely to have a serious defect, or the pregnancy is the result of rape or incest. This pattern of opinion has been reasonably stable over the past decade.

The other dimension relates to the personal preferences of the mother. Americans are divided on whether a legal abortion is acceptable when the family has a low income and does not want any more children or when the mother is unmarried and does not want to marry the father.

Although the accompanying tables do not reveal intensity, the patterns in boxes a, b, and c show agreement, or consensus, whereas boxes d, e, and f reveal disagreement, or conflict.

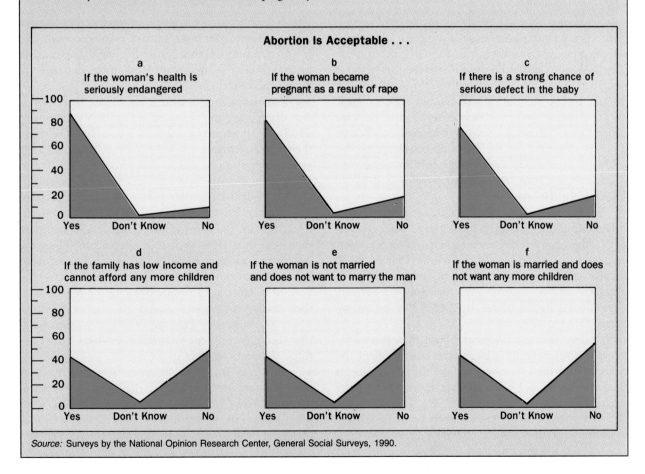

Abortion Is Acceptable . . .

a — If the woman's health is seriously endangered
b — If the woman became pregnant as a result of rape
c — If there is a strong chance of serious defect in the baby
d — If the family has low income and cannot afford any more children
e — If the woman is not married and does not want to marry the man
f — If the woman is married and does not want any more children

Source: Surveys by the National Opinion Research Center, General Social Surveys, 1990.

books in advanced grades often present idealized versions of the way government works and exaggerated views of the responsiveness of government to citizen participation.

Schools appear to foster pride and compliance, but they are less successful in teaching political participation skills and support for democratic values. Only a minority of a sample of 17-year-olds could list four or more ways to influence politics. Sixty percent of a sample of high school seniors favored allowing the police and other groups to censor books and movies.[19]

Nor does the curriculum make much difference. Civics instruction has only a modest impact on knowledge of and interest in politics, sense of political efficacy (feelings that one can influence government), levels of tolerance, and political trust.[20] Nor do teachers generally have much impact, though there is evidence that they have more impact if they are believable.[21]

The failure of the schools to develop participation skills and commitment to democratic values often is attributed to the "hidden curriculum."[22] Schools are run by teachers and administrators with little input from students. In such an environment, it is not surprising that students fail to develop democratic, participatory orientations.

Education—the skills that it provides and experiences it represents—does make a difference, however. People who have more years of formal education are generally more interested in and knowledgeable about politics.[23] They are also more likely to participate in politics and to be politically tolerant.

The major impact of schooling is that it helps create "good" citizens. Citizens are taught to accept political authority and the institutions of government and to channel political activity in legitimate and supportive ways. Thus, the schools provide a valuable function for the state.

Studies have shown the liberalizing influence of a college education. Many go to college to get a job that pays a high salary. Some attend to expand their knowledge and understanding of the world. Others enroll because their parents want them to or simply because everyone else is. Probably no one goes to become more liberal in his or her opinions. But becoming more liberal is often the result.[24]

College students are more liberal than the population as a whole, and the longer they are in college the more liberal they become. Seniors are more liberal than freshmen, and graduates are more liberal than undergraduates.

Why does college lead to liberal opinions? One explanation is that a college education leads to greater political awareness. College graduates are more knowledgeable about politics and more likely to follow politics on television and in newspapers and magazines. As a result, they are more likely to sense changes in society and identify with them. Support for change is a component of liberalism.

A closely related explanation is that college leads to a broadened perspective on the world. Individuals begin to look beyond their immediate environment and see themselves as part of a larger world community. This leads to an increased tolerance of different opinions and an awareness of the conditions that are faced by the less fortunate; both are components of liberalism.

A third possible explanation is that liberal college professors indoctrinate students. A Carnegie Commission survey showed that 64% of the social science faculty in the nation's colleges identified themselves as liberal and only 20% regarded themselves as conservative. Faculty in other disciplines are much less likely to be liberal, however. For example, 30% of the business and 55% of the natural science faculty identified themselves as liberal. Thus, although the potential for influence exists, and college professors, no doubt, affect some students, the impact is exaggerated. The broadened outlook that leads to greater tolerance of ideas is likely to make students more resistant to indoctrination.

Evidence also suggests that students' orientations vary over time. During the height of the Vietnam War, 1968–1971, students were more likely to identify themselves as liberal in outlook than students in the early 1960s and late 1970s. Data from the 1980s also show a considerable move to the center on the part of college students. For example, 24% of college freshmen identified themselves as liberal in 1990 compared to 38% in 1970. Over the same time period, however, there was only a 2% shift to conservatism. Thus, the big change was from liberal identification to middle of the road. At the same time, college faculty changed very little. Thus, students are not simply a reflection of their college classroom teachers. At large universities, where the largest percentage of students attend college, the environment is sufficiently diverse to reinforce all points of view.

Although students are more conservative than they were in the late 1960s, they remain predominantly liberal. In 1984, for example, 76% were prochoice on the abortion issue, whereas only 43% of the adult population approved of abortion on demand. Fifty-seven percent of the students agreed that the United States was spending too much on defense, compared to 40% for the population as a whole. A comparison of college and noncollege youth also revealed substantial differences. Eighteen percent of college youth agreed that money is very important, compared to 40% of the noncollege youth. Thirty-six percent of the college students responded that abortion is morally wrong; 64% of the noncollege youth took that position.

Still another explanation for the liberalizing influence of college is that it attracts those who are more liberal in the first place. Some evidence suggests that this may be true for some issues. Whereas 68% of 1990 college freshmen thought the courts treat criminals too leniently, 83% of the public thought so. Fifty-six percent of college freshmen favored busing to achieve racial balance in the schools, whereas only 33% of the adult population favored it.

Thus, although some liberals attend college and have their opinions reinforced, and others are influenced by college faculty, most likely, liberal opinions result from increased political awareness and a broadened world perspective.

Peers.   In many instances, peers simply reinforce the opinions of the family or school. When there is a conflict between peer and parental socialization, peers sometimes win out but only on issues of special relevance to youth. For example, peer influence is more important than family influence on the issue of whether 18-year-olds should be allowed to vote, but parental influence appears to be more significant with respect to partisanship and vote choice.[25] Peers have the most influence when the peer group is attractive to the individual and when the individual spends more time with the group.

Mass Media.   The primary effect of the media on children is to increase their level of information about politics. For adults the media primarily influence what people think about, that is, the issues, events, and personalities they pay attention to,[26] but the media also influence opinions about issues and individuals. Research shows that changes in public opinion tend to follow sentiments expressed by television news commentators.[27] We will examine the impact of the media in more detail in chapter 8.

Adult Socialization.   Not all political socialization occurs in childhood. It is a lifelong process; opinions change as we have new experiences.

Citizens' encounters with government have the potential to change their opinions about politics. Many Americans who were particularly hard hit by the depression, for example, became active in the political

process for the first time. Most of these new voters voted Democratic in 1932, and many have voted Democratic ever since. The war in Vietnam was another event that influenced masses of people. Some took to the streets to protest the war; others rejected their country and traveled to Canada to avoid the draft. Watergate was yet another event that affected the opinions of millions of Americans.

Opinions also change with changed personal situations. Marriage, divorce, unemployment, or a move to a new location can all have an impact on political opinions.[28]

Impact of Political Socialization

Each new generation of Americans is socialized to a large extent by the preceding generations. In many ways each new generation will look and act much like the one that came before. In this sense, political socialization is biased against change. Typically it leads to support for and compliance with government and the social order. Although many disagree with particular government policies, few question the basic structure of government.

Yet the impact of political socialization is not the same for all groups of people. The socialization experiences of poor minority children are different from those of rich white ones. Children from low-income families are more cynical about government; black children feel less able to influence government and are less inclined to trust it.[29]

Measuring Public Opinion

Public opinion typically is measured by asking individuals to answer questions in a survey. If done properly, this is probably the most accurate way to measure public opinion. Before the use of polls, other techniques were employed: elected officials relied on opinions of people who wrote or talked to them; journalists tried to gauge public opinion by talking selectively to individuals; letters written to newspaper editors or newspaper editorials were thought to reflect public opinion.

These techniques can lead to distortions, however. Letters to public officials and newspapers are more likely to come from people with extreme opinions[30] or from those with writing skills, that is, people with more education. Nor will opinions culled from a few conversations match the pattern of opinion for the nation as a whole. Editorial opinion is even less likely to provide an accurate picture of public opinion because most newspaper publishers tend to be conservative, which often is reflected in their editorials. In most presidential elections in this century, newspapers have favored the Republican candidate by about three to one.[31]

Polling to measure public opinion is an obvious improvement, but the result of a poll cannot be equated with public opinion. A poll is an instrument for measuring public opinion, and whenever something is measured, there is always the possibility of mistakes.

Early Polling Efforts

The first attempts to measure popular sentiments on a large scale were the **straw polls** (or unscientific polls) developed by newspapers in the nineteenth century.[32] In 1824 the *Harrisburg Pennsylvanian,* in perhaps the first poll assessing candidate preferences, sent reporters to check on support for the four presidential contenders that year. In July, the paper reported that Jackson was the popular choice over John Quincy Adams, Henry Clay, and William H. Crawford. Jackson also received the most votes in the election, but John Quincy Adams was elected president after the contest was decided in the House of Representatives. Toward the end of the nineteenth century, the *New York Herald* regularly tried to forecast election outcomes in local, state, and national races. During presidential election years, the paper collected estimates from reporters and political leaders across the country and predicted the Electoral College vote by state.

Straw polls are still employed today. Some newspapers have interviewers who ask adults at shopping centers and other locations to cast simulated ballots. Other newspapers have readers return coupons printed in the papers. Television and radio stations often ask questions and provide two telephone numbers for listeners to call: one for yes, one for no. The votes then are electronically recorded.

The major problem with straw polls is that there is no way to ensure that the sample of individuals giving opinions is representative of the larger population. Generally speaking, they are not.

The famed *Literary Digest* poll is a good example. This magazine conducted polls of presidential preferences between 1916 and 1936. As many as 18 million ballots were mailed out to persons drawn from telephone directories and automobile registration lists. Although the purpose was less to measure public opinion than to boost subscriptions, the *Digest* did have a pretty good record. It predicted the winners in 1924, 1928, and 1932. However, in 1936, the magazine predicted Alfred Landon would win when Franklin Delano Roosevelt won by a landslide. The erroneous prediction ended the magazine's polling, and in 1938 the *Digest* went out of business.

A bias in the *Digest*'s polling procedure that the editors failed to consider led the magazine to predict Landon as the winner. At the time, owners of telephones and automobiles were disproportionately middle- and high-income individuals who could afford a telephone or car in the depths of the depression; these people were much more likely to vote for Landon (a Republican) than lower-income people.[33]

Emergence of Scientific Polling

Scientific polling began after World War I, inspired by the new field of business known as marketing research. After the war, demand for consumer goods rose, and American business, no longer engaged in the production of war materials, turned to satisfying consumer demand. Businesses used marketing research to identify what consumers wanted and, perhaps more important, how products could be packaged so consumers would buy them. For example, the American Tobacco Company changed from a green to a white package during World War II because it found that a white package was more attractive to women smokers.[34]

Also important to the development of scientific polling was the application of mathematical principles of probability. To check for rates of defects in manufactured products, random or spot inspections of a few items, called a sample, were made. From these, projections of defects among the entire group of items could be made. From this use of sampling, it was a small step to conclude that sampling a small number of individuals could provide information about a larger population.

In the early 1930s, George Gallup and several others, using probability-based sampling techniques,

AMERICAN DIVERSITY

The Gender Gap

If women alone had voted in 1988, Michael Dukakis might be president. Men gave George Bush his winning margin. Women split their vote almost evenly between the two candidates, with some polls showing women giving the edge to Dukakis.[1] These rather startling findings illustrate a gender gap in partisanship and political opinions.

Until the 1970s, the attitudes of men and women about politics were basically the same. Women were somewhat less inclined to support the use of armed forces around the world and capital punishment at home. However, on most other issues the attitudes of men and women were about the same, and their voting choices were also similar.

In the mid-1970s differences began to appear on many issues, and in the 1980s they increased. The differences are modest but consistent. Women continue to be less supportive of the use of force abroad and at home. For example, they are more likely to favor gun control laws and oppose capital punishment, Star Wars (SDI), increased spending for the military, and a tougher stand against the Soviets.

On many social issues (sometimes called compassion issues), women are more apt to favor government inter-

vention to relieve the plight of the elderly, handicapped, ill, and financially needy. Women are more likely to favor government action to relieve unemployment, to spend for Social Security, and to improve conditions of minorities and the poor. Women are also more supportive of environmental regulations and protections. Women are less confident than men that the nation is moving in the right direction and are more likely to respond that the economy is not doing very well.

On some issues, however, few differences of opinion between men and women remain. Ironically, these include "women's" issues, such as abortion. They also include busing for racial integration, spending for education, and crime control.

Will the gender gap persist? Women are increasingly politically active and aware of women's lower economic status in society. As long as these differences persist, particularly the latter, the gender gap is likely to remain.

[1] Poll reference is to Cable News Network/*Los Angeles Times* Exit Poll reported in *National Journal*, November 12, 1988, p. 2855.

Examples of the Gender Gap

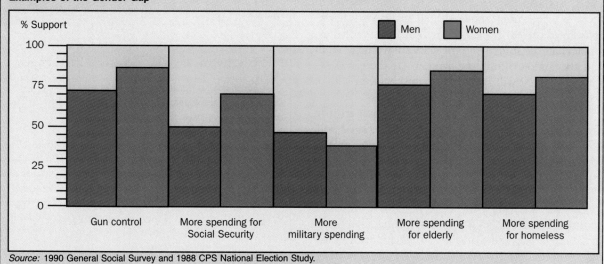

Source: 1990 General Social Survey and 1988 CPS National Election Study.

began polling opinions on a wide scale. In 1936, Gallup predicted that the *Literary Digest* would be wrong and that Roosevelt would be reelected with 55.7% of the vote. Roosevelt received 62.5%.

Increasingly, polls were used by government. In 1940, Roosevelt became the first president to use polls on a regular basis, employing a social scientist to measure trends in public opinion about the war in Europe. Most major American universities have a unit that does survey research, and there are hundreds of commercial marketing research firms, private pollsters, and newspaper polls.

Polling Procedures

Opinion polling involves (1) drawing a sample or subset of individuals from a larger population; (2) presenting a question or statement to individuals in the sample regarding their opinions; and (3) analyzing the results.

Sampling.   Most commercial pollsters draw samples of 1,000 to 1,500 adults. Surveys of this size are able to measure accurately the opinions of all adults in the United States because of **random sampling;** that is, everyone has a known chance of being included in the sample.

To understand what random sampling is, assume that you want a sample of 33 students from a class of 100. The name of each student in the class is placed on a separate slip of paper, the papers are put in a hat and mixed up, and 33 are drawn. The characteristics of those selected, the sample, should reflect the characteristics of the entire class, the population. If, for example, half the students in the class are women, about half the sample should be women. If the sample is large enough, it will approximate the characteristics of the larger population from which it comes.

Nonrandom sampling can be a source of error in measuring public opinion. In the *Literary Digest* poll, voters with telephones and automobiles had a greater chance of being in the sample, whereas those without a telephone or automobile had virtually no chance. The sample was biased, that is, not representative of all voters, and the picture of public opinion it presented was inaccurate. Phone-in polls often conducted by radio and television networks are a contemporary example of nonrandom polls. Those who happen to be listening to radio or watching television and who are motivated to call in their preferences have a greater

chance of being included than others. "Instant" polls taken overnight after presidential debates are often biased because the pollsters do not have time to call back people who are not at home. The sample may be biased in favor of those not working night shifts, the middle-aged, and others likely to be home in the evening. Similarly, those motivated to respond to questionnaires mailed by members of Congress typically are not representative of the entire state or district.

Even when samples are drawn randomly, however, there is some error because not everyone in the population is included in the sample. This is **sampling error.** Although all samples have sampling error, it is possible to calculate sampling error in random samples and specify a range of accuracy for sample results. A surprising feature of sampling error is that its magnitude depends on sample size and not population size. This means that a sample of 1,500 of the residents of Buffalo, New York, will have the same error as a sample of 1,500 citizens of the United States. A sample of 1,200 to 1,500 is large enough to approximate the characteristics of any large population—city, state, or nation—with only a small error.

Sampling error decreases as the sample size gets larger. For populations of more than 10,000, the sampling error associated with samples of 1,000 is about

---

Examples of Biased Survey Questions

The leading question: "You don't favor a policy of disarmament, do you?" (An answer is suggested by the question.)

The overly technical question: "Do you think that the oil depletion allowance should be repealed or not?" (The question concerns a subject about which most people have little knowledge.)

The biased alternative question: "Do you think that food stamp aid should be increased so children do not starve or do you think that food stamp aid should not be increased?" (The question offers one biased alternative.)

The ambiguous question: "How do you feel about President Bush and his policies in the Persian Gulf?" (The question focuses on more than one subject, the president and his policies in the Persian Gulf.)

These kinds of questions will not provide an accurate picture of public opinion.

election, some voters may believe that they do not need to vote. As polls become more accurate and more numerous, they will be more likely to have this effect.

Polls also may corrupt the political process. They contribute to the marketing of an image of political candidates that fits voters' expectations. Thus, elections may turn more on image than on substance. The democratic process suffers when voters are deceived, and the deception leads to a loss of respect for the electoral process.

How Informed Is Public Opinion?

Many Americans are ignorant of elementary aspects of American government. For example, in a 1978 poll, more than half did not know that two senators were elected from their state.[46] Forty-one percent did not know which party had the most members in the House of Representatives in 1988[47] (see table 2).

Many Americans are also unable to identify prominent political personalities. In 1986, six years after George Bush was elected to the vice-presidency, 23% could not identify him.[48] Six times as many people can identify the judge on the television show "The People's Court" than can identify the chief justice of the United States.

Table 2 ■ Political Ignorance of the Public

	Percentage Unable to Identify
Vice-president (1986)	23
Limit on presidential terms (1970)	33
Party with most members in the House before election (1988)	41
Party with most members in the Senate before election (1988)	46
Number of senators elected from each state (1978)	48
Secretary of state (1988)	61
Candidates for the House and their party (1988)	62
Name of the Speaker of the House (1988)	86
Chief justice of the United States (1988)	96

Source: National Opinion Research Center, General Social Surveys and Center for Political Studies, American National Election Studies.

Many Americans are uninformed about current issues, and a large number have no opinion at all on many issues.[49] Evidence suggests that from 15% to 25% of the population have not thought enough about most issues to venture an opinion when asked. For example, in a 1988 study, 17% had no opinion on whether the United States government should cooperate more with the Soviet Union, and 21% had no opinion on whether the government should cut services and reduce spending. Others offer "doorstep" opinions; they give an opinion even though they have thought very little or not at all about the issue.

Individuals tend to think most about those issues that are important to them, such as family and work. Most people view politics as irrelevant to their personal concerns and therefore not very important. The lack of public concern often leads government to be responsive to special interests at the expense of the public. Thus public inattentiveness is an important factor in making government less responsive to public opinion.

Before we conclude that the public is incompetent, however, we need to consider the standard by which the public should be judged.

Some political scientists argue that individual citizens know in general what they like and dislike and can make sound political judgments on this basis.[50] It is probably unreasonable to expect most people to have an opinion on all issues. Those who have the greatest stake in an issue will be most likely to have an opinion on it. Moreover, many citizens make voting decisions based on government performance in important policy areas such as the economy. And many have at least a general idea of the relative positions of the major candidates on the issues.

We also need to consider the failure of public officials to educate the public on many issues. Politicians often do not like to discuss issues, especially controversial ones. When they do, public awareness does increase. After former President Reagan made an issue of American support for the Nicaraguan contras, awareness of the issue and the side the United States was supporting jumped from 25% to 59%.[51]

Public Opinion

There are many aspects of public opinion. Public opinion polls cover virtually every aspect of American

Figure 3 ■ Ideological Self-Identification, 1974–1990

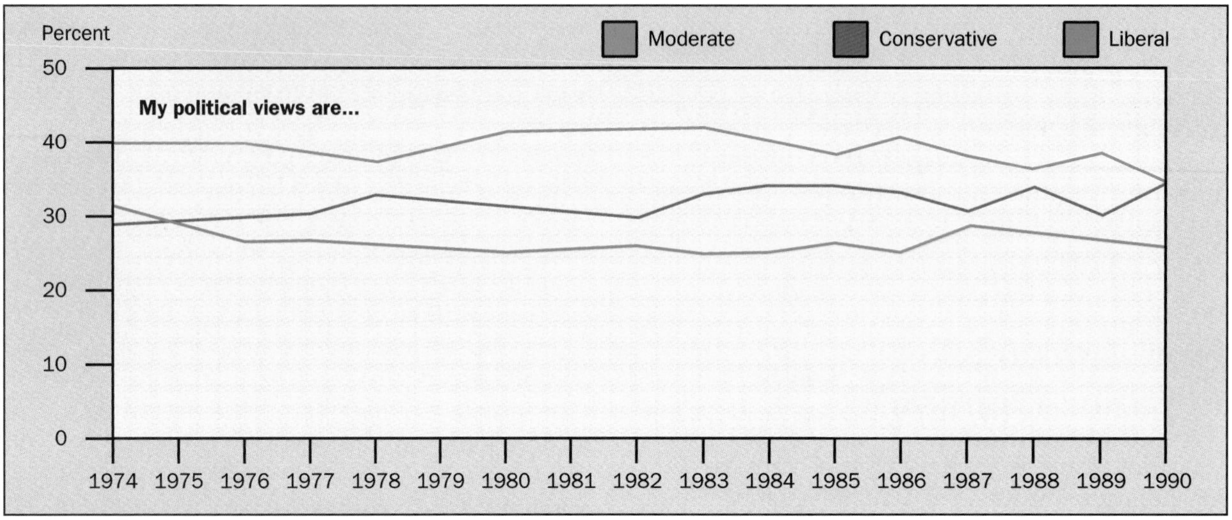

Source: Surveys by National Opinion Research Center. General Social Survey.

life. Polls have reported the number of California drivers with paraphernalia hanging from their rearview mirrors and Iowans with ornaments on their lawns. Political polls examine opinions about political issues and political candidates, whether the American people are liberal or conservative, and whether this influences their positions on issues and preferences for political candidates. While it is important to know how Americans stand on current issues and how they feel about political candidates, it is also important to know what they think about government: its founding principles, political institutions, and political leaders. How Americans feel about government influences whether they will participate in and accept the government as it is or reject and work to change it.

We will use ideology as a way to examine public opinion. We begin by asking whether Americans identify themselves as liberal or conservative. We then look at how ideology relates to opinions on specific issues such as social welfare, social issues, and race. We also explore how ideology is related to political tolerance, whether Americans are willing to extend rights and liberties to individuals who do not share their opinions. Finally, we look at trust in government: Do Americans trust their government to do the right thing, and are liberals more trusting than conservatives?

Ideology

The term **ideology** refers to a highly organized and coherent set of opinions. In the extreme, one who is ideological takes a position on all issues consistent

with his or her ideology. Liberalism and conservatism are terms used to describe the current major ideologies in American politics. A **liberal** is someone who believes in a national government active in domestic policies, providing help to individuals and communities in areas such as health, education, and welfare. A **conservative** is someone who believes that the domestic role of government should be minimized and that individuals are responsible for their own well-being. In foreign policy, liberals currently are more inclined to seek cooperation abroad and emphasize diplomacy rather than military force. Conservatives are more suspicious of the Communist world and hostile toward it, and they tend to favor "big government" in military spending. Liberals are sometimes identified by the label "left," and conservatives by the label "right."

To what extent are Americans ideological? Do the ideological labels liberal and conservative describe the opinions of the American people? One way to find out whether a person is liberal or conservative is to ask. The greatest percentage of Americans opt for the middle, identifying themselves as moderate or centrist. Comparing the percentage of liberals to conservatives reveals conservatives to be slightly more numerous. These distributions have changed very little in the past 15 years (see figure 3).

Self-identifications are helpful, but one cannot be sure that individuals actually know what the label means or that they support the positions identified with the label. To determine whether the labels distinguish Americans in terms of issue positions, we need to look at specific issues.

The Ups and Downs of the "L" Word

One of the tactics of the Bush presidential campaign in 1988 was to label Michael Dukakis a "liberal." Dukakis denied the label until the closing days of the campaign. Polls show that the Bush tactic succeeded in changing some voters' perceptions. The proportion of the public saying Dukakis was "too liberal" doubled to 32% between May and October.

Why has liberalism become something of a dirty word? The answer lies in the contemporary meaning of liberalism.

During the American Revolution, liberalism meant rejecting absolute monarchy and aristocracy in favor of equality and individual rights. Liberalism was identified with limited government and capitalist economy. These are ideas identified with contemporary American conservatism. In fact, Barry Goldwater, the Republican presidential nominee in 1964, once argued that American conservatives are the real liberals.

Liberalism took on another meaning in the twentieth century, particularly in the United States. Liberalism came to refer to the use of government authority to expand opportunities to the poor and powerless and to improve the quality of life for all. This was the liberalism of Roosevelt, Truman, Kennedy, and Johnson. With this as their platform, the Democrats came to power in the 1930s and dominated American politics through the 1960s.

When Dukakis acknowledged that he was a liberal in the 1988 campaign, it was the policies of Roosevelt, Truman, Kennedy, and Johnson with which he wished to be identified. The problem, however, was that since the 1960s liberalism has been identified with some less popular policies. Liberalism was linked to the civil rights policies of the Democrats in the 1960s and 1970s. These policies threatened the white-dominated social order in the South and white ethnic communities in the North. Blacks rallied to the Democratic party, and many whites, especially in the South, were driven away.

The term also was linked to the anti–Vietnam War protests and the presidential campaign of George McGovern in 1972. In the Vietnam era, many who were liberals in the Roosevelt tradition rejected the label and called themselves neoconservatives. They believed that liberals no longer supported an anti-Communist foreign policy.

Liberalism also was identified with Supreme Court decisions that expanded the rights of persons accused of crimes, legalized abortion, and barred mandatory prayers in public school. The term also was identified with big government, high taxes, and the runaway inflation of the late 1970s.

"Should anyone inquire, Harrington, our portions are generous, not liberal."

Over the years, the "L" word—the phrase used by Bush in 1988 so he would not have to utter the "dirty word" liberal—has come to mean different things to different people. Even John Kennedy wanted to avoid the label when he referred to himself as a fighting conservative in his first congressional election. However, he offered the following clarification in his 1960 run for the presidency. Asking what opponents mean when they apply the label liberal, he said, "If by liberal, they mean someone who is soft in his policies abroad, against local government, and unconcerned with the taxpayer's dollar, then the record shows we are not that kind of liberal. But, if by a liberal, they mean someone who looks ahead, welcomes new ideas, cares about the welfare of the people, believes that we can break through the suspicions that grip our policies abroad, then I'm proud to say that I'm a liberal."[1]

Unfortunately for Dukakis, the first of these definitions is what most voters had in mind in 1988.

[1] E. J. Dionne, Jr., "Meaning of Liberalism Shifted to an Unpopular Connotation," *Lincoln Journal*, November 11, 1988, pp. 1, 5.

Drawing by Lorenz; © 1988 The New Yorker Magazine, Inc.

Social Welfare and the Proper Role of Government

Government programs to help individuals deal with economic hardship started during the Great Depression in the 1930s. These included programs to provide aid for the elderly (Social Security), unemployed, and poor (Aid to Dependent Children). Most Americans supported government assistance of this kind in the 1930s and support it today.

Polls show that Americans favor increased government spending for Social Security and aid to the poor.[52] In 1987, 70% supported the notion that government should insure that everyone who wants to work has a job, slightly below the 77% who endorsed the idea in 1935.[53] A majority of Americans do draw the line, however, on the government providing everyone with a good standard of living or guaranteed income. Even so, 40% endorse this idea.

In addition to support for those in need, Americans accept government involvement in a number of other areas. Americans approve increased spending for education, health care, the environment, drug rehabilitation, and crime and law enforcement.[54] For example, well over a majority, 60% to 80%, have also consistently endorsed the idea that government should "help people get doctors and hospital care at low cost." While less than a majority, sizable numbers favor increased spending for the nation's cities, highways and bridges, mass transportation, and parks and recreation. Only small minorities, less than 10%, oppose additional funding in these areas.[55]

There are limits to popular support for "big government," however. While Americans do not reject the idea of taxes to support government, most (60%) think that taxes are too high.[56] And from one-third to one-half respond that the government is too strong for the good of the country.[57]

Liberals and conservatives tend to disagree on both social welfare policies and the role of government. Liberals are more likely to favor spending for Social Security, health care, education, and the environment. They are also more likely to favor spending to combat drugs and for aid to the poor and minorities (see figure 4). They are less likely to think that the government is too powerful.

Thus Americans have ambivalent attitudes about government. They want it to do more to deal with social and economic problems, but they feel negatively about the intrusion and dependence that government assistance implies.

Social Issues

Beginning in the 1960s, so-called social issues have been important sources of political debate. These issues generally relate to family, school, and church.

Figure 4 ■ Self-identified Liberals Are More Liberal on Most Social Welfare Issues

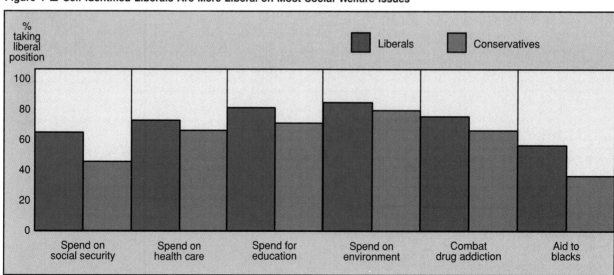

Source: 1990 General Social Survey.

A Comparative Perspective: Support for Social Welfare

Although the United States has a variety of government assistance programs for the needy, the elderly, those in poor health, and others, Americans have been slower than citizens in other western democracies to adopt, and less likely to support, social welfare programs. Some European countries began experimenting with social welfare programs in the late nineteenth century, and most had developed major programs before the beginning of World War I (1914). Germany, for example, introduced public health insurance, public pension, and maternity benefits in the 1880s. Britain adopted these programs between 1908 and 1912, though a full-fledged program of health insurance was not adopted until 1948. In contrast, the United States did not introduce programs for the unemployed or for families with no income until the 1930s. It still does not have a public health insurance program that covers everyone; as chapter 16 points out, only the elderly and the very poor are covered, and 40 million people are without either private or public health insurance.

We also spend relatively less of our income on social welfare programs. The ratio of the cost of government to the size of the economy is lower in the United States (around 30%) than in any other major Western democracy (most range from 40% to 50% and some as high as 60%). Moreover, a larger part of our government expenditure is on the military and less is for domestic purposes.

These variations reflect the attitudinal differences between Americans and those in other industrial democracies about the roles and responsibilities of government. Some of these differences are illustrated in the table, which indi-

Americans Are Less Likely than Britons or Germans to Believe Social Problems Are Government Responsibilities

	United States	Great Britain	West Germany
Problem			
Providing good education	47	68	55
Providing medical care	42	74	63
Looking after old people	41	58	51
Guaranteeing jobs	34	55	60
Providing adequate housing	25	60	39
Reducing income inequality	13	25	29

Note: Numbers are the percent who think the problem is a government responsibility. Source for opinion data: Russel J. Dalton, Citizen Politics in Western Democracies, (Chatham: N.J.: Chatham House, 1988), p. 100. Other sources: Richard Rose, "Common Goals but Different Roles," in Richard Rose and Rei Shiratori, The Welfare State East and West (Oxford: Oxford University Press, 1986), pp. 13–39.

cates that fewer Americans than Germans or Britons believe government has a responsibility to take care of a wide variety of social and economic problems. With the exception of taking responsibility for education, British and German beliefs about the proper role of government are closer to each other than to Americans' views.

More specifically, they include opinions on abortion, prayer in public schools, restrictions on pornography, tolerance of homosexuals, crime, and the role of women in society.

Social issues have led to a clash of values between those seeking to preserve traditional moral standards and those seeking to establish new ones. Many Americans feel that government policy has encouraged the decline in moral standards and increased permissiveness. Spurred by a rising crime rate in the 1960s and 1970s, Americans felt increasingly that the courts were not being severe enough with criminals. Forty-eight percent responded that the courts were not

harsh enough with criminals in 1965; 82% felt this way in 1990.[58] Increasing numbers of Americans, 71% in 1990, were also willing to endorse the death penalty for murder.[59]

The position of liberals and conservatives on social issues is opposite of what it is on social welfare. On social welfare issues, liberals are likely to support government action, but on social issues they are more likely to reject government involvement. Liberals generally prefer to leave questions of religious belief and sexual morality to individuals to decide for themselves, while conservatives are more willing to call upon government to enforce particular standards of behavior.

Figure 5 ■ Liberal-Conservative Differences on Social Issues

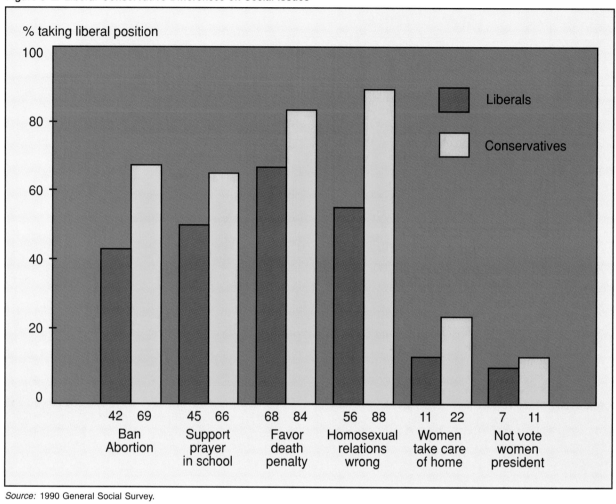

Source: 1990 General Social Survey.

Conservatives, for example, are more likely to favor a ban on abortion and to require prayer in public schools (see figure 5). They are more willing to support capital punishment. Conservatives are considerably more likely than liberals to respond that homosexual relations are always wrong and somewhat more likely to subscribe to the traditional roles for women. For example, conservatives are more likely to feel that women should take care of the home and leave running the country to men.

Liberals and conservatives do not differ on all social issues, however. They are similar in their attitudes about whether they would vote for a woman president; a high percentage of both liberals and conservatives say they would. Nor is there much difference between them in their strong support for the death penalty.

Race

Public opinion has influenced the progress of the black struggle for equality as well as responded to it. Although the historical record extends to colonial times, the polling record begins in the 1940s. It shows white America increasingly opposed to discrimination and segregation, at least in principle.[60] In fact, the change might be characterized as revolutionary. For example, whereas only one-third accepted the idea of black and white children going to the same schools in 1942, in the 1980s more than 90% approved. The

find important in life falls outside of politics. We are concerned about our families and jobs, which for most are not directly and immediately affected by government. Lack of interest leads to lack of intensity. Even where majorities of liberals and conservatives disagree, as, for example, on abortion, prayer in school, and busing, feelings are not very intense, perhaps because most are not touched by these issues.

Second, political candidates and parties do not mobilize their followings with ideological or issue appeals. Both candidates and parties try to be all things to all people, for reasons we will discuss more fully in chapter 6, and often blunt the ideological or issue content of their message in order to attract support from both the right and the left.

Third, there is widespread agreement on how the game of politics is played. Commitment to the basic rights and freedoms for individuals, while not fully endorsed by everyone in all contexts, is an important part of the socialization process in the United States.

Public Opinion and Public Policy

Our interest in public opinion stems in part from the belief that in a democracy government should be responsive to the wishes of the people. But is it? Political scientists have had only limited success answering this question because of the difficulty in measuring influence.

The most direct way to assess whether public policy is responsive to public opinion is to compare changes in policy with changes in opinion. The largest study of this type examined several hundred public opinion surveys done between 1935 and 1979. From these surveys, the researchers culled hundreds of questions, each of which dealt with a particular policy and had been asked more than one time. On more than 300 of these questions, public opinion had changed. The authors of the study compared changes in these 300 opinions with changes, if any, in public policy. They found congruence between opinion and policy changes in more than two-thirds of the opinions. Congruence was most likely when the opinion change was large and stable and when the opinion moved in a liberal direction.

The authors acknowledged that in about one-half of the cases, the policy change may have caused the

opinion change, but in the other half the opinion change probably caused the policy change or they both affected each other. Although in many instances policy was not congruent with public opinion, on important issues, when changes in public opinion were clear-cut, policy usually became consistent with opinion.[87]

Although policy usually changes with changes in opinions, sometimes it does not. One reason is that reelection does not rest with the entire public but with the voting public, and those who vote often differ in their policy preferences from those who do not.[88] To the extent that elected public officials are responsive to voters, and voters differ from nonvoters, public policy will not reflect public opinion.

Then, too, elected public officials must not only pay attention to the direction of public opinion but also to its intensity as well. It may be advantageous for an elected official to vote in support of a minority opinion that is intensely held. A minority with intense feelings is more likely to vote against a candidate who does not support its position than is a group with weak preferences. When elected officials are confronted with an intense minority—for example, the gun lobby—public policy may not reflect public opinion.

Moreover, public opinion is not the only influence on public policy, nor is it necessarily the most important. Interest groups, political parties, other institutions of government, and public officials' own preferences also influence policy, and they may or may not agree with public opinion. Where the preferences of the various influences do not agree, policy generally will reflect a compromise among them.

Finally, there is nothing sacred about public opinion. Even when a majority of the public favors a course of action, one should not assume that this is the most desirable course; the public can be wrong. It is this possibility that led the Founders to establish a government that was partially insulated from the influence of public opinion. In other words, we do not have complete and immediate correspondence between opinion and policy because the Founders did not want instant government responsiveness. They built a federal system with separation of powers and many checks and balances to ensure that the majority could not steamroll the minority. Thus, one should not expect public policy to reflect public opinion perfectly. The fact that policy usually comes to reflect large and stable majorities does indicate, however, that government is eventually responsive on important issues.

Conclusion: How Responsive Should Government Be to Public Opinion?

Although there are difficulties in measuring public opinion and assessing its influence on public policy, one can find some correspondence between the two in the United States.

Several of the drafters of the Constitution were suspicious of public opinion. They saw the public as uneducated, ill-informed, and incapable of governing itself. Because of these misgivings, the Founders tried to create a system of government that limited the public's role.

It is unclear to what extent these institutional checks have limited the public's influence in politics. Contributing as much or more is a socialization process that instills a strong commitment to governmental institutions and directs the public to participate largely through the regulated and legitimate mechanism of elections. Moreover, many issues that might serve to mobilize the public are regarded as matters of personal rather than public concern.

On the whole, government policy is responsive to public opinion when that opinion is strong and stable. However, the lack of concern for politics on the part of the public means that many issues are decided on bases other than public opinion. These include the preferences and interests of elites and interest groups, which may not be consistent with pubic opinion. Decisions made on these bases are not necessarily bad; yet in a democracy one expects some correspondence between the wishes of the public and the direction of public policy. If over a long period of time, there is none, one can raise the question of whether the government is a democracy.

If decisions fail to respond to public opinion or if they disregard it, and if the government performs poorly by the public's standards, we can expect support for the government to decline. This has occurred over the past two decades. Should support fall too low, we might expect the public to begin agitating for political, economic, and social change.

EPILOGUE

America Finds Military Victory Easy, Peace Difficult

On January 16, 1991, the president ordered an attack on Iraq. Americans rallied to the cause, as they always do early in military conflicts. During the first week, polls showed 80% of the public approved the war. The continued outpouring of support led one columnist to conclude that "Americans love war." Fortunately for the president and the troops, the war was short and casualties minimal. In six weeks, Iraq was defeated. The president's gamble appeared to have paid off. Although some Americans protested the war, the quick victory precluded the development of any kind of major protest or questioning by the media. Most Amer-

U.S. soldiers arriving in Saudia Arabia.

icans seemed delirious with joy over the victory. The president's popularity reached record high levels toward the end of the war and immediately after.

Though the president declared that Iraq was not another Vietnam and that the victory put the Vietnam syndrome behind us, it was not clear exactly what that meant. Like Vietnam, Iraq was a Third World country with a fifth-rate economy. Unlike Vietnam, Iraq's armed forces were mediocre, they had no military allies, they were competing with a multinational coalition, and they were completely vulnerable to American and allied air power because they had no cover in which to hide. We were able to bomb them back to a premodern state within days. Nonetheless, as the weeks passed, we were less sure we won a total victory. Tens of thousands of American troops found themselves watching while Saddam Hussein's army used brutal force to put down revolts by minorities within Iraq. Instead of stabilizing the Middle East, the situation seemed as unstable as ever, with Iraq destroyed as a modern nation; Iran and Syria, both recent foes of the United States, strengthened; and Hussein remained in power.

KEY TERMS

public opinion

political socialization

agents of political
    socialization

straw polls

random sampling

sampling error

ideology

liberal

conservative

political tolerance

FURTHER READING

Herbert Asher, *Polling and the Public: What Every Citizen Should Know* (Washington, D.C.: CQ Press, 1988). *An introduction to polling methodology and the influence of polls on American politics as well as advice to citizens on how to evaluate polls.*

Irving Crespi, *Public Opinion, Polls, and Democracy* (Boulder, Colo.: Westview Press, 1989). *An authority on polling, the author discusses how public opinion polls can benefit democracy. Crespi was employed by the Gallup organization for 20 years.*

Celinda Lake, *Public Opinion Polling: A Handbook for Public Interest and Citizen Advocacy Groups* (Washington, D.C.: Island Press, 1987). *A step-by-step treatment for lay audiences on how to conduct a public opinion poll.*

Herbert McClosky and John Zaller, *The American Ethos: Public Attitudes toward Capitalism and Democracy* (Cambridge, Mass.: Harvard University Press, 1988). *An extensive review of citizens' opinions toward democracy and capitalism.*

Jerry Yeric and John Todd, *Public Opinion: The Visible Politics* (Itasca, Ill.: Peacock, 1988). *This text focuses on the public's impact on public policy.*

NOTES

1. For a discussion of how public opinion has been defined, see B. Hennessy, *Public Opinion*, 4th ed. (Monterey, Calif.: Brooks/Cole Publishing Co., 1983), p. 2.

2. R. Cook, "Topsy-Turvy Polls: Medium Is the Message," *Congressional Quarterly Weekly Report*, September 17, 1988, pp. 2559–62.

3. T. E. Cook, "The Bear Market in Political Socialization and the Costs of Misunderstood Psychological Theories," *American Political Science Review* 79 (December 1985): 1079–93.

4. S. W. Moore et al., "The Civic Awareness of Five and Six Year Olds," *Western Political Quarterly* 29 (August 1976): 418.

5. R. W. Connell, *The Child's Construction of Politics* (Carlton, Victoria: Melbourne University Press, 1971).

6. F. I. Greenstein, *Children and Politics* (New Haven, Conn.: Yale University Press, 1965), p. 122; see also F. I. Greenstein, "The Benevolent Leader Revisited: Children's Images of Political Leaders in Three Democracies," *American Political Science Review* 69 (December 1975): 1317–98; R. D. Hess and J. V. Torney, *The Development of Attitudes in Children* (Chicago: Aldine, 1967).

7. Hess and Torney, *Development of Attitudes in Children*; Connell, *Child's Construction of Politics*.

8. Greenstein, *Children and Politics*; Greenstein, "The Benevolent Leader"; and Hess and Torney, *Development of Attitudes in Children*.

9. Connell, *Child's Construction of Politics*.

10. F. C. Arterton, "The Impact of Watergate on Children's Attitudes toward the President," *Political Science Quarterly* 89 (June 1974): 269–88; also F. Haratwig and C. Tidmarch, "Children and Political Reality: Changing Images of the President," paper presented at the 1974 Annual Meeting of the Southern Political Science Association; J. Dennis and C. Webster, "Children's Images of the President and Government in 1962 and 1974," *American Politics Quarterly* 4 (October 1975): 386–405; R. P. Hawkins, S. Pingree, and D. Roberts, "Watergate and Political Socialization," *American Politics Quarterly* 4 (October 1975): 406–36.

11. M. A. Delli Carpini, *Stability and Change in American Politics: The Coming of Age of the Generation of the 1960s* (New York: New York University Press, 1986), pp. 86–89.

12. R. Merelman, *Political Socialization and Educational Climates* (New York: Holt, Rinehart and Winston, 1971), p. 54.

13. R. Sigel and M. Hoskin, *The Political Involvement of Adolescents* (New Brunswick, N.J.: Rutgers University Press, 1981).

14. J. Citrin, "Comment: The Political Relevance of Trust in Government," *American Political Science Review* 68 (September 1974): 973–1001; J. Citrin and D. P. Green, "Presidential Leadership and the Resurgence of Trust in Government," *British Journal of Political Science* 16 (1986): 431–53.

15. It is plausible to assume that the content of early political socialization influences what is learned later, but the assumption has not been adequately tested. Thus, we might expect the positive opinions toward government and politics developed early in childhood to condition the impact of traumatic events later in life. D. Easton and J. Dennis, *Children and the Political System: Origins of Regime Legitimacy* (New York: McGraw-Hill, 1969); R. Weissberg, *Political Learning, Political Choice and Democratic Citizenship* (Englewood Cliffs, N.J.: Prentice-Hall, 1974). See also D. D. Searing, J. J. Schwartz, and A. E. Line, "The Structuring Principle: Political Socialization and Belief System," *American Political Science Review* 67 (June 1973): 414–32.

16. D. Jaros, H. Hirsch, and F. Fleron, Jr., "The Malevolent Leader: Political Socialization in an American Subculture," *American Political Science Review* 62 (June 1968): 564–75.

17. K. Tedin, "The Influence of Parents on the Political Attitudes of Adolescents," *American Political Science Review* 68 (December 1974): 1579–92.

18. On the impact of the public schools and teachers on political socialization, particularly in the area of loyalty and patriotism, see Hess and Torney, *Development of Attitudes in Children.*

19. The study of 17-year-olds is reported by E. Shantz, "Sideline Citizens," in Byron Massiales, ed., *Political Youth, Traditional Schools* (Englewood Cliffs, N.J.: Prentice-Hall, 1972), pp. 69–70; the study of high school seniors is reported by H. H. Remmers and R. D. Franklin, "Sweet Land of Liberty," in H. H. Remmers, ed., *Anti-Democratic Attitudes in American Schools* (Evanston, Ill.: Northwestern University Press, 1963), p. 62.

20. K. Langton and M. K. Jennings, "Political Socialization and the High School Civics Curriculum," *American Political Science Review* 62 (September 1968): 852–77.

21. D. Goldenson, "An Alternative View about the Role of the Secondary School in Political Socialization: A Field Experimental Study of the Development of Civil Liberties Attitudes," *Theory and Research in Social Education* 6 (March 1978): 44–72.

22. R. Merelman, "Democratic Politics and the Culture of American Education," *American Political Science Review* 74 (June 1980): 319–32.

23. G. Almond and S. Verba, *Civic Culture* (Boston: Little, Brown, 1965).

24. Material for this section is drawn from E. C. Ladd and S. M. Lipset, *The Divided Academy* (New York: McGraw-Hill, 1975); C. Kesler, "The Movement of Student Opinion," *The National Review,* November 23, 1979, p. 29; E. L. Boyer, *College: The Undergraduate Experience in America* (New York: Harper & Row, 1986); "Fact File: Attitudes and Characteristics of This Year's Freshman," *The Chronicle of Higher Education,* January 11, 1989, pp. A33–A34; General Social Survey, National Opinion Research Center, 1984, p. 87.

25. M. K. Jennings and R. G. Niemi, *The Political Character of Adolescence* (Princeton, N.J.: Princeton University Press, 1974), p. 243.

26. M. McCombs and D. Shaw, "The Agenda Setting Function of the Media," *Public Opinion Quarterly* 36 (Summer 1972): 176–87.

27. B. I. Page, R. Shapiro, and G. R. Dempsey, "What Moves Public Opinion?" *American Political Science Review* 81 (March 1987): 23–44.

28. H. Weissberg, "Marital Differences in Voting," *Public Opinion Quarterly* 51 (1987): 335–43.

29. P. R. Abramson, *Political Attitudes in America* (San Francisco: Freeman, 1983), pp. 150, 213; see also Paul R. Abramson, *The Political Socialization of Black Americans* (New York: Free Press, 1977).

30. P. E. Converse, A. R. Clausen, and W. Miller, "Electoral Myth and Reality," *American Political Science Review* 59 (1965): 321–26.

31. J. P. Robinson, "The Press as Kingmaker: What Surveys Show from the Last Five Campaigns," *Journalism Quarterly* 49 (Summer 1974): 592.

32. For a review of the history of polling, see Hennessy, *Public Opinion,* pp. 42–44, 46–50. See also C. Roll and A. Cantril, *Polls: Their Use and Misuse in Politics* (New York: Basic Books, 1972), pp. 3–16.

33. P. Squire, "The 1936 Literary Digest Poll," *Public Opinion Quarterly* 52 (1988): 125–33; see also Don Cahalan, "The Digest Poll Rides Again," *Public Opinion Quarterly* 53 (1989): 107–13.

34. Hennessy, *Public Opinion,* p. 46.

35. B. Sussman, "On 'Star Wars,' It all Depends on How You Ask the Questions," *Washington Post National Weekly Edition,* November 25, 1985, p. 37.

36. R. Morin, "The Perils of All This Polling," *Washington Post National Weekly Edition,* October 3, 1988, p. 42.

37. R. Morin, "Women Asking Women about Men Asking Women About Men," *Washington Post National Weekly Edition,* January 15, 1990, p. 37.

38. I. A. Lewis and W. Schneider, "Is the Public Lying to the Pollsters?" *Public Opinion Magazine* (April/May 1982): 42–47. See also A. Clausen, "Response Validity and Vote Report," *Public Opinion Quarterly* 32 (1968): 588–606.

39. H. Asher, *Polling and the Public* (Washington, D.C.: CQ Press, 1988), pp. 113–14.

40. H. Mendelsohn and I. Crespi, *Polls, Television, and the New Politics* (Scranton, Penn.: Chandler Publishing Company, 1972), pp. 125–28.

41. B. Sussman, "In Pollsters We Trust," *Washington Post National Weekly Edition,* August 25, 1968, p. 37.

42. M. C. Shelley and H. Hwang, "The Mass Media and Public Opinion Polls in the 1988 Presidential Election," *American Politics Quarterly* 19 (January 1991): 59–79.

43. Roll and Cantril, *Polls,* p. 23; Mendelsohn and Crespi, *Polls, Television, and the New Politics,* p. 130.

44. Roll and Cantril, *Polls,* p. 24.

45. J. Klapper, quoted in B. Sussman, "Some Answers to the Polls' Critics," *Washington Post National Weekly Edition,* November 12, 1984, p. 37.

46. 1978 National Election Study, Center for Political Studies, University of Michigan.

47. 1988 National Election Study, Center for Political Studies, University of Michigan.

48. 1986 National Election Study, Center for Political Studies, University of Michigan; "Wapner Top Judge in Recognition Poll," *Lincoln Star,* June 23, 1989, p. 1 (*Washington Post* syndication).

49. M. J. Robinson and M. Clancey, "Teflon Politics," *Public Opinion* 7 (April/May 1984): 14–18.

50. V. O. Key, *The Responsible Electorate* (Cambridge, Mass.: Harvard University Press, 1966); N. Nie, S. Verba, and J. R. Petrocik, *The Changing American Voter* (Cambridge, Mass.: Harvard University Press, 1976), chapter 18.

51. B. Sussman, "When Politicians Talk about Issues People Listen," *Washington Post National Weekly Edition,* August 18, 1986, p. 37.

52. R. Niemi, J. Mueller, and T. Smith, *Trends in Public Opinion* (New York: Greenwood, 1989), pp. 89–90.

53. R. Erikson, N. Luttbeg, and K. Tedin, *American Public Opinion* (New York: Macmillan, 1988), p. 77.

54. Niemi, pp. 79–80, 82–84.

55. Neimi, pp. 81, 91.

56. Neimi, p. 76.

57. Neimi, p. 33.

58. Neimi, p. 136.

59. Neimi, p. 138.

60. This section draws heavily on H. Schuman, C. Steeh, and L. Bobo, *Racial Attitudes in America* (Cambridge, Mass.: Harvard University Press, 1985); data summaries are drawn from the General Social Surveys of the National Opinion Research Center, University of Chicago, and National Elections Studies of CPS, University of Michigan; see also L. Sigelman and S. Welch, *Black Americans' Views of Racial Inequality* (Cambridge, Mass.: Cambridge University Press, 1991).

61. *Washington Post National Weekly Edition,* October, 30, 1989, p. 37.

62. "Whites Retain Negative Views of Minorities, a Survey Finds," *New York Times,* January 10, 1991, p. C19.

63. M. Jackman, "General and Applied Tolerance: Does Education Increase Commitment to Racial Inequality?" *American Journal of Political Science* 22 (1978): 302–24; M. Jackman, "Education and Policy Commitment to Racial Equality," *American Journal of Political Science* 25 (1981): 256–69; D. Kinder and D. Sears, "Prejudice and Politics," *Journal of Personality and Social Psychology* 40 (1981): 414–31.

64. "Whites Retain Negative Views."

65. H. Schuman and L. Bobo, "Survey-Based Experiments on White Attitudes toward Residential Integration," *American Journal of Sociology* 94 (1988): 272–94; W. R. Merriman and E. Carmines, "The Limits of Liberal Tolerance: The Case of Racial Politics," *Polity* 20 (1988): 519–26; see also Schuman, Steeh, and Bobo, *Racial Attitudes.*

66. L. Sigelman and S. Welch, "A Dream Deferred: Black Attitudes toward Race and Inequality," unpublished manuscript, 1989. Al-most all blacks support school integration, only 50% to 60% support busing.

67. "1990 General Social Survey."

68. ABC/*Washington Post* Poll, 1981.

69. ABC/*Washington Post* Poll, 1981 and 1986.

70. J. Sullivan, G. Marcus, S. Feldman, and J. Pierson, "Sources of Political Tolerance: A Multivariate Analysis," *American Political Science Review* 75 (March 1981): 92–106.

71. S. Stouffer, *Communism, Conformity, and Civil Liberties* (New York: John Wiley and Sons, 1954).

72. R. W. Jackman, "Political Elites, Mass Publics, and Support for Democratic Principles," *Journal of Politics* 34 (August 1972): 753.

73. H. McClosky and J. Zaller, *The American Ethos: Public Attitudes toward Capitalism and Democracy* (Cambridge, Mass.: Harvard University Press, 1986).

74. C. Z. Nunn, H. H. Crockett, Jr., and J. A. Williams, *Tolerance for Nonconformity* (San Francisco: Jossey-Bass, 1976).

75. J. Sullivan, J. Pierson, and G. Marcus, "An Alternative Conceptualization of Tolerance: Illusory Increases 1950s–1970s," *American Political Science Review* 73 (September 1979): 781–94. For a critique of this study, see P. M. Sniderman, P. E. Tetlock, J. M. Glaser, D. P. Gress, and M. Hout, "Principled Tolerance and the American Mass Public," *British Journal of Political Science* 19 (January 1989): 25–46.

76. P. Abramson, "Comments on Sullivan, Pierson, and Marcus," *American Political Science Review* 74 (June 1980): 780–81.

77. 1990 General Social Survey.

78. Almond and Verba, *Civic Culture,* pp. 64–68.

79. A. Miller, "Political Issues and Trust in Government, 1964–1970," *American Political Science Review* 68 (September 1974): 951–72.

80. T. J. Lowi, *The Personal President* (Ithaca, N.Y.: Cornell University Press, 1985), pp. 64–68.

81. S. M. Lipset and W. Schneider, *The Confidence Gap* (New York: Free Press, 1983), pp. 63–64.

82. A. Miller and S. Borrelli, "Confidence in Government During the 1980s," *American Politics Quarterly* 19 (April 1991): 147–73.

83. 1990 General Social Survey.

84. R. Dalton, *Citizens Politics in Western Democracies* (Chatham, N.J.: Chatham House, 1988), p. 231.

85. Dalton, pp. 231–32.

86. Dalton, pp. 236–37.

87. Benjamin Page and Robert Shapiro, "Effects of Public Opinion on Policy," *American Political Science Review 77* (March 1983): 175–90. See also Robert Weissberg, *Public Opinion and Popular Government* (Engelwood Cliffs, N.J.: Prentice-Hall, 1976); Alan D. Monroe, "Public Opinion and Public Policy, 1960-1974," paper delivered at the American Political Science Association meeting, New York, 1978.

88. Sidney Verba and Norman H. Nie, *Participation in America: Political Democracy and Social Equality* (New York: Harper & Row, 1972), chapter 15.

89. Edward Gargan, "Kuwait Deeply Split on Vision of a Post-Occupation Order," *New York Times,* May 19, 1991, p. 1.

90. Jack Kelley, "Dream of 'New Kuwait' Dying," *USA Today,* May 22, 1991, p. 2.

91. *Time,* June 3, 1991, p. 19. A Yankelovich poll.

5 | Interest Groups

In the U.S., groups form to promote just about every cause and interest imaginable. Many groups verbally fence with other groups over public issues. This group fences more literally.

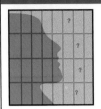

Should You Battle Bork?

You are Ralph Neas, lobbyist and executive director for the Leadership Council on Civil Rights, a coalition of 185 civil rights groups.[1] You joined the Leadership Council in 1981 and have become one of the best-known civil rights lobbyists in Washington.

The Reagan years have not been good for civil rights, but you have held your own. You won the fight against eliminating affirmative action goals in companies doing work for the federal government. You also managed to save the Civil Rights Commission from efforts to dismantle it. You succeeded in winning congressional support for fair housing and against age discrimination.

These, however, are minor compared to the battle looming now in 1987. Supreme Court Justice Lewis Powell has suddenly announced his retirement, so President Reagan will have an opportunity to appoint a replacement. The news is extremely disturbing to you because Powell was a moderate, who generally supported civil rights, whereas Reagan has appointed conservatives. Given that the Court is already divided, its ideological makeup is at stake. Another conservative justice could move the Court majority sharply to the right and undermine the policies you have struggled for. The new justice's effect would last far longer than Reagan's presidency.

Your worst fears are realized when the president nominates federal court of appeals judge Robert Bork to fill the vacancy. Bork is very conservative. In the past he opposed some major advances in civil rights, including outlawing restrictive covenants, poll taxes, literacy tests, and discrimination in public accommodations and private housing. Though he recanted some of his controversial positions, he still opposes affirmative action. He is conservative in other areas as well. He believes that states should be able to ban abortions and that governments should be able to impose more restrictions on speech and demonstrations than the Court allows now.

Yet there is no question about Bork's technical qualifications. He was a distinguished professor of law at Yale and a high-ranking official—solicitor general—in Nixon's Justice Department. He was appointed to the court of appeals by Reagan. Recently, the American Bar Association gave him its highest rating—"exceptionally well qualified" to serve on the Court.

It is clear that the White House is going to do everything possible to secure Bork's confirmation by the Senate. Not only is control of the Court at stake, but the president wants to show that he still can work the magic that brought him so many victories in the early years of his administration. Most think Bork will be confirmed.

So what do you do? Do you oppose him on ideological grounds, even though he is highly qualified in other respects and even though you seem to have little chance to defeat him? Your organization—low-budget crusaders working out of a dingy townhouse basement—would be like David opposing the administration's Goliath.

You have three choices. You can do nothing. You can provide token opposition, conserving your limited resources for battles you can win. Or you can throw all your resources and efforts into defeating the nomination.

OUTLINE

In 1773 a group of colonists organized to protest British taxes on tea by throwing tea into Boston Harbor. In 1989 groups organized to protest a congressional pay increase by sending teabags to their representatives in Washington.

In the United States everything from fruits to nuts is organized. From apple growers to filbert producers, every interest has an organization to represent it. These organizations touch every aspect of our lives; members of the American College of Obstetrics and Gynecology bring us into the world, and members of the National Funeral Directors Association usher us out.

Organizations that try to achieve at least some of their goals with government assistance are called **interest groups.** Fruit and nut growers want government subsidies and protection from imported products; doctors and funeral directors want to be free of government controls. The efforts of interest groups to influence government are called **lobbying.** Lobbying may involve direct contact between a lobbyist, or group representative, and a government official, or it may involve indirect action, such as attempts to sway public opinion, which will in turn influence officials.

People organize primarily because organization is a way for them to enhance their influence. The old adage "in numbers there is strength" is true. When people pool their resources, they enhance the possibility of success.

The Founders feared the harmful effects of interest groups. Madison was intent on "curing the mischiefs of faction" through separation of powers, checks and balances, and federalism. Today, many people bemoan the "mischiefs of faction" or "special interests" because they seem to block government actions favoring the larger interests of society.[2] Sometimes it seems that everyone is represented in Washington but the people.

Do interest groups undermine the people's interests? Or do they make government more responsive by giving people greater representation in the political process? These are the difficult questions we explore in this chapter.

Group Formation

There are thousands of groups in the United States. Americans seem to be "joiners." As early as the 1830s, the Frenchman Alexis de Tocqueville, who traveled in America, noted the tendency of Americans to join groups: "In no country in the world has the principle of association been more successfully used or applied to a greater multitude of objects than in America."[3] Americans are even now more likely to belong to groups than citizens of other countries.[4]

The United States provides an especially fertile soil for the growth of groups. Our diversity of races, religions, and national origins makes us more heterogeneous than people in some countries. This diversity prompts people to organize to protect their interests.[5]

Groups can organize because of the freedom to speak, assemble, and petition government, guaranteed

For the Right to Undress, Nudists Are Flexing the First Amendment Right to Redress

Have you ever had the urge to go skinny-dipping in the public pool or to get a tan in the nude at the neighborhood park? If you tried it, chances are you would get a quick visit from a fully clothed police officer. The 17,000-member Naturalist Society, the nation's most politically active organization of nudists, is out to change this.

While the government has no policy for or against nudism on public lands, and the National Park Service allows nude beaches in remote areas, members are lobbying to keep from getting kicked off public lands when conflicts occur between "textile beaches" and "clothing-optional" beaches. Members argue that they "are tired of always moving farther down the beach." To protect their right to clothing-optional recreation, as members call it, the organization retained a Washington lobbyist to make its case to Congress.

Politically, nudists are divided between conservatives and liberals. Conservatives tend to join the Florida-based sunbathing association, which claims 36,000 members. They prefer to be left alone and gravitate toward private clubs. Liberals are more likely to join the Naturalist Society and use public beaches. If a nude nudist ever testifies on Capitol Hill, it is likely to be one of the public beachgoers.

Besides beach access, nudists are addressing other issues as well, including child custody and jobs. Many have lost children and jobs because of their penchant for nude recreation.

The first task of their newly hired lobbyist is make the issue less attention grabbing. The strategy is to become just another pestering group in Washington. When the smirks fade from the faces of official Washington, the group believes it will be taken more seriously.

Source: "The Right To Undress," *Common Cause Magazine* (January/February 1991): 6–7.

The groups that formed during the revolutionary war period did not confine themselves to writing pamphlets and making fiery speeches. Tarring and feathering was a common form of protest activity. Happily this form of protest is not so common now, though many French women who collaborated with the Nazis during World War II were tarred and feathered after France was liberated.

Our federal structure also encourages the proliferation of groups. It is not enough to have a national organization. Because state and local governments have significant power, groups also must be organized at those levels to protect their interests.

Why Groups Form

The formation of groups occurs in waves.[6] In some periods formation is rapid and extensive, whereas at other times there is very little activity.

Social and economic stress often account for these surges.[7] The stress of the revolutionary war period activated groups for and against independence. The slavery controversy in the decades before the Civil War

in the First Amendment to the Constitution. Without such freedom, only groups favored by the government—or groups whose members are willing to be punished for their actions—could exist.

Brewing Conflict

Many things become the focus of political competition and group activity. Beer is a case in point. Brewers, distributors, retailers, and drinkers are involved. The distributors, or wholesalers, buy large quantities of beer from the brewers and sell it to retailers. Each distributor has a fixed territory in which to operate and is authorized by the brewers to sell certain labels.

Each group has a different view of how the system should work. Retailers want to buy beer from distributors as cheaply as possible to maximize their profits. Sometimes the cheapest price is offered by distributors outside the territories where their stores are located.

Distributors naturally are concerned with their own profits and want retailers to buy within their territory. These opposing points of view brew conflict.

The distributors have organized a political action committee, Six-Pac, to distribute campaign donations to key members of Congress. The Six-Pac lobby has worked to get legislation passed permitting distributors to have exclusive marketing territories without violating antitrust regulations. The brewers supported them because they liked the prospect of higher, more stable prices for their product.

Six-Pac's initial efforts were bottled up by a coalition of consumer (The Consumer Federation of America and Congress Watch) and retailer groups. Consumers feared higher prices, and retailers feared less business caused by higher prices. The Justice Department and Federal Trade Commission also opposed the distributors and brewers.

These political actors view the world through their self-interest. How the rest of us feel about it is also subjective, depending on whether we are filling, selling, or emptying the bottle.

---

energized groups on both sides of the issue. After the war, rapid industrialization led to the formation of trade unions and business associations. Economic problems in agricultural areas spurred the development of farm groups.

The greatest surge in group formation occurred between 1900 and 1920. Stimulated by the shocks of industrialization, urbanization, immigration, and the government's response to them, groups such as the United States Chamber of Commerce, American Medical Association, American Farm Bureau Federation, National Association of Colored People (NAACP), Socialist and Communist parties, and countless others formed.[8]

The 1960s and 1970s witnessed an interest group explosion, directed primarily toward Washington. As the national government expanded in power and influence in the post–World War II period, it increasingly became the center of interest group efforts to satisfy demands for favorable public policy. Spurred by the success of civil rights and war protest movements in the 1960s, other groups representing racial minorities, women, consumers, the poor, the elderly, and the environment organized. Business lobbying surged in the late 1970s as a response to the successes of consumer and environmental groups in prompting government to increase the regulation of occupational safety and environmental standards.[9]

Technological changes also accelerate group formation. A national network of railroads and the telegraph contributed to the surge in the early 1900s. Computers and WATS lines (wide-area telephone service) increased the ability of groups to mobilize and communicate with members in the 1960s and 1970s. The number of groups increased by 60% between 1960 and 1980, and the number sending representatives to Washington doubled.[10]

Group organizers also play a role in group formation.[11] These entrepreneurs often come from established groups. They gain experience and then strike out on their own. Many civil rights activists of the 1950s and early 1960s founded organizations in the late 1960s. Some used their skills to organize groups against the war in Vietnam and later to organize groups for women's rights and environmental causes.[12] Thus the formation of one group often opens the door to the formation of others.

The government is also important to group formation. Government attempts to deal with perceived problems often generate organized opposition groups, such as the increase in business lobbying in response to environmental lobbying. In addition, government provides direct financial assistance to some groups, particularly nonprofit organizations. Groups as diverse as the American Council of Education, the National Governors Association, and the National Council of Senior

Members of the American Association of Retired People use phone banks to recruit new members and raise money.

(CDF) have formed, but they are small by comparison. AGE has 700 members. As benefits to the elderly continue to increase and the burden on younger Americans becomes more severe, groups like AGE and CDF are likely to become more active in lobbying policymakers to gain their share of government benefits.

Foreign Governments.   Foreign interests also lobby in Washington. Most countries recruit lobbyists from the ranks of former members of Congress and the bureaucracy. One-third of the 45 top officials who left the Office of U.S. Trade Representatives during the Reagan administration are now working for foreign governments, the most prominent for Japan.[36] In one recent year, the Japanese spent more than $60 million to lobby in the United States, twice as much as any other country.

Public Interest Groups

Public interest groups, more than 2,500 with 40 million members,[37] lobby for benefits that cannot be limited or restricted to their members. Although nearly all groups think of themselves as pursuing the public interest, the label applies only to those providing public interest benefits. "Public interest" does not mean that most or even a majority of the public necessarily favors the goals of these groups.

The Sierra Club lobbied successfully to preserve the redwood trees in California and won benefits not limited to members alone. The National Taxpayers Union lobbies for reduced taxes not only for themselves but for everyone who pays taxes. Amnesty International lobbies for the rights of political prisoners around the world even though none of its members are prisoners. All are public interest groups.

Public interest groups are not new, but their numbers and size increased dramatically during the late 1960s and early 1970s. Several factors account for this surge. Americans were becoming increasingly distrustful of government, which appeared to favor special interests over more general interests. The need for a balance between the two led many to join public interest groups. Many middle-class Americans also had the financial means to support public interest groups. The new technology mentioned earlier also made it possible to reach and mobilize large numbers of them.[38]

While many of the public interest groups that were established during the 1960s and 1970s were "shoestring" operations staffed by idealistic social reformers with few professional skills, the public interest organizations of today have larger budgets and memberships and a cadre of professionals—attorneys, management consultants, direct-mail fund raisers, and communications directors—handling day-to-day operations and seeking to influence government with a variety of strategies and tactics.[39]

Multiple-Issue Groups. Some public interest groups are multiple-issue groups, involved with a broad range of issues. Others have a narrower focus and are often referred to as single-issue groups.

Consumer Groups.   One of the more famous consumer organizations is the network founded by Ralph Nader. Author of *Unsafe at Any Speed,* a book exposing safety defects in Corvair automobiles, Nader testified before Congress, which was considering the Auto Safety Act in 1965. Nader became famous practically overnight when it was revealed that General Motors had hired a private detective to try to collect evidence that could discredit him. Greatly embarrassed when this ploy became known, GM had to pay Nader an out-of-court settlement for harassment. No "dirt" was ever found—Nader then and now lives a Spartan life and is apparently totally devoted to his work.

With the settlement and funds from book royalties and lecture tours, Nader founded a wide variety of public interest organizations, the most famous of which is called Public Citizen. Nader's staff members, called "Nader's Raiders" to characterize their zeal, accept low wages and work long hours. Their reward is the chance to influence government to pass and enforce laws protecting consumers and workers and reducing government waste.

Nader's organizations research and publicize problems and lobby in Congress. Current causes include problems in the nuclear industry, costs of health care, consumer protection, and congressional campaign finances.

Although consumer groups achieved many of their objectives in the 1960s and 1970s, in the 1980s they had less success. Their main target, business, reasserted its usual political dominance.

Women's Groups.   Groups advocating women's equality have mushroomed in the past two decades and range from large, mass-based organizations with a broad agenda such as the National Organization for Women (NOW) to much smaller groups with very specific interests such as women's athletics or electing women to office.

NOW is the largest women's group with 150,000 members in all 50 states.[40] With a national board made up of regional representatives and national salaried officers, NOW is well organized. It has field representatives and organizers, researchers, lobbyists, and specialists in various policy areas such as reproductive freedom and economic rights.

NOW is funded largely from membership dues but has actively solicited funds by mail. It also receives income from subscriptions and selling such things as T-shirts and posters. One unique idea to raise money was the Adopt-a-Picket program used in California. Members would adopt a prolifer who picketed outside Planned Parenthood clinics and donate every time their adopted picket showed up. Private foundations interested in promoting women's rights also provide significant funding.

Although NOW began as a protest movement, today its focus is on lobbying at the national, state, and local levels. It provides leadership training and education for local and state groups and works with a shifting coalition of other women's rights groups.

The activities of the women's movement have shifted from Washington, where funds are scarce, to state governments, where resources are more plentiful. Family and child care have joined more confronta-

tional issues such as abortion as major concerns.[41] Though the women's movement has had only mixed success in getting its legislative agenda passed, and it was defeated in its move for an Equal Rights Amendment, the tide of public opinion continues to move in its favor. A 1985 poll showed 73% of the public favoring a stronger role for women in society compared to 44% in 1970.

Religious Groups.   Religious groups often lobby on political issues. The National Council of Churches, representing liberal Protestant denominations, has spoken out on civil rights, human rights, and other social issues. Catholic groups have been active in both antiabortion and antinuclear movements. Jewish groups have been involved in lobbying for liberal issues, such as the rights of workers and minorities.

Jewish groups have been particularly active in lobbying for Israel. Since its beginning in 1951, the pro-Israel lobby has lost on only three key decisions, all involving the sale of U.S. arms to Egypt and Saudi Arabia. The success of Jewish groups in lobbying for Israel reflects their commitment, organization, and political skill and an opposition Arab lobby that is weak by comparison.[42]

Identified by a "born again" experience, a desire to win converts to Jesus Christ, and a literal interpretation of the Bible, members of the Christian right, sometimes called fundamentalists, spurred by what they saw as a decline in traditional values, became active in politics in the 1970s.[43] Opposed to abortion, divorce, homosexuality, and women's rights, conservative Christians were the major force behind the effort of television evangelist Pat Robertson to win the Republican presidential nomination in 1988. Local churches worked to secure names on endorsing petitions and funds. The campaign raised $30 million in contributions and matching funds, second only to George Bush. Although he did not win nomination, Robertson did win a number of delegates to the Republican National Convention. He also established a formidable network of state organizations that continues to battle traditional Republicans for control of the party. While little of the Christian right's agenda has been enacted into law, many drawn to politics in the 1970s remain active and involved.[44]

A church network also provided Jesse Jackson with needed support during his campaign for the Democratic presidential nomination in 1988. Black ministers endorsed his candidacy, urged their members to vote for him, and raised funds. Black churches throughout the nation served as the basic political units for the Jackson effort, particularly during the early stages of the campaign.[45]

Other Multiple-Issue Interest Groups. Common Cause, a multiple-issue interest group established in 1970 by John Gardner, attracted nearly 100,000 members in the first six months of its existence. Much of the group's lobbying program has been directed toward improving the accountability of government. The group successfully lobbied for the 1974 Campaign Reform Act, which placed stricter rules on reporting campaign expenditures and contributions and provided public financing for presidential elections. The organization also supports further finance reform, including public funding of congressional elections.

Environmental groups are another example. Earth Day 1970 marked the beginning of the environmental movement in the United States. Spurred by an oil spill in California, what was to be a "teach-in" on college campuses mushroomed into a day of national environmental awareness with an estimated 20 million Americans taking part. A minority movement in the 1970s, the environmental lobby today is large and active and its values are supported by most Americans.[46]

Some environmental groups, such as the National Audubon Society, Sierra Club, and the Natural Resources Defense Council, have permanent offices in Washington with highly skilled professionals who carry out a full range of lobbying activities. All experienced substantial growth in membership and finances during the 1980s, when the Reagan administration threatened to undo the environmental gains of the 1970s.[47]

The so-called Greens are environmental groups that shun conventional lobbying approaches and are more confrontational. Groups like Greenpeace, Earth First!, and the Sea Shepherds seek a "green cultural revolution." Local citizen groups have also organized in support of local environmental concerns such as the location of toxic or nuclear waste dumps. Citizens, skeptical of government and corporate claims that such facilities are safe, want them located elsewhere.[48]

Single-Issue Groups.   **Single-issue groups** pursue public interest goals but are distinguished by their intense concern for a single issue and their unwillingness to compromise. Members of the National Rifle Association (NRA) passionately oppose any form of

The right-to-life movement is considered a single issue group.

government control of firearms. For years, in spite of a majority of Americans who support gun control, the NRA has successfully lobbied Congress to prevent it. The group has members in every congressional district and is well organized to mobilize them. The NRA spent $4 million in 1987 to defeat a bill that required gun dealers to wait seven days, time enough to allow the police to run a check on the buyer, before completing the sale of a handgun. The money was used to urge its three million members to write and phone their representatives. The group was dealt a setback, however, in 1991, when the House approved a waiting period. The NRA vowed to make a major effort to defeat supporters of the bill in the 1992 congressional elections.

The abortion controversy has generated a number of single-issue groups. The National Right to Life Committee seeks a constitutional amendment banning all abortions. The committee has worked to elect candidates who favor such an amendment and defeat those who do not. After the 1989 Supreme Court decision allowing more state regulation of abortion, the committee and other pro-life groups turned their attention to state legislatures.

Operation Rescue is a more confrontational antiabortion group that attempts to prevent women seeking abortions access to abortion clinics across the country. Many "rescuers" have been arrested and jailed because of their activity. The founder and leader, Randall Terry, a former used-car salesman, in testimony at his own trial for illegal activities, equated the movement with the civil rights movement, identifying himself with Dr. Martin Luther King, Jr. and Rosa Parks.

Members of the national Abortion Rights Action League and Planned Parenthood are equally fervently committed to protecting women's right to abortion. Planned Parenthood is the oldest, largest, best-financed, and most powerful single advocate of reproductive freedom for women, including birth control and abortion. Under the leadership of Faye Wattleton, the organization has become more vocal in recent years, particularly on the issue of abortion.[49] Planned Parenthood was part of the 125-group coalition that opposed the nomination of Judge Bork to the Supreme Court because of his position on abortion.

Since 1988, the organization has mounted a major effort to win policymakers to the pro-choice point of view. Using the theme that Americans want abortion to be safe and legal, ads were placed in national newspapers such as the *New York Times* and the *Washington Post*. Local and state press were informed about the impact of illegal abortion. Testimony was provided by physicians who treated botched abortions in the days when abortion was illegal, by clergy involved in counseling, and by women who underwent illegal abortion because they had no choice. At the national level, briefings with reporters and editors were held on abortion-related cases before the Supreme Court and on the latest health and safety information on abortion. Three months before the 1989 Supreme Court decision allowing state regulation of abortion (for more on this see chapter 14), 300,000 pro-choice activists staged a march in Washington. Calling the event the "March for Women's Lives," the goal was to recast the issue in terms of freedom and choice rather than abortion. The march slogan, "Who Decides, You or Them?" became the rallying cry in several state elections in 1989. The three-day event received substantial

publicity and demonstrated to members of Congress that the movement could mobilize a large number of supporters.[50]

Since the decision, both pro-choice and pro-life groups lobbied the states and tried to elect candidates sympathetic to their point of view. The pro-choice side won major electoral victories in gubernatorial elections in Virginia and New Jersey and defeated several bills restricting abortion in Florida. Pro-life groups won major restrictions on abortion in Pennsylvania and barely missed in Idaho, where a bill passed by the legislature was vetoed by the governor.[51]

Single-issue groups have increased in number since the mid-1960s. Some view this with alarm, because when groups clash over a highly emotional issue and are unwilling to compromise, government cannot resolve the issue.[52] The issue commands excessive time and energy of policymakers at the expense of broader issues that may be more important.

On the other hand, single-issue groups have always been part of politics.[53] These groups may even be beneficial because they represent interests that may not be well represented in Congress. Fears about single-issue groups may result from their own exaggerated claims of influence and their heavy media coverage.

Tactics of Interest Groups

Interest groups engage in a variety of tactics to secure their goals. Some try to influence policymakers directly, whereas others seek to mold public opinion and influence policymakers indirectly. Sometimes interest groups form broad coalitions or engage in protest activity, both of which involve direct and indirect techniques.

Direct Lobbying Techniques

Direct lobbying techniques involve personal encounters between lobbyists and public officials.

Making Personal Contacts.   Making personal contacts, in an office or in a more informal setting, is probably the most effective lobbying technique. Compared to other forms of lobbying, direct personal contact is relatively inexpensive, and it minimizes prob-

lems of misinterpretation by allowing questions to be answered on the spot.

Lobbyists know that contacting every legislator is unnecessary, whereas contacting key legislators, those who sit on the committees having jurisdiction over matters of interest to the lobbyists, and staff serving those committees, is critical.[54] Conventional wisdom also suggests that only those legislators who support a group's position or who are known to be undecided should be contacted directly.[55] Putting undue pressure on known opponents may jeopardize prospects for working together in the future on other issues.

Most lobbyists are honest. Dishonesty can hurt their cause. Willingness to compromise is another mark of a good lobbyist. Lobbyists who are less than honest or who refuse to compromise may throw away victory. One example is the 1983 fight of tobacco lobbyists against strengthening the warnings about the effects of smoking on cigarette packages. Going into the fight, the tobacco industry seemed to have the clout to get its way. But the lobbyists alienated congressional allies by spreading stories to congressional staffers that several senators had accepted a compromise bill favorable to the tobacco industry. "Under the bizarre misapprehension that the staff members would not compare notes, they left a messy, bipartisan trail of conflicting, fanciful tales depicting platoons of senators poised to champion their compromise.[56] When the committee writing the bill offered the lobbyists the compromise, they publicly rejected it, in hopes of getting something better, humiliating the committee chair, who had thought that the industry supported the compromise. One observer said the chair was "absolutely livid."

After also backing out of a previously agreed-to compromise bill in the House, the tobacco lobbyists so enraged the chair of the House committee considering the bill that he put his committee's chief staffer to work on the issue. The staffer's strategy: "The way to deal with these people is to have at them with an axe." Not unexpectedly, the tobacco industry lost, and new, more severe warnings were added to cigarette packages.

Providing Expertise.   Some lobbying groups do research and present their findings to public officials. One of the major strengths of Ralph Nader's organization, and the public interest movement in general, is the ability to provide public officials, particularly Congress, with accurate and reliable information.

Lobbyists often have a great deal of knowledge and expertise that is useful in drafting legislation. A legislator may ask a lobbyist to draft a bill or both may work together in drafting legislation. Sometimes interest groups themselves draft legislation and ask a sympathetic legislator to introduce it. General Electric drafted a tax reform measure that saved it millions in taxes. There is nothing illegal about this.

Testimony at Hearings.   Testimony at congressional hearings is designed to establish a group's credentials as a "player" in the policy area as well as to convince their own constituents that they are doing their job. It can also provide free publicity. However, testimony rarely persuades committee members. Sometimes a group must testify to counter opposition testimony. Because of the media value of hearings, staging often occurs. A lobbyist might request a sympathetic legislator to ask certain questions that the lobbyist is prepared to answer or to indicate in advance what questions will be asked. Sometimes celebrities are invited to testify. To encourage media coverage of the farm issue, Jane Fonda and others who starred in movies dealing with the farm crisis testified on the plight of farm families.

Giving Money.   Lobbyists try to ensure access to legislators, and giving money is one way to guarantee this. Justin Dart, a longtime financial backer of Ronald Reagan, once said that having a dialogue with a politician is fine, "but with a little money they hear you better."[57] One Democrat commented in a similar

AMERICAN DIVERSITY

Take Your
Pick of PACs

There seems to be a political action committee (PAC) for everybody. There is a FishPAC, BeefPAC, LardPAC, and yes, a BackPAC. Cigar smokers are represented by Cigar-PAC, beer drinkers by Six-PAC. Sports lovers have the American Fishing Tackle Manufacturers Association PAC, the California Motorcyclist PAC, and the Hawaii Golfers for Good Government PAC.

Some PACs strike an upbeat note, including committees for A Stronger Future, Better Political Choices, Hon-

esty and Integrity, and Morality and Decency. One visionary organization is called the Committee for the Twenty-First Century. Other PACs, however, seem to have expectations that exceed reality, such as the Committee Urging Reduced Bureaucracy.

Source: Dom Bonafide, "Some Things Don't Change—Cost of 1982 Congressional Races Higher Than Ever," *National Journal,* October 1982, p. 1835.

vein, "Who do members of Congress see? They'll certainly see the one who gives the money. It's hard to say no to someone who gives you $5,000."[58]

The primary way groups channel money to legislators is through campaign contributions. Groups, including businesses and unions, may set up political action committees (PACS) to give money to campaigns of political candidates.

The number of PACs has grown dramatically in the past decade as has the amount of money they have contributed. (We discuss PACs more fully in chapter 9).

Lobbying the Bureaucracy. For lobbyists, the battle is not over when a bill is passed. Lobbyists also must influence bureaucrats who implement policy. For example, regulations outlawing sex discrimination in educational institutions were drafted largely in the Department of Education with only very broad guidelines from Congress. Both women's rights groups and interests opposing them lobbied for years to influence the regulations.

In influencing bureaucrats, interest groups use most of the tactics already described. They also try to influence who gets appointed to bureaucratic positions. Someone opposed by the major agricultural interest groups is not likely to be appointed secretary of agriculture. Nor is someone unsympathetic to labor apt to be appointed head of the Labor Department. Of course, groups do not always succeed in their opposition. President Reagan appointed as heads of sev-

eral agencies persons strongly opposed by interest groups sympathetic to the agency's activities. He appointed a secretary of the interior opposed to many governmental efforts to protect public land and an Environmental Protection Agency head who opposed most government efforts to protect the environment.

The influence of groups in the appointment process is especially crucial in the case of appointments to regulatory agencies such as the Food and Drug Administration. By influencing appointments to an agency, the regulated industry can improve its prospects of favorable treatment.

Interest groups often develop strong ties to both the executive agency and the congressional subcommittee with responsibility in the policy area. **Iron triangles,** sometimes called subgovernments, refer to the mutually supportive and advantageous relationships that exist between interest groups, executive agencies, and congressional subcommittees. Interest groups seek favorable decisions from both congressional committee members with information, advice, and campaign support. Likewise, interest groups are a source of information for agencies as well as allies in securing favorable votes from Congress. Agencies aid committee members by providing information and assistance with constituents' problems. Committee members respond by supporting higher funding levels for agencies. The triangles make policy with little interference from agents and interests outside the network, including Congress and the president.

Iron triangles exist in several policy areas. Some policy areas, however, have become more open in recent years. Agriculture, for example, is no longer dominated by a few major farm groups, the House and Senate Agriculture committees, and the Department of Agriculture. One study identified 215 organizations active in agriculture policy, including farmers, farm suppliers, food industries, financial institutions, consumers, environmentalists, the poor, state and local government, and many more.[59] Moreover, their lobbying efforts extended to numerous congressional committees and several agencies and departments.

The change reflects the greater complexity of agriculture and government's role in it. It also illustrates greater sharing of congressional power and influence, which allows members other than committee chairs to play a role in policymaking. The opening of agriculture and other policy areas to many competing interests has injected a degree of uncertainty into the policy process. In an effort to minimize competition and reduce the prospects of being challenged on issues, many interest groups have narrowed their agendas to a few issues on which they can claim expertise and maximize their influence.[60]

Lobbying the Courts.   Like bureaucrats, judges also make policy. Some interest groups try to achieve their goals by getting involved in cases and persuading courts to rule in their favor. Although most groups do not initiate litigation, some use it as their primary tactic. Litigation has been employed extensively by civil liberties organizations, particularly the American Civil Liberties Union (ACLU), civil rights organizations like the NAACP, environmental groups like the Sierra Club, and public interest groups like Common Cause. Litigation often is used by groups that lack influence in Congress and the bureaucracy.

Groups can file civil suits, represent defendants in criminal cases, or file friend of the court briefs, which are written arguments asking the court to decide a case in a particular way.[61]

Some groups use the courts to make their opponents negotiate with them. Environmental groups frequently challenge developers who threaten the environment in order to force them to bear the costs of defending themselves and to delay the project. The next time, developers may be more willing to make concessions to avoid lengthy and costly litigation.

Groups try to influence the courts indirectly by lobbying the Senate to support or oppose judicial nominees, as we saw in the You Are There at the beginning of this chapter.

Indirect Lobbying Techniques

Traditionally, lobbyists employed tactics of direct persuasion almost exclusively—providing advice, information, and occasionally pressure. More recently, interest groups are going public, that is, mobilizing their own activists and molding and activating public opinion. A recent study of 175 lobbying groups found that most were doing more of all kinds of lobbying activity, but the largest increases were in going public.[62] Talking with the press and media increased the most, and mobilizing the grass roots to inspire letter-writing, telegram, and telephoning campaigns was second. On occasion, groups will fly influential group members to Washington to lobby their representatives and senators. Several groups have enjoyed quick success using public strategies.

Mobilizing the Grass Roots.   The constituency of an interest group—the group's members or those whom the group serves—can help communicate the group's position to public officials. The National Rifle Association is effective in mobilizing its members. The NRA can generate thousands of letters within a few days. As one senator remarked, "I'd rather be a deer in hunting season than run afoul of the NRA crowd."[63]

In one Common Cause "action alert," letters were sent to 60,000 citizens in congressional districts of members who were wavering on an issue involving funds for a new missile. The mailing generated hundreds of letters to members of Congress within a few days.[64]

Appeals to write or phone policymakers often exaggerate the severity of the problem and the strength of the opposition. Only the threat of imminent failure or a monstrous adversary with superior resources is sufficient to move the membership. Because of the difficulty in mobilizing members and the cost in time and money, grass-roots efforts are typically a last resort. Besides, as one lobbyist put it, members of Congress "hate it when you call in the dogs."[65]

To be successful, mass letter writing and phone calls must look sincere and spontaneous. Groups often send members sample letters to help them know what to write, but letters that appear unique are most effective. Campaigns producing thousands of postcards

An Old War Story: The Iron Triangle

Four major groups, with a combined membership of more than five million, represent the interests of American war veterans: the American Legion, Veterans of Foreign Wars, Disabled American Veterans, and American Veterans of World War II. Over the years these groups, with the help of the Veterans Administration and the veterans' committees in Congress, have channeled billions of dollars of benefits—$28 billion in 1988—to veterans; these benefits include free health care in veterans' hospitals, pension and disability benefits, guaranteed home loans, life insurance, and a hiring preference for federal jobs.

Because of the special place accorded veterans by Congress and because veterans reside in every congressional district, this iron triangle rarely has been challenged and has gone about its business free of outside interference.

The strength of the network was revealed in 1981. When much of the federal budget was being slashed by the Reagan administration, the Veterans Administration was untouched. In 1985, David Stockman, Reagan's budget director, spoke out against veterans' pensions, but neither Reagan nor Congress paid much attention.

In 1988, the Veterans Administration was elevated to cabinet rank—the Department of Veterans Affairs. Few in the Reagan White House or Congress were enthusiastic about the change, but it passed anyway. Reagan, who pledged to eliminate Carter's departments of Energy and Education to reduce the size of government, not only failed in his promise but added a department of his own. The change may give veterans' groups even more power and benefits.

The Iron Triangle

The Iron Triangle

Department of Veterans Affairs — Provides Information and Assistance with Constituent's Problems / Provides Higher Funding Levels — Veterans Affairs Committees of the House and Senate

Provides Veterans' Benefits / Offers Support in Securing Favorable Decisions in Congress

Authorizes Veterans' Benefits / Provides Information and Campaign Support

Veterans' Interest Groups

generally are not effective unless representatives do not hear from the other side.

Molding Public Opinion.   Groups use public relations techniques to shape public opinion through the media. Ads in newspapers, magazines, and on television supply the public with information, foster a positive image of the group, or promote a public policy. By themselves ads have little impact in moving policymakers to action or shifting public opinion dramatically in the short run. They are most effective in combination with other tactics.

Groups also may stage events such as rallies or pickets to attract media coverage to their cause. For example, those opposing racial segregation in South Africa have won considerable attention picketing and protesting outside the South African embassy in Washington, D.C. They were especially effective because they enlisted members of Congress, community leaders, and other celebrities in their protests. Arrests for trespassing by members of Congress and other celebrities kept the issue in the limelight for months.

A tactic increasingly used by interest groups to influence public opinion is rating members of Congress. Groups may choose a number of votes crucial to their concerns such as abortion, conservation, or consumer affairs. Or they may select many votes reflecting a liberal or conservative outlook. They then publicize the votes to their members with the ultimate objective of trying to defeat candidates who vote against their positions. The impact of these ratings is probably minimal unless they are used in a concerted effort to target certain members for defeat.

Coalition Building. Coalitions, networks of groups with similar concerns, help individual groups press their demands. Coalitions can be large and focus on many issues or small and very specific. For example, 7-Eleven stores, Kingsford charcoal, amusement parks, and lawn and garden centers joined the Daylight Saving Time Coalition to lobby Congress to extend daylight saving time. All wanted additional daylight hours to snack, grill, play, or till the soil, which would mean more money in their pockets.

Coalitions demonstrate broad support for an issue and also can take advantage of the different strengths of groups. One group may be adept at grass-roots lobbying, another at public relations. One may have lots of money, another lots of members.

The growth of coalitions in recent years reflects a number of changes in the policy process.[66] For one thing, issues have become increasingly complex. Legislation often affects a variety of interests, which makes it easier to form coalitions among groups representing the interests. In addition, changes in technology make it easier for groups to communicate with each other and with constituents. And the number of interest groups is larger than it used to be, especially the number of single-issue and public interest groups. Many such groups have limited resources, and coalitions help them stretch their lobbying efforts. The decentralized Congress and weak political parties also have led to coalition building to win needed majorities at the various stages of the policy process.

Coalitions vary in their duration—some are short term whereas others are permanent. The International Ladies Garment Workers Union (ILGWU) joined with the southern-based textile industry to fight for a rollback on imports. The coalition could not be expected to last long, given the many conflicting interests of the two groups. Textile manufacturers have fought efforts by the ILGWU to organize southern textile workers.

Another short-term coalition was formed to win federal aid for highway construction. These groups, including state and local government, highway builders, highway users, and transportation labor unions, presented a united front in testimony before the House Public Works and Transportation Committee and in other lobbying efforts.[67]

On the other hand, the Leadership Conference on Civil Rights (see You Are There) is a permanent coalition of 185 civil rights, ethnic, and religious and other (Elks, Actors Equity, YMCA, and the National Funeral Directors and Morticians Association) groups. Unlike short-term coalitions, permanent ones need to be sensitive to how today's actions will affect future cooperation. Some issues may be avoided even though a majority of coalition members want to deal with them. When a coalition is unified, it can be formidable, however. The Leadership Conference on Civil Rights was united in opposing Bork and winning renewal of the 1965 Voting Rights Act in 1981.

In elections, coordination among PACs in channeling money to political candidates is widespread. Business PACs, for example, take their lead from the Business-Industry Political Action Committee (BIPAC). Information is shared on candidates' issue positions, likelihood of winning, and how much they need and when.

Protest and Civil Disobedience

Groups that lack access or hold unpopular positions can protest. They can target policymakers directly or indirectly through public opinion. In recent years, issues as diverse as abortion, American support for the contras in Nicaragua, busing to promote school integration, nuclear weapons, and the poor farm economy in the Midwest have generated protest marches and rallies.

Peaceful but illegal protest activity, where those involved allow themselves to be arrested and punished, is called civil disobedience. Greenpeace is an environmental and peace group that practices civil disobedience. It started in 1971 when a group of environmentalists and peace activists sent two boats to Amchitka Island in the Aleutians to protest a U.S. underground nuclear weapon test. The boats were named "Greenpeace," linking the ideas of peace and the environment. Although the boats failed to reach the island, the publicity generated by the affair led Washington to cancel the test.

Throughout the 1970s and 1980s, Greenpeace has staged a number of such protests. To protest dumping of toxic wastes and sewage in the ocean, 13 Greenpeace activists lowered themselves from a New York bridge and hung there for eight hours, preventing any sewage barges from carrying wastes out to sea. All were arrested. To protect endangered whales, members have placed themselves in the path of a harpoon, narrowly missing being struck. Others have clung to nuclear-powered ships on the high seas to protest nuclear weapons or parachuted over coal-powered power plants to protest acid rain. The goal is to generate publicity and dramatic photographs that will activate the general population.

Protest can generate publicity and awareness regarding an issue, but to be successful, it must influence public opinion or political elites. Often it is the first step in a long struggle that takes years to resolve. Sometimes the first step is to create hostility toward the group using it. Antiwar protest by college students in the 1960s and 1970s angered not only government officials, who targeted the leaders for harassment, but also many citizens. In the early years of the women's movement, the media labeled many female protestors "bra burners" even though it is not clear if any woman ever burned a bra.

Greenpeace attempts to influence public opinion with dramatic events. Here, Greenpeace protests dumping of nuclear waste at sea, while dumpers prepare to drop a barrel of waste on the Greenpeace protestors.

Extended protests are difficult because they demand more skill by the leaders and sacrifices from the participants. Continued participation, essential to success, robs participants of a normal life. It can mean jail, physical harm, or even death and requires discipline to refrain from violence, even when violence is used against them.

The civil rights movement provides the best example of the successful use of extended protest and civil disobedience in twentieth-century America. By peacefully demonstrating against legalized segregation in the South, black and some white protestors drew the nation's attention to the discrepancy between the American values of equality and democracy and the southern laws that separated blacks from whites in every aspect of life. Protestors used tactics such as sit-ins, marches, and boycotts. Confrontations with authorities often won protestors national attention and public support, which eventually led to change.

Success of Interest Groups

Although no interest group gets everything it wants from government, some are more successful than others. Politics is not a game of chance, where only luck determines winners and losers. Many factors influence success. Knowing what to do and how to do it—strategy and tactics—are important, as are resources, competition, and goals.

Resources

Although large size does not guarantee success, large groups have a number of advantages. They can get the attention of public officials by claiming to speak for more people or even threaten officials by mobilizing members to vote against them.

The geographical distribution of members of a group is also important. Because organized labor is concentrated in the Northeast, its influence is less elsewhere. The Chamber of Commerce, on the other hand, has members and influence throughout the country.

Other things being equal, a group with well-educated members has an advantage because highly educated people are more likely than others to communicate with public officials and contribute to lobbying efforts.

Honey Producers Sting Uncle Sam

Since 1981 the federal government has owned millions of pounds of honey. Even Uncle Sam's sweet tooth is not that large; it can hardly be argued that honey is crucial to the national defense. So why the stockpile?

The answer is that lobbyists for beekeepers have won government price supports for honey. Beekeepers get loans from the federal government, and the government takes the honey as collateral. By 1987, however, the market price of honey was 28¢ per pound less than what the government pays, so beekeepers found it better to let the government have their honey than to sell it on the open market. Meanwhile, the taxpayers paid $90 million each year to support less than 3,000 beekeepers, and foreign beekeepers gained a large part of the U.S. honey market.

This situation, coupled with the spiraling costs of the program (from $8 million in 1981 to $90 million in 1984) led one member of Congress to call the program a "sweet little rip-off."[1] This view was shared by most members of Congress, which in 1986 changed the program. Now, instead of selling to the government, beekeepers sell on the open market. However, the government pays the difference between the market price of honey and the support price, around 63¢ per pound. Instead of paying the full 63¢ as before, the taxpayers now only pay about half that. Unfortunately, by 1988, the cost of the program had risen to $100 million, about $50,000 a year for each of the 2,000 commercial beekeepers in the United States.

Some members of Congress question why we support beekeepers at all. But, even though beekeepers are a small group, organizing and lobbying won them a substantial government benefit. Even though many Americans might oppose this subsidy, few have ever heard of it, and few but beekeepers are abuzz about it.

1. Jonathan Rauch, "Why the Honey Bees Aren't Laughing," *National Journal,* July 4, 1987, p. 1737: Jonathan Rauch, "A Federal Honey Program Drones On," *National Journal,* April 1, 1989, p. 807.

Group cohesion and intensity are also advantages. Public officials are unlikely to respond to a group if it cannot agree on what it wants or if it does not appear to feel very strongly about its position.

A large **market share,** the number of members in a group compared to its potential membership, is another advantage. For years the American Medical Association enrolled a large percentage (70% or more) of the nation's doctors as members. As its membership as a percentage of the total number of doctors has declined, so too has its influence.

The more money a group has, the more successful it probably will be. Not only does money buy skilled lobbyists and access to elected officials, it is also necessary for indirect lobbying efforts.

Knowledge is a major resource too. If leaders of a group are experts in a policy area, they are more apt to get the attention of public officials. Knowledge of how things get done in Washington is also helpful, which is why many groups employ former members of Congress and the executive branch as lobbyists.

Finally, public image is important. A negative public image often troubles new, change-oriented groups, such as the civil rights and antiwar movements of the 1960s. Many of the country's traditional interest groups, big business and organized labor, also suffer from a poor image, being viewed as too powerful and self-serving.

Few groups are blessed with all resources, but the more resources a group has, the better its chances of getting what it wants from government.

Competition and Goals

Success also depends on group competition and goals. When a group competes with other groups of nearly equal resources, the outcome is often a compromise or a stalemate.

Many lobbying groups are successful because they face weak opponents. Supporters of gun control have public opinion on their side, but their main organization, the National Council to Control Handguns, has only 160,000 members and an annual budget of less than $1 million, a fraction of what the NRA spends. It is not surprising, therefore, that it has not been able to get Congress to adopt gun control legislation.

Used-car dealers successfully lobbied against "the lemon law," which would have required them to tell consumers of any defects in cars. Few lobbyists represented the other side. These mismatches between groups occur most often on highly technical issues (such as business taxes) where one side has more expertise or on issues that are not very important to the general public.

The Clean Air Act was not rewritten for years because the auto industry, which wants a weaker law, and the environmental lobby, which wants a tougher one, have been about equal in strength. The increased clout of the proenvironmental forces finally led to a strengthening of the law in 1990.

Groups that work to preserve the status quo are generally more successful than groups promoting change; it is usually easier to prevent government action than to bring it about.

Conclusion: Do Interest Groups Help Make Government Responsive?

Interest groups provide representation that helps make government more responsive. Although elected officials are representatives, they cannot adequately represent all interests in our diverse society. Interest groups pick up some of the slack by representing the views and opinions of their members and constituents and communicating these to political decision makers. This does not mean that all members agree with everything group leaders say or do, or that group leaders are accountable to their members. Group leaders often develop perspectives somewhat different from those of their members. In most instances, however, groups do represent and speak for at least some of the interests of their members. In voluntary organizations particularly, leaders are likely to reflect the interests of their members. If they do not, members can simply exercise their option to leave. Even "checkbook" members can withhold their support if they disagree with group leaders.

Interest groups do not represent, however, all interests or all interests equally. In 1960, E. E. Schattschneider described the pressure system as small in terms of numbers and biased toward business and the wealthy. At that time no more than 1,500 groups were included, and more than 50% represented either corporations or trade and business associations.[68] Few groups represented consumers, taxpayers, the environment, women, and minorities.

The pressure system has changed since Schattschneider wrote, but its bias remains. The number of interest groups exploded in the 1960s and 1970s, with many of the new groups representing consumers, environmentalists, minorities, and other nonbusiness interests, but these were more than offset by an increase in the number of corporations in the pressure system.

AMERICAN DIVERSITY

Organizing Protest: The Montgomery Bus Boycott

The 1955 Montgomery, Alabama, bus boycott was the first successful civil rights protest, and it brought its 26-year-old leader, Dr. Martin Luther King, Jr., to national prominence. Montgomery, like most southern cities, required blacks to sit in the back of public buses while whites sat in the front. The dividing line between the two was a "no man's land" where blacks could sit if there were no whites. If whites needed the seats, blacks had to give them up and move to the back.

One afternoon, Rosa Parks, a seamstress at a local department store and a leader in the local chapter of the National Association of Colored People (NAACP), boarded the bus to go home. The bus was filled and when a white man boarded, the driver called on the four blacks behind the whites to move to the back. Three got up and moved, but Mrs. Parks, tired from a long day and of the injustice of always having to move for white people, said she did not have to move because she was in "no man's land." Under a law that gave him the authority to enforce segregation, the bus driver arrested her.

That evening a group of black women professors at the black state college in Montgomery, led by Jo Ann Robinson, drafted a letter of protest. They called on blacks to stay off the buses on Monday to protest the arrest. They worked through the night making 35,000 copies of their letter to distribute to Montgomery's black residents. Fearful for their jobs and concerned that the state would cut funds to the black college if it became known they had used state facilities to produce the letter, they worked quickly and quietly.

The following day black leaders met and agreed to the boycott. More leaflets were drafted calling on blacks to stay off the buses on Monday. On Sunday, black ministers encouraged their members to support the boycott, and on Monday 90% of the blacks walked to work, rode in black-owned taxis, or shared rides in private cars.

The boycott inspired confidence and pride in the black community and signaled a subtle change in the opinions of blacks toward race relations. This was obvious when, as nervous white police looked on, hundreds of blacks jammed the courthouse to see that Rosa Parks was safely released after her formal conviction. And, it was obvious later that evening at a mass rally when Martin

Rosa Parks being fingerprinted after her arrest.

Luther King cried out, "There comes a time when people get tired of being trampled over by the iron feet of oppression. There comes a time when people get tired of being pushed out of the glittering sunlight of life's July, and left standing amidst the piercing chill of an Alpine November." After noting that the glory of American democracy is the right to protest, King appealed to the strong religious faith of the crowd, "If we are wrong, God Almighty is wrong. . . . If we are wrong, Jesus of Nazareth was merely a utopian dreamer. . . . If we are wrong, justice is a lie." These words and this speech established King as a charismatic leader for the civil rights movement.

Each day of the boycott was a trial for blacks and black leaders. Thousands had to find a way to get to work, and black leaders struggled to keep a massive carpool going. However, each evening's rally built up morale for the next day's boycott. Later the rallies became prayer services, as the black community prayed for strength to keep on walking, for courage to remain nonviolent, and for guidance to those who oppressed them.

continued on next page

The city bus line was losing money. City leaders urged more whites to ride the bus to make up lost revenue, but few did. Recognizing the boycott could not go on forever, black leaders agreed to end it if the rules regarding the seating of blacks in "no man's land" were relaxed. Thinking they were on the verge of breaking the boycott, the city leaders refused. Police began to harass carpoolers and issue bogus tickets for trumped-up violations. Then the city leaders issued an ultimatum: settle or face arrest. A white grand jury indicted over 100 boycott leaders for the alleged crime of organizing the protest. In the spirit of nonviolence, the black leaders, including King, surrendered.

The decision to arrest the leaders proved to be the turning point of the boycott. The editor of the local white paper said it was "the dumbest act that has ever been done in Montgomery."[1] With the mass arrests, the boycott finally received national attention. Reporters from all over the world streamed into Montgomery to cover the story. The publicity brought public and financial support. The arrests caused the boycott to become a national event and its leader, Martin Luther King, a national figure. A year later, the U.S. Supreme Court declared Alabama local and state laws requiring segregation in buses to be unconstitutional, and when the city complied with the Court's order, the boycott ended.

Rosa Parks became a hero of the civil rights movement. She has been honored many times since then, and millions saw her appearance at the 1988 Democratic National Convention.

1. Taylor Branch, *Parting the Waters, America in the King Years* (New York: Simon and Schuster, 1988), p. 83.

Source: Taylor Branch, *Parting the Waters,* chapters 4 and 5; and Juan Williams; *Eyes on the Prize* (New York: Viking Press, 1987).

Figure 3 shows that business interests still dominate. Indeed, business had a greater presence in Washington in the 1980s than it did in the 1960s. Nearly two-thirds of the groups that lobbied in Washington in the 1980s represented either corporations or trade associations. Groups representing civil rights concerns, minorities, women, the poor, and elderly are less than 10% of all groups with an office in Washington and only 5% of all groups that lobby.

To the extent that interest groups influence public policy, this bias in the pressure system is a big advantage for business and wealthy interests.

This bias may be increasing. Over the past three decades, business groups have increased in numbers and influence relative to other groups. Labor unions, a strong supporter of legislation to improve the welfare of the working class, often in opposition to business and wealthy interests, have declined in influence. Although business interests need to be represented in the political process, the pressure system seems to give them greater weight and priority than other interests. The growing gap between rich and poor is one reflection of this.

Interest group strength is relevant to the debate between those who think our system reflects pluralism and those who think it is run by elites. People who argue that we have a pluralist system emphasize group competition and the ability of individuals to organize themselves to influence government. Those who think we have an elitist government point to the inequality of group competition. On some issues, such as those involving economic benefits for workers, there is competition among groups. On other issues, such as tax policy, there is little.

There may, however, be a waning of interest group influence overall. One study argues, for example, that interest groups are not as influential as often portrayed. Rather than pursuing their well-defined interests, interest groups spend a lot of time trying to assess whether they have an interest in a particular policy and what that interest is. The study contends that a number of factors, including the myriad special interests competing with each other, have reduced the influence of interest groups. Despite impressive resources, even those groups that are assumed to be the most influential in a policy area do not have the capacity to get involved in all issues of significance to them.[69]

James Madison foresaw the inevitable development of interest groups and wanted to create a government that would hold them in check. That is, he wanted government to prevent one or more of them from doing harm to others or to the nation as a whole. Madison thought a system of checks and balances and competition among groups would accomplish this. Just as he thought, competing groups can slow the political process. But when there is no competition, the nation suffers. Similarly, it suffers when so many interests are involved in politics that it is difficult for government to take action. Government's capacity to

Figure 3 ■ Business Interests Dominate the Contemporary Pressure System

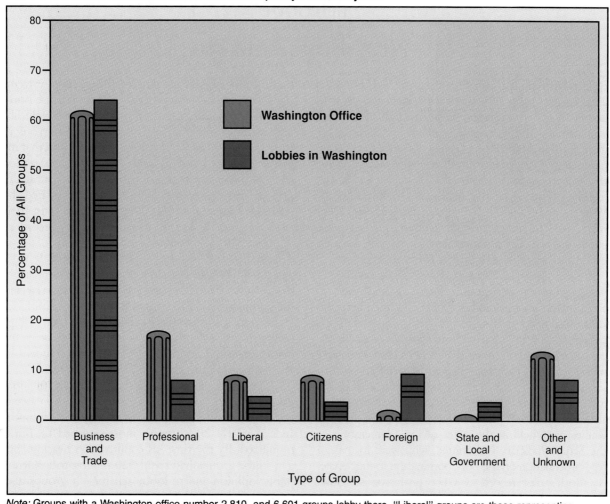

Note: Groups with a Washington office number 2,810, and 6,601 groups lobby there. "Liberal" groups are those representing women, minorities, civil rights concerns, the poor, unions, and the elderly.

Source: K. L. Schlozman and J. T. Tierney, *Organized Interests and American Democracy* (New York: Harper & Row, 1986), p. 67.

do its job is limited by both the bias in the pressure system and the large number of interest groups. Moreover, the built-in checks and balances that Madison thought would preserve the system threaten it by allowing groups to block needed action.

How can we preserve the constitutional rights of interest groups to form and petition government and still keep government responsive to the needs of unorganized or poorly organized interests that lack the resources to press their demands? Recognizing and correcting imbalances in group strength is not simple or easy. Groups currently enjoying an advantage will fight to keep it.

Neas Beats Goliath

Ralph Neas pulled out all the stops. The potential costs to his group and its coalition were too great to accept Bork's confirmation without a fight. He began with a rally of civil rights, women's, and consumer groups. Benjamin Hooks, chair of the Leadership Council and director of the National Association for the Advancement of Colored People; Elinor Smeal, former president of the National Organization for Women; and Ralph Nader were all present. Neas identified the struggle as "the most important legislative battle the civil rights movement has fought, because everything else we have fought for is at stake."

Neas developed a four-part strategy involving media, grass-roots organization, lobbying, and research. Each group in the coalition alerted its members and stimulated letter-writing campaigns to senators. Press conferences were held and newspapers were bombarded with opinion pieces. Southern black ministers mobilized their congregations to write letters to conservative Democratic senators who were predisposed toward Bork on ideological grounds but concerned about the electoral support of their black constituents. Rallies were held in the states of the 14 members of the Senate Judiciary Committee, who were to make a recommendation on the Bork nomination to the Senate.

Bork's past record as a law professor, solicitor-general, and judge was thoroughly analyzed. Certain of his opinions seemed to mark him as more of a radical than a traditional conservative. So Neas's media and lobbying efforts portrayed Bork as an extremist. Then public opinion began moving against Bork. Although the administration predicted that only liberals would oppose Bork, others became nervous at the prospect of his confirmation. They realized that his views challenged doctrines they had considered settled and might reopen battles few wanted to fight again. Despite the efforts of the president, who invited the undecided senators to the White House to twist their arms, senators gradually began to go on record as opposed to Bork's confirmation.

Finally, the Judiciary Committee voted 9 to 5 against Bork. Rather than withdraw the nomination, the president forced a Senate vote, but it too rejected the nominee, 58 to 42, with 6 Republicans joining 52 Democrats to defeat the nomination. Southern Democrats, so important to the president's success in his first term, voted against him. Although infrequent in Washington, in this case David beat Goliath.

The Bork fight demonstrates how individual groups that lack resources can join together in a coalition with other groups to increase their strength. Indeed nearly 200 groups, most opposed to Bork, mobilized. By the time his confirmation hearings began, these groups had spent $20 million to influence public opinion and to lobby senators. If groups also can mobilize the public on behalf of their causes, public officials will listen.

KEY TERMS

interest groups

lobbying

political action
   committees (PACs)

private interest groups

public interest groups

single-issue groups

iron triangles

coalitions

market share

FURTHER READING

Jeffrey M. Berry, *The Interest Group Society* (Boston: Little, Brown, 1984). *A general survey of interest groups in American politics. It covers political action committees, lobbyists and lobbying, the internal dynamics of groups, and the problems that interest groups present to society.*

Mark Green, *The Other Government* (New York: W. W. Norton, 1975). *An examination of the role of Washington lawyers in representing clients before the government.*

Michael Pertschuk, *Giant Killers* (New York: W. W. Norton, 1986). *How low-budget lobbies can sometimes defeat the big guys by superior organization, tactics, and luck.*

E. E. Schattschneider, *The Semi-Sovereign People* (New York: Henry Holt & Company, 1975). *A classical statement on how interest group politics benefit business and corporate interests by limiting the involvement of citizens in the political process.*

Ernest Wittenberg and Elisabeth Wittenberg, *How to Win in Washington: Very Practical Advice About Lobbying, the Grassroots and the Media* (Cambridge, Mass.: Basil Blackwell, 1989). A "How To" book for average citizens.

NOTES

1. Much of the material for this You Are There is drawn from L. Romano, "Leading the Charge against Bork," *Washington Post,* September 15, 1987, pp. D1, D10–D11.

2. M. A. Peterson and J. L. Walker, "Interest Group Responses to Partisan Change: The Impact of the Reagan Administration upon the National Interest Group System," in A. J. Cigler and B. A. Loomis, eds., *Interest Group Politics,* 2nd ed. (Washington, D.C.: CQ Press, 1987), p. 162.

3. A. de Tocqueville, *Democracy in America* (New York: Knopf, 1945), p. 191.

4. G. Almond and S. Verba, *Civil Culture* (Boston: Little, Brown, 1965), pp. 266–306.

5. D. Truman, *The Governmental Process* (New York: Knopf, 1964), pp. 25–26.

6. Truman, *Governmental Process,* p. 59.

7. Ibid., pp. 26–33.

8. J. Q. Wilson, *Political Organization* (New York: Basic Books, 1973), p. 198.

9. G. K. Wilson, *Interest Groups in America* (Oxford: Oxford University Press, 1981), chapter 5; see also G. K. Wilson, "American Business and Politics," in Cigler and Loomis, *Interest Group Politics,* pp. 221–35.

10. K. L. Schlozman and J. T. Tierney, "More of the Same: Washington Pressure Group Activity in a Decade of Change," *Journal of Politics* 45 (May 1983): 335–56.

11. R. H. Salisbury, "An Exchange Theory of Interest Groups," *Midwest Journal of Political Science* 13 (February 1969): 1–32.

12. J. M. Berry, *The Interest Group Society* (Boston: Little, Brown, 1984), pp. 26–28.

13. J. L. Walker, "The Origins and Maintenance of Interest Groups in America," *American Political Science Review* 77 (June 1983): 398–400; see also *National Journal* (August 1981): 1376.

14. Wilson, *Political Organization,* chapter 3.

15. C. Brown, "Explanations of Interest Group Membership Over Time," *American Politics Quarterly* 17 (January 1989): 32–53.

16. C. Brown, "Explanations of Interest Group Membership." The National Rifle Association. Annual Meeting of Midwest P. S. Association, 1987.

17. National Opinion Research Center, General Social Surveys, 1987.

18. N. Babchuk and R. Thompson, "The Voluntary Associations of Negroes," *American Sociological Review* 27 (October 1962): 662–65; see also P. Klobus-Edwards, J. Edwards, and D. Klemmach, "Differences in Social Participation of Blacks and Whites," *Social Forces,* 56 (1978): 1035–52.

19. M. T. Hayes, "The New Group Universe" in Cigler and Loomis, *Interest Group Politics,* pp. 133–45.

20. C. Tomkins, "A Sense of Urgency," *New Yorker,* March 27, 1989, pp. 48–74.

21. Walker, "Origins and Maintenance of Interest Groups."

22. E. E. Schattschneider, *Semi-Sovereign People* (New York: Holt, Rinehart, and Winston, 1960), p. 118.

23. "Business Roundtable: New Lobbying Force," *The Washington Lobby,* 3rd ed. (Washington, D.C.: Congressional Quarterly, 1979), pp. 121–25; Wilson, *Interest Groups,* chapter 2.

24. P. E. Johnson, "Organized Labor in an Era of Blue Collar Decline," in A. J. Cigler and B. A. Loomis, eds. *Interest Group Politics,* 3rd ed. (Washington, D.C.: CQ Press, 1991), pp. 33–62.

25. Ibid., p. 47.

26. Ibid., p. 51.

27. A. J. Cigler and J. M. Hansen, "Group Formation Through Protest: The American Agriculture Movement," in A. J. Cigler and B. A. Loomis, eds., *Interest Group Politics* (Washington, D.C.: CQ Press, 1983), chapter 4.

28. A. J. Cigler, "Organizational Maintenance and Political Activity on the Cheap: The American Agriculture Movement," in Cigler and Loomis, *Interest Group Politics,* pp. 81–108.

29. On the AMA, see L. H. Zeigler and G. W. Peak, *Interest Groups in American Society,* 2nd ed. (Englewood Cliffs, N.J.: Prentice-Hall, 1972), pp. 225–58.

30. For a discussion of the ABA, see M. Green, "The ABA: The Rhetoric Has Changed But the Morality Lingers On," *Washington Monthly* (January 1974): 21–27.

31. The education lobby is treated in R. Stanfield, "The Education Lobby Reborn," *National Journal,* August 9, 1983, pp. 1452–56.

32. J. Tierney, "Old Money, New Power," *New York Times Magazine,* October 23, 1988, p. 52.

33. "Grays on the Go," *Time,* February 22, 1988, p. 69.

34. "Gray Power," *Time,* January 4, 1988, p. 36.

35. "Our Footloose Correspondents," *New Yorker,* August 8, 1988, p. 70.

36. "Grapevine," *Time,* November 28, 1988, p. 24.

37. A. S. McFarland, *Common Cause* (Chatham, N.J.: Chatham House, 1984); see also A. S. McFarland, *Public Interest Lobbies: Decision Making on Energy* (Washington, D.C.: American Enterprise Institute, 1976).

38. R. G. Shaiko, "More Bang for the Buck: The New Era of Full Service Public Interest Groups," in Cigler and Loomis, *Interest Group Politics,* p. 109.

39. Ibid., p. 120.

40. For a discussion of the evolution of NOW and its success in lobbying Congress, see A. N. Costain and W. D. Costain, "The Women's Lobby: Impact of a Movement on Congress," in Cigler and Loomis, *Interest Group Politics.*

41. C. F. Steinbach, "Women's Movement II," *National Journal,* August 29, 1987, pp. 2145–49.

42. E. M. Uslaner, "A Tower of Babel on Foreign Policy," in Cigler and Loomis, *Interest Group Politics,* p. 309.

43. K. Wald, *Religion and Politics* (New York: St. Martin's Press, 1985), pp. 182–212.

44. A. D. Hertzke, "The Role of Churches in Political Mobilization: The Presidential Campaigns of Jesse Jackson and Pat Robertson," in Cigler and Loomis, *Interest Group Politics*, pp. 185–91.

45. Ibid., p. 180–85.

46. C. J. Bosso, "Adaption and Change in the Environmental Movement" in Cigler and Loomis, *Interest Group Politics*, pp. 155–56.

47. Ibid., p. 162.

48. Ibid., p. 169.

49. P. Span, "Meet Ms. Family Planning," *Washington Post National Weekly Edition*, November 2, 1987, pp. 8–9.

50. A. Rubin, "Interest Groups and Abortion Politics in the Post-Webster Era," in Cigler and Loomis, *Interest Group Politics*, pp. 241–48.

51. Ibid., pp. 249–51.

52. D. Broder, "Let 100 Single-Issue Groups Bloom," *Washington Post*, January 7, 1979, pp. C1–C2; see also D. Broder, *The Party's Over: The Failure of Politics in America* (New York: Harper & Row, 1972).

53. Wilson, *Interest Groups*, chapter 4.

54. P. M. Evans, "Lobbying the Committee: Interest Groups and the House Public Works and Transportation Committee, in the Post-Webster Era," in Cigler and Loomis, *Interest Group Politics*, pp. 257–76.

55. Berry, *Interest Group Society*, p. 188.

56. M. Pertschuk, *Giant Killers* (New York: W. W. Norton, 1987). This anecdote is based on chapter 3. The quotations are from pp. 59, 60, and 76.

57. E. Drew, *Politics and Money: The New Road to Corruption* (New York: Macmillan, 1983), p. 78.

58. Ibid.

59. W. P. Brown, "Issue Niches and the Limits of Interest Group Influence," in Cigler and Loomis, *Interest Group Politics*, p. 348.

60. Ibid., see also R. H. Salisbury, "Putting Interests Back into Interest Groups," in Cigler and Loomis, *Interest Group Politics*, pp. 371–84.

61. For an article dealing with the success of interest group ligating at the district court level see L. Epstein and C. K. Rowland, "Debunking the Myth of Interest Group Invincibility in the Courts," *American Political Science Review* 85 (March 1991): 205–20.

62. S. Kernell, *Going Public* (Washington, D.C.: CQ Press, 1986), p. 34.

63. R. Harris, "If You Love Your Grass," *New Yorker*, April 20, 1968, p. 57.

64. Pertshuk, *Giant Killers*, p. 205.

65. Evans, "Lobbying the Committee," p. 269.

66. Much of the information in this section is taken from B. A. Loomis, "Coalitions of Interests: Building Bridges in the Balkanized State," in Cigler and Loomis, *Interest Group Politics*, 2nd ed., pp. 258–74.

67. Evans, "Lobbying the Committee," p. 261.

68. Schattschneider, *Semi-Sovereign People*, chapter 2.

69. Salisbury, "Putting Interests Back," p. 381.

6 Political Parties

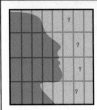

YOU ARE THERE

To Switch or Not to Switch

You are Phil Gramm, a Democrat from Texas, elected to the House of Representatives in 1978. Your legislative goals are a government with low taxes, limited social welfare responsibilities, the world's strongest military, and a balanced budget. Although these goals are out of step with the national leadership of your party, they are in line with your conservative district. Stretching from east-central Texas to the Dallas–Fort Worth area, the district has been represented by Democrats since statehood.

Soon after your election you showed your concern for government spending by proposing an amendment to require a balanced budget. The amendment was rejected. In 1980 you demonstrated your concern for a strong military by opposing your own party and trying to transfer $5.1 billion from domestic to military spending. It too failed. Although your own party was upset with you, you were reelected in 1980 with 71% of the vote.

In 1981 you sought a seat on the prestigious Budget Committee. In addition to support from conservative southern Democrats, you were able to win over fellow Texan Jim Wright, the Democratic majority leader. In exchange for your commitment to support the party's position on the budget, you were given a committee seat. A month later you cosponsored a bill with Wright calling for automatic cuts if the budget is not balanced. This measure failed, opposed by many in your own party.

Failing to win the party to your goals, you cosponsored and worked for the 1981 Reagan budget, which drastically cut domestic spending and dramatically increased defense spending. You also informed the Republicans of the Democrats' budget bill plans.

Although you were labeled a traitor by many of your fellow Democrats, in 1982 you won reelection with 95% of the vote after the Republican candidate withdrew.

Now, with the start of the 1983 session, Democrats, still rankled by your collaboration with the Republicans, vote to remove you from the Budget Committee.

What do you do? One option is to take your punishment. Working secretly to pass information on the Democrats' proposals to the White House was a severe breach of party discipline. Besides, the punishment is not particularly severe. You could have lost all your seniority or even been kicked out of the party. And in time you may be able to work yourself back into the good graces of the party and try again for a seat on this committee.

Another option is to switch parties. Party switching by elected officials is unusual but not unknown. Normally, party loyalties run deeper than issue positions, but philosophically you are closer to the Republican party. Last year you voted with the majority of Democrats only 10% of the time, and you supported Reagan 84% of the time. Switching parties, however, has risks. You may not be able to win reelection as a Republican from your Democratic district. Even if you get elected, the Republican leadership in Congress may not treat you very well or trust you. What do you do?

OUTLINE

What Are Political Parties?

Development and Change in the Party System
Preparty Politics: The Founders' Views of Political
    Parties
First Party System: Development of Parties
Second Party System: Rise of the Democrats
Third Party System: Rise of the Republicans
Fourth Party System: Republican Dominance
Fifth Party System: Democratic Dominance
Has the Fifth Party System Realigned?

Characteristics of the Party System
Two Parties
Fragmentation
Moderation
Minor Parties in American Politics

Party in the Electorate
Party Identification
Characteristics of Democrats and Republicans

Party in Government

Party Organization
National Party Organization
State and Local Party Organizations
Big-City Party Organizations

The Nominating Process
Caucuses
Conventions
Primaries

**Conclusion: Do Political Parties Make Government
More Responsive?**

George Washington warned against the "baneful" effects of parties and described them as the people's worst enemies. More recently, a respected political scientist, E. E. Schattschneider, argued that "political parties created democracy and that democracy was impossible without them."[1] The public echoes these contradictory views. Many believe that parties create conflict where none exists, yet most identify with one or another of our two major parties.[2]

These same feelings exist among candidates for office. They often avoid political parties by establishing their own personal campaign organizations and raising their own funds. If elected, they often do not follow the party line. At the same time, candidates for national and state offices are nominated in the name of political parties, they rely on parties for assistance, and they have little chance of winning unless they are Democrats or Republicans.

In this chapter, we examine American political parties to see why they are important and why many observers believe that if they become less important and effective, our system of government may not work as well as it does.

What Are Political Parties?

Political parties are a major link between people and government. They provide a way for the public to have some say about who serves in government and what policies are chosen. Political parties generally are defined as organizations that seek to control government by recruiting, nominating, and electing their members to public office. They consist of three interrelated components: the **party in the electorate,** those who identify with the party; the **party in government,** those who are appointed or elected to office as members of a political party; and the formal **party organization,** the party "professionals" who run the party at the national, state, and local levels (see figure 1).[3]

In linking the public and government policymakers, parties serve several purposes. They help select public officials by recruiting and screening candidates and then providing campaign resources. They help empower citizens by activating and interesting them in politics. Individually, citizens have little power, but collectively, through parties, they can make their wishes felt.

Parties help people vote on the basis of issues. Parties are associated, however dimly, in the voters' minds with issues. In the recent past, the Democratic party has favored an expanded role for the national government in maintaining the economic well-being of Americans, whereas the Republican party has supported a more limited role. Most voters understand this difference. Knowing that a candidate belongs to a particular party is a clue to the candidate's general stand on the issues, and voters therefore do not need to study each candidate's position in great detail.

The party in government plays an important role in organizing and operating government; it formu-

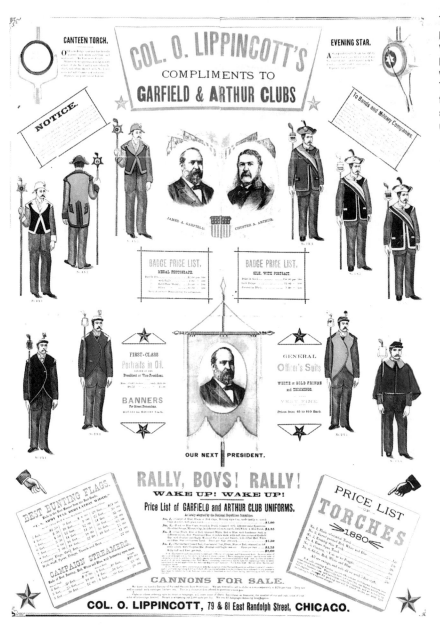

Today, most citizens take part in political activities as "couch potatoes" watching television. During the third party era, most eligible voters (largely white males) participated actively. Torchlight parades and rallies were frequent, and businesses sprung up to supply the necessary torches, banners, uniforms, and flags.

reform, which reduced political patronage. These reforms, intended to check corruption, all weakened the political parties. They gave parties, and their bosses, less control over elections and jobs.

Fifth Party System: Democratic Dominance

In the 1920s, the Republicans began to lose support in the cities. The party ignored the plight of poor immigrants and in Congress pushed through quotas limiting immigration from southern and eastern Europe. After the depression hit in 1929, these immigrants, along with many women voting for the first time, joined traditional Democrats in the South to elect Franklin Roosevelt in 1932. This election reflected another party alignment.

The **New Deal coalition,** composed of city dwellers, blue-collar workers, Catholic and Jewish immigrants, blacks, and southerners, elected Roosevelt to an unprecedented four terms. The coalition was an odd alliance of northern liberals and southern conservatives. It stuck together in the 1930s and 1940s because of Roosevelt's personality and skill and because northerners did not seriously challenge southern racial policies. But the coalition came unglued after Roosevelt's death. The Republicans, by nominating a popular war hero, General Dwight D. Eisenhower, won the presidency in 1952 and 1956. Although the Democrats regained the White House in 1960, the civil rights movement and the Vietnam War divided them sharply, and they lost again in 1968 and 1972.[7] They won in 1976, but only because they nominated a southerner—Jimmy Carter—and the Republicans suffered from the Watergate scandal. Even though the Democrats continue to dominate Congress, they have not won the presidency since 1976, nor have they come close, leading to speculation that the fifth party system has ended.

Has the Fifth Party System Realigned?

Many of the signs that preceded major realignments of the party system have been present for some time. **Ticket splitting,** voting for a member of one party for one office but a member of another party for a different one, is at a high level. In the 1980s, ticket splitting was two to three times that in the 1950s.[8] This is most

evident at the national level: Republicans have controlled the White House since 1968, except for 1977–1980; the Democrats have controlled the House of Representatives during that time and the Senate for all but four years.

Another sign of change is the increased number of citizens who do not choose to identify or align with any political party. Many new voters eligible to vote for the first time have not been attracted to either the Democrats or Republicans, and some older voters have not formed firm allegiances.

Realigning periods also are characterized by compelling issues that fracture the unity of the major party and sometimes the minority party too.[9] In the years before 1860, slavery was such an issue. It destroyed the Whigs, divided the Democrats, and led to the emergence of the Republicans. In 1932, economic issues led many Republicans away from their party and, along with most new voters, to the Democrats. As the depression generation dies and the children of this generation grow older, the influence of depression-era economic issues may decline, opening the door to the possibility of a realignment based on other issues (see table 1).

Have the elections of the 1980s signaled a major party realignment? The answer is no. By the end of the 1980s, most polls showed the Democrats still ahead in

Table 1 ■ Impact of the Depression and the New Deal Fades
Those individuals who became eligible to vote in the 1930s are more Democratic than those who became eligible in the 1920s and after the depression and the New Deal. Democratic allegiance of those first voting during the Reagan years is the weakest. This group is also more likely to be independent than earlier generations.

First Eligible to Vote in	Democrat (percent)	Republican (percent)	Independent (percent)	Percentage Point Difference between Republicans and Democrats
1920–1929	44	35	23	9
1930–1939	47	26	24	21
1960–1970	38	25	35	13
1980–1988	26	28	47	2

Source: 1988 CPS National Election Study.

party identification in spite of the three Republican presidential election victories during the decade. Although the gap between the parties narrowed, the Democrats continued to control the House of Representatives and the Senate and to dominate the state legislatures and gubernatorial offices.[10]

There is also little evidence that the electorate has been attracted to the conservative issue positions identified with Reagan and Bush. On balance, the electorate remains predominantly middle of the road but prefers the government to do more in a number of policy areas rather than less (see chapter 4). Indeed, the efforts of the Republican party to define itself ideologically as the party of the right may be retarding movement into its ranks.[11] Although support for moral issues such as abortion and prayer in schools may win conservatives on the far right, it is unlikely to attract others drawn to the Republicans because of economic policies.

The Republican party represents an uneasy coalition of traditional conservatives, motivated primarily by a desire to minimize government intervention in the economy, and new conservatives, motivated primarily by a desire to institutionalize their religious and moral values. The new conservatives want to increase government intervention in such areas as abortion, prayers in school, and pornography. Compounding this ideological split are class differences. Many traditional conservatives are upper-middle and upper class, while many new conservatives are lower-middle class. Yet the two factions were united in their hate for communism and brought together by the popularity of Reagan. But now the weakened Soviet Union and disintegrated Communist bloc pose less threat, and

Reagan is gone, so disagreements between the factions have reemerged. One Republican observer sarcastically expressed the party's problem: "[Y]ou don't get the Bubba vote with capital formation strategies. It's going to be fun to see all the Bushies . . . when they have to deal with the Polyester Legions again."[12]

A modest realignment, however, confined principally to the South, has occurred. Long a bastion of Democratic party strength, the South began to drift away in the 1950s and showed major signs of change in 1964. For the first time in a century, the Republicans carried Alabama, Georgia, Louisiana, Mississippi, and South Carolina in the presidential election. Upset with the civil rights policies of the national Democratic party, many white southerners voted for Barry Goldwater, the Republican nominee.

Since 1968 Republicans have carried the South in all presidential elections, except for Jimmy Carter's election in 1976. Although the Georgian carried the region, a majority of white southerners voted for Ford. Carter won the region on the strength of the black vote.

White southerners increasingly vote for Republicans in congressional races too, though the Democrats still capture the votes of most.

Today the Republican party is competitive in the South in statewide races and, measured in terms of voter registration and party identification, is equal to the Democrats.[13]

The change in party identification among white southerners is the main reason that polls have shown a decline in Democratic loyalties nationwide (see figure 3). The shift of white southerners to the Republican party makes the South a lot more like the rest of the country in

Development of Partisanship among Newer Asian and Latino Americans

Native-born citizens tend to adopt the partisan identifications of their parents. But new immigrants must use other cues. The millions of newcomers who arrived in the United States in the 1970s and 1980s provide an opportunity to see how newer Americans choose partisan identifications.

One study, based on a survey of Californians, examined two possible patterns of partisan identification among Latinos and Asian Americans. One pattern is that partisan identities follow class lines, as they do for longer-term residents. As immigrants move up the economic ladder, they increasingly become Republican. Another possibility, however, is that as members of a nonwhite (Asians) or non-Anglo (Hispanics) minority group their partisan loyalties will remain with the Democrats, who are seen as more sympathetic to the needs of outgroups in society.

Partisan patterns among Hispanics support both possibilities. Among first-generation Hispanic Americans, the longer their residence in the United States, the more Democratic they are. Second- and third-generation Hispanics are more Democratic than immigrants despite the fact that they have higher incomes and more education. Thus, socialization into minority status seems to increase Democratic partisanship. However, within each generation, Latinos who are better off economically are more likely to vote Republican, thus suggesting that economic factors also affect partisan loyalties.

On the other hand, the partisan loyalties of Asian Americans do not reflect a minority group basis for partisanship and reflect only partly an economic one. Asian Americans are more likely to be Republican than other nonwhite or non-Anglo minority groups such as African-Americans or Hispanic Americans. This might be expected, since Asian Americans are economically better off than other minority groups. However, among Asians, there is little relationship between Republican identification and income or educational levels. The Democratic affiliation of Asian immigrants increases with length of residence in the United States, but the increase is very gradual and the gap between the proportion of Democrats and the proportion of Republicans is small. Second- and third-generation Asian-Americans are also only slightly more likely to be Democrats than Republicans. Within the Asian-American community, those who immigrated from Communist or former Communist regimes are more likely to be Republican than Democratic, likely reflecting a belief that Republicans have taken a stronger anti-Communist foreign policy stance than Democrats.

These patterns remind us that in our increasingly multicultural society, it is not very useful to make generalizations about "minority groups," because different groups have different characteristics, and within each group, economic and other differences insure that the groups will not be politically homogeneous.

Source: Bruce Cain, D. Roderick Kiewiet, and Carole Uhlaner, "Acquisition of Partisanship by Latino and Asian Americans," *American Journal of Political Science* 35 (May 1991): 390–422.

terms of its politics. The change also gave the party system a somewhat more ideological look. The southern Democrats who changed tend to be conservatives and are more ideologically compatible with policies of the Republican party.

The race issue, which spurred this realignment, continues to play a role. Where white southerners in the 1950s and 1960s claimed "betrayal" by the national Democratic party for its policies urging equality for blacks, they now say they object to its policies accepting affirmative action for minorities. The polarization between the races has sharpened the realignment between the parties to such an extent in some places that whites who are asked their party affiliation sometimes retort, "I'm white, aren't I?" meaning "I'm Republican."[14]

Blue-collar ethnics and Catholics also have found the Democrats less attractive since the 1960s.[15] As New Deal policies succeeded in providing many blue-collar workers with economic security, other issues became more important. Social issues surfaced and benefited the Republicans. Moral issues such as abortion led many Catholics to vote Republican. Divisions in the Democratic party over the Vietnam War pushed many who were in favor of the war, particularly union households, to the Republicans.

Other changes also occurred. Northern white Protestants and white-collar workers are somewhat

Figure 3 ■ Southern Whites' Allegiance to the Democratic Party Has Declined, Except in 1976

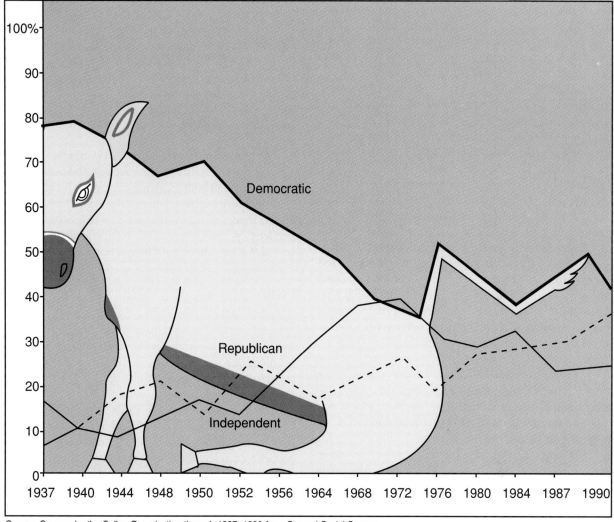

Source: Surveys by the Gallup Organization through 1987; 1990 from General Social Survey.

less Republican than they used to be. Many of them are employed by government and more sympathetic to government spending than before. Issues appear to be contributing to a minor realignment, with parties becoming slightly more homogeneous.[16]

There also has been some **dealignment**.[17] More individuals have opted for independence as parties become less and less relevant. Party voting has declined and split ticket voting has increased. Candidates and issues have become more important.

Dealignment has occurred at the same time as a minor realignment. Dealignment may be preventing a major realignment. That is, some people who might have switched parties do not care enough about them to switch.

Characteristics of the Party System

The American party system is characterized by a number of intriguing and in some instances unique qualities.

Two Parties

First, the American party system is a **two-party system**. Only two parties win seats in Congress, and only two parties compete effectively for the presidency. The development and perpetuation of two parties is somewhat rare among the nations of the world.

In Western Europe, for example, **multiparty systems** are the rule. Italy has 9 national parties and several regional parties; France and West Germany have 4. Great Britain, long considered a predominantly two-party system, now has at least 3 parties. Multiparty systems also are found in Canada, which has 3 parties, and Israel, which has more than 20.

Why do we have a two-party system? The most common explanation is the nature of our election system.[18] Public officials are elected from **single-member districts** under a **winner-take-all** arrangement. This means that only one individual is elected from a district or state: the individual who received the most votes. This contrasts with **proportional representation** election schemes, where seats in the national legislature go to political parties roughly according to the proportion of the popular vote the parties' candidates received.

In single-member district, winner-take-all systems, only the major parties have much chance of winning legislative seats. Without much hope of developing a base to build on, minor parties tend to die off or merge with one of the major parties.

However, this explanation might not account for the difference. It may be the party system that influences the election system rather than the reverse. Where only two parties exist, it is to their advantage to maintain an election system that undermines the development and growth of minor parties. For example, legislatures, controlled by the two parties, have tried to make it as difficult as possible for third parties to get on the ballot (though the courts have struck down much of this restrictive legislation). Where several parties exist, it is to their advantage to establish an election system that benefits many parties.[19]

Fragmentation

The federal system, with its fragmentation of power between state and national levels, leads to fragmentation within parties. State and local parties have their own resources and power bases separate from those of the national parties.

Power also is fragmented at each level. At the national level, power is shared among the president and members of Congress. No one controls the party. Presidents often have a difficult time winning support for their policies among their party members in Congress. The Democratic-controlled Congress failed to ratify many of Carter's proposals, and the Republican-controlled Senate failed to support some of Reagan's policies. In 1990, House Republicans supported George Bush 63% of the time, Senate Republicans 70%.[20]

To be reelected, members of Congress have to satisfy only a plurality of the voters in their district or state, not the president. American political parties are a combination of individuals and organizations (national, state, and local) that are to a large extent independent of each other. This independence makes it very difficult to have a unified national party.

Moderation

American political parties are moderate; there are no extremely liberal or extremely conservative major parties. One reason for this is that the people themselves are moderate (see figure 4). To attract the most voters, the parties try to appear moderate.

Because parties try to attract many voters, both have liberals as well as conservatives, though the Democratic party has more liberals and fewer conservatives than the Republican party. This combination prompts parties to moderate their appeals and nominate moderate candidates. When liberal or conservative candidates do get nominated, they usually move toward the middle on some issues or at least portray themselves as moderate. Even Reagan, when running for reelection, embraced a conciliatory stance toward the Soviet Union in contrast to his earlier "evil empire" posture.

Minor Parties in American Politics

Sometimes called "third parties," minor parties are as varied as the causes they represent. Some are one-issue parties, like the Prohibition party (1869 to the present), which campaigns to ban the sale of liquor, and the American Know-Nothing party (1856), which ran on a platform of opposing immigrants and Catholics.

Other parties advocate radical change in the American political system. Economic protest parties, such as the Populist party of 1892, sometimes appear

Figure 4 ■ Parties Aim Their Campaigns to the Middle, Where the Voters Are

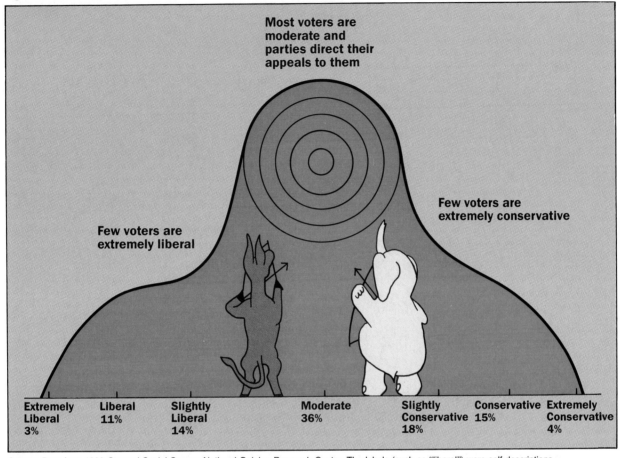

Most voters are moderate and parties direct their appeals to them

Few voters are extremely liberal

Few voters are extremely conservative

| Extremely Liberal 3% | Liberal 11% | Slightly Liberal 14% | Moderate 36% | Slightly Conservative 18% | Conservative 15% | Extremely Conservative 4% |

Source: Data from 1990 General Social Survey, National Opinion Research Center. The labels (such as "liberal") were self-descriptions.

when economic conditions are especially bad and disappear when times improve. Since the 1920s, the Communist party has espoused the adoption of a Communist system.

Finally, many minor parties are factions that have broken from a major party. The States' Rights Dixiecrats left the Democrats in 1948 and mounted a presidential campaign on a segregationist states' rights platform. In 1968, George Wallace split from the Democratic party to run for president as the candidate of the conservative American Independent party.

Minor parties face many obstacles in trying to establish themselves. Because a sizable portion of the electorate is firmly attached to the existing parties, minor party candidates find it difficult to attract voter support and money and to develop lasting state and local organizations. Even voters who favor the ideas or

candidates of a minor party often will not vote for them because in a close race between the major party candidates, a vote for a minor party is seen as a "wasted" vote.

Because most policymakers are also members of the Democratic or Republican parties, they have erected substantial barriers to prevent minor party candidates from getting on the ballot. Excessive numbers of signatures of registered voters are required of minor party candidates seeking to be placed on the ballot. However, court decisions have made it easier for minor party candidates to qualify for office, and campaign finance laws give some boost to minor parties that can win 5% of the popular vote.

Minor parties often lose ground because one or both major parties adopt their ideas. After Prohibition became law, the Prohibition party lost support, and

FOCUS ON AN ISSUE

Does the United States Need a Multiparty System?

Since the nation's founding, the United States has had a two-party system. Most Americans are attached to the idea; third or minor parties seem out of place—somehow un-American. Voters typically fail to support them, and most disappear before the next election.

But is a two-party system really good for the United States?

Would Three or More Parties Provide Voters More Choice?

The Republican and Democratic parties often are criticized for not providing voters much choice. The labels Tweedledum and Tweedledee, used by critics, suggest that the two major parties are more alike than different. George Wallace justified his 1968 third party presidential campaign by noting: "There's not a dime's worth of difference between the Democrats and Republicans." Although there is much more difference than Wallace observed, a third and possibly a fourth party could provide considerably more choice to the voters.

Would a Multiparty System Increase Voter Turnout?

Nonvoters often explain their lack of participation by complaining that there are no good candidates to vote for and elections do not make any difference. In fact, most working-class and poor Americans no longer vote. Turnout among all voters, and especially working-class voters, is much higher in multiparty systems such as France and West Germany than in the United States.

If parties in the United States represented the views of diverse groups of voters more clearly and actively, which happens in multiparty systems, turnout in elections would be likely to increase. A party catering to working-class voters, for example, might raise their low voting rates. A party speaking primarily for the poor might encourage them to go to the polls.

Would a Multiparty System Result in More Issue-Oriented Campaigns?

In a multiparty system, parties take more specific issue positions and campaign on them. They do not try to be all things to all people. Campaigns are likely to deal with real rather than manufactured issues, and elections are likely to provide voters with clear choices. Moreover, a party's emphasis on issues is likely to drive those who disagree out, insuring that the party will continue to represent the specific interests of those who remain. This also may stimulate the formation of more parties as those who leave start new ones.

With just two parties, the need to establish a large winning coalition obscures differences within the parties. Disagreement drives potential supporters away. Campaigns often focus on style and image rather than issues.

Would Three or More Parties Make It Difficult for Voters to Hold Government Accountable?

In a two-party system, responsibility is fixed. Voters can punish the party in control for poor decisions by voting for the opposition in the next election. In a multiparty system with no clear majority, party coalitions among parties form

---

the Socialist party lost supporters after New Deal social legislation was passed in the 1930s.

Party in the Electorate

The party in the electorate, those individuals who identify with a political party, are a party's grass-roots supporters. **Party identification** is a psychological link between individuals and a party similar to the

identification they feel toward religious, ethnic, and racial groups. One may, for example, identify as an Italian or a black; no formal or organization membership is necessary.

Party Identification

A majority of Americans identify with a political party (see table 2). In 1988, 35% said they were Democrats, 28% Republicans, and 36% independent.

on specific issues, then may disappear. This makes account-ability to the voters difficult.

However, even in a two-party system, accountability is not easy. The president may be of one party and Congress of the other. Party members do not all vote the same way. Moreover, regardless of how many parties there are, the president and his party are likely to be held responsible when things go wrong. The desire to win and hold onto the presidency will lead to accountability whether or not there are two or more parties competing.

A multiparty system might provide greater responsibility. Parties with a more specific focus could be held accountable on policies reflecting this focus.

Does a Two-Party System Promote Majoritarian Government?

An advantage of a two-party system is that it promotes majoritarian government. Because there are only two parties, one is certain to win a majority of the votes and seats in Congress. There will be no deadlocks caused by several minority parties. The two-party system also enhances government's legitimacy. Winning a majority of the votes means that a party has a clearer mandate to govern.

In contrast, multiparty systems rarely find a single party in control. In Italy, for example, no party is close to having a majority; control passes from different ruling coalitions several times a year. In Israel, neither of the major parties controls a majority, and both are forced to bargain with extremely conservative religious parties, which results in tilting national policy in a direction the majority of voters oppose.

However, even in a two-party system, the president must put together a majority coalition by bargaining and compromise. Even when his own party is a majority, it is unheard of for the president to win a vote with only his party's support. There is no built-in majority in Congress ready to do the president's bidding.

Does a Two-Party System Moderate Conflict?

Many people believe that one of the advantages of a two-party system is its moderating influence. Because there are only two parties, widely disparate interests have to come together within each party and be willing to compromise. In the process, severe conflict is checked. In a multiparty system, there is no incentive to come together. Indeed, pressures push in the opposite direction. Thus intraparty cleavages are diminished, but interparty conflict increases.

On the other hand, although two parties may moderate political conflict, there is no reason to believe that three or even four parties could not do the same thing. To be a viable choice in an election and to mount an effective campaign for the presidency, parties would still need to form large electoral coalitions, which would require compromise, though not to the degree as in a two-party system.

Would a Multiparty System Increase Citizens' Interest and Support for Government?

If political parties provide citizens with more choice, interest in politics and turnout for elections are likely to rise. If citizens are better able to see how their votes relate to what political parties and the government do, this may lead to greater citizen support and trust of government.

If, however, a multiparty system leads to deadlock through an absence of majority control of government, people might lose interest and grow more cynical about government.

For a discussion of the advantages of a multiparty system in the United States, see Theodore J. Lowi, *The Personal President: Power Invested, Promises Unfulfilled* (Ithaca, N.Y.: Cornell University Press, 1985).

In chapter 4, we discussed how political socialization leads to party identification early in childhood. Political scientists used to think that changes in party identification after childhood were rare except for those that occurred during major party realignments. But in fact people change their party identification more often. This can happen because they change their job or residence, or because they develop policy views that conflict with their original party. As we have seen, for example, the national Democratic par-

ty's increased support for civil rights and other liberal policies caused many white southerners to leave the party.

Characteristics of Democrats and Republicans

Although people from all walks of life are found in each party, individuals with certain characteristics are more likely to be found in one than the other (see table 3). Blacks and Hispanics are more likely than non-Hispanic whites to be Democrats. Jews and Catholics are more likely than Protestants to be Democrats.

High-income professionals and those in business are most apt to be Republicans; low-income blue-collar workers are most likely to be Democrats. Skilled blue-collar workers and white-collar workers are in between.

In chapter 4 we called attention to the gender gap—differences between men and women on a number of issues. The gap is reflected in party affiliation as well. Women are more likely than men to be Democrats. Except for gender, most of the differences revealed in table 3 have their origins in the depression and New Deal.

Table 2 ■ Party Identification, 1960–1988

Affiliation	1960	1972	1980	1988
Strong Democrat	21	15	18	17
Weak Democrat	25	25	23	18
Independent Democrat	8	11	11	12
Independent	8	13	13	11
Independent Republican	7	11	10	13
Weak Republican	13	13	14	14
Strong Republican	14	10	9	14
Apolitical, do not know	4	2	2	2

Source: University of Michigan Survey Research Center/CPS/NES.

Party in Government

Nationally, the party in government is the party's elected members of Congress and, for the party that occupies the White House, the president. The party in government links the party in the electorate to their government. The job of the party in government is to enact policies that party voters favor. This seems like a simple idea, but political scientists have waged great debates over how close the link between the party in government and the party in the electorate should be.

Proponents of a **responsible party government** believe that parties should take clear and contrasting positions on issues and enforce them on their mem-

bers. "Responsible" party government would be responsible in that:

- voters would have a choice between parties advocating different programs;
- a party would make sure that its members in office vote for these programs;
- therefore, if a party had a majority, it would enact its program into law.

Under these conditions, voting for one party rather than another would have definite policy consequences. It would increase the prospects for popular control of government because a voter would know what a vote for one party means for public policy. Great Britain is an example of responsible party government. Political parties there are heavily involved in developing, articulating, and implementing public policy. If a party member defects too often from important policy positions, party leaders can deny him or her the right to stand for reelection as the party's candidate.

The American system is not a responsible party government. Political parties do not always offer clear and contrasting positions. When they do, party leaders are limited in authority to ensure that members support the "party," that is, the position of the president or party's leaders in Congress.

Although the American system is not a responsible party government, it has some elements of party responsibility. The party links presidents with the members of their party in Congress. Parties also have important organizational and leadership functions in Congress. Party influence is visible in congressional voting.[21] More than one-third of all roll calls find a majority of one party opposed to a majority of the other, and the proportion of members voting with

Source: Tony Auth, Universal Press Syndicate. Reprinted with permission.

Table 3 ■ Characteristics of Republicans, Democrats, and Independents

	Republican (percent)	Democrat (percent)	Independent (percent)
TOTAL*	32	36	32
East	33	39	28
Midwest	36	28	36
South	33	42	25
West	29	35	36
Age 18–29	37	23	40
30–49	29	35	36
50 and over	34	46	22
Less than high school education	23	43	35
High school graduate	30	40	30
Some college	37	30	33
College graduate	41	29	31
Men	34	31	35
Women	32	39	29
White	36	32	32
Black	12	62	26
Protestant	37	34	30
Catholic	31	42	29
Professional and business	37	31	32
Other white collar	35	34	31
Blue collar	26	42	32
Skilled worker	35	33	32
Unskilled worker	35	43	31
Union households	24	47	29
Nonunion households	33	36	32
Under $15,000	24	44	32
$15,000–$24,999	30	36	34
$25,000 and over	37	33	30
Conservative	51	25	24
Middle of the road	25	36	39
Liberal	20	49	31

*The overall percentages differ somewhat from those in table 2 because of the somewhat different wording of questions in the two different polls. The polls were also done at different times.

Source: General Social Survey 1990.

their party is increasing (see figure 5). Party unity tends to be particularly high on economic and social welfare issues.

Some people would like to increase the level of party responsibility in American politics. This would require significant changes in the operation of government. In Congress, for example, party leaders would have to be given more power to maintain party discipline. A greater tie between the president and Congress also would be required. This could be accomplished

Figure 5 ■ Party Unity is on the Rise in Congress

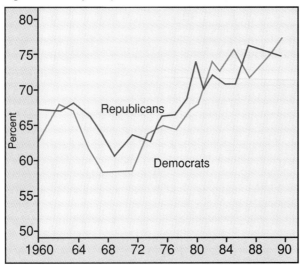

The percentage of times the average Democrat or Republican in Congress voted with his or her party majority on votes where a majority of Democrats opposed a majority of Republicans.
Source: Party unity voting studies in *Congressional Quarterly Almanac* for the respective years, Washington, D.C.: Congressional Quarterly.

on a continuing basis only through a constitutional change providing for a parliamentary system similar to Britain's, in which Congress would elect the president. Such a change is unlikely.

Party Organization

The party organization is the third component of the political party. The major levels of party organization—national, state, and local—coincide with political units responsible for administering elections. Within the local parties there are further subdivisions. The smallest unit is usually the precinct-level organization. Several precincts comprise a ward or district; several wards comprise the city or county organization.

Although party organization seems hierarchical (organized from the top down), it is not. Party organization is a layered structure with each layer linked to, but independent of, the others. Higher levels cannot dictate to or impose penalties on lower levels to ensure compliance.

Party organization is only loosely connected with the party in government. This contrasts with the British system, in which the party leaders in Parliament try to maintain a tight grip on the party organization.

National Party Organization

The head of the party organization is the national chair. Although selected by the party's presidential nominee, the national chair is not a major political figure.

Responsibilities of the national party chair include managing the national headquarters, overseeing the national party apparatus, planning the national convention, and coordinating the presidential campaign efforts of the national organization with those of the nominee's personal organization. Fund raising and promotion of the party also fall on the chair.

Members of the **national committee** are selected by state party committees or conventions, and membership usually is awarded on the basis of service to the party. Duties of the committee are few but important: it chooses the site of the national convention and the formula for determining the number of delegates each state sends to it.

Both parties also have two national campaign committees that are growing in influence. In the 1980s both parties raised more money than ever before from a variety of sources. The Democrats topped the $100 million mark, and Republicans tripled that amount (see figure 6). Money came from PACs and large and small contributors. Both party organizations opened permanent headquarters and expanded their staffs.[22]

The national party organizations have become increasingly active in recruiting candidates to run for office. The Republicans' programs to help their candidates are better developed, but the Democrats are catching up. Since 1984, the Republican organization has provided every female Senate primary candidate a $1,500 campaign contribution once a similar amount has been raised by the candidate. Specific candidates have been encouraged to run. In an effort to convince a Nebraskan to run for the Senate, the Republican national organization invited her to Washington to tour the capital, dine with senators, and see what life in the Senate is like (she ran and lost). Occasionally, the organizations have discouraged individuals from running, especially where another candidate appeared to have a better chance of winning.

Training in managing a campaign is also available from the national party organizations. Both parties hold how-to seminars and help candidates design campaign strategies; they help research issues and write speeches; and they conduct polls and work with state and local party organizations to get out the vote.

- 9:00 P.M. At the clubhouse again. Spent $10 for a church excursion. Bought tickets for a baseball game. Listened to the complaints of a dozen pushcart peddlers who said they were being persecuted by the police. Promised to go to police headquarters in the morning and see about it.

- 10:30 P.M. Attended a Hebrew wedding reception and dance. Had previously sent a handsome wedding present to the bride.
- 12:00 P.M. In bed.

Source: Alistair Cooke, *Alistair Cooke's America* (New York: Alfred A. Knopf, 1973), pp. 290–91; adapted from William L. Riordon, *Plunkitt of Tammany Hall* (New York: E. P. Dutton, 1963), pp. 91–93.

George Washington Plunkitt holds forth in his unofficial office, a bootblack stand at the New York County Court House.

number of Democratic candidates, sometimes the winner of the primary did not have a majority of the vote. In those cases, some southern states used a run-off election between the two highest vote-getters in the primary.

Although primaries have increased citizen participation in nominations, turnout in primaries is quite low, averaging 15% to 30%, and unrepresentative of the public at large. Voters in primaries tend to have higher incomes and education and to be older, more interested in politics, and more partisan.[25]

The primary also hurts the party organization and undermines the party in government. Candidates can bypass party leaders and appeal directly to voters. Candidates who oppose the party's issue positions can run and win the party's nomination, especially in elections in which voters do not know much about the candidates. In 1988, a Klu Klux Klan member won the Louisiana Republican nomination for a state legisla-

tive seat much to the embarrassment of Republican leaders, including President Reagan, who endorsed his opponent.

Conclusion: Do Political Parties Make Government More Responsive?

Although the Founders had little use for political parties, parties did develop, and during the nineteenth century they were the major link between the public and government. Following the Progressive reforms of the early twentieth century, the importance of parties began to decline.

Compared to a century ago or even a few decades ago, party decline is visible in each of the components

Why Not Return to the "Smoke-Filled Rooms"?

In addition to attracting a small and unrepresentative group of voters to the ballot box, primaries have other flaws. In some ways, the primary process is less responsive to voters than party conventions, where candidates were once selected by a small group of party leaders meeting in smoke-filled hotel rooms.

Primaries do not necessarily provide voters with much choice. Many primaries are uncontested. Often the presence of an incumbent deters challengers, or at least strong challengers. In either case, incumbents are generally renominated.

Primaries also may make the general election less competitive. The minority party (that is, the party less likely to win the general election) often has no strong candidate who can mount an effective campaign in the general election. In preprimary days, party leaders generally made sure that there were strong candidates running in the general election regardless of election prospects.

Another problem with primaries is that the electorate may nominate a candidate known by his or her party peers to be incompetent, difficult to work with, or lacking in character and integrity. Although the convention system does not guarantee that such candidates will be avoided, party leaders are more likely to know the real strengths and weaknesses of potential candidates than are voters, who must rely on the media for information. Indeed, voters have so little information about primary candidates that success often turns on name recognition. For example, several John Kennedys, none related to the president, were nominated for state and local offices in the early 1960s.

Primaries hurt the most, however, by freeing candidates from supporting the party's program. It is nearly impossible for party leaders to withhold nominations from candidates who are party members in name only or who often vote with the other party. Thus, the party bonds are weakened and members can feel free to vote and act however they want.

This might seem desirable. But when candidates vote completely independent of their party, it is more difficult for voters to cast an informed vote. When parties offer a clear choice, voters know what they are voting for and can reward or punish the parties for what they do or plan to do in office. Thus, party voting can make government more responsive to the voters.

Some commentators have advocated returning to convention nominations. If we did so, the abuses that we associate with the smoke-filled rooms of a century ago are less likely to occur today because of the greater likelihood of exposure by the media and consequent hostile voter reaction. In states and localities where the parties are competitive, it is likely that conventions would produce strong candidates. This would give voters a real choice in the general election. However, in locales dominated by one party, the convention system would not necessarily produce stronger candidates than a primary.

Why haven't we returned to the convention system? Primaries are widely accepted. They *seem* more democratic because more people are involved than in conventions, where only party activists participate. But the sheer number of people involved is only one aspect of democracy and probably not the most important. Democracy also implies that those making the nominations are representative of the public; primary electorates are not. Moreover, a democratic process must offer some choice, and primaries adversely affect competition.

Although it is unlikely that we will abolish primaries and return to conventions, in recent years party leaders have asserted more control in some states through preprimary endorsements. Parties endorse candidates for nomination. The endorsed candidates are listed first on the primary ballot or are simply publicized as the "official" party candidate. Although on occasion the preferred candidate is defeated, the voters usually go along with the party's choice. Such arrangements promote party strength and ultimately responsiveness to voters.

of political parties. Fewer individuals identify with a party; party organization has lost many of its functions to interest groups and campaign consultants; and because television allows candidates to appeal directly to voters, party workers are less relevant today. Freed from reliance on party organization for campaign resources and less able to mobilize voters on the basis of party appeals, those who serve in the govern-

ment are less committed to their party than officeholders were decades ago. Diminished party influence means increased nonparty influence, namely interest group and constituency pressure.

The past decade and a half, however, has seen a resurgence in party influence. The growth in independents has halted. Party organizations are adapting to the current political environment and are now playing a significant role in the recruitment, funding, and campaign strategies of candidates. This is particularly true of the national parties, whose support is increasingly necessary to the success of aspiring congressional candidates. And party loyalty in terms of voting is on the upswing in Congress. It is too soon to say "The Party's Over," the title of a text on parties published twenty years ago.

Despite these reversals in the decline of parties, politics is more fragmented than it was a half century ago. Split ticket voting and the divided government it produces make it unclear how one's vote will affect what government does. It is hard for voters to reward or punish officeholders for what they do. If each officeholder stands alone, there are no unifying and simplifying forces allowing voters to throw the incumbents out when they are ready for a change. Elections become less meaningful because voters have little idea what they are voting for. And because elections are the chief means by which most voters can influence government, government may become less responsive to the average voter. Citizens have a greater prospect of influencing the direction of government if they elect party loyalists to office. This factor is what led E. E. Schattschneider to reflect on the inevitability and necessity of parties in our American democracy.

EPILOGUE

Phil Gramm Switches

In a seemingly risky move, Phil Gramm decided to resign his House seat, return to Texas, and seek election to the House as a Republican. His gamble paid off, because he regained his seat, defeating 10 opponents. A month after he lost his seat on the Budget Committee, he was back in the House, the first Republican ever to represent his district. Moreover, the Republicans put him back on the Budget Committee, where he continued to work for a balanced budget and his conservative views. In 1984 he ran for the Senate and was elected by the largest margin ever received by a Republican for statewide office in Texas.

Gramm's switch to the Republican party can be seen as part of a minor realignment of party loyalties.

Many white southern Democrats, especially those with conservative views, have switched to the Republican party, finding it more ideologically congenial. Although most of the realignment has taken place among rank-and-file voters, a few elected officials have switched and have been reelected to office, including Senator Strom Thurmond (R-S.C.) and former Representative Andrew Ireland (R-Fla.). Democrats outside the South who have switched to the Republican party have not been very successful in winning. For most party activists and elected leaders, party loyalties supersede issue opinions, and switching is uncommon.

KEY TERMS

party in the electorate	ticket splitting	proportional	patronage
party in government	dealignment	representation	caucus
party organization	two-party system	party identification	direct primary
realignment	multiparty systems	responsible party	closed primary
political machines	single-member districts	government	open primary
New Deal coalition	winner-take-all	national committee	

FURTHER READING

David S. Broder, *The Party's Over: The Failure of Politics in America* (New York: Harper & Row, 1972). *Argues that the only way America will be able to meet the difficult challenges of the future is for the political parties to assert themselves and exercise more influence in American politics.*

Paul Herrnson, *Party Campaigning in the 1980s* (Cambridge, Mass.: Harvard University Press, 1988). *Documents the revival of the national parties in the 1980s.*

Edwin O'Connor, *The Last Hurrah* (New York: Bantam Books, 1957). *A warm, intimate novel, set in Boston in the 1950s, which contrasts the old-style party election campaigns with new media-oriented ones.*

William L. Riordan, *Plunkitt of Tammany Hall* (New York: Dutton, 1963). *A series of witty talks by a ward boss of New York City's Democratic party machine. A slice of Americana, this book discusses "honest graft" and other aspects of "practical politics" and in the process demonstrates why political machines flourished.*

Mike Royko, *Boss: Richard J. Daley of Chicago* (New York: New American Library, 1971). *An intriguing account of how the Chicago political machine operated under the late mayor Richard J. Daley.*

James L. Sundquist, *Dynamics of the Party System* (Washington, D.C.: Brookings Institution, 1973). *Analyzes the concept of realignment based on a review of the major party realignments in America history.*

NOTES

1. E. E. Schattschneider, *Party Government* (New York: Holt, Rinehart & Winston, 1960), p. 1.

2. Jack Dennis, "Trends in Public Support for the American Party System," in Jeff Fishel, ed., *Parties and Elections in an Anti-Party Age* (Bloomington: Indiana University Press, 1978).

3. Frank Sorauf, *Political Parties in the American System,* 4th ed. (Boston: Little, Brown, 1980).

4. Richard Hofstadter, *The Idea of Party System: The Rise of Legitimate Opposition in the United States, 1780–1840* (Berkeley: University of California Press, 1969).

5. Theodore J. Lowi, *The Personal President: Power Invested, Promise Unfulfilled* (Ithaca, N.Y.: Cornell University Press, 1985).

6. James MacGregor Burns, *The Vineyard of Liberty* (New York: Knopf, 1982).

7. Kevin Phillips, *The Emerging Republican Majority* (New York: Doubleday, 1969).

8. Everett Carll Ladd, *Where Have All the Voters Gone?* (New York: W. W. Norton, 1982), p. 78; 1984 and 1988 data are from the 1984 and 1988 CPS National Election Study.

9. James L. Sundquist, *Dynamics of the Party System: Alignment and Realignment of Political Parties in the United States* (Washington, D.C.: Brookings Institution, 1973).

10. Nelson Polsby, "Did the 1984 Election Signal Major Party Realignment?" *The Key Reporter* 50 (Spring 1985): 2.

11. Ibid.

12. D. Sarasohn, "Wall Falls on Reagan Coalition," *Lincoln Sunday Journal-Star,* February 18, 1990, p. 4C.

13. David Broder, "The New Politics of Dixie," *Washington Post National Weekly Edition,* June 2, 1986, pp. 6–7; John Petrocik, "Realignment," *Journal of Politics* 49 (May 1987): 347–75.

14. Petrocik, "Realignment"; George Rabinowitz, Paul-Henri Gurian, and Stuart MacDonald, "The Structure of Presidential Elections and the Process of Realignment," *American Journal of Political Science* 28 (November 1984): 611–35; D. Broder, "The GOP Plays Dixie," *The Washington Post National Weekly Edition,* September 12–18, 1988, p. 4; T. B. Edall, "A Serious Case of White Flight," *The Washington Post National Weekly Edition,* September 10–16, 1990, p. 13.

15. John R. Petrocik and Frederick T. Steeper, "The Political Landscape in 1988," *Public Opinion Magazine* (September/October 1987): 41–44; Helmurt Norpoth, "Party Realignment in the 1980s," *Public Opinion Quarterly* 51 (Fall 1987): 376–90.

16. See Edward Carmines, John McIver, and James Stimson, "Unrealized Partisanship," *Journal of Politics* 49 (May 1987): 376–400; Paul Abramson, John Aldrich, and David Rohde, *Change and Continuity in the 1984 Elections* (Washington, D.C.: CQ Press, 1987).

17. Walter Dean Burnham, *Critical Elections and the Mainstream of American Politics* (New York: W. W. Norton, 1970); Helmut Norpoth and Jerrold Rusk, "Partisan Dealignment in the American Electorate," *American Political Science Review* 76 (September 1982): 522–37.

18. Maurice Duverger, *Political Parties* (New York: John Wiley & Sons, 1963). See also Edward R. Tufte, "The Relationship between Seats and Votes in Two-Party Systems," *American Political Science Review* 67 (1973): 540–54.

19. See also Lowi, *Personal President,* where he makes the point that two parties survived in the United States despite the use of multimember districts in elections for Congress in the nineteenth century.

20. *Congressional Quarterly Weekly Report,* November 10, 1988.

21. William R. Shaffer, *Party and Ideology in the United States Congress* (Lanham, Md.: University Press of America, 1980).

22. Frank J. Sorauf, *Money in American Elections* (Glenview, Ill.: Scott, Foresman, 1988), pp. 121–53; Paul Herrnson, *Party Campaigning in the 1980s* (Cambridge, Mass.: Harvard University Press, 1988).

23. Xandra Kayden, "The Nationalization of the Party System," in Michael Malbin, ed., *Parties, Interest Groups, and Campaign Finance Laws* (Washington, D.C.: American Enterprise Institute, 1980).

24. Milton L. Rakove, *Don't Make No Waves, Don't Back No Losers* (Bloomington, Ind.: Indiana University Press, 1975).

25. Austin Ranney, *Participation in American Presidential Nominations, 1976* (Washington, D.C.: American Enterprise Institute, 1977). See also Austin Ranney, "Parties in State Politics," in Herbert Jacob and Kenneth Vines, eds., *Politics in the American States,* 3rd ed. (Boston: Little, Brown, 1980), pp. 61–99.

Voting and Elections

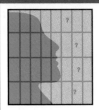

High Road
or Low Road?

You are George Bush. It is June 1988, and you are faced with one of the biggest decisions of your life. The polls show you far behind your Democratic presidential opponent. Now your campaign strategists tell you that to get back into the race you must launch a hard-hitting set of ads and speeches attacking Michael Dukakis as soft on crime and unpatriotic.

You believe that you and your party should win the election. The country is prosperous and experiencing steady economic growth. Typically, the incumbent party does well in times of economic growth, especially when no foreign crises threaten. Though many economists are warning that this growth is based on a flimsy foundation of borrowing and huge budget deficits, these over-the-horizon problems do not seem as important to voters as the real increases in their incomes.

In addition to economic growth, another factor working in your favor is the warming of relations between the United States and the Soviet Union. After treating the Soviets as the arch-enemy for most of his first term, President Ronald Reagan has signed an agreement with Soviet leader Mikhail Gorbachev to remove many nuclear missiles from Europe. The Democrats mostly support the agreement, thus removing it as an election issue.

And finally, you believe you should have an edge because the incumbent is so popular. Reagan's popularity has rebounded since the Iran-contra affair. You believe that some of his popularity reflects positive feelings toward the Republican party and will spill over to you too.

Given this election setting, why are you behind? Political experts think it is because you are not a very good candidate. Your advisers tell you that your "negatives" in public opinion are extremely high. A *Newsweek* cover story was entitled "Can Bush Overcome the Wimp Factor?" Media observers as well as your opponents portray you as a wimp; they point to your eastern establishment upbringing, your tendency to dress and speak like a "preppy" (the "We're in deep doo-doo" phrase belongs to you), and your repeated disavowals of any involvement in many of the controversial issues of the Reagan presidency, such as the Iran-contra affair, which makes you look weak. Opponents also portray you as a wimp because despite your many years of public service it is difficult to find any consistent pattern in your political beliefs. Though you have sometimes been regarded as a moderate Republican, after you became vice president, you adopted the policies and seemingly the principles of the Republican right wing. Even so, the Republican right still distrusts you.

Now the polls are showing you trailing Michael Dukakis, by as many as 17 points. Indeed, in the late spring, for every two good things people said about you, they said three negative things.[1] One poll even showed you running behind Soviet leader Mikhail Gorbachev in public esteem.[2] Your advisers say you cannot win with that kind of image, and they present you with a new strategy to consider.

They tell you that despite Dukakis's high standing in the polls, and the public's perception of him as competent and nonideological, he is not very well known. Your campaign could redefine him in the public's mind as a far-left liberal, soft on crime, and not very patriotic. As one adviser said, "If you have high negatives the only way to beat him is to get his negatives higher than yours."[3]

Your advisers believe they have found some "soft" spots in Dukakis's record that will make this redefinition possible. As governor of Massachusetts, Dukakis vetoed a bill that would have required teachers to lead the Pledge of Allegiance in schools each day. And he had initially resisted altering the state's prison furlough plan. Massachusetts, like 40 other states (and the federal government), had a plan to

(continued on next page)

give some prisoners furloughs to go home occasionally. Unfortunately, one of the furloughed prisoners in Massachusetts, Willie Horton, raped a woman and terrorized her and her fiancé.

Your advisers know that these issues will have a powerful appeal to the public. Earlier, your aides had previewed their campaign material with 30 Democratic voters who had voted for Reagan. When the sessions began, these Democrats thought that Dukakis was more conservative than Bush, tougher on drugs, and more in tune with their own values. However, when the Republican consultants talked about Dukakis's veto of the Pledge of Allegiance bill, his stance against capital punishment, and the furlough program, they found that voters became antagonistic toward him. The furlough program struck an especially hostile chord among the voters when the Republican advisers told them about the Willie Horton rape. Many voters left the focus groups believing that Dukakis was a radical who was soft on crime. Half of the 30 had decided to vote against him.[4]

Based on these groups, your aides decided that these very emotional issues would greatly damage Dukakis. Indeed, one adviser commented that by election day, "Willie Horton" would be a household name. Your advisers tell you that you must come out strongly and negatively to portray Dukakis as a radical whose values are way out of the mainstream. Aides show you a videotape of the session with the voters, showing that the furlough and Pledge issues played a major role in changing these perceptions.

But do you want to take that road? On the one hand, you are regarded generally as a decent person. You have never run a campaign by attacking your opponent's character. You have never liked the grubbier side of politics. And you had been heard to say that Dukakis is a decent and able man.[5] You know that Dukakis is no less patriotic and no less concerned about crime than you are. Dukakis vetoed the Pledge bill because he thought it was unconstitutional, and he accepted the prison program, which had been initiated by his Republican predecessor and was much like the one Governor Ronald Reagan had in California, because criminologists recommended the program.

On the other hand, you badly want to win and it looks like you will not if you do not do something drastic. There is evidence that a negative campaign might help. In recent elections, the press and other political analysts have complained about negative campaigning, but the public responds to it anyway. Says one political consultant, "The man on the street always says he doesn't like dirty politics. Then he goes home and watches it with relish on television.[6]

You also believe that the voters are uninformed about Dukakis. You think that they need to be told about his record.

In light of these considerations, what do you decide?

eral Democratic southern senators. In these cases, the majority of whites voted for the Republican, but a huge majority of blacks voted Democrat.

The Voting Rights Act was renewed and expanded in 1970, 1975, and 1982. It now covers more states and other minorities, such as Hispanics, Asians, native Americans, and Eskimos, and thus serves as a basic protection for minority voting rights. For example, states must provide bilingual ballots in counties in which 5% or more of the population does not speak English.

In 1982, southern representatives sought to scrap the provision for federal approval of changes in election procedures because they felt it singled out southern states for federal interference. Although they claimed that there was no longer any discrimination, hence no need for the provision, considerable evidence suggested otherwise. For example, the federal government had vetoed more than 800 proposed changes in election laws and electoral districts. Some local governments in the South were still trying to dilute the black vote by changing election district boundaries, by switching from district-based to at-large elections (where a solid black minority could be continually outvoted by a white majority), and by other means. Eventually, however, Congress rejected efforts to narrow and weaken the act.

Women and the Right to Vote

When property ownership defined the right to vote, women property owners could vote in some places. When property requirements were removed, suffrage came to be seen as a male right only. Women's right to vote was reintroduced in the 1820s in Tennessee school board elections.[13] From that time on, women had the vote in some places, usually only at the local level or for particular kinds of elections.

The national movement for women's suffrage did not gain momentum until after the Civil War. Before and during that war, many women helped lead the campaign to abolish slavery and establish full political rights for blacks. When black males got the vote after the Civil War, some women saw the paradox in their working to enfranchise these males when they themselves lacked the right to vote. Led by Susan B. Anthony, Elizabeth Cady Stanton, and others, they lobbied Congress and the state legislatures for voting rights for women.

The first suffrage bill was introduced in Congress in 1868 and each year thereafter until 1893. Most members were strong in their condemnation of women as potential voters. One senator claimed that if women could hold political views different from their husbands it would make "every home a hell on earth."

When Wyoming applied to join the union in 1889, it already had granted women the right to vote. Congress initially tried to bar Wyoming for that reason but then relented when the Wyoming territorial legislature declared, "We will remain out of the Union 100 years rather than come in without the women." Still, by 1910 women had complete suffrage rights in only four states.

Powerful interests opposed suffrage for women. Liquor interests feared that women voters would press for prohibition because many women had been active in the temperance (antiliquor) movement. Other businesses feared that suffrage would lead to reforms to improve working conditions for women and children. Southern whites feared that it would lead to voting by black women and then by black men. Political bosses feared that women would favor political reform. The Catholic church opposed it as contrary to the proper role of women. According to some people, suffrage was a revolt against nature. Pregnant women might lose their babies, nursing mothers their milk, and women might grow beards or be raped at the polls (then frequently located in saloons or barber shops).[14] Others argued less hysterically that women should be protected from the unsavory practices of politics and should confine themselves to their traditional duties.

About 1910, however, the women's suffrage movement was reenergized, in part by ideas and tactics borrowed from the British women's suffrage movement. A new generation of leaders, including Alice Paul and Carrie Chapman Catt, began to lobby more vigorously, reach out to the working class, and engage in protest marches and picketing, new features of American politics. In 1917, when the National Women's party organized around-the-clock picketing of the White House, their arrest and forced feeding during jail hunger strikes embarrassed the administration and won the movement some support. These incidents, plus contributions by women to the war effort during World War I, led to adoption of the Nineteenth Amendment guaranteeing women the vote in 1920. Although only 37% of eligible women voted in the 1920 presidential election, as the habit of voting spread, women's rates of voting equaled those of men.

Women's contributions to the war effort during World War I helped lead to the ratification of the women's suffrage amendment in 1920. Here Broadway chorus women train as Home Guards during the war.

Other Expansions of the Electorate

Federal constitutional and legislative changes extended the franchise to young adults. Before 1971, many states required a voting age of 19 or more. The service of 18-year-olds in the Vietnam War brought protests that if these men were old enough to die for their country, they were old enough to vote. Yielding to these arguments and to the general recognition that young people were better educated than in the past, Congress adopted and the states ratified the Twenty-sixth Amendment giving 18-year-olds the right to vote.

Only convicted felons, the mentally incapable, noncitizens, and those not meeting minimal residence requirements are unable to vote now. Voting has come to be an essential right of citizenship rather than a privilege just for those qualified by birth or property. Paradoxically, however, as the *right* to vote has expanded, the proportion of eligible citizens *actually* voting has contracted.

Voter Turnout

Political Activism in the Nineteenth Century

In 1896, an estimated 750,000 people—5% of all voters—took train excursions to visit presidential candidate William McKinley at his Ohio home during the campaign.[15] This amazing figure is but one indication of the high level of intense political interest and activity in the late nineteenth century.

In those days, politics was an active, not a spectator, sport. People voted at high rates, as much as 80% in the 1840 presidential election,[16] and they were very partisan. They thought independents were corrupt and ready to sell their votes to the highest bidder. Elaborate and well-organized parties printed and distributed the ballots. Voters, after being coached by party leaders, simply dropped their party's ballot into the box. Split-ticket voting and secrecy in making one's choice were impossible.

AMERICAN DIVERSITY

Women in Office

Even before women were given the right to vote nationally, they held political office. Women officeholders in colonial America were rare but not unknown. In 1715, for example, the Pennsylvania Assembly appointed a woman as tax collector.[1]

Elizabeth Cady Stanton, probably the first woman candidate for Congress, received 24 votes when she ran in 1866.[2] It was not until 1916 that the first woman member of Congress, Jeannette Rankin (R-Mont.), was actually elected. In 1872, Victoria Claflin Woodhull ran for president on the Equal Rights party ticket teamed with abolitionist Frederick Douglass for vice president.

More than 17,000 women now hold elective office, but many of these offices are minor. Inroads by women into major national offices have been slow. Geraldine Ferraro's 1984 vice presidential candidacy was historic but not victorious. Women have barely increased their membership in Congress; it is now 6% after hovering around 5% for years.

Real progress has been made in state and local governments. Women hold 18% of all statewide elective offices, including three governors, Joan Finney (R-Ka.), Ann Richards (D-Tx.) and Barbara Roberts (D-Ore.), and six lieutenant governors.[3] In 1965, only 5% of state legislators were women; today 18% are. There is tremendous variation among the states. Nine have legislatures with more than 25% women (New Hampshire, Vermont, Colorado, Washington, Maine, Arizona, Idaho, Hawaii, and Kansas), whereas three have less than 6% (Louisiana, Kentucky, and Alabama).

More than 20% of the city council seats in medium and large cities are now occupied by women, a proportion that is steadily growing. Ten percent of the mayors of cities of 30,000 and more are women. These include San Francisco and Houston.

Does it make a difference in terms of policy to have women officeholders rather than men? Studies of the be-

Ann Richards and campaign workers celebrate her election as governor of Texas.

havior of women members of Congress and other legislative bodies indicate that they are, on the whole, more liberal than men.[4] Women tend to give issues relating to women, children, and the family higher priority than male legislators do.[5] Women are also less likely to be involved in corrupt activities.

More and more women are getting graduate and professional education and working outside the home. These changes, coupled with increased public support for women taking an active role in politics, suggest that the trend toward more women in public office will continue.

1. Joseph J. Kelley, *Pennsylvania: The Colonial Years* (Garden City, N.Y.: Doubleday, 1980), p. 143.
2. Elisabeth Griffin, *In Her Own Right* (New York: Oxford University Press, 1983).
3. Data are from Center for the American Woman and Politics, National Information Bank on Women in Public Office, Rutgers University, Fact Sheets 1991.
4. Susan Welch, "Are Women More Liberal Than Men in the U.S. Congress?" *Legislative Studies Quarterly* 10 (February 1985): 125–34.
5. Sue Thomas and Susan Welch, "The Impact of Gender on the Priorities and Activities of State Legislators," *Western Political Quarterly,* 1991.

Progressive Reforms

The **Progressive reforms** of the early twentieth century brought radical changes to election politics. Progressive reformers, largely professional and upper middle class, sought to eliminate corruption from pol-

itics and voting. But they also meant to eliminate the influence of the lower classes, many of them recent immigrants. These two goals went hand in hand, because the lower classes were seen as the cause of corruption in politics.

In the nineteenth century, politics involved most people, and political parades and festivities were common. Here a torchlight parade in Buffalo honors Grover Cleveland in the late 1880s.

The Progressive movement was responsible for several reforms: primary elections, voter registration laws, secret ballots, nonpartisan ballots (without party labels), and the denial of voting rights for aliens, which removed a major constituency of the urban party machines. The movement also introduced the merit system for public employment to reduce favoritism and payoffs in hiring.

The reforms, adopted by some states at the beginning of the century, and by others much later, were largely effective in cleaning up politics. But the reformers also achieved, to a very large extent, their goal of eliminating the lower classes from politics. Taking away most of the reason for the existence of the political parties—choosing candidates and printing and distributing ballots—caused the party organization to decline, which in turn produced a decline in political interest and activity on the part of the electorate. Without strong parties to mobilize voters, only the most interested and motivated participated. The new restrictions on voting meant that voters had to invest more time, energy, and thought in voting. They had to think about the election months in advance and travel to city hall to register.

As a consequence, politics began to be a spectator activity. Voter turnout declined sharply after the turn of the century.

Turnout figures from the nineteenth century are not entirely reliable and not exactly comparable with today's. In the days before voter registration, many aliens could vote and some people voted twice. In some instances more people voted in a state election than lived there! Nevertheless, it is generally agreed that turnout was very high in the nineteenth century and that it has diminished substantially; it dropped from more than 77% from 1840–1896 to 54% in the 1920–1932 era, when the Progressive reforms were largely in place. During the New Deal era, when the

Democratic party mobilized new groups of voters, turnout rose again, but it has never achieved anything close to the levels of the nineteenth century.

Recent Turnout

Since 1964, turnout in presidential elections has continually declined. In the 1980s, barely half the eligible electorate (that is, all citizens who could have registered and voted) voted. This means that even in a landslide election, like that of 1984, less than one-third of all potential voters actually voted for Ronald Reagan.

The turnout for off-year congressional elections is even lower. It has not exceeded 45% since World War II, and in 1986 it was 33%. Turnout in primary elections is even lower. In 1986 it was an astoundingly low 10%.

Although nations count their turnouts differently, it is clear that Americans vote in much lower proportions than citizens of other Western democracies (figure 1). Only Switzerland, which relatively recently gave women the right to vote, approximates our low turnout levels.

Within the United States, turnout varies greatly among the states. In the 1988 presidential election, for example, 65% of Minnesota's citizens voted, but only 38% of Georgia's did. Turnout tends to be lower in the South and higher in the northern Plains and Mountain states.[17]

These differences suggest that not only are there certain kinds of people who are unwilling to vote, but there are also certain kinds of laws and political traditions that depress voting turnout.

Who Does Not Vote?

Before we can explain why some people do not vote, we need to see who the nonvoters are. The most important thing to remember is that voting is related to education, income, and occupation, that is, to socioeconomic class. For example, if you are a college graduate, the chances are about 80% that you will vote; if you have less than a high school education, the chances are only about half that.[18] Differences between higher- and lower-income people are also quite large. Two out of three nonvoters have incomes below the average.[19] This class gap in turnout is widening. Although voting among all groups of Americans has declined in the past 30 years, the proportion of

Figure 1 ■ Turnout in the United States Is Lower Than in Most Other Democracies

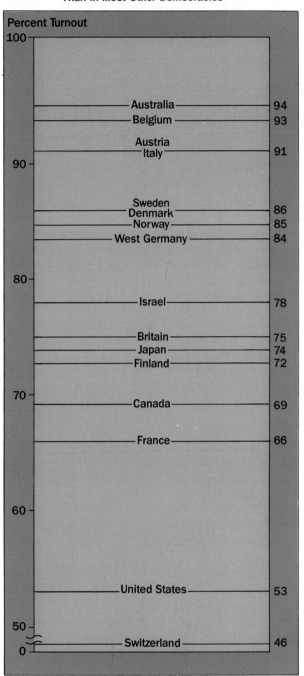

Source: Data are from national elections between 1986 and 1989. Richard Flickinger and Donley Studlar, "The Disappearing Voter?" *West European Politics,* forthcoming 1992.

college-educated persons who participated fell by less than 10% while that of high-school-educated persons dropped by nearly 20%.

Though many people take it for granted that those in the working class vote at lower rates than those in the middle and upper classes, these differences in the United States are far wider than in other nations[20] and far wider than in nineteenth-century America. So there appears to be something unique about the contemporary American political system that inhibits voting participation of all citizens, but particularly those whose income and educational level are below the average.

Voting is also much more common among older than younger people (see figure 2). The popular impression that young people often participate in politics was reinforced during the Vietnam years, when college campuses exploded with antiwar dissent. In fact, however, young people vote much less than their elders. The middle-aged—the highest participators—have established themselves in a career and a family, and they

have more time and money to devote to voting and other political activities. They also have not reached the stage where poor health limits their activities.

Why Turnout Is Low

There are a number of possible reasons why more Americans, especially low-income and young Americans, do not vote.

Satisfaction Among Voters. One reason sometimes given for low rates of voter turnout is that nonvoters are satisfied; not voting is a passive form of consent to what government is doing.[21] This argument falls flat on two counts. First, voter turnout has decreased in an era when public trust in government has decreased, not increased. And second, voter turnout is lower precisely among those groups of citizens who have least reason to be content, not those who have most reason to be so. If staying at home on election day was an indication of satisfaction, one would expect turnout to be lower among the well-off, not among the working class and the poor.

Voters are "Turned Off" by Political Campaigns. About one-third of a group of nonvoters in the 1990 election, when asked why they did not vote, gave reasons suggesting they were disgusted with politics.[22] In explaining the low turnout in the 1988 campaign, one analyst commented. "The media consultants, media and politicians gave this nation an awful election, and the public responded with appropriately awful turnouts."[23] The analyst was condemning the lack of real issues in the campaign, the negative advertising, and the constant attention paid by television to the polls telling people how they were going to vote (in 1988, there were 140 campaign polls, according to one count).[24] These analyses surely contain some grains of truth, but how many? After all, people who are most likely to pay attention to the media, watch the ads, hear about the polls, and follow the campaigns are the most likely to vote, not the least. It is possible that the increasingly media-oriented campaigns have decreased overall turnout during the past generation (and we will have more to say about these campaigns later in the chapter). In fact, there is some evidence that turnout is inversely related to media spending; the more the candidates spend, the lower the turnout.[25] However, negative advertising and other media attention cannot explain the class bias in nonvoting.

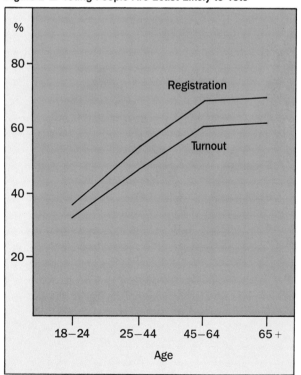

Figure 2 ■ **Young People Are Least Likely to Vote**

Source: Data for the 1988 election were reported by the Census Bureau and found in *Lincoln Journal*, March 8, 1989, p. 36.

Source: Reprinted by permission: Tribune Media Services.

In addition to the *quality* of the campaigns, some people think that turnout has declined because our elections are so frequent, campaigns last so long, and so many offices are contested that the public becomes bored, confused, or cynical.[26] At the presidential level, the sheer quantity of coverage, much of it focused repetitively on "who's winning," may simply bore people.

At the local level, voters elect so many officeholders, all the way down to weed and mosquito control commissioners, that many have no idea for whom or what they are voting. This proliferation of elective offices, thought by some to promote democracy and popular control, may promote only voter confusion and alienation. The problem is compounded because elections for different offices are held at different times. For example, most states have decided to hold elections for governor in nonpresidential election years. This decision probably reduces presidential election turnout by 7% and may reduce by one-third the number of those who vote for governor in those states.[27]

Primary elections are another problem. One estimate is that holding primary campaigns diminishes the general election turnout by 5%.[28]

By contrast, in Britain the time between calling an election (by the current government) and the actual election is only a month. In May 1987, Prime Minister Margaret Thatcher called the election; in June it was held. All campaigning is done during that time. There are no primaries. Moreover, as in most other parliamentary democracies, British citizens vote only for their representative in parliament and (at one other time) for the local representative. Voters are not faced with choices for a myriad of offices they barely recognize.

Barriers to Registration. The necessity to register is a major impediment to voting. About one-quarter of nonvoters surveyed in 1990 indicated they did not vote because it was too difficult. As one commentator put it, "The United States is the only major democracy where government assumes no responsibility for helping citizens cope with voter registration procedures."[29] In many other nations, voter registrars go door to door to register voters, or voters are registered automatically when they pay taxes or receive public services. Difficult registration procedures have a special impact on low-income Americans, who were 17% less likely to vote in states with difficult registration procedures than in other states.[30] Some states make it more convenient to register by having registration periods lasting up to election day (most states require registration at least 25 days before the election), registration in precincts or neighborhoods instead of one county office, registration by mail, registration offices open in the evenings and Saturday, and a policy of not purging voters who fail to vote from the registration lists. One estimate is that voting turnout would be 9% higher if all states' procedures were similar to those of states that try to facilitate voter registration.[31]

Regardless of whether the laws themselves encourage or discourage voting, voters are on their own in taking the initiative to register to vote, unless they are contacted through the sporadic efforts of private groups focusing on particular segments of the voting-age population. For example, the Jesse Jackson campaigns of 1984 and 1988 concentrated on registering blacks; the United States Student Association focused on college students; and the American Coalition for Traditional Values, a group formed by the Moral Majority and other Christian Right organizations, attempted to sign up hundreds of thousands of Christian fundamentalists.

Even in states with fairly open registration laws, efforts of these groups or of citizens acting alone can be frustrated. For example, allowing people to register by mail does little good if the necessary forms are only available at the registration office or if the location of the forms is a well-kept secret. In some jurisdictions, voter registrars try to hinder groups working to increase registration. They may refuse to allow volunteers to register voters outside the registration office or let only selected volunteers handle registration (for example, allowing members of the League of Women Voters or the Christian Right as volunteers but not the NAACP or organizations targeted toward registering lower-income groups).[32]

A number of proposals to make registration easier are now pending in Congress. One would allow citizens to register when they go to the polls to vote. A proposal more likely to be adopted, given the administrative problems of same-day registration, would allow people to register at public offices; this is called agency registration. One form of agency registration is the "motor voter" plan whereby citizens can register when they get their drivers' licenses.[33] This has increased registration in the few states that allow it, although motor voter plans are limited in that only half of the adults in the nation's poorest families have driv-

Registering Republicans

Old-time politicians knocked on doors to encourage voters to register. Now, computers and phone banks are standard tools of the voter registration trade. One of the most efficient users of these tools is the Republican party.

Many observers predicted that voting by "have-nots" would increase after 1980 in response to Reagan policies and the high unemployment of the early 1980s. Several groups worked to register low-income people in time for the 1984 presidential election. In response to predictions by Republican analysts that perhaps 10 million more voters might vote in 1984, most of them Democrats, the Republican party decided to mount a registration campaign itself.

The Republicans appeared to face an uphill battle in registering new voters because, as we have already seen, most nonvoters are Democrats or Independents. Thus registration drives without specific targets might register more Democrats than Republicans. But with millions of dollars to spend, Republicans could use sophisticated technology to pinpoint potential Republican voters. They purchased computer tapes from the Census Bureau, voter registration bureaus, and private firms such as mail-order houses, financial magazines, and motor vehicle registration agencies. Using these tapes, analysts were able to identify people living in affluent neighborhoods who themselves seemed affluent—they owned a new automobile or subscribed to magazines for people with money to spend and invest—and were unregistered.

These pinpointed households were called and residents were asked if they thought Reagan was doing a good job. If the response was positive, they were sent registration cards.

Republican leaders claimed to have made more than two million phone calls, mainly in the large states of Illinois, Texas, California, and Florida. Some estimated the cost of the drive at $5 per registered voter. Whatever the cost, however, this drive, along with efforts made by the Christian Right and other conservative groups, meant that the number of new voters registered by nonpartisan, liberal, and Democratic groups was matched or even exceeded by the number registered by Republican sympathizers.

Source: Frances Piven and Richard Cloward, *Why Americans Don't Vote* (New York: Pantheon, 1988), chapter 6.

er's licenses.[34] Thus such plans go only part way toward remedying the class bias in voting.

Most agency registration plans include other government agencies as registration sites, such as libraries, day-care centers, and welfare and employment offices. These plans, however, have met with strong resistance, especially from Republicans. In New York, after the governor announced that state agencies could assist voters in registering, Republicans persuaded the courts that state employees should neither ask citizens if they wanted to register to vote nor answer questions about registration forms. They could, however, leave the forms lying around on tables in waiting rooms.[35]

A related proposal suggests that change of address cards filed with the post office be accompanied by cards that go to the voting registration offices in the voter's former residence and new residence. Registration in the new residence would be automatic. One estimate is that the mobility of our society reduces voting by as much as 9%. The proposal also would reduce election fraud by removing names of residents who move from voting rosters.[36]

The U.S. House passed a bill in 1990 authorizing mail registration and agency registration. The bill failed in the Senate, however.

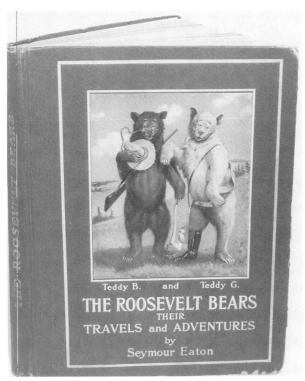

Voter turnout was higher in the days when campaigns were more fun and involved more people. Songs were often written about the candidates, and, here, a book about teddy bears reflects Theodore (Teddy) Roosevelt's popularity.

Failures of Parties to Mobilize Voters. The lack of interest by the political parties in mobilizing millions of nonvoters, most of them working class or poor, is another reason for low voter turnout. Because of their low income, most of these nonvoters are Democrats. If mobilized, they would probably vote for Democrats, although in some elections the preferences of nonvoters have simply reflected the preferences of voters.[37]

Republicans are most fearful of this potential electorate. One conservative analyst wrote that a national registration plan, by tapping the voting power of the poor, "has the potential for altering the American party system."[38]

Even some Democrats are wary. In the 1960s and 1970s, the party embraced social and economic reforms that attracted many middle-class and some business groups. The goals of these groups sometimes conflict with those of the poor, and the party's leaders do not want to threaten these constituencies. Moreover, in recent years, as the terms "liberal" and "big government" have become negative symbols, the party has muted its appeals to the working class. This further reduces the incentives of working-class people to vote.

And incumbents of both parties are reluctant to approve new registration plans that might change the nature of the electorate. As one observer commented, "Incumbents generally don't want change."[39]

Recently, however, support for federal legislation has increased among Democrats. The 1988 Democratic platform, for example, called for mail registration, election day registration, and agency registration.

Voting as a Rational Calculation of Costs and Benefits. Nonvoting also may be the result of a rational calculation of the costs and benefits of voting. Economist Anthony Downs argues that people vote when they believe the perceived benefits of voting are greater than the costs.[40] If a voter sees a difference between the parties or candidates, and favors one party's position over the other, that voter has a reason to vote and can expect some benefit from doing so. For that reason, people who are highly partisan vote more than those less attached to a party, and people with a strong sense of political efficacy, the belief they can influence government, vote more than others.

Voters who see no difference between the candidates or parties, however, may believe that voting is not worth the effort it takes and that it is more rational to abstain. And in fact, 40% of nonvoters in 1990 gave only the excuse that they were "too busy," suggesting a large degree of apathy.[41] Nevertheless, some people will vote even if they think there is no difference between the candidates because they have a sense of civic duty, a belief that their responsibilities as citizens include voting.

Downs assumes that the costs of voting are minimal, but, in reality, for many people the time, expense, and possible embarrassment of trying to register are greater than the perceived benefits of voting. This is especially true for lower-income people who perceive that neither party is attentive to their interests. Moreover, it is possible that the frequency, length, and media orientation of campaigns lower the perceived benefits of voting for people of all incomes by trivializing the election and emphasizing the negative.

litical participation aside from voting, whereas those with college education participated in 3 to 4. Those with some college education actually had increased their participation over the past 20 years, whereas those with less than a high school education had decreased theirs. Thus the class bias in participation, as in voting alone, has increased over time.[43]

Gender, race, age, and regional differences in participation also appear. Even taking education into account, men usually participate slightly more than women, whites somewhat more than blacks, older people more than younger people, and southerners more than northerners. But these differences change over time. Young people participated more than their elders, and blacks more than whites, during the late 1960s and early 1970s.[44] These were times of heightened interest in politics generally, and the anti–Vietnam War and civil rights movements drew many young and black people into political activity.

Other Campaign Participation

We have seen that only about half of all Americans vote in presidential elections, and even fewer vote in off-year congressional races. Still fewer participate actively in political campaigns. For example, in a recent year, about one-quarter of the population said that they worked for a party or candidate. About an equal proportion claimed that they contributed money to a party or candidate. Smaller proportions attended political meetings or actually belonged to a political club.

Unlike voting, rates of participation in campaigns have not declined over the past 20 years. This suggests that people are not less political than they used to be, but that something about elections themselves has decreased voter turnout. Indeed, more people give money to candidates and parties than they used to, probably because, unlike 20 years ago, candidates and parties now use mass mailing techniques to solicit funds from supporters.[42] Hundreds of thousands of potential donors can be reached in a very short time.

Just as there is a strong class basis to voting, there is also a strong class basis to participation in campaign activities. Those with more education and income are more likely to participate. A recent study found that those with only eight grades of education or less participated, on average, in only one of 12 types of po-

Presidential Nominating Campaigns

Many Americans believe in the Horatio Alger myth, that with hard work anyone can achieve great success. This myth has its parallel in politics, where it is sometimes said that any child can grow up to be president. In fact, only a few run for that office and even fewer are elected.

Who Runs for President and Why?

In deciding whether to run for president, individuals consider such things as the costs and risks of running and the probabilities of winning.[45] Most people have little chance of being president: they are unknown to the public, they do not have the financial resources or contacts to raise the money needed for a national campaign, they have jobs they could not leave to run a serious campaign, and their friends would probably ridicule them for even thinking of such a thing.

But a few people are in a different position. Take, for instance, a hypothetical U.S. senator from Texas or a governor of California. By their vote-gathering ability in a large state, they have demonstrated some possibility that they could win. Their decision to run might hinge on such considerations as whether they think they could raise the money necessary to run a

COMPARATIVE PERSPECTIVE

Could Proportional Representation Make a Difference?

Electoral systems comprise the rules for conducting elections, including procedures for deciding who is eligible to vote, for choosing candidates, and for translating votes into legislative seats. Despite their procedural nature, many of these rules have excited considerable controversy over the past decades; examples include who should vote and how difficult it should be, how we should nominate presidential candidates, and whether we should have a direct election of the president. However, one major element of our electoral system, the **single-member district**, has received very little national debate.

We have not always used the single-member district, which is a procedure where voters in each electoral unit, such as a congressional district, elect only one representative. In the nineteenth century, many members of Congress were elected from districts with more than one representative, and this is true today for about one-third of our state legislators and over half our local council members. Yet, in our national legislative elections and in most of our state elections, we take the single-member district for granted. We go to the polls and choose between candidates, usually one Democrat and one Republican. Then we hear that one received more votes than the other and was elected.

This system, sometimes called first-past-the-post, is a relatively unusual way of electing members of national legislatures. The single-member district system is used mostly in Britain and its former colonies, such as Canada, India, and New Zealand. But almost all other industrial democracies, such as Denmark, Sweden, Germany, Italy, and Japan, use **proportional representation** (PR) to elect their legislators.

Proportional representation, as its name suggests, allocates seats in the legislature in proportion to the vote received by each party. PR systems have multi-member districts (since there is no way to divide one representative). For example, representatives from a major metro area might be chosen from a five-member district. If the Democrats got 60% of the votes and the Republicans

40%, the Democrats would get three of the seats and the Republicans two. In general, the larger the number of representatives, the more proportional the vote division could be.

Many analysts think that PR is a fairer system than single-member districts. One reason is that single-member districts tend to overrepresent the majority party. In the U.S. Congress, for example, the Democrats hold a greater proportion of the seats than their percentage vote. With proportional representation, the overall composition of a legislative body is much closer to the votes received by the parties. Moreover, PR systems may allow more proportional representation of underrepresented groups such as women and racial and religious minorities. Thus, women are much better represented in the national legislatures of countries with PR systems than those with single-member district systems. And countries with severe religious divisions, like Northern Ireland, have found PR useful in representing the minority religious group.

The major criticism leveled against PR is that it tends to encourage more political parties. There is a strong relationship between having a PR system and having a multi-party rather than a two-party system, although analysts do not always agree that the PR system *causes* the growth of new parties. And some observers believe that the growth of new parties is a healthy development, not a negative one, because it can promote voter interest and participation.

It is unlikely that the United States will adopt the PR system for congressional elections in the near future, or maybe ever. A number of cities have adopted it for elections to their city councils, though most dropped it, some precisely because it did allow for representation of small, non-mainstream parties. However, in this era of concern over falling voter turnouts and representation of diverse groups in our population, interest in PR is increasing.

Sources: Martin Harrop and William L. Miller, *Elections and Voters* (London: Macmillan Education Ltd., 1987); Enid Lakeman, *How Democracies Vote* (London: Faber, 1990).

campaign, whether they are willing to sacrifice a good part of their private life and their privacy for a few years, and whether they would lose the office they currently hold if they run and lose.

These calculations are real. Most candidates for president are, in fact, senators or governors.[46] Vice

presidents also frequently run, but until George Bush's victory, they had not been successful in this century.

Why do candidates run? An obvious reason is to gain the power and prestige of the presidency. But they may have other goals as well, such as to gain

AMERICAN DIVERSITY

Can a Black Person Be Elected President?

The Jesse Jackson campaigns of 1984 and 1988 again raised the question of whether a black person can be elected president. Or, more generally, will the American presidency continue to be held only by white, non-Jewish males?

These questions sound familiar. In 1960, some doubted that a Catholic could ever be elected president. At that time, only 71% of all voters said they would vote for a Catholic for president.[1] The only previous major-party Catholic candidate, Alfred Smith, had been soundly defeated by Herbert Hoover in 1928. But then John F. Kennedy was elected. Since then, two Catholics, Geraldine Ferraro and Sargent Shriver, have run as vice presidential nominees without much attention paid to their religion.

But race has been a more pronounced cleavage in American society than religion. Racism persists, and race influences all kinds of political debates, from welfare reform to the all-volunteer military. The minor party realignment that has occurred in the South is shaped by racial as well as class issues.[2] A majority of white southerners, resentful of the Democratic party's support of the civil rights struggle, has turned to the Republican party.

Race was important in the 1988 campaign. It surfaced when the Republicans succeeded in tying Willie Horton to Dukakis. It also came up when Jesse Jackson's prominence in the Democratic party was highlighted and made to seem somehow illegitimate and frightening. One Republican governor called the alliance among Dukakis, Lloyd Bentsen, the Democratic vice presidential nominee, and Jackson a "three-headed monster."[3] A campaign letter from the California Republican party asked, "Why is it so urgent you decide now? . . . Here are two [reasons]." Below were two photos, one of Bush and Reagan, the other of Jackson and Dukakis. "If [Dukakis] is elected to the White House," it continued, "Jesse Jackson is sure to be swept into power on his coattails."[4]

This is not to say that all of those who voted against Jackson in the primaries or against the Democrats in the general election are racists. Many argue that it might very well be possible for a black to be elected president, but not Jesse Jackson. In foreign as well as domestic policy, Jackson has been identified with the most liberal wing of the Democratic party. He is undoubtedly more liberal than George McGovern, the defeated Democratic presidential candidate of 1972, from whom many Democrats are eager to distance themselves. And his public career has largely been in the civil rights movement rather than in government. All of these things would work against any candidate.

Shirley Chisholm was the first African-American to campaign for a major party presidential nomination. She is shown with George McGovern at the 1972 Democratic National Convention, where her name was placed in nomination. Jesse Jackson and his family appeared at the 1988 Democratic National Convention.

Declining Numbers Oppose Blacks, Women, and Jews for President

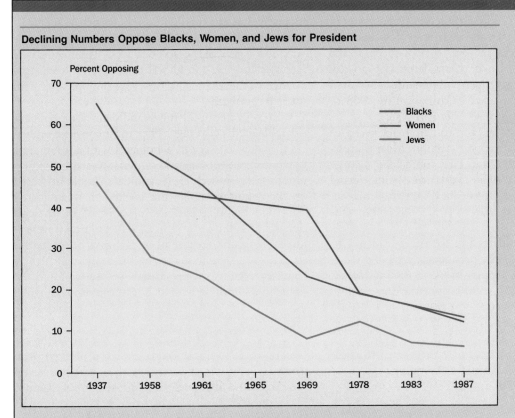

Source: Gallup Polls. The question asked was, "If your party nominated a generally well-qualified man for president and he happened to be a black [Jew], would you vote for him?" or, "If your party nominated a woman for president, would you vote for her if she were qualified for the job?" No questions were asked about blacks until 1958. The 1961 data for blacks are from 1963.

For many, perhaps most, blacks, however, Jackson has become a symbol of their hopes that a black might one day be president. In a 1988 poll, almost two-thirds of all blacks said that Jackson should run again in 1992. Some blacks interpret any anti-Jackson sentiment as a sign of racism, but others believe that blacks should not place all of their electoral aspirations in Jackson.[5] Although no other blacks have the national visibility of Jackson, a number of popular black local and state officials have demonstrated that they can win white as well as black votes. One, Douglas Wilder, governor of Virginia, has been on journalistic lists of "potential" Democratic contenders for 1992.

The differing views of the black and white communities are a microcosm of the racial gulf that divides us. Undoubtedly there will come a time when a black man or woman will be president, just as will white women, Jews, and others who are not white, Christian males. And the forecast is not all bleak. As the figure shows, 12% to 13% of the public say they would not vote for a black or a woman who was their party's nominee, and a slightly lower proportion say they would not vote for a Jew. Although 12% to 13% is a sizable bloc of voters, more people today say they would vote for a black, Jew, or woman than said they would vote for a Catholic in 1960. John Kennedy's victory suggests that 12% to 13% is not an insurmountable barrier.

1. Barry Sussman, "A Black or Woman Does Better Today Than a Catholic in '60," *Washington Post National Weekly Edition*, November 21, 1983, p. 42.
2. Earl Black and Merle Black, *Politics and Society in the South* (Cambridge, Mass.: Harvard University Press, 1973).
3. Thomas Edsall, "Race Continues to Be a Wild Card in American Politics," *Washington Post National Weekly Edition*, August 8–14, 1988, p. 12.
4. Through This Be Meanness, Yet There is a Method in It," *Washington Post National Weekly Edition*, October 10–16, 1988, p. 26.
5. Juan Williams, "How Reagan and Jackson Managed to Isolate Blacks," *Washington Post National Weekly Edition*, November 28-December 4, 1988, p. 33.

support for a particular policy or set of ideas. Ronald Reagan, for example, clearly wanted to be president in part to spread his conservative ideology. Jesse Jackson wants to be president in part to help those at the bottom of the social ladder. Candidates with no real hope of winning a major party nomination also often have policy goals. Eugene McCarthy ran in 1968 to challenge Lyndon Johnson's Vietnam policy.

Sometimes candidates run to gain name recognition and publicity for the next election. Most successful candidates in recent years have run before. George Bush lost the nomination in 1980 before being elected in 1988; Ronald Reagan lost in 1976 before his victory in 1980; Richard Nixon lost in 1960 before winning in 1968.

Sometimes candidates run for the presidency to be considered for the vice presidency, probably viewing it as an eventual stepping-stone to the presidency. But only occasionally, such as when Reagan chose Bush in 1980 or Kennedy chose Johnson in 1960, do presidential candidates choose one of their defeated opponents to run as a vice presidential candidate. In 1988, both nominees passed over their defeated rivals in choosing a vice presidential running mate.

How a Candidate Wins the Nomination

Presidential candidates try to win a majority of delegates at their party's national nominating convention in the summer preceding the November election. Delegates to those conventions are elected in state caucuses, conventions, and primaries. Candidates must campaign to win the support of those who attend caucuses and conventions and of primary voters.

Normally, candidates formally announce their candidacies in the year preceding the presidential election year. Then their aim is to persist and survive the long primary and caucus season that begins in February of election year and continues until only one candidate is left. Candidates use a number of methods to try to maximize their chances of survival. They carefully choose the primaries they will enter and to which they will devote their resources. Candidates must enter enough primaries so they are seen as national, not regional, candidates, but they cannot possibly devote time and resources to every primary or caucus. Especially important are the early events—the Iowa caucus and the New Hampshire primary—and the larger state events in the middle of the season.

Candidates also try to survive by establishing themselves as *the* candidate for a particular policy or other constituency. In 1988, Pat Robertson hoped to win the loyalties of the new Christian Right within the Republican party, but he was unsuccessful in enlisting enough of these voters to offset his unpopularity with other Republicans.

To compete successfully, candidates also need considerable media coverage. They must convince reporters that they are serious candidates with a real chance of winning. Journalists and candidates establish expectations for how well each candidate should do based on the results of polls, the quality of a candidate's campaign organization, the amount of money and time spent in the campaign, and the political complexion of the state. If a candidate performs below expectations, even though garnering the most votes, it may be interpreted by the press as a weakness and hurt the campaign. On the other hand, a strong showing when expectations are low can mean a boost to a candidate's campaign.

Consequently, candidates try to lower media expectations. It is not enough to win a primary; you have to win by at least as much as the media claims you should, or you will be seen as a loser. In the Republican race in 1988, Pat Robertson's organizers tried to counter media predictions for the Iowa caucuses by urging supporters to tell pollsters that they were not going to attend the caucuses. Because pollsters do not count people who do not plan to vote, this tactic could result in an artificially low prediction—and then a surprisingly high vote.[47]

Sometimes even losers are portrayed as winners if they do better than expected. For example, in 1968 in the New Hampshire primary, antiwar candidate Senator Eugene McCarthy won 40% of the vote against President Johnson, who had become increasingly unpopular because of the Vietnam War. Although McCarthy did not win, he did much better than expected, and the press interpreted the vote as a repudiation of Johnson's leadership.

In sum, then, the primary season is a game among the media, the candidates, and the voters, with the candidates trying to raise voter enthusiasm and lower media expectations simultaneously.

But even though the media are influential participants in the process, especially at the beginning and in multi-candidate races, they do not determine the winner. In 1988, for example, the most favorable media coverage was given to Jesse Jackson and Bruce

The Election of 1988

In an election with the lowest presidential voting turnout since 1924, George Bush won 40 states and 426 Electoral College votes, and Dukakis won 10 states and 112 Electoral College votes. The popular vote margin was a fairly substantial 54% to 46%. Although Dukakis captured more Electoral College votes than any Democratic candidate since 1964, with the exception of Jimmy Carter, Bush swept the South and most of the West. Dukakis captured only 2 industrial states that any Democratic candidate must have to win (Massachusetts and New York). Dukakis also picked up 3 western states (Hawaii, Oregon, and Washington), 3 states of the upper Midwest (Wisconsin, Iowa, and Minnesota), along with West Virginia, Rhode Island, and the District of Columbia.

Voting patterns were much the same as in the past several elections. There was a sizable gender gap: women split their votes evenly between the two candidates, but men gave Bush a healthy majority. Almost 60% of non-Hispanic whites voted for Bush, but only 11% of blacks and 38% of Hispanics did so. Votes of the unmarried went to Dukakis, the married to Bush.

In 1984, Republicans had been encouraged because they believed that they were winning the allegiance of young and other first-time voters. In 1988, however, new voters cast only 43% of their votes for Bush, and voters under 30 were only about as likely to vote for Bush as their older cohorts.

Social and economic class played an important role in the voting. Families making less than $25,000 favored Dukakis: those making more favored Bush. Dukakis was able to win a healthy majority of voters in households with a union member, reversing the pattern of the Reagan years.

Dukakis entered the campaign thinking he could appeal to many Democrats who had voted for Reagan. These individuals were working-class or poorly paid white-collar workers who identified with Reagan's pride in America but were falling behind economically. He hoped that his proposals for helping lower-middle-class people send their children to college and making health care and housing more accessible would appeal to them. But he was never able to turn the campaign discussion to these issues. Thus, although Bush did do considerably worse among those with less-than-average incomes than Reagan did in 1984, the majority of families making $25,000 to $35,000, the lower middle class, voted for Bush, as did people of higher incomes in even greater proportions.

Issue Reasons for the 1988 Voting Choice

Issue	% Saying Most Important	% Voting for	
		Dukakis	Bush
National defense	23	15	84
Taxes	15	29	70
Crime	18	31	67
Abortion	20	36	63
Foreign trade	5	42	57
Drugs	14	58	41
Budget deficit	25	60	39
Unemployment	10	64	35
Ethics in government	17	67	31
Environment	11	70	28

Sources: Cable News Network-Los Angeles Times exit polls, reported in *National Journal,* November 12, 1988, p. 2854; CBS-*New York Times* exit polls, *New York Times,* November 10, 1988. See also Michael Nelson, ed., *The Elections of 1988* (Washington, D.C.: CQ Press, 1989), especially chapters 3 and 5.

(continued on next page)

Michael Dukakis campaigning in Cerritos, California.

Party loyalties and ideology played a big part in the voting decision. Ninety-one percent of those who consider themselves Republican voted for Bush, and 82% of those who call themselves Democrats favored Dukakis. Independents gave 55% of their votes to Bush. Conservatives voted overwhelmingly for Bush, liberals for Dukakis.

Bush captured the voters' preferences on some specific issues, but Dukakis appealed to them on about an equal number. Voters concerned about drugs, ethics in government, the environment, unemployment, and the budget deficit voted strongly for Dukakis. Voters concerned about taxes, national defense, crime, abortion, and foreign trade voted for Bush. Perceptions of the candidates' competence gave neither candidate an edge. Given these trends, why did Bush win? The most in-depth analyses of voter surveys suggests it was because of overall satisfaction with the Reagan administration and the condition of the country.[1]

Though Bush himself was reelected by a substantial margin, his **coattails** (that is, his ability to help other Republicans win election) appeared nonexistent. Indeed, Republicans actually lost seats in both the House and the Senate. The last newly elected president whose party lost seats in both the Senate and the House was John Kennedy in 1960, and before that Grover Cleveland in 1892. Thus, though Bush continued the 20-year string of Republican presidential victories (broken only by the victory of Carter in 1976), the long-heralded major realignment of the national political party system was no closer than since 1964. However, the election, like those of 1980 and 1984, gave further evidence that the realignment in the South is for real. Bush won every southern and border state except West Virginia.

1. J. Merrill Shanks and Warren E. Miller, "Partisanship" Policy and Performance: The Reagan Legacy in the 1988 Election," *British Journal of Political Science* 21 (April, 1991); pp. 129–197.

finance health care, and send their children to college were lost in the din.

Issue appeals are usually general, and often candidates do not offer a clear-cut choice even on the most important controversies of the time. For example, the 1968 presidential election offered voters little choice on Vietnam policy, because the positions of candidates Nixon and Humphrey appeared very similar.[57] Voters who wanted to end the war by withdrawing and others who wanted to escalate the war had no real choice of candidates.

Ideally, the major campaign themes and strategies have been put into place by the end of the summer, but these themes and strategies are revised and updated on a daily, sometimes hourly, basis as the campaign progresses. Decisions are made not just by the candidate and the campaign manager but by a staff of key advisers who include media experts and pollsters. Sophisticated polling techniques are used to produce almost daily reports on shifts in public opinion across the nation and in particular regions. Thus, media ads can be added and deleted as polls reflect their impact. Campaign trips are modified or scratched as the candidate's organization sees new opportunities. And media events can be planned to complement the paid advertising the candidate runs.

The Electoral College

All planning for the campaign has to take into account the peculiar American institution of the **Electoral College.** In the United States we do not have a direct election of the president, although this may surprise those who thought they voted for Bush or Dukakis. In

Figure 5 ■ Electoral Votes per State, 1988

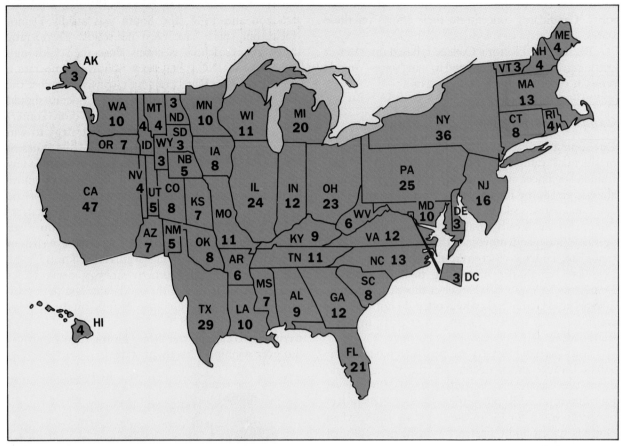

States are drawn in proportion to their number of electoral votes, of a total of 538 electoral votes. The state totals will change following a reapportionment in 1991 (explained in chapter 10).

fact they voted for Bush's or Dukakis's electors who formed part of the Electoral College.

Electors are party notables who gather in each state capitol in December after the presidential election to cast their votes for president and vice president. Each state has as many electors as its total representation in Congress (House plus Senate). The smallest states (and the District of Columbia) have 3, whereas the largest state—California—had 47 in the 1980s and will have more in the 1990s after reapportionment (figure 5).

With the exception of Maine, which divides its Electoral College votes according to who wins in each congressional district, all of each state's electoral votes go to the candidate winning the most votes in that state. If one candidate wins a majority of the electors voting across the United States, that candidate wins. If no candidate wins a majority, the election is

decided in the House of Representatives, where each state has one vote and a majority is necessary to win. This has not happened since 1824, when John Quincy Adams was chosen. If voting in the Electoral College for the vice president does not yield a majority, the Senate chooses the vice president; again each state has one vote.

The Founders assumed that the Electoral College would have considerable power, with each elector exercising independent judgment and choosing from among a large number of candidates. They did not foresee the development of political parties. As state parties developed, the electors became part of the party process, pledged to party candidates. Thus, electors usually rubber stamp the choice of voters in each state rather than exercise their own judgment.

Because of the winner-take-all feature of the Electoral College, the system gives an advantage to large states and their urban populations. The 11 largest states have 267 of the 538 votes, just short of a majority. Candidates concentrate their efforts on these states.

Because the Electoral College is based on states, it encourages campaigns designed to win "states." In this sense, it reinforces the federal system.

Campaign Strategies

Developing a strategy is an important element of a presidential campaign. But every strategy is surrounded by uncertainty, and even political pros cannot always predict the impact of a particular strategy.

Candidates seek to do three things: mobilize those who are already loyal to them and their party; persuade independent voters that they are the best candidate; and try to convert the opposition. Most candidates emphasize mobilizing their own voters. Democrats have to work harder at this than Republicans because Democratic voters often do not vote and are more likely to vote for the other party than are Republicans.

Both parties must try to persuade independent voters because independents are the swing voters; their votes determine the outcome. In 1964, when Johnson trounced Republican Goldwater, 80% of Republicans voted for Goldwater. And in 1988, when Dukakis was soundly beaten by Bush, over 80% of Democrats voted for Dukakis. It was the independent voters who determined the outcomes.

The crucial strategic question is where to allocate resources of time and money: where to campaign, where to buy media time and how much to buy, and where to spend money helping local organizations. Candidates must always remember that they have to win a majority of the Electoral College vote. The most populous states, with the largest number of electoral votes, are vital. Prime targets are those large states that could go to either party, such as Illinois, Texas, California, and New York.

Candidates also have to expand their existing bases of support. Most of the western states are solidly Republican in their presidential loyalties (see figure 6). It is nearly impossible for a Democratic presidential candidate to carry them. Republicans can build on their solid western base and their strength in the South. They only have to carry a few of the large industrial states to win.

Democrats have a strategic problem given the western Republican bloc. Between the end of Reconstruction and 1948, the South was solidly Democratic, but there have been no solidly Democratic states in presidential elections since then (although Washington, D.C., has been solidly Democratic). Since 1976, the Democrats have consistently lost the South. Some strategists believe the Democrats should try to win back the South by choosing more conservative candidates. Others argue for a strategy to win without the South, aiming for the industrial states of the East and Midwest along with California and a few other states of the West. This approach seems more likely to succeed without alienating the base of the Democrats' supporters. Indeed, carrying out this strategy did seem within Dukakis's reach; he won three western states and came close in California as well as in the industrial states of Pennsylvania and Illinois.[58] The success of this non-southern strategy depends, of course, on the nature of the candidates and the times, but it was a strategy used successfully by the Republicans between the 1870s and the 1920s, when they were able to capture the White House regularly without ever winning a southern state.

Soliciting votes by giving speeches and making appearances was once considered beneath the dignity of the presidential office. William Jennings Bryan was the first presidential candidate to break this tradition. In 1896 he traveled more than 18,000 miles and made more than 600 speeches in an effort to win voters. Although Bryan lost the election to William McKinley, his approach to campaigning became the standard.

Figure 6 ■ The Democrats Have Done Poorly in the West and South in the Past Twenty Years

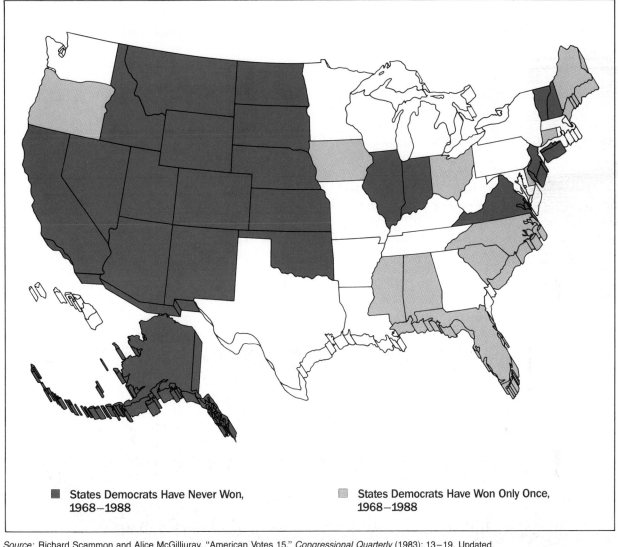

■ States Democrats Have Never Won,
1968–1988

░ States Democrats Have Won Only Once,
1968–1988

Source: Richard Scammon and Alice McGilliuray, "American Votes 15," *Congressional Quarterly* (1983): 13–19. Updated.

The Media Campaign

Campaigns are expensive because they rely so heavily on the media to get the candidate's message to the voters. As one observer argued, "Today's presidential campaign is essentially a mass media campaign. It is not that the mass media entirely determine what happens. . . . But it is no exaggeration to say that, for the large majority of voters, the campaign has little reality apart from the media version."[59]

Impact of the Media. The media, both through news coverage and paid advertisements, help shape voters' opinions and choices in three ways. They inform, they help set the campaign agenda, and they help persuade voters.

Media provide information about the candidates and issues.[60] Much information is simply about the candidates and whether they can win. For example, after the New Hampshire primary in 1984, all Democratic voters interviewed could offer opinions about

Gary Hart's prospects for winning the nomination. Only three-fourths could offer opinions about his policy positions.[61] But voters learn about issues too. For example, during the 1988 campaign, voters' awareness of Bush's and Dukakis's issue positions increased during the campaign. Those who read newspapers increased their awareness more than those who watched television, but even television viewers gained information.[62] Even paid ads increase voter awareness about candidates and issues. For the uninformed, particularly, ads provide more information about candidates and issues than does much news coverage.

A second way the media help shape voter preferences is through setting the agenda. By focusing attention on certain topics, the media influence the topics that voters believe are important.[63] Experimental studies, as well as survey research, have shown that when the media focus on an issue such as crime, for example, more of the public believe that crime is an important problem. Moreover, the media influence the weight voters give these topics when they vote. For example, not surprisingly voters vote for candidates whom they evaluate positively; when they receive media information about the candidates, the impor-

tance of these personal evaluations on vote choice increases substantially.[64] In primary elections, voters' perceptions of a candidate's chances to win are strongly affected by media coverage. These perceptions, in turn, affect the vote.[65]

Finally, the media can persuade voters directly. Early researchers on the effects of media on vote choice found few direct effects; they argued that the media mostly reinforce preexisting attitudes. For example, most voters who watch presidential debates believe that the candidate they favored initially won the debate. However, more recent studies have found that some voters are persuaded by the media; these voters tend to be those with moderate, but not low, educational levels and incomes and those with some interest in politics but without strong partisan ties.[66]

Most people get their campaign information from television rather than from newspapers and magazines. And often we hear that television has been responsible for deteriorating quality of political campaigns. However, two common perceptions about the negative impact of television are untrue. Common wisdom suggests that television more than other media emphasizes the "horse race" aspect of political campaigns. This is not so, however. The emphasis on who is winning and losing relative to issues is about the same in newspapers and magazines as on television.[67]

Other common wisdom suggests that this focus on the "horse race" in all media has come about because of the modern television age. However, a careful analysis of newspaper coverage of presidential election campaigns since 1888 indicates that coverage has changed very little over the course of the century.[68] The major media focus in 1888 as in 1988 and every year between was on campaign activity: where the candidates are and what they are spending, doing, and saying (figure 7). This emphasis encourages candidates to provide more colorful media events and fewer serious issue discussions, but this has been true for decades. Surprisingly, issues get the second largest amount of coverage; moreover, there is relatively more coverage of issues today than in the "good old days" 100 years ago. The candidates' traits and other characteristics receive no more coverage today than in the past. Thus, the television age has not brought a new emphasis on personality, contrary to popular wisdom.

Analysis of the "horse race" aspect of the campaign, who is ahead and behind, did increase in 1988 compared to previous campaigns. The authors of this study argue that much of that increase stems not from

Bush's emphasis on the symbols of patriotism—flags and pledging allegiance to the flag at openings of meetings and rallies—boosted his public image throughout the summer of the 1988 campaign. He downplayed this emphasis after his visit to a flag factory generated criticism that his campaign lacked substance and focused only on symbols.

**Figure 7 ■ Coverage of Campaign Activities Has Always Comprised the Biggest Share
of Media Coverage in Presidential Elections**

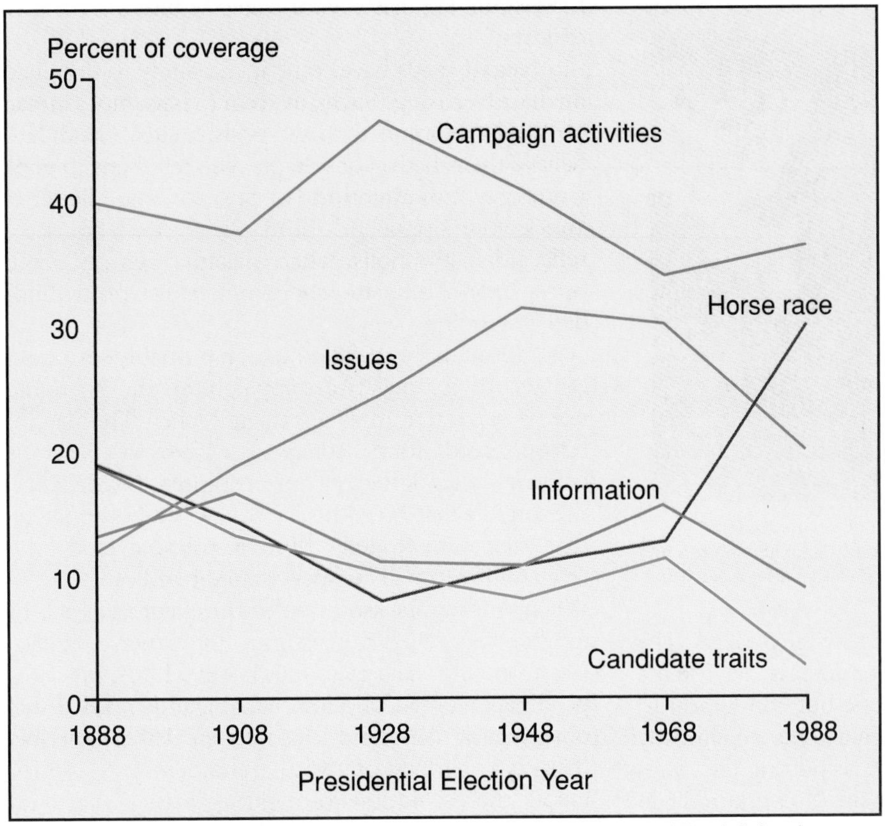

Source: Lee Sigelman and David Bullock, "Candidates, Issues, Horse Races, and Hoopla," *American
Politics Quarterly* 19 (January 1991): 5–32.

television but from the development of national polls, which provide dozens of poll results during the course of the campaign. The poll results become news, which are then covered by the press.

Use of the Media.   Candidates try to use the media to their advantage by staging media events that allow them to be photographed doing and saying noncontroversial things in front of enthusiastic crowds and patriotic symbols. As Bush campaign strategist Roger Ailes proclaimed 20 years ago, "This is the beginning of a whole new concept. This is the way they'll be elected forevermore. The next guys will have to be performers."[69]

Candidates and their advisers try to design settings that will encourage television reporters to focus their stories on the candidate and put his or her policies in the best light.[70] George Bush almost literally wrapped himself in the flag, frequently "pledging allegiance," until negative media reaction led his advisers to decide that they were overdoing it.

Candidates spend most of their time going from media market to media market, hoping to get both national and local coverage.[71] Some candidates are much better than others at using the media. Gerald Ford was plagued by media coverage that seemed to emphasize his bumbling.

Paid advertisements allow candidates to focus on points most favorable to their case or to portray their opponents in the most negative light. Most political ads are quite short, 30 or 60 seconds in length. Television ads were first used in the 1952 campaign. One, linking the Democratic Truman administration to the unpopular Korean War, showed two soldiers in combat talking about the futility of war. Then one of the soldiers is hit and dies. The other one deliberately

Few Americans see candidates in person anymore. Most people see the candidates, such as Bruce Babbitt, who ran in 1988, only on television.

Some ads are issue oriented. In 1988, for example, one Dukakis ad focused on the Democrat's plans for helping families pay for college education for their children.

Negative ads have come increasingly to dominate media advertising. Such ads seem to have more impact on public opinion than do positive ads. Candidates believe their media consultants who tell them, "People won't pay any attention [to positive ads]. Better to knock your opponent's head off."[74] And they see it reflected in the polls, where negative ads can sometimes have a dramatic short-term effect on a candidate's standing.

Although the 1988 campaign probably set a modern record for negative campaigning, the phenomenon is as American as apple pie. When Thomas Jefferson faced John Adams in 1796, a Federalist editorial called Jefferson "mean spirited, low-lived . . . the son of a half-breed Indian squaw" and prophesized that if he were elected, "Murder, robbery, rape, adultery and incest will be openly taught and practiced."[75] When Andrew Jackson ran for president in 1832, his mother was called a prostitute, his father a mulatto (someone of mixed races, black and white), his wife a profligate woman, and himself a bigamist.[76] A British observer of American elections in 1888 described them as a "tempest of invective and calumny . . . imagine all the accusations brought against all the candidates for the 670 seats in the English Parliament con-

exposes himself to the enemy and is also killed. The announcer's voice says, "Vote Republican."[72] Today's ads are perhaps less melodramatic but still appeal to viewers' emotions. In 1984, Reagan's ads were mostly a "soft sell," depicting his policies as putting the country on the road to greatness again ("It's morning in America").[73]

Source: Bob Gorrell, The Richmond News Leader. Used with permission.

FOCUS ON AN ISSUE

Should the Electoral College Be Abolished?

Critics frequently suggest that the Electoral College, a complex and sometimes puzzling institution, should be reformed or abolished. One reform would keep the overall system but eliminate electors as individuals; electoral votes would automatically be cast according to a state's popular vote.

A second reform, changing the way Electoral College votes are allotted, is unlikely. It would divide the Electoral College vote in each state in proportion to the popular vote or according to the number of congressional districts won by each candidate. This would undermine the advantages of the largest states.

Abolishing the Electoral College in favor of a direct popular election is a third reform idea that has some support. Votes would be counted nationwide; state totals would not matter. This proposal has been offered as a constitutional amendment in Congress several times but has never won approval. Even if passed in Congress, it probably would fail to obtain ratification by the necessary three-fourths of the state legislatures because large states would oppose it.

To decide whether you favor this reform or not, consider the following questions.

Is the Electoral College Democratic?

If democratic is defined as popular sovereignty and majority rule, there are some undemocratic aspects to the Electoral College—just as the Founders intended. The Electoral College makes it possible for the candidate with the most popular votes to lose the election. This has occurred three times: John Quincy Adams (1824), Rutherford B. Hayes (1876), and Benjamin Harrison (1888).

Critics of the Electoral College argue that these anomalies should not happen; in a democratic system, the person with the most votes should win.

Supporters usually do not defend the minority winner situation, but they point out that it has not happened for 100 years. Further, the Electoral College often converts candidates with a plurality but not a majority of the popular vote into majority winners in the Electoral College. This may give a greater legitimacy to the winners. In 1960 John F. Kennedy won only 49.7% of the popular vote but a substantial 56% of the Electoral College vote. Substantial margins of popular votes can be turned into the appearance of consensus too. For example, in 1984 President Reagan won 59% of the popular vote, but because he won in 49 states, he won 97% of the Electoral College vote.

Another undemocratic feature of the current system is the **faithless elector,** an elector who decides to cast a vote for a personal choice, not for that of his or her state's voters. Occasionally electors do stray from their pledge—in 1988 a West Virginia elector voted for Lloyd Bentsen for president and later said she wished she had voted for Kitty Dukakis. Even though the intent of the Founders was to allow electors to cast their votes any way they desired, many people believe that in our more democratic era electors should be bound by the wishes of the voters. However, no faithless elector has ever made a difference in the outcome of an election.

(continued on next page)

centrated on one man, and read . . . daily for three months."[77]

In the old days, newspapers were the main medium of negative campaigning, but now television is.

People's tolerance for negative advertising is quite high. Few people complain even when the ads are downright false. One Republican consultant noted, "It used to be that one error will sink you; now, one provable fact will get you by the critics."[78] One Bush ad, attacking Dukakis for Boston's dirty harbor, showed sludge and polluted material near a sign reading "Danger/Radiation Hazard/No Swimming." The sign had nothing to do with Dukakis or Boston harbor; it warned people not to swim near an area where nuclear submarines had undergone repair.[79]

Some people blame the media, the campaign advisers and consultants, and the candidates themselves for negative advertising. But really the finger should be pointed at the public itself. If issues, rather than negative advertising, boosted candidates in the polls,

Is a Direct Election Simpler?

Supporters argue that direct election of the president is simpler because it eliminates the faithless elector and the problem of winner-take-all in the states and it is more consistent with majority rule. In other words, it is a more understandable system.

Supporters of the Electoral College argue that direct popular election is not as simple as it sounds. When no candidate receives a majority of the popular vote, how will the system choose a winner? There are, of course, many rules that could be adopted to take care of this, including a run-off between the top two candidates if neither has a majority. Formulating rules to deal with nonmajority situations makes the popular vote alternative seem more complicated than at first glance.

Should Urban Interests Receive an Advantage in the Presidential Election Process?

This question gets to the heart of support for and opposition to Electoral College reform. In the current system, voters in large states receive more attention from candidates. A 1-vote margin in Pennsylvania yields the candidate 29 votes, a 1-vote margin in North Dakota only 3. So it is more important to get that extra vote in Pennsylvania than in North Dakota. Rational candidates and parties will direct their resources and perhaps tailor their policy views accordingly.

Although political scientists have debated the actual extent of the large state bias in the current system, most believe it does exist and is significant.[1] Urbanites, especially central city residents, have more clout in the Electoral College system than they would have under a direct election system. Minority groups benefit, too, because they are disproportionately located in urban areas. However, one should not overstate this clout. After all, more liberal candidates, presumably those favored by the more urban interests, have lost most presidential elections since 1968.

Is the urban advantage fair? Opponents of the system argue that it is not; each person's vote should count as much as any other person's.

Supporters of the system argue that this bias is fair when viewed in the context of our other political institutions. The Senate, for example, overrepresents the interests of smaller, rural states because each state, regardless of population, has two votes. Many of the institutions of Congress, too, work in a way that gives an advantage to more conservative interests, often identified with rural America. The complex committee system and diffused power structure make dramatic changes in the status quo difficult.

Defenders of the Electoral College argue that to abolish it would remove a balance that exists in American politics: the conservative, rural bias of Congress on the one hand and the liberal, urban bias of the Electoral College on the other.

How Important Is Tradition?

Supporters of the existing system argue that it has worked well. Despite potential difficulties, in practice it has not produced scandal or a series of unpopular minority presidents. Supporters argue, "If it ain't broke, don't fix it."

Opponents of the current system counter that the potential for trouble is inherent in it and we should change it before disaster strikes.

1. Lawrence Longley and James Dana, Jr., "New Empirical Estimates of the Biases of the Electoral College for the 1980s," *Western Political Quarterly* 37 (March 1984): 157–75.

---

negative advertising would disappear. And if voters started to punish candidates who used negative advertising, it would disappear even more quickly.

But why does negative advertising work when most people say they do not like it? People may say they like to hear about issues, but their actions belie their words. Politics is just not that important to most people, and indeed many are woefully ignorant about specific issues. If one out of seven Americans cannot find the United States on a world map, how interested are they going to be in a discussion of foreign policy?[80] This is not to say that the voters are fools; indeed most people have a pretty good general picture of where the parties stand on a whole variety of general issues. But they are not particularly attuned to listening to debates on specifics, and the candidates realize this.

Thus, although the voters say that they deplore negative advertising, their actions contradict their words. Sixty percent of the voters thought Bush waged a "dirty" campaign, but a good many must have voted for him anyway (40% thought Dukakis waged a dirty campaign).[81] As one prominent political scientist commented, "We had real political junk food this year, and I'm afraid that if you liked 1988, you're going to love 1992."[82]

Some political observers think that there will be a backlash against negative ads as they become more

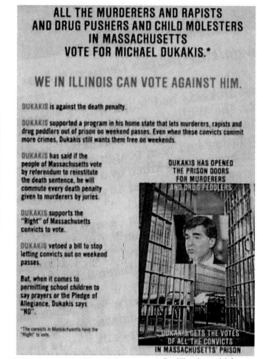

The Democratic party in Massachusetts paid for the anti-Bush ad: the Republican party in Illinois paid for the anti-Dukakis one.

and more common. Others do not fear the impact of negative campaigns because they believe that negative ads are more informative and that there are checks on them.[83] One check is the press, which could point out errors of fact. A second is the voter, who might become outraged. The third is the candidate under attack, who in most cases will hit back.[84] Still, one expert who argued in 1984 that these checks exist decided that in 1988 at least, they were insufficient. In her opinion, "Never before in a presidential campaign have televised ads sponsored by a major party candidate lied so blatantly."[85] The press was lax in pointing out factual errors in ads, the public apathetic, and the candidate under attack—Dukakis, unaggressive. Some journalists have called for the press to be more critical in evaluating candidates' ads, to evaluate the truthfulness and reasonableness of the ads just as they would a campaign speech. Instead of calling an ad "cynical" or "negative" it should be labeled "racist" or "dishonest" if that is what it is.[86]

Given the success of negative ads in 1988, therefore, we can expect them to be an important part of campaign strategies. And perhaps that is what voters now want. As one observer commented, "The voters are often less interested in being well governed than in being entertained or excited, less intent on putting a 'leadership team' in the White House than in living out a wish-fulfillment fantasy."[87]

Campaign Funding

Success in raising money is one of the keys to a successful political campaign. Although some of the money for presidential campaigns comes from public funds, much is raised privately. In chapter 9 we will discuss campaign funding and its impact on politics.

Voting

For 40 years political scientists have argued about how voters make their choices. Are parties most important? Issues? Personalities? Political scientist Stanley Kelley has argued that voters go through a simple process in deciding how to vote: they add up the things they like about each candidate and party and they vote for the candidate with the highest number of "likes." If there is a tie, they vote on the basis of their party identification, if they have one. If they do not, they abstain.

On the basis of this simple idea, Kelley explains more than 85% of the variation in voting choice.[88]

In making these calculations, then, voters consider three things:

■ The party of the candidate, which has a great effect on how the voter views everything else about him or her.
■ The candidate's personality, style, and appearance.
■ The issue stands of the candidates and parties.

Despite considerable disagreement as to exactly how each of these is weighted in the voter's mind, political scientists can offer some general conclusions.

Party Loyalties

One's party loyalty, called party identification, is probably the most important factor influencing a person's vote: Democrats tend to vote for Democrats and Republicans for Republicans. This is most true for lower-level contests such as state legislative elections, but it is also true for presidential races because party preference influences how a voter perceives a candidate's personality and issue stance. For some people, party identification is their only source of information about candidates, and they vote on the basis of it alone.

However, since the turn of the century, and even since the 1950s, party has become less important to voters. There are more independents and more people who vote contrary to their partisan loyalties. Party loyalties seem to be in flux, and parties themselves have been weakened by competition from the media and interest groups. Nevertheless, if you are guessing how a person will vote, the best single bit of information to have is the person's party identification.[89]

Candidate Evaluations

Candidates' personalities and styles have had more impact as party influence has declined and as television has become voters' major source of information about elections. Reagan's popularity in 1984 is an example of the influence of a candidate and his personality. The perceived competence and integrity of candidates are other facets of candidate evaluation. Voters are less likely to support candidates who do not seem capable of handling the job, regardless of their issue positions. Jimmy Carter suffered in 1980 because of voter evaluations of his competence and leadership.

Issues

Issues are a third factor influencing the vote. Although Americans are probably more likely to vote on issues now than they were in the 1950s, issues only influence some voters some of the time. In 1988, for example, 18% of those voters who considered themselves liberal voted for George Bush, and 19% of those who considered themselves conservative voted for Michael Dukakis. And both in 1984 and 1988, voters' issue positions overall were closer to the positions of Mondale and Dukakis than to Reagan or Bush. This certainly suggests that factors other than issues influence some voters.

To cast an issue vote, voters have to be informed about issues and have opinions. In recent elections, more than 80% of the public could take a position on issues such as government spending, military spending, women's rights, and relations with the Soviet Union.[90] Knowledge about these issues may have been vague, but individuals were able to understand the issues enough to define their own general positions.

Also, for voters to cast issue votes, candidates must have detectable policy differences. A substantial minority of voters are able to detect some differences among presidential candidates. In recent elections the percentages able to identify correctly general differences between the major party candidates varied between 36 and 62%.[91]

In the 1972 through 1988 elections, more than 70% of those who could correctly identify the positions of the candidates as well as their own position on an important issue cast a vote consistent with their own position.[92] We call this issue voting. Issues with the highest proportion of issue voting were those that typically divide Republicans and Democrats, such as government spending, military spending, and government aid to the unemployed and minorities. However, because only one-third to two-thirds of the electorate was able to define both their own and the candidates' positions on each issue, the proportion of the total electorate that can be said to cast an "issue vote" is usually less than 40%, and for some issues it is much less.[93]

Some scholars have suggested that issue voting is really more of an evaluation of the current incumbents. If voters like the way incumbents, or the incumbent's party, have handled the job in general or in certain areas—the economy or foreign policy, for example—they will vote accordingly, even without much knowledge about the specifics of the issues.

Voting on the basis of past performance is called **retrospective voting.** There is good evidence that many people do this, especially according to economic conditions.[94] Voters support incumbents if national income is growing in the months preceding the election. Unemployment and inflation seem to have less consistent effects on voting, and economic conditions two or three years before the election have little impact on voting.[95] The recession in the early Reagan years hurt Republicans in the congressional elections of 1982, but the recovery helped Reagan get reelected in 1984 and helped put Bush in the White House in 1988.

Parties, Candidates, and Issues

All three factors—parties, candidates, and issues—clearly matter. Party loyalties are especially important because they help shape our views about issues and candidates. However, if issues and candidates did not matter, the Democrats would have won every presidential election since the New Deal. Republican victories suggest that they often have had more attractive candidates (as in 1952, 1956, 1980, and 1984) or issue positions (in 1972 and in some respects in 1980). However, the Democrat's partisan advantage shrunk throughout the 1980s. Though there are still more Democrats than Republicans, the margin is very small.

Partisan loyalties are important, but they are even more important in voting for Congress (where Democrats have controlled the House for most of the past 40 years) and for state offices than for president.

Elections as Mandates?

In a democracy, we expect elections to allow us to control government. Through them we can "throw the rascals out" and bring in new faces with better ideas, or so we think. But other than to change the party that controls government, do elections make a difference?

In the popular press, we hear a lot about "mandates." A president with a **mandate** is one who is clearly directed by the voters to take some particular course of action—reduce taxes or begin arms control talks, for example. George Bush had a substantial majority in his 1988 victory. But did he have a mandate?

If so, what for? The campaign hardly talked about the budget deficit even though the election-day polls showed that this was the issue of concern to the largest group of voters. They, in turn, gave an overwhelming majority of *their* votes to Dukakis. On other issues, such as protecting the environment, Bush portrayed himself as a liberal (without, however, using the dreaded *l*-word. On many issues, ranging from abortion to day care to defense policy, the two candidates clearly differed. But did Bush's victory mean that he was to limit abortions, leave it to the states to fund day care, or continue the Reagan defense policy? Did he have a mandate on any of these issues?

Like most things in politics, the answer is not simple. Sometimes elections have an effect on policy, but often their effects are not clear-cut. In 1988, some voters chose a candidate on the basis of the national defense issue, others the budget deficit issue, others on taxes, and so on. Only one issue (the deficit) was the primary concern of even a quarter of the voters.

Typically, presidents are given a very vague mandate. Reagan's huge election victory in 1984 did not mean that the public agreed more with him than with Mondale on the issues, but mainly that they liked him and approved of the upturn in the economy. Still, over time a rough agreement develops between public attitudes and policies, which is usually consistent with majority public opinion.[96]

It is primarily political parties that translate the mix of various issues into government action because voters' issue positions influence their party loyalties and their evaluations of candidates. A vote for the candidate of one's own party is usually a reflection of agreement on at least some important issues.[97] Once in office, the party in government helps sort out the issues for which there is a broad public mandate from those for which there is not.

Elections that appear to be mandates can become "mandates for disaster." More than one observer has pointed out that every twentieth-century president who has won election by 60% or more of the popular vote soon encountered serious political trouble. After his landslide in 1920, Warren Harding had his Teapot Dome scandal involving government corruption. Emboldened by his 1936 triumph, Franklin Roosevelt tried to pack the Supreme Court and was resoundingly defeated on that issue. Lyndon Johnson won by a landslide in 1964 and was soon mired in Vietnam. Richard Nixon smashed George McGovern in 1972 but then had to resign because of Watergate. Ronald

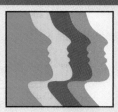

AMERICAN DIVERSITY

Voting Ethnic

Although in many ways America has been a melting pot of different races and religions, we have not melted so far as to be indistinguishable. One visible sign of ethnic and cultural differences is in voting behavior. In general, socioeconomic class is a very important predictor of the vote: the lower the income, the more likely to vote Democrat. But this general rule is cross-cut with distinctive ethnic patterns (we use ethnic here to refer to differences of religion, national origin, and race).

For example, Jews are much more likely to vote Democratic than other whites of similar income. On the whole, they have a higher-than-average income yet in 1988, about three-fourths of Jewish voters voted Democratic. As a group, they were exceeded in their Democratic allegiance only by blacks.

Catholics used to be predominantly Democratic. They still are, but not consistently. Although 60% supported Democratic congressional candidates in 1986, only half voted for Dukakis and a majority voted for Reagan in 1980 and 1984.

Blacks are probably the most distinctive group politically. About 90% consistently vote Democratic, and this loyalty has increased over the past 25 years.

Hispanics, who also have lower-than-average incomes, are not as universally Democratic as blacks and have voted Republican in significant numbers in recent elections. Although almost three-quarters voted Democratic in the 1986 congressional elections, just about 60% voted for Dukakis in 1988.

Hispanics vote Republican more than they previously did for several reasons. One is that many Hispanics are moving into the middle-class. Another is that Republicans have made a great effort to lure Hispanic voters. Moreover, a growing number are Cuban-Americans, largely located in Florida, whose most intense political opinion is anticommunism. Cuban-Americans are much more likely to be Republican than either Mexican-Americans or Puerto Ricans.

White Protestants generally give a majority of their vote to the Republicans and have done so for decades. However, as for other groups, income differences are important in determining the vote of Protestants.

Why is ethnicity important in determining the vote? There is nothing genetic about it. Rather, ethnicity is a shorthand term for many other factors influencing political behavior—class, historical treatment within the society, and basic culture and values. Jews are predominantly Democratic, for example, because as a persecuted minority

This year I'm not getting involved in any complicated issues. I'm just voting my straight ethnic prejudices.

throughout much of their history, they have learned to identify with the underdog, even when their own economic circumstances move them into the middle or upper class. Catholics were sometimes discriminated against too; this discrimination plus their working-class status propelled them to the party of Roosevelt. As Catholics have moved into the middle class and as tolerance toward Catholics has grown, Catholics, like Protestants, have tended to vote their income.

Source: *Washington Post National Weekly Edition,* April 9, 1984; *National Journal,* November 10, 1984, p. 2132; 1988 Cable News Network—*Los Angeles Times* exit poll summarized in *National Journal,* November 12, 1988, p. 2855. Lee Sigelman, "If You Prick Us, Do We Not Bleed? If You Tickle Us, Do We Not Laugh? Jews and Pocketbook Voting" paper prepared for presentation at the 1990 American Political Science Meeting; Susan Welch and Lee Sigelman, "The Politics of Hispanic Americans," *Social Science Quarterly,* 1991.

Source: Drawing by Whitney Darrow, Jr.; © 1970 The New Yorker Magazine, Inc.

Reagan's resounding victory in 1984 (a shade less than 60%) was followed by the blunders of the Iran-contra affair. Of these presidents, only Roosevelt was able to recover fully from his political misfortune. Reagan regained his personal popularity but seemed to have little influence on policy after Iran-contra. One recent observer has argued that these disasters come because "the euphoria induced by overwhelming support at the polls evidently loosens the president's grip on reality."[98]

Conclusion: Do Elections Make Government Responsive?

The right to vote in the United States is nearly universal, but many Americans do not exercise that right.

Those of below-average income and education are especially unlikely to vote.

Election campaigns are far less successful in mobilizing voters and ensuring a high turnout today than they were in the past century. The passive medium of television has supplanted old-style campaigns that involved voters more directly.

Elections can point out new directions for government and allow citizens to make it responsive to their needs, but the fact that many individuals do not vote means that the new directions may not reflect either the needs or wishes of the public. The necessity for large amounts of money to run campaigns may mean that government is more responsive to those with resources. Elections promote government responsiveness to those who participate in them.

EPILOGUE

The Low Road

Bush, realizing that he was far behind, accepted the negative campaign strategy and in early June unveiled a strong attack on Dukakis at a Texas Republican meeting (figure 8). As one commentator wrote, the Bush campaign began the "un-Americanization of Michael Dukakis,"[99] an effort to show that Dukakis was "not a patriot, no believer in law and order, no manly man, no lover of family . . . one of those loose lovers of 'them' and 'their' ways."[100]

During the early summer, before the parties' national conventions, the Republicans began to run ads featuring Willie Horton and giving the impression that Dukakis had started the furlough program (it was established by a previous Republican governor in Massachusetts), that hundreds of furloughed prisoners had raped and murdered while on furlough (Horton was the only one), and that Dukakis somehow approved of criminals (in fact, though Dukakis initially supported the program, he changed it after the Horton tragedy). The ads played not so subtly on a racist theme as well, since Horton was black and his rape victim was white.

These ads were used heavily in key states, such as Texas, Ohio, and California. And Bush and his staff talked constantly about Horton and the furlough issue. In a crude, though far from the crudest, comment on the issue, Lee Atwater, Bush's campaign manager, tried to link Dukakis, Jackson, and Horton, suggesting that Horton might be Dukakis's running mate, "I saw in [Dukakis's] driveway of his home Jesse Jackson. So anyway, maybe he [Dukakis] will put this Willie Horton on the ticket after all is said and done. And Willie Horton is the fellow who was a convicted murderer and rapist."[101] Bush supplemented these attacks by criticizing Dukakis for vetoing the mandatory Pledge of Allegiance bill and began to say the Pledge at his own rallies and public appearances.

As his lead in the polls began to melt, many of Dukakis's advisers urged him to respond, especially to the furlough issue. After all, Dukakis had a sound record because Massachusetts had one of the lowest crime rates of any industrialized state. One version of his convention acceptance speech also included a section pointing out that he was hardly soft on crime; his

Figure 8 ■ Dukakis Starts Strong, Then Slides Until Mid-September

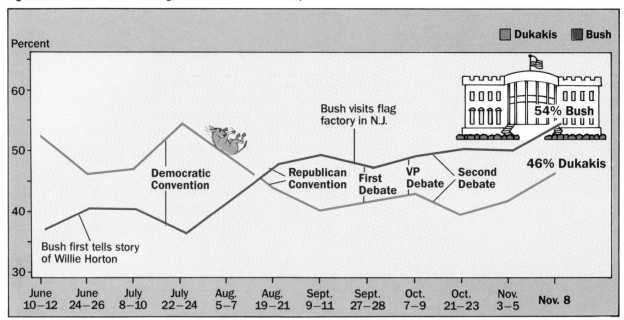

Source: Data are from the Gallup poll, Christopher Blumrich; adapted from *Newsweek,* November 21, 1988, p. 14.

own father had been a victim of a beating, and his brother was killed by a hit-and-run driver. But Dukakis did not give this response until well into October. Nor did he respond to the attacks on his patriotism until the first debate with Bush in September. Meanwhile his lead steadily dwindled as the Republican campaign worked the Pledge and furlough issues daily on the campaign. As one Democratic activist noted, "They [the Republicans] woke up every morning this summer and this fall and they've been able to say to themselves, 'Hey, this furlough stuff is still working. Let's keep doing it.' "[102] The Republican campaign advisers themselves did not think that these issues would be useful throughout the campaign. They saw them as opening shots to which Dukakis would respond, after which the campaign would move on to new issues.[103]

One of the interesting questions of the campaign is why Dukakis did not respond to these attacks; as political pros generally agree, unless you are far in front and quite well known, an unanswered smear by an opponent usually is believed. Dukakis was particularly vulnerable because he was not widely known outside Massachusetts. Apparently not recognizing his danger, he insisted that his campaign remain positive. One of his advisers commented, "At first, we used to

read this stuff [about the furlough and pledge of allegiance] and laugh and say '. . . why would people take this stuff seriously.' "[104] Dukakis greatly overestimated the voters' level of information, sophistication, and interest in issues. Because he did not take these attacks seriously, he did not believe the public took them seriously either. In that sense, he was out of step with the values of Americans, not because he did not believe in them, but because he did not realize the importance of symbols.

We all know that George Bush won the election. But would he have won anyway? Obviously, we will never know for sure. Political pollsters and media experts like to think that they determine the outcome of elections, when in fact they may have had only a small effect, or none at all.

In 1988, based on the state of the economy and the popularity of President Reagan, many political scientists had predicted a Republican victory even when Dukakis was running ahead in the polls in the summer. Indeed, one said, "Any GOP presidential nominee in 1988 would have had to work awfully hard to lose the election."[105] Reagan's job approval by November was extremely high—60%. No president with that kind of approval rating has ever seen his party lose the White House.[106] Given all this, even the best-run

Democratic campaign might not have won. But clearly the Dukakis campaign was not the best run, and in light of the inherent weaknesses of Bush as a candidate, it is reasonable to think that Dukakis should have done better.

Some observers of American national politics are worried that this election may mean that all barriers have fallen in the use of negative campaign tactics.[107] Political pundits argue that voters are turned off by such tactics and point to the ever lower voter turnout rates as evidence. Lee Atwater himself, as he was dying of brain cancer, apologized for the cruelty and racism of his role in the campaign.[108] Because voters obviously responded to the negative campaigning of 1988, some analysts fear that future presidential campaigns will all be negative. A somewhat more sanguine view was expressed by a Republican campaign expert who said, "My concern is that a lot of political professionals will conclude that you don't need to talk about issues, that you need to attack your opponent early and often. But that's not the lesson. The lesson is that, in Dukakis, you have a candidate who, when a match was lit in his vicinity, poured gasoline all over himself."[109]

KEY TERMS

suffrage

Reconstruction

literacy tests

grandfather clause

poll tax

white primary

Voting Rights Act

Progressive reforms

Single-member districts

proportional representation (PR)

presidential preference primaries

Super Tuesday

coattails

Electoral College

faithless elector

retrospective voting

mandate

FURTHER READING

Lucius Barker, *Our Time Has Come: A Delegate's 'Diary' of Jesse Jackson's 1984 Presidential Campaign* (Urbana, Ill.: University of Illinois Press, 1988); Adolph Reed, *The Jesse Jackson Phenomenon* (New Haven: Yale University Press, 1986). *Barker provides a unique account of Jackson's 1984 campaign from his viewpoint as a political scientist and Jackson delegate. Reed's account of Jackson is relatively unsympathetic.*

Taylor Branch, *Parting the Waters: America in the King Years* (New York: Simon & Schuster, 1988). *An excellent, readable account that illustrates the impact of political protest in changing America's race laws and to a considerable extent its attitudes about race.*

Robert Darcy, Susan Welch, and Janet Clark, *Women, Elections, and Representation* (New York: Longman, 1987). *An examination of the potential barriers faced by women candidates.*

Kathleen Hall Jamieson, *Packaging the Presidency* (New York: Oxford University Press, 1984). *The history and impact of presidential campaign advertising. Jamieson changed her views about the benign nature of negative advertising after the 1988 campaign.*

Allan Lichtman and Ken De Cell, *The Thirteen Keys to the Presidency.* (Madison Books, 1990). *Focusing on 13 factors—"Keys"—that help explain presidential election outcomes, these authors correctly predict every election since 1860.*

Frances Fox Piven and Richard Cloward, *Why Americans Don't Vote* (New York: Pantheon, 1988). *The authors attribute nonvoting to restrictive registration laws and the disinterest of parties in mobilizing the working class.*

Theodore H. White, *The Making of the President,* 4 vols. (New York: Atheneum Publishers, 1961, 1965, 1969, 1973). *Journalistic accounts of presidential elections from 1960 to 1972. White was the first journalist to travel with the candidates and give an inside view of campaign strategy.*

NOTES

1. Paul Taylor and David Broder, "How the Presidential Campaign Got Stuck on the Low Road," *Washington Post National Weekly Edition,* November 7–13, 1988, p. 14.

2. See *Newsweek,* November 21, 1988, p. 100.

3. Elizabeth Drew, "A Letter from Washington," *The New Yorker,* December 12, 1988, p. 126.

4. Taylor and Broder, "How the Presidential Campaign Got Stuck on the Low Road," p. 14.

5. "Elephants on Parade," *Newsweek,* November 21, 1988, p. 100.

6. Quoted in *Newsweek,* October 31, 1988, p. 18.

7. William Flanigan and Nancy H. Zingale, *Political Behavior of the American Electorate* (Boston: Allyn and Bacon, 1972), p. 13. See also Chilton Williamson, *American Suffrage from Property to Democracy* (Princeton, N.J.: Princeton University Press, 1960).

8. James MacGregor Burns, *Vineyard of Liberty* (New York: Alfred A. Knopf, 1982), p. 363.

9. August Meier and Elliot Rudwick, *From Plantation to Ghetto* (New York: Hill and Wang, 1966), p. 69.

10. Robert Darcy, Susan Welch, and Janet Clark, *Women, Elections, and Representation* (New York: Longman, 1987).

11. Grandfather clause: *Guinn v. United States,* 238 U.S. 347, (1915); white primary: *Smith v. Allwright,* 321 U.S. 649, (1944).

12. Data on black and white voter registration in the southern states are from the *Statistical Abstract of the United States* (Washington, D.C.: U.S. Bureau of the Census, various years).

13. Darcy, Welch, and Clark, *Women, Elections and Representation*.

14. The discussion in this paragraph is drawn largely from Lois Banner, *Women in Modern America* (New York: Harcourt Brace Jovanovich, 1974), pp. 88–90.

15. Richard Jensen, "American Election Campaigns: A Theoretical and Historical Typology," paper delivered at the 1968 Midwest Political Science Association Meeting, quoted in Walter Dean Burnham, *Critical Elections and the Mainsprings of American Politics* (New York: W. W. Norton, 1970), p. 73.

16. Frances Fox Piven and Richard A. Cloward, *Why Americans Don't Vote* (New York: Pantheon, 1988), p. 30.

17. Daniel Elazar, *American Federalism: A View from the States* (New York: Thomas Y. Crowell, 1972).

18. Piven and Cloward, *Why Americans Don't Vote*, p. 162. See also G. Bingham Powell, Jr., "American Voter Turnout in Comparative Perspective," *American Political Science Review* 80 (March 1986): 17–44.

19. Piven and Cloward, *Why Americans Don't Vote*, pp. 17–18. Data are from 1980.

20. Powell, "American Voter Turnout," p. 30; Piven and Cloward, *Why Americans Don't Vote*, p. 119.

21. George Will, "In Defense of Nonvoting," *Newsweek*, October 10, 1983, p. 96.

22. Richard Morin, "The Dog Ate My Forms, and, Well, I Couldn't Find a Pen," *Washington Post National Weekly Edition*, November 5–11, 1990, p. 38.

23. Curtis Gans, quoted in Jack Germond and Jules Witcover, "Listen to the Voters—and Nonvoters," *Minneapolis Star Tribune*, November 26, 1988.

24. Ibid.

25. Priscilla Southwell, "Voter Turnout in the 1986 Congressional Elections," *American Politics Quarterly* 19 (January 1991): 96–108.

26. Curtis B. Gans, "The Empty Ballot Box," *Public Opinion* 1 (September/October 1978): 54–57. See also Austin Ranney, *Channels of Power* (New York: Basic Books, 1983); and Richard Boyd, "The Effect of Election Calendars on Voter Turnout," paper presented at the Annual Meeting of the Midwest Political Science Association, April 1987, Chicago, Illinois.

27. Boyd, "The Effect of Election Calendars."

28. Ibid.

29. Piven and Cloward, *Why Americans Don't Vote*, p. 17.

30. Benjamin Ginsberg, *The Consequences of Consent: Elections, Citizen Control and Popular Acquiescence* (Reading, Mass.: Addison-Wesley, 1982), p. 37.

31. Raymond Wolfinger and Steven Rosenstone, *Who Votes?* (New Haven: Yale University Press, 1980), table 6.1.

32. See Piven and Cloward, *Why Americans Don't Vote*, pp. 196–97 for illustrations of these kinds of informal barriers.

33. James A. Barnes, "In Person: Marsha Nye Adler," *National Journal*, February 18, 1989, p. 420.

34. "Poorest" is defined here as family income less than $10,000, "richest" as more than $40,000.

35. Piven and Cloward, *Why Americans Don't Vote*, pp. 230–31.

36. Peverill Squire, Raymond Wolfinger, and David Glass, "Residential Mobility and Voter Turnout," *American Political Science Review* 81 (March 1987): 45–66. See also Samuel C. Patterson and Gregory A. Caldeira, "Mailing in the Vote: Correlates and Consequences of Absentee Voting," *American Journal of Political Science* 29 (November 1985): 766–88.

37. For a recent review of this literature, see John Petrocik, "Voter Turnout and Electoral Preference," in Kay Schlozman, ed., *Elections in America* (Boston: Allen & Unwin, 1987).

38. Kevin Phillips and Paul Blackman, *Electoral Reform and Voter Participation* (Stanford, Calif.: American Enterprise System, 1975).

39. Ibid.

40. Anthony Downs, *An Economic Theory of Democracy* (New York: Harper & Row, 1957).

41. Morin, "The Dog Ate My Forms."

42. Norman H. Nie, Sidney Verba, Henry Brady, Kay Lehman Schlozman, and Jane Junn, "Participation in America: Continuity and Change," paper presented at the Annual Meeting of the Midwest Political Science Association, Chicago, Illinois, April 1988. The standard work on American political participation is Sidney Verba and Norman Nie, *Participation in America* (New York: Harper & Row, 1972).

43. Ibid.

44. Paul Allen Beck and M. Kent Jennings, "Political Periods and Political Participation," *American Political Science Review* 73 (1979): 737–50; Nie et al., "Participation in America."

45. The following discussion draws heavily from John Aldrich, *Before the Convention* (Chicago: University of Chicago Press, 1980).

46. Ibid. See also David Rohde, "Risk-Bearing and Progressive Ambition: The Case of Members of the United States House of Representatives," *American Journal of Political Science* 23 (February 1979): 1–26.

47. "Political Grapevine," *Time*, February 8, 1988, p. 30.

48. Media Monitor, Center for Media and Public Affairs, based on "clearly positive and clearly negative statements of candidates' desirability" on ABC, CBS, and NBC evening news from February 8 to June 7, 1988, as reported in David Shaw, "Television," *Los Angeles Times*, August 15, 1988.

49. "The Fall Campaign," *Newsweek*, Election Extra (November/December 1984): 88.

50. Bruce Babbitt, "Bruce Babbitt's View from the Wayside," *Washington Post National Weekly Edition*, February 24–March 6, 1988, p. 24.

51. New York Times Delegate Survey, reported in *New York Times*, August 14, 1988, p. 14.

52. Gerald Pomper and Susan Lederman, *Elections in America* (New York: Longman, 1980), chapter 7.

53. Michael J. Robinson, "Where's the Beef," in Austin Ranney, ed., *The American Election of 1984* (Durham, N.C.: Duke University Press, 1985).

54. "Squall in New Orleans," *Newsweek*, November 21, 1988, p. 103.

55. "Conventional Wisdom Watch," *Newsweek*, November 21, 1988, p. 18.

56. See *Congressional Quarterly*, July 23, 1988, p. 2015.

57. Benjamin Page and Richard Brody, "Policy Voting and the Electoral Process," *American Political Science Review* 66 (1972): 979–95.

58. David Mayhew and Bruce Russett, "How the Democrats Can Win in 1992," *New Leader*, January 9, 1989, p. 13.

59. Thomas E. Patterson, *Mass Media Elections* (New York: Praeger, 1980), p. 3.

60. The discussion of the functions of the media relies heavily on the excellent summary found in Stephen Ansolabehere, Roy Behr, and Shanto Iyengar, "Mass Media and Elections," *American Politics Quarterly* 19 (January 1991): 109–39.

61. Larry Bartels, *Presidential Primaries and the Dynamics of Public Choice* (Princeton, N.J.: Princeton University Press, 1988).

62. Bruce Buchanan, *Electing a President: The Markle Commission Report on Campaign '88* (Austin, Tex.: University of Texas Press, 1990); Montague Kean, *30-Second Politics* (New York: Praeger, 1989). Marion Just, Lori Wallach, and Ann Crigler, "Thirty Seconds or Thirty Minutes: Political Learning in an Election," paper presented at the Midwest Political Science Association Meeting, April 1987, Chicago, Illinois.

63. Shanto Iyengar and Donald Kinder, *News that Matters* (Chicago: University of Chicago Press, 1987).

64. Iyengar and Kinder, *News that Matters,* chapter 11.

65. Henry Brady, "Chances, Utilities, and Voting in Presidential Primaries," paper delivered at the Annual Meeting of the Public Choice Society, Phoenix, Arizona, cited in Ansolabehere, Behr, and Iyengar, "Mass Media and Elections;" Bartels, *Presidential Primaries,* 1988.

66. John Zaller, *Elite Discourse and Public Opinion* (Cambridge: Cambridge University Press, forthcoming).

67. Thomas Patterson, *The Mass Media Election* (New York: Praeger, 1990); Doris Graber, *Mass Media and Presidential Politics* (Washington D.C.: CQ Press, 1980).

68. Lee Sigelman and David Bullock, "Candidates, Issues, Horse races and Hoopla," *American Politics Quarterly* 19 (January 1991): 5–32.

69. *Congressional Quarterly Weekly Reports* July 30, 1971, p. 1622 quoted in Stephen Ansolabehere, Roy Behr and Shanto Iyengar, "Mass Media and Elections," p. 109.

70. Martin Schram, *The Great American Video Game: Presidential Politics in the Television Age* (New York: William Morrow, 1987).

71. Patterson, *Mass Media Election,* p. 4.

72. Robert McNeil, *The Influence of Television on American Politics* (New York: Harper & Row, 1968), p. 182.

73. Elisabeth Bumiller, "Selling Soup, Wine and Reagan," *Washington Post National Weekly Edition,* November 5, 1984, pp. 6–8.

74. Paul Taylor, "Pigsty Politics," *Washington Post National Weekly Edition,* February 13–19, 1989, p. 6.

75. Eileen Shields West, "Give 'em Hell These Days Is a Figure of Speech," *Smithsonian* (October 1988): 149–51. The editorial was from the *Connecticut Courant.*

76. Charles Paul Freund, "But Then, Truth Has Never Been Important," *Washington Post National Weekly Edition,* November 7–13, 1988, p. 29.

77. Quoted in Freund, "But Then, Truth Has Never Been Important," p. 29.

78. Taylor, "Pigsty Politics," p. 7.

79. Kathleen Hall Jamieson, "Is the Truth Now Irrelevant in Presidential Campaigns?" *Washington Post National Weekly Edition,* November 7–13, 1988, p. 28.

80. Freund, "But Then, the Truth Has Never Been Important," p. 29.

81. Richard Morin, "Relieved Rather than Elated," *Washington Post National Weekly Edition,* November 7–13, 1988, p. 42.

82. Walter Dean Burnham quoted in Paul Taylor, "The Dull Election of '88: Who Gets the Blame?" *Washington Post National Weekly Edition,* November 21–27, 1988, p. 25.

83. One of those observers is political scientist Michael Robinson. See Taylor, "Pigsty Politics," p. 7. In her book, *Packaging the Presidency* (New York: Oxford University Press, 1984), Kathleen Jamieson also argued that there are checks on misleading advertising, but later ("Is the Truth Now Irrelevant in Presidential Campaigns?") she argued that these checks did not work well in 1988.

84. Jamieson, "Is the Truth Now Irrelevant in Presidential Campaigns?"

85. Ibid. Jamieson is quoted in Lawrence Zuckerman, "The Made-for-TV Campaign," *Time,* November 14, 1988, p. 68.

86. Daniel Slocum Hinerfeld, "How Political Ads Subtract," *Washington Monthly.* May 1990, pp. 12–22; David Broder, "How

to Stop a Political Mudbath in Five Easy Steps," *Washington Post National Weekly Edition,* January 22–28, 1990, p. 23.

87. Godfrey Hodgson, "Maybe No President Could Govern under This Constitution," *Washington Post National Weekly Edition,* May 21, 1984, p. 34.

88. Stanley Kelley, Jr., *Interpreting Elections* (Princeton, N.J.: Princeton University Press, 1983); Stanley Kelley, Jr., Richard Ayres, and William G. Bower, "Registration and Voting: Putting First Things First," *American Political Science Review* 61 (June 1967): 359–79.

89. J. Merrill Shanks and Warren E. Miller, "Partisanship, Policy and Performance: The Reagan Legacy in the 1988 Election," *British Journal of Political Science* 21 (April, 1991): 129–197; Eugene DeClerq, Thomas Hurley, and Norman Luttbeg, "Voting in American Presidential Elections," *American Political Quarterly* 3 (July 1975), updated and reported in David B. Hill and Norman Luttbeg, *Trends in American Electoral Behavior,* 2nd ed. (Itasca, Ill.: F. E. Peacock, 1983), p. 50.

90. Paul Abramson, John H. Aldrich, and David Rohde, *Change and Continuity in the 1988 Elections* (Washington, D.C.: CQ Press, 1990), p. 172.

91. Ibid., p. 165.

92. Ibid.

93. Ibid, p. 170.

94. Morris Fiorina, *Retrospective Voting in American National Elections* (New Haven: Yale University Press, 1981).

95. Edward Tufte, *Political Control of the Economy* (Princeton, N.J.: Princeton University Press, 1978); Douglas Hibbs, "The Mass Public and Macroeconomic Performance," *American Journal of Political Science* 23 (November 1979): 705–31; John Hibbing and John Alford, "The Electoral Impact of Economic Conditions: Who Is Held Responsible," *American Journal of Political Science* 25 (1981): 423–39.

96. Benjamin I. Page and Robert Shapiro, "Effects of Public Opinion on Policy," *American Political Science Review* 77 (March 1983): 175–90.

97. Abramson, Aldrich, and Rohde, *Change and Continuity.* See also Benjamin Page and Calvin C. Jones, "Reciprocal Effects of Party Preferences, Party Loyalties and the Vote," in Richard Niemi and Herbert Weisberg, *Controversies in Voting Behavior,* 2nd ed. (Washington, D.C.: CQ Press, 1984).

98. Arthur Schlesinger, Jr., *Wall Street Journal,* December 5, 1986.

99. "Elephants on Parade," p. 100.

100. Gus Tyler, "After the Brawl Was Over," *New Leader,* November 28, 1988, p. 7.

101. Thomas Edsall, "Race Continues to Be a Wild Card in American Politics," *Washington Post National Weekly Edition,* August 8–14, 1988, p. 12.

102. Quoted in Taylor and Broder, "How the Presidential Campaign Got Stuck on the Low Road," p. 14.

103. Drew, "A Letter from Washington," p. 122.

104. Tyler, "After the Brawl Was Over," p. 7.

105. Greg Markus, quoted in David Broder, "Bush Gets Big Prize but It's a Split Decision," *Washington Post National Weekly Edition,* November 14–20, 1988, p. 10.

106. *National Journal,* November 11, 1988, p. 2855.

107. See Jamieson, "Is the Truth Now Irrelevant in Presidential Campaigns," p. 28.

108. Anna Quimdlen, "No Thanks for the Memories," *Lincoln Star,* February 8, 1991, *New York Times* Syndicate.

109. Taylor and Broder, "How the Presidential Campaign Got Stuck on the Low Road," p. 15.

The Media

Reporters zero in on Senator Dan Quayle as he runs for vice president in 1988.

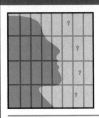

Should You Broadcast from Baghdad?

You are Peter Arnett, war correspondent for the Cable News Network (CNN), and it is January 1991. Just days ago you arrived in Baghdad, Iraq, as the United Nations' deadline for Iraq to remove its troops from Kuwait approached. When the deadline passed and allied planes began bombing Baghdad, most Western journalists headed to a bomb shelter under their hotel in the center of the city. But you and two colleagues with CNN remained in your room. Leaning out your window observing the bombardment, you gave live telephone reports to the world: "They're coming over our hotel. You can hear the bombs now." But 16 hours later, after American officials said they could tell how accurate the bombing was from CNN's coverage, Iraqi officials pulled the plug.

Now it was obvious that Iraq was not going to allow uncensored reporting. Other Western correspondents, including your two colleagues, decided to leave the next day. Should you also leave, or should you stay and carry on under the restrictions of censored reporting?

Should you worry about your safety? With the allies' relentless bombardment and with Iraq's dictatorial government, you could lose your life from either side with one misstep. Yet you have put your life on the line many times before, covering 16 wars and insurrections in 30 years. You were in the thick of fighting in Angola, El Salvador, and Nicaragua. You survived Beirut and a fistfight with KGB agents in Moscow. You covered the Vietnam War from the beginning to the end. After American troops withdrew from South Vietnam and the country began to fall to North Vietnam in 1975, you remained while more prudent reporters left. As North Vietnamese troops overran the South Vietnamese capital of Saigon, you sat at your desk and typed your story.

When a North Vietnamese major marched in, you offered him a Coke and a cookie, interviewed him, and filed your story before the wires were cut.[1]

Should you put your commitment to getting the news ahead of other concerns? As an Associated Press (AP) correspondent in Vietnam, you refused to rely on press briefings by government officials or secondhand accounts from other reporters. You followed troops into the jungles and through the rice paddies to see for yourself. You heard an American major justify a bombing attack by saying, "It was necessary to destroy the village in order to save it."[2] You challenged the government's optimistic reports about the progress of the war. Your reporting prompted President Lyndon Johnson to call you a Communist and try to get you fired, but it also got you a Pulitzer Prize.

But can you get the news with Iraq's censorship? You would be restricted in your movements—you could go only to places where officials took you—and you would be restricted in your broadcasts—you could say only what officials permitted. You would not be allowed to report any information, whether military or civilian, that reflected poorly on Iraq's policies or favorably on the allies' progress.

In fact, you would be used by Iraqi officials to disseminate information and film that they wanted the world to see, information and film that would serve their propaganda campaign to discredit the allies' assertions that they were targeting just military facilities and not hurting civilians or trying to destroy the country. Iraqi officials are well aware that CNN provides news to 103 countries around the world. Previously they gave CNN access to phone lines that they denied the three major U.S. networks.

With these thoughts in mind, do you stay to get the news? If so, do you broadcast what you get?

A "medium" transmits something. The **mass media**—which include newspapers, magazines, books, radio, television, movies, and records—transmit communications to masses of people.

Although the media do not constitute a branch of government or even an organization established to influence government, such as a political party or interest group, they have an impact on government. In addition to providing entertainment, the media provide political information, sometimes directly in a newscast, other times indirectly in a program or story addressing a public problem such as crime or drugs. Either way, people obtain most of their information about government and politics from the media.

The Media State

The media have developed and flourished to an extent the Founders could not have envisioned. As one political scientist noted, the media have become "pervasive . . . and atmospheric, an element of the air we breathe."[3] Without exaggeration, another observer concluded, "Ancient Sparta was a military state. John Calvin's Geneva was a religious state. Mid-nineteenth century England was Europe's first industrial state, and the contemporary United States is the world's first media state."[4]

American adults spend nearly half their leisure time exposed to the media.[5] Seventy-seven percent read newspapers; the average person does so for three-and-a-half hours a week. The average person also reads two magazines for one-and-a-half hours a week.[6] Eighty-eight percent of American homes have a radio, and 98% have a television. More homes have a television than a toilet.[7] The average adult watches television three hours a day and the average child four. By the time the average child graduates from high school, he or she has spent more time in front of the tube than in class.[8] By the time the average American dies, he or she has spent one-and-a-half years just watching television commercials.[9]

Development of the Media

It is no accident that the United States became the world's first media state. The greater democratization of American society created the climate for a free press and a mass audience. And the greater technological advancement produced the means to gather the news and to disseminate it more widely and quickly.[10]

Print Media. The first newspaper in the United States was published in 1690.[11] Although it was suppressed, other papers appeared not long after, and when the Declaration of Independence was adopted, these papers conveyed it to the people. The Founders recognized the value of the press and included a provision for freedom of the press in the First Amendment of the Bill of Rights.

In the young republic, political parties created and controlled most newspapers. The Federalists established one, then the Jeffersonians another in opposition. Parties sponsored other papers and even put the journalists on the government's payroll. Naturally, the papers echoed the parties' views and the journalists bowed to the parties' leaders. The editor of one Democratic party paper made sure a pail of fresh milk was left on the White House doorstep for President Andrew Jackson every morning, even if the editor had to deliver it himself.[12]

Many people could not read, and because the process of printing and delivering papers was slow and expensive, most people could not afford them (figure 1). Consequently, these party papers were read by only a small circle of people—the political and commercial elites.

Publishers filled their pages with statements by the party and stories from other papers in other cities

Figure 1 ■ News Traveled Slowly in 1790

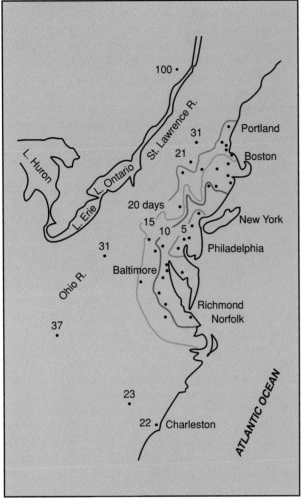

In 1790 news from an outlying place traveled slowly to Philadelphia, where it was published. The lines on the map indicate in days how long this process usually took.

Source: Atlas of Early American History (1976), p. 69. Adapted from map in Allan R. Pred, *Urban Growth and the Circulation of Information: The United States System of Cities,* 1790–1840 (Cambridge, Mass.: Harvard University Press, 1973), p. 37.

or countries. But in the 1830s newspapers began to emphasize local rather than national or foreign news and to focus on human interest aspects of the news. At the same time, they reduced the price, from six cents to one cent, and had newsboys hawk the papers on the street corners.

These penny papers attracted many more readers than the party papers. Expansion of public education meant more people could read, and improvement of home lighting—from candles to oil, and then to gas—meant they could read at night more easily. And advancements in technology enabled papers to be printed more quickly and cheaply.

In the 1840s invention of the telegraph permitted news dispatches to be sent across the country quickly and led to the development of the wire services—Associated Press (AP) and United Press International (UPI)—which provided timely news of national events.

During the Civil War reporters went to the battlefields and reported what they themselves saw and heard rather than relying on what others wrote. After the war a reporter conducted the first interview of a president—Andrew Johnson.[13] Both these techniques of gathering news provided more news, and more timely news, than before. And both were popular, so they attracted more readers.

In addition to these techniques, papers began to engage in **yellow journalism**—sensationalizing news, especially of crimes and scandals—and **muckraking**—exposing corruption, particularly in city governments and big businesses. Muckraking was a forerunner of what is now called investigative reporting. Sometimes papers combined the two practices in order to crusade for causes they advocated. These practices, along with their excesses, enlivened the papers and attracted more readers.

The first political magazines in the United States were published in the mid-nineteenth century, and muckraking magazines appeared by the end of the century. Newsweeklies arose to summarize and comment on the news of the week in the 1920s. Magazines grew in number and importance because of the increase in leisure time and education—some were pitched directly to college graduates.

Broadcast Media.   Development of the broadcast media enabled politicians to reach people who could not or did not read, and it allowed them to reach people more directly. No longer did they have to go through political parties or editors.

Radio became popular in the 1920s, and people planned their schedules around their favorite programs. Station KDKA in Pittsburgh broadcast on-the-spot returns in the presidential election of 1920, and President Calvin Coolidge used radio in his presidential campaign in 1924.

But President Franklin D. Roosevelt was the first to use radio effectively. During his four terms he was opposed by most newspaper owners, yet he succeeded because he took his case directly to the people in a series of **fireside chats** on the radio. He had a fine voice but, more important, a superb ability to speak informally—he would comment about his family, even his dog, in such a way as to appeal to average people. He drew so many listeners that he was given as much air time as he wanted, but he was shrewd enough to realize that too much would result in overexposure.

Television became available in the late 1940s, and sales zoomed in the 1950s. During some weeks in the 1950s, 10,000 people a day bought their first television.[14] People bought a television to watch entertainment programs, but they also began to watch newscasts and news specials.

Yet people did not watch the networks' evening newscasts widely for some years. The newscasts, lasting only 16 minutes and consisting solely of an anchor and a few correspondents talking, were not compelling. But in 1963 CBS expanded its show to 30 min-

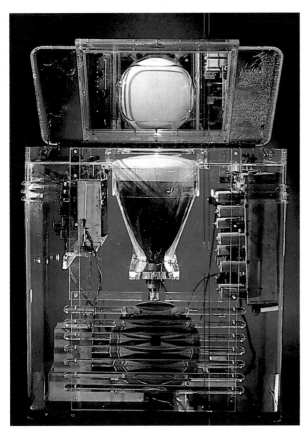

This television made its debut in the Hall of Television at the New York World's Fair in 1939. President Franklin Roosevelt opened the fair by appearing on the tiny screen (*top*).

utes in an effort to top NBC in the ratings. The other two networks followed suit. The additional time required a new format, so the networks emphasized visual interest in the news stories. This approach drew more viewers. This year, for the first time, people reported they got more of their political information from television than from any other source.

As television grew in popularity, newspapers waned. They found it useless to print "Extra" editions for late-breaking news. Although they began to provide in-depth analysis of news, which television did not, they struggled for readers and advertisers, and some folded.

These trends have continued. In the 1970s and 1980s, the number of adults in the country increased 34% and the number of households 41%, but the circulation of daily newspapers remained stagnant (see figure 2).[15]

Consequently, television has become the most important of the media for politics. According to surveys, people pay more attention to it and put more faith in it than in other media. This makes positive coverage on television essential for politicians.

Nevertheless, television has not fully eclipsed newspapers. Most people who say that they get the bulk of their political information from television admit that they do not watch the news daily, whereas more people who get the bulk of their political information from newspapers read the news sections daily. Because newspapers require more effort or provide more depth, they leave a longer-lasting impression; people remember what they read in newspapers better than what they watch on television.[16]

Moreover, national newspapers such as the *New York Times* and *Washington Post*, which blanket the country with in-depth international and national news, influence opinion leaders who, in turn, influence other persons.

Coverage of the Persian Gulf War reflected the contemporary role of both broadcast and print journalism. As the war began people were riveted to their television sets. Though the networks had little film footage of the war itself, they provided immediacy and drama. When the Scud missile attacks threatened, reporters were edgy with anticipation: "There go the sirens. We'll probably have an attack here in five minutes." In Israel, where poison gas attacks were feared, reporters were shown putting on gas masks or scurrying to sealed rooms. The live reports, beamed via satellite, often were unedited and rough yet compel-

Figure 2 ■ Newspaper Circulation Has Remained Flat While Regular Readership Has Declined

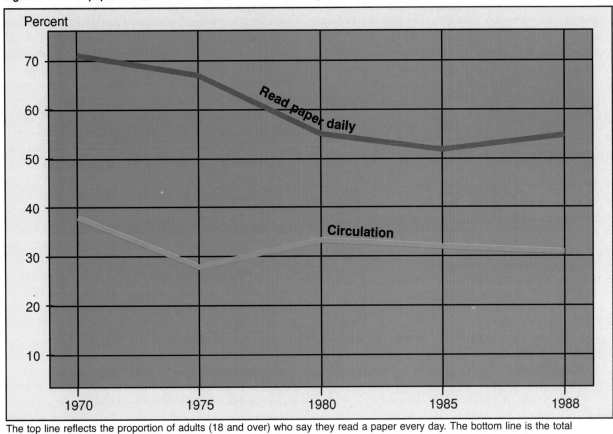

The top line reflects the proportion of adults (18 and over) who say they read a paper every day. The bottom line is the total newspaper circulation as a percentage of the total adult population.

Source: Statistical Abstract of the U.S., 1990, Table 914. NORC, General Social Survey Trend Tape Marginals, 1988.

ling. They were hypnotic for many viewers. But they were also fragmentary and sometimes contradictory. Newspapers presented more complete and accurate accounts the next day.

Concentration of the Media

While development of the media has led to the mass media, concentration of the media has led to a national media.

Alexis de Tocqueville, the Frenchman who traveled through the United States in the 1830s, found a flourishing newspaper in every hamlet he visited. Due to freedom of the press, the government could not restrict the number of papers the way European governments could and did. Yet de Tocqueville observed that the proliferation of papers presenting different news and views limited their potential power.

This diversity continued into the twentieth century. The media were local media. But in the 1930s economic pressures began to force many newspapers out of business and others into the arms of chains. Newsmagazines began to expand their circulation. In the late 1940s and early 1950s, television networks began to sign up local stations as affiliates. The networks were large enough to finance the development of entertainment programs, so the local stations came to depend upon their news shows as well. By the late 1950s and early 1960s, then, a national media had developed.[17]

Although media in this country, compared with those in other Western democracies, are relatively decentralized—in the United States there are approximately 1,700 daily newspapers, 10,000 radio stations, and 1,600 television stations[18]—these numbers are misleading. Newspaper chains own papers with more than 70% of the circulation in the country.[19] Media conglomerates own newspapers, magazines, radio stations, and television stations (although the Federal Communications Commission forbids them from owning more than one AM radio station, one FM radio station, and one television station in the same market, or more than twelve of each throughout the country). The result is that just 10 corporations control the following:

- 58 newspapers, including the *New York Times, Washington Post, Los Angeles Times,* and *Wall Street Journal;*
- 59 magazines, including *Time* and *Newsweek;*
- 41 book publishers;
- 3 major radio and television networks;
- 62 radio stations;
- 34 television stations;
- 201 cable television systems; and
- 20 record companies.[20]

Similarly, a small number of businesses garner a disproportionate amount of revenue. Six magazine companies, among 11,000 in the country, account for half the magazine revenue, and 6 book publishers, among 2,500 in the country, account for more than half the book revenue.[21]

These trends are likely to continue because the media business is big business. In the 1980s all three major networks were bought by giant corporations. In addition, Time, Inc., and Warner Communications, Inc., merged to become the world's largest media conglomerate. One economic analyst predicted "a frighteningly powerful company."[22]

Local television stations with satellite-linked vans can provide coverage of events independent of the television networks.

Just as important as the growth of chains and conglomerates is the dominance of a few sources of news. Two wire services—Associated Press (AP) and United Press International (UPI)—supply the international and national news for most newspapers. Three magazines—*Newsweek, Time,* and *U.S. News and World Report*—control the market of newsmagazines. Four radio networks—ABC, CBS, NBC, and Mutual—furnish the news for most radio listeners, and four television networks—ABC, CBS, NBC, and CNN—furnish the news for most television viewers. Consequently, the media present quite homogeneous international and national news.

Despite these trends toward concentration, there are some trends in the opposite direction. Magazines have become more specialized, with opinion magazines for readers all along the spectrum. Television also promises to become more specialized, with cable television offering a multitude of channels and network television losing its dominance. Increasingly, viewers are getting their news from local television. Local stations can join a consortium of other stations across the country and, linked by satellite, share coverage of events of national interest. This development allows the stations to put together their own newscasts independent of the networks. Even so, the media are far more centralized today than in de Tocqueville's time. Many of them represent a national media that presents a more uniform message and exercises a more powerful influence.

Relationship Between the Media and Politicians

"Politicians live—and sometimes die—by the press. The press lives by politicians," according to a former presidential aide. "This relationship is at the center of our national life."[23]

Journalists and politicians are preoccupied with each other. Journalists have to cover government, and politicians have to assess the impressions the media give the public because these impressions affect politicians' ability to accomplish their goals. Presidents, members of Congress, or their aides scan the major newspapers in the morning and the network newscasts in the evening. President Lyndon Johnson watched the three network newscasts on three televisions simultaneously.

The pervasiveness of the media has increased tremendously. Andrew Jackson was the first president to have his photograph taken. Modern presidents, such as Gerald Ford, must expect to have their photograph taken almost anywhere at almost any time.

The close relationship between the media and politicians is both a **symbiotic relationship,** meaning they use each other for their mutual advantage, and an **adversarial relationship,** meaning they fight each other.

Symbiotic Relationship

The media inform politicians of current events and public attitudes and provide politicians with opportunities to reach the public. In exchange, politicians give the media information to fill their news columns and newscasts.

To cover politicians, some reporters are assigned to monitor **beats.** Washington beats include the White House, Congress, Supreme Court, State Department, Defense Department, and some other departments and agencies. Other reporters are assigned to cover specialized subjects, such as economics, environmental problems, and energy issues, which are addressed by several branches, departments, or agencies.

The government has press secretaries and public information officers who provide reporters with ideas and information for stories. The number of these officials is significant; in one recent year the Defense

Department employed almost 1,500 people just to handle press relations.[24]

The government supplies reporters with a variety of news sources, including copies of speeches, summaries of committee meetings, news releases, and news briefings about current events. Officials also grant interviews, hold press conferences, and stage "media events." The vast majority of reporters rely on these sources rather than engage in more difficult and time-consuming investigative reporting.

Interviews show the symbiotic nature of the relationship between reporters and politicians. During the early months of the Reagan presidency, *Washington Post* writer William Greider had a series of 18 off-the-record meetings with budget director David Stockman. Greider recounted:

Stockman and I were participating in a fairly routine transaction of Washington, a form of submerged communication which takes place regularly between selected members of the press and the highest officials of government. Our mutual motivation, despite our different interests, was crassly self-serving. It did not need to be spelled out between us. I would use him and he would use me. . . . I had established a valuable peephole on the inner policy debates of the new administration.

And the young budget director had established a valuable connection with an important newspaper. I would get a jump on the unfolding strategies and decisions. He would be able to prod and influence the focus of our coverage, to communicate his views and positions under the cover of our "off the record" arrangement, to make known harsh assessments that a public official would not dare to voice in the more formal setting of a press conference, speech, or "on the record" interview.[25]

Interviews can result in **leaks**—disclosure of information officials do not want disclosed at that time. Leaks are rarely accidents. They are usually efforts by high-level officials in the administration, Congress, or bureaucracy to use publicity to help them accomplish some immediate aim. They might leak information about a proposed policy to test the water for it, without committing themselves or their offices to it in case intense opposition surfaces. Or, engaged in infighting with other officials, they might leak information to make the competitors or their policies look bad.

As the Republican Convention of 1988 neared, there was much speculation about whom George Bush would choose to be his running mate. Bush's campaign manager, James Baker, leaked the fact that Senator Dan Quayle was one of the finalists. Baker saw this as a way to discourage Bush from choosing Quayle; he thought once the *New York Times* published this fact, there would be so much opposition that Bush would have to select someone else. (Baker's ploy failed because the press did not take the idea seriously enough to criticize it.)[26]

When the congressional Iran-contra committees completed their reports assessing the Reagan administration's handling of the affair, Republicans on the committees leaked the minority report (Republican version) the day before the committees were scheduled to release their majority report. The Republicans' purpose was to confuse the public about an affair that was complicated but potentially highly damaging to President Reagan and Vice President Bush. After the *New York Times* printed the minority version, other media followed and included statements by the Republicans. As a result, the media were filled with attacks on a majority report that neither they nor the public had seen and that neither could evaluate yet. The *New York Times* recognized the Republicans' aim but let itself be used in order to be the first with the story.[27]

When reporters get information before other reporters, they can **scoop** them. In 1980 NBC correspondent Chris Wallace scooped his colleagues in reporting that Reagan would choose Bush as his running mate. Although Wallace was first by just seconds, this helped him win a promotion to NBC White House correspondent.[28] Usually, however, reporters are reluctant to be out front if their information is controversial. Most are more comfortable following their fellow reporters than scooping them.[29]

The interdependence between reporters and politicians can result in less news for the public. Reporters who want to continue to receive information and rub shoulders with powerful politicians may feel obligated to treat their sources favorably or at least not as skeptically as they treat others. When the Watergate burglary occurred, most newspapers dismissed it as an inconsequential "caper." With their close ties to high officials, reporters in the Washington press corps did not dig to unearth the story behind the burglary. Instead, two young reporters—Bob Woodward and Carl Bernstein—who covered local news for the *Washington Post* got the story. As one of the *Post's* editors noted, they were not part of "the Establishment"; they did not mind embarrassing administration officials.

Before the Iran-contra affair came to light, some reporters relied on Lt. Col. Oliver North for information. Although many reporters suspected that North was involved in supplying the contras with arms despite congressional restrictions on such aid, North had been a valuable source and, as one reporter remarked, "his romantic derring-do and colorful antics made him more fun to talk to than other bureaucrats."[30] Reporters did not investigate North's involvement until the story broke in an obscure Lebanese magazine. If they had been willing to sacrifice their access to him, they could have publicized the affair far sooner.

Press conferences also show the symbiotic nature of the media-politician relationship. Theodore Roosevelt started the **presidential press conference** with irregular and informal sessions, often while being shaved. Later presidents, uncomfortable with what they regarded as cross-examination, held fewer sessions and demanded questions in advance.

Franklin Roosevelt realized that the press conference could help him reach the public, much as his fireside chats had, even though many newspaper owners detested him and criticized him in editorials. By holding sessions twice weekly and allowing reporters

Teddy Roosevelt called the presidency a "bully pulpit" at which he could speak, through the press, to the people to persuade them to support his programs.

to pop questions on the spot, he provided a steady stream of news, which editors felt obligated to publish. This kept him in the public eye. Thus, his strategy was to circumvent the owners but still gain access to their audience.

John Kennedy allowed television to broadcast his press conferences live. Instead of informal sessions around the president's desk, the conference became a formal event, complete with a seating chart for reporters. Because it was televised, it provided the president an even greater opportunity to reach the public; editors could not filter his remarks. At the same time, the president could not be as open, he could not commit himself to a policy prematurely, and he could not allow himself to make a gaffe in front of a huge audience.

As a result, presidents and their aides transformed the conference into a carefully orchestrated media show. Now an administration schedules a conference when it wants to convey a particular message. It might

even limit questions to that topic. Aides identify potential questions, and the president rehearses appropriate answers. Aides occasionally have friendly reporters ask questions the president wants to answer. During the conference, the president calls on the reporters he wants. Although he cannot ignore those from the major media, he can call disproportionately on those he knows will ask soft questions. Consequently, the conference usually helps the president.

The introduction of television cameras to the press conference has made it less of a news source than the informal exchange around the president's desk, which used to reveal his thinking on plans and decisions. At most, the conference is an opportunity for the public to assess the president's ability to react to a few tough questions on the spot.

The transformation of the press conference has frustrated reporters and prompted them to act as prosecutors. As one presidential press secretary observed, reporters play a game of "I gotcha."[31] Still, reporters value the conference and criticize presidents who hold sessions infrequently. Editors consider the president's remarks news, so the conference helps reporters do their job. It also gives them a chance to bask in the limelight. Hence the jockeying for attention.

Media events also show the symbiotic nature of the media-politician relationship. These events are designed to convey an image of a politician's position on some issue. Whether simple announcements or more action-oriented performances, they are visually interesting to attract television cameras. For example, President Bush announced his clean air proposal in front of the Teton Mountains in Wyoming.

Media events do not feature classical orations or even cogent addresses with a beginning, middle, and end. Instead, they offer informal speeches emphasizing a few key words or phrases or sentences—almost slogans, because a television news story has time for only a short **sound bite.** As a former presidential aide explained, "A lot of writers figure out how they are going to get the part they want onto television. They think of a news lead and write around it. And if the television lights don't go on as the speaker is approaching that news lead, he skips a few paragraphs and waits until they are lit to read the key part."[32] This does not result in coherent speeches. But the

people watching on television will not know, and the few watching in person do not matter because they are just props anyway.

Media events do not always convey an accurate impression. When polls showed that the public thought Reagan slighted education because he cut federal money for student loans and for schools, he traveled across the country to meet with teachers and students in a series of media events covered by television. Then, according to an aide, "The polls absolutely flip-flopped. He went from a negative rating to a positive rating [on education] overnight."[33] Yet he did not change his policies at all. Bush unveiled his anticrime package at a police academy, but later it was noticed that his budget proposed cutting funds for this academy.[34]

Perhaps more than any other source of news, media events illustrate the reliance of politicians on television, and of television on politicians. The head of CBS News said, "I'd like just once to have the courage to go on the air and say that such and such a candidate went to six cities today to stage six media events, none of which had anything to do with governing America."[35] Yet television fosters these events, and despite occasional swipes by correspondents networks continue to show them.

Adversarial Relationship

Although the relationship between the media and politicians is symbiotic in some ways, it is adversarial in others. Since George Washington's administration, when conflicts developed between Federalists and Jeffersonians, the media have attacked politicians, and politicians have attacked the media. In John Adams's administration, Federalists passed the Sedition Act of 1798, which prohibited much criticism of the government. Federalists used the act to imprison Jeffersonian editors. Not long after, President Andrew Jackson proposed a law to allow the government to shut down "incendiary" newspapers. Even recently a former press secretary commented, "There are very few politicians who do not cherish privately the notion that there should be some regulation of the news."[36]

The conflict stems from a fundamental difference in perspectives. Politicians want the media to help them accomplish their goals, so they hope the media will pass along their messages to the public exactly as they deliver them. But journalists see themselves as servants not of the government but of the public. At least sometimes they question officials until the public

Sometimes media events are used to overcome a negative image. In the 1988 presidential campaign, Michael Dukakis was perceived by the public as weak on defense, so advisers had him strap on a helmet and ride in a tank. But this attempt was so transparent that it backfired.

"Hey, do you want to be on the news tonight or not? This is a sound bite, not the Gettysburg Address. Just say what you have to say, Senator, and get the hell off."

knows enough about a matter to hold the officials accountable. In this role they must be skeptical. According to ABC correspondent Sam Donaldson, "My job is not to say here's the church social with the apple pie, isn't it beautiful?"[37]

In contemporary society, information is power. The media and the government, especially the president, with the huge bureaucracy at his disposal, are the two primary sources of information. To the extent that the administration controls the flow of information, it can achieve its policy goals. To the extent that the media disseminate contradictory information, they can ensure that the administration's policy goals will be subject to public debate.

Inevitably politicians fall short of their goals. When they blame the media for their failures, many are confusing the message and the messenger, like Czar Peter the Great, who, when notified that the Russian army had lost a battle in 1700, promptly ordered the messenger strangled.

When President Kennedy became upset by the *New York Times* coverage of Vietnam, he asked the paper to transfer the correspondent out of Vietnam. (The paper refused.) When President Nixon became angry with major newspapers and networks, he had Vice President Agnew lash out at them. He also ordered the Department of Justice to investigate some media companies for possible antitrust violations and the Internal Revenue Service to audit a newspaper and a reporter for possible income tax violations.

The wariness between the media and politicians has increased since the Vietnam War and Watergate scandal fueled cynicism about government's performance and officials' truthfulness. Today the media are less trusting of politicians and less trusted by them.

Even so, it would be incorrect to think that the relationship between the media and politicians usually is adversarial. In fact, it normally is symbiotic. Although journalists like to think of themselves and try to portray themselves as adversaries who stand up to politicians, most rely upon politicians most of the time.[38]

Thus, despite the impression created by media coverage of Watergate, few journalists engage in investigative reporting. An examination of 224 incidents of criminal or unethical behavior by Reagan administration appointees found that only 13% were uncovered by reporters. Most were discovered through investigations by executive agencies or congressional committees, which then released the information to the press. Only incidents reflecting personal peccadillos of government officials, such as sexual offenses, were exposed first by reporters.[39] A $2-billion scandal involving influence peddling at the Department of Housing and Urban Development (HUD) went unnoticed by nearly all reporters until the department's inspector general and a congressional committee probed the payoffs. Yet HUD had been considered "a feeding trough" by Washington insiders for several years.[40]

Relationship Between the Media and the Reagan and Bush Administrations

The relationship between the media and the Reagan and Bush administrations, like that between the media and politicians generally, has been both symbiotic and adversarial.

No president used the media as extensively and effectively as Reagan. Before losing his effectiveness during his second term, the media dubbed Reagan the Great Communicator for his uncanny ability to communicate his broad themes.

The Reagan administration approached its relationship with the media as "political jujitsu."[41] A jujitsu fighter tries to use the adversary's force to his or her own advantage through a clever maneuver. The administration knew the media would cover the president extensively to fill their news columns or newscasts. Aide Michael Deaver explained the strategy: "The media, while they won't admit it, are not in the news business; they're in entertainment. We tried to create the most entertaining, visually attractive scene to fill that box, so that the networks would have to use it."[42]

Deaver spared no effort or expense to satisfy the demands of television and enhance the image of the president at the same time. Deaver sent advance agents days or weeks ahead of the president to prepare the "stage" for media events—the specific location, backdrops, lighting, and sound equipment. A trip to Korea was designed to show "the commander in chief on the front line against communism." The advance man went to the demilitarized zone separating North and South Korea and negotiated with the army and the Secret Service for the most photogenic setting possible. He demanded that the president be able to use the most exposed bunker, which meant that the army had to erect telephone poles and string 30,000 yards of camouflage netting from them to hide Reagan from North Korean sharpshooters. The advance man also demanded that the army build camera platforms on a hill that remained exposed but offered the most dramatic angle to film Reagan surrounded by sandbags.

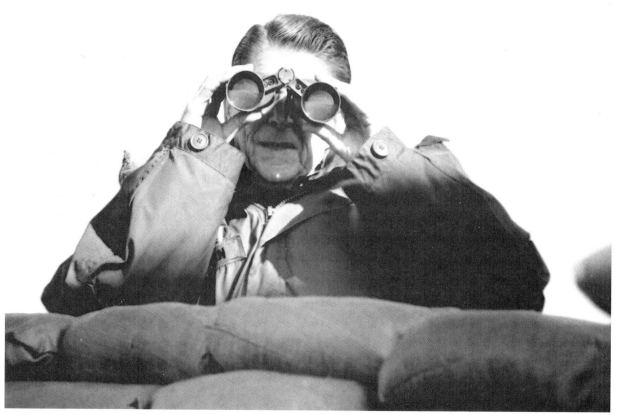

President Reagan, staged to reflect "American strength and resolve" in Korea.

Although the Secret Service wanted sandbags up to Reagan's neck, the advance man insisted that they be no more than four inches above his navel so viewers would get a clear picture of the president wearing his flak jacket and demonstrating "American strength and resolve."[43]

It did not seem to matter that there was little connection between what the president was doing and what actually was happening. When U.S. planes shot down two Libyan jets, Reagan was helicoptered to the deck of an aircraft carrier—off the coast of California, not Libya—for a triumphant photo opportunity.[44]

On a day-to-day basis, the administration planned its operations around its relationship with the media. In the morning aides met to plan public relations strategy for the day. They determined what "the line of the day"—the message—would be. They considered what questions the president would be asked and what answers he should give, and then they briefed him. Later in the day, after all his appearances, aides called each network to learn what stories about the president or his policies it was going to use on its evening newscast. If they were not satisfied, they tried to convince the network to change its lineup. At night aides met to evaluate the success of their strategy. They often called each network to praise or criticize its coverage.[45]

To set the agenda, and to prevent the media from doing it, the administration tried to control the president's appearances and comments. Aides especially worried that Reagan's off-the-cuff comments would reveal his limited command of the facts and details behind his policies or would result in a blooper, such as the time he said that trees cause most air pollution. To keep such comments from damaging his image or at least overshadowing his message for the day, aides provided few opportunities for reporters to ask questions. When reporters asked questions inside a building, aides frequently demanded the television lights be shut off so that any answers could not be televised; outside they often ordered the helicopter's engines revved up so that the questions would be drowned out. Aides had Secret Service agents push reporters away from the president at the same time they allowed strangers to approach and shake hands with him. Once when a reporter got close enough to ask a question, Reagan revealed the strategy: "If I answer that question, none of you will say anything about what we're here for today. I'm not going to give you a different lead."[46]

Reagan's press conferences were also infrequent. With about six a year, he held far fewer than other recent presidents except Nixon.[47] Although press conferences normally benefit presidents, they are subject to less control than media events. Reagan's aides considered them too risky.

Paradoxically, Reagan was the most visible but least accessible president in modern times. By alternately using and avoiding the media, his administration succeeded in managing the news more than any other administration.

Perhaps the clearest example of the administration's efforts to manage the news occurred when Reagan ordered the invasion of Grenada in 1983. The administration excluded reporters from the invasion force and turned back reporters who arrived on the island on their own. For two days the only news that reached the public came from the administration, and it was uniformly positive about both the need for the invasion and its success.

The Bush administration generally has taken a different approach. Although the president has some of the same advisers, he does not have the same ability to appeal to the public on television. So the administration has tried to deemphasize television appearances in favor of more informal get-togethers with reporters, where his grasp of issues comes across. Bush has held frequent press conferences—more in his first year and a half than Reagan held in his eight years—and many mini–press conferences. He has even telephoned reporters to talk and invited them to jog with him. In these ways he has tried to reach the public indirectly—by impressing the reporters and hoping they will give him favorable coverage.

For the invasion of Panama in 1989 and war with Iraq in 1991, however, the Bush administration insisted on strict control and censorship rather than accessibility and openness. In response to media criticism that reporters were excluded from Grenada, the Pentagon established a pool system for future wars. Pools, representative groups of reporters, would be assigned to cover the action and share their reports with other media. The military could transport and protect a few pools more easily than a huge number of individual journalists. Also, it could restrict release of sensitive information more surely.

But military incompetence and political resistance prevented the pool system from working when the United States invaded Panama to force General Manuel Noriega from office. Reporters were delayed arriving in Panama and then delayed transmitting their dispatches back to the United States. They were prevented from seeing most battles out of fear that they would witness civilian casualties. Consequently, despite later indications of many civilian casualties, we may never learn what really happened in this operation.[48]

Yet because there were few negative news stories, the Pentagon and Bush administration were satisfied with the results and used a similar system when the United States fought Iraq. Approximately 800 reporters tried to cover the war. About 100 at a time were escorted to locations where American troops were living or fighting. Reporters were permitted to interview soldiers only when supervised by their officers. Reporters who ventured off on their own were arrested, detained, and threatened with the loss of their credentials. Even one caught interviewing Saudi Arabian shopkeepers was treated this way by U.S. officials.[49]

Before dispatches could be sent back to the United States, they had to be cleared by military censors. Though the stated purpose was to prevent release of information that could jeopardize the safety of U.S. troops, sometimes the apparent purpose was to prevent release of information that could put the U.S. military in a bad light. One censor blocked a story that

said pilots were watching pornographic movies before bombing missions, while another changed a story that said pilots were "giddy" after a mission. (Instead, the censor described them as "proud.")[50] Yet, according to reporters, censorship was not nearly the problem as lack of access and information.

The Pentagon was most sensitive about casualties, whether American or Iraqi. Officials' concern went far beyond the possibility that television might show a dead soldier before his or her kin could be notified. They worried that pictures of dead or wounded Americans would cause the public to turn against the war. Likewise, they worried that information about injured Iraqi civilians or destroyed homes would weaken support for the war. Little information has been released about the extent of casualties and destruction in Iraq.

One example indicates the conflicting positions and the self-serving nature of both the administration and the media. In other recent wars, the dead bodies of American troops were flown back through Dover Air Force base in Delaware where the military held a brief ceremony for the families. The media were permitted to view, and photograph, the ceremony and

Source: Don Wright, The Palm Beach Post.

Due to military restrictions, reporters, such as these in a hotel in Saudi Arabia, had to rely on television newscasts for much of their information about the Persian Gulf War.

closed caskets. In this war, the administration eliminated the ceremony and the opportunity to photograph the caskets. The alleged reason was "national security," though journalists were allowed on base other times. The real reason was that officials shuddered at the thought of pictures of caskets piled high. The media complained that they were denied access to news. Actually, they wanted pictures they could get easily and use for human interest stories rather than focus on more substantial news about the war.

As a result of the administration's management of the news, television showed film of one precise bombing attack after another. Commentators lauded the "smart" bombs that were so accurate it was like having them "delivered by Federal Express." On television the war looked like a Nintendo game—without real casualties. Yet after the war one official said only 7% of the bombs dropped were "smart" bombs, and another said only 25% of the other bombs hit their targets. This means that at least 61,000 tons of bombs landed where they were not supposed to.[51]

Although the public was engrossed in media coverage of the war, polls showed that most Americans approved the military's control of the news, and a majority even thought the military should have more control of the news. Only 19% thought the military was "hiding bad news from the public."[52] People almost seemed to think that if they did not hear bad news, it meant that there was none.

The military used the media in a more direct way as well. By lying to or misleading reporters, they deceived the Iraqis. Early during the buildup of U.S. forces in the region, they announced larger numbers

of troops than existed, so Iraq would not attack Saudi Arabia. The CIA planted a false report that 60 Iraqi tanks and their crews had defected to prompt some to do so. Days before the ground war began, the military took pools to see amphibious landing rehearsals for a landing that the military did not plan, so Iraq would expect the allies to move this direction. Unlike the restrictions on access and the censorship, however, the military's use of the media in these ways reflected real security concerns.

Bias of the Media

Every night Walter Cronkite, former anchor for CBS Evening News, signed off, "And that's the way it is." His statement implied that the network reported the news exactly the way it happened, that the network held a huge mirror to the world and reflected it to the viewers—without any distortion.

Yet the media do not act like a mirror. They act more like a searchlight that seeks and illuminates some things instead of others.[53]

From all the events that occur in the world every day, the media can report only a handful as the news of the day. Even the fat *New York Times,* whose motto is "All the News That's Fit to Print," cannot include all the news. The media must decide what events are newsworthy. When the Wright brothers invited reporters to Kitty Hawk, North Carolina, to observe the first plane flight in 1903, none thought it was newsworthy enough to cover. After the historic flight, only seven American newspapers reported it, and only two reported it on the front page.[54]

After the media decide what events to report, they must decide where to report them—on the front page or top of the newscast, or in a less prominent position. Then they must decide how to report them. Except for magazines, most media attempt to be "objective"; that is, they try to present facts rather than their opinions. Where the facts are in dispute, they try to present the positions of both sides. They are reluctant to evaluate these positions, although sometimes they do explain or interpret them.

In making these decisions, it would be natural for journalists' attitudes to affect their coverage. As one acknowledged, a reporter writes "from what he hears and sees and how he filters it through the lens of his own experience. No reporter is a robot."[55]

The Power of Pictures

During the 1984 presidential campaign, CBS aired a tough commentary by correspondent Lesley Stahl. The four-and-a-half-minute piece accused the Reagan administration of using media events "to create amnesia" about the president's political record:

> He's been criticized as the rich man's president, but the TV pictures say it isn't so. At 73, Mr. Reagan could have an age problem. But the TV pictures say it isn't so. Americans want to feel proud of their country again, and of their president. And the TV pictures say you can.

Then Stahl said the administration "tried to counter the memory of an unpopular issue with a carefully chosen backdrop that actually contradicts the president's policy." She noted that he had tried to cut funding for programs for the disabled and housing for the elderly, while appearing on television greeting handicapped athletes in wheelchairs and cutting the ribbon at a nursing home. She said the administration also tried to distance the president from bad news by having him "disappear, as he did the day he pulled the marines out of Lebanon. He flew off to his California ranch, leaving others to hand out the announcement."

She concluded:

> President Reagan is accused of running a campaign in which he highlights the images and hides from the issues. But there's no evidence that the charges will hurt him because when people see the president on television, he makes them feel good, about America, about themselves, and about him.

While Stahl was talking, television was showing a montage of visuals to illustrate her piece: Reagan pumping iron; throwing a football with Secret Service agents; hugging Olympic gold-medal winner Mary Lou Retton; paying tribute to American servicemen who died at the D-Day landing on Normandy beach in World War II; mingling with blacks in an inner city and whites in a suburb; talking with farmers in a field; receiving a birthday cake and a kiss from Nancy; and standing in a sea of supporters while red, white, and blue balloons floated to the sky.

"I thought it was the single toughest piece I had ever done on Reagan," Stahl said. "The piece aired, and my phone rang.

> "[The Reagan aide] said, 'Great piece.'
> "I said, 'What?'
> "And he said, 'Great piece.'
> "I said, 'Did you listen to what I said?'

"He said, 'Lesley, when you're showing four and a half minutes of great pictures of Ronald Reagan, no one listens to what you say. Don't you know that the pictures are overriding your message because they conflict with your message? The public sees those pictures and they block your message. They didn't even hear what you said. So, in our minds, it was a four-and-a-half-minute free ad for the Ronald Reagan campaign for reelection.'

"I sat here numb. I began to feel dumb 'cause I'd covered him four years and I hadn't figured it out."

Source: Hedrick Smith, *The Power Game* (New York: Random House, 1988), pp. 412–14.

Political Bias

Historically, the press was politically biased. The party papers, which were established by political parties, parroted the party line. Even the independent papers, which succeeded them, advocated one side or the other. Publishers', editors', and reporters' attitudes seeped—sometimes flooded—into their prose. But papers gradually abandoned their ardor for editorializing and adopted the practice of objectivity to retain as many of their readers as possible.

Yet the public thinks that the press is still biased. According to one survey, 41% think that the press is "out to get" the groups they identify with: executives believe the press is out to get businesses, and laborers believe it is out to get unions. Liberals believe it is biased against liberals, and conservatives believe it is biased against conservatives.[56]

Bias for Established Institutions and Values. The media generally do reflect a bias for established institutions and values. This should not come as a surprise. Because the media are major businesses owned by large corporations, and because they need to retain their readers and viewers to make a profit, they consciously or unconsciously mirror the mainstream.

The media have a long history of bias against other ideologies, such as communism or even democratic socialism. The failures of noncapitalist economic systems are played up, the successes played down. In foreign policy matters, the U.S. government line usually is adopted. During the cold war, this meant harsh attacks on the Soviet Union, and in recent years, it often has meant sharp criticisms of leftist Latin American countries.[57]

Correlated with the media's support for established institutions and values is their reliance upon government officials for their news. A study of front-page stories from the *New York Times* and *Washington Post* over two decades found that 74% were based on statements by U.S. government officials.[58] This is striking considering that these papers have far more staffers and resources to do investigative journalism than other papers. Such heavy reliance upon government officials means that the stories are likely to bear their strong imprint. Similarly, a study of ABC's "Nightline," which features news and interviews, found that 80% of the Americans interviewed on the program were from the government or corporate establishment (and 90% of these were white males). The watchdog group Fairness & Accuracy In Reporting (FAIR) found that representatives from peace, environmental, consumer, or labor groups were "hardly visible."[59]

Bias for Particular Candidates and Policies.   Most debate about media bias revolves around charges that the media exhibit a preference for particular candidates and policies over others. Conservative groups, in particular, claim that the media are biased toward liberal candidates and policies, and they have gone so far as to mount an effort to buy CBS in order to change its newscasts.

In studying media bias, social scientists have examined the characteristics and behavior of journalists. They have found that journalists are not very representative of the public. They are disproportionately white males from the upper middle class with a college degree. Further, they are disproportionately urban, especially from the Northeast, and secular, rather than rural and religious. Moreover, they identify themselves disproportionately as Democrats or independents leaning to the Democrats, rather than Republicans or independents leaning to the Republicans. Likewise, they identify themselves disproportionately as liberals rather than conservatives.[60]

But journalists do differ among themselves. Those who work for the prominent, influential organizations—large newspapers, wire services, newsmagazines, and radio and television networks—are more likely to be Democrats and liberals than those who work for nonprominent organizations—small newspapers and radio and television stations.[61]

As would be expected, journalists in prominent organizations are more likely than the public to support the liberal position on issues. Large majorities support homosexuals' right to teach in public schools and affirmative action. They are also suspicious of big business, believing it is the sector of society that exerts the most influence but should exert much less.[62] At the same time, they support capitalism. Large majorities think businesses should be owned privately rather than publicly; businesses should be regulated less than they are; and businesses are fair to their workers. According to one study, 73% do not think that our institutions "need overhaul."[63] Thus, although these journalists are likely to be liberals, they are hardly extreme liberals or radicals.

These findings might seem to support the charge that the media are biased against conservatives, but this assumes that journalists' attitudes necessarily color what they report. Several factors mitigate the effect of journalists' attitudes. For one thing, journalists do not seem to have intense opinions. Most did not become journalists because of a commitment to political ideology but because of the opportunity to rub elbows with powerful people and be close to exciting events. "Each day brings new stories, new dramas in which journalists participate vicariously."[64] As a result, most "care more about the politics of an issue than about the issue itself,"[65] which makes them less likely to voice their views about the issue.

In addition, media organizations pressure journalists to muffle their views, partly out of a conviction that it is more professional to do so and partly out of a desire to avoid the headaches that could arise otherwise—debates among their staffers, complaints from their local radio and television affiliates, complaints from their audience, perhaps even complaints from the White House, Congress, or the Federal Communications Commission (FCC), which licenses them. Sometimes media executives or editors pressure reporters because they have contrary views. Reporters learn not to explore certain subjects, not to ask certain questions. Reporters who pursue the stories regardless might find their copy edited, with the most critical portions deleted. The *New York Times,* despite its liberal reputation, has altered reporters' stories on foreign affairs to hew more closely to the administration's line.[66] CBS toned down correspondents' stories about Reagan's economic policies.[67] Reporters who pursue the stories might find themselves transferred to another beat. One who covered El Salvador for the *New York Times* wrote a series of reports about the government's massacre of nearly a thousand peasants. The reports contradicted Reagan's assertions that the nation was making great strides in human rights. Under pressure, the *Times* pulled him off this beat.[68] Ultimately, reporters who pursue the stories could find themselves fired.[69]

For all of these reasons the media do not exhibit nearly as much **political bias** as would be expected from their journalists' attitudes. Although they do show a bias for established institutions and values, they do not show much bias for particular candidates in elections.

To measure bias, researchers use a technique called "content analysis." They scrutinize newspaper and television stories to determine whether there was an unequal amount of coverage, unequal use of favorable or unfavorable statements, or unequal use of a positive or negative tone. They consider insinuating verbs ("he conceded" rather than "he said") and pejorative adjectives ("her weak response" rather than "her response"), and for television stories they evaluate the announcer's nonverbal communication—voice inflection, eye movement, and body language.

Studies of the coverage of several presidential campaigns by the television networks and a wire service found relatively little bias. The media typically gave the two candidates equal attention and rarely made a favorable or unfavorable statement about them or used a positive or negative tone discussing them.[70]

At most, the studies found some bias against incumbents, front-runners, or emerging challengers. That is, the media might have stricter standards for the top dogs.[71] During the campaign for the Democratic presidential nomination in 1988, reporters treated Jesse Jackson favorably as a spokesman for the oppressed and as a power broker between competing factions in the party. But once Jackson won the Michigan caucuses, reporters began to ask pointed questions about his "administrative inexperience," "ties to the Arab world," and other vulnerabilities.

If the media find a real weakness, they might continue until the victim erases their doubts or the public

loses interest. During the presidential campaign in 1988, reporters suggested that Dan Quayle had too little experience and too few qualifications to be vice president. The charges continued through the campaign, because his behavior did little to dispel them.

Overall, however, political bias for or against candidates during election campaigns seems insignificant. When candidates complain, they usually are objecting to reports of bad news.

There are two exceptions to this generalization. First, the media usually give short shrift to third-party candidates. Second, newspapers traditionally print editorials and columns that express opinions. In editorials before elections, papers often endorse candidates. Most owners are Republican, and this is one time many seek to influence the content of their papers. Since the first survey in 1932, more papers have endorsed the Republican presidential candidate, except in the election between Democratic President Lyndon Johnson and Republican Senator Barry Goldwater in 1964.

The relative lack of bias in coverage of elections does not necessarily mean there is a lack of bias in coverage of other events. Because elections are highly visible and candidates are very sensitive about the coverage, the media might take more care to be neutral here than elsewhere. Researchers have not examined coverage of other events as much. Some think that journalists' liberal attitudes do surface. A study of coverage of nuclear energy found an evolution from slightly pro- to strongly anti-nuclear power during the 1970s,[72] while one of school busing found a tilt for busing during the same decade.[73] Yet an analysis of news about the Iranian hostage seizure and the Soviet invasion of Afghanistan, both in 1980, revealed a slight conservative bias by CBS and UPI.[74]

Bias Against All Candidates and Policies.   Some critics charge that there is a general bias against all candidates and policies—a negative undercurrent in reporting about government, regardless of who or what is covered. President Nixon's first vice president, Spiro Agnew, called journalists "nattering nabobs of negativism." Critics think that this bias increased after the Watergate scandal made reporters more cynical.

There seems to be some validity to this charge. Analyses of newspapers, magazines, and television networks show that the overwhelming majority of the stories about government are neutral.[75] However, the rest of the stories are more often negative than positive.[76]

Despite a tendency toward negativism, the tone appears to vary depending on the medium and the institution covered. Television is more critical than newspapers and magazines,[77] and Congress is more criticized than the president.[78] For example, after reporting that the Supreme Court gave Congress 30 days to revamp an independent regulatory commission, NBC anchor David Brinkley remarked, "It is widely believed in Washington that it would take Congress 30 days to make instant coffee."[79] The tone also appears to vary from the national media to the local media. The national media, whose reporters are better educated and more experienced in national affairs, are far more critical.

The emphasis upon the negative rather than the positive has led some researchers to conclude that newspapers and especially television foster **media malaise** among the public.[80] This is a feeling of cynicism and distrust, perhaps even despair, toward the government and its officials. Although this feeling probably originates among people who are politically unsophisticated, and therefore more easily disillusioned, researchers think that the feeling eventually infects others too.

Commercial Bias

Except for public radio and television networks and stations, American media are private businesses run for a profit. To make a profit, they must sell subscriptions and advertising. The larger the audience, the higher the price they can charge for advertising. A change of 1% in the ratings of a television news program in New York City, for example, can mean a difference of $5 million in advertising revenues for a station in a year.[81] The potential to make a profit is so enormous that CBS's "60 Minutes," the most watched program during some recent years, made more money in its first decade on the air than the entire Chrysler Corporation in the same decade.[82]

The need to attract an audience shapes the media's presentation of the news tremendously. In this sense there is a **commercial bias** in the news. Sometimes this means that the media deliberately print or broadcast what advertisers want. At the request of the gas company sponsoring the drama "Judgment at Nuremberg," one network bleeped the words "gas ovens" from descriptions of the Nazis' war crimes.[83] Other times the media censor themselves. When the auto industry was pressuring Congress to repeal seat-belt

and air-bag regulations in 1973 and 1974, the *New York Times* publisher urged the editors to present the auto industry position because it "would affect the advertising."[84] Numerous magazines have avoided references to the dangers of smoking in articles broadly focused on health for fear of losing advertising from tobacco companies. *Ms.* magazine, generally attentive to women's health, even avoided references to the increased dangers of smoking during pregnancy (at a time when it was still accepting advertising).[85]

Usually, though, commercial bias means that the media must print or broadcast what the public wants, and this means that the media must entertain readers and viewers. This creates a "conflict between being an honest reporter and being a member of show business," network correspondent Roger Mudd confessed, "and that conflict is with me every day."[86]

The dilemma is most marked for television. Many people who watch television news are not interested in politics; in fact, a majority say it covers too much politics.[87] Some watch the news because they were watching another program before the news and left the television on, others because they were going to watch another program after the news and turned the television on early. Networks feel pressure "to hook them and keep them."[88]

Therefore, networks try to make the everyday world of news seem as exciting as the make-believe world they depict in their other programs. One network instructed its staff: "Every news story should, without any sacrifice of probity or responsibility, display the attributes of fiction, of drama. It should have structure and conflict, problem and denouement, rising action and falling action, a beginning, a middle and an end."[89] As one executive says, television news is "info-tainment."[90]

Although television anchors and newscasters help determine the content of their newscasts, they are not hired strictly for their journalistic experience and ability but partly for their appearance and personality. They become show business stars. To enhance their appeal, networks and stations shape their image, ordering them to change their hairstyle and even, with tinted contact lenses, their eye color. They set up clothes calendars so newscasters will rotate their outfits regularly.

Although appearance is important for both men and women newscasters, it is especially crucial for women. While viewers accept men aging on the screen, they do not seem to accept women aging. As one woman anchor commented, "The guys have got white hair, and the girls look like cheerleaders."[91]

The commercial bias of the media has a number of consequences. The primary one is emphasis on human interest stories. In 1980 UPI and CBS carried seven times more stories about President Jimmy Carter's beer-drinking brother, Billy, than about the Strategic Arms Limitation Talks (SALT) between the United States and the Soviet Union.[92] By 1990, the networks had mentioned President Bush's dog, Millie, in more stories than three cabinet secretaries.[93] In 1988 a pair of whales got trapped under ice in the Arctic. Their plight and rescue efforts, which took three weeks, new technology, and cooperation with the Soviet Union, received daily coverage. Yet efforts to restrict whaling, which results in the slaughter of many whales, receive less attention because they involve more complex policies and less human interest.

The emphasis on human interest stories also means an emphasis upon crime and sex. During the 1976 presidential campaign, Carter gave an interview to *Playboy* magazine and, in a short portion of the long interview, admitted that he had "looked on a lot of women with lust. I've committed adultery in my heart many times." The media seized upon this quotation and ignored the rest of the interview. In fact, they gave more play to Carter's comments about sex than *Playboy* itself did.

Source: BIZARRO cartoon by Dan Piraro, reprinted by permission of Chronicle Features, San Francisco, California.

The emphasis on human interest stories also means a focus on which candidate in an election is going to win, rather than on the issues and which candidate should win. The media cover elections as horse races, with "front-runners" and "dark horses" (see table 1).

The emphasis upon human interest stories and horse-race aspects of an election led one observer to summarize the 1976 presidential campaign as follows:

> I saw President Ford bump his head leaving an airplane. . . . I saw Carter playing softball in Plains, Georgia. I saw Carter kissing [daughter] Amy, I saw Carter hugging [mother] Lillian. I saw Carter, in dungarees, walking hand in hand through the peanut farm with [wife] Rosalyn. I saw Carter going to church, coming out of church. . . . I saw Ford misstate the problems of Eastern Europe—and a week of people commenting about his misstatement. I saw Ford bump his head again. I saw Ford in Ohio say how glad he was to be back in Iowa. I saw marching bands and hecklers, and I learned about the size of crowds and the significance of the size of crowds. . . .
>
> But in all the hours of high anxiety that I spent watching the network news, never did I hear what the candidates had to say about the campaign issues. That was not news.[94]

In the 1988 presidential campaign, the focus on the horse race accounted for the bulk of the coverage.[95] Even during the primaries, one-third of all network stories on the campaign referred to candidates' poll standings.[96] This is remarkable so early in the campaign, when most citizens know little about most candidates. It is likely that many citizens exposed to this coverage knew where the candidates were running in the race but not where they stood on the issues.

Contrary to common perceptions, this focus is not confined to television. It is typical of print media as well. An examination of coverage of presidential campaigns by five metropolitan newspapers from 1888 through 1988 demonstrates that the emphasis on horse-race aspects of campaigning was a staple of journalism long before the advent of broadcast media.[97]

This focus continues even after the election. During Reagan's first term, social programs were cut, taxes were cut significantly, and military spending was increased sharply, but the main theme of media coverage was whether Reagan was "winning" or "losing" his battles with Congress and the bureaucracy.

Another consequence of commercial bias is emphasis upon conflict rather than consensus. Stories

Table 1 ■ Presidential Election News Emphasizes the Horse Race

According to a study of the 1976 presidential campaign, the media devoted considerably more attention to the horse-race aspects than the substance. But note the differences among the media.

Subject of Coverage	Los Angeles Times	Time, Newsweek	ABC, CBS, NBC Evening News
Horse race	51%	54%	58%
Winning and losing	20	23	24
Strategy and logistics	19	22	17
Appearances and hoopla	12	9	17
Substance	35	32	29
Issues	21	17	18
Candidates' characteristics and records	8	11	7
Endorsements	6	4	4
Other	14	14	13

Source: Thomas E. Patterson, *The Mass Media Election* (New York: Praeger, 1980), p. 24.

with conflict, protest, and violence generate more drama. During the urban unrest in the late 1960s, one reporter noted that the media "placed a premium on the rhetoric of violence. Black leaders who talked thoughtfully, at press conferences, about hopes and plans for peaceful change tended not to make it on the evening news; those who warned of riots and destruction often had greater success."[98]

The commercial bias of the media leads to certain consequences for television specifically. One is emphasis on events, or those parts of events, that have visual interest. The networks have people whose job is to evaluate all film for visual appeal. Producers seek the events that promise the most action; camera operators shoot the parts of the events with the most action; and editors select the portions of the film with the most action.[99] Television thus focuses on disasters, crimes, and protests far more than these actually occur, and when it covers other events, it focuses on the most exciting aspects of them. It distorts reality in order to hold the viewers' attention. In the summer of 1988, fires raged through Yellowstone National Park. Television showed a wall of flame night after night and called the park "a moonscape." As one lifeless scene followed another on the screen, NBC's Tom Brokaw intoned, "This is what's left of Yellowstone tonight." The effect, according to a journalism study, was to create the impression that our first national park was completely burned. Yet three-fourths of the park, including its famed geysers and waterfalls, was nearly unscathed. And, according to biologists, fire plays a

natural and necessary role in the ecosystem of the park.[100]

For the environment, this emphasis on visual interest results in coverage of disasters over more important news. The Alaska oil spill, with its ooze and otters, took precedence over such hazards as ozone depletion and global warming, which are too gradual to offer many photo opportunities. (A frustrated environmentalist asked, "How do you take a picture of the earth getting hotter?") Despite scientists' repeated statements, it took the hellishly hot summer of 1988, whose heat probably was coincidental rather than the result of global warming, for the media to take notice of the greenhouse effect.[101]

For many matters, the emphasis on visual interest results in coverage of the interesting surface of events over the underlying substance—the protest but not the cause. When blacks rioted in the 1960s, the burning and looting were extensively covered, but the conditions in the ghettos that fueled the riots were barely noted. When Iranians seized the American embassy and employees, the demonstrators discovered television's appetite for visual interest and teased it almost every night for more than a year. As the cameras arrived, they erupted with wild chants and threats, hung Jimmy Carter effigies, and shredded American flags. Yet the reasons for the seizure were only briefly mentioned.

The pressure for visual interest even led ABC to show staged footage in 1989. When American diplomat Felix Bloch was suspected of spying for the Soviet

Yellowstone National Park springs back to life after the fire.

Union, the network simulated an incident that was being investigated. Shot to look as if it came from a hidden camera, the film showed a man who looked like Bloch hand a briefcase to another man, while a voice-over said that intelligence sources believed that Bloch had delivered a briefcase of sensitive information to a KGB agent. It appeared that the camera had recorded an actual crime instead of a simulation of an alleged incident.

Another consequence of commercial bias for television is that it can cover the news only briefly. In a half-hour newscast, there are only 22 minutes without commercials. In that time, the networks broadcast only about one-third as many words as the *New York Times* prints on its front page alone. Television conveys additional information visually, but even so, the contrast in the amount of information these media transmit is striking.

The stories are short—about one minute each— because the time is short and because the networks think viewers' attention spans are short. Indeed, a survey found that a majority of 18- to 34-year-olds who have remote controls typically watch more than one show at once.[102] Thus, networks do not allow leaders or experts to explain their thoughts about particular events or policies. Instead, networks take sound bites to illustrate what was said. Although correspondents themselves take more time to talk, usually they do not have enough time to explain the events or policies or to provide background information about them. The newscast is essentially a headline service, which for many viewers amounts to a bewildering variety of short snippets not developed enough to be understood.

A network correspondent stationed in Lebanon was asked what went through his mind when he signed off each night. "Good night, dear viewer," he said. "I only hope you read the *New York Times* in the morning."[103]

The networks have tried to expand to a full hour newscast, but local affiliates have resisted because the networks would sell commercials for the extra time and the affiliates would lose revenue they generate during this period. Regardless, there is no guarantee that a longer newscast would be a better newscast. It might be just more of the same.

Altogether these factors mean that television news tends to be superficial. As former NBC anchor John Chancellor acknowledged, "Politicians deal in a world of complexity . . . [but] television deals in a world of simplicity."[104]

Aside from the need to appeal to the average viewer, there is no inherent reason that television news must simplify things. With its visual capability, it has the potential to explain things well. Occasionally it fulfills this potential, usually in a special report or documentary. Yet local affiliates often choose not to run these because they think that they can draw more viewers with reruns or old movies.

In sum, the commercial bias of the media, especially television, limits the quality of the news presented. This, more than any political bias, makes it difficult for citizens, particularly those who rely on television, to become well informed.

Impact of the Media on Politics

It is difficult to measure the impact of the media on politics. Different media provide different coverage and reach different though overlapping audiences. Because other factors besides the media influence people's knowledge, attitudes, and behavior toward politics, it is exceedingly difficult to isolate the impact of particular media on particular groups of people. But there is considerable agreement that the media have a substantial impact on the public agenda, political parties and elections, public opinion, and policies.

Impact on the Public Agenda

The most important impact of the media is in **setting the agenda**—influencing the process by which problems are considered important and alternative policies are proposed and debated.[105] The media publicize an

their personalities? Is it appropriate to speak of winning and losing when governing a democratic society requires mostly negotiating and compromising? Yet, according to the media, debates are akin to boxing matches. "There is talk of keeping the pressure on, of pounding away at this issue or that, of drawing blood, even of scoring a knockout."[2]

Consequently, even before the debates begin, the contenders engage in skirmishes over the schedule and format. In 1988 Dukakis, who was considered a better debater, wanted three 90-minute debates, whereas Bush wanted two 60-minute debates. Then Dukakis wanted one to focus on foreign affairs and the other on domestic matters. Bush, who was more experienced in foreign affairs, insisted that both be on a variety of issues. He feared that if Dukakis held his own during an entire debate on foreign affairs, claims that Bush was more experienced would lose their impact.

The candidates even engage in skirmishes over the props. In 1976 Ford, who was tall, wanted both candidates to use a tall podium so that Carter, who was shorter, would seem even shorter than he was. Carter wanted both candidates to use a short podium, so he would seem taller than he was. (They agreed to a medium-size podium.)

In preparation for debates, the candidates are coached to modulate their voice, make eye contact with the audience, and use appropriate body language. They are confronted by a stand-in for their opponent. The candidates practice their answers and even their jokes. In 1980 Reagan used the line, "There you go again," as though he caught Carter lying or at least exaggerating about Reagan's statements and proposals. The line was devastating, in part because it seemed spontaneous, as though Reagan had finally had enough and could no longer contain his exasperation. But in practice Reagan had tried several cracks, settled on this one, and rehearsed it. The line lingered as one of the most memorable aspects of the debate.

Once debates begin, the candidates engage in still more skirmishes unrelated to the substance of the debates. For the vice presidential debate in 1984, George Bush

asked to be addressed as "Mr. Vice President," and Geraldine Ferraro asked to be addressed as "Congresswoman Ferraro." Yet throughout the debate Bush called her "Mrs. Ferraro" to diminish her stature in the eyes of the viewers. In 1988 the tables were turned when Dukakis called the vice president "George."

The emphasis on winning is all the more troubling because "winning" is sometimes defined in such trivial terms. It might be based on which candidate looks or sounds better or which one seems more comfortable and therefore, somehow, more presidential. It might depend on which is quicker with the sidestep or comeback. Or it might come down to a gaffe.

In 1988, according to polls, Dukakis won the first debate, but Bush won the second debate big. The reason? He "triumphed in the congeniality competition."[3] He seemed more warm and likeable.

Do Debates Symbolize Important Values?

Perhaps debates symbolize to Americans and others that we have free speech and that we do not think the most important person in the country is too lofty to be confronted by a challenger. A letter to the editor from a recent immigrant suggests that the debates symbolize such important values:

> I arrived in this strange land as a student three years ago, and am delighted and bemused to see the two presidential candidates tear each other apart, especially in the debates. I do not know which man is better. But I do know I like the U.S. because all this is happening without a single stone being thrown.[4]

1. George J. Church, "Fast and Loose with Facts," *Time,* November 5, 1984, p. 22.
2. Hugh Sidey, "The Big Fight Syndrome," *Time,* October 29, 1984, p. 32.
3. Walter Sharpiro, "Bush Scores a Warm Win," *Time,* October 24, 1988, pp. 18–20.
4. "Letters," *Time,* November 19, 1984, p. 5.

---

concluded that government and military statements could not be believed and that the war could not be won. When he returned to the United States, he wrote a half-hour news special reflecting these views. He said that the United States had to start planning to get out. This was a major departure from his practice of trying to remain as neutral as possible. As one observer noted, this was "the first time in American history a war had been declared over by an

anchorman."[130] (American troops continued to fight for seven more years, however.) President Johnson said that he thought Cronkite represented the center of the electorate and his switch was a sign that Johnson had lost the center. The president admitted that this was instrumental in his decision not to seek a second term.[131]

After CBS switched directions, the other networks followed. An ABC executive sent a memo to his

Although television showed little blood from the war, newspapers and magazines portrayed considerable gore. Here the chief of police for Saigon executes a Vietcong guerilla. Dubbed "the shot seen 'round the world," this and other photographs might have contributed to the shift in public attitudes toward the war.

and more the same, with neither side gaining a decisive advantage. As one observer concluded, "The war played in American homes and it played too long."[136]

Whether because the media adopted a more pessimistic tone, or because television showed a seemingly endless war, or both, the media evidently affected people's attitudes, which changed about the same time the media coverage switched. This was especially true of upper- and lower-middle-class persons

staff: "I think the time has come to shift some of our focus from the battlefield . . . to themes and stories under the general heading: We Are on Our Way out of Vietnam."[132]

Many newspapers and magazines reached the same conclusion at the same time. Five of seven major mass circulation magazines that had vigorously supported the war before switched directions in 1968: *Newsweek, Time, Life, Look,* and *Saturday Evening Post* (but not *U.S. News and World Report* or *Reader's Digest*).[133]

In addition to the shift in media coverage after the Tet offensive, the nature of television coverage likely had an impact. Television made Vietnam the first "living room war," the first war that came into people's homes every night. The networks focused on battles rather than on stories about more complex conditions and events, although the cameras did not fill the screen with blood. "We go on the air at suppertime," they explained, and they did not want viewers to change channels.[134] Instead, the cameras typically panned scenes of helicopters taking off and landing, soldiers jumping on and off and fanning out across the countryside, with the occasional sound of a ping in the distance.[135] Thus the probable effect of television was not to horrify viewers and thereby turn them against the war. Rather, it was to show a seemingly endless war, as the coverage of battle after battle looked more

Figure 3 ■ Editorial Comments by Television Journalists About the Vietnam War Changed After the Tet Offensive

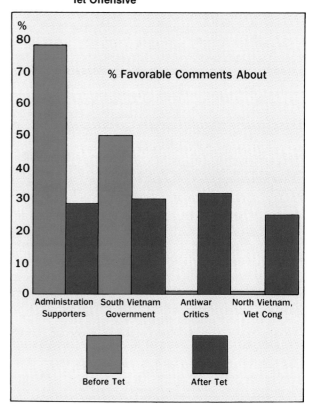

Content analysis of the television networks' evening news stories about the Vietnam War from 1965 to 1973 shows a marked change after the Tet offensive. Even so, the editorial comments occurred in less than 6% of the stories about the war before Tet and in less than 10% after, so there were no editorial comments in the overwhelming majority of the stories. The comments did not demonstrate much support for the antiwar critics or North Vietnam and the Vietcong either.

Source: Daniel C. Hallin, "The Media, the War in Vietnam, and Political Support," *Journal of Politics* 46 (February 1984): 12–24.

who read both newspapers and magazines regularly.[137] Although it is possible that the media and the public shifted independently of each other, in response to the increasing number of critics and the steady stream of young Americans in pine boxes, it seems likely that the media did have an effect on the public.[138]

Even so, it would be erroneous to conclude that the media "lost" the war. U.S. political and military officials had unrealistic views of the nature of the conflict and the ways to resolve it, as chapter 19 explains.

Conclusion: Are the Media Responsive?

The media have to be responsive to the people to make a profit. They present the news they think the people want. Because they believe the majority desire entertainment, or at least diversion, rather than education, they structure the news toward this end. According to a number of studies, they correctly assess their consumers.[139] For the majority who want entertainment, network television provides it. For the minority who want education, the better newspapers and magazines provide it. Public radio, with its hour-and-a-half nightly newscast ("All Things Considered"), and public television, with its hour nightly newscast ("MacNeil/Lehrer News Hour"), also provide quality coverage. The media offer something for everyone.

When officials or citizens get upset with the media, they pointedly ask, "Who elected you?" Journalists can reply that the people—their readers or listeners or viewers—"elected them" by paying attention to their news columns or newscasts.

To say the media are responsive, however, is not to say they perform well. Giving the people what they want most is not necessarily serving the country best. As one reporter lamented, "People seem to 'know' everything now—hearing the same news bulletins repeated around the clock—but they seem to understand precious little of what's really going on."[140] The media personalize and dramatize the news. The result is to simplify the news. Superficial coverage of complex events leaves the public unable to understand these events and, ultimately, unable to force the government to be responsive.

The media's shortcomings are aggravated by a declining interest in politics and decreasing number of people who read newspapers or, to a lesser extent, watch newscasts. Although the public is better educated now than in the 1960s, it is less likely to follow the news and less able to answer questions about the government.[141] People under 35 especially reflect these trends. To keep these vanishing readers, many newspapers have revamped their formats. While some have improved their quality, more have emulated *USA Today* and reduced their substance to hold the attention spans of younger readers weaned on television. This has disturbing implications. Citizens who are not aware of the news or who do not understand it cannot fulfill their role in a democracy.

These trends come at a time when the media, despite their shortcomings, provide more news than ever and—with journalists better educated and better able to address complex topics—more effective news than ever. Because the media are responsive enough and effective enough, they have become powerful enough to serve as a check on government in many situations. This was evident during the major crises of recent decades. During the war in Vietnam, the media stood up to two presidents when Congress and the courts were relatively passive. During the Watergate scandal, the media led Congress and the courts in standing up to a president. The media serve as a check on the government in countless other situations. As a former government official noted, "Think how much chicanery dies on the drawing board when someone says, 'We'd better not do that; what if the press finds out?'"[142]

EPILOGUE

Arnett Broadcasts from Baghdad

When all other Western journalists left Baghdad, Peter Arnett and his small crew remained and reported despite the heavy hand of censorship. Iraq did try to use Arnett for its purposes. Officials restricted his movements and statements. They refused to show him targeted military facilities and instead took him to bombed neighborhoods and buildings where civilians lived and worked, so the sight of dead and maimed civilians would arouse sympathy around the world and opposition against the war in the United States. Saddam Hussein granted him a televised interview, so the Iraqi president could present his views and try to improve his image—from a vicious dictator to a benign leader solely concerned about his country's survival and well-being.

Peter Arnett, in front of a bombed bridge in Baghdad.

Although Arnett reported only what he himself saw or heard, and CNN noted each time that his reports were subject to censorship, many Americans vented anger at Arnett and CNN for "letting themselves be used." Calls and letters poured into CNN headquarters in Atlanta. Representative Lawrence Coughlin (R-Pa.) said Arnett was to Hussein what Goebbels was to Hitler—his minister of propaganda.[143] Senator Alan Simpson (R-Wy.) called Arnett an Iraqi "sympathizer." Then, because Arnett had a Vietnamese wife, Simpson implied that the reporter had been a Vietcong sympathizer in the Vietnam War. (Yet, earlier in the year Simpson had rebuked Arnett and other journalists for their critical portrayals of Hussein. Simpson had visited Hussein and assured him that government officials considered him a friend of the United States.)[144]

Arnett was disappointed with the criticism but continued to broadcast. "I've taken some flak. So what else is new?"[145] Arnett said he thought it was better to report partial news than no news. Moreover, he found some ways to alert viewers and circumvent the censorship. For instance, officials took him to a factory the allies demolished because they said it produced biological weapons but that Iraqis said made baby formula. When Arnett and his photographer arrived, a sign in the ruins said in English, as well as Arabic: "Baby Milk Factory." The officials did not explain why a sign to the factory would be printed in English. Without saying the sign was a crude attempt to mislead viewers—such a statement would have been censored—Arnett managed to call attention to the language on the sign.

What Arnett's critics failed to mention was that the allied officials also restricted reporters' movements and censored their stories, although to a lesser degree.

Arnett's critics did raise a troubling question about democracy. Essentially, they said: "I am smart enough to put all this information in its proper perspective, but other people are stupider than I. I will sort out the facts from the propaganda . . . but other people won't. I can absorb the emotional impact of the terrible imagery of war without losing my ability to reason, but other people cannot."[146] While this may occur sometimes—people are irrational at times—if it does often, then democracy is in serious trouble.

KEY TERMS

mass media

yellow journalism

muckraking

fireside chats

symbiotic relationship

adversarial relationship

beats

leaks

scoop

presidential press
   conference

media events

sound bite

political bias

media malaise

commercial bias

setting the agenda

selective perception

FURTHER READING

The print media themselves are the primary sources for further reading. A good metropolitan newspaper or a weekly newsmagazine is essential. For political junkies, the *Washington Post National Weekly Edition,* a compilation of the newspaper's best articles and cartoons about politics during the week, is wonderful.

W. Lance Bennett, *News: The Politics of Illusion,* 2nd ed. (New York: Longman, 1988). *A critical examination of the superficiality of the news and its implications for democracy.*

Timothy Crouse, *The Boys on the Bus* (New York: Random House, 1972). *An irreverent account of press coverage of elections by a writer who reported on the reporters rather than on the candidates along the presidential campaign trail in 1972.*

Edwin Diamond, *The Spot* (Cambridge, Mass.: MIT Press, 1984). *A history of political ads on television.*

Mark Hertsgaard, *On Bended Knee* (New York: Farrar, Straus & Giroux, 1988). *An indictment of media coverage of the Reagan presidency. The author's thesis is that Reagan turned news hounds into lap dogs.*

Kathleen Hall Jamieson and David S. Birdsell, *Presidential Debates* (New York: Oxford University Press, 1988). *A history of presidential debates and a set of proposals for their reform.*

Joe McGinniss, *The Selling of the President 1968* (New York: Simon & Schuster, 1969). *An account of the often-comical efforts by Richard Nixon's advisers to transform him into a media candidate.*

NOTES

1. William Prochnau, "If There's a War, He's There," *New York Times Magazine,* March 3, 1991, pp. 30–34.

2. Ibid.

3. James David Barber, *The Pulse of Politics* (New York: W. W. Norton, 1980), p. 9.

4. Kevin Phillips, "A Matter of Privilege," *Harpers,* January 1977, pp. 95–97.

5. Doris A. Graber, *Mass Media and American Politics* (Washington, D.C.: Congressional Quarterly, 1980), pp. 2–3.

6. Thomas R. Dye and L. Harmon Zeigler, *American Politics in the Media Age* (Monterey, Calif.: Brooks/Cole Publishing, 1983), pp. 123–24.

7. Edwin Diamond, *The Tin Kazoo* (Cambridge, Mass.: MIT Press, 1975), p. 13.

8. Graber, *Mass Media,* p. 2.

9. William Lutz, *Doublespeak* (New York: Harper & Row, 1989), pp. 73–74.

10. S. Robert Lichter, Stanley Rothman, and Linda S. Lichter, *The Media Elite* (Bethesda, Md.: Adler & Adler, 1986), pp. 2–3.

11. Benjamin M. Compaine, *Who Owns the Media?* (White Plains, N.Y.: Knowledge Industry Publications, 1979), p. 11.

12. Thomas Griffith, "Leave Off the Label," *Time,* September 19, 1984, p. 63.

13. Bernard Roshco, "The Evolution of News Content," in Doris A. Graber, ed., *Media Power in Politics* (Washington, D.C.: Congressional Quarterly, 1984), p. 15.

14. Theodore H. White, *America in Search of Itself* (New York: Harper & Row, 1982), p. 65.

15. Richard Harwood, "Nobody Reads Anymore," *Washington Post National Weekly Edition,* December 26, 1988–January 1, 1989, p. 29.

16. Thomas E. Patterson, *The Mass Media Election* (New York: Praeger, 1980), pp. 58–60, 62–63.

17. J. Fred MacDonald, *One Nation Under Television: The Rise and Decline of Network TV* (New York: Pantheon, 1991); Lichter et al., *The Media Elite,* pp. 5–7.

18. Otto Friedrich, "Edging the Government Out of TV," *Time,* August 17, 1987, p. 58.

19. Benjamin M. Compaine, *Who Owns the Media?* (White Plains, N.Y.: Knowledge Industry Publications, 1979), pp. 11, 76–77.

20. Michael Parenti, *Inventing Reality* (New York: St. Martin's, 1986), p. 27.

21. Paul Farhi, "You Can't Tell a Book by Its Cover," *Washington Post National Weekly Edition,* December 5–11, 1988, p. 21.

22. "Time, Warner Plan To Merge," *Lincoln Sunday Journal-Star,* March 5, 1989.

23. Dom Bonafede, "Press Paying More Heed to Substance in Covering 1984 Presidential Election," *National Journal,* October 13, 1984, p. 1923.

24. Charles Peters, *How Washington Really Works* (Redding, Mass.: Addison-Wesley Publishing, 1980), p. 18.

25. William Greider, "Reporters and Their Sources," *Washington Monthly* (October 1982): 13–15.

26. Elizabeth Drew, "Letter from Washington," *New Yorker,* September 12, 1988, p. 92.

27. Tom Collins, "GOP's 'Good Leaks' Exploit Media," *Lincoln Journal,* November 24, 1987.

28. William A. Henry III, "Scrounging for Good Air," *Time,* September 3, 1984, p. 7.

29. Timothy Crouse, *The Boys on the Bus* (New York: Random House, 1972).

30. Jonathan Alter, "When Sources Get Immunity," *Newsweek,* January 19, 1987, p. 54.

31. Dom Bonafede, " 'Mr. President,' " *National Journal,* October 29, 1988, p. 2756.

32. Lance Morrow, "Time Essay," *Time,* August 18, 1980, p. 78.

33. Steven R. Weisman, "The President and the Press," *New York Times Magazine,* October 14, 1984, p. 71.

34. Ronald H. Brown, "Republican Baloney About Crime," *Washington Post National Weekly Edition,* April 30–May 6, 1990, p. 29.

35. David Halberstam, "How Television Failed the American Voter," *Parade,* January 11, 1981, p. 8.

36. George E. Reedy, *The Twilight of the Presidency* (New York: New American Library, 1970), p. 112.

37. Thomas Griffith, "Winging It on Television," *Time,* March 14, 1983, p. 71.

38. W. Lance Bennett, *News: The Politics of Illusion* (New York: Longman, 1988).

39. John David Rausch, Jr., "The Pathology of Politics: Government, Press, and Scandal," *Extensions* (University of Oklahoma), Fall 1990, pp. 11–12.

40. Michael Riley, "Where Were the Media on HUD?" *Time,* July 24, 1989, p. 48.

41. Hedrick Smith, *The Power Game* (New York: Random House, 1988), p. 403.

42. Timothy J. Russert, "For '92, the Networks Have To Do Better," *New York Times,* March 4, 1990.

43. Smith, *Power Game,* p. 420.

44. Adam Hochschild, "All the President's Patsies," *Mother Jones,* July/August 1988, p. 52.

45. Weisman, "The President and the Press," pp. 71–72; Dick Kirschten, "Communications Reshuffling Intended to Help Reagan Do What He Does Best," *National Journal,* January 28, 1984, p. 154.

46. Weisman, "The President and the Press," p. 72.

47. Smith, *Power Game,* p. 442.

48. Patrick J. Sloyan, "The War the Administration Isn't Going To Let You See," *Washington Post National Weekly Edition,* January 21–27, 1991, p. 23; Vicki Kemper and Deborah Baldwin, "War Stories," *Common Cause,* March/April 1991, p. 18; Stanley W. Cloud, "How Reporters Missed the War," *Time,* January 8, 1990, p. 61.

49. Howard Kurtz, "The Press Pool's Chilling Effect on Covering the War," *Washington Post National Weekly Edition,* February 18–24, 1991, p. 12.

50. Howard Kurtz, "Keeping It All Pretty Quiet on the Mideastern Front," *Washington Post National Weekly Edition,* February 4–10, 1991, pp. 34–35.

51. Calculated from David Sarasohn, "Not So Smart," *Lincoln Journal* (Newhouse News Service), April 2, 1991.

52. Richard Morin, "The New War Cry: Stop the Press," *Washington Post National Weekly Edition,* February 11–17, 1991, p. 38.

53. Edward Jay Epstein, *News from Nowhere* (New York: Random House, 1973), p. 13.

54. Graber, *Mass Media,* p. 62.

55. Milton Coleman, "When the Candidate Is Black Like Me," *Washington Post National Weekly Edition,* April 23, 1984, p. 9.

56. Roper Organization, "A Big Concern about the Media: Intruding on Grieving Families," *Washington Post National Weekly Edition,* June 6, 1984.

57. Parenti, *Inventing Reality,* chapters 7–11; Charles E. Lindblom, *Politics and Markets* (New York: Basic Books, 1977); MacDonald, *One Nation Under Television.*

58. Leon V. Sigal, *Reporters and Officials* (Lexington, Mass.: D. C. Heath, 1973), pp. 120–21.

59. Lucy Howard, "Slanted 'Line'?" *Newsweek,* February 13, 1989, p. 6.

60. Lichter et al., *The Media Elite,* pp. 21–25.

61. John Johnstone, Edward Slawski, and William Bowman, *The Newspeople* (Urbana, Ill.: University of Illinois Press, 1976), pp. 225–26.

62. Stanley Rothman and S. Robert Lichter, "Media and Business Elites: Two Classes in Conflict?" *The Public Interest* 69 (1982): 111–25.

63. S. Robert Lichter and Stanley Rothman, "Media and Business Elites," *Public Opinion* (October/November 1981): 44.

64. Stephen Hess, *The Washington Reporters* (Washington, D.C.: Brookings Institution, 1981), p. 89; Lichter et al., *The Media Elite,* pp. 127–28.

65. James Fallows, "The Stoning of Donald Regan," *Washington Monthly* (June 1984): 57.

66. Parenti, *Inventing Reality,* pp. 38, 56–57.

67. Mark Hertsgaard, "How Ronald Reagan Turned News Hounds into Lap Dogs," *Washington Post National Weekly Edition,* August 29–September 4, 1988, p. 25.

68. Joel Millman, "How the Press Distorts the News from Central America," *Progressive* (October 1984): 20.

69. Epstein, *News from Nowhere,* pp. 206–7.

70. C. Richard Hofstetter, *Bias in the News* (Columbus, Ohio: Ohio State University Press, 1976); Michael J. Robinson, "Just How Liberal Is the News?" *Public Opinion* (February/March 1983): 55–60; Maura Clancy and Michael J. Robinson, "General Election Coverage: Part I," *Public Opinion* 7 (December/January 1985): 49–54, 59; Michael J. Robinson, "The Media Campaign, '84; Part II," *Public Opinion* 8 (February/March 1985): 43–48.

71. Clancy and Robinson, "General Election Coverage"; Robinson, "The Media Campaign '84"; Michael J. Robinson, "Where's the Beef? Media and Media Elites in 1984," in Austin Ranney, ed., *The American Elections of 1984* (Durham, N.C.: Duke University Press, 1985), p. 184; Michael J. Robinson, "News Media Myths and Realities: What Network News Did and Didn't Do in the 1984 General Campaign," in Kay Lehman Schlozman, ed., *Elections in America* (Boston: Allen & Unwin, 1987), pp. 143–70.

72. Stanley Rothman and S. Robert Lichter, "The Nuclear Energy Debate," *Public Opinion* 5 (August/September 1982): 47–48; Stanley Rothman and S. Robert Lichter, "Elite Ideology and Risk Perception in Nuclear Energy Policy," *American Political Science Review* 81 (June 1987): 383–404.

73. Lichter et al., *The Media Elite,* chapter 7.

74. Robinson, "Just How Liberal Is the News?" p. 59.

75. Hofstetter, *Bias in the News.*

76. Robinson, "Just How Liberal Is the News?" p. 58; Arthur H. Miller, Edie N. Goldenberg, and Lutz Erbring, "Type-Set Politics," *American Political Science Review* 73 (1979): 69.

77. Michael Baruch Grossman and Martha Joynt Kumar, *Portraying the President* (Baltimore: Johns Hopkins University Press, 1981).

78. Michael J. Robinson and Margaret A. Sheehan, *Over the Wire and on TV* (New York: Russell Sage Foundation and Basic Books, 1983).

79. Michael J. Robinson, "Three Faces of Congressional Media," in Doris A. Graber, ed., *Media Power in Politics,* (Washington, D.C.: Congressional Quarterly, 1984), pp. 215–16.

80. Michael J. Robinson, "Public Affairs Television and the Growth of Political Malaise," *American Political Science Review* 70 (1976): 409–32; Miller, Goldenberg, Erbring, "Type-Set Politics."

81. "Anchorwoman Verdict Raises Mixed Opinions," *New York Times*, August 9, 1983.

82. Theodore H. White, *America in Search of Itself*, (New York: Harper & Row, 1982), p. 186.

83. George F. Will, "Prisoners of TV," *Newsweek*, January 10, 1977, p. 76.

84. Parenti, *Inventing Reality*, p. 48.

85. David Owen, "The Cigarette Companies: How They Get Away with Murder, Part II," *Washington Monthly* (March 1985), pp. 48–54.

86. Martin A. Linsky, ed., *Television and the Presidential Elections* (Lexington, Mass.: D. C. Heath, 1983).

87. Barry Sussman, "News on TV: Mixed Reviews," *Washington Post National Weekly Edition*, September 3, 1984, p. 37.

88. Bill Carter, "Networks Fight Public's Shrinking Attention Span," *Lincoln Sunday Journal-Star* (New York Times), September 30, 1990.

89. Epstein, *News from Nowhere*, p. 4.

90. William A. Henry III, "Requiem for TV's Gender Gap," *Time*, August 22, 1983, p. 57.

91. Tom Jory, "TV Anchorwoman's Suit Exposes Subtle Bias in Hiring," *Lincoln Journal*, July 31, 1983, p. 1A.

92. Robinson, "Just How Liberal Is the News?" p. 60.

93. [no author], "Tidbits of Outrages," *Washington Monthly* (February 1990): 44.

94. Parenti, *Inventing Reality*, p. 15, quoting Malcolm MacDougall, "The Barkers of Snake Oil Politics," *Politics Today* (January/February 1980): 35.

95. Stephen Ansolabehere, Roy Behr, and Shanto Iyengar, "Mass Media and Elections: An Overview," *American Politics Quarterly* 19 (January 1991): 119.

96. S. Robert Lichter, Daniel Amundson, and Richard Noyes, "The Video Campaign: Network Coverage of the 1988 Primaries (Washington, D.C.: American Enterprise Institute for Public Policy Research, 1988), p. 65.

97. Lee Sigelman and David Bullock, "Candidates, Issues, Horse Races, and Hoopla: Presidential Campaign Coverage, 1888–1988." *American Politics Quarterly* 19 (January 1991): 5–32.

98. Daniel Schorr, "Is There Life After TV?" *Esquire*, October 1977, p. 160.

99. Epstein, *News from Nowhere*, pp. 179, 195.

100. T. R. Reid, "Media Wrong About Yellowstone," *Lincoln Journal* (Washington Post), July 24, 1989.

101. Mark Hertsgaard, "Covering the World; Ignoring the Earth," *Greenpeace* (March/April 1990): 16.

102. John Horn, "Campaign Coverage Avoids Issues," *Lincoln Sunday Journal-Star*, September 25, 1988.

103. John Eisendrath, "An Eyewitness Account of Local TV News," *Washington Monthly* (September 1986): 21.

104. Linsky, *Television*, p. 12.

105. Donald L. Shaw and Maxwell E. McCombs, *The Emergence of American Political Issues: The Agenda-Setting Function of the Press* (St. Paul, Minn.: West, 1977). For a review of agenda-setting research, see Everett M. Rogers and James W. Dearing, "Agenda-Setting Research: Where Has It Been, Where Is It Going?" *Communication Yearbook* 11 (Newberry Park, Calif.: Sage, 1988), pp. 555–94.

106. Lutz Erbring, Edie N. Goldenberg, and Arthur H. Miller, "Front-Page News and Real-World Clues: A New Look at Agenda-Setting by the Media," *American Journal of Political Science* 24 (February 1980): 16–49.

107. Michael Bruce MacKuen and Steven Lane Coombs, *More Than News* (Beverly Hills: Sage, 1981), p. 140; Rogers and Dearing, "Agenda-Setting Research," pp. 572–76; G. E. Lang and K. Lang, *The Battle for Public Opinion* (New York: Columbia University Press, 1983), pp. 58–59.

108. Shanto Iyengar and Donald R. Kinder, *News That Matters* (Chicago: University of Chicago Press, 1987), pp. 42–45.

109. Erbring et al., "Front-Page News," p. 38; MacKuen and Coombs, *More Than News*, pp. 128–37.

110. Lichter et al., *The Media Elite*, p. 11.

111. Rogers and Dearing, "Agenda-Setting Research," p. 569; MacKuen and Coombs, *More Than News*, p. 101; Erbring et al., "Front-Page News," p. 38.

112. Rogers and Dearing, "Agenda-Setting Research," p. 577, citing Jack L. Walker, "Setting the Agenda in the U.S. Senate," *British Journal of Political Science* 7 (October 1977): 423–45.

113. Robinson and Sheehan, *Over the Wire*; Robinson, "The Media Campaign, '84," pp. 45–47.

114. Thomas Whiteside, "Annals of the Cold War: The Yellow-Rain Complex—II," *New Yorker*, February 18, 1991, pp. 44–68.

115. Doris A. Graber, "Kind Pictures and Harsh Words: How Television Presents the Candidates," in Kay Lehman Schlozman, ed., *Elections in America* (Boston: Allen & Unwin, 1987), p. 141.

116. Ibid., p. 116.

117. David Paletz and Robert Entrum, *Media—Power—Politics* (New York: MacMillan, 1981), pp. 35ff.

118. Ansolabehere et al., "Mass Media and Elections," pp. 128–29; Christine F. Ridout, "The Role of Media Coverage of Iowa and New Hampshire in the 1988 Democratic Nomination," *American Politics Quarterly* 19 (January 1991): 45–46, 53–54.

119. Lee Sigelman and Carol K. Sigelman, "Judgments of the Carter-Reagan Debate," *Public Opinion Quarterly* 48 (1984): 624–28.

120. Theodore H. White, *The Making of the President 1960* (New York: Atheneum House, 1961), p. 333.

121. For a review, see MacKuen and Coombs, *More Than News*, pp. 147–61.

122. Robert S. Erickson, "The Influence of Newspaper Endorsements in Presidential Elections," *American Journal of Political Science* 20 (May 1976): 207–33.

123. MacKuen and Coombs, *More Than News*, p. 222.

124. Benjamin I. Page, Robert Y. Shapiro, and Glenn R. Dempsey, "What Moves Public Opinion?" *American Political Science Review* 81 (March 1987): 23–43.

125. For an example of research assessing this influence, see Stephen Erfle, Henry McMillan, and Bernard Grofman, "Testing the Regulatory Threat Hypothesis: Media Coverage of the Energy Crisis and Petroleum Pricing in the Late 1970s," *American Politics Quarterly* 17 (April 1989): 132–52.

126. Susan Welch, "The American Press and Indochina, 1950–1956," in Richard L. Merritt, ed., *Communication in International Politics* (Urbana, Ill.: University of Illinois Press, 1972), pp. 207–31; Edward Jay Epstein, "The Selection of Realty," in Elie Abel, ed., *What's News?* (San Francisco: Institute for Contemporary Studies, 1981), p. 124.

127. David Halberstam, *The Powers That Be* (New York: Dell, 1980), pp. 642–47.

128. Daniel C. Hallin, *The "Uncensored War": The Media and Vietnam* (New York: Oxford University Press, 1986).

129. Peter Braestrup, *Big Story*, vols. I and II (Boulder, Colo.: Westview Press, 1979).

130. Halberstam, *The Powers That Be,* p. 716.

131. Ibid., pp. 716–17.

132. Epstein, *News from Nowhere,* pp. 17–18.

133. James D. Wright, "Life, Time and the Fortunes of War," *Transaction* 9 (January 1972): 43–44.

134. Epstein, *News from Nowhere,* pp. 17–18.

135. Michael Arlen, "The Air," *New Yorker,* August 16, 1982, p. 73.

136. Halberstam, *The Powers That Be,* p. 291.

137. Wright, "Life, Time and the Fortunes of War," p. 47.

138. One study strongly suggests that the public's shift cannot be accounted for by the increases in the number of troops sent to Vietnam or the number of casualties there. MacKuen and Coombs, *More Than News,* pp. 84–87.

139. Graber, *Mass Media,* p. 244.

140. Greider, "Reporters and Their Sources," p. 19.

141. Stephen Earl Bennett, "Trends in Americans' Political Information," *American Politics Quarterly* 17 (October 1989): 422–35; Richard Zoglin, "The Tuned-out Generation," *Time,* July 9, 1990, p. 64.

142. Peters, *How Washington Really Works,* p. 32.

143. Prochnau, "If There's a War," p. 34.

144. "Sen. Simpson and Peter Arnett," *Washington Post National Weekly Edition,* February 18–24, 1991, p. 28 (Sen. was abbreviated, and no author); "Arnett Tells of Reporting in Iraq," *Lincoln Journal* (Los Angeles Times), March 20, 1991.

145. Prochnau, "If There's a War," p. 31.

146. Michael Kinsley, "Trusting Ourselves with the News," *Time,* February 25, 1991, p. 80.

Money and Politics

Charles Keating and a Phoenix resort he built for a reported $142 million.

correlation between where money goes and the legislative actions of recipients doesn't do much for public confidence in Congress' dedication to the public interest."[2] Other papers headlined their stories about AMA contributions: "Medical lobby gifts linked to FTC bill," "Doctoring the Anti-Trust Laws," "Doctors in the House." The New York Times declared, "This is one doctor's bill there is no reason to pay."[3]

In its releases, Congress Watch pointed out exactly which members were taking campaign money from the AMA. These names often were picked up by the members' home media, which editorialized against them. A New York representative was narrowly defeated in the primary election after his links with the AMA were exposed. This defeat led the New York Times to say: "Opportunistic congressmen who flack for special interests may wind up paying for their jobs."[4] Copies of the editorial were distributed to congressional offices by the anti-AMA lobby.

Gradually, the AMA lost its reputation as a group of selfless individuals interested in the public's health and began to be tagged as a greedy group interested in its own economic health. This perception was helped along by a Congress Watch news release pointing out that the average doctor earned more than $86,000 the year before.

Meanwhile, Congress Watch accompanied its publicity campaign with one-on-one lobbying of members of Congress. Soon, members who originally cosponsored the AMA bill decided to back off.

When the Senate vote was to be taken, Senator Warren Rudman (R-N.H.) said that he "noticed something very interesting in the last week. For the first time in 20 years doctors are making house calls. They made house calls in the Dirksen [Senate] Office Building. They made house calls in the Russell Office Building."

The vote, which went overwhelmingly against the AMA, was greeted with approval by the press. As one editorial noted: "The vaunted AMA was reeling from severe legislative contusions."

This outcome illustrates a key point about the influence of campaign money. It is more influential when the issue is not well publicized. When AMA foes were able to spotlight the money generously flowing from the AMA to those willing to do its bidding in Congress, the AMA's money began to be seen as a liability rather than an asset. When Congress Watch and other groups were able to focus the debate on the public interest versus the special interest, and to show members that their home constituents were watching, members opted for the public interest.

1. This example is drawn from Michael Pertschuk (former chair of the Federal Trade Commission and now involved in public interest lobbying), Giant Killers (New York: Norton, 1986), chapter 4.

2. Ibid., p. 100.

3. Ibid., p. 108.

4. Ibid.

tainly affected by the Watergate scandal, and it is likely that revelations about big money lobbying activity since then have not improved the public's view of the honesty of public officials.

There is some evidence that the public is reacting against the growth of big money in campaign finance. Most of the few members of the House who were defeated in 1988 and 1990 had some conflict-of-interest allegations leveled against them.

Many members have been unhappy with the campaign finance system, and the rising cost of campaigns and the intensive intertwining of fund raising and congressional activity have increased the number of members seriously discussing campaign finance reform.

Several proposals to reform the system have been offered, most focusing on congressional campaign spending.[55] One of the major proposals, a combination of public financing and limits on spending, is discussed in this chapter's Focus on an Issue. Other ideas include strengthening the parties' role in financing elections by allowing them to give more to candidates; raising the amounts individuals can contribute (inflation has eroded the value of the limits set in the

early 1970s) and limiting further the amount PACs can give; forcing PACs to disclose more about their operations; or giving tax credits for campaign contributions given only to candidates of one's own state (or to presidential candidates).

The most drastic proposed reforms try to limit campaign spending by reducing campaign costs. Currently, between 60% and 80% of campaign money is spent on television.[56] If this spending were curtailed, campaigns would cost significantly less.

Some proposals would allow candidates free media time and prohibit purchase of additional time as is common in other nations (this would also deal with independent spending). See the Comparative Perspective box for a discussion of this. Candidates would be given time and must use it in slots of at least 5 or 10 minutes with this proposal. No 30-second slash-and-burn commercials would be allowed. Proponents believe that the proposal would not only decrease the impact of money on winning elections, it would encourage more discussion of the issues by forcing candidates and parties to put together at least a 5-minute statement.

Opponents point out the practical difficulties of this kind of reform in a federal system in which each congressional candidate must appeal to his or her own constituency. Unlike Western European nations, where citizens vote primarily for the national party, not for their local candidate, politics in the United States is decentralized. But this roadblock to reform may not be insuperable, for, as Senator Robert Dole (R-Kan.) said, "If they can figure out the tax code, they can figure this out."[57]

Walter Lippman, a famous American journalist, once said that American communities govern themselves "by fits and starts of unsuspecting complacency and violent suspicion." We think nothing is wrong, and then we think everything is wrong. So it is with our views of campaign money. For several years after the 1974 reforms, we thought things were going along pretty well. Today many are convinced that the nation is in terrible jeopardy because of the influence of money. Whether we are overreacting or not, the issue of campaign finance reform is again on the public agenda.

Conflicts of Interest

In addition to money's influence on political campaigns, it also leads to **conflicts of interest.** This term refers to officials making decisions that directly affect their own personal livelihoods or interests. The campaign contribution system we have just described is certainly a huge conflict of interest. Presidents and members of Congress make decisions about policies affecting those who give them campaign money. But conflicts of interest are not confined to decisions involving sources of campaign money. As Madison noted, almost every decision involves potential conflicts of interest. Decisions made by presidents, bureaucrats, and members of Congress can affect their personal financial interests (including stocks, bonds, or other investments).

Conflict-of-Interest Reforms

The 1970s brought about not only reform in campaign finance but also new rules about financial interests within government. Ethics committees had been part of Congress since 1964, when the Senate established one, followed by the House in 1968, in the wake of financial scandals. Until 1976, this House committee, the Committee on Standards of Official Conduct, made no formal investigations. But then it investigated a widely publicized sex and payroll scandal. This scandal, following Watergate by only two years, led both the House and the Senate to rewrite and tighten their codes of conduct. These codes include limits on outside income the member can earn and restrictions on the amount of gifts that can be accepted from lobbyists, as well as provisions for public disclosure of financial interests.

In addition to rewriting their codes of conduct, Congress also passed the Ethics in Government Act in 1978. This legislation was designed to prevent employees of the executive branch (Congress exempted itself from the act) from leaving government and then using their inside knowledge to benefit their new private employers. Thus, the act bars former public servants from lobbying their former agencies for a year and on matters in which they "personally and substantially" participated as public officials, for life. Current employees also are prohibited from participating in decisions affecting interests with which they are negotiating about future employment. Thus, the act tries to prevent federal employees from using their government positions to profit themselves or future employers.

Congress

Despite the ethics codes, in 1981, six House members and one senator were convicted in an FBI undercover operation known as Abscam. Several members of Congress were approached by undercover FBI agents who offered to introduce them to wealthy Arabs. Members were asked to use their influence to help these "Arabs" secure certain benefits. Five of the seven were videotaped accepting cash. Incidents of outright bribery such as this are rare. What is more common is conflict of interest, where the issues are less clear-cut.

Congress has not dealt successfully with the question of conflict of interest. Many members vote on issues in committee and on the floor that might benefit their personal financial interests. Committee members often have a direct financial interest in the legislation they consider. For example, most members of the Agriculture Committee have agribusiness interests, members of the Banking Committee banking interests, members of the Armed Services Committee interests in military contractors, and so forth.[58] Some observers have suggested that members be required to divest themselves of any financial interests likely to come before the committees on which they serve, but Congress remains unwilling to agree.

FOCUS ON AN ISSUE

Should Congressional Campaigns Be Publicly Financed?

The idea of publicly financing part of the cost of congressional campaigns is not new. In 1907 President Teddy Roosevelt, a Republican who was strongly influenced by Progressive sentiment, argued that one way to reduce graft in Congress would be to provide public funding so that members would not need, or would not be allowed, to raise huge sums of money.

The idea languished until the early 1970s, when Congress enacted public funding for presidential elections but rejected it for congressional elections. Now proposals for funding of congressional elections, currently pending in Congress, have support from across the ideological spectrum, ranging from labor organizations to the American Bar Association. But they also have opposition from both liberal and conservative groups. A small majority of the public favors such public funding.

Most proposals for public funding of congressional elections have at least two key components: public funds and some limitation on private contributions. For example, one bill would provide public funds for Senate candidates willing to abide by a spending limit (set differently for each state depending on its population) and would restrict the amount of money candidates could accept from PACs. Similar proposals have been made for House elections.

Would Public Funding Be Too Expensive?

Public funding of congressional campaigns would be costly, especially if it were generous enough to reduce private donations significantly. One estimate is that it would cost nearly $90 million for the two candidates for each of the 435 House seats and perhaps an additional $10 million per election year for Senate races (only one-third of the Senate seats are contested each election year, but Senate races in large states are quite expensive).[1]

Obviously, if public funds were more generous, the cost would go up. It also would go up if the public were to fund candidates in primary elections. One hundred million dollars is a lot of money, but it is only 1/10,000 of our national budget. It is also less than corporations spend to advertise soap or cereal. Whether it is too much depends on how bad we think the current situation is, what the probabilities are that public funding could fix some of the current problems, and what else we might spend this money for.

The Puck cartoon "Jack and the Wall Street Giants" shows a brave but tiny Theodore Roosevelt challenging the large corporations of his time. Removing their influence in elections was but one way Roosevelt fought the trusts.

Should a Provision for Public Funding Include Ceilings on Spending?

Public funding could occur with or without a ceiling on spending. We might say, for example, that candidates can spend only public money and matching money from individuals. This would eliminate the direct role of PACs in congressional campaign financing. Alternatively, we could allow candidates to spend a fixed amount more than their public funding or even put no ceiling on spending at all. However, public funding provisions without a ceiling

(continued on next page)

would not deal with the perceived problem of too much special interest money in congressional campaigns.

Is Public Funding an "Incumbent Protection Act"?

Some people have called plans for public funding and ceilings on spending "incumbent protection acts" because challengers to congressional incumbents must spend a lot of money to be as well known as incumbents. A ceiling on campaign spending would deter them more than incumbents, who are already widely known.

Although that argument is plausible, the facts suggest that incumbents are already very well protected by the current laws. As we will see in the next chapter, most incumbents who run are reelected. In fact, in 1986, 1988, and 1990 nearly 98% of all House incumbents were reelected. It is hard to see how a change in the law could make incumbents safer than they already are.

Senate incumbents usually are reelected but not as consistently as their House counterparts. Their challengers usually are already well known, as former governors, members of the House, or other public figures. For that reason, Senate challengers may not need the extra advantage of money that House challengers do.

Would Public Funding Benefit One Party More Than Another?

Because Congress must approve any public financing scheme, its members must be persuaded that the law will not be detrimental to them personally or to their party. Some Republicans believe that public funding will be beneficial to Democrats because the majority of Democrats are incumbents. However, as we just saw, incumbents are already so safe that it is hard to see how they could be more so. Some Democrats have opposed public funding because they believe that it gives more resources to challengers, who are more often Republicans.

Republicans traditionally have opposed ceilings on spending and public funding primarily because they are able to raise more money than Democrats and because they fear that incumbents will benefit. Republicans have believed that their traditional advantage in raising money must be maintained to offset the Democrats' incumbency advantage. But now many Republicans believe that the current system favors the Democrats because PACs overwhelmingly support incumbents. This perception may increase Republican support for a change in the campaign finance system.

Would Public Funding and Caps on Individual Donations Eliminate the Influence of Money on Members of Congress?

Clearly no system would completely eliminate the influence of money on the behavior of all public officials. But providing a substantial part of the cost of campaigns through tax money, and setting limits on how much more members could spend, would take away some of the anxiety that members feel about raising money. As one observer noted, "A kind of fever takes over. Members hear that someone else is raising $500,000, and they think they have to raise $500,000, and soon everyone thinks he has to raise $500,000."[2] This anxiety preoccupies members of Congress with fund raising and leads them to consider the impact of their decisions on their ability to raise funds. This is clearly an unhealthy situation.

What Are Some Other Effects of Public Funding?

One of the few clear aspects of campaign financing reform is that we cannot always foresee what the impact of changing the rules would be. No one imagined in 1974 that PACs and Washington lobbyists would come to dominate fund raising and have the influence they do today. Those now considering campaign finance reform are therefore more cautious than they were a decade ago. As Terry Dolan, the now-deceased director of a successful conservative PAC, said in 1983, "Whatever changes they make in the law, we'll turn them to our advantage."[3]

One feared effect of either candidate spending limits or limits on the amounts that PACs can give to candidates is that it would increase "independent" spending. Given the Supreme Court's current view of independent spending, that will be difficult to regulate. Many people believe that it is better to have PACs contributing openly than to have independent spending accountable to no one.

Sources: Larry Sabato, *PAC Power* (New York: W. W. Norton, 1984), chapter 9; Gary Copeland, "The House Says 'No' to Public Financing of Congressional Campaigns," *Legislative Studies Quarterly 9* (August 1984): 487–504; Alan Abramowitz, "The Root of all Evil," paper presented at the 1988 Hendricks Symposium, Lincoln, Nebraska.

1. Kenneth John, "Don't Give Away the Store," *Washington Post National Weekly Edition,* May 4, 1987, p. 39.
2. Elizabeth Drew, *Politics and Money* (New York: Collier Books, 1983), p. 51.
3. Sabato, *PAC Power,* p. 172.

Gerrymanders

The practice of "gerrymandering" is probably as old as elections. The name originated in 1812 when the Massachusetts legislature carved out a district that historian John Fiske said had a "dragonlike contour." When painter Gilbert Stuart saw the misshapen district, he drew in a head, wings, and claws and exclaimed, "That will do for a salamander!" Editor Benjamin Russell replied, "Better say Gerrymander," after Elbridge Gerry, then governor of Massachusetts.

Gerrymanders are not historical relics, as the diagrams of Los Angeles County indicate. Before the 1982 redistricting, the districts were relatively contiguous and were part of a statewide districting plan that left the California congressional delegation nearly evenly divided between Republicans and Democrats. A 1981 gerrymander, masterminded by California Democratic congressman Phillip Burton, with the help of one aide and a pocket calculator, maximized the number of safe Democratic seats in the state. As one observer noted, districts resembled a "mosaic of bizarre fishhooks, meanders and cul-de-sacs." Burton, now deceased, liked to say it was his "contribution to modern art." This contribution also ensured that Democrats dominated the California delegation during the 1980s.

Source: *Guide to Congress,* 2nd ed. (Washington, D.C.: Congressional Quarterly Inc., 1976), p. 563. Quotes from "A Not So Simple Game," *Newsweek,* January 14, 1991, p. 20.

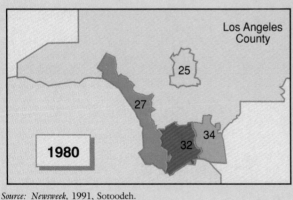

Source: *Newsweek,* 1991, Sotoodeh.

reelection is an important objective for almost all members of Congress and *the* most important objective for many, members work at being reelected throughout their terms. Most are successful, though as we have seen, the electoral fortunes of senators are not as secure as those of members of the House. In recent years, as few as 55% and as many as 97% of

senators have won reelection, while the success of House incumbents varied from only 88% to 98%.

The Advantages of Incumbency

Before they even took the oath of office, newly elected representatives in 1990 were given an introduction to the advantages of incumbency. At meetings arranged by the Democratic and Republican leadership and by the House Administrative Committee, new members heard about free mailing privileges, computers and software to help them target letters to specialized groups of constituents, facilities to make videotapes and audiotapes to send to hometown media, and other "perks" designed to keep members in touch with their constituencies and, equally important, to ensure reelection.

Incumbents win because, partly through these methods, they are better known than nonincumbents and voters evaluate them more positively. Almost all voters can recognize the name of their representatives, they have seen them on television or received mail from them, and they can give a general rating of their performances (see figure 1).[14] Although most voters can correctly identify their representatives as liberal or conservative, only a small minority know how their representatives voted on any issue.[15] Therefore, representatives have the advantage of name recognition without the disadvantage of having voters know how they really voted.

Representatives' high level of public recognition is not so surprising given that members of Congress spend most of their time and energy looking for and using opportunities to make themselves known to their constituents. Members visit their home districts or states an average of 35 times a year—at taxpayers' expense.[16]

Sometimes members take unusual steps in an attempt to become better known. A representative from Detroit gained publicity by being a disc jockey for a radio program in his district on weekends. One member stood on the Capitol steps "dressed in an exterminator's outfit with plastic cockroaches glued to his shoulders." He then jumped up and down, shouting "squash one for the Gipper." This was to endear himself to owners and workers of an insecticide manufacturer in his district.[17]

Constituency Service. Members of Congress make themselves known in more routine ways. One is by providing **constituency service:** answering questions and doing personal favors for constituents who write or call for help.

This function, also called **casework,** is crucial for members and their staffs, who function as red-tape cutters for everyone from elderly citizens having difficulties with Social Security to small-town mayors trying to get federal grants for new sewer systems. Representatives provide information to students working

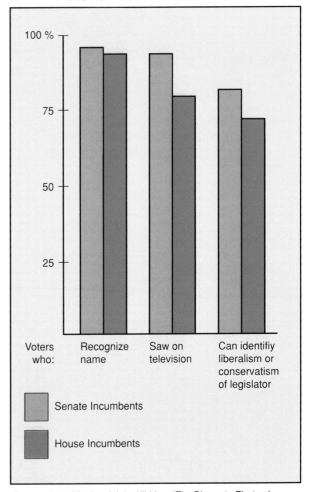

Figure 1 ■ Senate and House Incumbents Are Well Known to Voters

Source: John Alford and John Hibbing, "The Disparate Electoral Security of House and Senate Incumbents," paper presented at the American Political Science Meetings, September 1989, Atlanta, GA.

on term papers and citizens puzzled about which federal agency to seek assistance from. Representatives can provide gifts of calendars, United States flags that were flown over the Capitol, and brochures and publications of the federal government.

Requests for service often come by mail. More than half the congressional office staffs work on the flood of mail that pours in. Members receive 300 million pieces of mail per year, skyrocketing from 15 million in 1970. Much of it simply expresses an opinion about an issue, but some offices get 5,000 to 10,000 requests per year for assistance.[18] In addition to handling casework in Washington offices, most representatives have one or more home district offices to deal personally with constituents and their casework, and senators have state offices for the same purpose. More than 40% of all representatives' staffs and more than 30% of senators' staffs are located in their home district or state.[19]

Citizens turn to their congressional representatives because they see them as allies in their struggles with bureaucracy.[20] Members of Congress, who are in large part responsible for the establishment of the huge Washington bureaucracy, are able to score with voters by helping them cope with the bureaucracy they have created.[21] Individual members may have limited power in trying to get important legislation passed, but in dealing with a constituent's problems, their power is much greater because of their clout with bureaucrats. A phone call or letter to a federal agency will bring attention to the constituent's problem.

Of course, not all casework is directed toward winning reelection. Some members say they enjoy their casework more than their policy roles, perhaps because the results of casework are often more immediate and tangible.

Members are aided in their casework and in their other attempts at recognition by free mail privileges called **franking.** In just six months during 1989, Senator Alphonse D'Amato (R-N.Y.) sent out nearly 17 million pieces of mail at a cost of $2.65 million. In 1988, Congress's postage bill was well over $100 million, about the same as the entire Peace Corps budget.

There are some restrictions on franking designed to make it less blatantly political. For example, mass mailings cannot be sent out close to an election. Regardless, one political consultant estimates that the frank is worth at least $350,000 in campaign funds.[22]

Franking privileges become even more useful when combined with sophisticated word processing systems to target very specific constituency groups with "personalized" letters. Members can maintain incredibly specialized lists, not just of Republicans and Democrats but of those living near federal prisons, small-business owners, veterans, teachers, and government employees, for example. No group is too specialized or ostensibly apolitical to be targeted. Charles

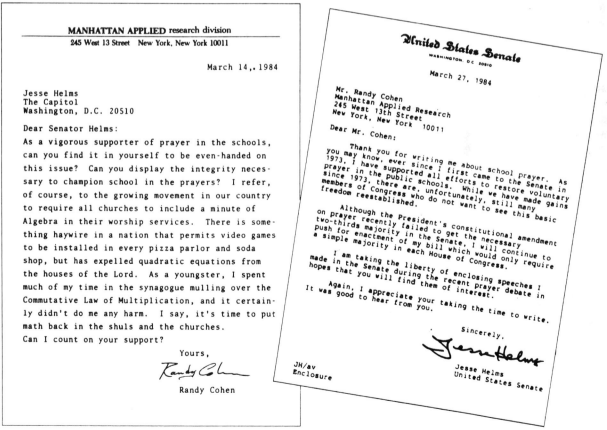

Even with computerized mailings, members' letters may not be specialized enough!
Source: Mother Jones, July 1984, p. 44. Reprinted by permission of Randy Cohen.

Figure 2 ■ Members of Congress Send More Mass Mail in Election Years

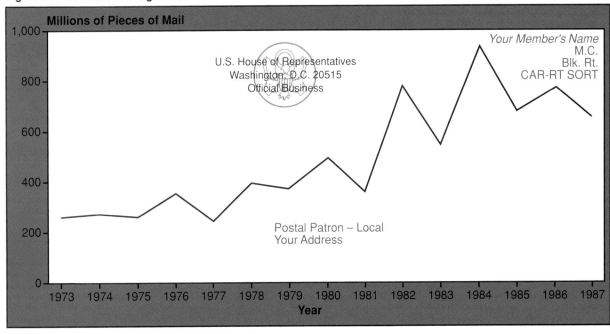

Source: Vital Statistics of Congress, 1989–1990. (Washington, D.C.: CQ Press, 1990), p. 164.

Grassley (R-Iowa) even sent a letter to a thousand Iowans with abbreviated intestinal tracts in honor of Ostomy Awareness Month.[23]

This system can help improve the representation of constituents. But the frank and the computer together have turned most congressional offices into full-time public relations firms. Their value in reelection is reflected in the fact that members send out much more mail in their reelection year than in other years (see figure 2).[24]

Pork Barrel. Another way that members gain the attention of constituents is to obtain funds for special projects, new programs, buildings, or other public works in their districts or states. Such benefits, often called **pork barrel** projects, are a constant feature of congressional policymaking. In the final days of one session of Congress, for example, a few of the last-minute pork barrel projects approved included a $3.6 million irrigation project for Maine's potato growers and a $400,000 fuel dock for a Hawaiian hotel.[25] These projects are desired by constituents because they provide jobs and business in the local district. Discussions of whether to continue a small federal agency, the Small Business Administration (SBA), have revealed that it is largely seen as a "petty cash

drawer for members of Congress, who pop it open whenever they need a few dollars for the folks back home."[26]

After the Reagan administration disbanded a committee of experts to evaluate possibilities for new additions to the nation's park system, Congress added numerous sites with no historic significance but that happen to be in the districts of powerful members. One is the former home of President William McKinley's in-laws. This home is in the district of Ralph Regula (R-Ohio), the ranking Republican on the subcommittee that oversees the national park service budget.[27]

Because pork barrel projects are considered crucial to reelection chances, there is little support in Congress for eliminating projects known to be unwise or wasteful. Both liberals and conservatives protect these kinds of projects. David Stockman, former president Reagan's director of the Office of Management and Budget, observed, "There's no such thing as a fiscal conservative when it comes to his district."[28]

Media Attention. To ensure that favors for the home state or district do not go unnoticed and that their legislative activities or popular positions on issues receive attention, members use increasingly sophisticated production equipment and technology to

Pork Barrel Science

Not only are legislators treating decisions about new dams, expanded military bases, and other such programs as pork barrel projects, but increasingly funds for basic scientific research are also being regarded as part of the pork.

Basic scientific research is largely done in universities and the federal government funds over 60% of that research.[1] Traditionally, scientific research has been funded through federal agencies, such as the National Science Foundation and the National Institutes of Health, that based their decisions, at least in theory, on merit. Merit was determined through a review of proposals by other scientists around the nation. Though agency directors had some influence, and a phone call from a member of Congress on an important project was hardly unheard of, scientists themselves largely determined who got funded.

But now, Congress is getting more involved in making the decisions about which scientific projects get funded. The reasons for the change are two. First, science costs more than it used to. A huge nuclear project is budgeted at $8 billion and one in biotechnology at $3 billion. Price tags like these get congressional attention; members see them as potential boons for their own districts. Moreover, expensive projects get the attention of state and local officials who see them as a way to stimulate and create economic development. Public officials think of California's Silicon Valley, where federal funding for scientific research at institutions such as the University of California at Berkeley and Stanford University stimulated the growth of new high-tech companies and a resulting economic boom. Thus, state and local officials want to fight for big science projects for their states and localities.

How is this changing funding for basic science? Under the old system, most research grants went to a relatively small number of universities, generally the most prestigious ones. In a recent year, the General Accounting Office reported that the top 20 universities received 42% of federal research funds. Most of the top 20 universities are major private institutions on the East Coast and the large public universities of the heartland and California. Thus, research money is not spent evenly among all or even most congressional districts.

The rationale for giving the money to the best universities is that these are the universities with the top rated scientists. Critics charge, however, that the peer review process is an "old boy network" and that getting grants depends on "who you know."[2] In the research grant process, the rich get richer, as those with grants have the time and resources to prepare other successful grants.

In the 1980s this peer review system has been eroded by the increased number of universities receiving funding from Congress earmarked for special projects. By 1988, over $200 million (of about $9 billion spent for basic research) was given this way, largely for facilities. Moreover, Congress directed the National Science Foundation to consider institutional and geographic balance in its distribution of funds. It is as though Congress suddenly realized that a lot of money over which it had little control was being spent. As former Senator Russell Long (D-La.) asked, "When did we agree that the peers would cut the melon or decide who gets this money? I have been around here for a while, I do not recall that I ever agreed to that."[3]

One effect of this new development has been to spread federal research money to more institutions. In 1986, for example, universities that ranked below the top hundred in federal research funding received only 14% of all federal research grants but 71% of earmarked funds.[4] Some people believe this spreading around will help lesser institutions develop a better capacity for scientific research.

But others see more negative side effects. They fear that decisions on science funding will increasingly be made on the basis of congressional pork barrel politics. If so, some believe that the overall quality of scientific research in the United States will be significantly lowered, a development we can ill afford. As the president of the Association of American Universities argues, "It is essential that steps be taken now to avoid sliding into decisions about what science will be done and who will do it that are based on which district has the most effective representative, or which institution has cultivated members most effectively, rather than which science should be done and who is best able to do it."[5]

1. This figure and those below are drawn from Mark V. Nadel, "The Rise of 'Political' Science," *G.A.O. Journal* (Winter 1988/1989): 47–53.
2. John Silber, quoted in ibid., p. 50.
3. Quoted in the *Washington Post,* March 22, 1988, p. A4.
4. Nadel, "The Rise of Political Science."
5. Robert Rosenzweig, testimony in a hearing before the Committee on Science, Space, and Technology of the House of Representatives, quoted in ibid., p. 47.

make television and radio shows to send home. For example, one evening in 1989, on any of three local television news shows, residents of Boise, Idaho, might have seen their congressional representative, Larry Craig (R-Idaho), state in an interview that he was strongly opposed to a pay increase for Congress and would not take it if it were passed. The viewers were not told that the "interviewer" was one of Craig's congressional staffers and that the camera crew was that of the Republican Congressional Campaign Committee, which also paid for the broadcast.[29]

Members also like to tape themselves at committee meetings asking questions or being referred to as "Mr. (or Madam) Chairman" (because many members are chairs of at least a subcommittee). The tape then is edited to a 30-second sound bite to be sent to local television stations. As one critic noted of this growing practice, "Short of scandalous senility, incumbents can easily persuade local unscrutinizing media that they are little Sam Rayburns" (a powerful House leader a generation ago).[30]

These productions are transmitted by satellite to local media within a few hours. Often stations run them as news and do not tell their viewers that they are essentially campaign features prepared by the members. But television is not alone in portraying members' self-publicity as "hard news." Congressional staffers write press releases about accomplishments of the member and fax them to local newspapers, which often print them as written. Local media, whether print or television, are often short of news with a local flavor and eagerly take whatever members give them.

There are now over 750 press secretaries in members' offices to help members get good coverage in the home district media.[31]

Unsafe at Any Margin?

Most members are reelected even if they have done relatively little constituency work or have obtained little federal money for their districts (see figure 3).[32] Still, incumbents believe that the best way to ensure victory is to be so good at constituency work, so successful in bringing pieces of pork to their districts, and so well known to the voters that no serious rival will want to run. Incumbents hope that potential rivals will bide their time and wait for a better year or run for some other office.[33]

Given their advantages, you may wonder why incumbents worry about losing. But worry they do. One political scientist proclaimed that members feel "un-

safe at any margin."[34] No matter how big their last victory, they worry that their next campaign will bring defeat. And despite the high reelection rate of incumbents, some are defeated. This fear prompts them to spend even more of their energies preparing for the next campaign.

But this fear is fairly remote. In 1988, only 10 of 400 House races involving incumbents were seriously contested. Only 6 incumbents lost, and 5 of them were accused of a major conflict of interest or other unethical conduct. What about 1990, supposedly an antiincumbent year? Fifteen incumbents lost out of 407 seeking reelection. Nine of the 15 were accused of unethical conduct or experienced personal scandals.[36] Though the average percent of the victory margin decreased for those members facing opposition, the proportion running unopposed increased.

Challengers

Another reason for the uneasiness of incumbents is that as their media and public relations sophistication has grown, so has that of challengers. Still, without

Until this television ad ran, former Senator Walter Huddleston (D-Ky.) was substantially ahead of his opponent. The ad pointed out that Huddleston had a poor attendance record (hence sending out bloodhounds to find him). When the local media focused on this ad, and it helped bring victory to his challenger, Mitch McConnell. A result of Senator McConnell's victory is that Senate attendance on roll-call votes has been at all-time highs.

Figure 3 ■ House Incumbents Have Had Secure Jobs in Recent Years

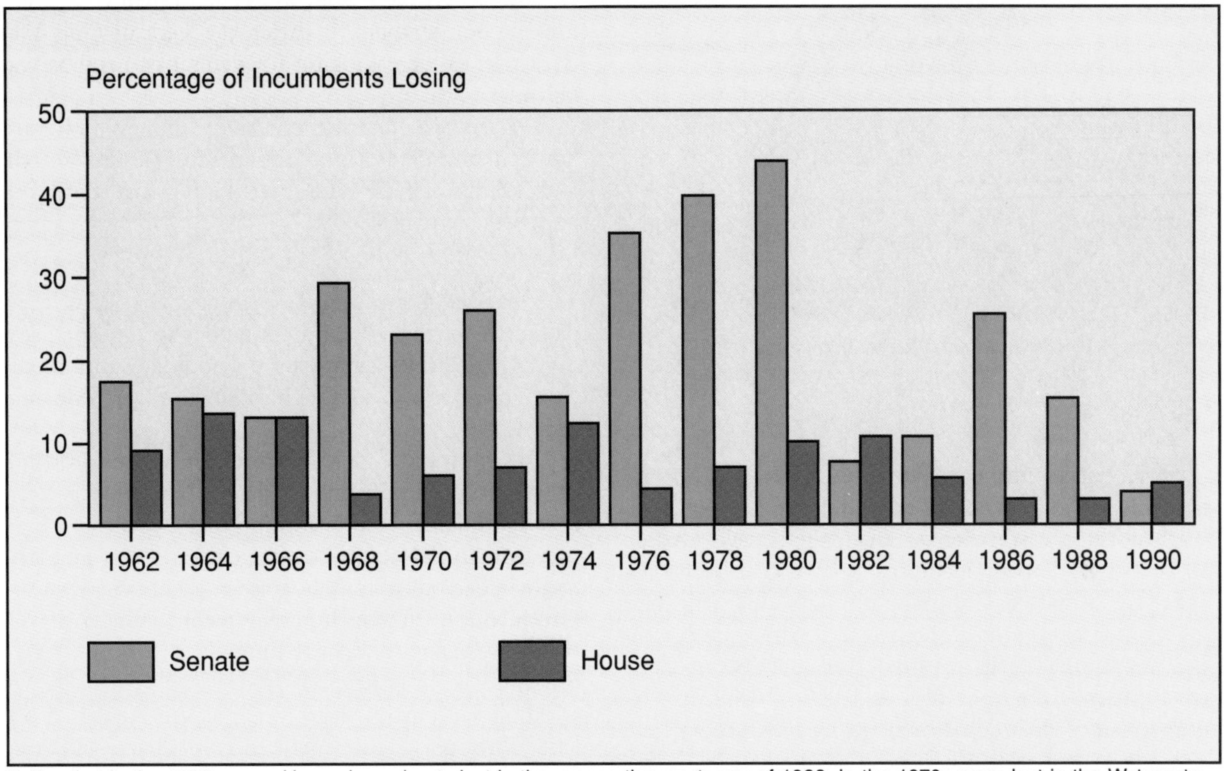

Percentage of Incumbents Losing

[bar chart with values on y-axis from 0 to 50, years 1962 through 1990 on x-axis]

Senate   House

Notice that in the 1980s more House incumbents lost in the reapportionment year of 1982. In the 1970s more lost in the Watergate year, 1974, when many Republican defenders of President Nixon were defeated. In the 1960s reapportionment did not start until after 1962, so the elections of 1964 and 1966 reflected reapportionment.
Source: Congressional Quarterly Weekly Report, November 19, 1988, p. 18, November 10, 1990, p. 3801.

the advantages of the free frank and other opportunities to become well known to constituents, challengers have a difficult time. The best advice to someone who wants to be a member of Congress is to find an open seat.

To beat an incumbent, challengers need money. The more they spend, the more likely they are to win. In recent House campaigns, a challenger needed to spend at least $250,000 to have even a one in four chance of winning—and the cost continues to rise.[36]

Spending is important for challengers because they must make themselves known in a positive way, and they must suggest that something is wrong with the incumbent. Usually challengers will charge incumbents with ignoring the district, being absent from committee hearings or floor votes, being too liberal or too conservative, or voting incorrectly on a key issue. Sometimes, of course, the incumbent has been involved in a scandal, which offers a ready target for the challenger.[37]

Sometimes challengers will try unusual tactics to make themselves known. Tom Harkin (D-Iowa) worked in a series of blue-collar jobs when running for the House to show people in his district that he understood their problems. Meanwhile he got a lot of free publicity. Dan Burton (R-Ind.) used a 1948 fire engine in his campaign.

Though the 1990 elections were an exception, Senate challengers usually fare better than House challengers. One reason is that there are stronger candidates to challenge incumbent senators because Senate seats are a bigger prize and because in a statewide constituency there are more potential challengers. Senate challengers are better known than House challengers.[38] They are often former governors or members of the House with a statewide reputation. For example, in 1988, about 80% of voters recognized the name of the person running against their incumbent senator; less than 60% recognized the challenger to

Kentucky GOP challenger (and former paratrooper) Will Scott jumped from planes to get publicity, but lost a close race to incumbent Carl Perkins (D-Ky).

their House incumbent.[39] Senate challengers can attract more money because they are better known.

Another reason Senate challengers have greater success is that most incumbents have constituencies (i.e., states) much larger than House districts. The greater population means that senators cannot have personal contact with as high a proportion of their constituents. Also they cannot satisfy as high a proportion since their constituencies are much more heterogeneous than House district constituencies.[40] Evidence indicates that senators from the largest states have about a six- or seven-point electoral disadvantage compared to senators from the smallest states. Senators from the smallest states do about as well as House members from their states.[41]

Campaigns

In the nineteenth century, political campaigns were organized largely by political parties, and the candidates had relatively little to do. Today, however, congressional campaigns are largely candidate centered. Most candidates hire workers, raise money, and organize their own campaigns. They may recruit campaign workers from local political parties; single-interest groups they belong to; unions; church, civic, or other voluntary organizations; or simply groups of friends and acquaintances.[42]

Political parties do have a significant role, however. Although most candidates put themselves forward or are recruited by friends and associates, national and local parties also recruit. Presidents make personal appeals to fellow party members who they think can run strong races, and national campaign committees also recruit aggressively. Said one Democratic congressional campaign chair, "I'm not looking for liberals or conservatives. That's not my bag. I'm looking for winners."[43] After the Persian Gulf War both parties were looking for veterans to run as war heroes.

Parties also provide campaign money and assistance to candidates for polling, mailing, issue research, and getting out the vote. That kind of assistance can be worth a great deal.[44]

The Media Campaign.   To wage a serious campaign, the challenger or a contender for an open seat must wage a media campaign. Candidates hire media consultants and specialists in polling, advertising, and fund raising.

With candidates establishing their own campaign organizations and hiring media specialists, fears grew that candidates were becoming less closely linked to parties than before and once elected, not as indebted to their party nor as obligated to reflect party views. Candidates *are* linked to their technicians who poll, plan advertising, and raise funds but who often have little interest in policies or governing.[45]

Political parties, however, recognized this problem. Throughout the 1980s, national parties increasingly provided useful services to congressional candidates: helping them manage their campaigns, develop issues, advertise, raise money, and conduct opinion polls. National parties also give substantial sums of money to congressional candidates.[46]

Media campaigning has attracted a new type of congressional candidate and hence a new type of congressional incumbent. The old-style politician who might have been effective in small groups but who cannot appear poised and articulate on television has given way to one who can project an attractive television image. Candidates are elected on the basis of their media skills, which may not be the same skills as those of a good lawmaker.

Campaign Money.   The old adage says, "Half the money spent on campaigns is wasted. The trouble is, we don't know which half." This bromide helps explain why congressional campaigns are expensive. There is a kind of "campaign arms race" as each candidate tries to do what the other candidate does and a little more, escalating costs year by year.

In 1988, winning House candidates spent $350,000 on average. Successful campaigns against incumbents and closely fought races cost much

The "Perks" of Office

The 1989 debate over whether to raise congressional salaries from $89,500 was long and loud; awash in a wave of public protest over that proposed raise, members of Congress first decided not to take it, then contented themselves with a raise to slightly less than $100,000. Salaries of members of Congress are high in comparison to the average American family income of around $28,000 a year. But they are low in comparison to elites in business and the professions. Presidents of some large corporations make millions per year, and the salaries of many lawyers and doctors are in the hundreds of thousands of dollars. Moreover, congressional salaries are quite low in comparison with the salaries of top officials of the interest groups that lobby Congress. Many of them make several hundred thousand dollars annually. For example, in 1987, the top officer's salary in 130 lobbying groups averaged about $200,000; the highest paid was the vice-president of the American Medical Association, who made around $700,000. Only 12 of the top executives of these special interest groups (who were mainly from public interest and consumer groups) made less than the $89,500 paid to members of Congress.

Yet the fringe benefits of members of Congress undoubtedly make the job more attractive and are probably competitive with the fringe benefits offered to high-ranking business executives. Moreover, many of the fringe benefits of members of Congress directly help them get reelected.

Creature Comforts

Creature comforts include:

- Free medical and dental insurance and free care at several Washington area hospitals.
- A generous retirement plan.
- Subsidized meals in the Senate and House dining rooms.
- Free parking at the Capitol, Washington airports, and on city streets.
- Free car washes.
- Free plants and flowers.
- Free prints from the National Gallery, framed free in the Capitol basement.
- Free recreational facilities in the Senate and House gymnasia.
- Free travel abroad at public expense, often in military planes; relatives travel free too if space is available, and, by happy coincidence, it usually is.

Benefits to Help Reelection Chances

Many benefits enable members to keep in close touch with constituents, either in person or by mail, and to

generate publicity back in the home district:

- An expense allowance averaging more than $430,000 for office expenses, staff, and travel. The size of senatorial allowances depends on the population of the senator's state.
- For senators, a generous allocation to rent space and buy furnishings for state offices.
- An additional $33,000 to $300,000 for "official" expenses.
- Television and radio recording studios in the Capitol, and professionals to assist members in producing their media spots.
- Freebies for constituents, like the "We the People" wall calendars, imprinted with the name of the member. The total cost of these wall calendars is more than $500,000. Members also can get free photos of themselves, surplus books from the Library of Congress, and copies of hearings and other congressional documents.
- Free WATS line in their home for unlimited long distance calls.
- Franking privileges are perhaps the most important congressional "perk."

The Final Perk

Should the free medical care fail, and the member die, there is a life insurance policy of about $92,000, partly paid for by the taxpayer. And, for the last journey, the sergeant-at-arms provides undertaker service to arrange for the funeral. Unlike most such services, this one is free.

Sources: Congressional Quarterly Almanac (Washington, D.C.: Congressional Quarterly, Inc., 1983) p. 578; "Are They Worth It," *Time,* January 23, 1989, p. 13.

more. Million-dollar campaigns are no longer un-usual. Because they are statewide, Senate races are much more expensive than House races. In 1988, winning Senate candidates spent more than $3 million, on average.

Voting

Just as for presidential elections, party loyalties, candidate evaluations, and issues are important factors in congressional elections.[47]

Party loyalties are even more important for congressional than for presidential elections because congressional elections are less visible, so more people base their vote on traditional party loyalties. Incumbency is also more important than in presidential races. The result is that increasingly, since about 1960, voters have split their tickets in voting for presidential and congressional candidates. This is both because voters favor congressional incumbents and because many Democrats desert their party when casting a vote for president but not for lesser offices. For example, one out of five Reagan voters in 1984 voted for a Democratic member of the House, leaving Reagan with only a 41% Republican House despite his commanding personal victory.

Normally, the party of a winning presidential candidate gains seats during a presidential election year and loses a substantial number of seats in the midterm election. This maintains a sort of equilibrium in party control of Congress.[48] In 1986, the Republicans lost 6 seats after gaining 16 in 1984. These swings are less pronounced then they used to be, reflecting the increased powers of incumbency.

The Representative on the Job

Informal Norms

In addition to the formal requirements of the representative's job—which are few—there are **informal norms** learned from colleagues, staff, and the press. Like the subtle socialization of young people, new members of Congress learn the ways of their elders.[49] These norms help keep the institution running smoothly by attempting to diminish friction and competition among members. Like other American institutions, the norms of Congress have changed.

Thirty years ago, the most important norm was **institutional loyalty,** the expectation that members would respect their fellow members and the Congress itself, especially their own house. Personal criticism of one's colleagues was to be avoided, and mutual respect was fostered by such conventions as referring to colleagues by title, such as "The Distinguished Senator from New York," rather than by name. Many believe that this norm has eroded in the last two decades.

Reciprocity ("you support my bill, and I'll support yours") is another norm that is increasingly threatened. It involves an exchange sometimes called **logrolling.** Sam Ervin, the late Democratic senator from tobacco-growing North Carolina, is reported to have told an audience from North Dakota, "I got to know Milt Young [then a senator from North Dakota] very well. And I told Milt, 'Milt, I would just like you to tell me how to vote about wheat and sugar beets and things like that, if you just help me out on tobacco'."[50] That is reciprocity—and logrolling.

Tied to the norm of reciprocity is the norm of **specialization.** Members cannot be knowledgeable in all areas, so they specialize in some area related to their committee work. The Senate traditionally has been more individualistic than the House and less willing to give priority to specialists. Many senators see themselves as potential presidential candidates who need to be well versed on a variety of issues. The Senate is also much smaller so there are fewer members to cover all the issues.

Specialization and reciprocity increase the influence of individual members but also facilitate the smooth running of the institution. By specializing, a member can become an expert. Reciprocity helps members' work be accepted by their colleagues.

Norms are changing as decentralization and a "go your own way" sentiment are becoming more common.[51] Open meetings and media scrutiny have made it more difficult for members to "go along" on bills unpopular in their constituency. The increased fears of members for their electoral security reaffirm this basic caution and individualism.

Members have also become more willing to challenge the work of their colleagues, making it difficult for anyone to control Congress and direct its energies to the solution of public problems. On the other hand, the decline of these norms means that the institution is more democratic, because new members can have influence without being under the thumb of more senior members.

Working Privately and "Going Public"

A member's routine traditionally involved bargaining with other members, lobbyists, and representatives of the administration. Working privately, one-on-one in small groups, or in committees, members and staff discussed and debated issues, exchanged information, and planned strategies. Twenty years ago most issues were probably resolved this way. Even though many issues still are resolved through these private channels, much has changed in the way Congress operates.[52]

Today members believe that it is as important to "go public" as it is to engage in private negotiation.[53] **Going public** means to carry an issue debate to the public through the media. Congress goes public by televising floor debates and important hearings, and leaders and individual members go public by using the media to further their goals.

Televised Proceedings.   After considerable controversy and anxiety, the House began routinely to televise its proceedings in 1979. Fearful of being overshadowed by the House, and mindful of Ronald Reagan's advice on how to deal with televised coverage ("Learn your lines, don't bump into furniture, and, in kissing, keep your mouth closed), in 1986 the Senate followed suit.[54] This coverage is available to more than 40 million people on cable television through C-SPAN. Estimates are that more than one-third of C-SPAN subscribers watch their legislators at least one hour a month.[55] Even more see them in session when network news programs use footage of members making speeches.[56]

C-SPAN coverage has had some influence on congressional behavior but probably not as much as either its supporters or opponents feared. The time that the House spends in session and the number of speeches have increased. The Senate tightened up its rules on debate. Members of both houses consulted media experts and found that they should wear blue shirts and red ties, speak in segments that are 20 seconds long (so the television networks can excerpt their speech for the evening news), gesture with their hands, hold their bodies still, and keep their aides out of the picture.[57]

The effect on others outside Congress is even more difficult to measure. Many important executive officials watch C-SPAN, as do state legislators and bureaucrats. Network news shows often provide a short segment for the national news. But most of the public is not watching. Perhaps for this reason, there is no evidence that televised coverage of congressional proceedings has increased reelection rates of incumbents.

Congress also has televised important hearings. The Watergate impeachment hearings and those for the Iran-Contra affair attracted heavy media attention and an extensive viewing audience.

Use of the Media.   During the 1980s, use of the media by congressional leadership increased tremendously.

The Democratic House leadership decided to use the media in reaction to former President Reagan's success in going public. In 1981 and 1982, Reagan was able to push many of his programs through Congress by bypassing members and appealing to the public. By influencing these constituents, the president was able to move Congress. In response, the congressional leadership now goes public too.[58] Leaders regularly call producers of television talk shows to suggest Democratic guests. They complain to editors of important newspapers if the Democratic response to the president's weekly radio show is not given enough attention. Each day before the House session, the Speaker meets with the press and usually has a prepared statement challenging the administration over a policy issue. Before important congressional votes on key issues, the leadership plans letters to the editor of important newspapers and floor speeches designed for maximum television coverage.

Some leaders want to be even bolder in their going public strategies. They have suggested that congress should meet five days a week instead of the Tuesday through Thursday routine it has adopted to allow members to go home and attend to constituents. A five-day week plus press conferences on the weekend would challenge the president's domination of the media on Friday through Monday, when Congress is not in session.

The more media-oriented among the rank-and-file members are experts in providing short and interesting comments for the nightly network news, writing articles for major newspapers, and appearing as commentators on news programs. One member, Charles Schumer (D-N.Y.), is on the "MacNeil-Lehrer News-Hour" so often "that it is sometimes hard to tell if he is a guest or host."[59]

Voting

We have seen that members of Congress represent their constituents through service and by obtaining special benefits for the district or state. A third major kind of representation is policy representation. In the eyes of most people, members are sent to Washington to make laws. By casting hundreds of votes each year, members try to represent the interests of their constituencies as they see them and in the process win support for reelection.

But constituency opinion is often uninformed, divided, or apathetic. Because most votes in Congress are not on subjects that the electorate knows much about, members cannot, and often do not want to, rely on a simple polling of constituents to tell them how to vote. The opinions of constituents do matter, but other influences are also important: the party, the president, the members' ideology, staffers, and other members' recommendations. Members look to these sources for cues as to how to vote.

Party. Forty to 60% of the ballots in Congress are party votes; that is, a majority of one party opposes a majority of the other. In these votes, party members support their party between 70% and 90% of the time. Party support increased during the 1980s and reached an all-time high in 1988 in the House.

There are several reasons for the continuing importance of party. All members of Congress are elected on a partisan ballot and many receive support from the party. Congress organizes itself on a partisan basis, and party leaders try hard to influence party members to vote the "right" way.

Most of the time this influence is low key, but sometimes party leaders turn on the heat. In a successful vote to override a Reagan veto in early 1987, Democratic Senate leaders adopted a "baby-sitting" strategy to make sure that wavering Democrats did not get near anyone who might persuade them to uphold the president's veto. These Democrats were accompanied at all times by two other Democrats with the "right" views. For their part, Republicans called on Reagan to make personal appeals to wavering Republicans.

When a member has no strong feelings, it is certainly in the member's interest to go along with party leaders, who have some "perks" to dispense. Then too, members tend to have policy views similar to others in their party, at least more similar than to those in the opposite party. Party votes reflect different constituency needs too, because Democratic and Republican constituencies are different.

Constituency. Members of Congress see their jobs as representing their constituencies. But the term

"constituency" is not as simple as it sounds. Members have several constituencies, including not only their entire district but also constituencies within the district, such as voters of their party, major socioeconomic groups, and their own personal supporters.[60] Sometimes these constituencies may be in conflict. The representatives' personal constituency may be more liberal or conservative than the district as a whole. When members vote in conflict with what seems to be the sentiments of the majority of voters in the district, it may be that they are responding to their own supporter or partisans. Of course, in those rare instances where most of the representative's constituents feel strongly about an issue, the member cannot buck an overwhelming majority and expect to win reelection.

Ideology. The member's own ideology usually reflects both the party and constituency, but it can be an independent influence.[61]

On the whole, Democrats vote for more liberal measures than do Republicans. Traditionally, southern Democrats often deserted the Democratic leadership and voted with Republicans because they shared the more conservative Republican outlook. This tendency has diminished and probably will dwindle further. With the growing strength of southern Republicanism, southern conservatives run as Republicans and have a good chance of winning. Also, many southern districts are increasingly urban and contain voters who are more liberal than they were 30 years ago. The enfranchisement of African-Americans also has been an important liberalizing influence on representatives from many southern districts.

The President. The president is also a factor in congressional voting, partly due to the position of party leader.[62] The president appeals to fellow partisans to support a program and tries to persuade those in the other party to go along as well. Presidents can win support by granting or withholding favors, such as support for a member's pet project in the district, and by mobilizing public opinion on behalf of their programs.

Interest Groups and Lobbyists. Interest group lobbyists are most effective when their interests overlap with constituency interests or when the issue is technical or little publicized.

Staffers. Staff can be a very important influence on a member's vote. Staff members are likely to have done

FOCUS ON AN ISSUE

Should Members of Congress Be Limited in the Number of Years They Serve?

In the Congress established under the Articles of Confederation, representatives were limited in the number of terms they could serve. The writers of the Constitution placed no limit on the number of terms members of Congress could serve, but it appears that they pictured a representative body of citizens who served temporarily. This vision was the reality until the Civil War.

Now members make a career of being members. There is little turnover, because most incumbents run for reelection and almost all in the House, and most in the Senate, win. This emphasis on a career in Congress makes reelection a priority. Important issues often are ignored as members invest time and energy in improving their reelection prospects through constituent service and home visits. Taking clear-cut stands on controversial issues is the last thing most want to do.

These new emphases on constituency service at the expense of legislation may be weakening Congress's policymaking ability and authority. Consequently, a reform limiting members to one longer term, probably six years, or limiting the number of shorter terms they can serve, is often suggested. These suggestions were widely publicized during and after the 1990 elections. Voters in California and Oklahoma approved a 12-year limitation on terms of office for their state officeholders, and Colorado voters endorsed an eight-year limitation for their state legislators and members of Congress. Most other state legislatures are considering term limitations as well.

On its face the proposal has some merit. A large majority of the public supports it, and many Republicans like the idea because they believe most Democratic incumbents can never be beaten. But is a limited number of terms really a good idea?

Are Limitations on Congressional Terms Constitutional?

We might first ask if state action limiting congressional terms is constitutional. Supporters say it is, claiming that states have the power to determine "the times, places, and manner" of elections of their representatives (Constitution, Article I, Section 4). On the other hand, opponents point to the fact that the Constitution sets congressional terms (Article I, Section 2), and there is no provision for states to change the terms. Clearly, the constitutionality issue will be determined by the courts. If they decide states cannot limit terms of their members of Congress, an amendment to the Constitution would be needed to make the change.

Will Limiting the Years Served Strengthen Congress?

One argument is that the reform will strengthen Congress's policymaking role by minimizing the nonlegislative

continued on next page

the research and briefed the member on an issue. They probably have the greatest influence on technical issues or those that the member does not care much about.

Other Members. Members also are influenced by other members of their party or their state's delegation. Members also may turn to colleagues whose judgment or expertise they respect or whose ideology or background they share. In fact, on most routine bills, cues from trusted fellow members are the most important influence on members' votes.

How Congress Is Organized

An institution of 535 members without a centralized leadership that must make decisions about thousands jobs, such as constituency service, a member must perform. Therefore, it should help focus the member's attention on legislating.

But opponents of the fixed term argue that the reform might make Congress weaker, not stronger. Government problems and their solutions are complex, and it takes time for new members to gain expertise. The executive branch is filled with career civil servants whom members of Congress must oversee; if Congress is filled with new members with little experience in government, it will not be able to match the executive branch in experience or expertise. Under the present rules, Congress has many specialists who know as much about agency issues as agency executives do. It would be almost impossible for members of Congress to develop this kind of expertise if they were limited to only a few years in office.

Members of Congress also might find themselves less knowledgeable than staff. Much of the work of Congress is now done by its staff. A continuous influx of new and inexperienced members would make Congress more dependent on staff, who have no direct responsibility to voters at all.

Will Limiting the Time Served Make the Institution More Democratic?

Supporters of the change believe it might free members from the influences of special interest groups that they rely upon for campaign funding. Because members could not run more than a few times, they would not be as obligated to special groups.

Opponents argue that, by the same token, the members who would not be running again would not need to listen to the voters. Members would perhaps be too independent and free to go their own way. In fact, they might be just as indebted to special interests as they are now, since they will be looking for postcongressional employment, possibly with those interests that are lobbying them.

Opponents also argue that it is not democratic to take away the choices of the voters. If they wish to keep sending old hands to Congress, they should be allowed to do so. It is the voters, after all, who keep reelecting the incumbents they claim they would like to throw out of office. Supporters of the proposed change point out that more than 30 years ago we decided to limit voters' choices by not allowing them to elect a president to a third term. They claim the advantages congressional incumbents have make it difficult to vote against them.

Might Other Consequences Result from Limiting Members to a Fixed Term?

Each reform of Congress has had consequences unanticipated by those supporting the reform. Supporters of the subcommittee reforms of the 1970s wanted to democratize Congress but perhaps not as much as they did. Limiting members of Congress to a fixed term would be a major change, which would make seniority and subcommittee reforms seem like "small potatoes." As one *Wall Street Journal* editor wrote, "The term limitation proposal is a bad idea that likely would have unintended consequences. It's another of those schemes to take politics out of politics."[1] Thus, it is difficult to anticipate exactly the changes in the institution that might result from such a dramatic shift in the rules of the game.

1. Albert R. Hunt, reprinted in Peter Montgomery, "Should Congressional Terms be Limited?" *Common Cause Magazine,* July/August 1990, p. 32.

of proposed public policies each year is not an institution that can work quickly or efficiently. Each year in the past 10, from 2,000 to 10,000 bills have been introduced in Congress, and 250 to 2,000 have been passed.

Although many of these bills are trivial, such as those proclaiming "National Prom Graduation Kickoff Day" or naming local courthouses, others deal with crucial issues. In addition to these bills, Congress must oversee the performance of the federal bureaucracy in implementing bills previously passed.

How Congressional Organization Evolved

The first House, meeting in New York in 1789, had slow and cumbersome procedures.[63] After discussions by the whole House, a committee was elected to draft each bill, and the House then debated it section by section. To speed things up, permanent committees were eventually created, each with continuing responsibilities in one area, such as taxes or trade.

After a short time the selection of the leader of the House, called the **Speaker of the House,** who appointed members to those committees, became a partisan matter. Beginning about 1811, Henry Clay became the leader of the Jeffersonian-Republicans in the House. As Speaker, he used his powers to appoint committee members and chairs to maintain party loyalty and discipline.

Although in these early years the House was the dominant branch, during the administration of Andrew Jackson its influence declined when it could not

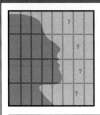

YOU ARE THERE

To Report or Not to Report

You are President Ronald Reagan. It is January 1986 and you must decide whether to tell Congress you are selling arms to Iran.

Over the 13 past months, eight Americans have been kidnapped and held hostage in Lebanon by Moslem extremist groups, some of whom get support from Iran and its leader, the Ayatollah Khomeini. One hostage, a Central Intelligence Agency (CIA) operative assigned to our embassy in Beirut, has already been killed. You are deeply troubled by the hardships and uncertainties the hostages and their families face. People look to you as president to gain the release of the hostages and to protect others from being kidnapped.

The situation is an embarrassment. In 1980, you belittled your predecessor Jimmy Carter for not being able to free hostages who had been kidnapped from the American embassy in Iran. In 1984, you campaigned for reelection using slogans such as "America is back, and standing tall." You know that the public dislikes Iran intensely.

On your desk, you have a two-and-a-half-page memorandum submitted by your new national security adviser, John Poindexter, and prepared by his subordinate, Lieutenant Colonel Oliver North. It seeks your approval to let the CIA sell arms to Iran. William Casey, the CIA director, is pushing the idea. He argues that Iran has a strategically important position in the world and we should try to reestablish normal relations with its government. He also thinks a moderate faction in the Iranian government might help us if we helped Iran in its war against Iraq. The memo notes that arms sales "may well be our way to achieve the release of the Americans held in Beirut."[1]

The memo maintains that both Secretary of State Schultz and Secretary of Defense Weinberger oppose the arms sale.[2] But it does not say why or describe their arguments. Neither does it offer you other options to consider for getting the hostages freed.

According to the Intelligence Oversight Act of 1980, you must sign this memo to approve the arms sales. The CIA cannot spend funds on a covert operation until the president "finds" that doing so "is important to the national security of the United States."[3] Your signature on the memo is the "finding" the act requires.

The act also requires you to notify in a "timely fashion" the House and Senate Intelligence Committees of the covert actions you approve. This is to hold intelligence agencies accountable. However, the act acknowledges the need to prevent disclosure of national security secrets, so it lets you define what "timely" means.

You decide to make the "finding" and approve the arms sales. You think people will applaud the sales when the hostages come home. But should you notify the Intelligence Committees as the law requires?

Lieutenant Colonel North advises you not to report the finding. In another memo, he argues that "the extreme sensitivity" of the matter requires you to "withhold notification . . . until such time as you deem appropriate."[4]

Most presidents have fought congressional limits on their self-defined constitutional authority in foreign policy matters. Likewise, you believe Congress should defer to your foreign policy leadership. Congress has difficulty keeping sensitive information secret. It cannot act quickly in response to events abroad, and it does not have all the information you have. You are elected by the entire country, so people look to you for leadership. Freeing the hostages would show that you are in charge and able to handle terrorism better than Carter.

No one is advising you to report, although you have not talked to Schultz or Weinberger. Your White House staff chief, Donald Regan, seems to support the arms deal and keeping it secret. However, you know that if the arms sale is discovered, it will certainly produce a lot of media coverage and criticism in Congress and around the country. What should you do?

OUTLINE

The president of the United States is one of the most powerful people in the world. His likes and dislikes, prejudices and preoccupations affect almost everyone. The scope of his power has led some observers to write about an "imperial" presidency.[5] People everywhere want to know what the president thinks and does; and his physical health, mental alertness, and stamina generate intense media coverage.

Yet all recent presidents have suffered reelection defeats or left office under a cloud. They have seemed powerless to shape events affecting the national interest and their own reputations. A conservative Congress frustrated John Kennedy's policy initiatives before his assassination. Lyndon Johnson's candidacy for reelection was killed by a war that took Richard Nixon six years to end. And Nixon had to resign from office because of his Watergate coverup. Gerald Ford and Jimmy Carter failed to get reelected, the latter hurt by serious economic problems and the Iran hostage crisis. And Ronald Reagan, one of our most popular presidents, was so frustrated by terrorism and Nicaragua that he condoned illegal activities, producing the Iran-contra scandal and a tarnished personal reputation.

Instead of an imperial presidency, we may have an "impossible" or "imperiled" presidency.[6]

We will consider the paradox of presidential power and presidential weakness. After describing the requirements for being president, we will examine the office's growth and see why modern incumbents are both powerful and vulnerable. We then will discuss the president's various responsibilities.

Presidential Job Description

Pharaohs, consuls, kings, queens, emperors, czars, prime ministers, and councils of various sizes served as executives in other governments before 1787. But no national government had a president, an elected executive with authority equal to and independent of a national legislature, until we did.

Qualifications

There are formal, constitutional qualifications to be president: one must be a "natural born citizen," at least 35 years old, and a resident of the United States for at least 14 years before taking office.

Informally, it also helps to be a white male with roots in small-town America, a Protestant of English, German, or Scandinavian background, from a state with a large population, and a good family man. In recent years, however, this profile has broadened considerably as society has become more tolerant of diversity, though gender and racial barriers still remain.

Tenure

Presidents have four-year terms. The Twenty-second Amendment limits them to serving two terms, or ten years if they complete the term of an incumbent who dies or resigns. Eight presidents have died in office from illness or violence. The first was William Harrison, who caught a fatal cold at his inaugural parade in 1841, and the last was Kennedy, who was assassinated in 1963. In 1974, Nixon was the first to resign.

Congress may remove presidents and other civil officers in a two-step process. The House decides questions of impeachment, or whether to bring charges of "high crimes and misdemeanors" (this phrase includes serious crimes and, depending on the mood of congressional majorities, political abuses). If a House majority favors impeachment, it notifies the Senate, which must mobilize a two-thirds majority to remove an accused president from office.

Two presidents have faced impeachment and removal. One vote in the Senate saved Andrew Johnson from removal after the Civil War. Nixon's role in Watergate crimes led the House Judiciary Committee to recommend his impeachment. He avoided it by resigning.

The Founders meant Congress's impeachment and removal power to be one of the checks and balances, a final weapon against executive unresponsiveness. However, the procedures involved are cumbersome. Presidents usually have enough clout to avoid them, so Congress has rarely used these powers.

Succession

The Constitution says only that presidential powers and duties "shall devolve on the Vice-President" if a president dies, resigns, or cannot execute them. It directs Congress to choose a successor if there is no vice-president. Congress passed the Presidential Succession Act of 1947 two years after Franklin Roosevelt's death in office. It lists the officers who become president, starting with the speaker of the House of Representatives and the president pro tempore of the Senate and ending with the head of the most recently created cabinet department.

The Succession Act has never been used because we have always had a vice-president when something happened to the president. The Twenty-fifth Amendment was ratified in 1967 to ensure, as much as possible, that this will always be the case. It directs that, if the office falls vacant, the president must name a new vice-president acceptable to majorities in the House and Senate. The amendment has been used twice. Nixon chose Gerald Ford to replace Spiro Agnew, who resigned after pleading no contest to charges of taking bribes when he was a public official in Maryland. Ford then named Nelson Rockefeller his vice-president after Nixon resigned.

A president's ability to do his job is not always clear. James Garfield was shot in July 1881 and did not die until mid-September. In 1919, Woodrow Wilson had a nervous collapse in the summer and a stroke in the fall and was incapacitated for many months. No one was sure about his condition, however, because his wife restricted access to him. In both cases, the

Many people believed that Edith Galt Wilson, the president's wife, was making the decisions during President Wilson's illness.

issue of who was or should have been acting as president was unclear.

Another section of the Twenty-fifth Amendment charges the vice-president and a majority of the cabinet (or some other body named by Congress) to determine if a president is able to do his job. The vice-president becomes "acting president" if they find the president incapacitated. The president resumes his functions after notifying Congress of his recovery. Reagan followed the spirit of this section in 1985. Before undergoing cancer surgery, he sent his vice-president, George Bush, a letter authorizing him to act as president while Reagan was unconscious.

Rewards

The president's salary of $200,000 a year is large by most standards but seems almost small compared to the job's other benefits. These benefits include living in one of the world's most famous houses, a rural retreat (Camp David) and fleets of aircraft and cars, and a generous pension after leaving office as well as money for an office and staff.

No one argues that the president's material rewards should be slight. However, there is some concern that daily life on Pennsylvania Avenue is too isolated from the daily realities of most citizens. Might a president come to think he is more special than we want him to be, that his views are better than others'?

Growth of the Modern Presidency

The Presidency Before the New Deal

Most presidents during the 1800s and early 1900s were "ordinary people with very ordinary reputations."[7] James Monroe, who served from 1817 to 1825, wore outdated knee breeches, silk stockings, ink-spotted clothing, and worn-down shoes. He looked, according to a European diplomat, like an unkempt clerk.[8] The nineteenth century was an age of legislative power. Indeed, Woodrow Wilson wrote a book calling national government in the 1880s "congressional government."

Although political scientists rank Jefferson as a great president, he did not consider the office, or his performance in it, very important. His instructions for an epitaph listed what he thought were his three main accomplishments in life: authoring the Declaration of Independence and a Virginia law guaranteeing religious freedom and founding the University of Virginia. He did not include his presidential office.

The Founders largely viewed the president as a presiding officer. Before 1932, most people saw Congress as the representative and policymaking part of government. They saw presidential leadership as a threat to responsive government. As a result, the office tended to attract individuals of average ability who did not try to be leaders and who regarded administering the law as their primary job. The powerful presidents before the New Deal were the exceptions and not the rule. Washington, Jackson, Lincoln, Teddy Roosevelt, and Wilson were all powerful. Washington set many important precedents. For example, he initiated meetings of department heads, or cabinet meetings. Jackson was the first to act assertively to fulfill the popular mandate he saw in his election—the first to veto a bill because *he* did not like it. Lincoln boldly and creatively interpreted the Constitution to say individual states could not legally leave the Union. Teddy Roosevelt understood our growing national power and sent a fleet halfway around the world to show off American strength, although he had only enough money to send it that far and Congress had to pay for bringing it home. Wilson was the first twentieth-century president to lead us into a major foreign involvement, World War I.

Someone once said Americans were lucky because we always got presidential leadership when we needed it: during the birth of the nation, the civil war, and foreign crises. This implies that our needs change, that we need more government and executive leadership during crises and little or none at other times. Presidential power was traditionally supposed to return to its "normal" low profile after we resolved special problems.

Development of the Personal Presidency

The presidency has grown considerably since the nineteenth century because people want more services from government and because they look to the president for leadership. Theodore Lowi believes that we have had a **personal presidency** since the New Deal.[9] He argues that, consciously or unconsciously, the American people have had a "new social contract" with the president since the 1930s. In return for getting more power and support from us than we give to

Vice-Presidency

Job

Vice-presidents of private corporations work on matters of importance to their firms. This has only recently been true of United States vice-presidents. Historically, the only jobs vice-presidents have had were to preside over the Senate and cast tie-breaking votes. Presidents have traditionally given vice-presidents little information and few opportunities for involvement. Truman did not know about the atom bomb when he became president after Franklin Roosevelt's (FDR's) death, but within months he had to decide about using it on Japan.

Gerald Ford's vice-president, Nelson Rockefeller, called the job "standby equipment." Others have been less charitable. John Adams wrote his wife, Abigail, that it is "the most insignificant office that ever the invention of man contrived or his imagination conceived." FDR's first vice-president, John Nance Garner, was less elegant in observing that his job was not worth a "pitcher of warm spit."

FDR had told Garner, "You tend to your office and I'll tend to mine." The problem was that there was little to tend. Historically, presidents have had difficulty delegating important jobs to their vice-presidents because they themselves have wanted to wield all the power of their administrations.

Until Carter, presidents asked their vice-presidents to deal mainly with partisan or ceremonial matters. Vice-presidents helped mend party fences and criticized the opposition in harsher terms than the president could use without damaging his image as president of all the people. Spiro Agnew gained considerable attention for calling Nixon's opponents "effete liberals," among other things.

Carter was the first president to use his vice-president, Walter Mondale, for important work. Carter had no national experience before his election and considered Mondale, a former United States senator, a major asset. Carter gave Mondale a White House office (as opposed to one in the Old Executive Office Building next door), scheduled weekly lunches with him, put him on all White House advisory groups, and had him attend all important meetings, lobby Congress, and read the paperwork that crossed Carter's desk. Ronald Reagan did much the same with George Bush, who is continuing this tradition of more vice-presidential involvement with Dan Quayle.

Although tensions sometimes exist between the vice-president's staff and the president's, as a reflection of their separate political careers, there is incentive for cooperation. Given the great public exposure of the White House, it is not to either offical's interest to appear on bad terms with the other.

Springboard to the White House?

George Bush was the first incumbent vice-president to win a presidential election since Martin Van Buren in 1836. That 34 men after Van Buren failed to win the presidency while serving as vice-president led to talk of a "Van Buren jinx." According to it, vice-presidents cannot win the White House because they are saddled with the negatives of their president's record without being able to take credit for his successes. Evidence for this are the failed presidential bids of Richard Nixon, Hubert Humphrey, and Walter Mondale. In 1960, Nixon received little help from the popular Dwight Eisenhower who preferred to avoid partisan battles and did not like Nixon personally. Opposition to the Vietnam War and Lyndon Johnson hurt Humphrey in 1968. And Reagan would not let Mondale escape Carter's shadow in 1984.

However, the "jinx" may be a fiction.[1] Only 7 of the 34 vice-presidents from Van Buren to Bush actually ran for president while they were vice-president. When Nixon lost in 1960 and Humphrey in 1968 (to former vice-president Nixon!), they lost by very little. In fact, recent history shows that vice-presidents do become presidential front-runners. Six of the last 8 vice-presidents were nominated to be president.

The caliber of people who have recently been vice-president indicates that the office may be more important now. Most have been seasoned public servants with considerable experience and personal records of achievement. That they were willing to take the job suggests it has become more than "standby equipment." Perhaps the furor over Quayle's qualifications (or lack of them) reflects the fact that the public thinks the vice-presidency is worth a highly qualified candidate.

1. Michael Nelson, *A Heartbeat Away* (New York: Priority Press, 1988). For more on the vice-presidency, see Paul C. Light, *Vice-Presidential Power: Advice and Influence in the White House* (Baltimore: Johns Hopkins University Press, 1984), and George Sirgiovanni, "The 'Van Buren Jinx': Vice Presidents Need Not Beware," *Presidential Studies Quarterly* 18 (Winter 1988): 61–76.

other parts of government, the president is supposed to make sure we get what we want from government.

Through the media, presidents amass tremendous personal power directly from the people. Presidents tell us what they think our needs are and give us an opportunity to accept or reject their views. Lowi argues that in the polling booth and in opinion polls we "vote" on each president and his policies. Our views shape presidential policy, power, and the workings of government.

Why did the personal presidency develop? We have already seen in chapter 3 that the New Deal brought about a large expansion in the role of government, especially the national government. In addition, it brought about a tremendous growth in presidential power. Franklin Roosevelt was elected president in 1932 because people thought he would help them. His policies, which he called the New Deal, put the national government and the presidency in direct contact with many citizens for the first time. People saw presidential leadership as a way to deal with national needs.

Other factors contributed to presidential power too. For example, political parties did not assume a more national character in response to the growth of the national government. As a result, they rarely provide national leadership, and few people look to them for answers to national problems.

Furthermore, Congress has been unable to provide national leadership. Made up of 535 individuals divided into two houses and hundreds of committees and subcommittees, it cannot develop, articulate, or keep its members faithful to national policy goals. It is also influenced by interest groups that have built effective national organizations. And, of course, Congress has strong representation from both political parties, another source of divisiveness.

In addition, enacting a flood of New Deal policies to combat Depression era problems led to the expansion of the executive branch. New agencies were created and new civil servants hired. This increased the president's power by making him more important as a manager and policymaker.

Finally, radio and television contributed to the expansion of presidential power. As an integral part of national life by the 1930s, broadcasting made the news seem more immediate and compelling. Along with the wire services, it gave people a way to follow presidents and a way for presidents to "sell" their policies and provide leadership. Because it is easier to

President Franklin Roosevelt gives a fireside chat.

follow one person than many (as in Congress), the media helped make the presidency the focal point of national politics.

Roosevelt's fireside chats were the first presidential effort to use the media to speak directly and regularly to the nation. They helped make him, and his office, the most important link between people and government. In a personalized style he began, "My friends. . . ." People felt Roosevelt was talking to each of them in their own homes, and they gathered around their radios whenever he was on. Whereas President Herbert Hoover had received an average of 40 letters a day, Roosevelt received 4,000 letters a day after beginning his chats.[10] He even received some addressed not to "The President" but simply to "My Friend, Washington, D.C." Currently, George Bush gets around 50,000 letters a week from adults, another 12,000 to 15,000 from children, and about 250,000 unsolicited telephone calls a year.

The personal presidency ties government directly to the people and can produce substantial benefits. For example, it gives us something to rally around during times of crisis. The public expressed loyalty to our system after Kennedy's assassination by supporting his successor, Johnson. The personal presidency also contributes to our ability to achieve national goals. Roosevelt was able to build support for New Deal programs because he articulated a persuasive view of what people expected government to do. He was the first president to use survey data to identify public needs and to use the media to tell people that he would give them what they wanted. Making himself the major link between public opinion and government often let him overcome the inertia and divisions associated with a system of fragmented powers.

However, Roosevelt's actions also revealed a cost of the personal presidency: presidents with great power often seek more. Roosevelt won reelection in 1936 by a landslide, confirming popular support for his New Deal. This led him to seek more power by trying to expand the size of an unfriendly Supreme Court so he could appoint judges who supported him. He also tried to get local and state parties to nominate certain congressional candidates by using federal funds as a carrot. The defeat of pro-Roosevelt congressional candidates in 1938 ruined both his plans. People did not want to politicize the Court. And state and local parties wanted to pick their own nominees. Nixon and Reagan also tried to wield too much power after their landslide reelections in 1972 and 1984. The Watergate and Iran-contra scandals were the results.

Incumbents of the personal presidency seek more power because they typically promise more than they can deliver. Their power is based on public support for their programs. The president can increase that support by promising to give people more. Presidents are tempted to do this because they need more power to compete successfully with other parts of government and maintain their public support. Thus, they are caught on a treadmill of making great promises, seeking more power to honor them, and making even greater promises to get more power. Inevitably, they promise more than they can deliver. Bush has promised to send astronauts to Mars, fight the drug problem, bail out failed savings and loan institutions, deploy the B-2 Stealth bomber, continue work on the Star Wars missile defense plan, do more to protect the environment, and be the "education president" while cutting the budget deficit without raising taxes.

Given this, Lowi may be right in calling the personal presidency the "victim" of democracy. After Roosevelt's death in 1946, only three of eight presidents left office without experiencing permanently lowered public opinion ratings: Eisenhower, Kennedy (who was assassinated in mid-term), and Reagan.[11]

Source: BERRY'S WORLD Reprinted by permission of NEA, Inc.

© 1978 by NEA, Inc.

"We never had winters like these past two before Carter took office."

If the personal presidency victimizes presidents, it also victimizes many others. Johnson's promise that he would not be the first president to lose a war not only caused his downfall but also had devastating consequences for many Americans and people in Southeast Asia.

Presidential Power

The presidency has formal powers deriving from the Constitution, acts of Congress, and judicial opinions interpreting them. Thus the Constitution charges presidents with nominating federal judges and members of their administrations, an act of Congress directs them to submit annual budget requests, and judicial decisions have directed presidents to spend money appropriated by Congress.

Although all modern presidents have had the same formal powers, each has used them more or less effectively depending on his native skills, the quality of the people serving him, and circumstances beyond his control.

Persuading the Washingtonians

To achieve their goals, presidents need more than their formal powers. They need the **power to persuade** people, whom Richard Neustadt called the **Washingtonians,** to support them.[12]

The Washingtonians are members of Congress who vote on a president's proposals, interest group leaders who can mobilize congressional and bureaucratic support, judges who consider challenges to presidential policies, and media leaders who influence public opinion. In short, they are the people the president needs to govern. Because the Washingtonians also need him to get what they want, a president can bargain and persuade.

The effective president is "one who seizes the center of the Washington bazaar and actively barters . . . to build winning coalitions."[13] Johnson told one member of Congress whose vote he was seeking, "You may need me some time, and I'll remember this if you'll do it." Presidents "remember" their friends by putting their pet projects in the budget, by campaigning for them, and by naming the people they want to public office.

A president's powers give him more favors and penalties to dispense than anyone else. As the chief foreign policymaker, he can seek support from Irish and Jewish Americans by promoting peace in Northern Ireland and giving aid to Israel. As commander-in-chief, he can help local economies by maintaining military bases in some places but not in others. And as chief budget maker, he has many favors to give and withhold. Reagan once traded funds for renovating the New Haven, Connecticut, train depot for a congressman's vote.[14]

Presidential persuasion does not always involve bargaining, however. Presidents also remind fellow Republicans or Democrats of the need to stick together to promote their party platform and achieve party goals. Bush used this tactic in 1990 when he asked former presidents and fellow Republicans Reagan, Ford, and Nixon to call House Republicans to urge them to vote for a budget plan supported by the White House. Bipartisan appeals can be effective too, especially in foreign affairs. In addition, presidents try to convince others of the merits of their positions. For example, having served many years in Congress, Johnson knew how to approach members and was a masterful lobbyist. In working for a foreign aid bill, he invited key members to the White House for one-on-one talks described by an aide as "endless talking, ceaseless importuning, torrential laying on of the facts . . . for several days."[15]

Sometimes presidents are more heavy-handed in seeking support. A Reagan aide described how the White House changed one senator's vote: "We just beat his brains out. We stood him in front of an open grave and told him he could jump in if he wanted to [oppose Reagan]."[16] Such tactics can succeed but make a president look bad. In 1990, Bush was criticized for the way White House staff lobbied Congress for a budget plan. His chief of staff, John Sununu, called Senator Trent Lott (R-Miss.) "insignificant" on television after Lott refused to support the plan, and Sununu alienated others with petty reprisals. For example, Representative Ralph Regula (R-Ohio) was offered the president's box at the Kennedy Center for a show but lost it after he decided to vote against the plan.

Presidents use the prestige of their office to get support too. In 1975, Ford persuaded 18 House members to change their votes to support one of his vetoes. He took them on his jet, *Air Force One,* and "lectured" them.[17] Because many members rarely, if ever, talk to a president, most consider these conversations memorable events and listen.

Presidents cannot always get the support of those they need, however. Members of Congress have their own constituencies and careers. Interest group leaders have to consider the views of their rank-and-file members. And other Washingtonians have interests that diverge from the president's.

Every president develops a track record of his effectiveness as a leader. Neustadt calls it the president's **professional reputation.**[18] A president with an effective reputation has a record of getting what he wants, helping his allies, and penalizing the opposition. This reputation contributes to his continuing ability to persuade.

A part of a president's professional reputation is based on how successful he is in getting congressional support. Reagan's effectiveness with Congress and his professional reputation were not as high as his personal popularity. His greatest success was in 1981, when he got Congress to make a major tax cut and raise military spending. However, this helped produce severe economic problems that hurt his persuasiveness. He also hedged on major issues, such as the possibility of a tax increase after the 1984 election, and

Presidential Personality

An individual's personality is a major influence on his style and approach to being president. James David Barber examines two sides of presidential personality: whether presidents tend to be active or passive and whether they enjoy being president.[1]

"Active" presidents try to control government's agenda. They have their own ideas and work hard to promote them. "Passive" presidents tend to react to developments rather than initiate them. For example, Calvin Coolidge was president from 1923 to 1929. He slept eleven hours a night, sat in a rocking chair on the White House porch in the evening, and napped a lot. Will Rogers, the great humorist, said "the country wanted nothing done, and he done it." Passive presidents permit others to do things for them. "Positive" presidents enjoy manipulating the strings of government. "Negative" presidents do not enjoy the push and pull, give and take, highs and lows of the presidency.

Barber combines these traits into four different personalities. "Active-positives" enjoy trying to be effective leaders. "Active-negatives" do not and end up craving more power to neutralize their critics. "Passive-positives" put a premium on getting approval from others. And "passive-negatives" want only the satisfaction of doing what they see as their duty.

On the basis of these characteristics, Barber believes we can predict a president's, or presidential candidate's, success in office. He thinks active-positives are likely to be the most successful and that passive-positives and negatives are likely to accomplish the least. Barber classifies Reagan as a passive-positive because he did not work as hard as many earlier presidents and leaned heavily on his aides. Yet he clearly enjoyed the job. And Barber thinks Bush is an

President Johnson was active in work and play.

active-positive because he likes politics, has a lot of energy, and has shown a capacity to learn and change.[2]

Barber warns against "active-negatives" whose activism seems compulsive because they do not get personal satisfaction from their work. This leads them, he concludes, to be isolated, frustrated, and rigid. Wilson's attempts to get Senate approval of United States membership in the League of Nations, Johnson's reaction to mounting criticism of the Vietnam War, and Nixon's handling of Watergate are examples of this.

Barber paints his presidential portraits with broad strokes by reducing complex personalities to just two dimensions. As a result, classifying some presidents is very hard. For example, contrary to Barber's categorization, many would classify Reagan as an "active" because of his commitments to cut domestic spending, raise military spending, and confront the "evil empire" of the Soviets. In addition, given popular demands for presidential leadership, it is hard to know whether presidential actions originate in the office or its incumbent. Still, although Barber's approach is imperfect, it highlights the importance of examining presidents' personalities.

1. James David Barber, *The Presidential Character: Predicting Performance in the White House*, 3rd ed. (Englewood Cliffs, N.J.: Prentice-Hall, 1985). For more on the impact of personality, see Erwin C. Hargrove, *Presidential Leadership: Personality and Political Style* (New York: Macmillan, 1966). For a more critical analysis, see Alexander George, "Assessing Presidential Character," *World Politics* 26 (1974): 234–82.

2. James David Barber, "George Bush: In Search of a Mission," *New York Times*, January 19, 1989, p. A31. See also Dom Bonafede, "Presidential Focus," *National Journal*, April 8, 1989, p. 890.

■ Barber's Presidential Personalities

	Active	Passive
Positive	F. D. Roosevelt	Taft
	Truman	Harding
	Kennedy	Reagan
	Ford	
	Carter	
	Bush	
Negative	Wilson	Coolidge
	Hoover	Eisenhower
	Johnson	
	Nixon	

he often seemed uninformed and uninvolved. As figure 1 shows, Reagan's congressional support dropped after 1981 and was low compared to other presidents. As one observer noted, "Reagan got his licks in early in 1981. By 1982, he had a hard time selling them [Congress] cheap lemonade."[19]

Franklin Roosevelt earned his professional reputation because he got Congress to enact much of his legislative program in the first 100 days of his administration. Since Roosevelt, the Washingtonians have expected presidents to make their marks early.

After his election, Bush's challenge was to put his imprint on the presidency without harming public perceptions of continuity with Reagan that had helped him win office.[20] Bush responded by taking symbolic actions to distinguish himself from Reagan, such as meeting with black leaders on Martin Luther King Day and holding more press conferences in his first 80 days than Reagan did in his last two years in office. Bush also tried to deal with such problems as bankrupt savings and loans, Latin American debt, and drugs. Some of his efforts were successful, but he was criticized for not emulating Reagan by capturing the public's attention with clear themes, what Bush once

called the "vision thing." His supporters defended him by arguing that he was a problem solver, not a visionary. He also was criticized for taking longer to fill jobs in his administration than any president before him.[21]

Bush's professional reputation as measured by congressional support scores was weak by his third year in office. Figure 1 shows that his first-year success with Congress was the lowest of any elected president since 1953, when scores were first computed. He also has the lowest two-year record. In part, these scores are products of partisanship. Bush has had fewer congressional Republicans to work with than any GOP president in this century. However, low support for Bush among congressional Republicans may result from the absence of a well-articulated White House legislative program.[22] His greater popularity in the months after the Persian Gulf War did not translate into more congressional support.

Persuading the Public

Presidents tried to generate public support before the growth of the personal presidency. Teddy Roosevelt called the presidency a "bully pulpit" from which to

Figure 1 ■ Presidential Success on Congressional Votes, 1953–1990

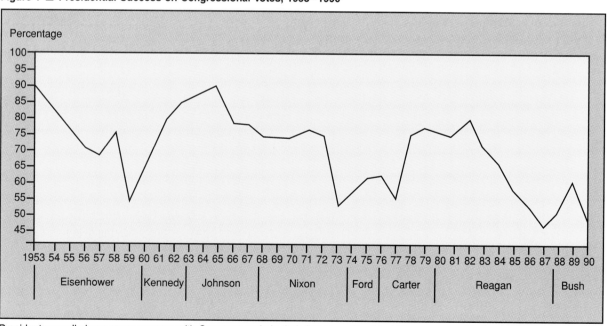

Presidents usually have more success with Congress early in their first term. President Reagan proved to be no exception.

Note: Precentages are based on votes on which presidents took a position.

Source: Congressional Quarterly Weekly Report, December 22, 1990, p. 4185.

(see figure 2).[28] Some polls ask people to rate presidential efforts on specific issues. Others ask more general questions such as: Do you approve or disapprove of the way President _____ has been handling his job?

Many people are predisposed to support the president. People tend to look at a president's efforts and positions more than his short-run success or how his policies affect them.[29] Failure on specific issues does not always produce low scores on general performance. For example, majorities of respondents simultaneously disapproved of Reagan's handling of environmental and foreign policy issues, which the public thinks are important, *and* registered approval of his overall performance. Bush's extremely high personal popularity is not matched by public support for his domestic policies either.

External conditions also affect presidential popularity. Dramatic international events like the 1989 invasion of Panama, called "rally events," are important.[30] Public support rises significantly at such times because people do not want to hurt the president, the symbol of national unity. However, the higher levels of support produced by rally events are rarely sustained.[31] Greater support among those who were critical of a president before the event tends to be brief; critics usually return to their earlier negative views shortly after it.

Increasing support for Bush's policies toward Iraq after its invasion of Kuwait demonstrates public readiness to rally around the president. In November 1990, the public was divided over Bush's decision to send more troops to the Persian Gulf, with 47% approving and 46% disapproving. By January 1991, after fighting began, almost 90% approved of the way he was handling the situation. As figure 2 shows, this increasing support helped raise Bush's general approval ratings from 54% in October to 89% in February. The

Figure 2 ■ Presidential Popularity Usually Declines over Time

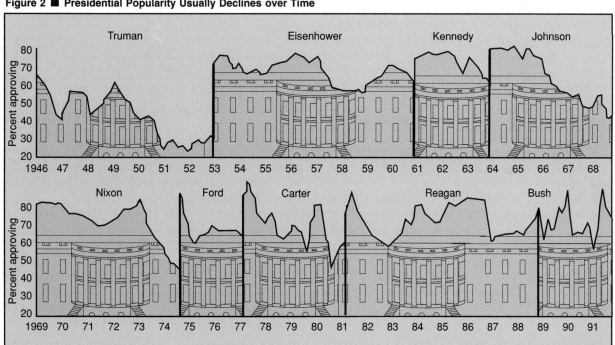

Eisenhower and to some extent Reagan are exceptions to the post–World War II tendency for presidential popularity to fall over time. Although Reagan's popularity plunged 20 points at the end of 1986 because of the Iran-contra scandal, it partly rebounded by the end of his term. Most commentators thought this reflected popular fondness for Reagan as a person and his early successes rather than policy achievements late in his term. Bush began his term with high ratings typical of new presidents; after falling in 1990, they rebounded to record heights during the Persian Gulf War.

Source: Caption: William Schneider, "Reagan Now Viewed as an Irrelevant President," *National Journal,* November 28, 1987, p. 3051. See also George Gallup, Jr. and Alec Gallup, "The Former President," *The Polling Report,* January 30, 1989, pp. 1 and 5. Figure data: Gallup Polls, reported in *Public Opinion,* January/February 1989, and updated. The question asked is: "Do you approve or disapprove of the way [name of president] is handling his job as president?"

unexpectedly swift defeat of Iraq with surprisingly few American casualties kept Bush's poll scores high for some time.[32]

Although many factors affect public opinion about presidential leadership, a positive image of leadership may be especially good at protecting a president's ratings from serious policy failure. Reagan's ratings survived policy failures because he already had such an image. However, they were lowered by the Iran-contra scandal, which cast serious doubts on his ability to lead. Carter's ratings receded as problems in gaining the release of Iranian hostages reinforced an earlier view of him as ineffective. Thus, although short-term crises or rally events can help a president's ratings, long-term ones that are not resolved successfully can lower them.

Limits of Presidential Power

Even persuasive presidents do not get everything they want. Given the pressures that modern presidents feel to satisfy public expectations, they can become very frustrated by limitations on their power, sometimes to the point that they may try to overcome their limitations with aggressive action, either overt or covert.[33] An example of overt action is Carter's failed attempt to free American hostages in Iran by force in 1980 after months of frustration.

The most famous examples of covert presidential action in the face of perceived frustrations are Nixon's secret attempts to know what his "enemies" were doing: invading individual privacy with phone taps, break-ins, and unauthorized reviews of income tax returns. Reagan, frustrated trying to free American hostages in Lebanon, authorized covert arms sales to Iran and supported covert and illegal aid to the Nicaraguan contras.

Roles of the President

We have seen that the president's role in government has grown with government's role in society. Here we examine the many roles of the president, sometimes called the president's many hats. Clinton Rossiter identified the president's roles in administrative, domestic and foreign policy leadership, military matters, promoting national unity, and party leadership.[34] Before discussing them, however, we will describe how

the president's own office has grown to handle the larger workload.

Growth of Presidential Staff

George Washington paid a nephew out of his own pocket to be his only full-time aide. Congress did not appropriate funds for a presidential clerk until 1857. Lincoln's staff "exploded" to four people, but he often opened and answered the daily mail himself. Cleveland answered the White House telephone, and Wilson typed many of his own speeches.[35] Today, demand for presidential leadership has produced a full-scale bureaucracy around the president, the Executive Office of the President (EOP), whose employees work directly for the president.

Franklin Roosevelt created the EOP by executive order in 1939 because New Deal programs had increased the number of federal agencies and workers and he needed help running a larger and more complex executive branch. The size of the EOP grew rapidly in the Nixon administration and has continued to grow. Bush's EOP employs more than 1,700 people, over 400 times as many as Lincoln had. The White House staff, a part of the EOP, has also grown. To put staff growth in perspective, Nancy Reagan's staff was larger than Roosevelt's at the height of the New Deal.[36]

Presidents have used different styles in running the EOP. Roosevelt and Kennedy cared little for rigid lines of responsibility. They gave staffers different jobs over time and fostered a competitive spirit: who could serve the president best?

Eisenhower and Nixon valued formal lines of authority. Eisenhower's military experience led him to rely on a chief of staff, Sherman Adams. Adams so dominated White House routine that one newspaper story was headlined, "Adams Insists Ike Is Really President."[37] Nixon's chief of staff, H. R. Haldeman, ran the White House for his president and took much of the heat when people did not get what they wanted. He saw his job this way: "Every president needs a son of a bitch, and I'm Nixon's. I'm his buffer and his bastard. I get done what he wants done and I take the heat instead of him."[38]

The Watergate scandal led presidents Ford and Carter to avoid the appearance of strong staff chiefs, although both eventually saw a need for a chief of staff to manage their schedules and the huge flow of paper that passes through the White House. Reagan prided himself on delegating authority to the best people and letting them do their work without interfering.[39] Consistent with this, he first used a three-person committee to head his staff, with each member having an area of responsibility. Serious problems developed, however, because none of them had enough authority to make final decisions on more important matters and Reagan was too removed from daily affairs to do so. He delegated considerable authority to his aides and preferred relaxing, reading his mail, and handling ceremonial tasks to reading reports. He once startled aides by confessing that he had watched *The Sound of Music* on television rather than read his briefing books before an economic summit meeting in 1983.[40] This detached management style had its costs, most noticeably the Iran-contra scandal.[41]

Problems produced by Reagan's detached management style led him to appoint a series of strong staff chiefs whose coordination of White House operations helped restore his image.

Bush's organization of the White House indicates that he understands the value of a strong chief of staff. His chief is former New Hampshire Governor John Sununu, a man known for loyalty, brains, and a short fuse. Senate minority leader Robert Dole (R-Kans.) called Sununu "the chief of chaff."[42] Bush has used

Sununu to control the White House. Bush's selection of mostly anonymous staffers for other White House jobs helped accomplish this too.[43] One senior White House official described Bush's staff as "nice people who will not handle him [Bush] or try to."[44]

Presidents seek advice from different people. Although their advisers differ from issue to issue, they consult some more than others. Thus, Reagan went to close friends from California when he was in particular need of good advice. Andrew Jackson was the first to call such groups of advisers "kitchen cabinets."

Members of the White House staff also have great influence on presidents because the president appoints them, works daily with them, and tends to trust them more than others. They are often people who helped him get elected or worked for him when he held other offices.

Other EOP members can also have influence on the president. For example, Reagan's and Bush's directors of the Office of Management and Budget have had tremendous influence on budget policy. Career civil servants have less influence because presidents tend to rely on their own staffs.

Today's EOP mirrors America's diversity of needs and interests. Its offices deal with national security, energy, economics, consumers, and drug abuse, for example. It employs special assistants with responsibilities for foreign trade, civil rights, the elderly, physical fitness, labor relations, women, Wall Street, and the District of Columbia, among others.

The growth of the EOP reflects the growth of government generally. Because departments and agencies often have policy interests independent of the president's, a president wants his "own" people around him, staffers he can trust. Many EOP jobs boil down to a ceaseless effort to monitor and control agency operations.

Administrative Leadership

Administrative powers were very important to the Founders. They expected a representative Congress to make policy and a representative president to administer it. Although they gave the president other tasks as well, they gave executive tasks the highest priority in creating the presidency.

The Constitution has very few provisions that describe the president's administrative duties. It does not call for the creation of bureaucratic departments and agencies directly, but it does invest the president with

Decisions ultimately rest on the president. Here President Kennedy is alone with his thoughts in the Oval Office.

executive power and authorizes him to demand written reports from his "principal officers." The Constitution also directs the president to nominate the most important officers of the executive branch.

Presidential control of the executive branch is difficult, however, because of Congress's legislative and budgetary powers, the huge number and diversity of executive jobs, and interest group influence. This difficulty and pressures associated with the need to attract popular support have led recent presidents to spend less time on the administrative side of their job.[45] Nevertheless, presidents have a number of ways to try to control executive agencies. They can appoint and remove key administrators, formulate budget recommendations, and reorganize agencies.

Appointing Officials.   The president nominates about 1,300 people to policymaking jobs in executive agencies and to positions as United States attorneys and marshals, ambassadors, and members of part-time boards and commissions. The Senate must confirm all of them, and, with a few exceptions, does. Another 1,140 presidential appointments to senior civil service jobs do not need Senate approval.[46]

Presidents have little freedom in naming people to many positions. The custom of **senatorial courtesy** gives senators of the president's party a virtual veto over appointments to jobs, including judicial appointments, in their states. Senatorial courtesy limits a president's ability to promote his policy preferences through his appointments because it gives senators

FOCUS ON AN ISSUE

Presidents or Prime Ministers?

Most democratic nations have **parliamentary governments,** that is, systems in which the executive is chosen by the legislature. Americans have long admired Britain's parliamentary system. Woodrow Wilson once proposed that members of the president's cabinet sit in Congress and be able to introduce bills like their British counterparts. Many Americans are frustrated by our system's fragmentation and by a lack of accountability among elected officials, as evidenced by the Watergate and Iran-contra scandals. They have looked enviously across the Atlantic where British heads of government, called prime ministers, seem to be better leaders *and* more accountable to the public.

Our government is fragmented in that Congress, the president, and the courts have independent, constitutionally protected roles. Also, members of Congress and the president are elected in different ways by different constituencies.

In contrast, the British government is marked by a unity of authority. The prime minister, or PM, is an elected member of the House of Commons, the lower house of Britain's national legislature called the Parliament. (Parliament's other house, the House of Lords, is unelected and has very little power.) The PM is elected like other members of the Commons by the voters of a constituency. A PM is chosen by the party as its leader. The PM is always the leader of the majority (or largest) party in the Commons and usually decides when elections to the Commons will occur. However, elections must take place within five years of the last election. As members of the Commons, the PM and the cabinet ministers appointed by the PM must argue for their policies and respond to criticism from minority party members in debate.

Rank-and-file members of the Commons have very little independent power and often do not live in the constituencies that elect them. National party organizations have a great deal of influence over who is selected to run for election to the Commons. Members who do not vote the party line sometimes lose their party's support for reelection. This helps explain why 97% of the bills sponsored by the PM and cabinet from 1945 to 1987 were enacted.[1]

Would changing our Constitution to institute a parliamentary system help us resolve any of our problems?

Would a Parliamentary System Make it Easier to Govern?

Our national government is often hamstrung by partisan differences which are exacerbated when different parties control the White House and Congress. Such divided control has been the case most years since World War II. Divided party control makes it more likely that the president and congressional leaders will advocate different policies and priorities. It also makes it easier for elected officials to avoid taking responsibility for failed policies and inaction.

Adopting the British system could help resolve these problems. Congress could eliminate divided party control by selecting the president. The majority party would choose one of its leaders who would be able to influence nominations for congressional office. Members of Congress would support the president to protect their nominations for reelection and because defeating a bill supported by the president could lead to a general election they might lose. This system would make it difficult for policymakers to play the "blame game"; the president and other party leaders would be responsible for government action or inaction.

Although this is an attractive picture in some respects, the Founders designed our system to represent the diverse interests of a large, heterogeneous population. While more effective leadership in government is appealing, greater centralization can mean less opportunity to accommodate diverse local interests. Many Americans would not like a party organization to have the major influence on nominations for congressional office. Some would also be angry if representatives advocated positions contrary to local majority opinion on an important issue. America is a much more diverse society than Britain which might make centralization less workable.

Diversity in America is also represented by powerful interest groups. Their close ties to congressional committees and subcommittees and executive branch officials give these interest groups considerable power to obstruct government. While these groups might be weakened by parliamentary-style arrangements, the interests they represent would still exist, as would iron triangle relationships and interest group vetoes.

(continued on next page)

Considering whether parliamentary forms would improve the workings of our government requires us to weigh some difficult trade-offs. Do we want to pay the costs of frequent gridlock and inefficiency to keep a system that is accessible to diverse local and other interests? Or do we want to sacrifice accessibility to government to have the efficiency of a stronger, more centralized system?

Some observers question whether the PM is really such a powerful leader. One student of British politics believes the PM is the "single most important person in government" but not "all-important or the cause of everything that is done."[2] Cabinet ministers make many important decisions without consulting the PM, and some PMs make staying in office their highest priority and give in to cabinet and other pressures.

Thus, like a president, a PM cannot do everything and must try to address problems that will allow him or her to build an effective reputation. This also suggests that a PM must generate support among the "Londoners" just as a president does among the Washingtonians. If this is right, the provision of strong executive leadership will be a challenge wherever citizens value democratic principles regardless of constitutional arrangements.

Would Adopting the British System Make the Presidency More Accountable?

Supporters of a parliamentary system argue that it is more accountable to the public than our system because PMs and cabinet ministers must defend their policies in debate. A member once noted that "the whole Watergate thing might not have gone along so far if the members of the President's Cabinet had been required to spend 40 minutes in Congress every day answering questions."[3] Would Johnson and Nixon have kept our troops in Vietnam for as long as they did or would we have had arms-for-hostages deals in the Reagan years if these presidents had had to explain and defend their actions in the wells of the House and Senate?

Accountability is also present in the British system, according to its advocates, because a PM may have to turn the leadership over to someone else or call for a general election if his or her policies fail, are unpopular, or are rejected by a vote in the Commons. Thus, Margaret Thatcher had to resign in 1990 because her unpopular local tax policies led not only to riots in the streets but also to greatly reduced support among her fellow Conservative party members.

By contrast, our system offers two remedies when a president's actions contradict strongly held public opinion:

we can impeach and remove the president or wait for his term to end. Neither offers the British system's flexibility. Impeachment and removal are only appropriate for crimes. And waiting for the end of a term may deprive us of effective leadership until the next election.

Supporters of our system argue that Americans do not want to pay the costs of adopting the British system. They say we do not want a president's reputation and effectiveness eroded by having to confront hostile questions from opposition party members more interested in embarrassing him than in making good policy. They also maintain that electing presidents for fixed terms lets them do what they think is necessary for the public interest. Allowing party leaders to replace presidents before an election could lead presidents to worry more about staying in office than providing leadership.

Would Stronger National Party Organizations Raise Levels of Political Participation?

The British system resembles the responsible party government model we discussed in chapter 6. British national party organizations give voters a relatively clear choice of programs that most of their members support. As a result, British voters know who is responsible for public policy. Voter turnout is much higher than in the United States. Advocates of this system believe that stronger national parties in the United States would produce the same increased participation.

Proponents of the British system argue that strong national parties would raise citizen confidence in government by reducing the influence of political action committees. Linking congressional elections to the selection of the president would also make elections more important. Political participation would grow because citizens would be excited by election contests between parties able to follow through on their competing platform promises.

Supporters of our system argue that strong national parties would reduce political participation. Displacing local nominating primaries with national party influences would resemble "backroom" politics and alienate many voters. Moreover, strong national parties would give members of Congress less incentive to stress constituency service. This, as well as the fact that strong national parties would be less representative of our national diversity, could also alienate people and reduce participation.

1. Richard Rose, *Politics in England: Change and Persistence,* 5th ed. (London: Macmillan Press, 1989), p. 113.
2. Rose, *Politics in England,* pp. 100–105.
3. Louis W. Koenig, *The Chief Executive,* 5th ed. (New York: Harcourt Brace Jovanovich, 1986), p. 398.

opportunities to push their own policy preferences, which might not be in tune with the president's.

Presidents have considerable discretion in filling jobs with national jurisdictions, such as cabinet jobs and seats on regulatory commissions. Several traditions govern those named to certain jobs (a westerner to be secretary of the interior and someone with union ties to be secretary of labor), but they are not confining. As a result, presidents can shape the direction and image of their administrations with their appointments. The reputations of Grant, Harding, and Nixon suffered because of the low quality of some of their appointees. Likewise, some of Reagan's appointees hurt his reputation. For example, a Justice Department report found that former Attorney General Edwin Meese had engaged in "conduct which should not be tolerated of any government employee."[47] Reagan aides, including Michael Deaver, John Poindexter, and Oliver North, admitted lying to Congress. And more than 100 high-ranking Reagan appointees resigned under suspicion of unethical behavior.[48]

Removing Officials. Although the power to remove political appointees is not in the Constitution, presidents have it. Their power to name people they trust implies a power to remove those they find wanting. In 1935 the Supreme Court tried to define this power by saying that presidents can remove appointees from purely administrative jobs but not from those with quasi-legislative and judicial responsibilities. Although this ruling protects many appointees, identifying quasi-legislative and judicial jobs can be subjective.[49]

Making the Budget. The Founders gave Congress, and particularly the House of Representatives, the power of the purse. However, the growth of the presidency has increased presidential power in this area.

Although the president is chief administrator, for many years he had a negligible role in managing executive branch funds. Agency budget requests went to the House unreviewed and unchanged by the White House. Until the turn of the century, Congress thought it could handle the budget, but by the end of World War I, a general awareness had developed that a larger government required better management. The Budget and Accounting Act of 1921 gave presidents important priority-setting and managerial responsibilities that contributed to the president's dominance in budgetary politics.

The 1921 act requires the president to give Congress annual estimates of how much money it will take to run the government during the next fiscal year. The president's budget message contains his recommendations for how much money Congress should appropriate for every program of the national government. Formulating the message requires the White House to examine all agency budget requests and to decide which to support or reject. This exercise gives the president a chance to activate public support by recommending budget policies consistent with public expectations. It also allows the president and his staff to initiate the annual budget debate on their own terms.

In addition, the act created the Bureau of the Budget, or BOB. Originally a part of the Treasury Department, BOB was meant to be the president's primary tool in developing budget policy. It was made a part of the newly created EOP in 1939. Nixon changed BOB's name to the Office of Management and Budget (OMB) to stress its function of helping the president manage the executive branch.

Employing hundreds of budget and policy experts, OMB works only for the president and is a powerful presidential resource. It begins evaluating agency budget requests more than a year before the start of each fiscal year and helps defend the president's budget message. OMB also regulates when agencies spend their money, what they do with it, what policy ideas they develop, and how they operate. The budget is a huge document allocating billions of dollars to thousands of programs. It is hard—if not impossible—to read and understand it systematically. Using OMB often gives the president an edge in dealing with Congress on budget issues.

Reorganizing Executive Agencies. Since the 1930s, presidents have had the authority to submit plans to Congress to reorganize parts of the executive branch. Reorganization means redrawing agency boundaries to promote coordination when their actions overlap or duplicate each other. This may involve merging or abolishing offices or creating new ones.

Presidents have also created councils or offices in the White House to oversee departments with overlapping responsibilities. For example, Nixon merged a number of offices to create the Domestic Council to improve White House coordination of domestic programs. Reagan reorganized the White House early in his second term for the same purpose.

Domestic Policy Leadership

Polls have consistently shown that Americans consider "leadership" very important in evaluating presidents.[50] Somewhat paradoxically in light of their fear of "big government," most people want a president who can get government to "do" things.

The Founders, who understood the need for national leadership, required the president to inform Congress and the country of the "State of the Union" and to recommend policies to better it. In the president's State of the Union address at the start of each congressional session, he lists past achievements as well as remaining and new problems.

The Founders' desire to have the president act for the entire nation is also evidenced in his constitutional authority to kill, or veto, bills passed by Congress. Once the president receives a bill from Congress, he can sign it into law, veto it and send his objections to Congress, or not do anything, in which case the bill becomes a law after 10 congressional working days. Congress can enact a vetoed bill if a two-thirds majority in each house votes to override the president's veto. Presidents can avoid override attempts at certain times, however. A bill reaching the president dies if he does not sign it and Congress adjourns within 10 working days. This way of killing a bill is called a pocket veto.

Given expectations of presidential leadership and the presence of White House supporters in Congress, mobilizing two-thirds majorities to override a veto is usually very hard. As a result, presidents can influence Congress to write bills in certain ways by threatening to veto them if they do not conform to presidential wishes.

Only eight presidents never vetoed a bill. Franklin Roosevelt, a very assertive president, holds the record with 635 vetoes in his 14 years in office. That Congress overrode only 9 of his vetoes shows the effectiveness of his leadership. Among more recent presidents, Eisenhower vetoed 181 bills in 8 years. Congress overrode only 2 of them even though his party was in the minority for 6 of those years. Reagan vetoed 78 bills with 9 overridden. In his first 2 years in office, Bush vetoed 16 bills and none was overridden.

Presidents must be careful about using the veto too often to avoid appearing isolated or uncooperative. Vetoes indicate that presidents have failed to win initial support for their positions. That presidents are rarely overridden reminds us of their power when they decide they really want something.

Executive orders are another vehicle of presidential leadership. Based on constitutional provisions and congressional acts, they are issued by the president and executive agencies and contain binding policy. Technological and other developments often require government to act quickly and flexibly. Having the president make policy when needed permits this. Thus, the Natural Gas Policy Act of 1978 authorizes the president to declare, through executive orders, natural gas emergencies in times of severe shortage and to allocate gas supplies for high-priority uses.

Presidential leadership also includes creating and promoting policy packages such as Teddy Roosevelt's Square Deal, Wilson's New Freedom, Franklin Roosevelt's New Deal, and Johnson's Great Society. In 1981, Reagan had a huge impact on policy although he did not use a catchy label. People often evaluate presidential leadership in terms of the content and impact of these programs.

Reagan's leadership style in dealing with Congress involved going public to pressure it for support. In contrast, Bush uses White House staff to negotiate policy matters directly with congressional leaders. This style has produced victories (such as a higher tax credit for poor families) as well as confusion (the White House position on reducing the capital gains tax changed three times in one week in 1990). Bush may prefer this style because he lacks Reagan's media skills and, as an insider, already has working relationships with many Washingtonians. This style also frees him to devote more time to foreign policy issues.

Foreign Policy Leadership

Although presidential leadership in domestic policy is important, presidents are even more dominant in foreign policy. Article II of the Constitution gives the president a number of foreign policy powers: to make treaties with other countries, with Senate approval; to appoint ambassadors and consuls to represent us abroad; and to receive ambassadors from other countries. This last power lets presidents recognize or not recognize other governments, an important decision. Recognition may show our approval of a government or a belief that it contributes to our national interest. Recognition is not, therefore, automatic. We did not recognize the Soviet government until 16 years after the Bolshevik Revolution of 1917 and that of the communist government of mainland China until almost 25 years after it took power.

The Constitution also contains implied powers, which were acknowledged by the Supreme Court in a 1936 decision.[51] Congress had authorized Franklin Roosevelt to ban arms sales to warring Bolivia and Paraguay, but a military aircraft manufacturer claimed that Congress lacked the constitutional authority to delegate such power. The Court ruled against the corporation, saying that every nation has implied powers to promote its interests in the world. The Court said that there is a logic behind presidential power in foreign policy. A nation's government must be able to speak with one voice; having more than one voice can produce confusion about our ends and actions.

Presidents have their own styles in making foreign policy.[52] Eisenhower preferred using the formal procedures of the National Security Council, Kennedy and Johnson liked face-to-face discussions with many different people, and Nixon isolated himself with staff reports. Bush has relied on four or five advisers who have worked together before and know each other well. Some observers are concerned that this approach ignores the expertise of other officials and inhibits constructive criticism and disagreement.

Over the years, the president has become more powerful than Congress in foreign policymaking, assuming powers that were not explicitly given to either the legislative or the executive branch. As one observer commented:

> The President's normal problem with domestic policy is to get congressional support for the programs he prefers. In foreign affairs, in contrast, he can almost always get support for policies that he believes will protect the nation—but his problem is to find a viable policy.[53]

Sometimes Congress will not support the president. For example, over President Reagan's veto, Congress passed a law detailing policy toward South Africa; it sometimes opposed Reagan's proposed aid to guerrillas fighting the Nicaraguan government; and it overrode President Wilson's desire for the United States to enter the League of Nations and ratify the Treaty of Versailles ending World War I. Usually, however, even ill-conceived presidential foreign policies win congressional support.

Vietnam is a good example of presidential dominance in foreign policy. Kennedy started sending troops there in the early 1960s. By 1968, public opinion polls reported considerable opposition to the war. Nevertheless, American involvement continued until the North Vietnamese victory in 1975. Presidential policy dominated even with demonstrations, mass arrests, opposing editorials, negative opinion polls, and congressional criticism.

President Bush's control of events leading up to the Persian Gulf War is another example of the effectiveness of determined presidential foreign policy leadership. He sent 250,000 troops to the gulf between August and November on his own authority. He also delayed announcing his decision to double this number until after the November elections, although he had made the decision in October. This kept the decision that changed our mission from defense (Operation Desert Shield) to offense (Operation Desert Storm) from becoming a campaign issue. And he mobilized United States and world opinion and gained United Nations support. By the time Congress authorized using force in January 1991, the question of whether to do so was, practically speaking, already decided. A rally effect supporting Bush's policies emerged after the fighting began.

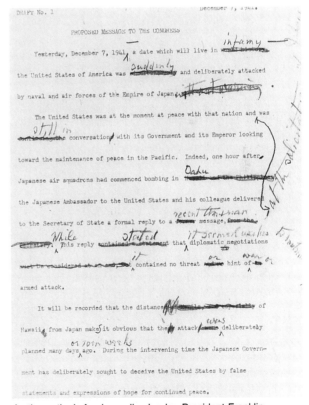

As the nation's foreign policy leader, President Franklin Roosevelt edited his own speech to Congress about the Japanese attack on Pearl Harbor. He added the word that made memorable his phrase, "a date which will live in infamy."

Since World War II, one of the president's most important foreign policy tasks has been to develop policy toward the Soviet Union. Early in his term, President Reagan took a hard line against the Soviet Union. But as pressure in the United States grew for more amicable relations between the superpowers, and as the Soviet Union moved toward a more open political system, Reagan began to negotiate seriously with Soviet leader Mikhail Gorbachev. Here, Gorbachev and Reagan are shown during Reagan's 1988 visit to Moscow.

One reason for this dominance is that in foreign policy, more than in domestic, the president has more information than others do. He can often stifle debate by saying, "If you knew what I knew, you would agree with me," because of classified or secret information from the CIA, Defense Department, State Department, and other agencies. The president can also share certain information with Congress (and the public) and try to withhold other information. Members of Congress must often rely on the media and are at a distinct disadvantage in dealing with the president. In 1984, the Reagan administration mined harbors in Nicaragua after telling the Senate Intelligence Committee it was not doing so. When the facts became known, the chair of that committee, Barry Goldwater (R-Ariz.) wrote a blistering public letter to the head of the CIA saying, not so formally, "I am pissed off."[54] Later the Iran-contra hearings revealed that administration officials deliberately lied to Congress about a whole series of actions taken with respect to Iran and Nicaragua.

The administration also has a large role in shaping the agenda of debate. Alternatives acceptable to the administration are advanced through public statements, background briefings of the press and Congress, and "national" newspapers such as the *New York Times* or *Washington Post*. Many reasonable alternatives may never be suggested or receive support. Thus, media outlets did little to initiate discussions of our goals in the Persian Gulf when they covered troop commitments largely as a logistical challenge and human interest story. Media acceptance of Pentagon restrictions on newsgathering also helped Bush generate support for his policies by producing news of successful, not unsuccessful, attacks and by concealing information describing casualties on both sides.

Although different presidential advisers sometimes advocate conflicting views publicly, it is much easier for a president to have a coherent policy than for Congress to do so. Thus, another advantage the president has over Congress is that he can act decisively, whereas Congress must talk in order to react. President Nixon preempted congressional opposition to warmer relations with the People's Republic of China (Communist China) by announcing in 1971 that he would visit there. Congressional opponents could do little but complain.

Because the president is one and Congress is many, the president is usually more effective in appealing for public support. There is almost always a "rally round the flag" effect on both Congress and the public when the president takes a strong stance in foreign policy, especially if troops are involved. Our 1989 invasion of Panama is a good example of this. There was very little negative media coverage of the invasion, and public opinion was strongly supportive.

A final advantage for the president is that members of Congress hesitate to oppose major presidential foreign or military policies because they fear that doing so may be seen by other nations as a sign of United States weakness.

Military Leadership

Using the military to achieve national goals is one way presidents conduct foreign policy. The Founders made the president "commander-in-chief." By this they meant that the president would be the "first general" and "first admiral," as Alexander Hamilton wrote in *Federalist #69.*

But the Founders did not want to give the president the sole power to make war. In the words of Connecticut's Roger Sherman, they believed that "the Executive should be able to repel and not to commence war." The founders feared that presidents, like the English kings from whom they had recently freed themselves, would be too eager to go to war.[55] So they gave Congress the power to declare war. James Madison expressed the view of several of the Founders when he argued that "the executive is the branch of power most interested in war and most prone to it. [The Constitution] has, accordingly, with studied care, vested the question of war in the legislature."[56] Thus, the Founders created a system of checks and balances in military affairs; the president commands the troops, but Congress has the power to declare war and, of course, decides whether to authorize funds to pay for it. Thomas Jefferson thought that this arrangement would be an "effectual check to the dog of war, by transferring the power of letting him loose from the executive to the legislative body, from those who are to spend to those who are to pay."[57]

Although every president is commander-in-chief, no president has ever led troops into battle. However, modern weapons have led to more presidential involvement. The decision to use certain weapons has become important politically as well as militarily. The decision to wage a "limited" war in Vietnam, that is, not to use nuclear weapons, was political and based on presidential beliefs that Vietnam was not worth a nuclear holocaust.

Other technological developments also have given presidents more military leadership opportunities. Johnson and Nixon used sophisticated communications equipment to select targets in Vietnam. While military commanders ran the Persian Gulf War, Bush was able to use modern transportation facilities to send large numbers of troops to the gulf quickly with the latest "smart" weapons. This allowed him to send a political message to Iraq indicating our commitment to protect gulf area states and to get Iraq out of Kuwait.

Despite congressional power in military affairs, presidential power is wide ranging and increasingly controversial as we more frequently use troops in situations when no war has been declared. Presidents have historically assumed the most military power during wars endangering our national survival. During the Civil War, Lincoln suspended the use of writs of habeas corpus, seized control of some eastern railroads, and blockaded southern ports. He did these things on his own authority as commander-in-chief and without congressional authorization. The war jeopardized national unity, and Lincoln believed he had to take extraordinary measures. Because most people in the North agreed with him, he was able to do what he thought necessary.

Acting under his self-defined authority as commander-in-chief, Franklin Roosevelt put 100,000 Americans of Japanese descent into camps during World War II. He had the government seize and operate more than 60 industries important to the war effort and vulnerable to union strikes. In addition, he created special agencies to control the consumption and price of important materials such as gasoline, meat, and shoes.

Wars not threatening our national survival do not tend to generate high levels of support for executive actions. When Truman had his secretary of commerce seize most of the nation's steel mills during the Korean conflict to keep them operating in the face of a possible labor strike, one of the steel companies took him to

President Lincoln, as commander-in-chief, consults his generals at the Antietam battlefield during the Civil War. Lincoln wanted a more active role in Civil War battles, but his generals worried about his safety and made sure he was gone when there was fighting. Limited by an inability to maintain close communications with field commanders, he could not direct ongoing battles as recent presidents have been able to do.

court to stop him. In 1952, the Supreme Court sided with the company by ruling that Truman had not exhausted other, legal remedies to the problem.[58]

The Vietnam War raised major questions about presidential authority in foreign and military policy. Although Congress never declared war in Vietnam, it routinely appropriated money for it. Nonetheless, many members of Congress believed the president exceeded his authority in pursuing the war. This painful experience led Congress to assert itself by trying to supervise presidential foreign and military policy more closely.

In 1973, Congress passed the **War Powers Resolution** to limit the president's ability to commit troops to combat. It says that the president can use troops abroad under three conditions: when Congress has declared war, when Congress has given him specific authority to do so, or when an attack on the United States or its military creates a national crisis. If a president commits troops under the third condition, he is supposed to consult with Congress beforehand, if possible, and notify it within 48 hours afterwards. Unless Congress approves the use of troops, the president must withdraw them within 60 days, or 90 days if he needs more time to protect them. Congress can pass a concurrent resolution (not subject to presidential veto) at any time ordering the president to end the use of military force.

Congress passed the War Powers Resolution over Nixon's veto. He believed it violated his constitutional authority to protect the nation from military threats. Although presidents have not questioned Congress's constitutional authority to declare war, all have fought congressional influence in the use of troops. As a result, enforcement of the resolution has been controversial. For example, President Carter did not inform, let alone consult, Congress before using United States troops in an attempt to free the Iranian hostages in 1980. Congress did not protest. Neither did it protest after Bush sent troops to invade Panama in 1989. Bush did not even refer to the resolution in the two-page letter he sent to Congress justifying the invasion 60 hours after it began. And no congressional leader demanded his compliance with its provisions.

On the whole, then, the War Powers Resolution has not stopped presidents from sending American troops abroad. This was certainly true in the Persian Gulf crisis. Bush did not refer to the resolution and ignored its procedures when he sent troops there. Few in Congress pressed him to do otherwise. It was not until five months after the crisis began that Congress authorized Bush to use force. By then, Bush's efforts to build public support for military action had succeeded and many members went along. Other members were ready to let Bush take responsibility for what they expected to be a long and unpopular war. Such an attitude among members is unlikely to produce more congressional influence.

In addition to passing the War Powers Resolution, Congress has sought to increase its power by trying to control CIA covert operations, by limiting the president's ability to make agreements with other nations without congressional approval, and by requiring congressional approval of major arms sales.

These efforts have had mixed success. On the one hand, Congress was more interested and involved in President Reagan's Middle Eastern and Central American policies than it was in presidential policies during the early years of involvement in Vietnam. On the other hand, the same forces that have promoted presidential dominance continue to exist.

Finally, congressional influence in foreign and military policy may be limited by presidents concerned about their popularity. Low presidential public opinion scores, especially before national elections, are related to the president's use of military force abroad.[59] Presidents may be tempted to use rally events to increase their popularity and congressional support for their policies. When Bush's scores were falling in 1990, his staff chief Sununu told associates that a short successful war against Iraq would guarantee Bush's reelection.[60] Historically, however, a president's use of military force tends to raise his congressional support for about a month.[61] For example, a White House aide acknowledged low presidential popularity in October 1983 and said Reagan needed "a major victory somewhere to show that we can manage foreign policy." Another added, "We need a win . . . whether it's in Central America, the Middle East or with the Russians."[62] We invaded Grenada that month. This led one observer to note that, based on our experiences in Vietnam and Grenada, presidents who start military actions abroad must win them in a hurry if they want to stay popular.[63] Presidents worried about their popularity must target weak nations that can be beaten quickly.

We want a president able to act decisively in international affairs. But we also want to make sure the president does not act against our wishes. Congress has historically served as the most important check on the president, but its clout in foreign and military policy is, as we have seen, limited. This uneasy balance between presidential powers adequate to do the job and controls necessary to maintain democracy will continue to concern us.

Symbolic Leadership

The president serves as a national symbol of collective unity and pride. Political scientists call this symbolic role **chief of state.**

In this role the president must say and do things on behalf of all Americans. Reagan opened the 1984 Olympic Games and welcomed athletes and spectators from abroad. Every president also attends the funerals of foreign leaders or sends a representative such as the vice-president. Bush's first trip abroad was to attend the funeral of Japanese Emperor Hirohito. Whether it involves phoning the winners of the Super Bowl or lighting the White House Christmas tree, all presidents perform symbolic tasks.

Knowing that symbolic responsibilities are very important, the Founders gave the president power to grant reprieves and pardons for crimes under national law. During the Civil War, Lincoln pardoned soldiers who were sentenced to die for sleeping on guard duty. Such humane acts allow presidents to express the sympathetic spirit of the nation. Ford used his authority to pardon Nixon for his part in the Watergate scandal. His justification was that trying Nixon would have served no useful purpose and divided the nation. He thought the pardon expressed a national feeling. However, opinion polls showed that most people disagreed, and the pardon hurt Ford in the 1976 election.

The more a president can link his personal reputation with popular feelings of patriotism and national

In their role as symbolic leaders, presidents, like Carter, often throw out the first ball of the baseball season.

To improve the electoral chances of their party, presidents try to help recruit good candidates for House and Senate races. In addition, presidents help raise money by being the guest star at fund-raising events, by staying on good terms with major contributors, and by looking like a winner generally. Thus, Bush raised $80 million at fund-raising events for Republican candidates in 1990. They also send their aides around the country to help fellow Democrats or Republicans with their campaigns and sometimes even go themselves. Seeing a president in person— seeing a little history in the making—is exciting and almost always draws a crowd and good media coverage. Candidates for any office are usually eager for a presidential visit, although Carter's unpopularity led some campaigning Democrats to discover "scheduling problems" ruling out a presidential visit in 1980. In 1990, the National Republican Congressional Committee told Republican congressional candidates that it was acceptable to distance themselves from Bush because of his falling popularity and his broken campaign promise on taxes.

This daily schedule of President Bush's indicates a variety of meetings and events, allowing him to play his roles as a symbolic leader as well as a policy leader. John Sununu is Bush's chief of staff. Brent Scowcroft is his national security adviser.

unity, the more persuasive he might be in getting support for his policies. The job of chief of state does not involve presidents in policy matters directly, but it can give successful practitioners more leverage in achieving their policy goals.

Party Leadership

In addition to roles representing the entire nation, the presidency includes a more partisan set of tasks. Presidents are elected only after being nominated by a political party. As "party leader," a president leads his party, confronts the opposition, and represents his party's interests when they are his own. For example, traditional Republican support for the Equal Rights Amendment changed when Reagan came out against it. In addition, a president seeking reelection typically has tremendous influence in writing his party's platform. In an extreme example of this, the 1972 Republican platform was mostly written in Nixon's White House and not at the party's convention.

Presidential partisanship has a purpose: the more members of a president's party who sit in Congress, the more support he gets for his policies. However, a president's support, when he chooses to give it, is no guarantee of electoral success for congressional candidates, especially in off-year elections (see table 1). Since 1932, the president's party has lost an average of 28 House and 3 Senate seats in off-year elections; in presidential election years, the average gains for the winning presidential candidate's party in Congress are almost a mirror image, 21 in the House and 3 in the Senate. The 1988 elections were highly unusual in that the winning presidential party lost 3 House seats and 1 Senate seat.

The president usually tries to camouflage his actions as party leader when trying to persuade people to support him or to vote for his party's candidates. People are more likely to listen to him when they see the president in terms of his other jobs, such as chief of state.

Few presidents were as good as Reagan at hiding their partisan performances. When he tilted his head, winked, and smilingly advised his audiences to ignore attacks on his policies, he implied that the attacks were clearly partisan and should be ignored. Moreover, he implied that he was above party differences, that his only concern was the national interest.

Conclusion: Is the Presidency Responsive?

The presidency has become the most consistently powerful part of government. Americans expect leadership from it because of societal changes resulting in more government and because of our larger interests abroad.

Neustadt called twentieth-century public opinion about the presidency "monarchical." Johnson's and Nixon's "imperial" styles certainly were consistent with it. After a ceremony for Marines going to Vietnam, Johnson was directed to a helicopter by an airman who said, "That's your helicopter over there, sir." Johnson responded, "Son, they are all my helicopters." He once called the State of the Union speech the "State of My Union address."

Most recent presidents eventually learned hard lessons about the limits of presidential power. Indeed, the moral of the personal presidency suggests we have

Table 1 ■ Congressional Candidates Fall Off the President's Coattails in Off-Year Elections

Year	President	Gains or Losses of Presidential Party in	
		House	Senate
1934	Roosevelt (D)	+9	+10
1938	Roosevelt (D)	−71	−6
1942	Roosevelt (D)	−45	−9
1946	Truman (D)	−55	−12
1950	Truman (D)	−29	−6
1954	Eisenhower (R)	−18	−1
1958	Eisenhower (R)	−47	−13
1962	Kennedy (D)	−4	+4
1966	Johnson (D)	−47	−3
1970	Nixon (R)	−12	+2
1974	Ford (R)	−48	−3
1978	Carter (D)	−11	−3
1982	Reagan (R)	−26	0
1986	Reagan (R)	−6	−8
1990	Bush (R)	−8	−1
Average, all off-year elections		−28	−3
Average, all elections in presidential election years		+21	+3

D = Democrat; R = Republican.

Source: Congressional Quarterly Guide to U.S. Elections, 1985, p. 1116; and Harold W. Stanley and Richard G. Niemi, Vital Statistics on American Politics, 2nd ed. (Washington, D.C.: CQ Press, 1989), table 3–11; and Congressional Quarterly Guide to Current American Government: Spring 1991 (Washington, D.C.: CQ Press, 1991), p. 1.

an "impossible" or "imperiled" presidency. Presidents who become popular by making exaggerated promises have trouble keeping them and their popularity in a system of fragmented power.

We have all become Washingtonians. We pay more attention to the president than to anyone else, and we link government's success to the effectiveness of his leadership. America was critical of the presidency in the 1970s. Vietnam and Watergate showed the dangers of placing too much faith in one part of government. By 1980, Americans were demanding presidential leadership again. They were still demanding it at the end of the decade when, after honesty, most people named leadership as the most important quality a president should have.[64] They were less concerned about policy. For many Americans, having presidential leadership is more important than where it takes them.

Is our personal presidency responsive? It is in that the president has an almost direct relationship with the public. Using the media, the president tells us what he wants. Through public opinion polls and the ballot box, we tell the president what we think. There are limits and dangers in this relationship, however. To remain popular, a president may seek short-term solutions to our problems and neglect our long-term interests. Short-term responsiveness catering to public opinion may not always represent responsiveness to our real needs.

EPILOGUE

The Beginning of the End

President Reagan approved covert arms sales to Iran in January 1986 and ordered the CIA not to inform Congress. When the Poindexter memo became public a year later, many, including some in the administration, were shocked that important policy was made on the basis of such superficial analysis.

As a result of Reagan's decision, 2,008 antitank missiles were sent to Iran along with parts for antiaircraft missiles.[65] Everything was kept secret until a pro-Syrian Lebanese publication broke the news in November. This led to more revelations. News surfaced that we had also shipped arms to Iran earlier, in September 1985. Robert McFarlane, then national security adviser, told a congressional committee the president had approved these sales orally. Reagan said he did not remember. And Attorney General Edwin Meese revealed that profits from the sales were used to aid the Nicaraguan contras.

Reactions were overwhelmingly negative. A poll taken in December reported that 47% of the people thought the president was handling his job well compared to 64% two months before. Even worse, most did not believe him when he said he did not know what was going on. Another poll found that Carter's handling of Iran rated almost twice as high as Reagan's.[66] Media analyses appeared comparing what was being called Irangate or Iranamok to Watergate. The public and Congress asked what the president knew and when he knew it. Comedians asked what he forgot and when he forgot it. Everyone wanted to know who did what. Robert McFarlane, John Poindexter, Oliver North, Donald Regan, William Casey, and George Bush were in the news daily. At first the president called North a "national hero." Then he fired him.

Reagan unsuccessfully tried to reclaim control of events in late November by appointing three respected elder statesmen, John Tower, Brent Scowcroft, and Edmund Muskie, to investigate White House operations. He told them he could not remember when he authorized arms sales to Iran and that he knew nothing of the diversion of funds to the contras. Three months later, the Tower Commission reported that he was too removed from daily business to be an effective leader. The commission criticized Reagan's management of foreign policy as lax and informal. It revealed that his staff chief Regan had been telling him what he wanted to hear rather than exposing him to legal and political realities. Under pressure from Nancy Reagan and other advisers, Reagan fired Regan.

A different picture of Reagan's role emerged in the summer of 1987 during almost three months of joint congressional committee hearings. A Poindexter memo reported a May 1986 conversation with Reagan in which Reagan declared his determination to aid the contras, even without congressional approval. The memo reported Reagan saying, "I want to figure out a way to take action unilaterally to provide assistance."[67] In a public statement in early 1987, Reagan contradicted his earlier claim that he did not know about efforts to aid the contras by declaring, "I was very definitely involved in the decisions about support to the freedom fighters [i.e., contras]—my idea to begin with."[68]

The congressional hearings produced considerable grist for the media that summer. More than two dozen witnesses testified publicly and many more testified privately. Answering committee questions and lecturing members about why they should support the contras, "Ollie" North achieved instant stardom. His secretary, Fawn Hall, justified violating congressional policy by arguing that "sometimes it is necessary to act above the written law." North, Poindexter, McFarlane, and Elliott Abrams, an assistant secretary of state, admitted lying to earlier congressional hearings regarding government support of the contras. Many people in and out of Congress thought some witnesses were still lying. In particular, Poindexter's testimony that he approved diverting arms sale profits to the contras without Reagan's knowledge sounded improbable given Poindexter's military background and history of following orders.[69]

Reagan's televised speech after the hearings did not clarify much. Although he promised to be candid ("You won't be able to shut me up"), he left many questions unanswered. For example, he failed to explain why he told the Tower Commission that he did not know about National Security Council support for the contras and then claimed credit for it later. As a result, opinion surveys continued to report that most people thought he was lying.[70]

The joint committee's hearings did not end things. A special prosecutor brought criminal charges against Poindexter, McFarlane, North, and others. In well-publicized trials, North and Poindexter claimed they had followed the orders of their superiors, including Reagan. North also said that Bush knew about illegal contra supply efforts and had helped get other countries to assist the contras in return for U.S. aid. Thus, the North and Poindexter trials also became Reagan's and Bush's. North's diaries, released later, indicated that Bush was party to arms-for-hostages discussions from the start.[71] More questions about Bush's role in the scandal were raised in 1990, when he vetoed a bill that would have required presidents to notify Congress when they ask other countries to conduct covert operations for us.[72]

In testimony taped for Poindexter's trial, Reagan still seemed out of touch with events, at best, or more involved than he would admit, at worst. He said he could not recall many "details" (like the name of his chairman of the Joint Chiefs of Staff) or that he never knew them. He maintained that he had not seen the Tower Commission conclusion that money from arms sales to Iran was diverted to the contras. After his testimony was televised, Reagan's popularity in the polls declined.

Regardless of who is president, the personal presidency imposes its own imperatives. Operating within a system of separation of powers and checks and balances, presidents never have enough power to keep all their promises. Although presidents have an inherent advantage over Congress in making foreign policy, they are not supposed to operate in defiance of Congress.

We can compare the Iran-contra affair to the earlier Watergate scandal when people asked whether Nixon ordered or knew about the illegal actions of his aides. During the Iran-contra hearings, people asked whether Reagan gave direct orders to violate a congressional ban on military aid to the contras. The answer to the question was as murky after the hearings as before them, but it was clear that the president knew of these activities. Moreover, it was also clear that the White House had learned important lessons from Watergate. One lesson was to cover its tracks. Nixon was nearly impeached on the basis of White House records. Reagan's aides shredded tons of paper after the arms sales and diversion of funds to the contras became public knowledge. Many observers worried that the lesson of Watergate seemed to be "destroy evidence" rather than "obey the law."

Another lesson from Watergate was to use aides with military backgrounds.[73] Many Nixon aides were civilians who cooperated early with investigators to protect themselves. Reagan aides with military careers were more interested in protecting the president and some lied to Congress. Yet even their loyalty had limits. McFarlane agreed to help prosecutors in return for a light sentence (two years on probation, 200 hours of community service, and a $20,000 fine). And North's courtroom defense was that he only followed Reagan's orders.

Unhappily, the Iran-contra scandal may provide lessons for future presidents too. One involves deniability or what Lowi calls "planned ignorance."[74] Confessions that aides acted without Reagan's approval let him deny knowledge of and responsibility for their actions. Although this exposed Reagan to charges of mismanagement, it let him avoid graver charges of breaking the law.

KEY TERMS

personal presidency

power to persuade

Washingtonians

professional reputation

going public

senatorial courtesy

executive orders

War Powers
    Resolution

chief of state

parliamentary
    governments

FURTHER READING

Theodore Draper, *A Very Thin Line: The Iran-Contra Affairs* (New York: Hill & Wang, 1991). *A detailed account of the Iran-Contra scandal, how it was investigated, and what it tells us about presidential and congressional roles in foreign policy matters.*

Richard E. Neustadt, *Presidential Power and the Modern Presidents* (New York: The Free Press, 1990). *The most cited book on the presidency, it argues that presidential power is based on the ability to persuade.*

Peggy Noonan, *What I Saw at the Revolution: A Political Life in the Reagan Era* (New York: Random House, 1990). *A lively description by a Reagan speechwriter of White House life and an analysis of why Reagan could not turn his election victories into a major party realignment.*

Bruce Oudes, ed., *From: The President: Richard Nixon's Secret Files* (New York: Harper & Row, 1989). *Memos, tape transcripts, and other communications from Nixon's White House express his complaints about rock bands playing on the Mall, the* Washington Post, *and many matters great and small.*

Bradley H. Patterson, Jr., *The Ring of Power: The White House Staff and Its Expanding Role in Government* (New York: Basic Books, 1988). *This book sees White House operations as so complex and involving so many officials that "the only decision a president carries out himself is to go to the bathroom."*

Bob Woodward, *The Commanders* (New York: Simon & Schuster, 1991). *An account of how Bush's White House brought the nation to war in the Persian Gulf that reveals divisions of high level opinions that did not surface in the months before the war.*

NOTES

1. Elizabeth Drew, "Letter from Washington," *The New Yorker,* February 16, 1987, pp. 95–107.

2. Ibid., p. 98.

3. Much of the information in this section comes from James M. McCormick and Steven S. Smith. "The Iran Arms Sale and the Intelligence Oversight Act of 1980," *PS* 20 (Winter 1987): 29–37.

4. Ibid., pp. 31–32.

5. Arthur M. Schlesinger, Jr., *The Imperial Presidency* (Boston: Houghton Mifflin, 1973).

6. Harold M. Barger, *The Impossible Presidency* (Glenview, Ill.: Scott-Foresman, 1984).

7. Theodore J. Lowi, *The Personal President* (Ithaca, N.Y.: Cornell University Press, 1985).

8. Paul F. Boller, Jr., *Presidential Anecdotes* (New York: Oxford University Press, 1981), p. 50.

9. Lowi, *The Personal President.*

10. David Halberstam, *The Powers That Be* (New York: Dell, 1980), p. 30.

11. Bush's ratings have fluctuated considerably. They achieved record highs during the Persian Gulf War after being fairly low in mid 1990.

12. Richard E. Neustadt, *Presidential Power: The Politics of Leadership from FDR to Carter* (New York: John Wiley & Sons, 1980).

13. Samuel Kernell, *Going Public: New Strategies of Presidential Leadership* (Washington, D.C.: CQ Press, 1986), p. 15.

14. Ibid., p. 135.

15. Reported in George C. Edwards III, *Presidential Influence in Congress* (San Francisco: W. H. Freeman, 1980), p. 125.

16. Quoted in Dick Kirschten, "Reagan Warms Up for Political Hardball," *National Journal,* February 9, 1985, p. 328.

17. Edwards, *Presidential Influence,* p. 127.

18. Neustadt, *Presidential Power,* p. 130.

19. Reagan's Support Index Up—But Not Much," *Congressional Quarterly Weekly,* November 19, 1988, p. 3324.

20. For an analysis of Bush's response, see James P. Pfiffner, "Establishing the Bush Presidency," *Public Administration Review* 50 (January/February 1990):64–73.

21. This is according to a study by G. Calvin Mackenzie as reported in Burt Solomon, "At This Point, Bush's Congeniality Seems to Be Offsetting His Inertia," *National Journal,* March 4, 1989, pp. 538–39.

22. "Presidential Support: Bush's Success Rate Sinks to Near-Record Low," *Congressional Quarterly,* December 22, 1990, pp. 4183–87.

23. Kernell, *Going Public.*

24. Ibid., p. 120.

25. Ibid., pp. 38–42.

26. "Notes and Comments," *The New Yorker,* November 7, 1988, p. 29.

27. Paul Taylor, "Pigsty Politics," *Washington Post National Weekly Edition,* February 13–19, 1989, p. 7.

28. Dennis M. Simon and Charles W. Ostrom, Jr., "The Politics of Prestige: Popular Support and the Modern Presidency," *Presidential Studies Quarterly* 18 (Fall 1988): 741–59.

29. George C. Edwards III, *The Public Presidency* (New York: St. Martin's Press, 1983), p. 253.

30. John Mueller, *War, Presidents and Public Opinion* (New York: John Wiley & Sons, 1970).

31. For example, see Edwards, *The Public Presidency,* pp. 239–47.

32. Poll scores reported here are from the following *National Journal* issues: December 8, 1990, p. 2993; January 19, 1991, p. 185; and February 16, 1991, p. 412.

33. Bruce Buchanan, *The Presidential Experience: What the Office Does to the Man* (Englewood Cliffs, N.J.: Prentice-Hall, 1978).

34. Clinton Rossiter, *The American Presidency* (New York: Harcourt Brace, 1956).

35. Thomas E. Cronin, *The State of the Presidency* (Boston: Little, Brown, 1975), p. 118.

36. James Reston, "Cut the Public Relations Budget," *Lincoln Star,* February 7, 1989, p. 6.

37. Fred I. Greenstein, *The Hidden-Hand Presidency* (New York: Basic Books, 1982), p. 139.

38. Quoted in Richard Pious, *The American Presidency* (New York: Basic Books, 1979), p. 244.

39. Ann Reilly Dowd, "What Managers Can Learn from Manager Reagan," *Fortune,* September 15, 1986, pp. 32–41.

40. Gerald M. Boyd, "The Bush Style of Management: After Reagan, It's Back to Details," *New York Times,* March 19, 1989, pp. 1 and 15.

41. For an analysis of White House staff, see John H. Kessel, "The Structures of the Reagan White House," *American Journal of Political Science* 28 (May 1984): 231–58.

42. Eleanor Randolph, "The Man Washington Loves to Hate," *Washington Post National Weekly Edition,* December 17–23, 1990, p. 7.

43. See "Sununu Seen Likely to Dominate Little-Known White House Staff," *National Journal,* January 7, 1989, p. 31; and Burt Solomon, "For Now, at Least, Collegiality Reigns Supreme among Bush Staff," *National Journal,* February 4, 1989, pp. 298–99.

44. Pfiffner, "Establishing the Bush Presidency," p. 67.

45. See Ronald Moe, "Traditional Organizational Principles and the Managerial Presidency: From Phoenix to Ashes," *Public Administration Review,* March/April, 1990, pp. 129–40.

46. "The First Hundred Days: Low Expectations," *National Journal,* November 12, 1988, p. 2839.

47. "Justice Says Meese's Conduct Intolerable," *Lincoln Journal,* January 17, 1989, p. 1.

48. "Beyond Sound Bites," *Newsweek,* October 17, 1988, pp. 27–28.

49. For discussion of the president's removal powers in light of a 1988 Supreme Court decision regarding independent counsels, see John A. Rohr, "Public Administration, Executive Power, and Constitutional Confusion" and Rosemary O'Leary, "Response to John Rohr," *Public Administration Review* 49 (March/April 1989): 108–15.

50. "Survey Finds Voters Stress Honesty Issue," *New York Times,* September 6, 1987, p. 19.

51. *United States v. Curtiss-Wright Export Corporation,* 299 U.S. 304 (1936).

52. For a discussion of these styles, see John P. Burke and Fred I. Greenstein, *How Presidents Test Reality: Decisions on Vietnam, 1954 and 1965* (New York: Russell Sage Foundation, 1989), and Burt Solomon, "Making Foreign Policy in Secret May Be Easy, But It Carries Risks," *National Journal,* January 12, 1991, pp. 90–91.

53. Aaron Wildavsky, "The Two Presidencies," *Transaction* 4 (December 1966): 6–7.

54. "A Furor over the Secret War," *Newsweek,* April 23, 1984, p. 22.

55. See the discussion in the *Federalist Paper #69,* written by Alexander Hamilton.

56. Quoted in "Notes and Comment," *New Yorker,* June 1, 1987, p. 23.

57. Ibid.

58. *Youngstown Sheet and Tube Co. v. Sawyer,* 343 U.S. 579 (1952).

59. Charles W. Ostrom, Jr. and Brian L. Job, "The President and the Political Use of Force," *American Political Science Review* 80 (June 1986): 541–66.

60. Elizabeth Drew, "Letter From Washington," *The New Yorker,* February 4, 1991, p. 83.

61. Richard J. Stoll, "The Sound of the Guns," *American Politics Quarterly* 15 (April 1987): 223–37.

62. Quoted in Lowi, *The Personal President,* p. 133.

63. Richard J. Barnet, *The Rockets' Red Glare: When America Goes to War—The Presidents and the People* (New York: Simon and Schuster, 1990).

64. "Survey Finds Voters Stress Honesty Issue."

65. Robert Pear, "The Story Thus Far: Assembling Some of the Pieces of the Puzzle," *New York Times,* December 14, 1986, Section 4, p. 1.

66. "Reagan's Crusade," *Newsweek,* December 15, 1986, pp. 26–28.

67. Elizabeth Drew, "Letter from Washington," *The New Yorker,* August 31, 1987, p. 72.

68. Ibid.

69. For a critique of the congressional hearings, see Seymore M. Hersh, "The Iran-Contra Committees: Did They Protect Reagan?" *New York Times Magazine,* April 29, 1990, pp. 46–78.

70. Louis Harris, "Iran-Contra Hearings Erode Faith in Reagan," *Lincoln Star,* May 25, 1987.

71. For more on North's diaries and other indications of Bush's role in the scandal see Tom Blanton, "Iran-Contradictions: It's Time to Ask Where George Was," *Washington Post National Weekly Edition,* June 18–24, 1990, pp. 24–25.

72. See Christopher Madison, "Reopened Wound," *National Journal,* December 15, 1990, p. 3056.

73. Francis E. Rourke, "The Iran-Contra Hearings and Executive Policymaking," *National Political Science Review* 1 (1989): 99.

74. Theodore J. Lowi, "Doin' the Cincinnati or What Is There about the White House That Makes Its Occupants Do Bad Things?" *National Political Science Review* 1 (1989): 94.

CHAPTER
12 The Bureaucracy

Millions of tax returns are stored on computer tapes at the Internal Revenue Service's Ogden, Utah offices.

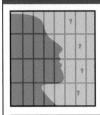

YOU ARE THERE

Attacking AIDS

You are the surgeon general of the United States, C. Everett Koop. It is 1986 and President Reagan has asked you, the government's top medical officer, to report to him on what has become a major problem, AIDS, or acquired immune deficiency syndrome. AIDS involves a virus that weakens the body's immunity, making it vulnerable to deadly infections.

There have been more than 35,000 cases of AIDS so far in the United States, 493 of them children. Those who contract AIDS inevitably die, as 20,000 Americans have so far. You estimate that 1.5 million people have been exposed to the virus and that 270,000 will develop AIDS by 1991.[1] In the United States, people with the most risk of getting it are intravenous drug users and homosexual men.[2] However, AIDs has begun to appear among heterosexual men and women through contact with intravenous drug users, prostitutes, bisexuals, and those who had multiple blood transfusions before the spring of 1985, when blood banks began testing for AIDS.

As long as the first two groups provided almost all the victims, most people did not worry about AIDS. As it began to spread, however, it became a major issue arousing considerable public anxiety. For example, real estate agents trying to sell Rock Hudson's house found that clients would not enter it because they knew he had died of AIDS. And some parents have tried to bar child victims of AIDS from the schools their children attend.

Now the president has asked for a report advising him what to do. You do not expect an effective vaccine to be available until the mid-1990s at the earliest. A major issue that your report must deal with is whether we should require mandatory testing for AIDS. A blood test can reveal exposure to the AIDS virus, but it cannot predict who will get the disease because some who carry the virus will not contract the disease. Still, finding out who has been

Former Surgeon General Koop visits an AIDS patient.

exposed to the virus can help limit the exposure of others to it.

Already, military recruits and Foreign Service officers must take a blood test to determine if they have been exposed to AIDS. Proposals have been made to test many others, such as convicted prostitutes and intravenous drug users, hospital patients from 15 to 49 years of age, venereal disease patients, and couples seeking marriage licenses. Secretary of Education William Bennett, whose views often echo the president's, also wants to include prison inmates and people planning to immigrate here. He says the government should notify spouses and past sexual partners if test results are positive, that is, if evidence of exposure to AIDS is found.

(continued on next page)

Many conservatives view AIDS as a moral issue. They think AIDS is a punishment for homosexuality and drug use. Some charge that public health officials are "intimidated by the homosexual lobby." One called AIDS the "first politically protected disease in the history of mankind."[3] They want you to recommend mandatory testing to identify who is infected so government can quarantine those who will not change their sexual or drug habits to protect society.

Most public health experts reject mandatory testing as unworkable. They argue that many people will go underground to avoid being tested. They also say mandatory testing of huge numbers of people will produce mistakes in test results. Further, most experts oppose mandatory testing as a violation of doctor/patient confidentiality and doubt that most people will identify their sexual partners. They add that mandatory testing will only increase discrimination against homosexuals and others who have been exposed to AIDS and who may or may not contract it.

Few experts agree with Secretary Bennett, who argues that the key to stopping AIDS is to teach sexual abstinence to our children. Most experts recommend educating young people about "safe sex" and contraception. They say abstinence as a policy is unrealistic given the emphasis on sex in our society, as illustrated by studies showing that television programming refers to sexual intercourse at least once an hour. Their views reflect Senator Paul Simon's (D-Ill.) remark that, "It's been too long since [Bennett] was a teenager."

Many conservatives object strongly to sex education in schools. Referring to "safe sodomy" instead of "safe sex," they say "condomania" means we have given up trying to raise our children properly.

The president is comfortable with conservative views on AIDS. When he appointed you, you were a surgeon in Philadelphia, known for having pioneered techniques to separate Siamese twins and for being a born-again Christian with conservative views on abortion and birth control. You know your views were more important to the president than your surgical innovations. You agree with him on many issues and want to write a report he will like. Your political instincts push you this way.

On the other side of the coin, and in government there is always another side to the coin, you are a doctor who respects the views of health-care professionals. You want to write a report that will help fight AIDS, without political interference. What should you do?

OUTLINE

An Agriculture Department employee recently spent almost a year trying to define what a good watermelon looks like. Another department project was devoted to producing oranges of the same size, and a third tried to find out how long Americans take to cook breakfast. Why should government focus on such trivia? Is this an example of furthering the public interest or of feathering a bureaucratic nest?

The federal bureaucracy, of which the Agriculture Department is a part, employs over three million civilians and over two million uniformed military personnel. The bureaucracy executes or enforces policies made by Congress and the president. Because policy-

presence of careerists can make the bureaucracy less responsive.

Bureaucracy also teaches citizens about government. First, it informs us about public policies and programs. For example, we contact the National Park Service if we want to know the rules governing camping in national parks. Second, the bureaucracy performs a socialization function. It helps us learn about government and our role as citizens.

Expectations About the Federal Bureaucracy

Historically, Americans have had two sometimes contradictory expectations about public bureaucracy. They have wanted bureaucracies to be responsive to their needs, which often means responsive to majority views. But they have also wanted bureaucracies to be competent enough to do an effective job. They want fair, apolitical competence applied so that, for example, Social Security recipients who are Democrats do not receive favors when Democrats are in office and Republican recipients do not receive favors when Republicans are in office. To have both political responsiveness and neutral competence is often difficult.

Responsiveness

Responsiveness refers to a democratic desire that public agencies do what we want. We have shown how highly we value bureaucratic responsiveness in three major ways.

First, Americans elect more bureaucrats than citizens of other nations do. By the mid-1800s voters were electing numerous state and local executive officers from ballots (called long ballots) having hundreds of names. Many states and localities still have long ballots electing not only chief executives, such as governors and mayors, but also treasurers, clerks, sheriffs, surveyors, auditors, engineers, and other administrative officers. Electing rather than appointing these officials is supposed to make them responsive, though in reality it may have the opposite effect by making it unclear who is really in charge.

The second way Americans have encouraged bureaucratic responsiveness is through **patronage**. Under the patronage system elected officials appoint their supporters to administrative jobs in order to build their own political strength. Newly elected presidents and other executives replace everyone appointed by their predecessors with their own supporters: "To the victor belong the spoils." Andrew Jackson's presidential election in 1828 was a watershed in using the patronage system. Jackson and others believed any white male citizen of average intelligence and goodwill could do a government job well. He reversed the existing practice of naming mostly well-off people from the East Coast by appointing less well-off supporters from frontier areas.

A major problem with patronage is that it can lead to corruption, in particular to deal making between candidates and voters or, more unfortunately, individuals who control blocks of voters. Voters may support candidates who promise them jobs or other favors. Such corruption increasingly sullied city councils, state legislatures, and Congress during the 1800s.

Another problem with patronage is incompetence. People got bureaucratic jobs because they supported winning candidates, not because they knew how to do the jobs. This became a major problem as government jobs became more technical.

The third way Americans have sought bureaucratic responsiveness is by giving legislatures great authority over the bureaucracy. Before the Revolution and for a long time after, the bureaucracy performed a few relatively simple jobs and was relatively easy to control. Now the job of controlling the bureaucracy is much more difficult as government has become larger and more complex.

Neutral Competence

Neutral competence can be a contradictory objective to responsiveness. It holds that bureaucrats should be uninvolved or neutral in policymaking and chosen only for their expertise in executing policy. It assumes there is no Republican or Democratic way to build a sewer, collect customs, or fight a war. In effect, it says politics has no place in bureaucracy. It also implies that bureaucrats should not profit personally from the decisions they make.

Woodrow Wilson, who was a major advocate of neutral competence, wrote that we can learn to execute policy both expertly and responsively.[21] He believed that government jobs are either political or administrative in nature, and that if we know which are which, we can create a bureaucracy policymakers can control. Most current observers believe it is impossible

Andrew Jackson opened the doors to the White House as well as to the government bureaucracy. The guests at a White House party open to the public consumed or carried away much of a 1400-pound cheese.

to separate the political from the administrative completely, however.

The first impact of the desire for neutral competence was the creation of the Civil Service Commission by the Pendleton Act in 1883. Patronage was a serious problem by the 1880s. Given the strength of political machines that had grown powerful through its use, it took the assassination of President James Garfield in 1881 by an unsuccessful job seeker to get Congress to do something.

The commission's job was to fill certain bureaucratic jobs with people who had proven their competence in competitive examinations. It was also supposed to protect these people from having to support or oppose particular candidates. The jobs under the commission's jurisdiction were part of the **merit system**.

The act authorized the president to extend merit system coverage to additional federal jobs by executive order. The merit system covered about 10% of the jobs in the federal bureaucracy in 1884. That figure is over 90% today; most of the remainder are covered by some other merit system such as that in the State Department's Foreign Service.

The important thing about the merit system is that it protects individuals from dismissal for partisan reasons. However, the system does not give "merit" a monopoly. The system favors veterans by adding a 5-point bonus to their test scores (disabled veterans get 10 points). People already in the system are also favored because they know about job openings first.

Sometimes, job descriptions are written to fit particular individuals.

The creation of independent regulatory boards and commissions was also a result of the push for neutral competence. In 1887, Congress created the Interstate Commerce Commission to decide, on the basis of expert, not partisan, factors, such things as interstate freight rates, railroad ticket prices, conditions of service, and which companies could operate between different places. Some partisan influences remain: the president names and the Senate confirms board and commission members, and Congress and the president determine their funding. But partisanship is supposed to end there.

Limits on the partisan political activities of federal workers are another result of attempts to achieve neutral competence. The **Hatch Act** of 1939 says federal employees can do very little in partisan campaigns, even in state and local ones. They can vote, attend rallies, and talk privately to others. But they cannot participate in party-sponsored voter registration drives, endorse party candidates, or work for or against them in any way. These prohibitions also apply to state and local government workers supported by federal funds.

The Hatch Act has been the subject of considerable controversy. Supporters argue that it protects the neutral competence of civil servants from partisan influences. Reminding us of past corruption when bureaucrats worked for party leaders, they argue that public employees should be concerned mainly with developing their job skills to promote the general welfare. Supporters also believe civil servants should not be able to sway the elections of those who make the laws they administer and appropriate the funds they spend.

Critics of the act say it makes civil servants second-class citizens by denying them the First Amendment guarantees of freedom of speech and association. They also argue that there is little gain in keeping civil servants from participating in state and local campaigns and that federal workers should get involved in local communities to get to know citizens and their needs better. They add that this would let citizens know and understand bureaucrats better too. Thus far, the Hatch Act has withstood attempts to kill it.

Neutral competence requires capable and experienced bureaucrats. One effort to increase bureaucratic competence was the 1978 establishment of the Senior Executive Service (SES). It was designed to attract the

A disappointed office seeker assassinates President Garfield.

very best and most experienced managers in the civil service by offering them challenging new jobs and giving them monetary rewards for exceptional achievement.

However, these hopes were disappointed by the policies of the Carter and Reagan administrations. Both allowed senior-level salaries to fall far behind comparable jobs in the private sector. SES morale was lowered and turnover increased when the Reagan administration put many SES members in jobs with little responsibility, placed unprecedented numbers of political appointees in relatively low-level jobs, and used the Office of Management and Budget to control agency policymaking.[22]

The 1980s were troubled years for the entire civil service. Reagan's belief that "government isn't the solution, it's the problem" endorsed negative views of the public service and indicated a commitment to cut government activity. This and publicity glorifying private business made hiring and keeping good people in government difficult; the work of many agencies suf-

fered. For example, the Food and Drug Administration (FDA) tests products that represent about a quarter of consumer spending. Yet in a decade that saw the onset of AIDS and the development of many new products, FDA staffing dropped 9% and food and drug inspections fell 40%. In 1990, the FDA took 31 months, not the 6 months required by law, to review new drug applications.[23]

Although Bush has noted his "very high regard for the overall competence of career civil servants and for [their] vital role,"[24] he has done little to overcome the trends of the 1980s. New workers will be in short supply in the 1990s when the "baby bust" generation enters the job market and when one-quarter of the federal work force will reach retirement age. Government will have trouble competing with the private sector for them because federal salaries lag over 22% behind comparable nongovernment jobs and this gap widens at higher levels.

Neutral competence also includes the idea that bureaucrats should not profit personally from their

FOCUS ON AN ISSUE

Should Civil Servants Be Tested for Drugs?

America has a drug problem. A recent poll found that one in three employees believes illegal drugs are sold where they work and one-fourth have seen or heard of illegal drug use at work.[1] Twenty-five million Americans have tried cocaine, including 6 million who use it at least once a month. Twenty million use marijuana as often. An estimated 10 million use prescription drugs without a prescription, and half a million are addicted to heroin. Drug abuse may cost the economy almost $100 billion a year in lost productivity.[2]

Some federal civil servants use drugs too. This creates problems. For example, no one wants air traffic controllers to work under the influence of drugs. Yet 60 of them were caught using illegal drugs in random drug tests. Likewise, no one wants national security compromised by drugs. However, 42 workers in a nuclear and chemical weapons program were caught too. Although government spokespeople said none of these workers alone could have caused a nuclear or chemical accident, this is hardly reassuring. The General Accounting Office found evidence of extensive drug use at the Los Alamos National Laboratory in New Mexico, where research on nuclear weapons occurs. A computer technician with a high-level security clearance was arrested carrying 207 pounds of marijuana in his truck.

In response to the drug abuse problem, President Reagan signed an executive order in 1986 ordering mandatory drug testing for those in "sensitive" federal jobs. The president's order included about 1.1 million civil servants. Its goal is to identify public workers using illegal drugs so they can be disciplined or put into rehabilitation programs. However, in 1987, concern for privacy rights of individual employees led Congress to direct federal agencies to halt most drug testing of civil servants until the agencies developed procedures protecting employees' rights. Several dozen individuals and employee groups also challenged the president by filing lawsuits to stop mandatory testing.

These actions illustrate the debate over drug testing. The public too is divided: 44% supported testing and 44% opposed it when Reagan signed his executive order.[3] Should we require drug testing of our civil servants? Here are some issues to consider in the debate that columnist William Safire called "Jar Wars."

Are Drug Tests Reliable?

Tests for evidence of drug abuse involve analyzing blood and urine samples. The most popular is a urine test that, its manufacturer claims, is accurate 95% of the time. Although these tests can produce signs of illegal drugs when someone has used over-the-counter legal drugs like Advil or Contac, or even eaten a poppy seed bagel, mandated follow-up tests are as reliable as any medical test can be. Still, without quality control safeguards and rules requiring follow-up tests, erroneous results could damage an employee's career. For this reason, Congress has directed agencies to develop strict quality control standards, though it is not clear how thoroughly they have been implemented. A federal study of 13 test laboratories found that 66% of their test findings were wrong.[4]

Does Drug Testing Violate the Constitutional Rights of Public Employees?

Opponents of testing say the Fourth Amendment which protects people from "unreasonable searches and seizures" applies. Drug testing is a type of search and seizure. Ordinarily law enforcement officials cannot engage in a search and seizure without a legitimate belief that an individual is hiding something illegal. Opponents of testing claim the amendment

Plainfield, New Jersey, firefighters offer their specimens for mandatory drug testing but are suing city government officials for invasion of privacy.

protects federal workers from tests when supervisors have no reason to think that they are using illegal drugs.

In 1989, two Supreme Court decisions indicated that, although individuals' rights to privacy are invaded by drug testing, such testing might still be legal. In these decisions the Court held that the government must weigh its interests in protecting public safety and security against individuals' privacy rights.[5] Dissenting justices argued that individuals' privacy rights should remain paramount. Justice Thurgood Marshall, for example, warned of suspending fundamental rights in the heat of the moment of concern about a specific issue: "Grave threats to liberty often come in times of urgency, when constitutional rights seem too extravagant to endorse."

There are other privacy issues too. Employees using illegal drugs may try to avoid detection by submitting someone else's urine for testing. Opponents of testing note that, as a result, workers will have to be followed into restrooms to make sure the urine they submit is their own.[6] These arguments raise the specter of "big brother" watching the most private actions of law-abiding citizens. A female Navy officer, a graduate of Annapolis, was court-martialed for not obeying an order to urinate "under the direct observation" of another woman. She agreed to submit a urine sample but argued that the order, meant to stop cheating, was "demeaning and degrading."[7]

Who Should Be Tested?

President Reagan ordered mandatory drug testing of federal employees in "sensitive" jobs. But what are sensitive jobs? Most people would agree that it is appropriate to test some kinds of employees for drugs. No one wants to be on an airplane flying over O'Hare Airport with air traffic routed by controllers high on drugs, for example. But what other federal employees, if any, should be tested? The Supreme Court, in two split votes, found that it was legal to do mandatory drug testing on federal employees involved with public safety or who have law enforcement responsibilities.[8] By a vote of six to three, it approved the testing of railroad crews involved in accidents, and by an even narrower five to four margin, it allowed the Customs Service to test applicants for drug enforcement jobs.

In these cases, the majority of the justices believed that threats to public safety outweighed individual rights. Not all justices agreed. Justice Antonin Scalia approved testing railroad workers but not customs officials. In the former case, only those who had already had accidents were involved, and the agency doing the testing had demonstrated a pattern of illegal drug use by railroad workers. In the case of customs officials, neither of these factors was present. Other justices opposed testing in both cases, defending individual rights of privacy.

Lower court decisions have been mixed. In one case, the testing of Chicago bus drivers was upheld, but in other cases the testing of school teachers, fire fighters, and prison guards was rejected.

Opponents acknowledge that it sounds reasonable to test employees with access to classified information, law enforcement people, and others whose jobs bear directly on public health and safety. However, they note that many people in agencies doing "sensitive" work do not themselves have sensitive jobs. One says, "The further you get away from the air traffic controllers and the closer you get to the typists, the murkier it gets."[9]

Is Drug Testing Worth the Cost?

Proponents say the Defense Department provides proof of testing's effectiveness. A 1980 Pentagon survey found that 48% of enlisted people ages 18 to 25 used drugs. After urinalysis testing began in 1982, the figure fell to 21.5% in 1984 and to under 10% by 1986. However, opponents note that agencies are required to give all employees who may be tested a 60-day notice that gives them time to stop using drugs and avoid incrimination.

Opponents also question whether the results of testing are worth the cost of paying for them. They point to a recent survey of 38 federal agencies that found that only 160 of 24,559 job applicants tested positive (an abuse rate of .7%) as did just 153 of 28,872 current employees (a rate of .5%). These tests cost $11.7 million or $77,000 per positive finding.[10] Critics ask if it is worth spending this much money to get such negligible results. They add that most drug users are young and uneducated, whereas federal workers tend to be educated and older. Test proponents counter that catching even a few drug users is good because it shows that tests are an effective deterrent.

1. Cindy Skrzycki, "Polls: Drugs in the Workplace," *The Washington Post National Weekly Edition,* January 1–7, 1990, p. 38.

2. Reported in Martin Tolchin, "The Government Still Waits to Test Millions for Drugs," *New York Times,* March 3, 1989, p. 5.

3. Pro & Con: Testing in the Workplace," *New York Times,* September 7, 1986, p. 6E, A *New York Times* CBS News Poll.

4. "Drug Testing Targeted by Federal Workers," *Public Administration Times,* March 15, 1986, p. 8. See also Irving R. Kaufman, "The Battle over Drug Testing," *New York Times Magazine,* October 19, 1986, p. 59.

5. *Skinner v. Railway Labor Executives' Assn.,* 109 S. Ct. 1402, 103 L.Ed.2d 639 (1989) and *National Treasury Employees Union v. Von Raab,* 109 S.Ct. 1384, 103 L.Ed.2d 685 (1989).

6. "Free the Federal 345,528," *Washington Post National Weekly Edition,* May 16–22, 1988, p. 24.

7. Lee Hockstader, "Behind Closed Doors," *Washington Post National Weekly Edition,* September 19–25, 1988, p. 33.

8. *Skinner v. Railway Labor Executives: National Treasury Employees Union v. Von Raab.*

9. Ruth Marcus, "Before You Get Your Drug Test . . . ," *Washington Post National Weekly Edition,* October 6, 1986, p. 33.

10. Reported in "Appeals Court Upholds Justice Department Drug Testing," *Lincoln Journal-Star,* March 30, 1991, p. 3.

decisions. Civil servants should be experts in what they do but should not have a personal stake in it. For example, bureaucrats who are stockholders in chemical companies should not make policy about chemical waste. Even if policymakers could completely divorce themselves from their financial interests, their ties with a regulated firm would still produce an appearance of conflict of interest. Critics of policy could point to it, lowering public confidence in government.

Responding to concerns about conflicts of interest, Congress passed the Ethics in Government Act in 1978. As explained in chapter 9, the act sought to prevent ex-public officials with inside information about specific issues from using it and their contacts to give their private employers an unfair competitive advantage. The act barred ex-public servants from lobbying their former agencies for one year and, on matters in which they "personally and substantially" participated as public officials, for life. In 1989, news that ex-Reagan officials had used their government service for substantial financial gain led to the passage of a law designed to strengthen the 1978 act. It will have little impact if it is enforced as weakly as its predecessor.[25]

Although responsiveness and neutral competence contribute to an effective bureaucracy, each has problems and ultimately works against the other. The most neutrally competent bureaucracy is not always the most responsive one and vice versa.

Controlling the Bureaucracy

To whom is the bureaucracy responsible? Although many bureaucratic decisions significantly affect our lives, most are not made in the public eye, and most citizens know little about them. No "ADM-SPAN" channel televises agency activities as C-SPAN covers Congress.[26] Nevertheless, many compete to influence public agencies: the president, parts of Congress, interest groups, and individual citizens. Whether they succeed depends on their resources, agency reactions, and agency ability to resist unwanted outside influence.[27]

President

The development of the bureaucracy led to demands for **executive leadership**. The president, constitution-

ally the "chief executive," has several tools to control the bureaucracy. One is budgeting. Presidents can try to limit agency appropriations to keep agencies from doing certain things, or they can tie conditions to appropriations to make them do things. Using these strategies effectively can be difficult, although President Reagan was able to weaken some regulatory agencies by significantly cutting their budgets.[28] President Bush's 1991 budget for the Internal Revenue Service proposed that the IRS target middle- and lower-income taxpayers for audits (to check the honesty of their tax returns) rather than wealthy individuals and companies. He cut the IRS's budget request to target rich tax cheats by over 90%.[29]

Second, presidents can try to control agencies by appointing people to them with views like their own. This is obvious in the case of cabinet departments. Reagan and Bush filled health care-related positions in the Department of Health and Human Services with people who were pro-life.[30] And it is also true in appointments to regulatory agencies. Republican presidents tend to appoint pro-business people and Democratic presidents pro-consumer and pro-labor individuals.[31] Reagan's appointees to regulatory agencies such as OSHA, the Consumer Products Safety Commission, and the EPA agreed with his goal of reducing government regulation.

Often, however, presidential appointees end up representing agency interests rather than presidential ones. This can happen because most appointees have less expertise and experience in agency operations than career civil servants and often come to rely on career officials for information about agency history, procedures, and policy questions.

Administrative reform is a third presidential opportunity to control the bureaucracy. Generally, the more sweeping a president's recommendation for change, the more he must anticipate congressional and interest group resistance. For example, Reagan wanted to abolish the Departments of Education and Energy and merge the Commerce and Labor Departments, but Congress would not support him.

Fourth, the White House can try to influence agencies not under presidential control by lobbying and mobilizing public opinion. For example, presidents try to influence Federal Reserve Board decisions on interest rates.

Despite these powers, there are many limits on the president's ability to control the bureaucracy. Given its size and complexity, the president cannot possibly control every important decision. Moreover,

The FBI Runs Amuck

J. Edgar Hoover helped the Federal Bureau of Investigation (FBI) develop a reputation for being *the* leading crime fighter in America. Hollywood made movies about the FBI and television carried a popular weekly series describing its exploits. What became known only later is that under Hoover's leadership the FBI consistently did things that were illegal and violated citizens' rights.

- It conducted over 500,000 investigations of "subversive" activity between 1960 and 1974, none of which resulted in a prosecution. Those investigated included Washington, D.C., high school students who had complained about the quality of school food, the women's liberation movement, all black student groups, and antiwar activists.
- It played "dirty tricks" on what it thought were subversive people. For example, it harassed Martin Luther King, Jr., by discouraging colleges from giving him honorary degrees; putting wiretaps and bugs in his hotel rooms, home, and offices; circulating information obtained with these devices to the media and executive branch officials; and mailing King a tape suggesting he kill himself or face public exposure of material on his extracurricular sex life the agency had collected about him. (After King's assassination, the FBI worked against congressional proposals to commemorate him with a national holiday.)
- Hoover "blackmailed" President Kennedy into signing an order permitting wiretapping of King by threatening to expose Kennedy's extracurricular sex life to the public. Hoover had gotten this evidence by tapping White House telephone conversations between Kennedy and a woman with Mafia ties.
- It conducted burglaries, forged letters, disrupted marriages, got people fired from jobs and ousted from apartments, and supplied violent groups like the Ku Klux Klan with arms and explosives.

The FBI's usual justification for doing these things was that they were necessary to fight those wanting to overthrow the government. But, in fact, the agency aimed its effort at anyone Hoover disliked—people such as Albert Einstein, Ernest Hemingway, and John Lennon. Hoover had the FBI keep files on leading political figures to protect himself and the agency from criticism.

Hoover led the FBI for 48 years, until 1972. Although his successors have acknowledged the need to prevent these kinds of abuses, progress is slow.

For example, from 1981 to 1985, the FBI harassed labor unions, churches, and individuals (including nuns and students) opposed to White House Central American policies. It infiltrated their meetings and took and circulated photographs of them without finding any criminal activity. In 1988, criticism that the FBI was violating pri-

J. Edgar Hoover.

vacy rights forced it to retreat from looking for Soviet spies by asking librarians to finger library users with foreign-sounding names or accents and those who acted in "suspicious" ways.[1] And, during the Persian Gulf crisis, FBI investigations into the political beliefs of Arab-Americans frightened many into recalling the internment of Japanese-Americans during World War II.

Hoover was a master organizer who created a paranoid agency environment that stifled those who disagreed with him or did not conform to his idea of what an FBI agent should do or look like. He hired agents who would adapt to this environment and, as an opponent of the civil rights movement, hired mostly whites. His preferences still dominate the agency. Even today, the FBI has few black (4.7%) and Hispanic (5.3%) agents and even fewer Asian and native American agents. Black agents resign at twice the rate of white agents. Only 10% of its agents are women.

In 1988, a federal judge ruled that the FBI had discriminated against Hispanic agents by giving them jobs unlikely to lead to promotion. The Justice Department also found that the FBI failed to stop racist harassment of a black agent by white agents.

Before we can control an agency, we need to know what it is doing. Most Americans had little idea these activities were taking place. This indicates that controlling the bureaucracy is a never-ending job.

1. Herbert N. Foerstel, *Surveillance in the Stacks* (Westport, Conn.: Greenwood Press, 1991).
Source: Robert Justin Goldstein, "The FBI and American Politics Textbooks," *PS* 18 (Spring 1985): 237–46. For more on Hoover and the FBI, see Taylor Branch, *Parting the Waters: America in the King Years, 1954–1963* (New York: Simon and Schuster, 1988), which examines the FBI and the civil rights movement; Herbert Mitgang, *Dangerous Dossiers* (New York: Donald I. Fine, 1988); and Kenneth O'Reilly, *"Racial Matters": The FBI's Secret File on Black America, 1960–1972* (New York: Free Press, 1989).

presidents have found it increasingly difficult to lead an executive branch containing large numbers of merit system employees deliberately insulated from presidential control.

Presidential control problems became much more serious in the 1930s with the establishment of many new programs and agencies. In 1935, Franklin Roosevelt appointed the Brownlow Committee, named after its chair and composed of public administration specialists, which wrote an excellent statement of the principles of executive leadership in its 1937 report.

The report was very influential. At its suggestion, the Bureau of the Budget, created in 1921, was put into the new Executive Office of the President to help the president cope with the bureaucracy. Congress also passed legislation in 1939 permitting the president to create, merge, or dissolve agencies subject to Congress's disapproval.

Since then, there have been many studies of the federal bureaucracy seeking to improve its management by increasing the president's influence. The Civil Service Reform Act of 1978, the latest major reform, replaced the Civil Service Commission with two agencies. One promotes executive leadership by working with the president in writing and administering civil service regulations. The other is supposed to protect civil servants from violations of these regulations. In addition, the act gave managers more opportunity to fire incompetent subordinates, authorized bonuses and a new pay scale for managers to encourage better performance, and created the Senior Executive Service (SES), whose problems we have already discussed.

Despite this legislation, executive leadership is still thwarted by the difficulty of removing incompetents from the civil service. Although job security is not meant to shield poor work by public servants, it does make firing incompetents difficult and time-consuming. The organization of public employees into unions contributes to this. The government's rate of discharging people for inefficiency is .01% a year. The 1978 reform has made little difference. As one public employee said, "We're all like headless nails down here—once you get us in you can't get us out."[32]

Another limit to presidential leadership is iron triangle relationships. Presidents have more success trying to control agencies that lack strong congressional allies and domestic clientele groups, such as the Treasury and State Departments, than agencies *with* such allies, such as the Agriculture and Health and Human Services Departments.

Congress

Creating and reorganizing agencies and enacting laws gives Congress opportunities to tell agencies what to do and how to do it. In recent years, Congress took away some of the powers of the Federal Trade Commission to regulate used-car sales, practices of the insurance industry, and children's television advertising. In doing so, Congress was responding to complaints (and campaign donations) from used-car dealers, the insurance industry, and other businesses who found their actions being circumscribed by the commission's new or proposed regulations. Despite these examples, however, the existence of complex, technical issues and generally stated congressional goals often gives agencies considerable leeway in doing their jobs.

Legislative oversight is another congressional tool of control, but it too has problems. Just as iron triangles can work to thwart presidential control, they can also limit congressional oversight. Iron triangles allow agencies to ally themselves with certain congressional committees and interest groups for mutual support; agencies adjust their actions to the preferences of the congressional committees that authorize their programs and appropriate their funds. For example, decisions by members of independent regulatory commissions are sensitive to the views of members of their congressional oversight committees. When the membership of the committees becomes more liberal, so too does voting by regulators.[33]

Constituent service is also a congressional tool for controlling the bureaucracy. Members of Congress often try to influence agencies on behalf of constituents. This becomes a problem when it leads to inefficiencies such as keeping unneeded military bases open to boost the economy of a member's district or when it impedes necessary government regulation, as it did when several prominent senators delayed investigation of corrupt and careless savings and loan operations.

Courts

The courts also influence the bureaucracy. Judicial decisions shape agency actions by directing agencies to follow legally correct procedures. The courts also help define congressional legislative intentions. Of course, the courts cannot intercede in an agency's decision making unless some aggrieved person or corporation files a suit against the agency. Nevertheless, in almost any controversial agency action, there will be ag-

AMERICAN DIVERSITY

Do Women Judges Make a Difference?

Some argue that more women judges are needed because women make up over half the population and are entitled to their "fair share" of all governmental offices, including judgeships. Others argue for more women judges because women have somewhat different views than men and might make somewhat different decisions than men.

A study of the votes of federal appellate court judges appointed by Jimmy Carter found that men and women were about equally liberal in criminal rights and racial discrimination cases.[1]

On the other hand, a study of the sentences of state trial court judges in a major metropolitan city in the Northeast found that women judges sentenced men defendants the same way men judges did, but they sentenced women defendants differently. Perhaps surprisingly, they sentenced women defendants to prison more frequently than men judges did. That is, in borderline cases, where judges could sentence defendants to prison or, instead, allow them to remain free on probation, women judges ordered women defendants to prison, while men judges gave them probation. Where women judges treated men and women defendants equally, men judges treated women defendants more leniently and more paternalistically, permitting them to avoid prison.[2]

In addition, women judges seem to make a difference in a less direct way. They help protect the credibility of women lawyers and witnesses. In court some men judges and lawyers refer to women lawyers and witnesses by their first names or by such terms as "honey" or "sweetie." Or the men, in the midst of the proceedings, comment upon the women's clothing or physical appearance. "How does an attorney establish her authority when the judge has just described her to the entire courtroom as 'a pretty little thing'?"[3] These remarks, whether purposeful or not, undermine the credibility of women lawyers and witnesses in the eyes of jurors. Women judges have attempted to squelch such remarks.[4]

1. Jon Gottschall, "Carter's Judicial Appointments: The Influence of Affirmative Action and Merit Selection on Voting on the U.S. Courts of Appeals," *Judicature* 67 (October 1983): 165–73.
2. John Gruhl, Cassia Spohn, and Susan Welch, "Women as Policymakers: The Case of Trial Judges," *American Journal of Political Science* 25 (May 1981): 308–22.
3. William Eich, "Gender Bias in the Courtroom: Some Participants Are More Equal Than Others," *Judicature* 69 (April-May 1986): 339–43.
4. Georgia Dullea, "Women on the Bench Increase," *New York Times,* April 26, 1984.

However, individual justices do not always reflect their group's views. In abortion cases Justice Sandra Day O'Connor has voted against the feminist groups' position, and former Justice William Brennan, a Catholic, voted against the Catholic Church's policy consistently. Sometimes groups have to satisfy themselves with the symbolic benefits of having a "member" on the Court.

Criteria Used by Senators   Although senators normally confirm presidential nominations to the lower courts, occasionally they refuse to confirm Supreme Court nominations. Because the high Court is more important and appointments to it are more visible, these nominations are more likely to become embroiled in politics. Since the late 1960s senators have rejected six nominations to the Court—two of President Lyndon

Johnson, two of President Nixon, and two of President Reagan.

Senators decide whether to confirm a nomination primarily on the basis of the qualifications and ideology of the nominee.[27] If the qualifications are good, they usually approve, regardless of the ideology. But if the qualifications are questionable, they often consider how closely the nominee's ideology matches theirs.

When Nixon chose Court of Appeals Judge G. Harold Carswell, law scholars familiar with his record were dismayed. At Senate hearings they testified that he was undistinguished, as well as opposed to civil rights. Nixon's floor manager for the nomination, Senator Roman Hruska (R-Neb.), blurted out in exasperation, "Even if he is mediocre there are a lot of mediocre judges and people and lawyers. They are entitled to a little representation, aren't they and a

Table 1 ■ Appointees of Democrats and Republicans Think Differently

A survey of the economic attitudes of federal lower court judges shows that most hold opinions accepting the economic status quo. Even so, there are significant differences according to the political party of the appointing president. Judges appointed by Republican presidents tend to think that individuals are largely responsible for their financial success or failure and that government should do less to equalize financial conditions.

	Percentage Who Agree		
	Democratic Appointees	Republican Appointees	Difference
Big corporations should be taken out of private ownership.	10%	2%	8%
U.S. institutions need complete restructuring.	24	13	11
The more able should earn more.	86	98	12
America would be better off if it moved toward socialism.	19	4	15
Private enterprise is fair to workers.	70	87	17
The poor are such due to circumstances beyond their control.	50	33	17
America offers an opportunity for financial security to all who work hard.	59	85	26
Government should ensure a good standard of living.	57	27	30
Less regulation of business is good for the country.	54	85	31
Government should not guarantee jobs.	36	70	34
Government should reduce the income gap between rich and poor.	78	44	34

Source: Althea K. Nagai, Stanley Rothman, and S. Robert Lichter, "The Verdict on Federal Judges," *Public Opinion* (November/December 1987): 54.

little chance? We can't have all Brandeises, Cardozos, and Frankfurters, and stuff like that there."[28] This was the kiss of death. Once Carswell's supporters admitted his mediocrity, senators who objected to his views on civil rights could vote against him more freely, and his nomination was doomed.

Yet when Nixon and Reagan nominated conservatives with unquestioned qualifications, they rarely faced a problem. One exception was Reagan's nomination of Robert Bork in 1987, as explained in chapter 5. Bork had criticized Court doctrine in his writings and speeches, and the debate focused on his ideology. In addition to rejecting a right to privacy, which was the basis of Court decisions allowing birth control and abortion, he had criticized Court decisions and congressional laws advancing racial equality. Bork's positions struck many Americans as extreme, and his nomination was voted down.

This battle prompted some observers to ask whether anyone with a record could be nominated again. Indeed, when Bush had a vacancy in 1990, he chose a man who had left no trail of controversial writings and speeches. David Souter, though a former New Hampshire attorney general and then state supreme court justice, was described variously as a "nineteenth-century man," "eighteenth-century man,"

"Nowhere Man," and as a "Stealth candidate."[29] Souter was a private person, living alone in a house at the end of a dirt road and not answering his neighbors' phone calls some nights. He had expressed few positions and made few decisions reflecting his views on federal constitutional doctrine. Even in his confirmation hearings he refused to reveal his views. It was assumed that he was another conservative, because of his life-style and because of his support from conservative aides to the president, yet he offered a small target and won confirmation easily.

When Bush had his second vacancy, in 1991, he had to replace the Court's first and only black, Thurgood Marshall, an ardent champion of civil rights and liberties. Bush chose Clarence Thomas, a black conservative Republican and a former head of the Equal Employment Opportunity Commission in the Reagan Administration. In that job Thomas criticized affirmative action and drew the ire of most black leaders. Some of his statements and writings also suggested that he opposed Court decisions making abortion legal.

Nominations to the Court, which were contentious during the nineteenth century but not during the first half of the twentieth century, have become contentious again partly because of the Court's activism—

Table 2 ■ Appointees of Democrats and Republicans Vote Differently

A study of the votes of federal appellate court judges appointed by Presidents Kennedy through Reagan (first term) shows marked differences according to the political party of the president. Judges appointed by Democratic presidents vote the liberal position on a variety of issues far more often than judges appointed by Republican presidents.

	Percentage Liberal* Votes By			
Issues	Kennedy/Johnson Appointees†	Nixon/Ford Appointees	Carter Appointees	Reagan Appointees
First Amendment	63%	26%	68%	35%
Criminal justice	56	23	61	31
Race discrimination	73	27	64	13
Sex discrimination	50	29	60	27
Welfare	74	32	67	23
Labor	69	28	75	23
Personal injury	53	31	65	55

*Liberal votes were defined as ones in favor of claimants of First Amendment protection in First Amendment cases, criminal defendants or prisoners in criminal justice cases, racial minorities or women in race or sex discrimination cases, welfare recipients in welfare cases, unions in labor cases, and persons injured in personal injury cases. Conservative votes were defined as the opposite.

†Appointees of Kennedy and Johnson were combined, and those of Nixon and Ford, to have enough to compare with the greater number of appointees of Carter and Reagan. The study includes all nonunanimous cases that involve these issues and were decided from July 1983 through December 1984.

Source: Jon Gottschall, "Reagan's Appointments to the U.S. Courts of Appeals: The Continuation of a Judicial Revolution," *Judicature* 70 (June/July 1986): 52.

both liberals and conservatives saw what the Court can do—and partly because of the struggle for control of the divided government since the late 1960s. Republicans have dominated the presidency while Democrats have dominated Congress, so both have fought over the judiciary to tip the balance. Republicans, especially, have been frustrated by their inability to push their civil liberties and rights policies through Congress, so they have hoped that their appointments to the Court would do what their members in Congress have not been able to do.

Results of Selection. Judges are drawn primarily from the lower federal and state courts, the federal government, or large law firms. These established legal circles are dominated by white men so, not surprisingly, most judges have been white men. Before President Jimmy Carter took office, only eight women had ever served on the federal bench.[30] Carter, however, made a concerted effort to appoint more women and racial minorities. Sixteen percent of his appointees were women, and 21% were racial minorities. President Reagan, despite the impression he created by naming a woman to the Supreme Court, named mostly white men to the lower courts. Eight percent of his appointees were women, and 6% were racial minorities.[31]

Most judges have been wealthy. Five percent of Carter's appointees were millionaires, and, during Reagan's first term, 23% of his appointees were.

Despite some efforts to balance representation on the Supreme Court, presidents have not sought actual representativeness of all socioeconomic groups. Throughout history, justices have come from a narrow, elite slice of society. Most have been born into families of Western European stock (especially English, Welsh, Scotch, and Irish), profess the Protestant religion (especially Episcopalian, Presbyterian, Congregational, and Unitarian), and are upper middle class or upper class. Moreover, they have been born into families with traditions of political or even judicial service, families with prestige and connections as well as expectations for achievement.[32]

With the power to nominate judges, presidents have a tremendous opportunity to shape the courts and their decisions. By the time Carter finished his term, he had appointed about 40% of the lower court judges, although he had no opportunity to appoint any Supreme Court justices. By the time Reagan completed his second term, he had appointed almost 50% of the lower court judges and three Supreme Court justices (in addition to elevating Rehnquist from associate to chief justice). Most of Carter's appointees were moderates or liberals, whereas most of Reagan's were conservatives (see tables 1 and 2).

Tenure of Judges

Once appointed, judges can serve for "good behavior." This means for life, unless they commit "high crimes and misdemeanors." These are not defined in the Constitution but are considered serious crimes or, possibly, political abuses. Congress can impeach and remove judges as it can presidents, but it has impeached only 11 and removed only 5.[33] The standard of guilt—"high crimes and misdemeanors"—is vague, the punishment drastic, and the process time consuming, so Congress has been reluctant to impeach judges.

As an alternative, Congress established other procedures to discipline lower federal court judges in 1980. Councils comprised of district and appellate court judges can ask judges to resign or can prevent them from hearing cases, but they cannot actually remove them. The procedures have been used infrequently, although their existence has prompted some judges to resign before being disciplined.

Qualifications of Judges

Given the use of political criteria in selecting judges, are judges well qualified?

Political scientists who study the judiciary consider federal judges generally well qualified. This is especially true of Supreme Court justices, apparently because presidents think they will be held responsible for the justices they nominate and do not want to be embarrassed by them. Also, because presidents have so few vacancies to fill, they can confine themselves to persons of their party and political views, and even to persons of a particular region, religion, race, and sex, and still locate good candidates. This is less true of lower court judges. Presidents and senators jointly appoint them, so both can avoid full responsibility for them. These judges are also less visible, so a lack of merit is not as noticeable.

Presidents do appoint some losers. President Truman put a longtime supporter on a court of appeals who was "drunk half the time" and "no damn good." When asked why he appointed the man, Truman candidly replied, "I . . . felt I owed him a favor; that's why, and I thought as a judge he couldn't do too much harm, and he didn't . . . he wasn't the worst court appointment I ever made. By no means the worst."[34]

Sometimes presidents appoint qualified persons who later become incompetent. After serving for many years they incur the illnesses and infirmities of old age, and perhaps one-tenth become unable to per-

form their job well.[35] Yet they hang on because they are allowed to serve for "good behavior." The situation has prompted proposals for a constitutional amendment setting a mandatory retirement age of 70. This would have a substantial impact because fully one-third of all Supreme Court justices, for example, have served past 75. But constitutional amendments are difficult to pass, and mandatory retirement ages are out of favor now. Further, some of the best judges have done some of their finest work after 70.

Independence of Judges

Given the use of political criteria in selecting judges, can judges be independent on the bench? Can they decide cases as they think the law requires? Or do they feel pressure to decide cases as presidents or senators want them to?

Because judges are not dependent upon presidents for renomination or senators for reconfirmation, they can be independent to a great extent. After surveying Warren and Burger Court decisions involving desegregation, obscenity, abortion, and criminal defendants' rights, one scholar observed, "Few American politicians even today would care to run on a platform of desegregation, pornography, abortion, and the 'coddling' of criminals."[36]

Presidents have scoffed at the notion that their appointees become their pawns. A study concluded that one-fourth of the justices deviated from their president's expectations.[37] Theodore Roosevelt placed Oliver Wendell Holmes on the Court because he thought Holmes shared his views on trusts. But in an early antitrust case, Holmes voted against Roosevelt's position, which prompted Roosevelt to declare, "I could carve out of a banana a judge with more backbone than that!"[38] Holmes had plenty of backbone; he just did not agree with Roosevelt's position in this case. Likewise, President Eisenhower placed Earl Warren on the Court, in part because he thought Warren was a moderate. But Warren turned out to be a liberal. Later Eisenhower said his appointment of Warren was "the biggest damn fool thing I ever did."[39] President Truman concluded that "packing the Supreme Court simply can't be done . . . I've tried it and it won't work. . . . Whenever you put a man on the Supreme Court he ceases to be your friend."[40]

Truman exaggerated, although some presidents have had trouble "packing" the courts. They have not been able to foresee the issues their appointees would have to rule on or predict the ways their appointees would change on the bench. Nevertheless, presidents who have made a serious effort to find candidates with similar views usually have not been disappointed.

Access to the Courts _____

In this litigation-prone society, many individuals and groups want courts to resolve their disputes. Whether these individuals and groups get their "day in court" depends on their type of case, their wealth, and the level of court involved.

Courts hear two kinds of cases. **Criminal cases** are those in which governments prosecute persons for violating laws. **Civil cases** are those in which persons sue others for denying their rights and causing them harm. Criminal defendants, of course, must appear in court. Potential civil litigants, however, often cannot get to court.

Wealth Discrimination in Access

Although the courts are supposed to be open to all, most individuals do not have enough money to hire an attorney and pay the related costs necessary to pursue a case. Only corporations, wealthy individuals, or seriously injured victims suing corporations or wealthy individuals do. (Seriously injured victims with a strong case can obtain an attorney by agreeing to pay him or her a sizable portion of what they win in their suit.) In addition, a small number of poor individuals supported by legal aid programs can pursue a case.

The primary expense is paying an attorney. A survey in 1984 found that lawyers charged an average of about $90 per hour for their services.[41] Other expenses include various fees for filing the case, summoning jurors, paying witnesses, and also lost income from the individual's job due to numerous meetings with the attorney and hearings in court.

Even if individuals have enough money to initiate a suit, the disparity continues in court. Those with more money can develop a full case, whereas others must proceed with a skeletal case that is far less likely to persuade judges or jurors. This is true not only for civil litigants but also for criminal defendants. Our legal system, according to one judge, "is divided into two separate and unequal systems of justice: one for the rich, in which the courts take limitless time to examine, ponder, consider, and deliberate over hundreds of thousands of bits of evidence and days of testimony, and hear elaborate, endless appeals and write countless learned opinions" and one for the non-rich, in which the courts provide "turnstile justice."[42] Consequently many individuals are discouraged from pursuing a case in the first place.

Interest Group Help In Access

Because of the expense of litigation interest groups, with greater resources than most individuals, have come to play a crucial role in helping individuals gain access. The groups sponsor and finance cases that relate to their goals. Some groups, especially civil liberties organizations such as the American Civil Liberties Union (ACLU), civil rights organizations such as the National Association for the Advancement of Colored People (NAACP), environmental groups such as the Sierra Club, and consumer and safety groups such as Ralph Nader's organizations, use litigation as a primary tactic to advance their goals. Interest groups have become so ubiquitous in the judicial process that most major court decisions involve an interest group. About 50% of all Supreme Court cases from 1969 to 1980 involved a liberal or conservative interest group.[43] Many lower court cases do as well.

Despite their activity and successes, interest groups can help only a small portion of individuals without the resources to finance their own suits.

Restrictions on Access

Even if litigants have enough wealth or interest group help, they must overcome various restrictions on access imposed by the courts. According to the Constitution, litigants can get access only for a "case" or "controversy." Courts interpret this to mean a real dispute—one in which the litigants themselves have lost rights and suffered harm. This major restriction is called **standing to sue**.

This principle is illustrated by a series of cases challenging Connecticut's birth control law. Passed in 1879, the law prohibited giving advice about, or using, birth control devices. Actually the law was not enforced much; women with a private doctor could get advice and a prescription. But the law effectively prevented opening birth control clinics that would help poor women without a private doctor or young women who did not want to go to their family doctor.

In the 1940s a doctor challenged the law, arguing that it prevented him from advising patients whose health might be endangered by childbearing. The courts said he did not have standing because he could not point to any injury he had suffered.[44] In the 1960s a doctor and two patients, who had had dangerous pregnancies in the past, challenged the law, claiming that it forced them to choose between stopping sexual activity or risking more dangerous pregnancies. Again the courts said they did not have standing because they could not point to any injury they had suffered, or would suffer, because the law was rarely enforced.[45] Finally, the head of Connecticut's Planned Parenthood League and the head of Yale's obstetrics and gynecology department opened a birth control clinic. Within days they were arrested. Although they could not get access in a civil suit, they could in the criminal case. In the process of defending themselves, they claimed that the law was unconstitutional, and the Supreme Court agreed.[46]

Proceeding Through the Courts

Individuals with a case normally start in the district courts. Those who lose have a right to have their case decided by one higher court to determine if there was a miscarriage of justice. They normally appeal to the courts of appeals.

Those who lose at this level can appeal to the Supreme Court, but they have no *right* to have their case decided by it. No matter how important or urgent an issue seems, the Court does not have to hear it. It can exercise almost unlimited discretion in accepting cases to review.

Litigants who want the Court to hear their case file petitions for review. Most petitions are for a **writ of certiorari** (Latin for "made more certain"). The writ is granted—that is, the Court agrees to hear the case—if four of the nine justices vote to do so. The rationale for this "rule of four" is that a substantial number, but not necessarily a majority, of the justices should think the case important enough to review. Generally the Court agrees to review a case when the justices think an issue has not been resolved consistently or satisfactorily by the lower courts.

From about 4,000 petitions each year, the Court selects less than one-tenth to hear, thus exercising considerable discretion. The oft-spoken threat, "We're going to appeal all the way to the Supreme Court," is usually just bluster. Likewise, the notion that the Court is "the court of last resort" is misleading. The vast majority of cases never get beyond a district court or court of appeals.

That the Supreme Court grants so few writs means that the Court has tremendous power to control its docket and therefore to determine which policies to review. It also means that the lower courts have considerable power because they serve as the court of last resort for most cases.

Deciding Cases

In deciding cases judges need to interpret statutes and the Constitution and determine whether to follow precedents. In the process they make law.

Interpreting Statutes

In deciding cases judges start with statutes—laws passed by legislatures. If the statutes are ambiguous, judges need to interpret them in order to apply them to their cases.

Sometimes statutes are ambiguous because of their nature. To be broad enough to cover many situations, their words and phrases must be so general that they might not be clear. Other times statutes are ambiguous because of the nature of the legislative process. To satisfy public demand for action on problems, legislators

Unlike the job of other politicians, the work of an appellate court judge, such as Supreme Court Justice Harry Blackmun, is very academic—pondering legal briefs and researching past decisions.

are urged to move quickly, even if they are not prepared. They are encouraged to act symbolically, even if they cannot alleviate the problems this way. They are pressed to compromise, even if they must include fuzzy provisions in statutes to avoid upsetting fragile agreements negotiated among themselves. These pressures tend to result in ill-conceived legislation.

When statutes are ambiguous, judges try to ascertain the legislators' intent in passing them. They scrutinize the legislators' remarks and debates. But they often find that different members said different things, even contradictory things, and most members said nothing about the provisions in question. This gives judges considerable leeway in construing statutes. A member of Congress admitted to Justice Harry Blackmun that they purposely use "unintelligible language" in statutes so the courts will "tell us what we mean."[47]

Interpreting the Constitution

After interpreting statutes, judges determine whether they are constitutional. Or, if the cases involve actions of government officials rather than statutes, judges determine whether the actions are constitutional. To do this they need to interpret the Constitution.

Compared to constitutions of other countries, our Constitution is short and therefore necessarily ambiguous. It speaks in broad principles rather than in narrow details. The Fifth Amendment states that persons shall not be "deprived of life, liberty, or property without due process of law." The Fourteenth Amendment states that persons shall not be denied "the equal protection of the laws." What is "due process of law"? "Equal protection of the laws"? Generally the former means that people should be treated fairly, and the latter means that they should be treated equally. But what is fairly? Equally? These are broad principles that need to be interpreted in specific cases.

Sometimes the Constitution uses relative terms. The Fourth Amendment provides that persons shall be "secure . . . against unreasonable searches and seizures." What are "unreasonable searches and seizures"? Other times the Constitution uses absolute terms. These appear more clear-cut but are deceptive. The First Amendment provides that there shall be "no law . . . abridging the freedom of speech." Does "no law" mean literally no law? Then what about the proverbial example of the person who falsely shouts "Fire!" in a crowded theater? Whether relative or absolute, the language needs to be interpreted in specific cases.

Occasionally politicians assert that judges ought to be "strict constructionists," that is, they ought to interpret the Constitution "strictly." This is nonsense. Judges cannot possibly interpret ambiguous language strictly.

When the language does not give sufficient guidance, judges try to ascertain the intentions of the framers by examining James Madison's notes of the Constitutional Convention or the *Federalist Papers*. Although these sources are considered the most authoritative, relying upon them is fraught with problems. Because Madison edited his notes many years after the convention, his experiences in government or lapses of memory in the intervening years might have colored his version of the intentions of the delegates. Because Madison, Hamilton, and Jay published the *Federalist Papers* to persuade New York to ratify the Constitution, their motive might have affected their account of the intentions of the delegates. Further, there were 55 delegates to the Constitutional Convention and many more to the state ratifying conventions, and the sources do not indicate what most of them thought about any of the provisions. Undoubtedly, all of them did not think the same.

When neither the language of the Constitution nor the intentions of the framers give sufficient guidance, judges try to distill the general meaning of the provisions and apply it to contemporary situations. The Fourteenth Amendment's equal protection clause does not refer to schools, and its framers did not intend it to relate to schools. However, they did intend it to grant blacks greater equality than before, and therefore the Court applied this meaning to segregated schools. Then the Court applied it to other segregated facilities, then to other racial minorities, and then to women. In short, the Court extracted the general meaning of equality and extended it to prohibit discrimination in many situations. In this way the Court put into practice Chief Justice Marshall's statement that the Constitution is "intended to endure for ages to come."[48]

When judges interpret the Constitution, they exercise discretion. As former Chief Justice Hughes candidly acknowledged, "We are under a constitution, but the Constitution is what the Supreme Court says it is."[49]

Restraint and Activism

All judges exercise discretion, but all do not engage in policymaking to the same extent. Some, classified as

FOCUS ON AN ISSUE

Restraint Versus Activism in Child Abuse Cases

A phone call told Melody DeShaney that her four-year-old son, Joshua, probably would not make it through the night. She had given him to his father after they were divorced three years before because she thought she was too young and poor to provide Joshua the life he deserved. She stayed in Wyoming while her son and his father moved to Wisconsin, and she had not seen them since. She thought Joshua was having "a nice kid life."

He was not. His father was physically abusing him. That night his father beat him so severely that, although he survived, he suffered brain damage that left him profoundly mentally retarded. He will have to live in an institution the rest of his life.

Melody DeShaney discovered that the Department of Social Services in the county where Joshua lived thought he was being beaten by his father. More than two years before, it had investigated a complaint by his father's second wife that there were beatings. Since then Joshua had been hospitalized three times, and the department had been notified by doctors that his injuries were likely from beatings. Officials of the department met with the father and proposed several measures to alleviate the situation, but the abuse continued. For six months a caseworker made periodic visits to the home and found Joshua with bumps and bruises, scratches and cuts, and even what appeared to be a cigarette burn on his chin. The day before the final beating the caseworker made a visit and was told that Joshua had fainted several days earlier and was napping. The caseworker did not ask to see him.

When Melody DeShaney learned all this, she decided to sue the county government. She maintained that the department should have taken Joshua away from his father (as it did once for three days) to protect him, because he could not protect himself. She sued for $50 million for his care and "to make sure that there is not another Joshua." And perhaps she sued to atone for her guilt.

She had faith in the legal system: "This is America, and you have to believe that what's right will happen in the end." However, the federal district and appellate courts ruled against her. She appealed to the Supreme Court, but it, too, ruled against her in *DeShaney v. Winnebago County Department of Social Services* in 1989. Was this the right decision?

Do Statutes Support DeShaney?

No federal statute explicitly authorizes suits against governmental officials for failure to protect victims of abuse. Although a Wisconsin statute might cover such suits in the state courts, it limits the amount litigants can recover to $50,000, which would pay for only a small portion of Joshua's care.

Does the Constitution Support DeShaney?

The Fourteenth Amendment's due process clause says "[n]o state shall . . . deprive any person of life, liberty, or property without due process of law." DeShaney claims that the department, by its inaction, deprived Joshua of his liberty. But the clause was intended to protect individuals against abuse of power by the government—not abuse by a private person, such as Joshua's father. DeShaney is asking the Court to extend the clause to cover inaction as well as action by the government.

Do Precedents Support DeShaney?

A federal appellate court in another circuit has held that once a state learns that a child is in danger of abuse and tries to protect the child, the state has a constitutional duty to protect the child adequately. But appellate court prece-

restrained, are less willing to declare statutes or actions of government officials unconstitutional, whereas others, classified as activist, are more willing to do so.

Restrained judges argue that the judiciary is the least democratic branch because judges are appointed for life rather than elected and reelected. Conse-

quently, they should be reluctant to overrule the other branches. "Courts are not the only agency of government that must be presumed to have the capacity to govern," Justice Harlan Stone said. "For the removal of unwise laws from the statute books appeal lies not to the courts, but to the ballot and the processes of dents do not bind the Supreme Court. In previous cases the justices have held that states have an obligation to provide medical care to prisoners and security to mental patients, but the justices have not ruled on any obligation to provide protection to abused children. The precedents, according to Justice Blackmun, "may be read more broadly or more narrowly depending upon how one chooses to read them."

Should the Justices Be Restrained or Activist?

In the absence of clear statutes, constitutional provisions, or precedents, the justices could be restrained; that is, they could rule for the county and thus refrain from making policy for welfare departments. Or they could be activist. They could rule for DeShaney and declare the department's inaction unconstitutional, thus involving themselves in policymaking. Such a ruling would force officials to take children away from abusive parents sooner than most do now.

Welfare officials urged the justices to be restrained. Otherwise welfare departments would have to shift some of their limited resources away from other programs, because abuse cases would require more time and effort in order to avoid lawsuits like DeShaney's. Children's advocacy organizations, on the other hand, urged the justices to be activist. They maintained that child abuse is too serious to be handled so carelessly.

A majority of six justices, including all three Reagan appointees, took a restrained stance. Chief Justice Rehnquist, writing for the majority, acknowledged that the case was "undeniably tragic" and admitted that the officials "stood by and did nothing when suspicious circumstances dictated a more active role for them." Still, Rehnquist said that judges should resist the impulse "to find a way for Joshua and his mother to receive adequate compensation for the grievous harm inflicted upon them." He insisted that the due process clause should not be expanded to create a new guarantee for children in these situations.

Justices Blackmun, Brennan, and Marshall dissented. They rejected the majority's restraint. Blackmun compared the ruling to "antebellum judges who denied relief to fugitive slaves." He said that "compassion need not be exiled

Melody DeShaney.

from the province of judging" and called the ruling "a sad commentary" upon American law. The result, Brennan noted, is to allow government "at the critical moment, to shrug its shoulders and turn away from the harm that it had promised to try to prevent."

Sources: 109 S. Ct. 998, 103 L.Ed.2d 249 (1989); William Glaberson, "Determined To Be Heard," *New York Times Magazine,* October 2, 1988, pp. 32–40.

democratic government."[50] These judges also contend that the judiciary is the branch least capable of making policy because judges are generalists. They lack the expertise and resources that many bureaucrats and legislators use to help make policy. Restrained judges further maintain that the power to declare laws unconstitutional is more effective if it is used sparingly. Justice Louis Brandeis concluded that "the most important thing we do is not doing."[51] That is, the most important thing judges do is declare laws constitutional and thereby build up political capital for the occasional times that they declare laws unconstitutional.

Activist judges do not share these qualms. Instead, they seem more outraged at injustice. Court of appeals judge David Bazelon, of the District of Columbia, said the test should be, "Does it make you sick?" If so, the law or action should be struck down.[52] These judges also seem more concerned about obtaining results than following technical procedures. Chief Justice Warren asked lawyers who emphasized technical procedures during oral arguments, "Yes, yes, yes, but is it right? Is it good?"[53] In addition, these judges seem more pragmatic. District court judge Frank Johnson, who issued sweeping orders for Alabama's prisons and mental hospitals, replied to critics, "I didn't ask for any of these cases. In an ideal society, all of these . . . decisions should be made by those to whom we have entrusted these responsibilities. But when governmental institutions fail to make these . . . decisions in a manner which comports with the Constitution, the federal courts have a duty to remedy the violation."[54]

The distinction between restrained and activist judges does not necessarily parallel that between conservative and liberal judges. In the 1950s and 1960s, it did; the Supreme Court was both activist and liberal. But in the early 1930s, the Court was activist and conservative; it struck down regulations on business. In the late 1930s, it was restrained and liberal; it upheld similar regulations on business.

But we should not make too much of the distinction between restraint and activism. It is probably more important to know if a judge is conservative or liberal. Sometimes a conservative who is restrained might vote differently than an activist conservative, but the two conservatives are likely to vote the same in most cases. A study of the justices appointed to the Supreme Court from 1953 through 1987 found that their conservative or liberal attitudes accounted for most of their individual votes, regardless of their restraint or activism (and regardless of the existence of relevant precedents or unique facts in the cases).[55] Some researchers conclude that "judicial restraint" is little more than "a cloak for the justices' policy preferences."[56] That is, justices justify their decisions on the basis of "judicial restraint" because that is considered appropriate by many people who do not think ideology or politics should play a role.

Following Precedents

In interpreting statutes and the Constitution, judges are expected to follow precedents established by their court or higher courts in previous cases. This is the rule of **stare decisis,** which is Latin for "stand by what has been decided."

The primary advantage of stare decisis is that it provides stability in the law. If different judges were to decide similar cases in different ways, the law would be unpredictable, even chaotic. "Stare decisis," Justice Brandeis said, "is usually the wise policy, because in most matters it is more important that the applicable rule of law be settled than that it be settled right."[57] Another advantage of this practice is that it promotes equality in the law, ensuring that judges treat comparable cases similarly. Otherwise, judges might appear to be arbitrary and discriminatory.

The primary disadvantage of stare decisis is that it produces excessive stability—and inflexibility—in the law when it is adhered to strictly. Times change and demand new law, but precedents of past generations bind present and future generations. Justice Holmes declared, "It is revolting to have no better reason for a rule of law than that it was laid down in the time of Henry IV. It is still more revolting if the grounds upon which it was laid down have vanished long since, and the rule simply persists from blind imitation of the past."[58]

Judges need to decide not only whether to follow precedents but also which ones to follow. There might not be any that are controlling but several that are relevant, and these might point in contrary directions. For some cases there are "plenty of precedents to go around," Justice Douglas remarked, and judges can use the ones they want to reach the results they want.[59]

Making Law

Many judges deny that they make law. They say that it is already there, that they merely "find" it or, occasionally, "interpret" it with their education and experience. They imply that they use a mechanical process. Justice Roberts wrote for the majority that struck down a New Deal act in 1936:

> It is sometimes said that the Court assumes a power to overrule . . . the peoples' representatives. This is a misconception. The Constitution is the supreme law of the land. . . . All legislation must conform to the principles it lays down. When an act of Congress is appropriately challenged in the courts as not conforming to the constitutional mandate, the judicial branch of government has only one duty—to lay . . . the Constitution . . . beside the statute . . . and to decide whether the latter squares with the former.[60]

In other words, the Constitution itself dictates the decision.

However, by now it should be apparent that judges do not use a mechanical process, and that they do exercise discretion. They *do* make law—when they interpret statutes, when they interpret the Constitution, and when they determine which precedents to follow or disregard.

In doing so, they reflect their own political preferences. As Justice Benjamin Cardozo said, "We may try to see things as objectively as we please. Nonetheless, we can never see them with any eyes except our own."[61] That is, judges, too, are human beings with their own perceptions and attitudes and even prejudices. They do not, and cannot, shed these the moment they put on their robes.

However, to say that judges make law is not to say that they make law as legislators do. Judges make law less directly. They make it in the process of resolving disputes brought to them. They usually make it by telling governments what they cannot do, rather than what they must do and how they must do it. More significantly, judges make law less freely. They do not start with clean slates but with established principles embodied in statutes, the Constitution, and precedents. They have to address these, and if they do not accept them, they have to state their reasons. If their reasons are not persuasive, they open themselves to criticism or political checks against their authority.

The Power of the Courts

Alexis de Tocqueville observed that unlike other countries, "Scarcely any political question arises in the United States that is not resolved, sooner or later, into a judicial question."[62] Because Americans are more inclined than other people to bring suits, courts have many opportunities to try to wield power.

This does not in itself guarantee that the courts can wield power, but they have been able to because the public venerates the Constitution and the courts interpret it, and because the courts enjoy relative, though not absolute, independence from the political pressures on the other branches.

The use of judicial review and the use of political checks against the courts reveal the extent of the power of the courts.

Use of Judicial Review

Judicial review—the authority to declare laws or actions of government officials unconstitutional—is the tool that courts use to wield power. When courts declare a law or action unconstitutional, they not only void that particular law or action, but they also might put the issue on the public agenda, and they might speed up or slow down the pace of change in government policies.

Judicial review, an American contribution to government, was for years unique to this country. Now it is used in numerous other countries but not as extensively and not with as great an effect as in the United States.

The Supreme Court alone has struck down more than 100 provisions of federal laws and more than 1,000 provisions of state and local laws. The Court has struck down more of the latter for several reasons: state and local legislatures enact more laws; they reflect parochial, rather than national, interests, so they enact more laws that the national Court considers in conflict with the national Constitution; and these legislatures are less risky to confront than Congress.

The number of provisions of laws that the Court has struck down, however, is not the true measure of the importance of judicial review. Instead, the ever-present threat that the Court could invalidate laws has undoubtedly prevented legislatures from enacting many laws that they believed the Court would strike down.

At times the Court has used judicial review as a brake to slow down change, as in the business regulation cases in the first third of the twentieth century. At other times it has used judicial review as a catalyst to speed up change, as in the desegregation cases in the 1950s. Then many in Congress favored desegregation, but the two houses were unable to act because they were dominated by southerners who, as committee chairs, blocked civil rights legislation. The Court's decisions broke the logjam.

By using judicial review to play a strong role in government, the Court has contradicted the Founders' expectation that the judiciary would be the weakest branch. Although it has been the weakest at times, it has been the strongest at other times. Arguably, these include the early nineteenth century, when the Court established national dominance; portions of the late nineteenth century and early twentieth century, when the Court thwarted efforts to regulate business; and the 1950s and early 1960s, when the Court extended civil liberties and rights.

Nevertheless, the extent to which the Court has played a strong role in government should not be exaggerated. The Court has not exercised judicial review over a wide range of issues; in each of the three eras of

The Supreme Court Decides a Case

When the Supreme Court agrees to hear a case, it asks the litigants to submit written arguments. These "briefs" identify the issues and marshal the evidence—statutes, the Constitution, precedents—for their side. After the Court receives the briefs, it sets a date for oral arguments.

On that date the justices gather in the robing room behind the courtroom. They put on their black robes and, as the curtains part, file into the courtroom and take their places at the raised half-hexagon bench. The chief justice sits in the center, and the associate justices extend out in order of seniority. The crier gavels the courtroom to attention and announces,

> The Honorable, the Chief Justice and Associate Justices of the Supreme Court of the United States! Oyez, oyez, oyez! [Give ear, give ear, give ear!] All persons having business before the Honorable, the Supreme Court of the United States are admonished to draw near and give attention, for the Court is now sitting. God save the United States and this Honorable Court.

The chief justice calls the case. The lawyers present their arguments. Those who read from a prepared text find the justices bored or even hostile; those who speak extemporaneously find them willing to engage in a lively dialogue. They interrupt with questions whenever they want. When Thurgood Marshall, as counsel for the NAACP, argued one school desegregation case, he was interrupted 127 times. Some lawyers are so unnerved by this practice that occasionally one faints on the spot.

The chief justice usually allots half an hour per side. When time expires, a red light flashes on the lectern, and the chief justice halts any lawyer who continues. Chief Justice Hughes was so strict he reportedly cut off one lawyer in the middle of the word "it."

The Court holds Friday conferences to make a tentative decision and assign the opinion. The decision affirms or reverses the lower court decision; it indicates who wins and who loses. The opinion explains why. It expresses principles of law and thereby establishes precedents for other cases, so it is very important.

A portrait of Chief Justice Marshall presides over the conference. To ensure secrecy, no one is present but the justices. They begin with handshakes. (During his tenure Chief Justice Marshall suggested that they begin with a drink anytime it was raining anywhere in the Court's ju-

Law clerks of the Supreme Court, recent law school grads who ranked high in their class, are chosen by the justices each year to help read petitions for review, research statutes and precedents, and draft opinions. Here two clerks meet with Justice John Paul Stevens.

risdiction. Perhaps this accounts for his extraordinary success in persuading his colleagues to adopt his views.) Then they battle. The chief justice initiates the discussion of the case. He asserts what he thinks the issues are and how they ought to be decided, and he casts a vote. The associate justices follow in order of seniority. The discussion might become heated. When the justices reach a tentative decision, if the chief justice is in the majority, he assigns a justice to write the opinion of the Court. If not, the most senior associate justice in the majority assigns one to write it.

These procedures reveal the chief justice's power. Although his vote counts the same as each associate justice's vote, his authority to initiate the discussion and assign the opinion is significant. The former can influence what the other justices think about the case; the latter can determine what the opinion expresses.

Before Marshall became chief justice, each justice wrote his own opinion. But Marshall realized that one majority opinion would have more clout. He often convinced the other justices to forsake their own opinions and subscribe to his; he authored almost half of the Court's approximately 1,100 opinions during his years. Chief Justices Warren and Burger assigned more than 80% of the Court's opinions during their years, though they wrote only some of them.[1] Burger reportedly used his authority to punish several colleagues who voted opposite him in other cases. Justice Powell told another justice, "I'm resigned to writing nothing but Indian affairs cases for the rest of my life."[2] Chief Justice Rehnquist is so conservative that he has dissented more than most chief justices and consequently has left the most senior associate to assign numerous opinions.[3]

After the conference the Court produces the opinion. This is the most time-consuming stage in the process. Because the justices are free to change their vote anytime until the decision is announced, there is much maneuvering and politicking. The justice assigned the opinion tries to write it to command support of the justices in the original majority and possibly even some in the original minority. The writer circulates the draft among the others. They suggest revisions. The writer circulates more drafts. These go back and forth, as the justices attempt to persuade or cajole, nudge or push their colleagues toward their position. Justice Brennan was especially adept at this and is considered by some scholars "the best coalition builder ever to sit on the Supreme Court."[4]

Source: Reproduced by special permission of *Playboy* Magazine. © 1972 *Playboy.*

"My dissenting opinion will be brief: 'You're all full of crap.' "

If the opinion does not command the support of some of the justices in the original majority, they write a concurring opinion. This indicates that they agree with the decision but not the reasons for it. Meanwhile, the justices in the minority write a dissenting opinion. This indicates that they do not agree even with the decision. Both concurring and dissenting opinions weaken the force of the majority opinion. They question the validity of it, and they suggest that at a different time with different justices there might be a different ruling.

The Court's own print shop in the basement prints the opinions. Then the Court announces the decision and opinions in the hushed courtroom.

1. David W. Rhode and Harold J. Spaeth, *Supreme Court Decision Making* (San Francisco: W. H. Freeman, 1976), p. 177; Harold J. Spaeth, "Distributive Justice: Majority Opinion Assignments in the Burger Court," *Judicature* 67 (December/January 1984): 299–304.
2. Nina Totenberg and Fred Barbash, "Burger's Colleagues Won't Be Sorry to See Him Go," *Washington Post National Weekly Edition*, July 7, 1986, p. 8.
3. Al Kamen, "The Scalia Surprise," *Washington Post National Weekly Edition*, March 23, 1987, p. 6.
4. Michael S. Serrill, "The Power of William Brennan," *Time*, July 22, 1985, p. 62.

its history, it has exercised review over one dominant issue and paid relatively little attention to other issues. Moreover, the one dominant issue always has involved domestic policy. Traditionally the Court has been reluctant to intervene in foreign policy. It has taken relatively few cases, and then it has usually upheld the government action.[63] For example, although the war in Vietnam was the hottest issue in the country for years and litigants challenged the constitutionality of presidents waging war without Congress declaring war, the Court never reviewed the issue.

Even when the Court has tackled an issue, it has been cautious; of the provisions of congressional laws held unconstitutional, more than half were voided more than 4 years after they had been passed, and more than one-fourth were voided more than 12 years after they had been passed.[64] These laws were voided years after many of the members of Congress responsible for them had left Congress; the Court confronted Congress when it was safer to do so.

Use of Political Checks Against the Courts

Although the courts enjoy relative independence from the political pressures brought to bear on the other branches, they by no means enjoy absolute independence. Because they are part of the political process, they are subject to political checks, which limit the extent to which they can wield judicial review.

Checks by the Executive.   Presidents can impose the most effective check. If they dislike judges' rulings, they can appoint new judges when vacancies occur.

Presidents and state and local executives, such as governors and mayors and even school officials and police officers, can refuse to enforce courts' rulings. School officials have disobeyed decisions requiring desegregation and invalidating class prayers. Police officers have ignored decisions invalidating some kinds of searches and interrogations.

Yet executives who refuse to enforce courts' rulings risk losing public support, unless the public also opposes the rulings. Even President Nixon complied when the Court ordered him to turn over the incriminating Watergate tapes.

Checks by the Legislature.   Congress and the state legislatures can overturn courts' rulings by adopting constitutional amendments or, sometimes, new stat-

utes. (When courts base decisions on particular interpretations of statutes, or when they make decisions in the absence of statutes, legislatures can pass new statutes to negate the decisions. In 1986 the Supreme Court ruled that the air force did not have to allow an ordained rabbi to wear his yarmulke with his uniform while indoors.[65] The next year Congress passed a statute permitting military personnel to wear some religious apparel while in uniform.) Legislatures can refuse to implement courts' rulings, especially when money is needed to implement them. The legislatures might simply fail to appropriate the money.

Although these checks are the most common, Congress has invoked others, although only rarely: it can alter the structure of the lower federal courts; it can limit the appellate jurisdiction of the Supreme Court; and it can impeach and remove judges.

Checks by the Public.   Judges come from the public, so it is not surprising that their decisions tend to reflect the views of the public. A study that compared 110 Supreme Court rulings from 1936 through 1986 with public opinion polls on the same issues found that the rulings mirrored the polls in 62% of the cases.[66]

But when court rulings do not reflect the views of the public, opinion toward the courts can turn negative. Although research shows that citizens know little about the cases, they do remember especially controversial decisions, and they do recognize broad trends in decisions. A study of opinion toward the Supreme Court from 1966 to 1984 found that opinion became more negative when the Court struck down more congressional laws and when it upheld more criminal rights. (On the other hand, opinion grew more positive immediately after Watergate; people saw the Court as the bastion of law in the face of the Nixon administration's efforts to circumvent the law.)[67]

When opinion toward the courts turns negative, the president or Congress is more likely to impose checks on the courts. This possibility has made the courts wary. As one political scientist concluded, the Supreme Court has "learned to be a political institution and to behave accordingly." It has "seldom lagged far behind or forged far ahead" of public opinion.[68] When it has, notably in the Dred Scott case and in the business regulation cases in the 1930s, it has lost some of its support and consequently some of its power.

In response to the occasional checks threatened or imposed on them, the courts have developed a strong sense of self-restraint to ensure self-preservation. This, more than the checks themselves, limits their use of judicial review.

Conclusion: Are the Courts Responsive?

The judiciary, appellate court judge Learned Hand said, stands as a bulwark against "the pressure of public panic." It provides a "sober second thought."[69] The Founders did not intend the judiciary to be responsive. Rather, they gave judges life tenure so courts would be independent to a large extent.

Indeed, the judiciary is more independent of pressures from the rest of the political process than the other branches are. Consequently, courts can act on behalf of the relatively powerless individuals and small groups that lack clout with the executive and legislative branches. Courts have extended important civil liberties and rights to these individuals and groups. However, even when courts act on behalf of nonelites, they rarely challenge the fundamental principles of society. They ordinarily uphold "the system." They simply give nonelites a place in it.

Although relatively independent, the judiciary is part of the political process and as such is sensitive to others in the process. It is responsive to the president and Congress—or at least to one of these—and to other elites. Eventually, it is responsive to the majority of the public. Thus, in most cases, decisions by the courts reflect the attitudes of society.

EPILOGUE

Exclusion of Japanese Upheld

In *Korematsu v. United States,* the Supreme Court, by a six to three vote, upheld the order excluding Japanese-Americans from the West Coast.[70] Justice Douglas voted against the order in conference but switched to the majority just before the Court announced its decision.[71] The Court noted that the president and Congress agreed that the order was necessary, and it emphasized that the government could take precautions to prevent espionage and sabotage during wartime.

Thus the majority was restrained, deferring to the combined force of the other two branches. These justices did not question the validity of officials' fear of espionage or sabotage or the scanty evidence of such acts by Japanese-Americans. Neither did they question the discrimination against these persons. In contrast, the minority was activist, challenging the other two branches. These justices disputed the charges of disloyalty and suspected that discrimination against these persons led to the order.

The minority raised the specter that the Court's ruling would set a dangerous precedent. "A military order, however unconstitutional, is not apt to last longer than the military emergency," Justice Robert Jackson wrote. "But once a judicial opinion rationalizes such an order . . . the Court for all time has validated the principle of racial discrimination . . . and of transplanting American citizens. The principle then lies about like a loaded weapon ready for the hand of any authority that can bring forward a plausible claim of an urgent need."

In December 1944—two-and-a-half years after it began the evacuation and one day before it heard the Court's decision—the military ordered release of all "loyal" Japanese-Americans.

Upon release they discovered that the government had failed to keep its promise to protect their property. Many of their possessions stored in warehouses had been vandalized or stolen. Some of their homes had been taken over by strangers, and some of their land had been seized for unpaid taxes.

"They did me a great wrong," Korematsu said. But he returned to live in the same town where he was arrested. "I love this country and I belong here."[72]

Near the end of his career, Justice Douglas expressed regret that he and others in the majority went along with the government. The case "was ever on my conscience."[73] Douglas did not live long enough to

A Japanese relocation camp in
Manzanar, California.

learn about research that revealed that the War Department had presented false information to the
Court. The department had altered some reports and
destroyed others demonstrating the loyalty of the
Japanese-Americans.[74] From Pearl Harbor until the
end of the war, the government had no record of a
single incident of sabotage by a Japanese-American
citizen or alien in this country.[75]

   With help from the lawyer who discovered the
false information, Korematsu reopened his case
through a rarely used procedure available only when
the original trial was tainted with prosecutorial misconduct and fraud. In 1983 a federal judge reversed
his conviction.[76]

   In 1988 Congress passed a law offering a public
apology for the internment and $20,000 compensa-
tion to each surviving internee.[77]

KEY TERMS

Korematsu v.
  United States
judicial review
Marbury v. Madison
court-packing plan
Warren Court
Burger Court
Rehnquist Court
district courts
courts of appeals

jurisdiction
habeas corpus
criminal cases
civil cases
standing to sue
writ of certiorari
restrained judges
activist judges
stare decisis

FURTHER READING

Peter Irons, *Justice at War* (New York: Oxford University
Press, 1983). *The story of Korematsu and other cases involving*
the Japanese-American relocation by the attorney who un-
covered the government's false information.

David M. O'Brien, *Storm Center,* 2nd ed. (New York: W. W.
Norton, 1990). *A lively account of the Supreme Court and its*
very human justices.

Bob Woodward and Scott Armstrong, *The Brethren* (New
York: Simon & Schuster, 1979). *Behind-the-scenes look at the*
politicking among Supreme Court justices for major cases during
the 1970s.

NOTES

   1. John W. Dower, *War without Mercy* (New York: Pantheon,
1986), p. 82.
   2. Ibid., p. 112.
   3. Peter Irons, *Justice at War* (New York: Oxford University Press,
1983), p. 269.
   4. John Hersey, "Behind Barbed Wire," *New York Times Maga-*
zine, September 11, 1988, p. 120.

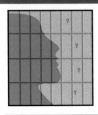
Should the Right to Abortion Continue?

You are Justice Sandra Day O'Connor of the Supreme Court. It is 1989, and you are facing a decision that could affect a right of every American woman of childbearing age. Since 1973, when the Court ruled in *Roe v. Wade* that women have a right to abortion during the first six months of pregnancy, controversy has swirled around the issue.[1] Critics have charged that the justices made law and in the process usurped states' prerogatives to regulate abortion. The Reagan administration tried to appoint justices who oppose abortion and the *Roe* decision. Now that the administration's third appointee is on the Court, many people think the Court may be ready to reverse *Roe*.

The Missouri legislature, which tried to restrict abortions before, thinks the time has come to try again. It has passed a law that bans use of public funds for abortion counseling; bans use of public clinics or hospitals for abortions, even for women who would pay the entire cost (except for those whose life is in danger); and requires doctors to conduct expensive tests to determine the viability of the fetus—ability to survive, with artificial help, outside the womb—on women who appear 20 or more weeks pregnant. These provisions would make abortions less available, especially for poor women. The law also declares that the "life of each human begins at conception," thus equating abortion with murder. Through these provisions the legislature is both restricting *Roe* and inviting the Court to overturn it.

When an abortion clinic challenged the statute the federal district court held most provisions unconstitutional, and when the state appealed the federal court of appeals agreed with the district court. Now the case of *Webster v. Reproductive Health Services* has reached the Supreme Court.

Your male colleagues appear deadlocked. Four—Blackmun, Brennan, Marshall, and Stevens—support abortion rights. Two, who dissented in *Roe*—Rehnquist

Justice O'Connor listens to oral arguments.

and White—surely will vote to uphold the statute. The two newest justices—Scalia and Kennedy—are Reagan appointees and very conservative, and they will likely vote to uphold the statute. That leaves you, the only woman justice in history, to cast the pivotal vote in the case. As one law professor observes, "If Justice O'Connor wants to continue protecting abortion rights, they will be protected. If she does not, they will not. It is her decision."[2]

You can affirm the right to abortion established in *Roe* and strike down the provisions of the statute.

(continued on next page)

Or you can reject the right to abortion established in *Roe* and let Missouri regulate or restrict the practice however it wants. Or you can take a middle course, accepting a right to abortion in principle but letting Missouri regulate or restrict the practice more than it can under *Roe*.

Your stance toward abortion has been ambivalent. Before appointment you assured President Reagan that you found abortion "personally repugnant." But as a state legislator you had voted to decriminalize abortion, prompting the right-to-life movement to oppose your nomination to the Court. Yet once on the Court, you have criticized *Roe* and voted to permit some restrictions on abortion.

Although in most matters you have been quite conservative, in sex discrimination cases you have been liberal. Do you consider the right to abortion essential to sexual equality, or do you consider it irrelevant to sexual discrimination?

You have also been a very restrained justice. But this case poses a dilemma: Upholding the state's statute would be a measure of restraint, but affirming the Court's own precedent would also be one. Which do you think is a more important measure of restraint?

You realize that the right to abortion has been the status quo for 16 years. About a million and a half women take advantage of this right each year, more than 4,000 every day. Almost 1 in 10 college women has had an abortion, and 1 in 4 of all women between the ages of 20 and 24 has had one. Many more see it as a symbol of women's struggle for equality.

The buildup has exceeded that for any other case in a decade. Hundreds of organizations have filed a record 78 "friend-of-the-court briefs" urging the justices to rule one way or the other. Briefs by feminist organizations assert that the right to abortion protects women's bodily integrity and their self-determination. Briefs by civil rights organizations note that elimination of the right would fall most heavily upon poor women, who would be less able to pay the higher cost or travel the greater distance to states or foreign countries where abortions would remain available. Many would induce their own abortions with wire coat hangers, knitting needles, or caustic douches as many did before *Roe,* or they would resort to untrained and unregulated illegal abortionists. Either way could jeopardize their health or even their lives. Briefs by medical organizations object to states' interference in the relationship between doctors and their patients.

On the other hand, briefs by right-to-life and some religious groups maintain that *Roe* was wrongly decided and that states have a compelling interest in protecting life before birth. A brief by the U.S. government, filed by the outgoing Reagan administration just days after the 1988 election (delayed to avoid offending pro-choice people planning to vote for Vice-President Bush), insists that the Court has usurped the state legislatures' responsibility to weigh competing ethical and scientific factors in a highly sensitive area.[3]

Pro-choice groups, for the first time fearing loss of the right, converged on Washington just two weeks before the oral arguments. More than 300,000 demonstrators sought to remind you of majority support for *Roe*. Some wrote about their own experience with abortion. "I was a 19-year-old college student in New York when I got pregnant in 1962," one wrote. "My boyfriend and I pooled our money and borrowed from friends, until we had the $460 necessary to pay for an illegal abortion. . . . When the operation was over, we took the elevator to the ground floor and found the street lined with police cars. The officers arrested me, my boyfriend and the physician."[4]

Right-to-life groups, sensing possible victory, have deluged you with letters and phone calls. (Televangelists apparently led viewers to think that the Court was conducting a public opinion survey on abortion.) The Court had to set up a rarely used third switchboard to handle all the calls.[5]

As the only justice who has experienced pregnancy, and the only one who has experienced the conflict between motherhood and a career, what is your decision?

- I vote to affirm the right to abortion as set forth in *Roe*.
- I vote to reject the right to abortion as set forth in *Roe* and let the states decide whether to allow it.
- I vote to narrow the right to abortion as set forth in *Roe* and let the states restrict it more but not abolish it.

Americans value their "rights." Eighteenth-century Americans believed that people had "natural rights" by virtue of being human. Given by God, not by government, they could not be taken away by government. Contemporary Americans do not use this term, but they do think about rights much as their forebears did.

Yet Americans have a split personality about their rights. As chapter 4 described, most people tell pollsters they believe in various constitutional rights in the abstract, but many do not accept these rights when applied to more concrete situations. For example, most people say they believe in free speech, but many would not allow Communists or atheists to speak in public.

Conflicts over civil liberties and rights have dominated the courts since the depression. This chapter, covering civil liberties, and the next, covering civil rights, describe how the courts have interpreted these rights and tried to resolve these conflicts. We will explain the most important rights and recount the struggles by individuals and groups to achieve them. We will see how judges act as referees between litigants,

brokers among competing groups, and policymakers in the process of deciding these cases.

The Constitution and the Bill of Rights _____

Individual Rights in the Constitution

Although the term *civil liberties* usually refers to the rights in the Bill of Rights, a few rights are granted in the body of the Constitution. The Constitution bans religious qualifications for federal office and guarantees jury trials in federal criminal cases. It bans **bills of attainder,** which are legislative acts rather than judicial trials pronouncing specific persons guilty of crimes, and **ex post facto laws,** which are legislative acts making some behavior illegal that was not illegal when it was done. The Constitution also prohibits suspension of the writ of habeas corpus, except during rebellion or invasion of the country. These rights are significant, but they by no means exhaust the rights people believed they had at the time the Constitution was written.

The Bill of Rights

Origin and Meaning. The Constitution originally did not include a bill of rights, but to win support for its ratification, the Founders promised to adopt amendments to provide such rights. James Madison proposed 12 amendments, Congress passed them, and in 1791 the states ratified the 10 that came to be known as the Bill of Rights.[6] Actually, just the first 8 grant individual rights. The Ninth says that the listing of these rights does not mean they are the only ones the people have; and the Tenth refers to the relationship between the federal and state governments.

The Bill of Rights provides rights against the government. According to Justice Hugo Black, it is "a collection of Thou shalt nots" directed to the government.[7] Actually it provides rights for a minority against the majority, because government policy concerning civil liberties tends to reflect the views of the majority. "The very purpose of a Bill of Rights," Justice Robert Jackson said, "was to withdraw certain subjects from the vicissitudes of political controversy, to place them beyond the reach of majorities." These rights "may not be submitted to a vote."[8]

Civil Liberties in the Bill of Rights

- First Amendment
  freedom of religion
  freedom of speech, assembly, and association
  freedom of the press
- Second Amendment
  right to keep and bear arms (for individuals in a militia at a time when there was no standing army to protect the country)
- Third Amendment
  forbids quartering soldiers in houses during peacetime
- Fourth Amendment
  forbids unreasonable searches and seizures
- Fifth Amendment
  right to grand jury hearing in criminal cases
  forbids double jeopardy (more than one trial for the same offense)
  forbids compulsory self-incrimination
  right to due process
  forbids taking private property without just compensation
- Sixth Amendment
  right to speedy trial
  right to public trial
  right to jury trial in criminal cases
  right to cross-examine adverse witnesses
  right to present favorable witnesses
  right to counsel
- Seventh Amendment
  right to jury trial in civil cases
- Eighth Amendment
  forbids excessive bail and fines
  forbids cruel and unusual punishment

The Founders set up a government that would protect minority rights. By this they meant property rights for the well-to-do against the jealous majority. Over the years, however, as the importance of property rights has declined and that of other rights has increased, the Bill of Rights has been used to protect the rights of the "have-nots" of society—the unpopular, powerless minorities in conflict with the majority.

Responsibility for protecting individual rights often falls on federal judges. Because they are appointed for life, they are more independent from majority pressure than elected officials are. In practice, the courts, especially the Supreme Court, define and protect individual rights.

Application. For many years the Supreme Court applied the Bill of Rights only to the federal government—not to state governments (or local governments, which are under the authority of state governments). The Court ruled that the Bill of Rights restricted only what the federal government could do.[9]

The Founders thought that the states, being closer to the people, would be less likely to violate their liberties. Also, they knew that about half the states had their own bills of rights, and they expected the rest to follow.

The Founders did not realize that states would actually come to violate people's liberties more frequently than the federal government. The state governments, representing smaller, more homogeneous populations, tended to reflect majority sentiment more closely than the federal government, and they often rode roughshod over criminal defendants or racial, religious, or political minorities. When disputes arose, the state courts tended to interpret their bills of rights narrowly.

However, starting in 1925[10] and continuing through 1972,[11] the Supreme Court gradually applied most provisions of the Bill of Rights to the states, using the Fourteenth Amendment's due process clause as justification. This clause, adopted after the Civil War to protect blacks from southern governments, reads, "Nor shall any state deprive any person of life, liberty, or property, without due process of law." The clause refers to states and "liberty." It is ambiguous, but the Court interpreted it to mean that the states too have to provide the liberties in the Bill of Rights.

The Court has applied all but three provisions of the First and the Fourth through the Eighth Amendments to the states: guarantee of a grand jury in criminal cases, guarantee of a jury trial in civil cases, and prohibition of excessive bail and fines. In addition, the Court has established some rights not in the Bill of Rights, and it has applied these to the states too: presumption of innocence in criminal cases, right to travel within the country, and right to privacy. Thus, most provisions in the Bill of Rights, and even some not in it, now restrict what both the federal and state governments can do.

To see how the Court has interpreted these provisions, we will look at three major areas—freedom of expression, rights of criminal defendants, and right to privacy.

Freedom of Expression

The First Amendment provides freedom of expression, which includes freedom of speech, assembly, and association;[12] freedom of the press; and freedom of religion.

The amendment states that "Congress shall make no law" abridging these liberties. The language is absolute, but few justices interpret it literally. They cite the example of the person who falsely shouts "Fire!" in a crowded theater and causes a stampede that injures someone. Surely the amendment does not protect this expression. So the Court needs to draw a line between expression the amendment protects and that which it does not.

Freedom of Speech

Freedom of speech, Justice Black asserted, "is the heart of our government."[13] First, by allowing an open atmosphere, it maximizes the opportunities for individuals to develop their personalities and potentials to the fullest. Second, by encouraging a variety of opinions, it furthers the advancement of knowledge and discovery of truth. Unpopular opinions could be true or partially true. Even if completely false, they could prompt a reevaluation of accepted opinions. Third, by permitting citizens to form opinions and express them to others, it helps them participate in government. It especially helps them check inefficient or corrupt government. Fourth, by channeling conflict toward persuasion, it promotes a stable society. Governments that deny freedom of speech become inflexible; they force conflict toward violence.[14]

Seditious Speech. The first controversies to test the scope of freedom of speech involved **seditious speech,** speech that encourages rebellion against the government. The government historically prosecuted individuals for seditious speech during or shortly after war, when society was most sensitive about loyalty.

The first prosecutions were just seven years after adoption of the First Amendment. The Federalists were in power, and Jeffersonian newspaper editors criticized them sharply about an apparent impending war with France. The Federalists were incensed. To silence the editors, the Federalist-dominated Congress and the Federalist president—John Adams—passed and signed the **Sedition Act of 1798,** which made it a crime to publish "false, scandalous, and malicious writing" against the government "with intent to defame the government" or "to excite against [it] the hatred of the people." In defense, individuals could try to prove that the claims in their writing were true, but this was so difficult to do that the act came very close to making it a crime to criticize the government. The Federalists justified this with what would become a familiar rationalization to punish speech: "national security." The war with France did not materialize, but the Federalists used the act anyway. They indicted 15 editors and convicted 10.

The act expired the day Jefferson became president, so the Supreme Court did not have an opportunity to determine its constitutionality. (In 1964, however, the Court declared that the act had been unconstitutional.[15])

More prosecutions came with World War I and the Russian Revolution, which brought the Communists to power in the Soviet Union in 1917. The Russian Revolution prompted a "Red Scare," in which people feared conspiracies to overthrow the U.S. government. Congress passed the Espionage Act of 1917, which prohibited interfering with military recruitment, inciting insubordination in military forces, and mailing material advocating rebellion; and the Sedition Act of 1918, which prohibited "disloyal, profane, scurrilous, or abusive language about the form of government, Constitution, soldiers and sailors, flag or uniform of the armed forces." Many states passed similar laws. In short, government prohibited a wide range of speech.

During the war the federal government prosecuted almost 2,000 and convicted almost 900 persons under these acts, and the states prosecuted and convicted many others. They prosecuted individuals for saying that war is contrary to the teachings of Jesus, that World War I should not have been declared until after a referendum was held, and that the draft was unconstitutional. Officials even prosecuted an individual for remarking to women knitting clothes for the troops, "No soldier ever sees those socks."[16]

These cases gave the Supreme Court numerous opportunities to rule on seditious speech. In six major cases, the Court upheld the federal and state laws and affirmed the convictions of all the defendants.[17] The

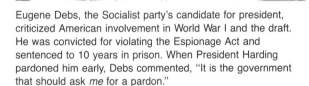

Eugene Debs, the Socialist party's candidate for president, criticized American involvement in World War I and the draft. He was convicted for violating the Espionage Act and sentenced to 10 years in prison. When President Harding pardoned him early, Debs commented, "It is the government that should ask *me* for a pardon."

defendants advocated socialism or communism, and some advocated the overthrow of the government to achieve these. Except for one—Eugene Debs, the Socialist party's candidate for president—the defendants did not command a large audience. Even so, the Court concluded that these defendants' speech constituted a "clear and present danger" to the government. Justice Edward Sanford wrote, "A single revolutionary spark may kindle a fire that, smouldering for a time, may burst into a sweeping and destructive conflagration."[18] In reality, there was nothing clear or present about the danger; the defendants' speech had little effect.

More prosecutions came after World War II. Congress passed the Smith Act in 1940, which was not as broad as the World War I acts because it did not forbid criticizing the government. But it did forbid advocating overthrow of the government by force and organizing or joining individuals who advocated overthrow.

The act was used against members of the American Communist party after the war. The uneasy alliance between the United States and the Soviet Union had given way to the Cold War between the countries.

Politicians, especially Senator Joseph McCarthy (R-Wis.), exploited the tensions. McCarthy charged various government officials with being Communists. He had little evidence, and his tactics were called "witch-hunts" and, eventually, **McCarthyism.** Other Republicans, too, accused the Democratic administration of covering up Communists. They goaded it into prosecuting members of the Communist party so it would not appear "soft on communism."

In 1951 the Court upheld the Smith Act and affirmed the convictions of 11 top-echelon leaders of the Communist party.[19] These leaders organized the party and the party advocated overthrowing the government by force, but the leaders had not attempted overthrowing it. (If they had, they clearly would have been guilty of crimes.) Even so, the Court majority concluded that they constituted a clear and present danger, and Chief Justice Fred Vinson wrote that the government does not have to "wait until the putsch is about to be executed, the plans have been laid and the signal is awaited" before it can act against the party. The minority argued that the Communist party was not a danger. Justice William Douglas said that the party was "of little consequence. . . . Communism has been so thoroughly exposed in this country that it has been crippled as a political force. Free speech has destroyed it as an effective political party."

Following the Court's decision, the government prosecuted and convicted almost 100 other Communists.

But the Cold War eased slightly, the Senate voted to condemn McCarthy, and two new members, in-

At congressional hearings Senator Joseph McCarthy identified locations of alleged Communists and "fellow travelers."

Television Blacklisting

The entertainment industry as well as government took action against alleged subversives following World War II. From 1950 to 1955 many performers suspected of having Communist sympathies were blacklisted from appearing on television or in movies. "Red Channels: The Report of Communist Influence in Radio and Television," published by an organization founded by former FBI agents was one commonly used **blacklist.** This publication informed television networks and program sponsors and their advertising agencies of "Communists" infiltrating the broadcast industry. The networks were expected to deny such performers any opportunities to appear on programs. If the networks were not sufficiently vigilant, the sponsors and their agencies were expected to pressure them by canceling their ads.

The publishers of blacklists cast their nets widely. "Red Channels," for instance, identified a panelist on the popular show "I've Got a Secret" as a Communist sympathizer because of his wife's politics. (And he was in the process of divorcing her partly because of her politics.)

According to a producer of television shows on CBS, the network had a full-time "security man." Before booking a performer, the producer had to send the performer's name to the security official. If the name was on any of the blacklists, the official would send word: "not cleared" or sometimes the code phrase "bad actor." The network never gave the actor an explanation. "The victim . . . seldom knew what hit him. He simply became unemployable."

The networks followed the lists because of the public's paranoia about communism. Even executives who disagreed with blacklisting ordinarily acquiesced; indeed, many helped implement the practice. An actress with the same name as a writer for the *Daily Worker,* a Communist newspaper, was listed by mistake. Yet executives of the ad agency for the sponsor of the program urged the producer to drop the actress. "We're already starting to get mail," they said, "and we can't let the sponsor be involved with protests."

In the rare case in which the networks used a performer whose name was on the lists, citizen groups pressured the sponsors. One group put stickers on store windows asking shoppers not to buy a brand of deodorant. One grocery store owner in Syracuse, New York, hung signs by a company's products, advising that the company was responsible for hiring "Communist fronters." Other stores removed the products from their shelves.

Source: Mark Goodson, " 'If I'd Stood Up Earlier. . . .' " *New York Times Magazine,* January 13, 1991, p. 22.

---

cluding Chief Justice Earl Warren, joined the Court. In a series of cases in the 1950s, the Court made it more difficult to convict Communists,[20] thereby incurring the wrath of the public, Congress, and President Eisenhower. In a private conversation, Warren asked Eisenhower what he thought the Court should do with the Communists. Eisenhower replied, "I would kill the S.O.B.s."[21]

The government took other action against Communists. The federal government ordered Communists to register, and then some state governments banned them from public jobs like teaching, or private jobs like practicing law or serving as union officers. Legislative committees held hearings to expose and humiliate them. The Court heard numerous cases involving these actions and usually ruled against the government.

The Vietnam War did not prompt the same fears that World Wars I and II did. Congress did not pass comparable laws, perhaps because many "respectable" people opposed this war and also because the Court in the 1950s and 1960s increasingly allowed seditious speech.

The Court developed new doctrine for seditious speech in 1969. A Ku Klux Klan leader said at a rally in Ohio that the Klan might take "revengeance" on the president, Congress, and Supreme Court if they continued "to suppress the white, Caucasian race." The leader was convicted under a statute similar to those upheld after World War I, but this time the statute was unanimously struck down by the Court.[22] The justices said that people can advocate—enthusiastically, even heatedly—as long as they do not incite illegal action. This broad protection for seditious speech remains in effect today.

Thus, after many years and many cases, the Court concluded that the First Amendment protects seditious speech as much as other speech. Justice Douglas noted that "the threats were often loud but always puny."[23] Even the attorney general who prosecuted the major Communist cases later admitted that the cases were "squeezed oranges. I didn't think there was much to them."[24] Nevertheless, the Court had permitted a climate of fear to overwhelm the First Amendment for many years.

Public Forum. People usually communicate with each other in private. But sometimes speakers want more listeners and they use public places where people congregate. This means speakers will be heard by some listeners who do not like their message or their use of public places to disseminate it, and it also means speakers might disrupt the normal purposes of these places.

The Court holds that individuals have a right to use public places, such as streets, sidewalks, and parks, to express their views on public issues. These places constitute the **public forum** and serve as "the poor person's printing press."

When speakers seek to use other public facilities, the Court has to determine which ones are also part of the public forum. It decided that federal and state capitol grounds,[25] Supreme Court grounds,[26] and public school grounds[27] are part of the forum. It decided that blacks could protest library segregation at a public library[28] and promoters could show the rock musical *Hair* at a public theater[29] because these too are part of the forum.

On the other hand, the Court decided that civil rights activists could not demonstrate against jail segregation outside a jail because of the need for security,[30] and Dr. Benjamin Spock—the baby doctor—and other antiwar activists could not encourage opposition to the Vietnam War at an army base because of the need for discipline in the army.[31]

Normally only publicly owned facilities are considered part of the public forum, but the proliferation of shopping centers and malls prompted speakers to use these privately owned facilities to reach crowds of shoppers. The Warren Court permitted them to do so, saying that shopping centers and malls are similar to downtown shopping districts where streets and sidewalks are part of the public forum.[32] But the Burger Court overruled the Warren Court, emphasizing property rights rather than First Amendment rights in this situation.[33]

Even in pubic forums people cannot speak whenever and however they want. The Court has divided speech into three kinds—pure speech, speech plus conduct, and symbolic speech—and established doctrine for each.

Pure Speech. **Pure speech** is speech without any conduct (besides the speech itself). Individuals can say what they want as long as they do not cause a breach of the peace or a riot, or hurl "fighting words" at specific persons, except at police officers, who are supposed to be trained and disciplined to take abuse.[34]

Before the Court's ruling in 1972, arrests for swearing were common. In the District of Columbia, for example, more than half of the 15,000 to 20,000 arrests for "disorderly conduct" each year involved swearing, usually at police.[35]

Individuals can use offensive language in many situations.[36] During the Vietnam War, a man walked through the corridors of the Los Angeles County courthouse wearing a jacket with the words "Fuck the Draft" emblazoned on the back. Police arrested him. The Court reversed his conviction, and 72-year-old Justice John Harlan remarked that "one man's vulgarity is another's lyric."[37]

The media, however, cannot broadcast some offensive language. A California radio station broadcast a monologue by comedian George Carlin. Titled "Filthy Words," it lampooned society's sensitivity to seven words that "you couldn't say on the public airwaves . . . the ones you definitely wouldn't say, ever." The seven words, according to the Federal Communications Commission report, included "a four-letter word for excrement" repeated 70 times in 12 minutes. In a close vote, the Court ruled that although the monologue was part of a serious program on contemporary attitudes toward language, it was not protected under the First Amendment because people, including children, tuning the radio could be subjected to the language in their home.[38]

Yet the Court struck down a Utah law restricting "indecent material" on cable television. The difference apparently is that people choose to subscribe and pay for cable television.[39]

Speech Plus Conduct. **Speech plus conduct** is speech combined with conduct that is intended to convey ideas—for example, a demonstration in which protesters chant slogans or carry signs with slogans (the speech) and march, picket, or sit in (the conduct).

Individuals can demonstrate, but they are subject to some restrictions. Places in the public forum are used for other purposes besides demonstrating, and individuals cannot disrupt these activities. They cannot, Justice Arthur Goldberg remarked, hold "a street meeting in the middle of Times Square at the rush hour."[40] To avoid this, governments can require them

to obtain a permit, which can specify the place, time, and manner of the demonstration. However, officials cannot allow one group to demonstrate but forbid another, no matter how much they dislike the group or its message. They cannot forbid the group even if they say they fear violence, unless the group actually threatens violence. In short, officials may establish restrictions to avoid disruption, but they may not use these restrictions to censor speech.

Accordingly, lower federal courts required the Chicago suburb of Skokie to permit the American Nazi party to demonstrate in front of the town hall in 1978.[41] About 40,000 of Skokie's population of 70,000 were Jews. Of these, hundreds had survived the German Nazi concentration camps during World War II, and thousands had lost relatives who died in the camps. The city, edgy about the announced demonstration, passed ordinances that prohibited wearing "military-style" uniforms and distributing material that "promotes and incites hatred against persons by reason of their race, national origin, or religion." These ordinances were thinly disguised attempts to bar the demonstration, and the courts threw them out. One quoted Justice Oliver Wendell Holmes's statement that "if there is any principle of the Constitution that more imperatively calls for attachment than any other it is the principle of free thought—not free thought for those who agree with us but freedom for the thought we hate."[42]

The Rehnquist Court, however, did uphold a Milwaukee suburb's ordinance that prohibited picketing at a residence.[43] The city passed the ordinance after anti-abortionists had picketed, six times in one month, the home of a doctor who performed abortions. Although protesters can march through residential neighborhoods, the Court said, a city can prohibit them from focusing on a particular home. Thus the Court emphasized the right to privacy at home over the right to demonstrate in this situation.

Symbolic Speech. Symbolic speech is the use of symbols, rather than words, to convey ideas.

During the Vietnam War, men burned their draft cards to protest the draft and the war. This was powerful expression, and Congress tried to stifle it by passing a law prohibiting destruction of draft cards. The Supreme Court was uncomfortable with symbolic speech and reluctant to protect it. Even Chief Justice Warren worried that this would mean that "an apparently limitless variety of conduct can be labeled 'speech.'" The Court upheld the law.[44]

One year later, however, the Court was willing to protect symbolic speech. A junior high and two senior high school students in Des Moines, Iowa, including Mary Beth Tinker, wore black armbands to protest the war. They were suspended, and they sued school officials. Public schools, Justice Abe Fortas said, "may not be enclaves of totalitarianism." They must allow students freedom of speech, providing students do not disrupt the schools.[45]

Mary Beth Tinker, here with her mother and brother, wore a black armband at school to protest the Vietnam War.

In the 1960s and 1970s, many students wore long hair or beards in violation of school policy. Some claimed they did so to protest "establishment culture." Blacks and Indians claimed they wore Afros and braids to show racial pride. Federal courts of appeals split evenly as to whether this was symbolic speech. The Supreme Court refused to hear any of these cases, so there was no uniform law across the country.

Some individuals treated the American flag disrespectfully to protest the Vietnam War. A Massachusetts man wore a flag patch on the seat of his pants and was sentenced to six months in jail. A Washington student taped a peace symbol on a flag and then hung the flag, upside down, outside his apartment. The Court reversed both convictions.[46]

When a member of the Revolutionary Communist Youth Brigade burned an American flag outside the Republican Convention in Dallas in 1984, the justices faced the issue of actual desecration of the flag. The Rehnquist Court surprisingly permitted this symbolic speech.[47] Two Reagan-appointed conservatives, Justices Anthony Kennedy and Antonin Scalia, joined the three most liberal members of the Court to forge a bare majority. The foremost free speech advocate on the bench, Justice William Brennan, wrote that the First Amendment cannot be limited just because this form of expression offends some people. "We do not consecrate the flag by punishing its desecration, for in doing so we dilute the freedom that this cherished emblem represents." The ruling invalidated laws of 48 states (not Alaska or Wyoming) and the federal government.

Chief Justice Rehnquist emotionally criticized the decision. He said the First Amendment should not apply because the flag is a unique national symbol. He then recounted the history of the "Star-Spangled Banner" and the music of John Philip Sousa's "Stars and Stripes Forever"; he quoted poems by Ralph Waldo Emerson and John Greenleaf Whittier that refer to the flag; and he discussed the role of the "Pledge of Allegiance."

Civil liberties advocates praised the decision. One lawyer for the defendant said, "If free expression is to exist in this country, people must be as free to burn the flag as they are to wave it." Another said that veterans should cheer the decision because it shows that the values in the Bill of Rights that they fought for are intact. Yet veterans groups were outraged.

After administration officials assessed public opinion by monitoring talk shows, President Bush stood in front of the Iwo Jima Memorial and proposed a constitutional amendment to override the decision.[48] Members of Congress, always anxious to appear patriotic, lined up in support. But some, especially Democrats, later came out in opposition. They criticized the proposal for creating an unprecedented exception to the First Amendment. Instead of the proposed amendment, Congress passed a statute prohibiting flag desecration. Apparently a majority felt that this less permanent substitute would be an adequate shield against the public's wrath. Yet in 1990, the justices, dividing the same way, declared the statute unconstitutional for the same reasons they reversed the Dallas conviction.[49] President Bush, this time waving a model of the Iwo Jima Memorial, proposed another constitutional amendment, and Senate Republican Leader Robert Dole (Kan.) warned Democrats that their opposition to the amendment "would make a good 30-second spot" for the upcoming elections, but Congress rejected the amendment. Members sensed less pressure from the public. By this second year of debate on this issue, the initial emotional reaction of the public had ebbed. More voices had spoken out against dilution of the First Amendment.

Protestors torch flags in Chicago.

Freedom of the Press

Unlike most civil liberties cases, which pit a relatively powerless individual or group against the government, freedom of press cases usually feature a more powerful publisher or broadcaster against the government. Even so, these cases still involve rights against the government.

Prior Restraint. The core of freedom of the press is freedom from **prior restraint**—censorship. If the press violates laws prohibiting, for example, libelous or obscene materials, it can be punished after publishing such materials. But freedom from prior restraint means that the press at least has the opportunity to publish what it thinks is appropriate.

Freedom from prior restraint is not absolute. At the height of the Vietnam War, the secretary of defense in the Johnson administration, Robert McNamara, became disenchanted with the war and ordered a thorough study of our involvement. The study, called "The Pentagon Papers," laid bare the reasons the country was embroiled—reasons not as honorable as the ones officials had been giving the public—and it questioned the effectiveness of military policy. The study was so revealing that McNamara remarked to a friend, "They could hang people for what's in

The chief of the presses of the *Washington Post* hails the Supreme Court's decision allowing publication of the Pentagon Papers.

there."[50] He printed only 15 copies and classified them "Top Secret" so few persons could see them. One of the 36 authors, Daniel Ellsberg, originally supported the war but later turned against it. In 1971 he photocopied the papers and gave them to the *New York Times* and *Washington Post,* which published excerpts.

The Nixon administration sought injunctions to restrain the newspapers from publishing more excerpts, but the Supreme Court refused to grant them.[51] Most justices said that they would grant injunctions if publishing the papers clearly jeopardized national security. But information in the papers was historical; it did not directly hinder the war effort. Thus, the rule remained—no prior restraint—but exceptions were possible.

The Rehnquist Court did approve prior restraint in a situation far removed from national security. When journalism students at a St. Louis high school wrote articles for their newspaper about the impact of pregnancy and of parents' divorce on teenagers, the principal deleted the articles and three of the students sued. The Court, noting that students below the college level have fewer rights than adults, decided that officials can censor school publications.[52]

Principals have exercised their authority typically over articles covering school policies or social issues. A Colorado principal blocked an editorial criticizing his study hall policy while allowing another editorial praising it. A Texas principal banned an article about the class valedictorian who succeeded despite the death of her mother, the desertion of her father, and her own pregnancy. An editorial urging students to be more responsible about sex was censored by a Kentucky principal, who feared it could be interpreted as condoning sex, while a survey on AIDS was censored by a Maryland principal, who prohibited students from defining the term "safe sex."

Despite these exceptions to freedom from prior restraint, the press in the United States is freer than that in Great Britain, where freedom from prior restraint began. Britain has no First Amendment and tolerates more secrecy. In 1987 the government barred publication of controversial and embarrassing memoirs by a former security service agent, even though they were being published in the United States at the time. A year later the government banned radio and television interviews with all members of the outlawed Irish Republican Army (IRA) and its political party, including its one representative in Parliament. The government even banned broadcast of a song by a

Leanne Tippell and Leslie Smart, two of the St. Louis high school students who sued their school for suppressing their student newspaper story, meet with their attorney Leslie Edwards.

popular folk group because the lyrics supported people convicted of IRA bombings. During the Persian Gulf War the French government banned sale of a song—"Go For It Saddam"—that criticized the West.

Restrictions on Gathering News.   Although prior restraint is an obvious limitation on freedom of the press, restrictions on gathering news in the first place are less obvious but no less serious. They also keep news from the public.

The Burger Court was not vigilant in guarding the press from these restrictions. Most important, it denied reporters a right to keep the names of their sources confidential. In investigative reporting, reporters frequently rely on sources who demand anonymity in exchange for information. The sources might have sensitive positions in government or relations with criminals that would be jeopardized if their names were publicized. A Louisville reporter was allowed to watch persons make hashish from marijuana if he kept their names confidential. But after publication of the story, a grand jury demanded their names. When the reporter refused to reveal them, he was cited for contempt of court, and his conviction was upheld by the Supreme Court.[53] The majority said reporters' need for confidentiality is not as great as the judicial system's need for information about crimes. So reporters either cannot guarantee potential sources anonymity, or reporters might have to choose between breaking their promise or being cited for contempt and jailed for an indefinite period of time.

Conflict with a Fair Trial.   The Sixth Amendment grants the **right to a fair trial,** including the right to impartial jurors. The right to a free press can conflict with this right when sensational crimes receive massive publicity that biases potential jurors. If the courts stress one right, they slight the other. English law emphasizes a fair trial; it forbids the press from publishing incriminating evidence against defendants before trial. American courts traditionally emphasized a free press, but both the Warren and Burger courts tried to bring the two rights into a more equal balance.

The Warren Court reversed several convictions in cases in which prejudicial publicity led to unfair trials.[54] In response, some judges issued gag orders prohibiting the press from publishing incriminating evidence against defendants before trial. The Burger Court said judges could impose gag orders rarely, if ever.[55] To overcome prejudicial publicity, judges could postpone the trial until the publicity subsides, move the trial to a location where the publicity does not extend, or question potential jurors and screen out those who seem affected by the publicity.

Unable to use gag orders, some judges closed pretrial hearings that determined the legality of evidence police obtained. Keeping the press from attending and learning about incriminating evidence served the same purpose as imposing gag orders, although it did not pose the same conflict with the press because it did not entail censoring information the press already had. In 1979 the Court, by a five to four vote, held that judges can close these hearings to preserve defendants' right to a fair trial.[56] The Court has tried to steer a middle course in this conflict between two constitutional rights.

Invasion of Privacy.   The right to a free press can also conflict with an individual's right to privacy when the press publishes personal information. The Supreme Court has permitted the press to publish factual information. For example, although a Georgia law prohibited the press from releasing names of crime victims to spare them embarrassment, an Atlanta television station announced the name of a high school girl who was raped by six classmates and left unconscious on a neighbor's lawn to die. The girl's father sued the station, but the Court said that the press needs freedom to publish information that is a matter of public record so citizens can scrutinize the workings of the judicial system.[57]

In 1975 a man in a crowd of people watching President Gerald Ford noticed a woman pull out a gun. He grabbed the gun and prevented the assassination. Reporters wrote stories about this hero, including the fact that he was a homosexual. This caused him embarrassment and some practical problems and he sued. The courts sided with the press again. The man's good deed made him newsworthy, whether he wanted to be or not.[58] Persons who become newsworthy are permitted little privacy. Justice Brennan said this is a necessary evil "in a society which places a primary value on freedom of speech and of press."[59]

Libel and Obscenity

Despite broad protection for the press overall, courts grant much less protection for libelous and obscene material. Traditionally, they considered such material irrelevant to the exposition of ideas and search for truth envisioned by the framers of the First Amendment. Whatever benefit such material might have was outweighed by the need to protect persons' reputations and morals. Courts thus allowed states to adopt and implement libel and obscenity laws as they saw fit.

Libel. **Libel** consists of printed or broadcast statements that are false and that tarnish someone's reputation. Victims are entitled to sue for money to compensate them for the damage.

The Warren Court decided that traditional state libel laws infringed on freedom of the press too much and forced radical changes in these laws. Its landmark decision came in *New York Times v. Sullivan* in 1964.[60]

The *Times* ran an ad by black clergymen who criticized Montgomery, Alabama, officials for their handling of racial protests. The ad contained some trivial inaccuracies. It did not mention any officials by name, but the commissioner of police claimed it referred to him implicitly, and he sued. The local jury ordered the *Times* to pay him a half million dollars! The Court could see that the law was used to punish a detested northern newspaper for an ad that criticized the handling of controversial civil rights protests. And the Court could not ignore the size of the award or the fact that another jury had ordered the *Times* to pay another commissioner a half million dollars for the same ad. It was apparent that libel laws could be used to wreak vengeance on the critical press.

The Court ruled against the police commissioner and made it harder for public officials to win libel suits. It said that officials must show not only that the statements about them were false but that they were

made with "reckless disregard for the truth." This provides the press some leeway to make mistakes and print false statements, as long as the press is not careless to the point of recklessness.

This protection for the press is necessary, according to Justice Brennan, because "the central meaning of the First Amendment" is that individuals should have the right to criticize officials' conduct. This statement prompted one legal scholar to herald the decision "an occasion for dancing in the streets."[61]

In later cases the Court extended this ruling to public figures—persons other than public officials who have public prominence or who thrust themselves into public controversies. The Court held several persons to be public figures: candidates for public office,[62] a retired general who spoke for right-wing causes,[63] a real estate developer,[64] and a university athletic director.[65] The Court justified making it harder for public figures to win libel suits by saying that they sometimes influence public policy as much as public officials do. They also are newsworthy enough to get coverage to rebut any false charges against them.

The Burger Court was less inclined to consider various persons public figures,[66] but it maintained the core of the Warren Court's doctrine, which shifted the emphasis from protection of personal reputation to protection of press freedom.

This shift in emphasis has aided the press tremendously at a time when its coverage of controversial events has angered much of the public. Increasingly since the 1960s, individuals and groups have sued the press not primarily to win compensation for damage to personal reputations but to punish it. A lawyer for a conservative organization admitted that the organization sought "the dismantling" of CBS by suing the network for its depiction of the army general commanding the U.S. military in Vietnam.[67]

Although the press has an advantage in the law when public officials or figures bring suits, lawsuits are expensive to defend against. A recent case cost the *Washington Post* more than a million dollars in defense expenses at the trial court level alone.[68] The expense puts pressure on the press to refrain from publishing controversial material. Large news organizations can withstand most of this pressure, but many small ones cannot. After 12 libel suits in as many years, the publisher of six weekly newspapers in suburban Philadelphia halted his papers' investigative reporting. "I found myself vigorously defending the First Amendment and watching my business go to hell," he said.

"Now the communities our papers serve no longer learn about the misconduct of their officials."[69]

Obscenity.   **Obscenity** also pits conservative groups against the media, albeit a small and specialized part of the media. Yet there are important differences. Whereas it is relatively clear what libel is, who the victim is, and why the law needs to deal with it, it is not at all clear what obscenity is, who, if anyone, the victim is, or why the law needs to deal with it. The justices themselves have disagreed, perhaps more than in any other area, and their decisions reflect this. They have been neither clear nor consistent.

The Warren Court decided that state obscenity laws infringed too much on freedom of the press. The Court thought the laws restricted publication of sexual material that should be allowed. While maintaining that the First Amendment does not protect obscenity, the Court narrowed the definition of obscenity in a series of cases in the 1950s and 1960s.[70]

The Burger Court, however, thought the Warren Court went too far. When a man and his mother received an ad for a book entitled *Orgies Illustrated*, their suit gave the justices an opportunity to broaden the definition of obscenity somewhat.[71] Now the Court defines obscenity as sexual material that is patently offensive to the average person in the community and that lacks any serious literary, artistic, or scientific value. The Court generally permits state legislatures and local juries, in passing statutes and deciding cases, to determine if this definition applies to certain types of material.

But some local officials get carried away. A prosecutor in Charlottesville, Virginia, announced that he would prosecute persons who sold *Playboy* magazine. Jurors in Albany, Georgia, convicted a theater manager who showed the movie *Carnal Knowledge*. The movie, which featured explicit language and occasional nudity, was nominated for an Academy Award as the best film of the year. The Burger Court reversed the conviction and announced that local communities have discretion but not "unbridled discretion."[72]

In 1990 a prosecutor in Cincinnati put the director of an art gallery on trial for an exhibit of photographs by Robert Mapplethorpe. The homoerotic pictures, which the director called "tough, brutal, sometimes disgusting," included three showing penetration of a man's anus with various objects. Yet the prosecutor could not prove that they lacked serious artistic value, because the photographer has received

After a gallery in Washington, D.C., canceled a show of works by Robert Mapplethorpe, protestors projected his photographs on the building.

praise from art critics and the pictures, of course, were displayed in an art gallery, so the jury acquitted the director.

The Burger Court did not succeed in its efforts to reduce the availability of sexual material. A survey asking prosecutors across the country to compare the years immediately before the Burger Court redefined obscenity with those immediately after found, surprisingly, that they prosecuted fewer cases. Prosecutors said that the public is less concerned about obscenity, so jurors are less likely to convict.[73]

The continuing flow and increasing violence of pornography prompted some radical feminists, in alliance with religious fundamentalists, to advocate new anti-pornography statutes. They maintain that pornography discriminates against women by degrading them and portraying them as willing targets for violent sex. In response, Indianapolis passed a statute that defined pornography as "the sexually explicit subordination of women"—material in which women were "sexual objects for domination . . . or use" or depicted in "positions of servility or submission or display." The statute allowed women who believed themselves victims of pornography to sue for a court order banning such material and, possibly, for monetary damages. The proponents' aim was to encourage enough women to sue to drive the purveyors out of business.

AMERICAN DIVERSITY

Can They Be "As Nasty As They Wanna Be"?

When the rap group 2 Live Crew released its album "As Nasty As They Wanna Be," a Florida lawyer who is a born-again Christian and a crusader against pornography sent copies of the lyrics to the governor and every sheriff in the state. The lawyer likens himself to Batman—he wears a Batman watch and distributes copies of his driver's license with Batman's photograph pasted over his own—and says he needs to help law enforcement officials. The Cuban-born Broward County sheriff, who as a public official has a history of flamboyant actions that attract publicity, mobilized his deputies to protect citizens against the album. They arrested a record store owner for selling the album and then arrested members of the group for singing lyrics from the album in an adult nightclub in Fort Lauderdale.[1]

Is the album obscene? According to current doctrine, it is obscene if it is patently offensive to the average person in the community and if it lacks serious artistic value. This doctrine from the Burger Court differs from that of the Warren Court primarily in its emphasis on the local community. Where the Warren Court based the definition on the views of the average person in the country, the Burger Court spoke of the average person in the community. The Warren Court reasoned, "It is, after all, a national Constitution we are expounding."[2] But the Burger Court countered that the Constitution should not require "the people of Maine or Mississippi [to] accept public depiction of conduct found tolerable in Las Vegas or New York."[3] So the decision in these cases would be made according to the views of the average person in Broward County.

Is the album patently offensive? The songs are about sex, and they feature explicit lyrics, including descriptions of oral sex, group sex, and masturbation, moans at appropriate moments, and a beat that mimics sexual passion. According to an evangelical group, the 79-minute album refers to genitalia 117 times (1.4 times per minute).[4] In addition, the songs are mean-spirited and sometimes violent; they exhibit, in the words of one critic, "a knuckle sandwich approach to women."[5] The rappers, who use "bitch" 163 times, speak of rape and ripping open women's vaginas.

Does the album lack serious artistic value? According to some students of African-American culture, the album reflects the vernacular tradition of this culture.[6] In particular, it reflects the oral tradition of inner-city speech, with its profanity, satire, and exaggeration. This tradition includes pretense—acting out the folklore of the streets. Other African-Americans, however, are offended by the lyrics and the depiction of women in them.

The residents of the county were called upon to decide. In a civil suit preceding the criminal cases, a Hispanic male judge found the album obscene, making it the first musical recording ever banned by a court in this country. Then a jury of six whites, mostly women, convicted the record store owner. Just two weeks later a jury of five whites and one black, also mostly women, acquitted the members of the group for their live performance. These jurors said they thought the album had artistic value.

These decisions have implications for the Court's obscenity doctrine. Is it possible to define a single "community standard" anywhere, let alone in cities or counties with ethnically and religiously diverse populations? Who or what determines a community standard? Men or women? Middle-class norms or those of the ghetto? When the jury convicted the record store owner, he yelled, "They don't know nothing about the . . . ghetto! They don't know where my record shop is. The verdict does not reflect my community standards as a black man in Broward County."[7] Even assuming it is possible to define a single "community standard," is it reasonable to expect laypersons to assess the artistic value of material they find offensive? Is it reasonable to ask a Hispanic judge and white jurors to gauge the artistic merit of black rap music?

Meanwhile, the controversy propelled the album toward the two-million sales mark.

1. Laura Parker, "How Things Got Nasty in Broward County," *Washington Post National Weekly Edition,* June 25-July 1, 1990, p. 10.
2. *Jacobellis v. Ohio,* 378 U.S. 184 (1964).
3. *Miller v. California,* 413 U.S. 15 (1973).
4. Paul Gray, "Grapevine," *Time,* July 2, 1990, p. 13.
5. Richard Lacayo, "The Rap Against a Rap Group," *Time,* June 25, 1990, p. 18.
6. For a good discussion see David Mills, "The Judge vs. 2 Live Crew," *Washington Post National Weekly Edition,* June 25-July 1, 1990, pp. 9-10.
7. "Which Community's Standards?" *Lincoln Journal,* October 10, 1990.

A coalition of book and magazine publishers, distributors, and sellers challenged the law. They said that it was so broad and vague it could apply to many nonpornographic books and magazines. The American Civil Liberties Union (ACLU) maintained that it could apply to books such as Ian Fleming's James Bond stories and movies like *Last Tango in Paris*. Some feminist writers said that it could apply to feminist literature.

The federal district court judge, a woman, ruled the statute unconstitutional. She said that its breadth and vagueness would prohibit much sexual material now permitted by the Supreme Court and would severely restrict the First Amendment. The Supreme Court affirmed the decision.[74]

Despite the Court's refusal to broaden its definition of obscenity further, it does allow cities, through zoning ordinances, to scatter "adult" theaters and bookstores to avoid seedy districts that might attract criminals, or to concentrate them to avoid location in neighborhoods where they might offend residents or passersby.[75] The Court acknowledged that such ordinances help preserve the quality of urban life.

Overall the Court seems close to saying, in the words of one scholar, "If people want it, they can have it. But they shouldn't subject everyone else to it."[76]

Freedom of Religion

Some people came to America for religious liberty, but once they got here many did not want to allow others this liberty. Some communities here were as intolerant as the ones in the Old World from which people had fled. But people came with so many different religious views that the diversity gradually led to tolerance, and by the time the Bill of Rights was adopted there was widespread support for religious liberty. The First Amendment states, "Congress shall make no law respecting an establishment of religion, or prohibiting the free exercise thereof." The two clauses concerning religion—the establishment clause and the free exercise clause—were intended to work in tandem to provide freedom of religion and, by implication, freedom from others' religions.

Thomas Jefferson said the clauses were designed to build "a wall of separation between church and state." Each would stay on its own side of the wall and not interfere or even interact with the other. However, as society became more complex and government became more pervasive, church and state came to inter-

The Supreme Court has exempted the Amish from high school attendance to help them preserve their semi-isolated agricultural life.

act, sometimes interfere, with each other. Inevitably, the high wall began to crumble, and courts had to devise new doctrine to accommodate both church and state.

Free Exercise of Religion. The **free exercise clause** allows individuals to practice their religion without government coercion. Government has occasionally restricted free exercise of religion directly. Early in the country's history, some states prohibited Catholics or Jews from voting or holding office, and as late as 1961 Maryland prohibited nonbelievers from holding office.[77] In the 1920s Oregon prohibited students from attending parochial schools.[78] More recently prisons in Illinois and Texas prohibited black Muslims and Buddhists from receiving religious publications and using the prison chapel.[79] The Supreme Court knocked down such barriers.

More frequently, government has restricted free exercise of religion indirectly. As society has become more complex, some laws inevitably have interfered with religion, even when not designed to. The laws usually have interfered with minority religions, which do not have many members in legislatures looking out for their interests.

At first the Court distinguished between belief and action: individuals could believe what they wanted, but they could not act accordingly if such action was against the law. In 1878 Mormons who believed that their religion required polygamy could not marry more than one woman.[80] The Court rhetorically asked,

"Suppose one believed that human sacrifices were a necessary part of religious worship?" Of course, belief without action gave little protection and scant satisfaction to the individuals involved.

In the 1960s the Warren Court realized this and began to broaden protection by granting exemptions to laws. A Seventh-Day Adventist who worked in a textile mill in South Carolina quit when the mill shifted from a five- to six-day workweek that included Saturday—her Sabbath. Unable to find another job, she applied for unemployment benefits, but the state refused to provide them. To receive them she had to be "available" for work, and the state said she was unavailable because she would not accept jobs that required Saturday work. The Court ordered the state to grant an exemption to its law.[81] Yet the Burger Court ruled that employers need make only a minimal effort to accommodate employees' requests to fit work schedules around their Sabbath.[82]

Amish in Wisconsin withheld their children from high school, although the law required attendance until age 16. The parents sent their children to elementary and junior high school to learn basic reading, writing, and arithmetic, but they complained that high school would subject their children to worldly influences that would interfere with their semi-isolated agricultural life. The Warren Court ruled that the Amish could be exempt from the additional one to

two years the law required beyond junior high school.[83]

Congress, too, has granted some exemptions. It excused the Amish from participating in the Social Security program, because the Amish support their own elderly. And in every draft law it excused conscientious objectors from participating in war.

The Court has been most reluctant to exempt individuals from paying taxes. It did not excuse either the Amish[84] or Quakers, who as pacifists tried to withhold the portion of their income taxes that would go to the military.[85] The Court worried that many other persons would try to avoid paying taxes, too.

The Rehnquist Court has been especially reluctant to grant exemptions.[86] The Native American church uses peyote, a hallucinogen from a cactus, in worship ceremonies. Members believe the plant embodies their deity and eating it is an act of communion. Although peyote is a controlled substance, Congress has authorized its use on Indian reservations and some states have authorized its use off reservations by members of the church. But when two church members in Oregon, a state that does not allow use of peyote, were fired from their jobs and denied unemployment for using the substance, the Court refused to grant them an exemption.[87] In an opinion with broad implications, a five-justice majority explicitly rejected the doctrine and precedents of the Warren and Burger courts.

The country's religious diversity has led to demands for some exotic exemptions. Inspired by the Bible's statement that Jesus' followers "shall take up serpents" and "if they drink any deadly thing, it shall not hurt them," members of the Holiness Church of God in Jesus' Name became enraptured and entranced to the point of hysteria, and some did die. In 1975 the Tennessee Supreme Court forbade such practices, saying that the state has "the right to guard against the unnecessary creation of widows and orphans." However, the practices continue in some places.

Justice Scalia, a Catholic, admitted that denying exemptions will put minority religions at a disadvantage but said that this is an "unavoidable consequence of democratic government." That is, denying minority rights is acceptable because of majority rule. This rationale, of course, could be used to emasculate not only the free exercise clause but other provisions of the Bill of Rights as well.

Adherents of minority religions have felt the effects of the ruling in various ways. Some families of deceased Jews and Laotian immigrants who reject autopsies on religious grounds have been forced to tolerate them. Muslim prisoners whose religion forbids them from eating pork have been refused other meat instead. Members of the Sikh religion, who wear turbans, were exempted from the federal law requiring construction workers to wear hard hats, but the Occupational Health and Safety Administration (OSHA) has rescinded the exemption in the wake of the ruling.[88]

Establishment of Religion.   Two competing traditions regarding the role of government have led to conflict over the **establishment clause.** Many early settlers in America wanted government to reinforce their religion, yet the framers of the Constitution were products of the Enlightenment, which deemphasized the role of religion. The two individuals most responsible for the religious guarantees in the First Amendment, Jefferson and Madison, wanted strict separation of church and state, advocating not only freedom *of* religion for believers but freedom *from* religion for others.[89]

Early decisions by the Supreme Court usually reflected the first of these traditions. In 1892 Justice David Brewer smugly declared that "this is a Christian nation."[90] But as the country became more pluralistic, the Court moved toward the second of these traditions. Since the early 1960s, the Court generally has interpreted the establishment clause not only to forbid government from designating an official church, like the Church of England in England, but also to forbid government from aiding one religion over another or even from aiding religion over nonreligion.

Courts have used the clause to resolve disputes about prayer in public schools. In 1962 and 1963, the

Source: Don Wright, The Miami News.

Supreme Court issued its famous, or infamous, prayer rulings. New York had students recite a nondenominational prayer at the start of every day, and Pennsylvania and Baltimore had students recite the "Lord's Prayer" or Bible verses. The Court, with only one justice dissenting, ruled that these practices violated the establishment clause.[91] The prayers technically were voluntary; students could leave the room. But the Court doubted that they really were voluntary. It noted that nonconforming students would face tremendous pressure from teachers and peers, and that leaving the room usually connotes being bad and being punished. Thus, said the Court, the prayers fostered religion. According to Justice Black, "Government in this country should stay out of the business of writing and sanctioning official prayers and leave that purely religious function to the people themselves and to those the people choose to look to for religious guidance." Schools could teach about religion, but they could not promote it.

Many people sharply criticized the rulings. A representative from Alabama lamented, "They put the Negroes in the schools, and now they've driven God out."[92] Actually, the justices had not driven God out because students could pray on their own anytime they felt the need.

A survey of teachers two years after the rulings found that prayers and Bible readings had decreased but by no means disappeared. Schools in the West, East, and, to a lesser extent, the Midwest generally complied with the rulings, but schools in the South overwhelmingly refused to.[93] For example, just 1 of 121 districts in Tennessee fully complied. A local official said, "I saw no reason to create controversy," and another asserted, "I am of the opinion that 99% of the people in the United States feel as I do about the Supreme Court's decision—that it was an outrage. . . . The remaining 1% do not belong in this free world."[94]

Despite the passage of time, periodic news reports indicate that many schools, especially in the rural South, still use prayers or Bible readings in violation of the Court's rulings.

Congress considered a constitutional amendment to overturn the rulings but did not pass one for several reasons. Some people support the rulings. Others support the Court and do not want to challenge its authority and thereby set a precedent for other groups on other matters. Some religious leaders are concerned that groups would never agree about specific prayers. America's religious diversity means that the

prayers would offend some students or parents. Prayers that suit Christians might not suit Jews; those that suit Jews might not suit persons of other faiths. Recent immigrants from Asia and the Middle East, practicing Buddhism, Shintoism, Taoism, and Islam, have made the country even more pluralistic. One observer commented that asking students in this country to say a prayer "is like asking the members of the United Nations to stand and sing the national anthem of one country."[95] Other religious leaders are concerned that officials anxious to avoid controversy would adopt the religious equivalent of canned peas—bland and watered down prayers.

In lieu of an amendment, almost half the states have passed laws providing for a "moment of silence" to begin each school day. Although the laws ostensibly are for meditation, some legislators admit they really are for prayer. In 1985 the Supreme Court invalidated Alabama's law that authorized a moment of silence "for meditation or voluntary prayer" because the wording of the law endorsed and promoted prayer.[96] Yet a majority of justices indicated that they would approve a moment of silence if students were not encouraged to pray.

On the other hand, the Court said that the University of Missouri at Kansas City had to make its meeting rooms available to students' religious organizations on an equal basis with other organizations, even if the religious organizations used the rooms for prayer or worship.[97] Otherwise, the university would be discriminating against religion. After this decision, Congress passed a law that requires public high schools as well to allow meetings of students' religious, philosophical, or political groups outside class hours. The Court accepted this law in 1990.[98] Justice O'Connor said high school students "are likely to understand that a school does not endorse or support student speech that it merely permits on a nondiscriminatory basis."

Despite its prayer rulings, the Court has been reluctant to invalidate traditional religious symbols. It has not questioned the motto "In God We Trust," on our money since 1865, or the phrase "One nation under God," in the Pledge of Allegiance since 1954.

The Rehnquist Court upheld the display of a nativity scene on government property, at least if it is part of a broader display for the holiday season.[99] Pawtucket, Rhode Island, had a creche, Santa Claus, sleigh with reindeer, Christmas tree, and talking wishing well. Although the nativity scene was an obvious symbol of Christianity, the Court said it was a traditional symbol of a holiday that has become secular as well as religious. Moreover, the presence of the secular decorations diluted any religious impact the nativity scene would have. A creche by itself, however, would be impermissible.[100]

Courts also have used the establishment clause to resolve disputes about teaching evolution in schools. In 1968 the Supreme Court invalidated Arkansas' 40-year-old law forbidding schools from teaching evolution.[101] Arkansas and Louisiana then passed laws requiring schools that teach evolution to also teach "creationism"—the biblical version of creation. In 1987 the Court invalidated these laws, because their purpose was to promote the fundamentalist Christian view.[102]

Courts also have used the establishment clause to resolve disputes about aid to parochial schools, most of which are Catholic. Millions of students attend, and their parents pay tuition and other expenses. In recent decades, costs have risen, and enrollments have dropped. Schools have asked legislatures to provide money to defray part of the costs of their nonreligious activities.

Students observe a "moment of silence" at their public school.

Courts have had to decide whether providing the money helps religion or whether denying it hinders religion. In addition, courts have had to determine if providing the money leads to excessive entanglement of church and state because of the monitoring required to ensure that the money is not spent for religious purposes.

In its first modern case, in 1947, the Court upheld New Jersey's program to reimburse both public and parochial students for bus fares to school.[103] Then the Court upheld New York's and Pennsylvania's programs to furnish textbooks to both public and parochial students.[104] Because the government already provided textbooks to public schools, the programs basically aided parochial schools, allowing them to use more of their scarce resources for religious purposes. But the Court said providing transportation and textbooks for all students is little different than providing police and fire protection for all schools.

The Court has struck down most other forms of aid, however.[105] Because these kinds of assistance have entailed sizable sums of money, the Court has said they could help Catholicism significantly and entangle church and state excessively. Yet the Court, reflecting shifting coalitions of justices, has not been consistent. The Burger Court, for example, struck down tax credits but upheld tax deductions to reduce tuition costs for parents.[106]

At the same time the Court struck down most forms of aid to parochial schools, it permitted aid to church-related colleges.[107] The Court noted that colleges are less likely to be under direct control of church officials and are less likely to try to indoctrinate college students, who are less impressionable than younger students.

Rights of Criminal Defendants

The Fourth, Fifth, Sixth, and Eighth Amendments provide **due process** rights for criminal defendants. When the government prosecutes defendants, it must give them the process—that is, the procedures—they are due; it must be fair and "respect certain decencies of civilized conduct,"[108] even toward uncivilized people.

One defense attorney said many of his clients "had been monsters—nothing less—who had done monstrous things. Although occasionally not guilty of the crime charged, nearly all my clients have been guilty of

Figure 1 ■ Number of Prisoners on Death Row Is Increasing Dramatically

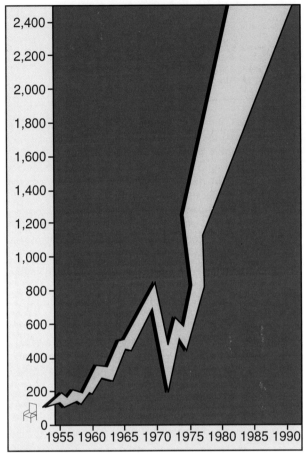

When the Supreme Court ruled capital punishment as then administered unconstitutional in 1972, all prisoners on death row were spared execution, but as the states passed new laws, the number on death row quickly shot up.

Sources: Report to the Nation on Crime and Justice: The Data (Washington, D.C.: U.S. Department of Justice, Bureau of Justice Statistics, October 1983), p. 83 for 1981–1985; *New York Times,* January 13, 1985, p. E4; *Newsweek,* May 4, 1987, p. 60; *Newsweek,* February 19, 1990.

Rights in Theory and in Practice

Although the Supreme Court has interpreted the Bill of Rights to provide an impressive list of rights for criminal defendants, all rights are not available for all defendants in all places. Some trial court judges, prosecutors, and police do not comply with Supreme Court rulings. If defendants appeal to a high enough court, they probably will get their rights, but most defendants do not have the knowledge, the resources, or the perseverance to do this.

When rights are available, most defendants do not take advantage of them. About 90% of all criminal defendants plead guilty, and many of them do so as part of a **plea bargain.** This is an agreement between the prosecutor, the defense attorney, and the defendant, with the explicit or implicit approval of the judge, to reduce the charge or the sentence in exchange for a plea of guilty. A plea bargain is a compromise. For officials it saves the time, trouble, and uncertainty of a trial. For defendants it eliminates the fear of a harsher sentence. However, it also reduces due process rights. A plea of guilty waives defendants' rights to a trial by a jury of their peers, in which defendants can present their own witnesses and cross-examine the government's witnesses, and in which they cannot be forced to incriminate themselves. A plea of guilty also waives the right to counsel to some extent because most attorneys appointed to represent defendants are overworked and inclined to pressure defendants to plead guilty so they do not have to prepare a defense. Despite these disadvantages for due process rights, the Court allows plea bargaining because of its practical advantages.[136]

Right to Privacy

Neither the Constitution nor the Bill of Rights mentions "privacy." Nevertheless, the **right to privacy,** Justice Douglas noted, is "older than the Bill of Rights,"[137] and the framers undoubtedly assumed that people would have it. The framers did include amendments that reflect a concern for privacy: the First Amendment protects privacy of association, the Third privacy of homes from quartering soldiers, the Fourth privacy of persons and places where they live from searches and seizures, and the Fifth privacy of thoughts from compulsory self-incrimination.

So far the Court's right-to-privacy doctrine reflects a right to autonomy—what Justice Brandeis called "the right to be left alone"—more than a right to keep things confidential. As noted earlier in the chapter, the Court has been reluctant to punish the press for invasion of privacy.[138]

Birth Control

The Warren Court established the right to privacy in 1965 when it struck down a Connecticut law that prohibited distributing or using contraceptives.[139] To

COMPARATIVE PERSPECTIVES

Are Americans More Vindictive than Citizens of Other "Civilized" Countries?

The Supreme Court allows capital punishment, and about three-fourths of the states authorize it. Public opinion polls show that the vast majority of Americans—from 70% to 80%—approve of capital punishment. It might surprise these Americans that most democracies and many other nations too reject capital punishment.

Western European countries began to reduce use of capital punishment in the mid-nineteenth century but, as they experienced increased crime rates as a result of the Industrial Revolution, increased use of the punishment later in the century. But in the twentieth century, they gradually reduced use of it again.

In the United States, the number of executions also decreased, beginning in the 1930s and continuing through 1972, when the Supreme Court invalidated capital punishment as it was then being administered. But as the United States experienced an increased crime rate during the 1960s, public opinion, which had opposed capital punishment for some years, began to reverse and some states reestablished the punishment. After the Court accepted the new laws in 1976, the states began to execute defendants again.

At the same time the United States has reestablished capital punishment, 28 countries in Western Europe, Central Europe, Central America, South America, and Asia have abolished it. These include impoverished Haiti and troubled Cambodia. They even include Australia, originally colonized by British convicts and still affected by a rough-and-tumble legacy like the American West.

Now 42 countries prohibit capital punishment for all crimes. Seventeen more prohibit it for all crimes except special crimes under military law or during wartime. These 59 countries encompass nearly all of the nations Americans consider democratic or enlightened.

Countries that continue to use capital punishment include Middle Eastern countries; some Communist countries, such as the Soviet Union, China, Vietnam, and Cuba; some African countries, such as South Africa; and some others scattered throughout the world. Ordinarily these are not countries Americans emulate.

Perhaps we cling to the death penalty because our murder rate is higher than in many of the countries that have abolished the death penalty. And just as American criminals are more violent than those in many other nations, so American citizens are as well.

Sources: "The Death Penalty," Amnesty International Publications, 1990 (based on data from 1986), printed in John Kaplan, Jerome H. Skolnick, and Malcolm M. Feeley, *Criminal Justice,* 5th ed. (Westbury, N.Y.: Foundation Press, 1991), pp. 605–6; Andrea Sachs, "A Fate Better Than Death," *Time,* March 4, 1991, p. 52; Al Kamen, "The Death Penalty Is a Solution the Country Hates to Face," *Washington Post National Weekly Edition,* November 13–19, 1989, p. 35.

---

enforce the law the state would have had to police people's bedrooms, and the Court said the very idea of policing married couples' bedrooms was absurd. Then the Court struck down Massachusetts and New York laws that prohibited distributing contraceptives to unmarried persons.[140] "If the right of privacy means anything," Justice Brennan said, "it is the right of the individual, married or single, to be free from unwarranted governmental intrusion into matters so fundamentally affecting a person as the decision whether to bear or beget a child."[141]

Abortion

When 21-year-old Norma McCorvey became pregnant in 1969, she was divorced and already had a 5-year-old daughter, and she sought an abortion. But Texas, where she lived, prohibited abortions unless the mother's life was in danger. She discovered, "No legitimate doctor in Dallas would touch me. . . . I found one doctor who offered to abort me for $500. Only he didn't have a license, and I was scared to turn my body over to him. So there I was—pregnant, unmarried, unemployed, alone, and stuck."[142]

Too poor to go to a state that permitted abortions, McCorvey decided to put her baby up for adoption. But the state law still rankled her. With the help of two women attorneys recently out of law school, she used her case to challenge Texas's law. She adopted the name Jane Roe to conceal her identity.

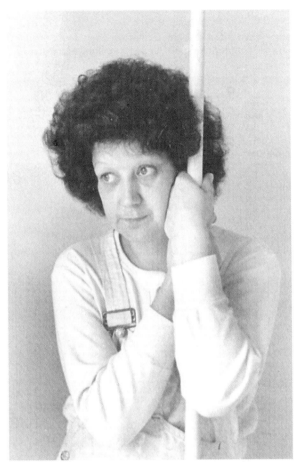

Norma McCorvey, alias "Jane Roe," 10 years after her suit prompted the Supreme Court to issue its landmark abortion ruling.

In *Roe v. Wade* in 1973, the Burger Court extended the right to privacy from birth control to abortion. The majority concluded that because doctors, theologians, and philosophers cannot agree when life begins, judges should not assert that life begins at conception, thus deeming a fetus a person and abortion murder. Amidst such uncertainty, the majority decided that a woman's right to privacy of her body is paramount.

The Court ruled that women can have an abortion during the first three months of pregnancy and, subject to reasonable regulations for health, during the middle three months. States can prohibit an abortion during the last three months. Thus the right is broad though not absolute.

The justices, as revealed in memos discovered years later, acknowledged that their division of preg-

nancy into trimesters was "legislative," but they saw this as a way to balance the rights of the mother in the early stages of pregnancy with the rights of the fetus in the later stage.[143]

The Court's ruling invalidated the abortion laws of 45 states (see figure 2). Far from settling the issue, however, it stimulated more controversy. The right-to-life movement, spearheaded initially by Catholics and later by fundamentalist Protestants, organized to protest the ruling. Activists picketed abortion clinics and harrassed women entering them. "Operation Rescue" engaged in civil disobedience and blockaded entrances to clinics so staff members and patients could

Figure 2 ■ The Number of Abortions Has Leveled Off

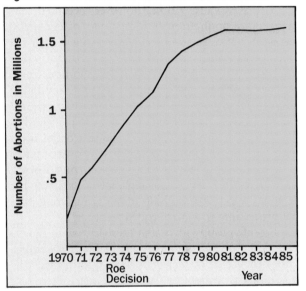

The number of abortions in the United States was already increasing before the Supreme Court's *Roe* decision because some states had liberalized their laws. After the *Roe* decision, the number increased sharply but leveled off in the 1980s.

The number of abortions is about 29% of all pregnancies (excluding miscarriages and stillbirths). This compares with 13% for West Germany, 14% for Canada, 27% for Japan, and 68% for the Soviet Union.

Sources: 1970–1972: Susan Hansen, "State Implementation of Supreme Court Decisions: Abortion Rates since *Roe v. Wade,*" *Journal of Politics* 42 (May 1980): 372–95; 1973–1981: Stanley K. Henshaw and Ellen Blaine, *Abortion Services in the United States, Each State, and Metropolitan Area, 1981–1982* (New York: Alan Guttmacher Institute, 1985), p. 64; 1982–1983: Stanley K. Henshaw, "Characteristics of U.S. Women Having Abortions, 1982–1983," *Family Planning Perspectives* 19 (1987): 6–7; 1984–1985: Stanley K. Henshaw, Jacqueline Darroch Forrest, and Jennifer Van Vort, "Abortion Services in the United States, 1984 and 1985," *Family Planning Perspectives* 19 (1987): 64; Richard Lacayo, "Whose Life Is It?" *Time,* May 1, 1989, p. 21.

not enter them. Fringe members of the movement vandalized and even bombed clinics.

The movement also pressured legislators to overturn or circumvent the ruling. Although Congress failed to pass a constitutional amendment banning abortions or allowing states to regulate them, many state legislatures did pass statutes restricting abortions in various ways.

The Burger Court invalidated most of these laws. It held that states cannot require a waiting period or counseling designed to change a woman's mind.[144] They cannot require abortions to be performed in hospitals rather than clinics, where they are cheaper.[145] They cannot require consent by either the parents of unmarried minors,[146] or the husband of married women (table 1 and figure 3).[147]

The Rehnquist Court, however, accepted laws that require notification of the parents of unmarried minors.[148] If a daughter does not want to tell her parents, she can try to get permission from a judge. She must convince the judge that an abortion would be in her best interest or that she is mature enough to make the decision herself. If she is not mature enough, she must become a mother. These laws, Justice Marshall wrote in dissent, force "a young woman in an already dire situation to choose between two fundamentally unacceptable alternatives: notifying a possibly dictatorial or even abusive parent or justifying her profoundly personal decision in an intimidating judicial proceeding to a black-robed stranger."

Pro-life groups advocated these laws with the expectation that they would result in fewer abortions. They believed many teenagers would go to their parents rather than face the forbidding atmosphere of a court hearing, and their parents would persuade or pressure them not to have the abortion. Some evidence indicates that the laws have had this effect.[149]

A different type of restriction on the right to abortion are laws that bar the use of government funds to pay for abortions for poor women. The Medicaid program, financed jointly by the federal and state governments, had paid for abortions for poor women. Before these laws, the program had paid for about one-third of the abortions in the country each year.[150] These laws put a safe abortion, by a doctor in a clinic or hospital, beyond the financial reach of some women. Regardless, a majority of the Burger Court ruled that governments have no obligation to finance abortions, even if this means that some women cannot take advantage of their right to have them.[151]

Table 1 ■ Why Women Have Abortions

Women gave these reasons for having abortions. Because many gave more than one, the percents total more than 100.

Reason	Percentage of Women
Child would change life (job, school)	76%
Cannot afford child	68
Problems with husband or partner, or do not want to be single parent	51
Do not want people to know I had sex or am pregnant	31
Too young, or cannot handle the responsibility	30
Husband or partner wants me to	23
Concerned for fetus's health	13
Concerned for own health	7
Pregnancy was due to rape or incest	1

Source: 1985 data from Alan Guttmacher Institute, published in *Lincoln Sunday Journal-Star*, April 30, 1989.

Congress and over half the states now prohibit use of their funds to pay for abortions for poor women, except for those whose pregnancy threatens their life. Although Congress voted to allow funds for those whose pregnancy is the result of rape, President Bush vetoed this extension in 1989. However, about a fifth of the states do provide funds for these women, and another fifth provide funds for all poor women who want abortions.[152]

The primary effect of the laws that bar use of government funds, according to one report from the District of Columbia, is to delay abortions, making them more risky and expensive, while the women search for the money themselves.[153]

Another type of restriction on the right to abortion is the policy adopted by the Reagan administration that bans family planning clinics (for example, Planned Parenthood) that receive any federal funds from telling pregnant women where they can get an abortion or even from discussing with them the option of abortion. In 1991 the Rehnquist Court, reflecting President Bush's appointment of Justice Souter, dismayed family planning clinics by voting five to four to uphold the ban.[154]

Figure 3 ■ Which Women Have Abortions

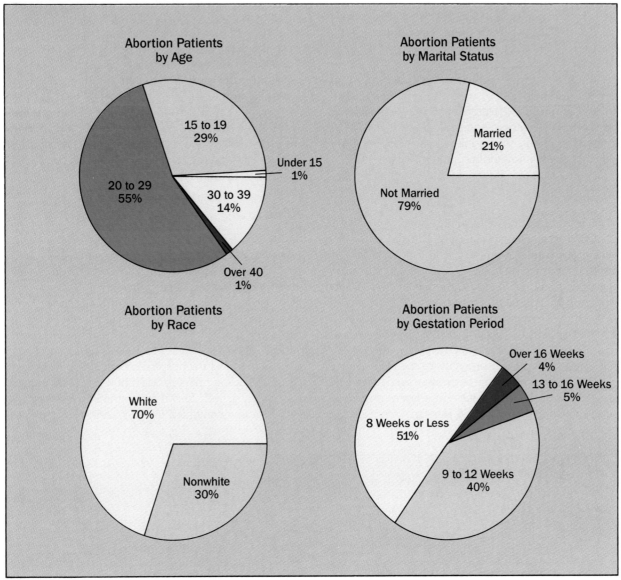

Women who have abortions tend to be young, unmarried, and white, though nonwhites have a higher rate per 1,000 women. Few abortions are done after the first trimester (about 12 weeks).
Source: "America's Abortion Dilemma," *Newsweek,* January 14, 1985, p. 24.

The precedent has disturbing implications for using federal funds to limit freedom of speech. If the government can use its funds as justification to curb speech about abortion, presumably it could use its funds to curb speech about other things. For example, schools receive federal money for many programs, while theaters and museums receive money for many shows; doctors get money from the Medicare and Medicaid programs, while farmers get money from assorted agriculture programs. The logical implications of the Court's decision are quite radical.

Since *Roe,* Justice Harry Blackmun, the author of the Court's opinion, has received death threats, and in 1985 he was shot at through the window of his home.

For most of these years, Norma McCorvey lived in relative anonymity. She claimed that her pregnancy, which led to the case, had been due to rape, when in reality it had occurred during an affair. Though ashamed of her lie, she was proud of getting the Court to make its ruling, so she decided to go public and confess. She said she had lied in "desperation," thinking it would help her obtain an abortion. Her decision to become a public symbol, however, has carried a cost. She has received hate mail, found baby clothes scattered across her lawn, and in 1989 was also shot at through the window of her home.[155]

Homosexuality

The Court has not extended the right to privacy to protect homosexual acts. Almost half the states have laws prohibiting sodomy—oral or anal sex. Although applicable to heterosexuals, these laws are seen as restrictions on homosexuals. Although they are primarily symbolic and rarely enforced, they can be applied at any time. For example, a case arose in Georgia in 1986 when police, delivering a summons to residents of a house, discovered two men violating the law. Police arrested them, but prosecutors declined to press charges. Nevertheless, one of the men sued to have the law declared unconstitutional. In a five to four decision, the Court refused to go this far.[156]

Justice Powell reportedly agreed during the Court's conference that the law was unconstitutional, but he changed his mind before the decision was announced because the man had not been prosecuted. Powell was leery of the Court issuing a highly controversial decision involving a law that might never be enforced. After retiring, however, he admitted making a mistake in the case.[157]

Despite the efforts of gay groups to have the laws repealed or declared unconstitutional, the appointment of conservatives to the bench and the spread of AIDS make extension of the right to privacy to homosexual acts unlikely anytime soon.

Right to Die

The Court has acknowledged a limited right to die, however. When Nancy Cruzan's car skidded off an icy road and flipped into a ditch in 1983, doctors were able to save her life but not her brain. She never regained consciousness. She lives in a vegetative state, similar to a coma, and is fed through a tube. Twenty-five at the time of the accident, she is expected to live another 30 years. When her parents asked doctors to remove the tube, the hospital objected and the state of Missouri, despite paying $130,000 a year to support her, also objected. This issue, complicated enough in itself, became entangled in other controversial issues.

Pro-life groups said denying life support was analogous to abortion; disability groups said her condition was merely a disability, and withholding food and water from her would lead to withholding treatment from other people with disabilities.[158]

In this case the Rehnquist Court established a right to die.[159] The justices ruled that individuals can refuse medical treatment, including food and water, even if this means that they will die. But the right is limited. It does not encompass suicide, and states can require individuals to make their decision while competent and alert. (Presumably individuals can also prepare a "living will" or designate another person as a proxy to make the decision in the event that they are unable to.)

The ruling did not help Cruzan or her parents. The justices, splitting five to four, held that Cruzan had not clearly expressed her wishes before her accident. Thus, Cruzan will continue in her present state, as will most of the approximately 10,000 Americans in irreversible comas who did not leave instructions beforehand.[160]

Conclusion: Are the Courts Responsive in Interpreting Civil Liberties?

The Supreme Court has interpreted the Constitution to provide many important civil liberties. The Warren Court in the 1950s and 1960s expanded civil liberties more than any other Court in history. It applied many provisions of the Bill of Rights to the states. It substantially broadened rights in the areas of speech, libel, obscenity, and religion. It enormously broadened rights of criminal defendants in the areas of search and seizure, self-incrimination, counsel, and jury trial. And it established a right to privacy.

Observers predicted that the Burger Court would lead a constitutional counterrevolution. However, it did not. The Burger Court in the 1970s and 1980s narrowed rights in the areas of freedom of the press, libel, and obscenity. It narrowed rights of criminal defendants in the areas of search and seizure, self-incrimination, and jury trial. And it narrowed opportunities for convicted defendants to appeal on the basis that their rights were violated.[161] But the Court accepted the core of the Warren Court's doctrine and, in fact, even extended it in two areas—right to counsel and right to privacy.

The Rehnquist Court, however, has narrowed rights in some areas further and could yet do what Republican presidents from Nixon through Reagan hoped the Burger Court would do.

The decisions of these Courts show the extent to which the Supreme Court is responsive to the majority in civil liberties cases. The majority of the people support civil liberties in general but not necessarily in specific situations. The elites support civil liberties more than the masses. As the Court has expanded civil liberties, it has not been very responsive to the majority. But it has been more responsive to the elites, and it has been very responsive to minorities.

The Court, given relative independence from the rest of the political process, was not intended to be responsive to the majority. Therefore, it does not have to mirror public opinion, although it cannot ignore this opinion either. It must stay within the broad limits of this opinion, or it will be pulled back. Thus, the Warren Court, which was not very responsive to majority opinion, went too far too fast for too many people. It produced a backlash that led to the Burger and Rehnquist courts, which have been more responsive to majority opinion.

EPILOGUE

Justice O'Connor Straddles the Fence

In *Webster v. Reproductive Health Services,*[162] O'Connor joined four other justices to rule in favor of Missouri and to reverse the lower federal courts. Yet the court majority sidestepped most issues in the case. They did not overturn *Roe v. Wade* or question the general right to privacy.

The majority did uphold the provision of the statute prohibiting use of public clinics or hospitals for abortions, but this will have little effect because private clinics perform most abortions. (The two public hospitals that accepted abortion patients performed less than 5% of Missouri's abortions.[163]) The majority also accepted the assertion by the state that it has a significant interest in the life of the fetus after the 20th week of pregnancy rather than after the 26th (that is, after the sixth month) as *Roe* stated. In this way the ruling does "modify and narrow *Roe,*" the justices acknowledged.

Although Justice Scalia said he wanted to overturn *Roe* directly, and three others hinted that they did, O'Connor refused to go so far. She wrote a separate concurring opinion criticizing her colleagues for reconsidering *Roe* as much as they did. She suggested, however, that she would approve further restrictions if they do not impose an "undue burden" on a woman's abortion decision. This implies that she accepts a basic abortion right.

Though the majority's decision in this case affected abortions relatively little, it sent a signal that states can impose more regulations. The ruling, then, is more important for what it portends than what it does now. As Justice Blackmun, in dissent, wrote, "For today, at least, the law of abortion stands undisturbed. For today, the women of this nation still retain the liberty to control their destinies. But the signs are evident and very ominous, and a chill wind blows."

The Court's rulings make state legislative elections more important for abortion rights than at any time since *Roe*. They will be more divisive. The director of the National Abortion Rights Action League (NARAL) vows, "To politicians who oppose choice, we say . . . , 'Take our rights, lose your jobs.'"[164] Indeed, one poll found that 32% of the public say that they would never vote for a politician who supports restrictions on abortion rights. Twenty-four percent say that they would never vote for a politician who supports abortion rights.[165] Another poll showed that 25% of the public vowed to take some sort of political action—for example, writing letters or donating money—because of the ruling.[166] Thus, the abortion issue promises to be an even more polarizing one.

KEY TERMS

bills of attainder
ex post facto laws
freedom of speech
seditious speech
Sedition Act of 1798
McCarthyism
blacklist
public forum
pure speech
speech plus conduct

symbolic speech
prior restraint
right to a fair trial
libel
obscenity
free exercise clause
establishment clause
due process
unreasonable searches
  and seizures

exclusionary rule
Miranda rights
right to counsel
right to a jury trial

cruel and unusual
  punishment
plea bargain
right to privacy

FURTHER READING

Dan T. Carter, *Scottsboro: A Tragedy of the American South* (Baton Rouge: Louisiana State University Press, 1979). *An examination of the infamous Scottsboro, Alabama, rape case that prompted the Supreme Court to begin to provide counsel to poor defendants.*

Fred W. Friendly, *Minnesota Rag* (New York: Random House, 1981). *A lively chronicle of the Court's first important freedom of the press case*—Near v. Minnesota *in 1927.*

Franz Kafka, *The Trial* (numerous editions, 1937). *One of the great novels of the twentieth century, which shows, perhaps more dramatically than anything else written, what life without due process rights would be like.*

James Kirby, *Fumble: Bear Bryant, Wally Butts, and the Great College Football Scandal* (New York: Dell, 1986). *Law for football fans—the story of the libel suit against a national magazine for writing that the coach of Alabama and athletic director of Georgia fixed a football game between the two schools. The author, a lawyer, was hired by the Southeastern Conference to determine what really happened in the dispute.*

Anthony Lewis, *Gideon's Trumpet* (New York: Vintage, 1964). *A wonderful account of Clarence Earl Gideon's suit and the Court's landmark decision.*

NOTES

1. 410 U.S. 113 (1973).
2. George Hackett and Ann McDaniel, "All Eyes on Justice O'Connor," *Newsweek*, May 1, 1989, p. 34.
3. Laura Mansnerus, "What Is Right and Wrong with *Roe v. Wade?* The View from Friends of the Court," *New York Times*, April 23, 1989.
4. Joan Biskupic, "Public Statements, Personal Pain," *Congressional Quarterly*, April 29, 1989, p. 974.
5. "All Eyes on High Court as Abortion Case Starts," *Lincoln Star*, April 26, 1989.
6. The states did not ratify a proposed amendment that would have required at least one representative in Congress for every 50,000 people. That amendment would have put about 5,000 members in today's Congress. The states did not ratify another proposed amendment that would have prohibited a salary raise for members of Congress from taking effect until after the next election to Congress.
7. *Reid v. Covert*, 354 U.S. 1 (1957).
8. *West Virginia State Board of Education v. Barnette*, 319 U.S. 624 (1953).
9. *Barron v. Baltimore*, 32 U.S. 243 (1833).
10. *Gitlow v. New York*, 268 U.S. 652 (1925).
11. *Argersinger v. Hamlin*, 407 U.S. 25 (1972).
12. Freedom of association is not listed in the First Amendment, but the Court has interpreted freedom of speech and assembly to imply such a right.
13. *Milk Wagon Drivers Union v. Meadowmoor Dairies*, 312 U.S. 287 (1941).
14. Thomas I. Emerson, *The System of Freedom of Expression* (New York: Random House/Vintage, 1971), pp. 6–8.
15. *New York Times v. Sullivan*, 376 U.S. 254 (1964).
16. Zechariah Chafee, Jr., *Free Speech in the United States* (Cambridge, Mass.: Harvard University Press, 1941), pp. 51–52.
17. *Schenk v. United States*, 249 U.S. 47 (1919); *Frohwerk v. United States*, 249 U.S. 204 (1919); *Debs v. United States*, 249 U.S. 211 (1919); *Abrams v. United States*, 250 U.S. 616 (1919); *Gitlow v. New York*, 268 U.S. 652 (1925); *Whitney v. California*, 274 U.S. 357 (1927).
18. *Gitlow v. New York*.
19. *Dennis v. United States*, 341 U.S. 494 (1951).
20. *Yates v. United States*, 354 U.S. 298 (1957); *Scales v. United States*, 367 U.S. 203 (1961).
21. Earl Warren, *The Memoirs of Earl Warren* (Garden City, N.Y.: Doubleday, 1977), p. 6.
22. *Brandenburg v. Ohio*, 395 U.S. 444 (1969).
23. *Brandenburg v. Ohio*.
24. *Esquire* (November 1974).
25. *Jeannette Rankin Brigade v. Chief of Capitol Police*, 409 U.S. 972 (1972); *Edwards v. South Carolina*, 372 U.S. 229 (1963).
26. *United States v. Grace*, 75 L.Ed.2d 736 (1983).
27. *Grayned v. Rockford*, 408 U.S. 104 (1972); *Tinker v. Des Moines School District*, 393 U.S. 503 (1969).
28. *Brown v. Louisiana*, 383 U.S. 131 (1966).
29. *Southeastern Promotions v. Conrad*, 420 U.S. 546 (1975).
30. *Adderley v. Florida*, 385 U.S. 39 (1966).
31. *Greer v. Spock*, 424 U.S. 828 (1976).
32. *Amalgamated Food Employees v. Logan Valley Plaza*, 391 U.S. 308 (1968).
33. *Lloyd v. Tanner*, 407 U.S. 551 (1972); *Hudgens v. NLRB*, 424 U.S. 507 (1976).
34. *Gooding v. Wilson*, 405 U.S. 518 (1972); *Lewis v. New Orleans*, 408 U.S. 913 (1972).
35. C. Herman Pritchett, *The American Constitution*, 2nd ed. (New York: McGraw-Hill, 1968), p. 476, n.2.
36. *Rosenfeld v. New Jersey*, 408 U.S. 901 (1972); *Brown v. Oklahoma*, 408 U.S. 914 (1972).
37. *Cohen v. California*, 403 U.S. 15 (1971).
38. *FCC v. Pacifica Foundation*, 438 U.S. 726 (1968).
39. *Wilkinson v. Jones*, No. 86–1125, 1987.
40. *Cox v. Louisiana*, 379 U.S. 536 (1965).
41. *Collin v. Smith*, 447 F.Supp. 676 (N.D. Ill., 1978); *Collin v. Smith*, 578 F.2d 1197 (7th Cir., 1978).
42. *U.S. v. Schwimmer*, 279 U.S. 644 (1929).
43. *Frisby v. Schultz*, 101 L.Ed.2d 420 (1988).
44. *United States v. O'Brien*, 391 U.S. 367 (1968).
45. *Tinker v. Des Moines School District*.
46. *Smith v. Goguen*, 415 U.S. 566 (1974); *Spence v. Washington*, 418 U.S. 405 (1974).
47. *Texas v. Johnson*, 105 L.Ed.2d 342 (1989).
48. Walter Isaacson, "O'er the Land of the Free," *Time*, July 3, 1989, p. 15; "What Price Old Glory?" *Time*, July 10, 1989, p. 23.
49. *U.S. v. Eichman*, 110 L.Ed.2d 287 (1990).
50. David Halberstam, *The Best and the Brightest* (Greenwich, Conn.: Fawcett, 1969), p. 769.
51. *New York Times v. United States*, 403 U.S. 713 (1971).
52. *Hazelwood School District v. Kuhlmeier*, 98 L.Ed.2d 592 (1988).
53. *Branzburg v. Hayes*, 408 U.S. 665 (1972).
54. *Irvin v. Dowd*, 366 U.S. 717 (1961); *Rideau v. La.*, 373 U.S. 723 (1963); *Sheppard v. Maxwell*, 384 U.S. 333 (1966).
55. *Nebraska Press Association v. Stuart*, 427 U.S. 539 (1976).
56. *Gannett v. DePasquale*, 443 U.S. 368 (1979).
57. *Cox Broadcasting v. Cohn*, 420 U.S. 469 (1975).
58. This was not a Supreme Court case.
59. *Time v. Hill*, 385 U.S. 374 (1967).

60. 376 U.S. 254.

61. Harry Kalven, "The *New York Times* Case: A Note on 'the Central Meaning of the First Amendment,'" *Supreme Court Review* 1964): 221.

62. *Monitor Patriot v. Roy*, 401 U.S. 265 (1971).

63. *Associated Press v. Walker*, 388 U.S. 130 (1967).

64. *Greenbelt Cooperative Publishing v. Bresler*, 398 U.S. 6 (1970).

65. *Curtis Publishing v. Butts*, 388 U.S. 130 (1967).

66. *Gertz v. Robert Welch*, 418 U.S. 323 (1974), and *Time v. Firestone*, 424 U.S. 448 (1976).

67. Eric Press, "Westmoreland Takes on CBS," *Newsweek*, October 22, 1984, p. 62.

68. William A. Henry III, "Libel Law: Good Intentions Gone Awry," *Time*, March 4, 1985, p. 94.

69. Ibid., p. 71.

70. *Roth v. United States*, 354 U.S. 476 (1957); *Manual Enterprises v. Day*, 370 U.S. 478 (1962); *Jacobellis v. Ohio*, 378 U.S. 184 (1964); *A Book Named "John Cleland's Memoirs of a Woman of Pleasure" v. Attorney General of Massachusetts*, 383 U.S. 413 (1966).

71. *Miller v. California*, 413 U.S. 15 (1973).

72. *Jenkins v. Georgia*, 418 U.S. 153 (1974).

73. "Project—An Empirical Inquiry into the Effects of *Miller v. California* on the Control of Obscenity" *New York University Law Review 52* (October 1977): 810–939.

74. *Hudnut v. American Booksellers Association*, 89 L.Ed.2d 291 (1986).

75. *Young v. American Mini Theaters*, 427 U.S. 50 (1976); *Renton v. Playtime Theaters*, 89 L.Ed.2d 29 (1986).

76. Richard Lacayo, "Give and Take on Pornography," *Time*, March 10, 1986, p. 67.

77. *Torcaso v. Watkins*, 367 U.S. 488 (1961).

78. *Pierce v. Society of Sisters*, 268 U.S. 510 (1925).

79. *Cooper v. Pate*, 378 U.S. 546 (1963); *Cruz v. Beto*, 405 U.S. 319 (1972).

80. *Reynolds v. United States*, 98 U.S. 145 (1879).

81. *Sherbert v. Verner*, 374 U.S. 398 (1963).

82. Although a congressional statute mandates "reasonable accommodation," the Court interpreted it so narrowly that it essentially requires only minimal accommodation. *T.W.A. v. Hardison*, 432 U.S. 63 (1977). For analysis see Gloria T. Beckley and Paul Burstein, "Religious Pluralism, Equal Opportunity, and the State," *Western Political Quarterly* 44 (March 1991): 185–208. For a related case see *Thornton v. Caldor*, 86 L.Ed.2d 557 (1985).

83. *Wisconsin v. Yoder*, 406 U.S. 205 (1972).

84. *United States v. Lee*, 455 U.S. 252 (1982).

85. *United States v. American Friends Service Committee*, 419 U.S. 7 (1974).

86. *Goldman v. Weinberger*, 475 U.S. 503 (1986); and *O'Lone v. Shabazz*, 482 U.S. 342 (1986).

87. *Employment Division v. Smith*, 108 L.Ed.2d 876 (1990).

88. Ruth Marcus, "One Nation, Under Court Rulings," *Washington Post National Weekly Edition*, March 18–24, 1991, p. 33.

89. William Lee Miller, "The Ghost of Freedoms Past," *Washington Post National Weekly Edition*, October 13, 1986, pp. 23–24.

90. *Church of Holy Trinity v. United States*, 143 U.S. 457 (1892).

91. *Engel v. Vitale*, 370 U.S. 421 (1962); *Abington School District v. Schempp*, 374 U.S. 203 (1963).

92. C. Herman Pritchett, *The American Constitution*, 3rd ed. (New York: McGraw-Hill, 1977), p. 406.

93. Kenneth M. Dolbeare and Phillip E. Hammond, *The School Prayer Decisions* (Chicago: University of Chicago Press, 1971).

94. Robert H. Birkby, "The Supreme Court and the Bible Belt," *Midwest Journal of Political Science* 10 (1966): 304–15.

95. Peter Cushnie, "Letters," *Time*, October 15, 1984, p. 21.

96. *Wallace v. Jaffree*, 86 L.Ed.2d 29 (1985).

97. *Widmar v. Vincent*, 454 U.S. 263 (1981). The law requires high schools that receive federal funds to allow meetings of students' religious, philosophical, or political groups if the schools permit meetings of any "noncurriculum" groups. Schools could prohibit meetings of all noncurriculum groups.

98. *Board of Education v. Mergens*, 110 S. Ct. 2356 (1990).

99. *Lynch v. Donnelly*, 79 L.Ed.2d 604 (1984).

100. *Allegheny County v. ACLU*, 106 L.Ed.2d 472 (1989).

101. *Epperson v. Arkansas*, 393 U.S. 97 (1968).

102. *Edwards v. Aguillard*, 1987.

103. *Everson v. Board of Education of Ewing Township*, 330 U.S. 1 (1947).

104. *Board of Education v. Allen*, 392 U.S. 236 (1968); *Meek v. Pittinger*, 421 U.S. 349 (1975).

105. *Lemon v. Kurtzman*, 403 U.S. 602 (1971); *Committee for Public Education and Religious Liberty v. Nyquist*, 413 U.S. 756 (1973).

106. Ibid; *Mueller v. Allen*, 463 U.S. (1983).

107. *Tilton v. Richardson*, 403 U.S. 672 (1971); *Hunt v. McNair*, 413 U.S. 734 (1973); *Roemer v. Maryland Public Works Board*, 426 U.S. 736 (1976).

108. *Rochin v. California*, 342 U.S. 165 (1952).

109. Seymour Wishman, *Confessions of a Criminal Lawyer* (New York: Penguin Books, 1981), p. 16.

110. *Stein v. New York*, 346 U.S. 156 (1953).

111. *Weeks v. United States*, 232 U.S. 383 (1914).

112. 367 U.S. 643 (1961).

113. *United States v. Leon*, 82 L.Ed.2d 677 (1984); *Massachusetts v. Sheppard*, 82 L.Ed.2d 737 (1984).

114. *Olmstead v. United States*, 277 U.S. 438 (1928).

115. *Katz v. United States*, 389 U.S. 347 (1967).

116. *Brown v. Mississippi*, 297 U.S. 278 (1936).

117. *McNabb v. United States*, 318 U.S. 332 (1943); *Mallory v. United States*, 354 U.S. 449 (1957); *Spano v. New York*, 360 U.S. 315 (1959).

118. *Ashcraft v. Tennessee*, 322 U.S. 143 (1944).

119. *Rogers v. Richmond*, 365 U.S. 534 (1961); *Lynumn v. Illinois*, 372 U.S. 528 (1963).

120. 384 U.S. 436 (1966).

121. *Johnson v. Zerbst*, 304 U.S. 458 (1938).

122. *Powell v. Alabama*, 287 U.S. 45 (1932).

123. *Gideon v. Wainwright*, 372 U.S. 335 (1963).

124. *Argersinger v. Hamlin*, 407 U.S. 25 (1972); *Scott v. Illinois*, 440 U.S. 367 (1974).

125. *Douglas v. California*, 372 U.S. 353 (1953).

126. *Baldwin v. New York*, 339 U.S. 66 (1970).

127. *Duncan v. Louisiana*, 391 U.S. 145 (1968).

128. *Taylor v. Louisiana*, 419 U.S. 522 (1975).

129. *Swain v. Alabama*, 380 U.S. 202 (1965).

130. *Wilkerson v. Utah*, 99 U.S. 130 (1878); *In re Kemmler*, 136 U.S. 436 (1890).

131. *Furman v. Georgia*, 408 U.S. 238 (1972).

132. *Gregg v. Georgia*, 428 U.S. 153 (1976).

133. *Woodson v. North Carolina*, 428 U.S. 289 (1976).

134. *Coker v. Georgia*, 433 U.S. 584 (1977).

135. *McCleskey v. Kemp*, 95 L.Ed.2d 262 (1987).

136. *Brady v. United States*, 397 U.S. 742 (1970).

137. *Griswold v. Connecticut*, 38 U.S. 479 (1965).

138. For a rare exception, see *Time v. Hill,* 385 U.S. 374 (1967).

139. *Griswold v. Connecticut.*

140. *Eisenstadt v. Baird,* 405 U.S. 438 (1972); *Carey v. Population Services International,* 431 U.S. 678 (1977).

141. *Eisenstadt v. Baird.*

142. Lloyd Shearer, "This Woman and This Man Made History," *Parade* (1983).

143. Bob Woodward, "The Abortion Papers," *Washington Post National Weekly Edition,* January 30–February 5, 1989, pp. 24–25.

144. *Akron v. Akron Center for Reproductive Health,* 76 L.Ed.2d 687 (1983).

145. *Akron v. Akron Center for Reproductive Health; Sendak v. Arnold,* 50 L.Ed.2d, p. N (1976).

146. *Akron v. Akron Center for Reproductive Health.*

147. *Planned Parenthood of Missouri v. Danforth,* 428 U.S. 52 (1976).

148. *Hodgson v. Minnesota,* 111 L.Ed.2d 344 (1990); *Ohio v. Akron Center for Reproductive Health,* 111 L.Ed.2d 405 (1990).

149. Margaret Carlson, "Abortion's Hardest Cases," *Time,* July 2, 1990, p. 24.

150. "The Supreme Court Ignites a Fiery Abortion Debate," *Time,* July 4, 1977, pp. 6–8.

151. *Beal v. Doe,* 432 U.S. 438 (1977); *Maher v. Roe,* 432 U.S. 464 (1977); *Poelker v. Doe,* 432 U.S. 519 (1977); *Harris v. McRae,* 448 U.S. (1980).

152. Carlson, "Abortion's Hardest Cases," p. 25.

153. Benjamin Weiser, "The Abortion Dilemma Come to Life," *Washington Post National Weekly Edition,* December 25–31, 1989, pp. 10–11.

154. *Rust v. Sullivan,* (1991). The Reagan administration's policy was put forth as an interpretation of a congressional law from 1970 that prohibits the use of federal funds "in programs where abortion is a method of family planning." Under previous administrations, doctors could discuss abortions but clinics could not use federal funds to pay for them.

155. Steven Waldman, "Attacking the Real 'Jane Roe,' " *Newsweek,* April 17, 1989, p. 22.

156. *Bowers v. Hardwick,* 92 L.Ed.2d 140 (1986); see also *Doe v. Commonwealth's Attorney,* 425 U.S. 901 (1976).

157. "Ex-justice's Second Thoughts To Make Heated Debate Hotter," *Lincoln Sunday Journal-Star,* October 28, 1990.

158. Al Kamen, "When Exactly Does Life End?" *Washington Post National Weekly Edition,* September 18–24, 1989, p. 31; Alain L. Sanders, "Whose Right to Die?" *Time,* December 11, 1989, p. 80.

159. *Cruzan v. Missouri Health Department,* 111 L.Ed.2d 224 (1990).

160. Otto Friedrich, "A Limited Right to Die," *Time,* July 9, 1990, p. 59.

161. *Stone v. Powell,* 428 U.S. 465 (1976).

162. 106 L.Ed.2d 410 (1989).

163. Cynthia Gorney, "*Roe v. Wade* Under Fire," *Washington Post National Weekly Edition,* April 24–30, 1989, p. 8.

164. "Four States Targeted for Passage of Legislative Restrictions," *Denver Post (Washington Post),* July 5, 1989; Margaret Carlson, "The Battle Over Abortion," *Time,* July 17, 1989, p. 63.

165. Carlson, "The Battle Over Abortion," p. 63.

166. "Abortion Edict Splits Nation," *Denver Post (Los Angeles Times),* July 5, 1989.

15 Civil Rights

A marine homebound from the Persian Gulf kisses the flag. Some blacks find more opportunity in the military than in civilian society, where discrimination remains widespread.

Forward March . . . Or Retreat?

You are Martin Luther King, Jr., a Baptist minister and head of the Southern Christian Leadership Conference. For a decade you have led the civil rights movement and have tried, through nonviolence, to bring about an end to laws that discriminate against African-Americans. A few weeks ago you were awarded a Nobel Peace Prize for your success in using nonviolence to bring about change in American race relations.

A new challenge to your nonviolent strategies has arisen in Selma, Alabama. You have come here to encourage black voter registration and to call national attention to the discrimination that blacks still suffer in trying to register to vote in the Deep South. The Fifteenth Amendment to the Constitution prohibits racial discrimination in voting, but in 1964, 94 years after its passage, only 13% of Alabama's blacks were able to register to vote. It is now 1965, and President Lyndon Johnson, after convincing Congress to pass the 1964 Civil Rights bill to open hotels, restaurants, and other public accommodations to blacks, and to outlaw discrimination in education and employment, has stated that the time is not ripe for a further bill to protect voting rights.

You are faced with a decision whether to march to Alabama's capital or to back down because of a court order banning the march. As you consider the decision, you reflect on recent events.

In Selma, as in other parts of the rural Deep South, white voting officials use harassment and intimidation to prevent blacks from registering. At meetings where civil rights workers explain to blacks how to register, local police show up to record names of those attending. Then their employers or landlords threaten to fire or evict them. Blacks brave enough to withstand these threats usually find the registration office closed. It opens only two days a month, and the registrar arrives late, leaves early, and takes long lunch hours, especially if blacks are waiting to register. Even if blacks get into the office to see the registrar, most of them "fail" the literacy tests, given and graded at the discretion of the registrar. They fail even if they are better educated than the registrar. In one recent incident, a black schoolteacher trying to register had to help a registration official who could not read the questions on the test. When the teacher said "those words are 'constitutionality' and 'interrogatory'," the registrar became angry and refused to register the teacher.

Recently, after demonstrators gathered at the courthouse to protest failure to register blacks and were harassed by the police, who jabbed at them with cattle prods, a state judge issued an order forbidding blacks to meet in groups of more than three people. The judge hoped to end demonstrations and publicity about black voting rights.

You, on the other hand, want to stimulate publicity. You hope that your presence in Selma, along with demonstrations by local voting rights groups, will focus national attention on the plight of southern blacks deprived of the vote. You hope that this attention will prompt the president and Congress to move a voting rights bill to the top of the national agenda.

In the past, you have gained national publicity when local citizens and even law enforcement officers reacted with violence to your group's nonviolent protest. Media attention pointed out the stark contradiction between American beliefs in democracy and equality and actual conditions in the South that you were protesting. Faced with this contradiction, public reaction led the president and Congress to act to defend your rights.

The black community in Selma has mobilized. Black schoolteachers have marched to the courthouse, startling the rest of the black community, because the teachers, fearful of losing their jobs, have

(continued on next page)

never done anything like this before. Then other groups, even black undertakers, have marched and protested. Although law enforcement officials at first seemed determined not to use physical force against demonstrators so that the national media would lose interest in the Selma voting rights story, Sheriff Jim Clark lost his cool and used force to arrest the growing number of demonstrators. One day he arrested you and 500 schoolchildren and the next day 400 more. Each evening, national television news covered the arrests and showed the children being led to jail. You wrote a letter from jail, published in the *New York Times,* noting that there are "more Negroes in jail with me than there are on the voting rolls." Fifteen members of Congress came to Selma to investigate.

Although you and many of the others were released from jail, the tension continued to mount. The sheriff punched a local civil rights leader in the mouth in front of national television cameras. A few days later, in a nearby town, a night march ended with the police killing a 26-year-old marcher, Jimmy Lee Jackson, and beating an NBC television reporter. That story, from the reporter who described the murder from his hospital bed, with his head bandaged and his words slurred, made compelling news.

The next day you flew to Washington to confer with the president. Despite Governor George Wallace's declaration that the state would not permit it, protesters began a march of 50 miles to the Alabama capital, Montgomery, to protest the killing of Jackson and to gain more support for a voting rights act. You planned to join the march later.

The marchers did not get far. As they approached the Edmund Pettus Bridge leading out of Selma, they met a sea of Alabama state troopers. Gas masks hung from their belts and billy clubs from their hands. The troopers demanded that the marchers disperse. No one moved. Seconds later, the commander of the troopers yelled "Advance!" A white, southern reporter for *Newsweek* described what happened next:

> The charge was swift and horrible. Impersonal behind their gas masks, the troopers clubbed their way through the screaming demonstrators. Blue-gray

clouds of eye-stinging tear gas were released. When the clouds lifted, I could see the full enormity of the brutality. Hurt and unconscious Negroes lay on the highway shoulder. A trooper walked by and dropped a tear-gas grenade by each fallen Negro. Across the highway, hundreds of white spectators cheered.[2]

The events at the bridge immediately reached the American public. On one television network, a movie, *Judgment at Nuremberg,* about Nazi brutality against Jews, was interrupted to bring news of the attack on the marchers. The attack was soon labeled "bloody Sunday," and as the mayor of Selma stated, "the wrath of the nation came down on us." Members of Congress denounced the terror. President Johnson conferred with the attorney general about what he should do, and even George Wallace called Sheriff Clark to his office for a scolding.

To protest this brutality, you sent telegrams to prominent clergy all over the nation asking them to join you at Selma for another march on Montgomery. Hundreds began arriving in Selma to take part in this protest. Two days later, however, U.S. District Judge Frank Johnson forbade the march until he could hold a hearing on its legality.

Now you are faced with a dilemma. Until now, the federal courts have been your allies. They have almost always sided with you, protecting your movement against illegal and violent actions by segregationists. This particular judge, a southerner, has always been fair to you. Further, the Justice Department also has asked you to reconsider. Nevertheless, you worry that it is too late to cancel. Your fellow clergy from across the nation are here. The march has been announced and hundreds are waiting to participate in it.

What do you do? Do you continue with the march, violate the court order, and risk conviction for contempt of court and possible imprisonment? Or do you call off the march, appear to be backing down to segregationist violence, and lose momentum for your movement?

OUTLINE

Civil rights refer to equality of rights for persons regardless of their race, sex, or ethnic background. The Declaration of Independence proclaimed that "all men are created equal." The author, Thomas Jefferson, knew that all men were not created equal in many respects, but he sought to emphasize that they should be considered equal in rights and equal before the law. This represented a break with England where rigid classes with unequal rights existed; nobles had more rights than commoners. The Declaration's promise did not include nonwhites or women, however. Thus, although colonial Americans advocated equality, they envisioned it only for white men. Others gradually gained more equality, but the Declaration's promise remains unfulfilled for some.

Virtually all minority groups in this country have suffered discrimination. Some religious groups, such as Catholics and Jews, and many ethnic groups, such as the Irish, Italians, and Poles, have made enormous progress against discrimination, but other groups have not. This chapter focuses on the struggle by racial minorities and women to overcome discrimination.

Race Discrimination

African-Americans, Hispanics, and native Americans all have endured and continue to face much discrimination.

Discrimination Against African-Americans

Slavery.   The first blacks came to America in 1619, just 12 years after the first whites. Like many whites, blacks initially came as indentured servants. In exchange for passage across the ocean, they were bound to an employer, usually for 4 to 7 years, and then freed. But later in the seventeenth century, the colonies passed laws requiring the blacks and their children to be slaves for life. Once slavery was established, the slave trade flourished, especially in the South.

As a result of the compromises between northern and southern states, the Constitution accepted slavery. It allowed the importation of slaves until 1808, when Congress could bar further importation, and it also required the return of escaped slaves to their owners.

Shortly after ratification of the Constitution, northern states abolished slavery. In 1808 Congress barred the importation of slaves but did not halt the practice of slavery in the South. Slavery became increasingly controversial, and abolitionists called for its end.

The Supreme Court tried to quell the antislavery sentiment in the **Dred Scott case** in 1857.[3] Dred Scott, a slave who lived in Missouri, was taken by his owner to the free state of Illinois and the free territory of Wisconsin and, after five years, was returned to Missouri. The owner died and passed title to his wife, who moved but left Scott in the care of people in Missouri. They opposed slavery and arranged to have Scott sue his owner for his freedom. They argued that Scott's time in a free state and a free territory made him a free man even though he was brought back to a slave state. The owner, also opposed to slavery, had the

Before the Civil War, most blacks were slaves on southern plantations. This Georgia family is picking cotton in the 1860s.

Dred Scott.

dent Lincoln's Emancipation Proclamation ending slavery. After the war, Congress passed and the states ratified three constitutional amendments: the Thirteenth prohibited slavery; the Fourteenth granted citizenship to blacks, thus overruling the Dred Scott decision, and also granted "equal protection of the laws" and "due process of law"; the Fifteenth provided the right to vote for black men. The **equal protection clause** eventually would become the primary guarantee that government would treat people equally.

Congress also passed a series of civil rights acts to reverse the "Black Codes" that southern states had enacted to deny the newly freed slaves legal rights. These civil rights acts allowed blacks to buy, own, and sell property; to make contracts; to sue; and to be witnesses and jurors in court. They also allowed blacks to use public transportation, such as railroads and steamboats, and to patronize hotels and theaters.[4]

Even so, most freed blacks faced bleak conditions. Without land or education, they had to work for their former masters as hired hands or sharecroppers. Leasing land and equipment from the plantation owner put sharecroppers so far in debt they had to give the owner most of their crops, leaving them few to sell to get out of debt.

During the period of Reconstruction, the Union army was supposed to enforce the new amendments and acts. To some extent it did. But in state after state, the South resisted, and the North capitulated. After a decade, the two regions struck a deal to end what was left of Reconstruction. The 1876 presidential election between Republican Rutherford Hayes and Democrat Samuel Tilden was disputed in some states. To resolve the dispute, Republicans, most of whom were northerners, and Democrats, many of whom were southerners, agreed to a compromise: Hayes would be named president, and the remaining Union troops would be removed from the South.

authority to free Scott, so the purpose of the suit was not to win his freedom. Rather, she and others sought a major court decision to keep slavery out of the territories. Scott, who desperately wanted to be free, was just a pawn in the contest.

In this infamous case, Chief Justice Roger Taney stated that no blacks, whether slave or free, were citizens, and that they were "so far inferior that they had no rights which the white man was bound to respect." Because Scott was not a citizen, he could not sue in federal court. This ruling could have ended the case, but Taney continued. He declared that Congress had no power to control slavery in the territories. This meant that slavery could extend into the territories Congress already had declared free. It also raised the possibility that states could not control slavery within their borders.

By this time, slavery had become the hottest controversy in American politics, and this decision fanned the flames. It provoked vehement opposition in the North and prompted further polarization, which eventually led to the Civil War. Meanwhile, Scott got his freedom from his owner.

Civil War Amendments and Reconstruction. The North's victory in the Civil War gave force to Presi-

Segregation In both the South and the North, blacks came to be segregated from whites.

Segregation in the South The reconciliation between Republicans and Democrats—northerners and southerners—was effected at the expense of blacks. Removing the troops meant that the South could govern itself again; it proceeded to reduce blacks to near-slave status.

Slavery itself kept blacks down, and segregation would have been inconvenient when blacks and whites needed to live and work near each other. There was no

AMERICAN DIVERSITY

Black Masters

Although most slaveowners were white, some were black. William Ellison, a free black slaveholder in South Carolina, was born a slave. He bought his own freedom and then his family's by building and repairing cotton gins. Over time he earned enough to buy slaves and operate a plantation. With 60 slaves, Ellison ranked in the top 1% of all slaveholders, black or white.

Ellison was unusual, but he was not unique. In Charleston, South Carolina, alone, more than 100 African-Americans owned slaves in 1860. Most, however, owned fewer than 4.

As part of the slave-owning class, black slaveholders were not much more acceptable to whites. Ellison's family was granted a pew on the main floor of the local Episcopal church, but they had to be on guard at all times. Failure to maintain the norms of black-white relations—acting deferentially—could mean instant punishment. As the Civil War approached, free blacks, even slaveholders, were seen as a growing threat by whites trying to preserve the established order. Harsher legislation regulated their lives. For example, they had to have a white "guardian" to vouch for their character, and they had to carry special papers to show their free status. Without these papers, they could be sold back into slavery.

Some black slaveowners showed little sign of shared concerns with black slaves. Indeed, Ellison freed none of his slaves.

Source: Michael P. Johnson and James L. Roark, *Black Masters* (New York: W.W. Norton, 1984).

---

residential segregation—not in rural areas, where former slaves' shacks were intermixed with plantation houses, and not in urban areas, where few blocks were solidly black. But after slavery, southerners established segregation as another way to keep blacks down. Initially, they did so haphazardly—one law here, another there. By the early 1900s, however, there was a pervasive pattern of **Jim Crow laws.**

Jim Crow laws segregated just about everything. Some segregated blocks within neighborhoods, others neighborhoods within cities. Laws in some small towns excluded blacks altogether. Some did so explicitly; others did so by setting curfews that required blacks to be off the streets by 10 P.M. Laws also segregated schools, which blacks had been allowed to attend during Reconstruction, and even textbooks (black schools' texts had to be stored separately from white schools' books). Many laws segregated public accommodations, such as hotels, restaurants, bars, and transportation. At first they required the races to sit in separate sections of streetcars; eventually they required them to sit in separate cars; finally they also forced them to sit in separate sections of waiting rooms. They segregated parks, sporting events, and circuses. Laws segregated black and white checkers players in Birmingham and districts for black and white prostitutes in New Orleans. They segregated drinking fountains, restrooms, ticket windows, entrances, and exits. They segregated the races in prisons and in hospitals and in homes for the blind. They even segregated the races in death—in morgues, funeral homes, and cemeteries.

Blacks were forced to defer to whites in all informal settings as well, and failure to do so could mean punishment or even death. They were "humiliated by a thousand daily reminders of their subordination."[5]

Meanwhile, northern leaders, who had championed the cause of the slaves before and during the Civil War, abandoned them a decade after the war; Congress passed no new laws, presidents did not enforce existing laws, and the Supreme Court gutted the constitutional amendments and civil rights acts. All acquiesced in "the southern way."

The Supreme Court struck down the civil rights act allowing blacks to use public accommodations, including transportation, hotels, and theaters.[6] Where the Fourteenth Amendment said that "no state" shall deny equal protection, the Court interpreted this to mean that "no government" shall, but private individuals—owners of transportation, hotels, and theaters—could. The Court's interpretation might seem plausible, but it was clearly contrary to Congress's intent.[7]

Then the Court upheld segregation. Louisiana passed "an Act to promote the comfort of passengers," which mandated separate accommodations in trains. New Orleans black leaders sponsored a case to test the act's constitutionality. Homer Adolph Plessy bought a ticket and sat in the white car. When the conductor ordered him to move to the black car, Plessy refused. Arrested and tried, he maintained that the act was unconstitutional under the Fourteenth Amendment. In *Plessy v. Ferguson* in 1896, the court disagreed, claiming that the act was not a denial of equal protection because it provided equal accommodations.[8] Thus the Court established the **separate-but-equal doctrine,** which allowed separate facilities if they were equal. Of course, government required separate facilities only because it thought that the races were not equal, but the Court brazenly commented that the act did not stamp "the colored race with a badge of inferiority" unless "the colored race chooses to put that construction on it." Only Justice John Harlan, a former Kentucky slaveholder, dissented: "Our Constitution is color-blind, and neither knows nor tolerates classes among citizens."

Three years later the Court accepted segregation in schools.[9] A Georgia school board turned a black high school into a black elementary school. Though the board did not establish a new high school for blacks or allow them to attend the ones for whites, the Court did not object. This set a pattern in which separate but equal meant separation but not equality.

Segregation in the North   Although Jim Crow laws were not as pervasive in the North as in the South, northerners imitated southerners to the point where one writer proclaimed, "The North has surrendered!"[10] Job opportunities for blacks were better in the North than in the South, but southern blacks migrating to northern cities for better jobs were forced to live in all-black ghettos both because they could not afford other housing and because they were discriminated against.

Denial of the Right to Vote.   With the adoption of the Fifteenth Amendment, many blacks voted and even elected fellow blacks to office during Reconstruction, but southern states began to disfranchise them in the 1890s (as explained in chapter 7). Although blacks

were a majority in some places, they were unable to elect black representatives or even pressure white officials to oppose segregation.

Violence.   To solidify their control, whites engaged in sporadic violence against African-Americans. In the 1880s and 1890s, whites lynched about 100 blacks a year. In the 1900s vigilante "justice" continued (table 1). For example, a mob in Livermore, Kentucky, dragged a black man accused of murdering a white man into a theater. The ringleaders charged admission and hanged the man. Then they permitted the audience to shoot at the swinging body—those in the balcony could fire once; those in the better seats could empty their revolvers.[11] In 1919 there were 25 race riots in six months. Mobs took over cities in the North and South, burning black neighborhoods and terrorizing black residents for days on end.[12]

The Ku Klux Klan, which began during Reconstruction and started up again in 1915, played a major

---

Table 1 ■ Why Whites Lynched Blacks in 1907

Whites gave the following reasons for lynching blacks, who may or may not have committed these acts.	Number
Murder	5
Manslaughter	10
Attempted murder	5
Rape	9
Attempted rape	11
Harboring a fugitive	1
Burglary	3
Theft of 75¢	1
Having debt of $3	2
Being victor over white man in fight	1
Insulting white man	1
Talking to white girls on telephone	1
Being wife or son of rapist	2
Being father of boy who "jostled" white women	1
Expressing sympathy for victim of mob	3
	56

Source: Adapted from Ray Stannard Baker, *Following the Color Line* (New York: Harper & Row, 1964), pp. 176–77. Copyright 1904, 1905 by S. S. McClure Co. Copyright 1907, 1908 by the Phillips Publishing Company. Copyright 1908 by Doubleday & Company, Inc.

Lynching occurred not only in the South but also in northern cities such as Marion, Indiana, in 1930.

role in inflaming prejudice and terrorizing blacks. It was strong enough to dominate many southern towns and even the state governments of Oklahoma and Texas. It also made inroads in some northern states.

Federal officials said such violence was a state problem—presidents refused to speak out and Congress refused to pass legislation making lynching a federal offense—yet state officials did nothing.

Overcoming Discrimination Against African-Americans

For at least the first third of the twentieth century, white supremacy reigned—in the southern states, the border states, and many of the northern states. It also pervaded the nation's capital, where President Woodrow Wilson instituted segregation in the federal government. Blacks fought white supremacy primarily in three arenas—the courts, the streets, and Congress. In general, they fought in the courts first and Congress last, although as they gained momentum they increasingly fought in all three arenas at once.

The Movement in the Courts.   The struggle in the courts revolved around African-Americans' efforts to convince the Supreme Court to overturn the separate-but-equal doctrine of *Plessy v. Ferguson.*

The NAACP   In response to white violence, a group of blacks and whites founded the **NAACP,** the National Association for the Advancement of Colored People, in 1909. In its first two decades, it was led by W.E.B. DuBois, a black sociologist. In time it became the major organization fighting for blacks' civil rights.

Frustrated by presidential and congressional inaction and its own lack of power to force action, the NAACP devised a winning strategy—to converge on the federal courts, which were less subject to pressures from the majority. The association assembled a cadre of lawyers, mainly from Howard University Law School, a black university in Washington, D.C., to bring lawsuits attacking segregation and the denial of the right to vote. In 1915 they persuaded the Supreme Court to strike down the grandfather clause (which exempted persons whose ancestors could vote from the literacy test),[13] and two years later they convinced the court to invalidate laws prescribing residential segregation.[14] But the Court continued to allow most efforts to segregate and most devices to disfranchise blacks.

In 1938 the NAACP chose a 30-year-old attorney, Thurgood Marshall, to head its legal defense arm. In the next two decades, presidents appointed more liberals to the Supreme Court. These two developments led to the NAACP's success in the courts.

Desegregation of Schools   Seventeen states and the District of Columbia segregated their schools. The states gave white students better facilities and paid white teachers more. Overall, they spent from 2 to 10 times more on white schools than on black ones.[15] Few of these states had graduate schools for blacks: as late as 1950 they had 15 engineering schools, 14 medical schools, and 5 dental schools for whites, and none for blacks; they had 16 law schools for whites and 5 for blacks.

The NAACP's tactics were first to show that "separate but equal" really resulted in unequal schools and then to attack "separate but equal" head on, arguing that it led to unequal status.

The NAACP began by challenging segregation in graduate schools. Missouri provided no black law school but offered to reimburse blacks who went to out-of-state law schools. In 1938 the Supreme Court said the state had to provide a black law school.[16] Texas then established a black law school clearly inferior to the white law school at the University of Texas in size of faculty, student body, library, and opportunities for students to specialize. In 1950 the Court said the black school had to be substantially equal to the white school.[17] Oklahoma allowed a black student to attend the white graduate school at the University of Oklahoma but designated a separate section of the classroom, library, and cafeteria for the student. The court said this too was inadequate, because it deprived the student of the exchange of views with fellow students necessary for education.[18] The Court did not invalidate the separate-but-equal doctrine in these decisions, but it made segregation almost impossible to implement in graduate schools.

The NAACP continued by challenging segregation in grade schools and high schools. Marshall filed suits in two southern states, one border state, one northern state, and the District of Columbia. The suit

Linda Brown's kindergarten class. Brown is in the back row, fourth from right.

Affirmative Action for . . . Alums' Children?

Critics of affirmative action by colleges and universities charge that preferential treatment for racial minorities means that many better-qualified whites are denied admission. Critics then claim that this lowers academic standards at the schools.[1]

But at most elite schools the number of students admitted through affirmative action does not come close to the number admitted because their parents are alums.[2] For more than 40 years, a fifth of Harvard's students have had preferential treatment in admission because their parents attended the school. In the 1980s Harvard's "legacies" were more than two times as likely to be admitted as blacks or Hispanics. A similar advantage exists at other Ivy League schools. Yale's legacies were more than two-and-a-half times as likely to be admitted as nonlegacies. A former dean of admissions at Princeton asserts that having one or both parents as alums "doubles, even trebles the chances of admission."

This advantage exists at other selective schools. Notre Dame reportedly reserves 25% of its openings for legacies. The Universities of Virginia and California-Berkeley treat out-of-state legacies as in-state students, which gives them a competitive edge because most state universities favor state residents.

Schools say legacies have such a high rate of admission because their parents provide the upbringing that makes their children more qualified than other students. Yet the U.S. Department of Education's Office of Civil Rights,

investigating Harvard for possible discrimination in admission, found that the average admitted legacy was significantly less qualified than the average admitted nonlegacy. In fact, the number of marginally qualified legacies was greater than the number of black, Mexican-American, Puerto Rican, and native American students combined.

Schools also justify their policies by saying they fear that alums will stop giving money if their children are denied admission. This probably is the main concern.

Regardless of the wisdom of the policies, hypocrisy toward affirmative action is widespread. Opponents ignore the many factors in addition to merit that have always gone into college admissions decisions. Some who have called for the end of affirmative action for minorities, such as a group of Dartmouth alumni, have at the same time demanded that it continue for their privileged children. Others have tried to pit minority groups against each other. They claim that affirmative action for blacks and Hispanics reduces the chance of admission for Asians, while defending the advantage for legacies that diminishes the chance of admission for all minorities and for other whites as well.

1. Thomas Sowell, *Preferential Policies: An International Perspective* (New York: Morrow, 1990); Dinesh D'Souza, *Illiberal Education* (New York: Free Press, 1991).
2. The remaining text is drawn from John Larew, "Why Are Droves of Unqualified, Unprepared Kids Getting into Our Top Colleges?" *Washington Monthly*, June 1991, pp. 10–14.

---

nomic reasons. Instead, the Court has accepted the traditional practice, based on seniority, that the last hired is the first fired.[91]

In 1989 the Rehnquist Court signaled a possible change of direction in affirmative action cases when it struck down a plan by Richmond, Virginia, to provide more construction contracts to minorities.[92] The majority said setting aside 30% of the contracts for minority-owned businesses, without showing a history of past discrimination in the construction industry in the city, was an invalid quota.

Affirmative action requirements are not enforced thoroughly. Federal officials are swamped with complaints about employers and are hard pressed to resolve them much less initiate their own investigations. And employers who are required to file an affirmative action plan but fail to reach their goals ordinarily need

to show only that they made a genuine effort to reach them. Employers are rarely penalized. Thus, compliance with affirmative action depends on the good faith of some employers plus the use of a few strategically chosen investigations and penalties to serve as a threat to others.

Although all three branches of government have authorized or encouraged affirmative action for most years in the past two decades, the policy remains controversial. Charges of quotas are especially volatile. In 1991, for example, civil rights groups proposed a bill to allow minorities and women to sue employers for discrimination more easily. A key provision put the burden of proof on employers to show that their hiring and promoting practices that have a negative effect on minorities or women are not discriminatory. Both parties agreed on the substance of such legislation. But

FOCUS ON AN ISSUE

Should the Government Require Affirmative Action?

To determine whether the government should have a policy of affirmative action, it is necessary to consider several issues.

Does Affirmative Action Help Minorities and Women?

According to most studies, affirmative action does help minorities and women. Companies that do business with the federal government, and therefore are subject to affirmative action, have shown more improvement in hiring minorities and women than other companies. And state and local governments, also subject to affirmative action, have shown more improvement in hiring than private companies. Organizations subject to affirmative action have shown even more progress in promoting minorities and women previously kept in low-level positions.

The state of Alabama, for example, made dramatic gains. After a finding that the state troopers had never employed any blacks, the Department of Public Safety was socked with a court order to hire one new black for every white until the force reached 25% black. The force reached 20% black within 12 years and became the most integrated force in the country. Faced with the threat of a similar order, other departments of the state government quickly hired more blacks at all levels. Mountain Bell of Denver, for another example, increased the number of minorities in managerial positions 7 times and the number of women in jobs traditionally held by men 15 times in just 5 years.

On the other hand, opponents, including a small number of black conservatives, claim that affirmative action hinders minorities by encouraging them to rely on government programs rather than themselves and by stigmatizing them. One black student complained, "I feel like I have AFFIRMATIVE ACTION stamped on my forehead."

Does Affirmative Action Result in Lower Standards and Lower Quality Employees?

Unlike changes in hiring and promoting, which can be measured objectively, "merit" is defined differently by different people.

Even so, affirmative action often is compared with traditional employment practices that are assumed to have been based squarely on merit. In reality, the practices were based only partly on merit. For government employment, many jobs were open only to those who already worked for that government. Other jobs were open to those who took exams and performed well, but the jobs did not necessarily go to the person who scored highest. Typically they went to the person among the three or five who scored highest and who had the desired political connections, personal connections, personality, or area of residence, or to the person who was a military veteran.

For faculty positions in colleges and universities, the "old boy network" of fellow faculty at other schools was the primary means of hiring. Departments seldom advertised their positions widely.

For private employment, vacancies were advertised by word of mouth to relatives or friends. Union membership was necessary for many skilled blue-collar jobs, and places were reserved for sons and brothers—rarely daughters and sisters—of members. Even when jobs were advertised, usually no effort was made to canvass the locality or region for the most meritorious candidate.

Because traditional practices were based on many factors along with or sometimes in place of merit, affirmative action should not be compared with an idealized version of past practices.

The Supreme Court's decision approving affirmative action for women illustrates this point. A woman who applied for a job as a dispatcher for the transportation agency of Santa Clara County, California, was one of nine considered qualified for the job. She scored 73, and a white man scored 75, on a subjective oral exam administered by a panel of men who had never hired a woman for a skilled position. When the county hired her for affirmative action, the man sued for reverse discrimination, but the Court upheld the hiring.

Nevertheless, there is a legitimate concern that affirmative action might result in lower standards and lower quality employees. Affirmative action undoubtedly pressures some employers into hiring some minorities and women who, due to past discrimination, lack adequate education, training, or experience. At the same time, affirmative action provides a larger pool of talent from which to choose. According to one executive, before affirmative action, "We were not using all the talent available." With

(continued on next page)

affirmative action, the company found a "gold-mine" of previously untapped talent.

Does Affirmative Action Result in Reverse Discrimination?

In compensating for discrimination against some, are others discriminated against? When the number of jobs is limited, if affirmative action provides more for minorities and women, it leaves fewer for white men. To determine if this is reverse discrimination, consider four possible outcomes of affirmative action in hiring or promoting: (1) Choosing a minority or woman who is more qualified than a white man. Although the principle of nondiscrimination should have led to this outcome, often it has not. Affirmative action has had a major impact in encouraging employers to hire and promote minorities and women who were more qualified and who should have been hired or promoted all along. (2) Choosing a minority or woman who is as qualified as a white man. This occurs frequently in less specialized jobs, where candidates do not differ clearly in qualifications, but rarely in more specialized jobs, where candidates do differ significantly. (3) Choosing a minority or woman who, though qualified, is less qualified than a white man. Here affirmative action is similar to past practices in that both select a person from among qualified candidates but according to some factor other than merit. (4) Choosing a minority or woman who is unqualified. Employers are not required to hire unqualified persons, but they undoubtedly do sometimes.

Of these four outcomes, only the last two actually result in reverse discrimination. When they occur, white men pay for the sins of their fathers and grandfathers. Yet the first two outcomes probably occur more often. Given the dominance of white men in the power structure, reverse discrimination is likely to be infrequent. If it were widespread, minorities and women would hold more jobs, at higher levels, than they do now. Despite gains, overall progress has hardly been meteoric. For instance, black employment by 40 cities between 1973 and 1980, the peak years for affirmative action, increased from 28% to 33% of the total employment by these cities. The number of black administrators increased from 9% to 16%, which was about half the proportion of black residents in these cities.

Does Affirmative Action Erode Traditional American Values?

A discussion of American values could be endless, but we should at least consider the effect of affirmative action on equality and individuality.

Affirmative action furthers equality of opportunity to the extent that it opens doors for people who found nothing but closed doors before. It furthers equality of results to the extent that it provides jobs for people who were entitled to them but did not get them before. It undermines equality to the extent that it provides jobs for people who are not entitled to them.

Affirmative action furthers individuality in that it helps minorities and women fulfill their potential and shows them that society values them, too. It undermines individuality in that it treats people not as individuals but as members of groups. Then, the policy helps group A (minorities or women today) by punishing B (white men today) for what C (white men yesterday) did to D (minorities or women yesterday). A white Chicago police officer complained, "I didn't own slaves, and I shouldn't be penalized for what happened hundreds of years ago." But a black Birmingham, Alabama, firefighter countered: "Say your father robs a bank, takes the money and buys his daughter a Mercedes, and then buys his son a Porsche and his wife a home in the high-rent district. Then they discover [his crime]. He has to give the cars and house back. And the family starts to cry: 'We didn't do anything.' The same thing applies to what the whites have to say. The fact is, sometimes you have to pay up. If a wrong has been committed, you have to right that wrong."

Affirmative action operates without regard to individual responsibility. But perhaps a group remedy is the only possible, or at least practical, solution to the group problem of discrimination and inequality.

In Light of These Considerations, What Policy Should We Have?

Obviously, the policy in the past should have been color blind. Just as obviously, the policy in the future should be color blind. But should the policy now be color blind or color conscious? Should it be nondiscrimination or affirmative action?

Sources: James E. Jones, "The Genesis and Present Status of Affirmative Action in Employment," paper presented at the American Political Science Association Annual Meeting, 1984; Robert Pear, *New York Times*, June 19, 1983; Nelson C. Dometrius and Lee Sigelman, "Assessing Progress Toward Affirmative Action Goals in State and Local Government," *Public Administration Review* 44 (May/June 1984):241–47; Peter Eisinger, *Black Employment in City Government* (Washington, D.C.: Joint Center for Political Studies, 1983); Milton Coleman, "Uncle Sam Has Stopped Running Interference for Blacks," *Washington Post National Weekly Edition*, December 19, 1983; Douglas B. Huron, "It's Fashionable to Denigrate Hiring Quotas—But It's Wrong," *Washington Post National Weekly Edition*, August 27, 1984, p. 23; Sylvester Monroe, "Does Affirmative Action Help or Hurt?" *Time*, May 27, 1991, pp. 22–23; *Johnson v. Transportation Agency*, 94 L.Ed.2d 615 (1987); William Bridges and Wayne Villemez, "Overqualified Minority Workers," in Michael Combs and John Gruhl, eds., *Affirmative Action in the '80s* (Jefferson, N.C.: McFarland, 1986); Thomas B. Edsall, "A Political Powder Keg," *Washington Post National Weekly Edition*, January 14–20, 1991, p. 6.

some Republicans saw an opportunity to score points with blue-collar workers who usually vote Democratic but feel threatened by minority progress. So President Bush called the proposal "a quota bill" and said it would lead to the use of more quotas by businesses that wanted protection against potential lawsuits. Actually, the bill discouraged the use of quotas, but the administration thought that if the president called it a quota bill often enough voters would believe him eventually. Then they would criticize the Democrats for a "radical" measure.

Executives from the Business Roundtable, a group of 200 major corporations, tried to work out a compromise between civil rights and business groups. When it appeared they would succeed, top aides to the president torpedoed the talks; the president could not convince voters the bill was a radical measure if business also supported it.[93]

Are Civil Rights Enough?

Although minorities and women have advanced toward legal equality, judicial decisions and legislative acts have not guaranteed social or economic equality. Despite increasing white acceptance of black and Hispanic equality and male acceptance of female equality, racist and sexist attitudes remain widespread.

In fact, there was a resurgence of racist behavior in the 1980s. The Justice Department's tabulation of various racial incidents nationwide showed an increase of more than 400% from 1980 to 1987.[94]

Lopsided economic inequality persists as well. Judicial decisions and legislative acts have opened many doors for minorities but primarily for those who are middle class. Overall, therefore, minorities continue to lag far behind whites in education, employment, income, housing, and longevity.

Blacks have illiteracy and poverty rates three times those of whites, a college graduation rate one-half that of whites, and unemployment and infant mortality rates twice those of whites. Their life expectancy is six years less than that of whites because of poorer living conditions and health care and greater drug use and violence in their communities.

The plight of young black men is worse than that of any other group in society. Almost one of every four black men between 20 and 29 is in prison or on proba-

tion or parole.[95] And a black man in Harlem has less chance of living past 40 than a man in Bangladesh.[96]

Although blacks made gains in the 1960s and, to some extent, the 1970s, they actually lost ground on some measures in the 1980s. They still suffer the lingering effects of slavery, and their color keeps them from blending in like other groups who fought discrimination in the past.

Many who live in the ghetto face a bleak future. After the riots in the 1960s, the Kerner Commission, appointed by President Johnson to examine the cause of the riots, concluded, "What white Americans have never fully understood—but what the negro can never forget—is that white society is deeply implicated in the ghetto. White institutions created it, white institutions maintain it, and white society condones it." After the riots, however, governments did little to improve the conditions that precipitated the riots. Now, a quarter of a century later, the conditions are about the same—except for the drug epidemic and the AIDS epidemic, which have combined to make life in the ghetto even more grim and dangerous than before.

Hispanics, too, remain disadvantaged. They earn considerably less than white non-Hispanics, though more than blacks.[97]

Native Americans, with a legacy of discrimination and coerced assimilation, continue to suffer extreme poverty and unemployment, which are exacerbated by high rates of alcoholism.

Women also have suffered. Although popular stereotypes associate poverty with racial minorities, women, like minorities, are more likely than others to be poor. Increasing proportions, now almost 40%, of all female-headed families are below the poverty line (see figure 2).

Despite the value of civil rights, it should be apparent from the current status of minorities and women that civil rights alone are not enough. As one black leader said, "What good is a seat in the front of the bus if you don't have the money for the fare?"[98]

Conclusion: Is Government Responsive in Granting Civil Rights?

Blacks and women have made tremendous progress in obtaining civil rights since the time when a federal official who fired competent blacks could insist, "A Negro's place is in the cornfield,"[99] or employers who

Figure 2 ■ Men Earn More than Women at Each Educational Level

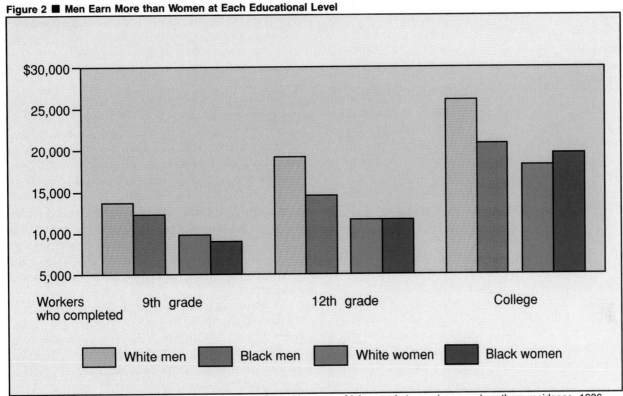

These data are for adults employed full time and are adjusted in years of labor market experience and southern residence. 1986 data.

Source: Reynold Farley, "After the Starting Line: Blacks & Women in an Uphill Race." *Demography* 25 (November 1988): 477–95.

refused to hire women could insist, "A woman's place is in the home." The black movement and the women's movement initiated the changes. They protested legal inequality and put the issue on the public agenda. As they grew and garnered support, they pressured the government to resolve it. Finally, approximately one century after the first significant agitations for change, the government responded.

Within the government, the Supreme Court exercised decisive leadership. Historically, the Court was both activist and restrained toward blacks— whichever was necessary to deny their rights—while it was restrained toward women. Then in the 1950s and 1960s, the Warren Court was activist in striking down segregation. In the 1970s and 1980s, the Burger Court was somewhat less activist in upholding limited busing and affirmative action. At the same time, it was activist in striking down sex discrimination. As with the Warren Court's decisions against race discrimination, the Burger Court's decisions

against sex discrimination may go down in history as its major achievement.

But the Court's rulings themselves did not guarantee the rights. Because the Court lacks the means to enforce its decisions, the president and Congress had to help overcome the resistance. The history of the government's efforts to grant civil rights, especially to blacks, shows both the power and the limits of the Supreme Court.

The changes in policy illustrate the responsiveness of government. In its subjugation of minorities until the 1950s and treatment of women until the 1970s, government was responding to the majority view. When minorities and women organized to protest their status, government began responding to them and to shifts in the majority view that their protest prompted.

In pressuring government to respond, blacks have benefited from being numerous, visible, and, with their common heritage of slavery and segregation, relatively cohesive. Their concentration in large northern cities and some southern states has helped them exercise political power. Their long history of discrimination, though, has fostered debilitating ghetto conditions and denied them resources to make quicker and greater progress.

Hispanics are less numerous but are growing in number rapidly. Their concentration in some western and southwestern states has enabled them to influence state and local governments. Their diversity and lack of cohesiveness, however, hinders their ability to influence the national government.

Native Americans are the smallest, most isolated, and least organized minority, so they have had the poorest success in pressuring government to respond.

As minority groups grow in size, they will be able to pressure governments more effectively. In the 1980s, blacks increased their population 13%, native Americans 39%, Hispanics 53%, and Asians 108%, while whites increased their population just 6%.[100]

But as minority groups expand, they will increasingly come into conflict with each other, especially if economic conditions remain stagnant. Competition for scarce resources will widen the cracks in the coalition. Already there are tensions. Some blacks resent the faster progress of Hispanics and Asians. Blacks say they were here before most Hispanics and Asians, they suffered more and struggled more, and so they should reap the rewards sooner. On the other hand, some Hispanic leaders resent the reluctance of black groups to help them with their civil rights problems.[101] Occasionally there are conflicts over issues. When Hispanics sought to repeal the sanctions on employers who hire illegal aliens, on the grounds that these penalties discourage employers from hiring legal residents who look foreign—that is, Hispanic—some blacks worried that employers once again would hire illegal aliens who would take jobs from them. Occasionally there have even been riots. Blacks have rioted in Miami from frustration with the Cuban-dominated leadership. And Hispanics have rioted in Washington, D.C. out of anger with their lack of city services and jobs and with gerrymandering by the black power structure.

Women were never subjugated as much as racial minorities, so they have had less to overcome. Moreover, they are a majority, they vote as frequently as men, and they have well-organized and well-funded interest groups. Consequently, since the 1970s they have made the greatest gains toward equality.

EPILOGUE

King Obeys the Court Order

As the Justice Department and Governor Wallace monitored the event by telephone, King led a crowd of 1,500 people out of the city to the Pettus Bridge, where the earlier violence had occurred. This time, when ordered to stop, the marchers sang "We Shall Overcome," the unofficial hymn of the movement, knelt and prayed, and then marched back to their church headquarters. Although many were upset and even felt betrayed, King believed that he must obey the court order not to march.

King asked marchers who had come from out of town to stay until the judge allowed the march to occur, and many did. That night, three of them, white Unitarian ministers, were attacked and beaten by local segregationists as they left a restaurant. Two days later, one died from the beating. Again, national outrage put pressure on the federal government to do something about voting rights. President Johnson announced that "the best legal talent in the federal government is engaged in preparing legislation which will secure the right (to vote) for every American."[102]

Within a week, the president addressed Congress in a speech watched by 70 million Americans. He announced his support for a voting rights bill and ended his speech with the words of the movement, "We *shall* overcome."

Finally, Judge Johnson announced that the planned Montgomery march could take place. President Johnson summoned Governor Wallace to Washington and gave him a strong dose of his persuasive powers, asking Wallace whether "we want to be remembered as petty little men, or . . . as great figures that faced up to our moments of crisis?"[103] Although Governor Wallace did nothing to hinder the marchers, he refused to provide police protection for them. President Johnson then federalized the Alabama National Guard and sent 2,000 Army troops and 200 FBI agents and federal marshals. The march took place without violence, and live television covered its final phase up the capitol steps in Montgomery.

But the violence was not over; one of the participants, Viola Liuzzo, a white housewife from Detroit, was murdered while driving some marchers back to Selma after the march.

This new violence increased the intensity of support for the bill proposed by President Johnson. Congress passed it, and, with King beside him when he signed it, President Johnson said, "The vote is the most powerful instrument ever devised . . . for breaking down injustice. . . . The Voting Rights Act is one of the most monumental laws in the entire history of American freedom."[104]

After receiving permission from the court, civil rights supporters march from Selma to Montgomery.

KEY TERMS

Dred Scott case

equal protection clause

Jim Crow laws

Plessy v. Ferguson

separate-but-equal doctrine

NAACP

Brown v. Board of Education

de jure segregation

de facto segregation

Civil Rights Act of 1964

restrictive covenants

steering

blockbusting

redlining

Civil Rights Act of 1968

Equal Pay Act

comparable worth

Equal Rights Amendment (ERA)

affirmative action

FURTHER READING

Margaret Atwood, *The Handmaid's Tale* (Boston: Houghton Mifflin, 1986). *A story of a society where women have no rights.*

Taylor Branch, *Parting the Waters: America in the King Years, 1954–63* (New York: Simon & Schuster, 1988). *Extremely readable account of Martin Luther King and the first decade of the civil rights movement.*

Ralph Ellison, *Invisible Man* (New York: Modern Library, 1963 [originally published in 1947]). *A classic novel with a nameless and powerless narrator who moves from the naivete of his childhood in the South to the cynicism of riot-torn Harlem.*

John Howard Griffin, *Black Like Me* (New York: Houghton Mifflin, 1960). *The true story of a white man who, with drugs, temporarily changed his skin to black and then traveled through the segregated South in the 1950s.*

N. Scott Momaday, *House Made of Dawn* (New York: Harper & Row, 1966). *A Pulitzer Prize–winning novel that shows a young Indian torn between tribal traditions and the materialism beckoning him from the city.*

Tomas Rivera, *And the Earth Did Not Part* (Berkeley, Calif.: Editorial Justa Publishers, 1977). *A collection of related stories that express the anger and alienation of the migrant farm worker.*

Alice Walker, *The Color Purple* (New York: Washington Square Press, 1982). *An acclaimed novel that tells the story, through letters written in black English, of an uneducated girl who triumphs over obstacles presented by her class, her race, and her sex.*

Juan Williams, *Eyes on the Prize* (New York: Viking, 1987). *Written to accompany the television series of the same name, this book recounts in sometimes moving prose the history of the civil rights movement from 1954 to 1965.*

NOTES

1. Much of the information on the Selma march is drawn from Juan Williams, *Eyes on the Prize* (New York: Viking, 1987), chapter 8; David Garrow, *Bearing the Cross* (New York: William Morrow, 1986) chapter 7.

2. *Newsweek,* March 22, 1965, p. 1, 18ff.

3. *Scott v. Sandford,* 19 How. 393 (1857).

4. Civil Rights Act of 1866; Civil Rights Act of 1871; Civil Rights Act of 1875.

5. C. Vann Woodward, *The Strange Career of Jim Crow,* 2nd ed. (London: Oxford University Press, 1966), p. 44.

6. *Civil Rights Cases,* 109 U.S. 3 (1883).

7. C. Herman Pritchett, *The American Constitution,* 3rd ed. (New York: McGraw-Hill, 1977), p. 486.

8. *Plessy v. Ferguson,* 163 U.S. 537 (1896).

9. *Cumming v. Richmond County Board of Education,* 175 U.S. 528 (1899).

10. Woodward, *Strange Career of Jim Crow,* p. 113.

11. Richard Kluger, *Simple Justice* (New York: Alfred A. Knopf, 1976), pp. 89–90.

12. Woodward, *Strange Career of Jim Crow,* p. 114.

13. *Guinn v. United States,* 238 U.S. 347 (1915).

14. *Buchanan v. Warley,* 245 U.S. 60 (1917).

15. Kluger, *Simple Justice,* p. 134.

16. *Missouri ex rel. Gaines v. Canada,* 305 U.S. 337 (1938).

17. *Sweatt v. Painter,* 339 U.S. 629 (1950).

18. *McLaurin v. Oklahoma State Regents,* 339 U.S. 637 (1950).

19. Earl Warren, *The Memoirs of Earl Warren* (Garden City, N.Y.: Doubleday, 1977), p. 291.

20. 347 U.S. 483 (1954).

21. *Holmes v. Atlanta,* 350 U.S. 879 (1955); *Baltimore v. Dawson,* 350 U.S. 877 (1955); *Schiro v. Bynum,* 375 U.S. 395 (1964); *Johnson v. Virginia,* 373 U.S. 61 (1963); *Lee v. Washington,* 390 U.S. 333 (1968).

22. *Brown v. Board of Education II,* 349 U.S. 294 (1955).

23. *Griffin v. Prince Edward County School Board,* 377 U.S. 218 (1964); *Norwood v. Harrison,* 413 U.S. 455 (1973); *Gilmore v. Montgomery,* 417 U.S. 556 (1974); *Green v. New Kent County School Board,* 391 U.S. 430 (1968).

24. James F. Simon, *In His Own Image* (New York: David McKay, 1974), p. 70.

25. William Cohen and John Kaplan, *Bill of Rights* (Mineola, N.Y.: Foundation Press, 1976), p. 622.

26. *Swann v. Charlotte-Mecklenburg Board of Education,* 402 U.S. 1 (1971).

27. *Columbus Board of Education v. Penick,* 443 U.S. 449 (1979); *Dayton Board of Education v. Brinkman,* 443 U.S. 526 (1979); *Keyes v. School District 1, Denver,* 413 U.S. 921 (1973).

28. *Milliken v. Bradley,* 418 U.S. 717 (1974).

29. Lee A. Daniels, "In Defense of Busing," *New York Times Magazine,* April 17, 1983, pp. 36–37.

30. *Board of Education of Oklahoma City v. Dowell,* (1991).

31. Daniels, "In Defense of Busing," p. 34.

32. Ibid., p. 97.

33. J. Harvie Wilkinson, *From Brown to Bakke* (New York: Oxford University Press, 1979), pp. 118–25.

34. Woodward, *Strange Career of Jim Crow,* p. 186.

35. *Norris v. Alabama,* 294 U.S. 587 (1935); *Smith v. Texas,* 311 U.S. 128 (1940); *Avery v. Georgia,* 345 U.S. 559 (1952).

36a. *Heart of Atlanta Motel v. United States,* 379 U.S. 421 (1964).

36b. William A. Henry III, "The Last Bastions of Bigotry," *Time,* July 22, 1991, pp. 66–67.

37. *Griggs v. Duke Power,* 401 U.S. 424 (1971).

38. *Washington v. Davis,* 426 U.S. 229 (1976).

39. *Firefighters Local Union v. Stotts,* 81 L.Ed.2d 483 (1984).

40. *Shelley v. Kraemer,* 334 U.S. 1 (1948).

41. Jerry DeMuth, "Fair-Housing Suits: Color Them Gold," *Washington Post National Weekly Edition,* August 11, 1986, p. 34.

42. Jonathan Kaufman, "In Big-City Ghettos, Life Is Often Worse Than in '60s Tumult," *Wall Street Journal,* May 23, 1980.

43. M. Barrera, *Race and Class in the Southwest: A Theory of Racial Inequality* (Notre Dame, Ind.: Notre Dame Press, 1979).

44. C. Davis, C. Haub, and J. Willette, "U.S. Hispanics: Changing the Face of America," *Population Bulletin* 38 (1983): 1–44.

45. Eloise Salholz, "The Push for Power," *Newsweek,* April 9, 1990, p. 18.

46. Guadaloupe San Miguel, "Mexican American Organizations and the Changing Politics of School Desegregation in Texas, 1945–1980," *Social Science Quarterly* 63 (1982): 701–15. See also Louis R. Fraga, Kenneth J. Meier, and Robert E. England, "Hispanic Americans and Educational Policy: Structural Limits to Equal Access and Opportunities for Upward Mobility," unpublished paper, University of Oklahoma, 1985.

47. San Miguel, "Mexican American Organizations," p. 710.

48. Leo Grebler, Joan W. Moore, and Ralph C. Guzman, *The Mexican-American People* (New York: Free Press, 1970), p. 157.

49. Fraga, Meier, and England, "Hispanic Americans," p. 6.

50. M. Weinberg, *A Chance to Learn: The History of Race and Education in the United States* (London: Cambridge University Press, 1977), p. 163.

51. *San Antonio Independent School District v. Rodriguez,* 411 U.S. 1 (1973).

52. *Plyler v. Doe,* 457 U.S. 202 (1982).

53. *Cherokee Nation v. Georgia,* 5 Peters 1 (1831); *Worcester v. Georgia,* 6 Peters 515 (1832).

54. Vine Deloria, Jr. and Clifford M. Lytle, *American Indians, American Justice* (Austin: University of Texas Press, 1983), p. 221.

55. Ibid., pp. 222–25.

56. Harvey Arden, "Who Owns Our Past?" *National Geographic,* March 1989, pp. 383, 388, 393.

57. Ruth B. Ginsburg, *Constitutional Aspects of Sex-Based Discrimination* (St. Paul, Minn.: West Publishing Co. 1974), p. 2.

58. Karen DeCrow, *Sexist Justice* (New York: Vintage, 1975), p. 72.

59. Barbara Sinclair Deckard, *The Women's Movement,* 2nd ed. (New York: Harper & Row, 1979), p. 303.

60. DeCrow, *Sexist Justice,* p. 119.

61. "A New Push to Raise Women's Pay," *New York Times,* January 1, 1984, p. F15.

62. "Battle of the Sexes Over 'Comparable Worth', " *U.S. News & World Report,* February 20, 1984, p. 74.

63. Bureau of Labor Statistics, March 1982.

64. Joyce Gelb and Marian Lief Palley, *Women and Public Policies* (Princeton, N.J.: Princeton University Press, 1982), p. 102.

65. For a discussion of these points, see Jane Mansbridge, *Why We Lost the ERA* (Chicago: University of Chicago Press, 1986); Mary Frances Berry, *Why ERA Failed* (Bloomington, Ind.: Indiana University Press, 1986); Janet Boles, "Building Support for the ERA: A Case of 'Too Much, Too Late'," *PS* 15 (Fall 1982): 575–92.

66. *Bradwell v. Illinois,* 16 Wall. 130 (1873).

67. *Muller v. Oregon,* 208 U.S. 412 (1908).

68. *Reed v. Reed,* 404 U.S. 71 (1971).

69. *Hoyt v. Florida,* 368 U.S. 57 (1961).

70. *Taylor v. Louisiana,* 419 U.S. 522 (1975).

71. *Stanton v. Stanton,* 421 U.S. 7 (1975).

72. *Phillips v. Martin-Marietta,* 400 U.S. 542 (1971).

73. *Cleveland Board of Education v. LaFleur,* 413 U.S. 632 (1974).

74. *Nashville Gas v. Satty,* 434 U.S. 136 (1977).

75. *Automobile Workers v. Johnson Controls,* 113 L.Ed.2d 158 (1991).

76. *Pittsburgh Press v. Pittsburgh Commission on Human Relations,* 413 U.S. 376 (1973).

77. *Dothard v. Rawlinson,* 97 S.Ct. 2720 (1977).

78. *Los Angeles Department of Water and Power v. Manhart,* 435 U.S. 702 (1978); *Arizona Governing Committee v. Norris,* 82 L.Ed.2d 462 (1983).

79. *Roberts v. United States Jaycees,* 82 L.Ed.2d 462 (1984); *Board of Directors of Rotary International v. Rotary Club,* 95 L.Ed.2d 474 (1987).

80. *Massachusetts v. Feeney,* 442 U.S. 256 (1979).

81. Judith Havemann, "Sexual Harassment: The Personnel Problem That Won't Go Away," *Washington Post National Weekly Edition,* July 11–17, 1988, p. 30.

82. Susan Benesch, "The Birth of a Nation," *Washington Post National Weekly Edition,* August 4, 1986, p. 12.

83. *California Federal Savings & Loan v. Guerra,* 93 L.Ed.2d 613 (1987).

84. *Craig v. Boren,* 429 U.S. 190 (1976).

85. *Orr v. Orr,* 440 U.S. 268 (1979); *Mississippi University for Women v. Hogan,* 458 U.S. 718 (1982).

86. *Rostker v. Goldberg,* 453 U.S. 57 (1981).

87. *Michael M. v. Sonoma County,* 450 U.S. 464 (1981).

88. Early decisions include *University of California Regents v. Bakke,* 438 U.S. 265 (1978); *United Steelworkers v. Weber,* 443 U.S. 193 (1979); *Fullilove v. Klutznick,* 448 U.S. 448 (1980).

89. *United Steelworkers v. Weber.*

90. *Sheet Metal Workers v. EEOC,* 92 L.Ed.2d 344 (1986); *Firefighters v. Cleveland,* 92 L.Ed.2d 405 (1986); *United States v. Paradise Local Union,* 94 L.Ed.2d 203 (1987).

91. *Firefighters v. Stotts* 467 U.S. 561 (1985); *Wygant v. Jackson Board of Education,* 90 L.Ed.2d 260 (1986).

92. *Richmond v. Croson,* 102 L.Ed.2d 854 (1989).

93. Anthony Lewis, "Bush Must Lack Empathy Gene," *Lincoln Journal (New York Times),* April 16, 1991.

94. Ted Gup, "Racism in the Raw in Suburban Chicago," *Time,* October 17, 1988, p. 25.

95. "A Lost Generation," *Time,* March 12, 1990, p. 25.

96. "Doctor: Harlem's Death Rate Worse Than Bangladesh's," *Lincoln Journal* (A.P.), January 18, 1990.

97. U.S. Census (Washington, D.C.: U.S. Government Printing Office, 1989), Statistical Abstract of the United States 1989, Table 713; Naomi Verdugo and Richard Verdugo, "Earnings Differentials among Mexican American, Black, and White Male Workers," *Social Science Quarterly* 65 (June 1984): 417–25; Allen Williams, Peter Beeson, and David Johnson, "Some Factors Associated with Income among Mexican Americans," *Social Science Quarterly* 53 (March 1973): 710–15.

98. *New York Times,* April 2, 1978.

99. Kluger, *Simple Justice,* p. 90.

100. Neal R. Peirce, "It's Later in the Day for a Nation Fashioned by European Immigrants," *Lincoln Sunday Journal-Star,* May 19, 1991.

101. Dick Kirschten, "Not Black-and-White," *National Journal,* March 2, 1991, pp. 496–500.

102. Williams, *Eyes on the Prize,* p. 275.

103. Ibid., pp. 227–78.

104. Ibid., p. 285.

PART FIVE

PUBLIC POLICIES

A federal inspector checks poultry in 1910.

16 Social Welfare Policy

Poverty is highest among female-headed families and among blacks and Hispanics. It is especially prevalent in black female-headed families.

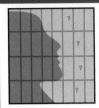

To Begin with ABC?

It is October 1988. You are Orrin Hatch, Republican senator from Utah. Since your election 12 years ago, you have received high ratings from conservative interest groups and have been a staunch supporter of Ronald Reagan. Like him you still would like to see the role of the federal government reduced. Nevertheless, when you were chair of the Senate's Labor and Human Resources Committee, you worked with more liberal members to revise rather than eliminate several human services programs.

You are facing a choice concerning a package of legislation relating to children, the most important part of which is the Act for Better Child Care Services, popularly known as the ABC bill. The bill, already approved by committees of the House and Senate, would give $2.5 billion to the states to help poor and lower middle-income families pay for child care and to train child-care providers, assist providers in meeting federal standards, and set up referral services to help parents find quality day care for their kids. Day-care centers receiving federal money would have to meet certain health and safety standards, such as having a high ratio of staff to children, hiring properly trained staff, and maintaining safe facilities.

Support for the bill is broad. Over 100 organized groups have endorsed the legislation. Over 60% of the public, including those who are not parents as well as those who are, believe the federal government should do something to make child care more available and affordable.[1] In this election year, both parties are seeking to show the public that they are concerned about children.

And in the America of 1988, there is much to be concerned about. One out of five children is poor. Nineteen percent of all white children, 30% of all Hispanic children, and 54% of all black children live in homes with only one parent.[2] The census projects

Policymakers at all levels of government are wrestling with the issue of making sure that day care is adequate, affordable, and available.

that only 39% of all children born in 1987 will live with both parents until they are 18. Growing numbers of children, many of them children of cocaine addicts, live with neither parent. And every night, 100,000 children are among the nation's homeless.[3]

To make matters worse, teenage pregnancy, higher than any other industrial nation in the world, is increasing, bringing a new cycle of poverty-stricken and often one-parent families. Unfortunately, children born into such homes are themselves likely to be poor, suffer ill health, bear children early, drop out of school, and end up on welfare or in prison.

And the nation is not even doing well at keeping children alive. The nation's infant mortality rate is disgracefully high. In 17 other countries, babies are more likely to survive than in the United States.

Contributing to these woes, the Reagan administration cut back many programs designed to help children, including Head Start, vaccination programs, school lunches and breakfasts, food stamps, and programs to provide nutrition and health care

(continued on next page)

for low-income pregnant women and their babies. But now, people are becoming concerned. As Jesse Jackson argued in most of his campaign speeches, "We can either fund Head Start and child care and day care on the front side of life, or welfare and jail care on the back side of life."[4] Conservatives and business people, normally against federal involvement in family life, have also decided that the problem of America's children can no longer be ignored. They realize that our society will not be able to function in the future, let alone be competitive in the international economic arena, with a generation of ill-fed, ill-educated, ill-trained young people outside the mainstream of society. A recent report of a group of major corporate executives called for drastic increases in funding of early childhood programs: "Such programs will be expensive . . . but if we fail to act, the true costs will be many times higher."[5]

Among the many needs of America's children, and their families, is quality day care. Over half of the women with children under 3 and almost three-quarters of women with children from 3 to 17 work in the paid labor force. And the number of working women increases each year as economic pressures force families to work harder to stay afloat. But many parents cannot afford day care and do not have trustworthy friends and relatives to baby-sit. Some go on welfare so they can stay home with their children, others leave their children in dirty or dangerous environments, and others worry constantly about tenuous day-care arrangements. And

even families that can afford day care cannot always find quality arrangements.

The ABC bill tries to increase the supply of day-care centers, increase their health and safety standards, and help families pay for them. You are in favor of these goals, but you are concerned about the contents of the ABC bill. It is costly. It sets up federal standards for health and safety which you strongly oppose. You believe such involvement will increase the size of the federal bureaucracy and cause problems for day-care providers. In addition, because of constitutional provisions mandating separation of church and state, the bill will not fund most day-care programs in churches, where over one-third of all day care is provided. You think this is a serious omission. The bill is also opposed by the right wing of the Republican party, one of whom thundered that it would "Sovietize the American family by warehousing babies."[6] Even though you think these views are a gross exaggeration, you still have serious reservations about the bill.

On the other hand, it is an election year and helping children is clearly an important political issue. Republicans like to consider themselves the party that is most in favor of family values, though this bill has more Democratic than Republican sponsors and supporters. You know that if Republicans vote against the bill, they could be labeled "antifamily." Thus there are a lot of pressures on you to support the bill.

What do you do?

The term "social welfare policies" generally brings to mind programs for the poor: welfare mothers, indigents receiving free cheese from government surplus, or people living in public housing. Yet government social welfare programs aid almost all groups—the rich as well as the poor and many in between. Indeed, most social welfare spending in the United States is not for the poor but for those of middle and upper income. Government aid provides $10.70 of every $100.00 in income Americans receive. Only $.60 of that is welfare for the poor and most of the rest is Social Security and pensions for government employees.

You are undoubtedly a beneficiary of federal social welfare programs yourself—programs that support students, aid farmers, help pay mortgages on homes, aid veterans, provide funds for the unemployed and elderly, or supply school lunches (figure 1). Most of these go to middle- or lower-middle-income people since poor people generally cannot buy homes, go to college, or get federal farm support, and they are less likely to have jobs entitling them to Social Security and unemployment compensation.

We do not have what is sometimes termed "a welfare state," where a coordinated set of income support programs provides help in a uniform way for those who need it. Instead, our social welfare programs are largely uncoordinated efforts designed to solve the particular problems of specific groups (e.g., college students, the poor, farmers, the elderly) by means that vary from program to program. The programs often have multiple goals. For example, the government provides cheese and other surplus commodities to the poor partly to ease the problem of food surpluses.

What Are Social Welfare Policies?

We use the term "social welfare policy" broadly to refer to direct or indirect government financial subsidies to individuals. People receive direct subsidies individually from the government by means of a check or other financial benefit. Social Security payments, surplus food, and subsidized student loans are direct subsidies. Indirect subsidies are not paid individually to beneficiaries. Instead, the government provides goods or services that are used collectively—for example, government supports education. Students receive

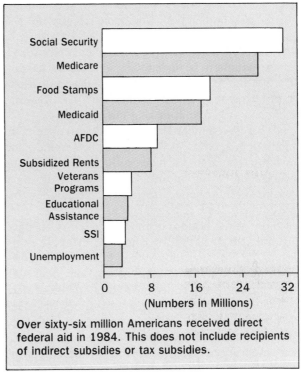

Figure 1 ■ One-Third of All Americans Receive Direct Federal Aid

(Numbers in Millions) — horizontal axis: 0, 8, 16, 24, 32

Programs (top to bottom): Social Security, Medicare, Food Stamps, Medicaid, AFDC, Subsidized Rents, Veterans Programs, Educational Assistance, SSI, Unemployment

Over sixty-six million Americans received direct federal aid in 1984. This does not include recipients of indirect subsidies or tax subsidies.

Source: Census Survey of Income and Program Participation, 1984. Reported in John Berry, "Uncle Sam Pays Nearly 3 in 10," *Washington Post National Weekly Edition,* October 15, 1984, p. 33.

a government service at only a fraction of its true cost because taxpayers in the school district, state, and nation pay.

A third kind of subsidy is one provided through tax benefits. A tax break subsidy permits some people and corporations to pay less in taxes than others of the same income. Most tax subsidies go directly to middle- and upper-income people or indirectly to them through corporate tax breaks. Since shareholders of corporations are usually upper-income people, they benefit the most from these tax subsidies.

Evolution of Social Welfare Policies

At the time the Constitution was written, no level of government was deeply involved in social welfare policies. Colonial local governments were responsible for the poor but gave little aid. Orphaned or destitute children were apprenticed to better-off families, where they worked as servants. Workhouses were established for the able-bodied poor, and some minimal aid was given to the old or sick.[7] Churches and other private charities helped the "deserving" poor and unfortunate. Those thought to be undeserving were treated harshly. These attitudes reflected the belief that individuals were mostly responsible for their own fate. Government had little role in making life better.

That government should provide extensive common public services such as education, hospitals, and asylums was largely a nineteenth-century idea. The concept of paying individuals benefits is mostly a twentieth-century one. Gradually the belief grew that government has a responsibility to help at least some of those at the bottom of the ladder. These changed attitudes led to state laws, beginning in 1911, establishing aid programs for poor children and their mothers. Fifteen years later, most of the states had such laws, replacing apprenticeship and poorhouses. Most of our major national social welfare programs were first developed in the 1930s as part of the New Deal and have expanded since then. Other major social welfare innovations, such as Medicare, began in the 1960s.

Social Welfare for Everyone

Social Security is a social welfare program for all classes of Americans who have worked or are dependents of workers. One of every 6 individuals now receives a Social Security payment, and 7 of 10 can expect to be covered now or in the future. Social Security payments account for 22% of federal spending, and Social Security taxes produce 32% of all federal revenues.

How Social Security Works

Social Security is not paid out of general revenues but is financed through a payroll tax on employees and employers paid to a special trust fund. In 1991, the tax was slightly over 7.65% of the first $51,300 of an employee's wages. Although employers contribute to the program, their cost is generally assumed to be passed on to the employee in the form of lower wages.[8]

Individuals collect their Social Security benefits upon reaching retirement age. Partial benefits can be collected before age 65, full benefits after (although this minimum age is being raised a month or so each year). Survivors (spouse and dependent children) of contributors to the program can also collect benefits.

Since only those who have paid into the program (and their survivors) can collect benefits, the program is regarded as a **social insurance** program. Those receiving payments believe they are not receiving "welfare" but only getting back what they paid into the program through payroll deductions. Unlike private insurance programs, however, Social Security pays its recipients far more than they paid it. Social Security recipients receive back their contributions and those of their employers in 3 years, while they typically receive Social Security for 14 years.[9] The program has stayed afloat because of ever-increasing numbers of people paying in at steadily rising rates. Thus workers today are supporting retirees of yesterday.

President Roosevelt and the other New Dealers who initiated the Social Security program would probably be astounded at its current magnitude. It was originally designed to ensure that the elderly would not live in poverty after retirement. Over the years, the disabled and survivors of those covered by Social Security have become eligible. Health benefits (Medicare) were also added. The program has therefore grown in size from about 220,000 recipients in

President Roosevelt signs the Social Security Act in 1935.

1940 to nearly 40 million today. The average benefit to a retired worker, a mere $18 per month in 1940, increased to over $600 in 1990.[10] Even taking inflation into account, real benefits have tripled.

In 1950, Social Security accounted for only 3% of all retirement income. It is now around 40%. Without Social Security almost half of our senior citizens would be poor; with it only 12% are.[11]

Problems with the Program

Social Security is a great public policy success story. Each year it lifts out of poverty about 15 million retirees, people with disabilities, and families with dependent children whose working parent has died. It is a major source of retirement income for many millions and a valuable supplement for millions more. Largely because of increased Social Security benefits, the poverty rate among the elderly is half what it was in 1965. Still, there are problems with the program.

The first is that Social Security pays benefits to those who do not need them, thus wasting resources. Sixty percent of Social Security payments go to those above the poverty line.[12] This problem is also an asset, however, since people do not have to show a financial need to receive Social Security; millions can accept it without the public stigma of being on welfare. This aspect of the program makes it politically popular.

Middle- and upper-income beneficiaries do pay taxes on half of their Social Security income, thus returning a portion of their payment to the government through taxes. Some suggest that the full benefits should be taxable.

A second problem is that retirement benefits are inadequate for poorly paid workers. While many who do not need it receive Social Security, others receive such small payments that they still live in poverty. The *average* payment of $600 is inadequate for those without other income, and about half the recipients receive less. Low payments go to workers who earned very low wages during their careers. These are the people most in need of a large Social Security income, as they are unlikely to have even modest private pensions or investment income. Poverty status follows them from their working lives to their retirements.

The dependence by the low-income aged on Social Security is illustrated by the fact that Social Security provides over 90% of the income for about one-quarter of the elderly.[13]

One of the success stories of American public policy, Social Security gives most elderly the freedom to swim in society's mainstream.

Some elderly are eligible for Supplemental Security Income (SSI), but many poor elderly "fall through the cracks" and are not eligible for these payments *or* for an adequate Social Security income.

A third problem is that lower-income workers are hardest hit by Social Security taxes. People earning high salaries pay taxes only on the first $51,300. Those earning less pay the tax on all they earn. Thus poorer workers are taxed at a higher real rate than wealthier ones. Although low-income workers receive more benefits relative to their earnings than do wealthier ones, Social Security has been called the poor person's welfare payment to the middle class.

A final problem with Social Security is that the president and the Congress are using today's surpluses to offset the nation's budget deficit. In recent years, the Social Security Trust Fund has had huge and growing surpluses. These surpluses are necessary in order to be prepared for the drain on Social Security that will occur in the next 20 or 30 years as the baby boom generation (born in the late 1940s and early 1950s) reaches retirement age. Yet, in order to make the budget seem less out of balance than it really is, policymakers are using Trust Funds for current bills. This casual use of funds designated for Social Security recipients leads to questions about whether Social Security will be solvent in a few decades. It is unlikely that Congress and the president would, in fact, allow the system to go bankrupt, though in the past decade, their stewardship of the nation's financial resources does not lead to an excess of confidence.

The Future of Social Security

Social Security costs are increasing, largely because our population is getting older. People 65 and older were only 11% of the population in 1980, but they are projected to be almost 20% in 2020. In the United States, as in most other industrial nations, the entry of most women into the work force, marriage at later ages, and contraception and abortion have lowered the fertility rate to less than the natural population replacement level.[14] Even though immigration is replacing some population, the population is aging and will do so at an even more rapid pace after 2000. By 2030, there may be only slightly over two active workers to support each Social Security retiree, compared to almost four in 1990.[15] This will put more of a strain on the system.

As a welfare program for everyone, Social Security continues to be politically popular among all groups. Everyone believes they will live to old age, and, as Daniel Moynihan (D-N.Y.) has pointed out, "Social Security has removed much of the fear of growing old."[16] Still, the program sometimes comes under attack. Though it is successful, its very success at reducing poverty among the elderly prompts some people to question whether we should be devoting so many of our resources to the no-longer-poor elderly and so few to the younger generation. Perhaps, given the wealth of our society, a more reasonable question is whether we can devise a program as successful at raising children out of poverty as Social Security is at doing so for the elderly. As one member of Congress commented, "We should be proud of what we have done for the elderly, and horrified at what we're doing to our children."[17]

Social Welfare for Some

In the United States, government aid for health care is a social benefit for some people of all income groups, but not for all people. Forty percent of all health care is paid for by the government.

The health-care system is paradoxical. Whether one measures it by the dollars we spend per capita or as a percentage of our national income, the United States spends more on health care than any country in the world. Yet, it is the only industrialized democracy that does not provide health insurance coverage or state-supported medical care for every citizen. Thus, compared to other nations, we spend more but help fewer. Partly because of this, the quality of medical care received in the United States can be the best in the world for those who can pay for it, but overall it lags behind much of the industrial world and some of the less-developed world too. Our infant mortality rates are higher than in 17 other nations, and our life expectancy is lower than Cuba's—and many other nations.[18] Fifty percent of pre-school children in the inner city are not immunized against common diseases. On some criteria of health care, black Americans, due to their on-average lower incomes than white Americans, are little better-off than people in the poor nations of Latin America, Asia, and Africa. In some central city neighborhoods, blacks are *worse* off than if they lived in those countries.

Our public hospitals in big cities are overflowing with people suffering from diseases we thought we had conquered, such as tuberculosis and the diseases caused by malnutrition and from the new diseases of AIDS and "crack babies." Our rural hospitals are closing daily, unable to make ends meet. To understand these problems, we need to understand government's role in the health-care system.

Federal Health-Care Programs

The federal government has been involved in some aspects of health care for decades, but before 1965 there was no general federal support for individual health care. In 1965, after years of debate over government's responsibility to fund health care, concern about the problems of inadequate health care among millions of Americans who could not afford it prompted President Johnson to propose and Congress to pass two programs, Medicare and Medicaid.

Medicare.   **Medicare** is a public health insurance program that funds many medical expenses for the elderly and disabled. It includes hospital insurance and additional, voluntary coverage that helps pay for physicians' services, outpatient hospital services, and some other costs.

Hospital insurance is paid for by Social Security taxes, while the other part is financed through general revenues and through the monthly premiums paid by participants. Those eligible for Social Security benefits are eligible for Medicare, and over 90% of Social Security recipients buy the optional insurance.

Although many factors affect our health, it is clear that Medicare has benefited the health of the elderly. Compared to the period before 1965, more people see

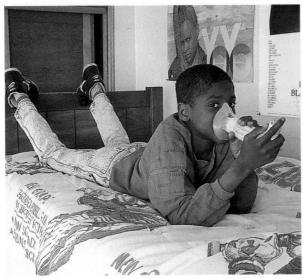

Like most individuals in middle class families, this young man gets good medical treatment for chronic illnesses, such as asthma. However, poverty stricken Americans are much more likely to die from lack of treatment of such diseases.

doctors now, and the elderly have more but shorter hospital stays. There have been declines in death rates from diseases affecting the elderly, such as heart attacks and strokes, and decreases in the number of days of restricted activity that older people have.[19]

Despite these substantial accomplishments, Medicare has not been a complete success. It is expensive, and many of those who need it have trouble paying for it. These same problems afflict the other major federal health-care program, Medicaid.

Medicaid. Medicaid is a federal-state program to help poor people pay their medical bills, but the program covers only about 40% of people below the poverty line. States are allowed to set their own Medicaid eligibility standards, within certain federal guidelines. In some states, almost all the poor are covered by Medicaid, but in other states relatively few are.

Medicaid covers many services, including hospitals, doctors, and laboratory tests. States may offer optional services such as nursing home and dental care, drugs, and eyeglasses, though few states offer all the options.

The Crisis in Health Care

There are two major problems in America's health-care system: one is that health care is increasingly expensive, and, second, as a consequence, growing numbers of

Americans have no access to even minimal care. Most observers believe we have a crisis in our health care system; some believe we are approaching catastrophe.

Cost. The overall cost of Medicare, Medicaid, and private health care has escalated rapidly. Spending for health comprised less than 5% of the federal budget in 1965 but 12% in 1990. Two-thirds is for Medicare. Health-care spending of state and local governments and of private consumers also rose dramatically in this period. States share much of the cost of Medicaid.

The cost of health care is increasing for several reasons. One is that the number of elderly is increasing, and the number of elderly elderly (those over 80) is increasing even faster. The elderly have more health problems than others, so as their numbers increase, the demand for medical services rises and Medicare costs increase.

A second reason is the growth of high technology in medicine. CAT scanners, dialysis equipment, intensive care units, and other sophisticated medical tools may cost millions of dollars, yet most hospitals and doctors want them and the taxpayers and patients pay for them. High technology has made possible organ transplants and other procedures unheard of a few years ago, but at a huge cost. The cost of the kidney dialysis program zoomed from $150 million a year in 1976 to over $2 billion per year a decade later, for example. Almost $3 billion is spent every year in infant intensive care units.

High-technology medicine also creates new demands for medical procedures. When better procedures become available, more people want them, so even if the new procedures are cheaper than the old, the total cost is higher. Surgery for cataracts, an eye

High-technology medicine has vastly increased medical costs.

disease affecting many elderly, is an example. Until a decade ago, surgery was both painful and often ineffective. Now new techniques and materials allow plastic lenses to be inserted into the eye surgically, greatly improving vision. As a consequence, in a recent year almost 1.5 million people received the surgery at a cost of $4 billion.[20] Many patients who would not have considered the old surgery have had the new. The number of these operations, most paid for by Medicare, has soared.

Some experts believe that with high technology, it will be impossible to contain costs without limiting medical services further. We are only now beginning to deal with the ethical and financial implications of this. Each day, doctors face the ethical question of whether to put dying, elderly patients on expensive life-sustaining equipment. Largely because of high-tech intensive care and procedures, 30% of all Medicare costs are paid to help people in the last year of their lives, much of that in their last month for what one doctor called $100,000 funerals.[21] In a nation where millions go without adequate health care, we must confront the question of whether this is a wise use of our health-care resources.

A third reason for rising health-care costs is the traditional way medical services are purchased. Because most health care is paid for not by individuals directly but by third parties—Medicare, private insurance, employers, or Medicaid—individuals have little stake in getting the cheapest medical care possible. Because they knew government or insurance would pay the bill, doctors and hospitals traditionally had no incentive to keep costs down. Indeed, since doctors charged a fee for each service performed, they had an incentive to do as many procedures as possible. The growing incidence of malpractice suits also prompted doctors to order even more tests and procedures to protect themselves.

A fourth cause of rising health-care costs is increasing poverty and social disorder. The decay of our inner cities has led to an epidemic of crime and disease that ultimately strains the health-care system. Hospital emergency rooms must take care of victims of knife and gunshot wounds, whether the victims are insured or not. "Crack babies," victims of their mothers' drug addiction, cost over $1,000 per day to treat. AIDS victims, now found disproportionately among drug addicts and their offspring, multiply each year. Babies born prematurely and underweight (who cost up to $2,500 per day to treat) increase in number because poverty-stricken, often teenaged mothers cannot get

adequate prenatal care and sometimes even adequate food. Increasing poverty coupled with cutbacks in Medicare and Medicaid also mean that people with "ordinary" diseases such as heart problems, high blood pressure, or diabetes do not get adequate early treatment, making their conditions harder, and often more expensive, to treat.

The spiraling costs brought about by these factors have led Congress, the states, and the health industry to make some rather dramatic changes in the way medical care is funded in order to contain costs (no one believes costs can be reduced). For example, private insurers try to limit unnecessary operations and provide incentives for outpatient care rather than hospital stays. Employers shop around for the best "deal" for insurance for their employees. Medicare sets limits on what it will pay for each procedure. New health-care organizations have sprung up to challenge the old fee-for-service practice. Called **health maintenance organizations (HMOs),** these groups of doctors agree to provide full health care for a fixed monthly charge. This system provides direct incentives for doctors to keep costs low, avoid unnecessary hospitalization and procedures, and emphasize preventive medicine. Unfortunately, most of these changes have been unsuccessful in halting cost increases and at the same time, some have limited access to medical care.

Problems of Access.   As efforts are made to control costs of Medicare and Medicaid, access to health care is increasingly limited. Medicare limits what it will pay doctors and hospitals for each type of procedure or treatment. In response, though, doctors have begun billing for more procedures and more expensive procedures, wiping out any cost savings to Medicare. Insurance companies, in attempts to cut their costs, are dropping from the insurance rolls people who they believe have a high risk of getting sick. Some states are throwing people off the Medicaid rolls too in order to control costs. In 1982, California dropped 270,000 people. One estimate is that about 5,000 to 10,000 people died annually as a direct consequence.[22] Some people simply could not afford to buy their medicine or to go to the doctor. People for whom a simple exam costs more than a week's food budget or a simple surgical procedure more than the rent are likely to sacrifice good health care.

Because of these factors and the decline in employment in businesses and industries that normally offered insurance as a fringe benefit, nearly 40 million

COMPARATIVE PERSPECTIVE

U.S. Lags Behind in Health Care

Infant mortality rates are one measure of the quality and avalibility of health care. On this measure, as on others, the U.S. lags behind all other western democracies and many other nations too. The table to the right provides a sampling. Within the U.S., the infant mortality rate for blacks is higher than any country shown, and double that for whites.

Table 1 ■ U.S. Infant Mortality Rates are High

Country	Deaths per 1,000 live births
Japan	5.0
Switzerland	6.8
Singapore	7.0
Canada	7.3
France	7.7
East Germany	8.1
United Kingdom	8.8
U.S.	10.0
Czechoslovakia	11.9
China	12.0
Nigeria	13.8

Sources: Statistical Office of the United Nations; National Center for Health Statistics

individuals in the United States are too poor to pay for medical care or insurance but are not eligible for Medicaid. These people are sometimes referred to as the **medically indigent.** Some states have tried to widen access by denying poor people the right to certain very expensive procedures, such as organ transplants, in order to pay for preventative and routine health care for more people. Oregon, for example, decided that instead of paying for extremely expensive organ transplants, it would pay for preventative care for thousands of children and women. Though denial of a life-saving procedure is often widely publicized and health-care "rationing" decried, the existing system whereby millions are deprived of even the most elementary medical services is in fact "rationing by wallet." Undoubtedly, as health-care costs rise, both the states and the federal government will examine more carefully their health-care spending priorities.

There are other problems of access too. The amount that Medicare patients themselves pay has in-

creased. This is undermining the very reason for the program, which was to rescue the elderly from huge health-care costs that send them close to the poverty line. Medicare patients pay one-quarter of their health-care costs out of their own pocket.

Moreover, many elderly contract "catastrophic diseases," that is, illnesses such as some kinds of cancer or heart diseases that require expensive, prolonged treatment. Often these illnesses and treatment drain a family's entire savings.

There are also real concerns about the quality of medical care given in an environment where cost-cutting seems to be the prevailing criterion. As one observer noted about the current trends, medical care is being seen as "an economic product rather than a social good . . . a commodity rather than a service available to everyone in need."[23]

The evidence is strong that uninsured patients enter the hospital sicker, receive fewer tests, and are dismissed sooner, unless they die, which is more likely for them than for insured patients.[24] Uninsured patients and those on Medicaid were significantly less likely to receive common surgical treatments for heart disease.[25] One interpretation is that many unnecessary tests and operations are being done on insured patients, but the other interpretation is that needed tests and surgery are not being done on poor patients. Neither interpretation speaks well for the effectiveness of the existing system.

National Health Insurance?

Our current health-care system is a crazy quilt of government and private funding. In itself, that is not bad. However, in our current system only the elderly and some of the very poor have access to government aid. Many nonelderly poor have no access to health care at all because they cannot afford it. Rapidly increasing costs are also making it difficult for businesses and middle-income people to cope. And even those covered by government programs find they must pay for a large amount of their care themselves, or in the case of Medicaid, find that they cannot get convenient, high-quality care at all (many private physicians will not take Medicaid patients at all).

There seem to be two possible alternatives. One is to adopt a national health insurance system like all other industrial democracies have done. Traditionally, most medical interests, especially doctors and insurance companies, opposed such a system. Many still do today. However, as the system becomes more expensive and less accessible, pressures for making dramatic changes increase. The American Medical Association

now has endorsed national health insurance. Seventy-five percent of the public favors a government-supported health insurance system,[26] as do many businesses, which cannot afford good health insurance for their employees; and unions, which have traditionally supported government-financed insurance.

The other alternative is to force private insurance companies to share the risk of insuring those most likely to be ill. Our existing system has been called "lemon socialism." Private enterprise insures those at least risk, the young, the well, and the well-off, while government—ultimately the taxpayer—pays for those most likely to be sick, the elderly and the poor. Such a system seems unlikely to last indefinitely.

Social Welfare for the Poor

How Many Are Poor?

We think of the United States as a rather egalitarian society, but in fact income is very unevenly distributed (table 1). The poorest 20% of families earn less than 5% of all income, and the richest 20% earn over 44% of the income. The gap between rich and poor widened noticeably in the 1980s.

Distribution of wealth, which includes homes, land, savings, and stocks and bonds, as well as cash, is even more skewed. One percent of Americans own 40% of all wealth and over half of all income-

Table 1 ■ Income Distribution Is Becoming More Lopsided

Percentage of Population	Percentage of Income Earned		
	1970	1980	1989
Lowest fifth	5%	5%	5%
Next lowest		11	11
Middle fifth	54	18 } 53	17 } 52
Next highest		24	24
Highest fifth	41	42	45
Top 5%	—	15	18

Since figures are rounded to the nearest percent, the drop in the proportion of income of the lowest fifth from 5.4% in 1970 to 4.6% in 1989 is not shown. The 4.6% is the lowest proportion ever since the Census Bureau started compiling these statistics in 1974.

Source: "Rich are Richer, Poor Poorer," *Lincoln Star,* November 22, 1986, p. 1; Bureau of the Census, Current Population Reports, Series P-60, no. 127, August 1981, p. 15 and no. 168, 1990, p. 29.

producing wealth, such as business investments, farms, and so forth. The bottom half of Americans own only 4% of the nation's wealth.[27]

The Census Bureau defines as poor anyone beneath a certain income. In 1989, this was about $12,700 for a family of four. Due to the booming economy and the Great Society programs of the 1960s, the proportion of poor people dropped from 22% in 1959 to 11% in 1973, the lowest point ever achieved in the United States. Since then, it has increased, peaking at over 15% in 1983, before declining slowly to 13% in 1989.

Not everyone agrees with the Census Bureau's estimates. Some conservatives argue that it overstates the number of poor because it does not take into account many "in-kind" benefits poor people receive, such as food stamps, housing, and medical care. Others think that the census understates the amount of poverty, because they believe the standard is based on costs for food, housing, and fuel that are inadequate.[28]

Not surprisingly, those who believe government should do relatively little to increase income equality tend to minimize the extent of the poverty problem; those who favor a more activist government usually have a higher estimate. What is beyond dispute, however, is that a sizable minority of the American population— anywhere from 10% to 25%—does not have enough money to live at a decent standard. By all measures, the number living in poverty increased in the 1980s.[29]

Many observers are quite concerned about the growing gap between rich and poor in America. Until 1979, that gap had stayed fairly steady since World War II. Between the war and the late 1970s, the rich grew richer, but so did the middle class. The amount of poverty shrunk. But during the 1980s, the gap opened. The poorest 20% saw their income drop 3%, while the richest 20% experienced an income gain of 32%. The richest 1% gained, over 80%.[30] Reasons include the loss of manufacturing jobs, unemployment, and declining real wages for workers; the lack of child support paid by fathers to an increasing number of divorced and unwed mothers; and the Reagan tax and spending policies, which redistributed the wealth upward by reducing taxes for the better-off and reducing spending for the poor.

Who Is Poor?

The *Wall Street Journal* commented on the growing gulf between rich and poor: "At the top is a growing

Motorcycle Helmets and Health Care

The fact that a large share of all health-care costs are paid by the government has far-reaching implications. For example, reformers have long fought for state laws mandating that motorcyclists wear protective helmets. They argue—and evidence seems to support them—that helmets prevent serious brain injuries in case of accident. Fatal or serious head injuries from motorcycle accidents are three times more common in states without helmet laws. Compared to helmeted riders in accidents, hospitalization of helmetless riders is longer, and disability is more common.

Those who oppose mandatory helmets argue that helmets are uncomfortable and that they limit vision and hearing. Ultimately, they argue, the government should let riders take risks. If riders fail to wear helmets and are severely injured, it is their own problem.

This may have been true in an earlier era. But public funding of much health care gives proponents of helmet laws another argument. They point out that taxpayers also suffer when an individual sustains a horrible injury and must receive prolonged hospital care and months or years of further treatment and care. Few individuals can afford such treatment, so Medicaid often foots the bill. Federal and state funds also pay for therapy, nursing home care, and other special treatment for brain-injured individuals, no matter what their age. One study showed that public funds pay 63% of the cost of medical care for victims of motorcycle accidents.

If an accident victim has a family and is disabled permanently or for a long time (which is frequent in these accidents), his or her family often collects Social Security benefits and sometimes, if they are poor, AFDC or SSI, representing a further drain on the tax dollar.

Thus, personal and family tragedies become part of the public cost of health care. One proponent of helmet laws in California, where injuries from motorcycle accidents are estimated to cost California taxpayers $100 million a year, remarks: "These guys argue it's their right to bash their head on a curb and kill themselves. I agree with 'em. But the bastards don't die, and the state has to pick up the tab."

Source: Gary Yarkony, "Nebraska Should Require Helmets for Motorcyclists," *Sunday Journal-Star,* February 3, 1985; "High Gear," *Time,* December 19, 1988, p. 65; "Real Men Don't Wear Hats," *California* (November 1988):18.

overclass of well-educated two income families. At the bottom is a growing underclass of single mothers, baby boomers stuck in low paying jobs, and children who inherited poverty from their parents."[31] With the important omission of race, the *Journal* description accurately depicts those most vulnerable to poverty.

Race, Family Status, and Sex.   Race, family status, and sex are important predictors of poverty. Whites are less likely to be poor than blacks. In 1988, about 32% of all blacks and 27% of Hispanics, but only 10% of all whites, were poor. Families headed by a married couple are much less likely to be poor than are single-parent families, especially those headed by a woman (see table 2).

Women and their dependent children are the single largest group of poor people in the United States. Female-headed families make up 20% of families with children. Yet they comprise 80% of people on Aid to Families with Dependent Children (AFDC), over 50% of food stamp users, and over 55% of households receiving Medicaid. Half of all poor people in the United States live in female-headed families. This has been called the **feminization of poverty.**

The number of people in female-headed families who are poor has grown for several reasons. The rate of poverty among female-headed families is actually much smaller than in the early 1960s before the Great Society programs. But the proportion of families headed by women has doubled since 1960.

Over half of black and Hispanic female-headed families fall beneath the poverty line, and over one-quarter of white female-headed families do so. For

	Percent in Poverty
Table 2 ■ Poverty Is Much More Common among Female-Headed and Minority Families	
All families	10
White	8
Black	28
Spanish origin	23
Married-couple families	6
White	5
Black	12
Spanish origin	16
Female-headed families, no husband	32
White	25
Black	47
Spanish origin	48

Source: U.S. Bureau of the Census, Current Population Reports, *Money Income and Poverty Status in the United States,* 1989, Series P-60, no. 168, 1990.

whites, the primary reason for the growth in poor female-headed families is divorce. When divorce occurs, even between a middle-class couple, often the women and children fall into poverty. The woman cannot earn enough to support a family, and child support from the man is typically erratic and inadequate. Less than half the children of divorced white women receive support payments.[32]

Children of black women who are divorced are even less likely than white women to receive support. However, among blacks the chief reason for the increase in poor female-headed families is the growing number of mothers who have never been married. Unwed teenaged mothers are likely to stay in poverty the rest of their lives; the younger a woman is when a child is born, the more children she is likely to have and the less likely she is to complete her education and thus be able to command a decent wage. Only a tiny proportion of children of unwed mothers receive support from the fathers.

Among blacks the feminization of poverty is especially acute. On average, black two-parent families have middle-class incomes; only 12% are poor. But as ever-larger proportions of black families are headed by women, ever-larger proportions of black children are born in poverty—today, more than half of all black children are born into poverty.

There are significant numbers of poor people in rural areas as well as in the cities.

Age. Due to Social Security, poverty among the aged has dramatically decreased, and only the very elderly (over age 85) who live alone have exceptionally high poverty rates compared to other groups.[33]

Geography. Despite the economic boom in the South in recent years, it has proportionally more poor than the North. And, of course, inner city poverty rates are much higher than those in the suburbs. Rural poverty is less serious, but 70% of all poor people live in cities.

The Causes of Poverty

Finding remedies for poverty depends primarily on diagnoses of what causes it. But individuals of different political ideologies disagree vehemently on the causes of poverty. In the following discussion we use the terms "conservative explanations" and "liberal explanations" broadly; not all conservatives agree with each other, nor do all liberals have the same views.

Conservative Explanations. Conservatives emphasize that people are poor because of their own failures. As one conservative argued, "The only dependable route from poverty is always work, family and faith."[34] He believes that the poor are poor because they do not work as hard as others, they are more likely to live in broken homes, and they lack faith in God, capitalism, and the future. Edward Banfield, another conservative scholar, argues that the poor do not rise out of poverty because they are too oriented to the present, rather than saving and working toward the future.[35]

Most conservatives are, of course, willing to admit that some people are poor through no fault of their own—the ill, the aged, children, and the handicapped—but their discussions of how to reduce poverty do not focus on these groups. In general, conservatives believe that the free market economy can provide jobs and adequate incomes for all who want them.

As a consequence, conservatives tend to oppose government programs for the able-bodied poor because they believe such programs weaken individuals' incentives to work. Conservatives also believe that government intervention into the economy—through minimum wages and mandatory social insurance programs like Social Security, for example—aggravates poverty by interfering with the natural workings of the market system.

Liberal Explanations. Liberals place less of the blame on the poor for their problems. As Michael Harrington noted:

> The real explanation of why the poor are where they are is that they made the mistake of being born to the wrong parents, in the wrong section of the country, in the wrong industry, or in the wrong racial or ethnic group. Once that mistake has been made, they could have been paragons of will and morality, but most of them would never have had a chance to get out of poverty.[36]

Liberals are more likely than conservatives to believe that at the heart of many poor peoples' problems is the lack of jobs paying wages adequate to support a family. Although millions of Americans have relatively secure and high-paying jobs in management, professional occupations, and blue-collar jobs where workers are protected by labor unions, other Americans do not. They have little job security, few hopes of advancement, and low-paying jobs like car washing, farm labor, private household work, hospital work, many clerical jobs, retail store sales, and nonunionized labor in rural and southern areas. Even with steady work, employees in these and similar occupations can hardly earn enough to keep a family above the poverty line. Indeed, about half of family heads of poor families work, but even working full-time at a minimum wage job yields an income less than $9,000, far below the poverty line for a family.[37] Employment is, unfortunately, not a cure-all for poverty.

Liberals believe that government should ensure those who have menial jobs a decent standard of living. Thus they favor minimum wage laws and mandatory fringe benefit programs. They also believe that government should help people obtain the education and training necessary to advance beyond these menial jobs, so they favor education and job-training programs. Liberals also usually believe that racial and sexual discrimination are partially responsible for the fact that women and minority males are the ones most frequently mired in poverty.

Public opinion on the causes of poverty reflects these basic divisions. About one-third adopt the more conservative view and believe that people are poor primarily due to lack of effort. Another third have a stance more common among liberals and believe that people are poor largely because of conditions beyond their control. The other one-third of the public believes both are reasons for poverty[38] (see figure 2).

Figure 2 ■ Republicans and Democrats Have Different Views about Poverty

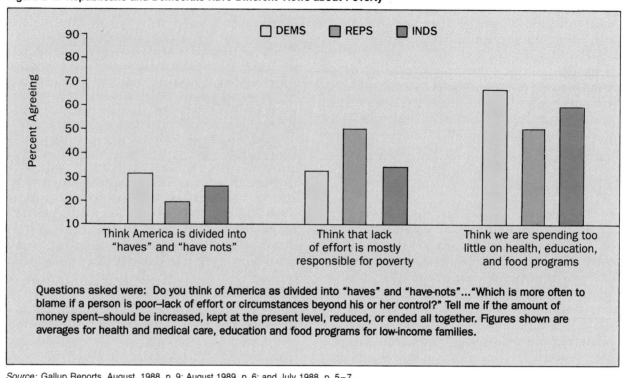

Questions asked were: Do you think of America as divided into "haves" and "have-nots"..."Which is more often to blame if a person is poor–lack of effort or circumstances beyond his or her control?" Tell me if the amount of money spent–should be increased, kept at the present level, reduced, or ended all together. Figures shown are averages for health and medical care, education and food programs for low-income families.

Source: Gallup Reports, August, 1988, p. 9; August 1989, p. 6; and July 1988, p. 5–7.

Basic Programs for the Poor

We have government programs to help the poor, just as we do to help the middle class and rich. But programs for the poor seem to be the target of substantially more criticism than programs for others. Liberals, for example, believe the programs provide inadequate support and are ineffective in moving people into the mainstream economy. Conservatives criticize the programs as an actual roadblock to self-sufficiency.

We have already discussed one important program for the poor, Medicaid, and will now examine three more: Aid to Families with Dependent Children (AFDC), Supplemental Security Income (SSI), and Food Stamps.

Aid to Families with Dependent Children (**AFDC**) originated in New Deal social security legislation providing income support for dependent children. Coverage was later added for mothers with dependent children and still later for both fathers and mothers with dependent children. Programs for the blind, elderly, and disabled, called **SSI**, also originated in the New Deal.

Both AFDC and SSI are **means test** programs; individuals who participate must periodically demonstrate eligibility by showing they are poor—they must have both limited income and few assets. For SSI, a couple may have up to $2,250 in liquid assets of cash or stocks—in other words, enough for a decent funeral. SSI recipients are automatically eligible for food stamps and Medicaid. Despite these benefits, most SSI recipients still remain in poverty in almost all states.

The SSI program is relatively uncontroversial because few people believe that the elderly, blind, or disabled should be forced to work to earn their government subsidy.

The AFDC program serves over twice as many people as SSI, costs 1.3 times as much, and probably receives 100 times the publicity. There are several reasons for the controversy:

■ Some recipients are able-bodied adults (the parents of dependent children).

AMERICAN DIVERSITY

The Homeless

Although millions of poor people are not homeless, growing numbers are. Indeed, homelessness has become a symbol of poverty in contemporary America. "Street people" used to be a phenomenon only of metropolitan America, but now in small and medium-size communities too, men and women search trash cans and families live in cars or temporary shelters and eat in soup kitchens.

How many are homeless? Lowest estimates, provided by the government, are that about 300,000 people are homeless. Higher estimates, provided by advocates for the homeless, range all the way to 3 million. A reasonable estimate might be that 600,000 people are homeless on any given night.[1]

Why has the problem of the homeless increased in intensity and visibility? One reason is our national housing shortage, affecting both middle- and low-income people. Younger, middle-income people cannot afford to buy homes because housing costs have risen much faster than earnings. They then occupy rental units that might other-

wise be available to slightly lower-income people and so on down the line. The inability of people to buy homes also drives up rental prices. In many cities, half of all renters cannot afford rent for a two-bedroom apartment. Eviction rates from rental apartments are up, and a growing number of "couch people" are moving in with friends and relatives or returning to their parental homes.

At the bottom end of the income ladder, the problems are even worse. There are 5 million households in the United States with annual incomes of less than $5,000 per year.[2] Many must depend on public housing. But there are 19 million more people eligible for public housing than there are units available, and 1 million people are on waiting lists. During the Reagan administration, the budget of the Housing and Urban Development agency was cut by more than half, and much of that was wasted because of corruption and political favoritism. Not only did construction of new units come to a standstill, but rehabilitation of existing units also pretty much stopped.

In the 1930s, homelessness was largely caused by the Great Depression. Here is photographer Dorthea Lange's historic photo of a homeless Oklahoma family during that era. Today the homeless population is increasing despite overall economic prosperity. Some live on the streets, and others live in cars or shelters. *(continued on next page)*

Currently, thousands of public housing units are standing vacant, but these cannot meet the needs of the homeless. Many of the units are unlivable. Some are in public housing projects that are unsafe and ridden with drug dealers and criminals. Others are in acceptable projects, but the individual units need rehabilitation. Some estimate that it will cost more than $10 billion to rehabilitate existing public housing.

Other problems have also contributed to the creation of the homeless. Funding has been cut back for community mental health centers and halfway houses. Two decades ago government and mental health professionals decided that it was better to treat most mentally ill people in community centers than in large institutions. So we emptied many mental institutions. But without adequately funded community mental health facilities, thousands of people do not have the support services they need to maintain a home and a job. So they wander the streets when formerly they would have been in institutions. To protect the civil liberties of these people, courts have held that unless they are a danger to themselves or others, the mentally ill cannot be institutionalized against their will. Other homeless have drug and alcohol problems that limit their abilities to function.

But half of all the homeless are families. Indeed women and children are the fastest growing segment of the homeless. Many of them simply cannot afford to pay rent and buy food with income from low-wage jobs or public assistance.

What can be done about the homeless? Most Americans want to increase spending to help them, even if it means raising taxes.[3] Though people are inclined to blame the homeless themselves for at least part of their plight,[4] average Americans now see the homeless in their own communities. It is harder, therefore, to ignore them than to ignore big city slums, the working poor, and other social problems.

Still, there is little agreement as to exactly what should be done. Conservatives resist building more public housing because they want the private sector to take care of the housing need. But although private markets are building tens of thousands of new apartments yearly, only a small proportion rent for less than $300 per month, about the maximum that a poor person can afford. Some Bush associates want to try privitization, selling public housing units to the poor, as the Thatcher government did successfully in Britain. In many cases, however, public housing projects here are probably too dangerous and run down to be sold to anyone, let alone poor people without many resources to use in fixing them up.

Congress may react to the problem of the homeless by embarking on a program of both building new housing units and helping more working- and middle-class people who want to buy homes. This might, in turn, stimulate the private housing market and through a combination of public and private efforts make some headway.

But any "solution" has also to take into account some deeper causes of homelessness. Funding for community-based mental health and drug treatment programs must be part of any solution, along with efforts at finding decent jobs for people with marginal skills and providing day care so poor mothers can work.

1. "Domestic Policy," *American Agenda: A Report to the Forty-First President of the U.S.A.* (1988), p. 3; Carol F. Steinbach, "Shelter-Skelter," *National Journal,* April 8, 1989, pp. 851–55.
2. Ibid., p. 853.
3. "Opinion Outlook," *National Journal,* February 4, 1989, p. 306.
4. "The Homeless at the Heart of Poverty and Policy," *New York Times,* January 29, 1989, p. 5.

- Over 11 million Americans—or 1 in 20—receive AFDC payments.
- Over 40% of the AFDC recipients are black, compared with only one-fourth of SSI recipients.

To be eligible for AFDC, individuals must reestablish eligibility monthly. In between times, any change must be reported to the welfare bureaucracy. This means not only major events such as births or deaths but also routine events such as moving or children leaving school. Even replacements of broken furniture must be approved by the welfare bureaucracy. In theory, and often in practice, almost every aspect of life is subject to scrutiny by welfare officials.

About 80% of families on AFDC are headed by a woman who is the mother of the dependent children. Only 4% are headed by fathers, and the rest by a grandparent or other relative of the children. Contrary to myth, the average AFDC family is not exceptionally large; over 70% have one or two children and only 14% have four or more.[39] Indeed the fertility rate of women on AFDC is lower than other poor women not on welfare.[40] Nor do most AFDC families stay on the welfare rolls indefinitely (see figure 3).[41]

Although in a 32-month period one-fifth of all families in the United States received some welfare, only a minority of AFDC families are permanently

Figure 3 ■ Many Americans Receive Welfare Some of the Time, but Few Receive It Regularly

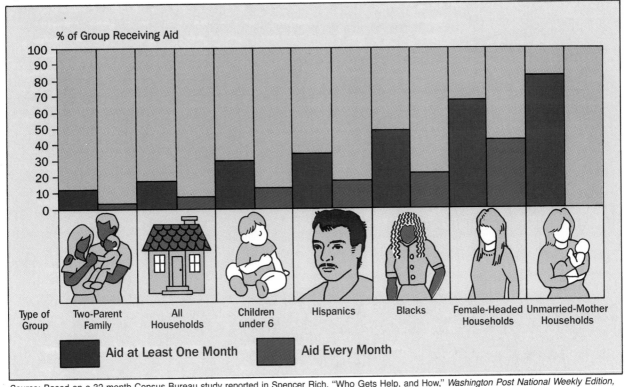

Source: Based on a 32-month Census Bureau study reported in Spencer Rich, "Who Gets Help, and How," *Washington Post National Weekly Edition,* May 15–19, 1989, p. 37. Welfare assistance includes AFDC, SSI, food stamps, rent assistance, Medicaid, and general assistance. "Aid Every month" data not available for unmarried mothers.

mired in poverty and need constant relief. A Census Bureau study found only about 3% received cash relief every month with about an equal number receiving food stamps each month.[42]

AFDC is administered by the states under strict federal guidelines. The states pay about one-third of the cost, the federal government slightly over half, and the local governments the rest. Local contributions are set by state law. In some states local governments pay nothing, in others quite a lot.

States determine who is eligible for AFDC assistance by determining a "standard of need," which varies widely from state to state (see figure 4). The average recipient received about $130 per month in 1988; the average family about $375.

How Successful Are Programs for the Poor?

Have Programs Achieved Their Goals? Scholars and politicians have waged a spirited debate over how successful our welfare programs have been. Some believe that the poverty programs of the Great Society (Johnson's programs of the 1960s discussed in chapter 3) were a success.[43] Beginning in the mid-1960s, poverty rates dropped and did not turn upward again until the high unemployment of the late 1970s and early 1980s. The people in programs where government benefits were most generous, such as the elderly, showed the greatest gains in income.

Smaller programs have also been successful. The program for health care for low-income pregnant women, for example, reduced infant mortality by

Figure 4 ■ Southern States Are Least Generous in AFDC Payments

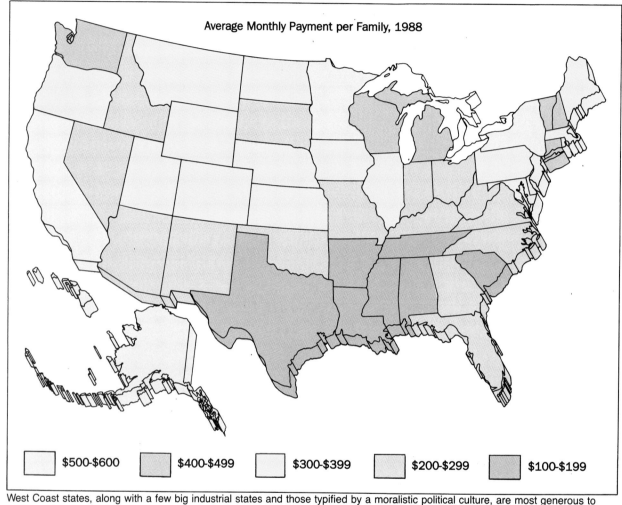

Average Monthly Payment per Family, 1988

$500-$600 $400-$499 $300-$399 $200-$299 $100-$199

West Coast states, along with a few big industrial states and those typified by a moralistic political culture, are most generous to AFDC recipients; southern states are the least generous.

Source: U.S. Census, Statistical Abstract of the United States (Washington, D.C.: Bureau of the Census, 1990), table 610.

20,000 to 35,000 deaths per year.[44] Medicare and Medicaid have improved health care for the poor and elderly.[45]

Those who argue that programs for the poor work point out that hardly any program for the poor actually has enough funds to allow the poor to participate (see figure 5). For example, only about 20% of children eligible for Head Start can be accommodated in the program, even though study after study shows that preschoolers with Head Start experience do much better in school than other poor children. Similarly, less than 60% of poor pregnant women can receive food supplements and prenatal care, even though it is

clear that the relatively cheap food supplements and prenatal care save thousands of dollars in treatment for each child born with problems because of the mother's poor health and nutrition.

On the other side are those who believe that welfare programs have actually worsened the condition of the poor, particularly the black underclass. They argue that our welfare system discourages the poor who try to work by making government assistance too easy to obtain and too lucrative.[46] In this view, welfare provides economic incentives for unwed women to have babies, fathers to desert their children, and neither to work.

Figure 5 ■ Most Programs for the Poor Reach Only a Minority of those Eligible

% of poor receiving

	Medicaid	Food stamps	AFDC and SSI*	School lunches	Public housing

*Also includes other cash assistance programs.
Source: Statistical Abstract of the U.S., 1990, table 579.

Actually, AFDC benefits in real dollars have decreased dramatically since 1970, yet the AFDC rolls have increased equally dramatically, especially during the 1970s. Moreover, the rising unemployment in the mid-1970s and 1980s and the decline in real wages have created more poverty, aside from the question of welfare benefits. And, there is no evidence that welfare causes fathers to leave their homes or unwed women to have babies, although it does encourage unwed mothers to establish separate residences rather than live with their parents.[47] The current system does clearly discourage part-time work, because women trying to get back in the labor force this way usually lose their welfare benefits and medical insurance, thus ending up worse off than if they did not work at all.

Another argument is that our current welfare system does not impose enough obligations on the recipients, that welfare does not make it clear that in an organized society one has obligations as well as rights—obligations to learn enough to support oneself, to work, to support one's family, and to be law abiding. To the extent that the welfare system erodes these obligations, then, in this view the system is eroding important values that are necessary for individuals to be productive members of society.[48]

Are Programs for the Poor Too Costly?   We have seen no scientific study of this attitude, but the average citizen appears to think that programs for the poor are

Source: By permission of Mike Luckovitch and Creators Syndicate.

FOCUS ON AN ISSUE

What Should We Do About Hunger in America?

In 1991, one out of every eight American children went hungry each day because their families could not afford to buy enough food. An equal number did not get enough to eat some of the time. These children, not surprisingly, tended to be sick, have trouble learning and paying attention, and miss school often. Poverty is taking its toll on America's children. But what can be done about it?

The major federal programs to combat hunger are federally supported, free and reduced-price school lunches for poor children and the **Food Stamp program.** With cutbacks in domestic programs in the 1980s, the number of children receiving free and reduced-price school lunches decreased. Only 2 million children of the 12 million who go hungry all or some of the time receive these lunches.

The Food Stamp program, for families and individuals, gives poor people coupons redeemable in grocery stores for food. The stamps may be used only to purchase unprepared food and cannot be used for eating out or for toilet or kitchen items, liquor, or tobacco. The only eligibility requirement for food stamps is to be poor.

The program, established nationwide in 1971, was spurred by an investigation of hunger in America demonstrating that tens of thousands of Americans were malnourished and many suffered from retarded growth, anemia, protein deficiencies, high rates of infant mortality, scurvy and rickets (from inadequate vitamin C and milk), and an impaired ability to learn. In other words, this "other nation" of the poor were subject to the same diseases and conditions that most Americans thought affected only poor people in Africa or Asia.

The establishment of a Food Stamp program also had support from those who saw it as one way to deal with the food surplus problem. Food stamps would allow more

A jobless breadwinner in Texas.

people to buy more food, and this would ultimately increase farm prices. For this reason the program was given to the Department of Agriculture to administer.

The Food Stamp program grew tremendously, but like the school breakfast and lunch programs it was cut back during the 1980s.

Despite public stereotypes that many food stamp benefits go to the nonpoor, analyses of the program have shown that most of the recipients are the poorest of the poor. In 1985, the average household income of users was $6,200.[1] Most of the recipients did not own a car, a home, or any other assets.

There is little doubt that food stamps helped raise the level of health and nutrition among the very poor and that cutbacks are creating more hungry people. In the first six

huge parts of the federal budget. In fact, while programs for the poor are not small change, they pale in comparison to spending on the middle class through Social Security and Medicare. The cost of AFDC, SSI, food stamps, and Medicaid amounts to only about 6% of the federal budget, compared to Medicare, which is 8%, and Social Security, which is over 22%. The military budget, now about 20% but during the Reagan years as high as 30% of the budget, overshadows all

social programs except Social Security. The MX missile program alone cost more than what we spend annually on AFDC.

Are Programs for the Poor Efficient?   A possibly more telling criticism of programs for the poor is that they are inefficient; for the money spent, the programs are not accomplishing what they should.

years of the program malnutrition among the poor decreased, and they had far fewer diseases caused by poor nutrition.[2]

Do we need the Food Stamp program and the other programs to provide food for poor adults and children? Consider these questions concerning what government should do about hunger.

Do We Have an Obligation to Keep People from Being Malnourished?

On the basis of their religious and ethical beliefs, people argue that we do have such an obligation. Supporters of democratic values agree. A democracy can function only when it has citizens who are able to take part, even if only indirectly and sporadically, in political affairs. A substantial minority mentally and physically disabled by hunger is not going to contribute to a well-functioning democracy. Such a group is also not going to be contributing at their full capacity to the economic development of our nation either. Some feel an obligation to the poor out of self-interest. It is in the interests of those better-off in society to keep those at the bottom from becoming too discontented.

On the other hand, a purely capitalist perspective might lead one to argue that while individuals may feel it appropriate to help others less fortunate than they are, government should not do so. From this perspective, private charity, not government help, is the only appropriate response.

If Government Does Help, What Is the Best Way?

To diminish malnutrition, should government simply give the poor more financial aid and let them spend it as they see fit? Or should the poor be given aid that can be used only to buy food, such as food stamps?

On the one hand, the poor should not be treated like children. Adults in poor families should be allowed to decide how they spend their family income and not be made more dependent on government than they already are.

Some may not spend it "wisely" as the larger public might define it, but neither do all other Americans. Then, too, the coupons themselves are a sort of stigma. Some people, particularly the needy elderly in rural communities, are too proud to use the stamps.

On the other hand, giving the poor food stamps ensures that money will be used for food. Extra money cannot be demanded by a landlord for rent, spent on other needed items, or wasted. Some, but not all, who argue in favor of food stamps rather than increased cash aid think the stigma of food stamps is good. It might deter some people from asking for aid when they do not really need it.

Who Should Get Food Stamp Help?

Most people seem to agree we should target food aid to pregnant women and to children. But what about other groups? The largest controversy surrounds those who are "temporarily" poor, people who are recently unemployed, those who are on strike and have no income, and students. If eligibility for food stamps means having very few assets, people temporarily down on their luck might not qualify. They might have a home, car, and some furniture but no current income. Is it a wise government policy to tell them they must sell their home, car, and other assets, use the funds, and then be eligible for food stamps? Some argue yes, that government aid should be only a last resort. Others argue no because that kind of disruption might cause more serious problems than unemployment.

Like other social programs, programs to combat hunger are beset by continuing controversy and declining budgets. Yet the problem of hunger in America is real and growing.

1. "Receipt of Selected Noncash Benefits," *Current Population Reports,* Consumer Income Series, P-60, no. 155 (1987).
2. Nick Katz, *Hunger in America* (New York: The Field Foundation, 1979). See also *Washington Post National Weekly Edition,* March 18, 1985, p. 27.

First, despite what is being spent on the programs, millions of poor, especially the working poor and their children and the childless poor, are not covered, as we saw in figure 5.[49]

Second, the programs are uncoordinated. Food stamps, SSI, Medicaid, and AFDC are administered by different federal agencies. In addition, responsibility for the programs is divided between the states and the national government.

Our attitudes toward the poor also lead to inefficiency. We do not want the poor to starve, but we also do not want to make government help too easy. We try to make the system fair and to give applicants full information and rights of appeal. Yet we want to reduce waste and to make sure no one receives benefits who is not both deserving and eligible (see table 3).

Every step we take to construct a system that screens out 100% of ineligibles also creates a system

The Ways of Welfare

Mrs. Santana, a New York welfare mother, had decided to move to another apartment and needed permission from the welfare agency. At 9:45 Mrs. Santana and Gabriel (her son) arrived at the welfare center. At 2:00, Mrs. Santana's name was called over a loudspeaker. After Mrs. Santana explained where she wanted to move and why, the social worker told her that "no one had been able to find her case record, that the rent ($195 in New York City in 1973 for a family of five) sounded excessive to her, and that she should return in a few days with some valid reason for moving.

The following Monday she returned. After another long wait, a male welfare worker escorted Mrs. Santana to his desk. When he asked her why she wanted to move, she said nothing about wanting to be nearer her friends and relatives. She just said that there were bad people in her building trying to foist drugs on her children. Years of dealing with welfare had taught her what welfare wanted to hear. The man nodded sympathetically. The welfare worker said that before he could approve the move Mrs. Santana would have to produce a two-year lease for the apartment. On Tuesday, Mrs. Santana obtained a two-year lease. She took it to the welfare center in the afternoon. Another worker—the third in a row that Mrs. Santana had never seen before—told her that the lease looked all right, but that she would have to bring in a copy of the broker's license before she could move. Mrs. Santana spent most of Wednesday obtaining a copy of the broker's license.

A few days later, when she returned to the center, the man to whom she handed the copy of the broker's license reviewed the matter and informed her she needed still another piece of paper: a declaration from the broker that there was no conflict of interest between him and the landlord.

Families often endure long waits for welfare.

Mrs. Santana sighed and observed to the man that this was the fourth time she had come to the welfare center about the move. She wasn't complaining, she was just stating a fact. The worker said to her, in a nasty tone, "I don't care if you come here 15 times. It's not my problem. You people always think you can get something for nothing." Mrs. Santana is a cheerful, considerate, unmalicious woman. Most people with whom she comes in contact respond warmly to her good nature. She was unprepared for the man's harsh attitude, and was stunned by his harsh words. Impulsively, she tore up the broker's license, threw it into a nearby wastebasket, called the man the worst obscenities she could think of—in English, so he would be certain to understand them—and walked out of the center.

Source: Reprinted in condensed form from Susan Sheehan, *A Welfare Mother* (Boston: Houghton Mifflin, 1976), pp. 61–63.

with ever greater amounts of red tape. More regulations defining eligibility and payment levels lead to more forms to fill out, the need for more government employees to read and process the forms, and more time spent on each case. Ultimately, then, attempting to screen out every ineligible person increases the cost of the program and the likelihood of errors in payments.

Thus, these programs create a paradox. The more we struggle to make them error and fraud proof, the

more complex they get and the more likely error is to creep in. But reducing their complexity and the demands that recipients continually prove eligibility lead to charges that people are being encouraged to go on welfare.

Reforming Welfare for the Poor

For many years, policymakers could reach no consensus on what should be done about AFDC. Conserva-

Table 3 ■ The Public Believes Welfare Recipients Should Live Simply

	Percentage Saying Welfare Recipients Should Have:
Two to three changes of everyday clothing and one "good" outfit	96
Telephone	89
Black-and-white television	79
Health insurance	75
Used car	68
Meal at fast-food restaurant once a week	66
More than one radio	63
Attend movies once a week	51
More than two to three changes of clothing and one "good" outfit	25
Color television	22
Stereo	7
More than one telephone in household	5
Meal at nice restaurant once a week	5
VCR or television recording equipment	0
New car	0

Source: Heritage Foundation Poll, *Washington Post National Weekly Edition*, September 23, 1985, p. 38. "In your opinion, should those recipients who are on public assistance receive enough assistance to enable them to afford any of the following household items?"

tives generally argued for mandatory work or no aid for adults on AFDC, while liberals argued for a guaranteed annual income program with few strings attached. Over the last few years, however, a modest consensus about appropriate strategies for welfare reform developed around three key points.

Consensus. The consensus, written into a welfare reform bill in 1988, incorporated the following ideas:

1. We should require work or work training by adults on AFDC (almost all of whom are women), called **workfare.** The consensus about requiring work has developed because societal norms about women working have changed. When AFDC was established, most

women did not work outside the home. Now that most women of all classes do, there is less resistance to requiring welfare women to work. As Daniel Moynihan said, "A program designed to pay mothers to stay at home with their children cannot succeed when we now observe most mothers going to work."[50]

Requiring welfare women to work meets the criticism that welfare has absolved recipients of obligations to the larger society. Workfare forms a sort of social contract, obligating the recipient to become part of the working class but obligating the government to help the recipient.

Workfare sounds good, but there are unresolved issues. We have to make work pay.[51] Many women on welfare are the least employable people in our work force. Some are school dropouts with no job training or experience. Jobs for such people are not easy to find, and jobs paying a living wage are nearly impossible to find (see figure 6). Thus, stating a work requirement and actually placing people in jobs are two different things. This leads to the second element of the developing consensus.

2. Government must provide assistance designed to allow welfare mothers to be financially better off by working. The most successful workfare programs provide job training, money for transportation to work, day-care services for children, and continuation of health insurance for the family. This latter is very important because AFDC families are eligible for Medicaid. In many states, those who leave AFDC lose their Medicaid eligibility. Most jobs available to unskilled workers do not have fringe benefits like health insurance.

3. We need some sort of national "family policy." This rather nebulous concept focuses on providing incentives for families to stay together. If that fails, supporters of family policy want to make sure that men support their children. Many AFDC families would not be on the rolls if fathers paid their court-ordered child support. In other cases, mothers lack the means to even go to court. Thus, devising a mechanism to mandate child support payments from all fathers who have incomes is another aspect of welfare reform.

The welfare reform legislation enacted in 1988 tries to implement these ideas. It requires states to provide assistance to poor two-parent families if they meet other guidelines, thus providing an incentive for the family to stay together (formerly, only about half

Figure 6 ■ Working at a Minimum Wage Job No Longer Is Enough to Support a Family

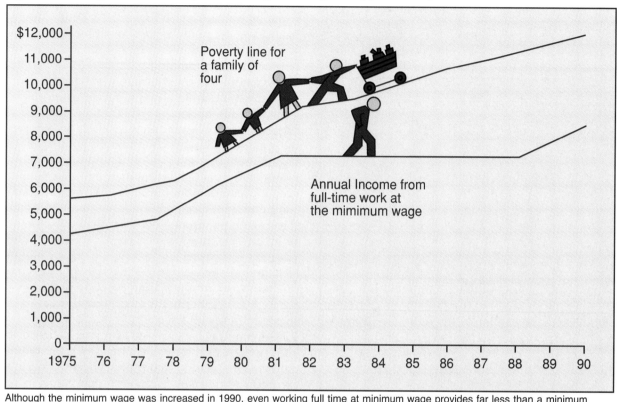

Although the minimum wage was increased in 1990, even working full time at minimum wage provides far less than a minimum standard of living.

the states provided welfare to husband and wife families). The act requires at least one parent to work at least 16 hours a week in these two-parent welfare households. In one-parent families, a woman must work or be enrolled in job training or education if her children are at least three years old. Finally, the legislation includes provisions for a tougher attempt to withhold child support payments from the paychecks of absent fathers.

The act sounds good, but the real question is how much money will be invested in carrying it out. Finding work and providing meaningful job training take money, and little new money is being put into the welfare reform. In addition, the implementation of the act does not require states to put the new work and training rules into effect for all their clients; only a few will come under the new rules in the next few years. Thus, although most people would agree the welfare reform is a step in the right direction, it is only a small step and its consequences remain to be seen.

Moreover, fundamental issues remain to be resolved. One is whether the federal government should be the employer of last resort. In other words, if a person on welfare cannot find a job in the private sector, should government guarantee a job? Some say that this would be an excellent policy, given the work that needs to be done in our schools, public buildings, day-care centers, and so forth. Making the government the employer of last resort increases the cost of the program, however.

Another issue is when women should be required to go to work. When their youngest child is three months old? a year? three years? Some argue that the age should be around three months; that raises the cost for day care but ensures that the women will be integrated into the work force faster. Others object to forcing mothers to leave young children.

Another issue involves helping those not even eligible for AFDC. Workfare does nothing for men who are the unemployed fathers of children on welfare. A

The Senator and an Advocate of Rugged Individualism

Mr. President, as a senator from the state of Ohio, I receive almost daily letters from constituents in my state denouncing price controls and price supports for farm products, and all welfare legislation. During the last two days, we have heard more talk in Washington to the effect that citizens are sick and tired of interference by the federal government in the daily lives of the people of our country.

In that connection I should like to tell a story about a young man who lived with his parents in a low-cost federal housing project in Hamilton County, Ohio.

He attended public school, rode the free school bus, enjoyed the free lunch program. Following graduation from high school, he entered the Army and upon discharge kept his National Service Life Insurance, as all of us who were in the armed services do, or should do. He then enrolled in an Ohio university, receiving regularly his GI check. Upon graduation, he married a Public Health nurse, bought a farm in southern Ohio with an FHA loan, and became a wheat farmer in my state. Later going into the feed and hardware business in addition to his farming, he secured help from the Small Business Administration when his business faltered. His first baby was born in the county hospital. This was built, in part, with federal funds. Then he bought considerable additional acreage adjoining the farm and obtained emergency feed from the government. He then put part of his land under the Soil Bank Program and used the payments from now growing crops

to help pay part of his debts. His parents, elderly by now, were living comfortably in the smaller of his two farm houses, using their Social Security and Old Age Assistance Check [now SSI]. Though electricity was at first lacking, the REA supplied the lines, and a loan from the Farmers Home Administration helped clear the land and secure the best from it. A Department of Agriculture agent suggested building a pond, and the government stocked it with fish for my constituent. The government guaranteed him a sale from his farm products. The county public library delivered books to his farm door. He, of course, banked his money in an institution which a government agency had insured up to $10,000 a depositor.

As the community grew, he signed a petition seeking federal assistance in developing an industrial project to help the economy of his area. About that time he purchased business and real estate at the county seat aided by a Federal Housing Administration loan.

He wrote me, as one of his two United States senators.

I believe in rugged individualism. People should stand on their own two feet, not expect government aid. I stand on my own two feet. I oppose all those socialistic trends you have been voting for and demand return to the free-enterprise system of our forefathers. I and my neighbors intend to vote against you next year.

Senator Stephen Young of Ohio

Source: Congressional Record 109, May 23, 1963, p. 9294.

---

major reason for rising rates of teenaged pregnancy and female-headed families in the black ghettos is the lack of employment opportunities for young black men. With unemployment rates over 30%, these men have little incentive to marry and undertake obligations to a family that they in all likelihood can never support. A workfare program for unemployed men is something that is not even contemplated by most welfare reformers, however. Workfare sounds good, but there are unresolved

Social Welfare for the Well-Off _____

Programs for the poor often produce outrage; even Medicare and other middle-class programs sometimes

are subject to scrutiny. But programs for the well-off are subjected to public debate less frequently, perhaps because benefits for the wealthy are less obvious and more diverse than benefits for the poor.

Tax Breaks

The biggest subsidies for the better-off often appear as tax benefits rather than as payment programs. The tax benefits for people who buy homes cost the United States Treasury over twice as much as AFDC payments. Because of tax benefits, households in the $50,000 and over income bracket, for example, can average a housing subsidy of nearly $2,000, whereas those in households earning less than $10,000 can average only a $211 subsidy.[52] Indeed, most of our

Figure 7 ■ A Comparison of the Cost of Programs for the Poor and Selected Tax Breaks for Middle-Income Individuals and the Rich

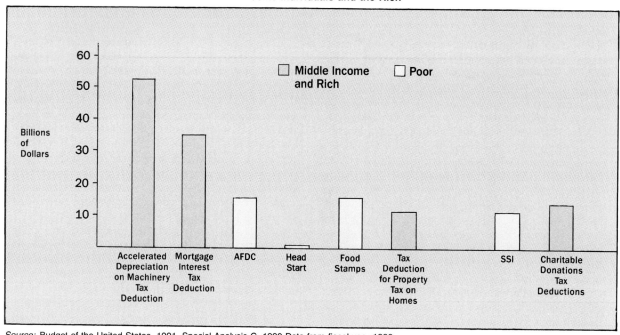

Source: Budget of the United States, 1991, Special Analysis G, 1990 Data from fiscal year 1990.

$40 billion housing subsidies annually go to middle- and upper-income people.

The tax write-off for property taxes on homes costs the taxpayers about as much as SSI, and tax write-offs for charitable deductions were about the same as the cost of food stamps (see figure 7). Tax breaks for corporations cost the Treasury billions of dollars more.

Farm Subsidies

Payments to the better-off segment of society are not just through tax breaks.

Agricultural subsidies have become a large part of the federal budget, and farming is undoubtedly the most heavily subsidized occupation in America. At a cost of nearly $50 billion each year, farm subsidies are larger than payments for AFDC, yet there are only about 1 million farmers (that have sales of $10,000 or more).

Farm subsidies occur because government pays producers of a particular commodity (e.g., corn, wheat, honey, or rice) more than the market price commands. Since the government pays more than the market price, farmers sell their crops to the government in return for the higher price. Farmers are also paid for not producing. For example, after accumulating thousands of tons of cheese, butter, and dried milk, Congress decided to pay dairy farmers to get out of business and stay out for five years. Thousands accepted at a cost of $1.8 billion to the federal government. We pay cotton farmers nearly $1 billion a year. Indeed, in some years during the 1980s, the federal government was contributing over half of all farmers' income, as high as 70% in some farm states. In theory, farm subsidies are not subsidies for the rich. But the subsidies go to wealthy farmers more than to small or middle-income farmers. In 1987, farmers with sales over $500,000 averaged over $60,000 in payments and over $100,000 in loans from Uncle Sam.[53] Pay-

Welfare Fraud

The "welfare queen," living high on the hog at taxpayers' expense, is a popular figure in American folklore. In fact, however, this kind of welfare fraud is quite rare. A study by the Department of Health and Human Services determined that only 3% of the waste and fraud in welfare programs could be attributed to clients. The rest was a result of management inefficiencies, fraud by others involved in welfare programs (such as doctors and hospitals), and failure of state legislatures and Congress to pass legislation enabling managers to control costs in programs like Medicaid.

Errors are more common than fraud. For example, in 1988, payment errors in AFDC were estimated at over 6%, a significant decrease from the 16% in 1973. Food stamp "over issuances" are greater but about on a par with error rates in other programs such as government payments to farmers.

Why do these errors occur? Minimizing fraud and errors costs money. A study by the Agriculture Committee concluded that a complete verification of food stamp applications would take 12 hours and cost eight times as much as it would save.

Minimizing waste and fraud means hassling clients and caseworkers, who are already overburdened. It also means decreasing service. Most people in agencies serving the poor define "helping the poor" as their appropriate mission and often resent extra hassles for them. One welfare worker asked

18 of his clients if they were cheating, and 12 said yes. They were not "welfare queens" but they had failed to report when a child moved out of the house or took a job or did not count their own irregular income, such as from baby-sitting. The caseworker did not report them because he feels that welfare grants are so low that clients could not live on them.

Errors also occur because the programs are large, fragmented, and complex: millions of people are in the programs, their circumstances are constantly changing, and the regulations are incredibly detailed, partially due to their intergovernmental status. One study showed that eligibility and payments were governed by over 2,000 pages of regulations, with more added each week. It is obvious that caseworkers cannot apply every rule to every particular circumstance of each client. They would never be able to handle their workload. Clients too make honest mistakes; over 50% of the mothers in AFDC do not have a high school education, and many have less than a ninth-grade one. Given the complexity of the rules, it is not surprising so many errors are found.

Source: Information in this box is drawn from John D. Young, "Reflections on the Root Causes of Fraud, Abuse, and Waste in Federal Social Programs," *Public Administration Review* 43 (July/August 1983); 362–69; *Common Cause* (May/June 1983): 39; Associated Press, January 5, 1983; Susan Sheehan, *A Welfare Mother* (Boston: Houghton Mifflin, 1976), p. 31; J. Gardiner and T. Lyman, *The Fraud Control Game: State Responses to Fraud and Abuse in Welfare and Medicaid* (Bloomington, Ind.: Indiana University Press, 1984).

---

ments over $1,000,000 are not unusual, leading farm state senator James Exon (D-Neb.) to call this "a major national disgrace."[54]

Other Programs for the Rich

Though the people of the western United States like to think of themselves as self-reliant, they spend billions of dollars of federal money to move and store water. Most water project costs are never repaid. For example, the water brought to California by the $8.8 billion California Central Valley Irrigation Project has created wealth for huge corporate as well as individual farms. But of the $36,000 cost per acre, the irrigators returned only $527 per acre to the government.[55]

Because of federal subsidies, water is cheap and consequently, waste is endemic. Golf courses water

their greens, suburbanites their lawns, and most important, farmers grow water-intensive crops, sometimes to be bought by the federal government through subsidies. Ironically, the most water used by California farmers is by those growing crops that can be grown more economically elsewhere, such as alfalfa, cotton, pasture for cows and sheep, and rice, which normally is only grown in very wet climates. These crops use far more water than the grapes, nuts, oranges, strawberries, and tomatoes we associate with California farming.[56]

At a cost of $17 billion annually, military pensions cost considerably more than AFDC payments. David Stockman, former President Reagan's budget director, called them a "scandal," partly because the typical beneficiary starts collecting at age 41. More than 60% of these benefits are paid to individuals in the richest

20% of the population. The bottom 20% get only 2% of the pension benefits.[57]

Conclusion: Are Social Welfare Programs Responsive?

Our social welfare system is extremely complex. The major beneficiaries of direct income support programs are the elderly of all classes, while programs for the poor are a much smaller part of all social welfare payments. Many programs also provide support for middle- and upper-income groups, including direct income supplements, tax breaks, and support for services largely used by the nonpoor.

These programs reflect the responsiveness of government to different groups. Most taxpayers define themselves as middle income, and they support services for themselves and others like them. Benefits to the upper classes are tolerated to a large extent because many of them go unnoticed or because the groups receiving them are powerful and respected in society. Those that do not go unnoticed, such as tax breaks, are resented, however.

Programs for the poor are both obvious and unpopular. The poor, although a sizable proportion of

Growing rice in the California desert—at taxpayer's expense.

the population, do not have the status or organization to win public support for programs benefiting them. In recent hard times, when support was most needed, programs for the poor took the brunt of budget cuts.

Not all Americans view politics only in terms of what they get. In the past, many religious, labor, civic, and business groups have rallied to the side of the poor. Now, some of these groups and others of the nonpoor are confronting the problems that the 1980s spawned. The nonpoor are finding out that the growth of the urban underclass harms not only those in it but also other citizens, who must pay for new jails, who are increasingly unable to buy reasonably priced health insurance, whose children are exposed to drug sellers, who see homeless on their way to work and in their neighborhoods, and who, in many cities, have become afraid to walk in their own neighborhoods or take public transportation. Businesses are discovering that the decay of public services, particularly schools, increases their costs when workers are ill educated and trained. Extreme inequality is exacerbating our racial problems too. Some blacks believe that the failure of government to deal with drugs and crime in inner-city ghettoes is part of a genocidal plot, while some whites see these same problems and use them to denounce civil rights and welfare. Increasing economic inequality seems to undermine our ability to deal with either poverty or racial issues.

But can we generate the will to act to save a generation of millions of children whose environments now provide them with little chance of developing into productive citizens? So far, we have not. We seem to have stopped trying to solve domestic problems. The problem is not money. We spent more in the first 28 hours of the Persian Gulf War than the federal government spends in a year for maternal and child health; we spent more in four days of that war than for Head Start in an entire year.[58] The money is there for programs we think are important. Thus, our social welfare policies illustrate the popular, if ungrammatical, saying: "Them that has, gets." Social welfare policies illustrate again that government is most responsive to those who are most organized and have the most resources.

EPILOGUE

Hatch Helps to Kill the Bill

Along with most other Republicans, Orrin Hatch decided to try to kill the bill. Using a variety of delaying tactics, they stalled the bill until the Democratic leaders called for a "cloture" vote, a vote to shut off debate on the bill and take a vote. Though 50 voted for cloture, 60 were needed, and with senators eager to return to their districts to campaign, the bill was dead for the 1988 session. Hatch was not among the 5 Republicans who voted for cloture. The vote seemed to confirm Pat Schroeder's (D-Colo.) comment that "There's no capital city in the world that talks more about family and does less."[59]

But the story was not over. After the election, Hatch, Barbara Mikulski, chair of the Labor Committee's Subcommittee on Children, and Christopher Dodd, the sponsor of the bill, worked out a series of compromises. A new ABC bill was one of the first introduced in 1989, joined by a proposal for a tax credit to help families pay for day care. Though both houses approved day-care bills in 1989, they could not reach agreement on details. Finally, at the end of the 1990 session, Congress passed the first significant child-care legislation in 19 years. The bill gave tax credits to low-income families for child care and grants and matching money to states to help pay for child care for lower income families, both those on welfare and those not. The bill also provided tax credits for poor families to purchase health insurance for their children.

In the end, Hatch voted against the bill. Because it was part of a much larger package designed to re-

Source: © 1989 Boston Globe. Reprinted by permission of Los Angeles Times Syndicate.

duce the deficit and raise revenues, it is not clear whether he favored or opposed the much changed child-care bill.

The program begins to deal with problems faced by children. Still, as Marian Wright Edelman, the director of the Children's Defense Fund, laments: "Children are dying of poverty every day in this country. They die in accidents that occur when no adult is watching over them; they die at birth, because of insufficient or nonexistent prenatal health care; they die of malnutrition or drugs, or preventable disease—but the root cause is poverty."[60]

KEY TERMS

Social Security

social insurance

Medicare

Medicaid

Food Stamp program

health maintenance organizations (HMOs)

medically indigent

feminization of poverty

AFDC

SSI

means test

workfare

farm subsidies

FURTHER READING

General

Michael Harrington, *The New American Poverty* (New York: Holt, Rinehart and Winston, 1984). *Harrington's earlier classic, The Other America* (New York: Macmillan, 1962) *alerted many Americans, including President Kennedy, to the extent of poverty in the 1950s. This newer book updates our knowledge of the extent of poverty and who is most likely to suffer from it.*

Lawrence Mead, *Beyond Entitlement* (New York: Free Press, 1986). *A critique of the welfare system for the poor from the perspective that individuals should have a sense of obligation to society as well as rights as citizens within it.*

Charles Murray, *Losing Ground: American Social Policy, 1950–1980* (New York: Basic Books, 1984). *Argues that social welfare programs for the poor have made things worse, not better.*

John E. Schwarz, *America's Hidden Success: A Reassessment of Twenty Years of Public Policy,* 2nd ed. (New York: Norton, 1988). *Argues that the Great Society programs of the 1960s and 1970s were largely successful in reducing poverty and achieving other goals.*

Topical

Joseph Califano, *America's Health Care Revolution: Who Lives? Who Dies? Who Pays?* (New York: Random House, 1986). *A former secretary of health and human services argues that America's health-care system is both wasteful and inadequate, providing too much for some and too little for others.*

Leon Dash, *When Children Want Children* (New York: Morrow, 1988). *A depressing account of some of the reasons for teenaged pregnancy based on the author's two-year investigation, living and talking with people in an urban slum.*

Nicholas Lemann, *The Promised Land* (New York: Knopf, 1991). *A readable account of the black urban underclass, told through the story of individuals who moved north to escape brutal conditions in Mississippi.*

Clifton Luttrell, *The High Cost of Farm Welfare* (Washington, D.C.: Cato Institute, 1989). *Taxing the poor to pay the rich through farm subsidies.*

Susan Sheehan, *Kate Quinton's Days* (New York: Houghton Mifflin, 1984). *An account of the life of one elderly, disabled woman and her dealings with the social welfare institutions designed to help her.*

William J. Williams, *The Truly Disadvantaged: The Inner-City, the Underclass and Public Policy* (Chicago: University of Chicago Press, 1987). *Argues that the worsening plight of the black underclass is due to the changing structure of the national economy, which is increasing the number of poorly paying jobs, and to the success of the black middle class, who when they leave the ghetto leave an ever more concentrated underclass behind.*

NOTES

1. *Congressional Quarterly Weekly Report,* July 2, 1988, p. 1834.
2. Spencer Rich, "More Kids Live in One-Parent Household," *Washington Post National Weekly Edition,* March 20–26, 1989, pp. 2934–39.
3. See Julie Kosterlitz, "Not Just Kid Stuff," *National Journal,* November 19, 1988, pp. 2934–29; Calvin Tomkins, "A Sense of Urgency," *New Yorker,* March 27, 1989, pp. 48–74; Ellen Goodman, "Tough Look at Spending on Children," *Lincoln Star,* March 21, 1989, p. 8.
4. "The Emerging Child Care Issue," *Time,* May 16, 1988, p. 42.
5. Julie Rovner, "Democrats Lining Up Behind 'Family' Banner," *Congressional Quarterly Weekly Report,* January 30, 1988, p. 188.
6. Antifeminist Phyllis Schlafly, quoted in "The Emerging Child Care Issue."
7. Patricia Dunn, "The Reagan Solution for Aiding Families with Dependent Children: Reflections of an Earlier Era," in Anthony Champagne and Edward Harpham, eds., *The Attack on the Welfare State* (Prospect Heights, Ill.: Waveland Press, 1984), pp. 87–110.
8. Harrell Rodgers, *The Cost of Human Neglect* (Armonk, N.Y.: M. E. Sharpe, 1982). The full name of Social Security is the Old Age Survivors Disability and Health Insurance Program.
9. Charles Peters, "Tilting at Windmills," *Washington Monthly* (June 1986): 10.
10. Peter Kilborn, "The Temptation of the Social Security Surplus," *New York Times,* December 27, 1988, p. 5.
11. Robert Pear, "U.S. Pensions to Lift Many of the Poor," *New York Times,* December 28, 1988, p. 1.
12. Melinda Upp, "Relative Importance of Various Income Sources of the Aged, 1980," *Social Security Bulletin* 46 (January 1983): 5.
13. Ibid.
14. Jonathan Rauch, "Growing Old," *National Journal,* December 31, 1988, p. 3235.
15. Ibid.
16. Paul Taylor, "Remember the Generation Gap?" *Washington Post National Weekly Edition,* January 20, 1986, p. 24.
17. Paul Taylor, "Like Taking Money from a Baby," *Washington Post National Weekly Edition,* March 4–10, 1991, p. 31.
18. Rodgers, *Cost of Human Neglect,* p. 91. Recent studies show that this continues to be true.
19. Clarke E. Cochran et al., *American Public Policy* (New York: St. Martins, 1982), p. 262. See also Spencer Rich, "Look Again: The Anti-Poverty Programs Do Work," *Washington Post National Weekly Edition,* May 21, 1984, p. 24.
20. Robert Samuelson, "Why Medical Costs Keep Soaring," *Washington Post National Weekly Edition,* December 5–11, 1988.
21. Charles Peters, "Tilting at Windmills," *Washington Monthly* (March 1985): 11.
22. Victor Cohn, "Rationing Our Medical Care," *Washington Post National Weekly Edition,* August 13–19, 1990, p. 11.
23. John Iglehart, "In a Land of Medical Plenty, More and More are Going Hungry," *Washington Post National Weekly Edition,* January 12, 1987, p. 23.
24. Malcolm Gladwell, "Health Insurance Warning Signs," *Washington Post National Weekly Edition,* January 28–February 3, 1991, p. 38.
25. "Health Care Varies With Ability to Pay," *Lincoln Star,* September 12, 1990, p. 30. From an Associated Press report.
26. Barbara Ehrenreich, "Our Health Care Disgrace," *Time,* December 10, 1990, p. 112.
27. David Gordon, "To Have and to Have Not," *Washington Post National Weekly Edition,* November 10, 1986, p. 23; and "Rich Are Richer, Poor Poorer, and Middle Class Is Vanishing," *Lincoln Star,* November 22, 1986; Daniel Patrick Moynihan, "Half the Nation's Children Born without a Fair Chance," *New York Times,* September 25, 1988.

28. Martin Anderson, *Welfare: The Political Economy of Welfare Reform in the U.S.* (Stanford: Hoover Institution, 1978); Richard Margolis, "The Arithmetic of Poverty," *The New Leader,* April 16, 1990, pp. 14–15; Julie Kosterlitz, "Measuring Misery," *National Journal,* August 4, 1990, pp. 1892–96; Jason De Parle, "In Debate Over Who is Poor, Fairness Becomes the Issue," *New York Times,* September 3, 1990, pp. 1, 10.

29. Aaron Freiwald, "Debut of Experimental Poverty Statistics Arouses Suspicions of Future Welfare Cuts," *National Journal,* August 18, 1984, pp. 1562–65.

30. "Share the Wealth," *National Journal,* April 21, 1990, p. 990; Julie Kosterlitz, "What's Fair," *National Journal,* December 8, 1990, p. 2957.

31. David Wessel, "U.S. Rich and Poor Increase in Numbers; Middle Loses Ground," *Wall Street Journal,* September 22, 1986, p. 1.

32. Data on feminization of poverty from Harrell Rodgers, *Poor Women, Poor Families* (Armonk, N.Y.: M. E. Sharpe, 1986) and Bureau of the Census, Current Population Reports, *Characteristics of the Population Below the Poverty Level 1984,* Series P-60, no. 152, 1986.

33. Bureau of the Census, *Demographic and Socioeconomic Aspects of Aging in the United States,* Series P-23, no. 138, U.S. Government Printing Office.

34. George Gilder, *Wealth and Poverty* (New York: Basic Books, 1981), p. 68.

35. Edward Banfield, *The Unheavenly City Revisited* (Boston: Little Brown, 1974). See also Charles Murray, *Losing Ground* (New York: Basic Books, 1984).

36. Michael Harrington, *The Other America: Poverty in the United States* (New York: Macmillan, 1962).

37. Isabel Sawhill, "Poverty and the Underclass," *American Agenda: A Report to the Forty-First President of the U.S.A.* (1988).

38. Gallup Polls, March 1985.

39. *Statistical Abstract of the United States* (Washington, D.C.: Bureau of the Census, 1984).

40. Mark Rank, "Fertility among Women on Welfare," *American Sociological Review* 54 (April 1989): 296–304.

41. Greg J. Duncan, *Years of Poverty, Years of Plenty* (Ann Arbor: Institute for Social Research, University of Michigan, 1983); Spencer Rich, "Who Gets Help and How," *Washington Post National Weekly Edition,* May 15–19, 1989, p. 37; "A Welfare State," *National Journal,* May 13, 1989, p. 1209.

42. "A Welfare State." Higher estimates are made by Anderson in *Welfare,* lower by Duncan in *Years of Poverty.*

43. John Schwartz, *America's Hidden Success,* 2nd ed. (New York: Norton, 1988).

44. Gary Copeland and Kenneth Meier, "Gaining Ground," *American Politics Quarterly* 15 (April 1987): 254–73.

45. Schwartz, *America's Hidden Success.*

46. Murray, *Losing Ground.*

47. Reported in the *Lincoln Star,* March 21, 1987, p. 2.

48. Lawrence Mead, *Beyond Entitlement* (New York: Free Press, 1986).

49. Ibid.

50. Daniel Moynihan quoted in "Fixing Welfare," *Time,* February 16, 1987, p. 20.

51. David Ellwood, *Poor Support* (New York: Basic Books, 1988).

52. Neal Pierce, "Tax Reform Proposal Exposes Subsidies," *Public Administration Times,* May 1, 1985, p. 2.

53. William Robbins, "Costly Farm Price Supports Are under Sharper Scrutiny," *New York Times,* December 5, 1983, pp. 1ff; Ward Sinclair, "Big California Farms Harvest Federal Cash," *Washington Post National Weekly Edition,* January 2, 1984, p. 30; data from Statistical Abstract of the United States, table 1127, 1991, p. 1.

54. Ward Sinclair, "The High Price of American Rice," *Washington Post National Weekly Edition,* July 21, 1986, p. 21; "Urban Solons Want Farm Policy Reforms," *Lincoln Star,* September 8, 1986, p. 1.

55. Molly McGregor, "Irrigation Farming: Subsidizing Mother Nature," *Journal of Freshwater* 6 (1982): 518–21.

56. "Nature Humbles a State of Mind," *New York Times,* February 10, 1991, E3. Marc Reisner, "The Emerald Desert," *Greenpeace,* July/August 1989, p. 7.

57. John Beckerman, "Stockman Is Right: Military Pensions Are a Scandal," *Washington Post National Weekly Edition,* April 1, 1985, p. 25.

58. Marc Kranowsky, "Military Costs Dwarf Domestic Programs," *Lincoln Star,* February 6, 1991, p. 28. This is based on an estimate of the cost of war at $500 million per day.

59. *Congressional Quarterly Weekly Report,* January 30, 1988.

60. Tomkins, *"A Sense of Urgency."*

Economic Policy

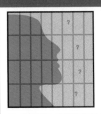

YOU ARE THERE

Stand By Your Man?

You are Newt Gingrich (Ga.), the Republican whip in the House. It is October 1990, and you are facing an important decision: whether or not to support a budget package worked out between the president and congressional leadership.

Though you have been in the House since 1978, you were long considered a gadfly, a conservative ideologue who cared more about getting publicity for your party and conservative causes than for getting legislation passed. Your opinion on pending legislation did not matter much. But in 1989, to the surprise of some, your fellow Republicans in the House chose you to be minority whip, their second most important leadership post. As whip, you are charged with rounding up support for bills supported by the president and the Republican House leadership. Many observers think you were elected whip because you challenged the Democrats aggressively rather than accepting minority status.

The situation facing you requires a simple decision, to vote yes or no. But the economic conditions facing the country are complex. In the 1980s, President Reagan pushed a tax cut through Congress, resulting in the loss of billions of dollars of revenue. At the same time he proposed dramatic spending increases for the military and other increases for entitlement programs such as Social Security, veterans benefits, and Medicare (though he cut some social programs for the poor). The combined effect of lower taxes and higher spending has caused a serious economic problem. Each year the Reagan administration spent $100 to $250 billion more than it received, creating a huge budget deficit. By the end of his second term, Reagan had nearly tripled the national debt. Now, almost 20% of our national budget goes to pay the interest on this debt.

Because of this huge debt, in 1985 Congress passed a bill, the Balanced Budget Act (sometimes called the Gramm-Rudman bill), which required that

Newt Gingrich.

the annual deficit be reduced each year until it disappeared in 1991. This law sounds good, but each year Congress and the president have evaded it, and the deficit has continued to grow. The public wants more government programs but does not want to pay for them, and neither Congress nor the president has been bold enough to tell the public that more programs will require more taxes. Now, in 1990, the economy has turned sour and put increased pressure on the budget. As one observer commented, "The combined executive and legislative branches got this country into such a horrendous fiscal mess over the past decade that they finally have to confront the result of their flight from responsibility."[1]

(continued on next page)

George Bush was elected pledging "no new taxes." His comment, "Read my lips, no new taxes," became a campaign classic. You wholeheartedly endorse this sentiment. Indeed, you have been busy promising campaign donors that you will continue to oppose new or higher taxes.

But since spring, it has been clear that a budget without some new source of revenue would be a budget further in the red than the current year's $250 billion deficit. Though the president proposed a budget, it was widely seen as unrealistic, and Democratic and Republican leaders sniped at each other over alternatives for several months. Finally White House and congressional leaders decided to try to negotiate their differences and began meeting to try to hammer out a budget that both branches and both parties could agree on. You thought the talks were "baloney," but as a Republican leader, you were included in them.[2]

The talks started badly. Bush proposed to reduce the capital gains tax, a tax that falls largely on the wealthy, and to cut some programs, though he offered few specifics. The Democrats, pointing out that taxes on the wealthy fell during the 1980s while taxes on the middle income and poor rose, opposed the capital gains tax cut. They also opposed cutting most social programs. The Democrats did not propose new taxes, fearing that Republicans like Gingrich would label them "big spenders."

Although the President adamantly opposed any new or higher taxes, he changed his mind after seeing gloomy budget forecasts; he admitted that new taxes were needed. Immediately most Republicans were in an uproar, since Bush had not consulted them. You and others attacked him for going back on his campaign pledge, and after a few days he seemed to change his mind.

Even though almost all negotiators agreed that some new revenue sources were needed, partisan conflict often caused the talks to degenerate into shouting matches.[3] Moreover, the Republicans and Democrats were both divided amongst themselves as to what to tax and what to cut. In the meantime, the president, by one count, changed his mind five times in three days about new taxes.[4] Neither the president, the congressional Democrats, nor the congressional Republicans wanted to take the lead in coming up with a realistic budget proposal that would include significant new taxes or significant spending

cuts because they feared that the other party would use it against them in the next campaign. Tensions were further inflamed by the high-handed behavior of the White House negotiators, Budget Chief Richard Darman and Chief of Staff John Sununu. Sununu, especially, insulted congressional leaders of both parties. Democratic Senator Robert Byrd (W.Va.) labeled Sununu and Darman "arrogant" and "rude." Senate Republican leader Robert Dole was also angered, and when the two men tried to sit at a table with congressional leaders he informed them, "Staff doesn't sit with the leadership."[5]

Though a Republican, you are often in opposition to the president and to the more moderate members of the Republican delegation. You earned the dislike of Republican as well as Democratic negotiators by not agreeing that new taxes were needed. In fact, during the negotiating sessions you called for tax cuts and blamed the Democrats for the recession.[6] You also annoyed your colleagues by reading books and magazines during bargaining sessions. You have been prominently featured in news coverage of the talks; one newsmagazine called you the "wild card."

Finally, the end of the government's fiscal year approached. Without a new budget, government operations could halt, inconveniencing millions of people and forcing government employees to go without pay. The media increasingly criticized both Congress and the president for their inaction. Given this pressure, the negotiators reached a compromise. They agreed to a small deficit reduction of $40 billion (in light of the projected $250 to $300 billion deficit) and some program cuts. The president gave up his insistence on reducing the capital gains tax, while Democrats gave up their insistence on making the increased taxes **progressive,** that is, taxes that would hit the rich harder than the poor. The Democrats agreed to a series of tax increases on beer, wine, cigarettes, and gasoline, which would hit the poor and middle-income taxpayer proportionally harder. Moreover, Medicare taxes were also to be raised. The rich were hit with some luxury taxes on pleasure boats, furs, and jewelry.

Few people are truly enthusiastic about the budget proposal, but most are relieved that something has been done. The president is lobbying hard for the bill, which must be approved by Congress to take effect.

Now what do you do? You basically oppose the agreement because it does raise taxes and does not significantly cut spending. You also think you might be able to make political capital by opposing the agreement; if Congress does not go along, you hope the public will blame the majority party Democrats for the stalemate. But you realize that the agreement has become the president's budget proposal now, and that if it is defeated, the president's clout will weaken. The negative effects also might spill over to congressional Republicans. The president has put his prestige on the line, and Sununu has threatened that the president would work against those Republicans who do not support the budget package.[7] Despite the threat, you want your party to look strong for the upcoming election.

You also feel pressure because of your leadership position. No longer just a gadfly buzzing here and there and irritating people, you are in a responsible position where you are expected to be a team player. Ordinarily members who participate in negotiations, and especially the leaders, feel obligated to support a proposal. Yet you have never been comfortable just going along or bashful about making waves.

Do you support the president and the agreement you have helped negotiate? Or do you stick to your original ideas and oppose the agreement because of its new taxes?

OUTLINE

Americans pride themselves on their free, private economy. Yet when economic problems occur, they want government to do something. The degree to which government should be involved in the economy is a perennial source of conflict.

Only a few people believe that government should not be involved at all. Most agree, for example, on the following:

1. Government, not volunteer efforts, must pay for a military force. Thus government must tax. We cannot individually decide whether to contribute to maintaining our nation's defense. If we did, some citizens would become "free riders."[8] Without paying, they would benefit from the voluntary contributions of others.
2. The market cannot determine which television or radio company should have the right to broadcast at a specific frequency. If broadcasting companies competed on the same frequency, none would be intelligible to listeners.
3. We cannot let market forces regulating supply and cost of food and lifesaving medicine determine whether some people will starve or die of treatable illnesses. Although many such deaths do occur, they are much less frequent than they would be without government aid to the poor and elderly.

Despite agreement on points such as these, there is much honest disagreement about how far government should go in regulating the economy and altering the distribution of wealth.

Types of Economic Systems

Capitalism

The role of government in the economy largely determines the kind of economic system we have. An economy in which individuals own businesses, factories, and farms is called a free market, free enterprise, or **capitalist economy.**

In a pure capitalist economy, prices, profits, working conditions, and wages would be totally determined by the market. Manufacturers would sell goods at what the market could bear, pay workers as little as possible, and manufacture products as cheaply as possible, concerned with health and safety only to the extent dictated by individual morality and the necessity to maintain consumer loyalty.

The idea that a capitalist economy would promote prosperity was popularized in 1776 by the British economist **Adam Smith** in *The Wealth of Nations.*[9] In his view, as each person seeks to maximize his or her own economic well-being, the collective well-being is enhanced. Businesses become more efficient, sell more at lower cost, hire more workers, and hence promote the economic well-being of the workers as well as the owners.

Socialism

Socialism is another kind of economic system. Although in theory it refers to collective ownership of factories, farms, and businesses by those who work in them, in practice it commonly refers to a system in which government owns the factories, businesses, and farms and has the power to control supply and demand for goods.

Sometimes in American public debate one candidate will accuse another of supporting "socialism"; in this context, socialism is often just a synonym for something a person does not like, especially bigger government.

Mixed Economies

In practice, there are no pure capitalist systems in the world and no pure socialist ones. In the United States, government owns some railroads as well as much land and power-generating dams, for example. It also owned part of the Chrysler Corporation when it was faced with bankruptcy. In other modern societies, such as Britain, France, Sweden, West Germany, and the former Communist nations of Eastern Europe, government has owned airlines, television networks, and telephone systems.

Just as all capitalist nations have socialist components, socialist nations have capitalist ones. Even before the reforms of the late 1980s, which led to Communist governments being swept away across Eastern Europe, most socialist nations found it useful

Adam Smith believed that a free market would best promote efficiency and individual economic well-being.

to tolerate or even encourage some private enterprises, and some, such as Hungary, had quite large private economies.

Most countries, then, have a **mixed economy.** Some are much more capitalist, others more socialist, but all have elements of both.

Government plays a large role in the economies of most mixed systems. For example, government directly influences the behavior of business and industry through regulation and taxation. Even Adam Smith believed that there was always some role for government in a capitalist system, such as to stop one business from dominating the market and to protect the nation against external threats.

Our own system is a mixture of free enterprise and a little government ownership combined with a good deal of government intervention through taxation and regulation.

In nineteenth-century America we had much less government involvement than we do today. We have moved toward a more active government economic role largely because of abuses by big business in the late nineteenth century: child labor was widely used; workers were paid a pittance; filthy and unsafe working conditions (as suggested by the term sweatshop) led to thousands of workers' deaths from industrial accidents; foods and drugs were often unsafe; and markets came to be dominated by a few large producers who controlled prices and wages. All of this produced public outcries, which led to increased government regulation of wages, working conditions, purity of foods and drugs, and much else.

Government also intervenes in the economy by redistributing wealth. By taxing and spending, government can make the rich richer and the poor poorer, or it can make the poor better off at the expense of the rich. Most Western democracies have fairly elaborate social welfare systems that redistribute some wealth from the rich to the poor in order to provide them with a minimal standard of living. In the United States, we do less of this than in most other industrialized nations.

Despite our mixed economy, we have a very individualistic, capitalistic ethic. The idea that individuals, not government, should provide services and that government should be small influences a wide range of public policies. The belief that individuals are poor because of their own failings limits our sense of responsibility to provide support for low-income families. The idea that private business is inherently self-regulating makes it difficult to enact higher standards for worker health and safety. The belief that private profit is not only the most important goal of business, but perhaps the only one, means that those fighting to protect the environment from abuse by industry have a difficult time.

Economic Systems and Political Systems

Economic distinctions between capitalism and socialism are not necessarily linked to gradations in democracy. Capitalist systems are not inevitably democratic. The most democratic systems in the world are mixed economies with strong elements of capitalism (such as Sweden, Britain, and Denmark), but many capitalist systems are undemocratic (the most blatant example being South Africa). Indeed, there is an inevitable tension between capitalism and democracy. The capitalist marketplace rewards and encourages inequities that, if unchecked, threaten democratic beliefs about individual equality. Socialist systems promote equality in wages, but in practice most Socialist systems have tolerated significant disparity in overall standard of living. Socialist theory also advocates democratic control

by workers, but in countries like the Soviet Union and China, the Communist party has used its dictatorial powers to deny individual freedom. Today in Eastern Europe and the Soviet Union, many of the political parties working to establish democratic governments hope to retain some elements of socialism in their economies.

Regulating the Economy ____

Economic cycles of boom and bust have been one of the constants of human history. Good times with rising living standards are followed by bad times when harvests are poor, people go hungry, unemployment is rife, and living standards decline. Until modern times, governments did little to regulate these cycles, although some tried to ease the consequences of the bad times by distributing grain to people who were starving or providing temporary shelters for the homeless. Only recently have governments tried, through economic policies, to prevent these cycles from occurring.

The idea that government intervention could ease the boom and bust cycle of the economy was revolutionary. Classical economists had argued that the market would adjust itself without government action. But in democratic societies, as government became larger and more powerful, people expected government to "do something" to alleviate economic problems.

Economic Problems

One of the familiar economic problems that modern government is expected to "do something" about is unemployment. Even in a "full employment" economy a few people will be out of work—people who quit their jobs to look for others, those just entering the work force, those unable to work, and those who do not want to work for one reason or another. But most Western countries experience periods when there are many people unemployed because the economy does not create enough new jobs. During the peak of the recession in 1981–1982, over 10% of the American work force was unemployed, and many others had only part-time work or had simply quit looking for work altogether. This did not approach the level of the Great Depression (1929–1935), when over one-quarter of the working population were without jobs. (A **depression** is a period of prolonged high unemployment.)

A second recurring economic problem is **inflation**—a condition of increasing prices. People begin to feel that their salaries will never catch up to the prices of goods they buy. So as a dollar becomes worth less, there is little incentive to save and great incentive to borrow. In the late 1950s and early 1960s, inflation in the United States was quite low, as little as 2% or 3% a year, but the Vietnam War and the energy crisis of the early 1970s stimulated a sharp rise. Inflation declined in the late 1980s, but began to rise again in the early 1990s.

Though some economists believe moderate inflation is not a bad thing,[10] many people feel threatened by it. It erodes the value of savings and gives people an incentive to consume rather than save. Bankers hate inflation because the dollar paid back to them in the future is going to be worth a lot less than the dollar

they lend today. Inflation drives interest rates up as banks charge higher and higher interest to compensate for the declining value of the dollar. Credit becomes more expensive, which makes it difficult for businesses and industries to expand. And, of course, inflation is bad because people think it is bad—they worry about it getting out of control.

A third economic problem is stagnant production, that is, the failure of the economy as a whole to produce increasing amounts of goods and services. Two or more consecutive quarters (a quarter is three months), of falling production are known as a **recession.**

Productivity, the amount of goods and services that can be produced by a fixed amount of labor and capital, increases when industries and businesses discover new ways to produce goods and services more efficiently, using less labor or machinery. To be competitive in the world market it is necessary to have a

In Germany in 1923 inflation was so high that a basket of money barely sufficed to buy a few groceries. The inflation was caused by the German government's printing ever more money to repay the victors of World War I the penalties they had assessed. The government finally ended the inflation by issuing new currency, one unit of which was equal to one trillion of the old. This made the lifetime savings of many people worthless.

steadily increasing rate of productivity, that is, for business to become increasingly more efficient. In Japan productivity has been increasing dramatically, but in the United States it has been increasing very slowly.

The ultimate goal in any economy is to have low unemployment, low inflation, and increasing productivity while total economic output grows steadily. Achieving all of this simultaneously is rare, however. Inflation is usually at its lowest when unemployment is high and production sags. Increasing employment often brings high levels of inflation. This means there usually is some trade-off among these three goals.

For example, one method to reduce inflation is to allow unemployment to increase and the economy to slow through fiscal and monetary policies (discussed later). This technique, which puts the burden of reducing inflation on the poor, was used by government to break inflation in the early 1980s.

An alternative means for reducing inflation is to balance the federal budget. This requires either dramatic spending cuts or huge tax increases, neither of which is acceptable to most people. It is politically more difficult for the president and Congress to elect this approach because it places the burden for reducing inflation on middle- and upper-income people, the largest part of the electorate.

Another measure used to reduce inflation is federally mandated ceilings on wages and prices. This requires a government monitoring system and usually meets with strong opposition from both business and labor. Some economists oppose such controls because they believe when the ceilings are lifted, wages and prices will soar. A new inflationary cycle may begin as workers and businesses try to make up lost ground.[11]

Government's Economic Tools

Government has two primary tools to help achieve its economic goals: fiscal policy and monetary policy.

Fiscal Policy. In 1935, John Maynard Keynes published *A General Theory of Employment, Interest and Money,* in which he argued that government could have an important role in shaping the economy.[12] His ideas, which revolutionized thinking about the role of government in the economy, are called, not surprisingly, **Keynesian economics.**

Keynes argued that government could stimulate the economy by increasing spending in a time of high unemployment. This would put more money into the economy, thus stimulating the demand for goods and

John Maynard Keynes's ideas revolutionized economics.

services and, in turn, causing factories to produce more and hire more workers.

Keynes's views ran counter to the conventional wisdom of the time. During the Great Depression, President Hoover believed that if the government went into debt it would make the depression worse, not better. His opponent in the 1932 election, Franklin Roosevelt, also ran on a pledge of a balanced federal budget. It was only after he was elected that Roosevelt adopted the Keynesian idea that government itself could help the nation get out of the depression by borrowing and spending money.

Since then it has been the accepted wisdom that government can have a substantial impact on the economy through its **fiscal policy,** that is, its decisions on how much money it will spend and how much tax it will levy. Increased government spending stimulates the economy and increases employment; lower government spending helps slow the economy and decreases inflation. Tax policy can also help regulate economic cycles. In bad times, when unemployment is high, tax cuts put more money back into the hands of the consumer, thus stimulating private spending and reducing unemployment. Increased taxes take more money out of the hands of the consumer, slow the economy, and thus reduce inflation.

Government's ability to regulate economic activity through spending and taxation, is limited however. Sometimes the economy responds to government changes too quickly, other times not quickly enough. International trends also affect our own economy, as we shall see in the next section.

Then, too, sometimes political factors constrain governments from pursuing needed economic policies. Because of the unpopularity of the Vietnam War, President Johnson did not want to increase taxes to fund it, so the government borrowed money, thus beginning the inflation that plagued us during the 1970s.

Who makes fiscal policy? In the United States, laws regarding taxation and spending are passed by Congress and approved by the president. In making his recommendations to Congress about taxes, spending, and other economic matters, the president is advised primarily by three people: the secretary of the treasury; the head of the Office of Management and Budget (OMB), who is responsible for preparing the annual budget message; and the chair of the Council of Economic Advisers, a group of economists who are specialists in fiscal policy matters. Sometimes, of course, these three advisers to the president are at odds with each other. Economics, like political science, is an inexact science!

Congress has its own fiscal specialists on committees such as Appropriations and Budget and relies heavily on the director of the Congressional Budget Office.

Monetary Policy.   Fiscal policy is one important tool in economic regulation; **monetary policy,** established by the Federal Reserve Board (Fed), is the other. The Fed controls the supply of money in the economy. Its members are appointed by the president for 14-year terms in order to minimize the effect of short-term political considerations on their decisions. The role of the Fed, as the nation's central bank, is crucial. As Will Rogers once said, "There have been three great inventions since the beginning of time: fire, the wheel, and central banking!"

The Fed controls the supply of money in several ways. It can buy and sell hundreds of millions of dollars of treasury notes and bonds. When it buys, it pumps money into other banks; when it sells, it depletes the money reserves of the banks and thus takes money out of the economy. The Fed also changes the interest rates it charges banks to borrow its money.

Low interest rates stimulate borrowing and put more money into the economy. As a last resort, the Fed can increase or decrease the amount of reserves it requires banks to have. If the reserve requirement is increased, banks take money out of circulation to build up their reserves. If the reserve requirement is decreased, banks take money out of the reserve and lend it to customers, thus increasing the money supply.

When the Fed makes money scarce, interest rates go up and the economy slows down. Businesses and industries are not able to borrow money for plant expansion, and production and inflation slow. When the Fed allows more money into the economy, interest rates go down and businesses can borrow for expansion.

Monetary policy is a dry subject, but its effects are dramatic. In the nineteenth century, "tight" money was often the main issue in elections. Today, the chair of the Federal Reserve Board is one of the most powerful people in the country. In 1982, when the Fed tightened the money supply, forcing interest rates down and unemployment and bankruptcy up, one man entered the offices of the Fed and tried to kill its chair.[13] Other groups drew up "wanted" posters for the board members. And still others, thrown out of work or off their farms, killed themselves. Yet, the effects of monetary policy are sometimes hard to predict and control. Like Congress and the president with fiscal policy, the Fed is limited in its ability to regulate economic cycles with monetary policies alone.

In the 1960s economists were optimistic that government could successfully regulate the economy to maintain high levels of employment and reasonable inflation. By the 1970s this confidence disappeared due to **stagflation,** a condition of simultaneous high unemployment and high inflation.

Contrary to Keynesian assumptions, with stagflation levels of unemployment and inflation were high and productivity was low. In the 1970s, neither monetary nor fiscal policies coped well with stagflation.

Managing the Economy for Political Purposes

Policymakers use knowledge of fiscal and monetary policy to improve the economy in election years by trying to increase the income of individual citizens and reduce inflation and unemployment. In his 1978 book, *Political Control of the Economy,* Edward Tufte finds that there is an observable relationship between trying to win elections and the kind of economic policy a president pursues.[14] Real changes in disposable income available to voters tend to be larger in election years than in other years. Unemployment tends to decrease in presidential election years, although not in off-year election years.

This suggests that presidents consciously work to manipulate the economy in ways that will benefit them. It also suggests that the timing of policies is crucially important. For example, the annual growth of the economy during the Carter administration was far higher than during the Reagan administration, yet voters punished Carter for his economic policies and rewarded Reagan for his. Part of the reason (aside from the fact that Reagan helped reduce inflation and Carter did not) was that in the 1980 election year, the economy had started to slump, while in 1984 and 1988, the economy boomed. In other words, voters have short memories. Carter's 1980 defeat and the Republicans' 1984 and 1988 victories had other causes, but economic factors were clearly important.

Cuts in government spending and increases in taxes reduce real personal income, so presidents usually do not make budget cuts or raise taxes in election years. Congress, too, responds to an electoral cycle. Spending on some benefit programs tends to increase somewhat in election years.[15]

Tufte and others have been critical of the use of economic policy for electoral purposes. He uses Nixon's attempt to increase real income before the 1972 election as an extreme example of the negative consequences of such attempts. Nixon attributed his loss to John Kennedy in 1960 to the faltering economy in the last year of the Eisenhower administration in which he was vice president. He was determined not to let the economy defeat him in 1972. So he pumped up the economy through a variety of spending programs and through pressure on the Federal Reserve Board to put more money into the economy. Many economists believe that these actions accelerated inflation.

There are partisan differences in the management of the economy. Conservatives and Republicans tolerate higher unemployment more easily than do liberals and Democrats, whereas liberals and Democrats are more tolerant of inflation.[16] The business and middle-class supporters of the Republican party are more concerned about inflation, whereas the working class have more to fear from unemployment and from attempts to "cure" inflation. Thus Republicans first try to bring down inflation, while Democrats first try to stimulate the economy.[17]

The Federal Reserve Board, although not under the direct control of the president, also tends to act in a partisan way in dealing with inflation and unemployment partially due to informal pressure from the administration. Over the past 30 years, the Fed was more concerned about controlling inflation during Republican administrations than under Democratic administrations. (The Kennedy and Nixon eras were significant exceptions to that generalization, however.[18]) The Federal Reserve Board also pumps up the economy around election time by lowering interest rates and allowing more money to circulate.[19]

The economy has an impact on the vote although it is not as simple as we might suspect. Those who have studied the impact of economic hard times on individual vote choices have reported that how people feel they are doing compared to a year or two before does have some mild influence on their presidential and congressional voting choice. If they feel things are improving, they are somewhat more likely to favor the incumbent; if they believe that their financial situation is eroding, they are somewhat more likely to vote against the incumbent. There is evidence that voters respond to changes in real per capita income in the few months before the election.[20] Voters are more concerned, however, with the state of the overall economy than with their own family's situation. Voters do not seem to respond to changes in unemployment or inflation levels, however. Nor is there much evidence that voters directly retaliate for increased taxes or specific cuts in benefits. Nevertheless, it is clear that economic policies are used for political purposes by members of both parties.

Taxing

Our Tax Burden

"Taxes are what we pay for a civilized society," argued Supreme Court Justice Oliver Wendell Holmes. Governments need revenue to protect their civilization, educate their citizenry, pay postal carriers, provide medical care for Social Security recipients, build roads, and do many other things. The federal government relies largely on borrowing and taxes for its revenue, especially personal income taxes and Social Security taxes (see figure 1).

Figure 1 ■ Federal Revenue Sources, 1992

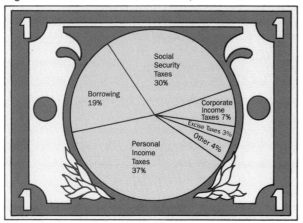

Though this estimated 1992 budget calls for 19% of U.S. income to be derived from borrowing, in past years proposed budgets have been inaccurate because of an unwillingness to budget large deficits. Thus, it is likely that borrowing will account for more than 20% of total revenue by year's end.
Source: Budget of the U.S. Government, 1992, p. 4–3, and *Budget in Brief 1992.*

The proportions shown in figure 1 represent rather substantial changes from previous years. The percent generated by the personal income tax is considerably less than a decade ago, mainly due to the large increase in borrowing and the cuts in income taxes during the Reagan administration. Social Security taxes have increased as a revenue source (they were less than 20% in 1960), corresponding to the increased spending on Social Security and related programs. There have also been dramatic decreases in the proportion of federal revenue contributed by corporate income taxes, which in the 1950s and early 1960s was about 25% of federal revenue.

We often believe that our tax rates are high, yet our tax burden is among the smallest in the industrial world. Reasons for this include our aversion to taxes and big government, our less than comprehensive social welfare system, and the lack of much government ownership of economic enterprises.

Recent Tax Policy

Our tax code is complex. President Franklin Roosevelt once stated that the tax code "might as well have been written in a foreign language," and the laws are dozens of times more complex now.[21] The complexity is because Congress and the president have designed a tax code to achieve a variety of social goals. The government wants to be fair to single people, so it sets tax rates for singles lower than for couples. Congress wants to encourage families where both parents work to have adequate care for their children, so it allows credits for child care. Policymakers want to encourage business investment, so they give credits and deductions for that. (A **deduction** is the amount taxpayers have spent for some item, such as mortgage interest or business equipment, that they are allowed by law to subtract from their income when filing their income tax reports.) Congress believes that voluntary giving to churches, synagogues, and charitable organizations is good, so it creates deductions for that too. Congress wants to help people buy homes and stimulate new housing construction, so deductions are allowed for interest on mortgage payments. Though these and hundreds of other exemptions and deductions may individually be desirable, together they create a tax code that is quite complex and favors the wealthy, who are able to take advantage of more loopholes.

Nonetheless, the tax code is probably somewhat fairer today than a decade ago. In 1986 Congress passed the Tax Reform Act to try to make the income tax structure fairer, simpler, and more efficient. It was also designed to be **revenue neutral,** meaning that the overall amount of revenue collected from the federal income tax was not supposed to change, although the impact on each income group would.

Some of these goals were achieved, at least in part.

Fairness.   The aim of fairness is to treat everyone equally and especially to make sure the rich pay their share of taxes.

One of the chief differences in the new and old tax structures is that the progressivity has been reduced on paper. (Recall that a *progressive* tax requires people to pay proportionately more as their incomes rise. A tax that requires the poor to pay proportionately more than those in middle- and upper-income brackets is a **regressive tax.**) The old tax structure had 15 different tax rates (counting the zero rate for those with almost no income); the higher a person's income, the higher the tax rate. The new tax plan has only 4 rates, again counting the zero rate. In one sense, this can be seen as a dramatic move away from progressivity, and hence away from what most would define as fairness. Most Americans opposed reducing the top rates for high-income people.[22]

However, the old tax law was so riddled with special exemptions and loopholes that it was no longer progressive. Poor people paid a higher proportion of their income in tax than the rich. Under the new tax rules, over six million of the lowest income Americans

Figure 2 ■ Billions of Dollars of Federal Revenue Are Still Lost Through Special Deductions

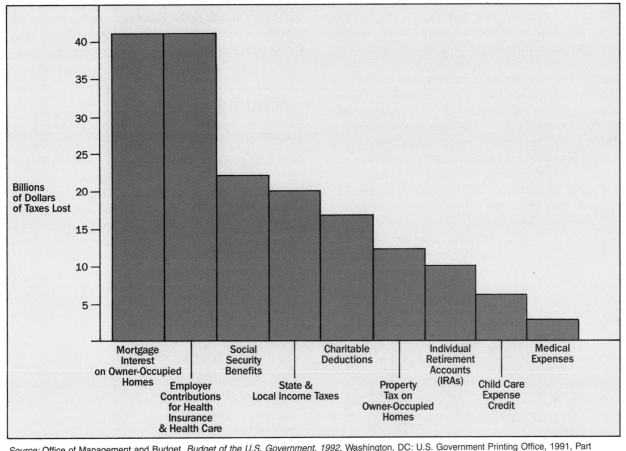

Source: Office of Management and Budget, *Budget of the U.S. Government, 1992,* Washington, DC: U.S. Government Printing Office, 1991, Part Three, Table XI–1. Data are for 1992.

no longer pay federal income taxes. If lawmakers can avoid writing new loopholes into the tax code, it may prove to be more progressive than the old law.

Most people's idea of fairness was also met by changes in the corporate tax. Although the top rate on corporate taxes was in fact lowered, the removal of several special tax breaks for business was designed to ensure that corporations actually pay more than in the recent past. So far this has happened: General Electric, which had received nearly $300 million in tax refunds from 1981 to 1983 with an income of over $6 billion, paid $744 million in taxes in 1987.[23] Similarly, other big corporations with large profits also paid substantial taxes.

Simplicity. The tax code is simpler in that many deductions and exemptions were eliminated. The 1986 law reduced the number of allowable deductions, including those for state sales taxes, interest paid on credit card bills, interest for mortgages on third and fourth homes, the special deduction allowed two-income married couples, and numerous others.

Of course, many exemptions and special provisions still remain. These are testimony to the power of a variety of interests. For example, middle-income Americans along with housing construction and real estate interests ensured that mortgage interest on first and second homes is still deductible, leaving a very large loophole in the new law.

Businesspersons can still charge the government for most of their meals and entertainment since 80% can be deducted. A recent advertisement for a medical convention in Mexico pointed out the attractions of ancient Mayan ruins, shopping, and the beautiful beaches but not the content of the symposium. The ad ended with "Remember, it's tax deductible!"[24] Thus, while tax reform closed many loopholes, it certainly did not close all (figure 2).

Efficiency. One aspect of efficiency is simply the time it takes the public to fill out the forms. Well over half of all Americans now have experts prepare their taxes. In addition, millions of hours of time are spent by highly paid accountants and lawyers figuring out how to evade taxes legally. Initially, backers of tax reform hoped that the new tax would be simpler, and that more taxpayers could do it themselves. Though some taxpayers have found their taxes easier to compute, for most the job is far from simple. Indeed in 1989, a mythical family's income and expenses were sent to 50 tax experts who calculated the family's taxes. They arrived at 50 different answers, ranging from a tax bill of $12,500 to nearly $36,000.[25] So the new tax code remains complex.

The public, although fed up with the old tax laws, is wary of the new.[26] After filing their taxes under the new system, over half said they believed it was less fair compared to only 14% who thought it was more fair.

Half also thought their taxes went up (even though tax rates were raised only for those in the top 2% of income).[27] These findings are not easy to explain except that many people may have noticed closed loopholes more than reduced tax rates.

Spending

Where the Money Goes

Although it raises over $1 trillion in revenue, the government now spends over $1.5 trillion a year, or about $199,000 per second of every working day.[28] How it spends this huge sum is a good indicator of national priorities. Although the government supports hundreds of programs, a very large proportion of the budget is consumed by a few. Figure 3 indicates the general categories of expenditures. Military spending and

---

Figure 3 ■ Federal Spending, 1992

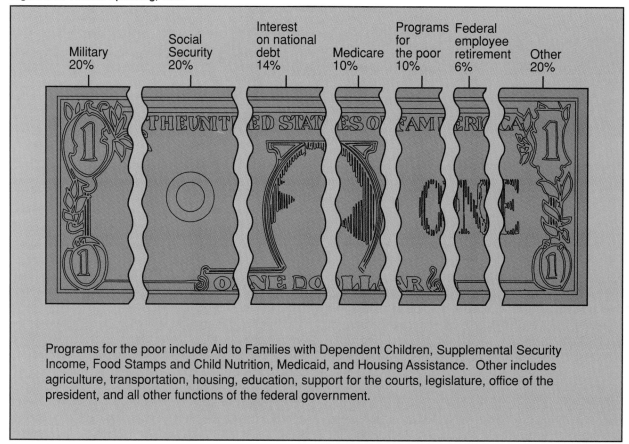

| Military 20% | Social Security 20% | Interest on national debt 14% | Medicare 10% | Programs for the poor 10% | Federal employee retirement 6% | Other 20% |

Programs for the poor include Aid to Families with Dependent Children, Supplemental Security Income, Food Stamps and Child Nutrition, Medicaid, and Housing Assistance. Other includes agriculture, transportation, housing, education, support for the courts, legislature, office of the president, and all other functions of the federal government.

Source: Compiled from Office of Management and Budget, Budget in Brief, fiscal year 1992.

Social Security comprise 40% of the budget. Interest on the national debt, Medicare, and retirement benefits for former government employees, civilian and military, represent other large chunks. These categories make up almost three-quarters of the national budget.

Welfare programs for the poor comprise a small part of the budget, about 6%, and are dwarfed by Medicare, Social Security, interest on the national debt, and military spending. The costs of Social Security and Medicare skyrocketed during the 1960s and 1970s and consume an ever-larger share of an ever-larger budget. Interest on the national debt surged in the 1980s as the nation rang up large deficits. The budget share consumed by military spending also grew considerably during the Reagan years, but has fallen since from over 30% to about 20%.

Spending for education, conservation of natural resources, farm subsidies, transportation and road construction, and other purposes together consume only about 17% of our total spending. When big budget cuts are made, budget makers must look first at military spending and social insurance, because these programs consume by far the largest proportion of our tax dollars. Not surprisingly, they are also the programs with the largest political support and are thus the most difficult to cut.

Controllables and Uncontrollables

Spending is often referred to as controllable or uncontrollable. **Uncontrollable expenditures** are those that Congress and the president can do little about—the interest on the national debt, for example. Once that debt is incurred, the interest must be paid. Similarly, pensions to veterans and other retired federal employees are uncontrollable; the government has a legal commitment to these individuals.

Payments to welfare and Social Security recipients are uncontrollable in a sense because Congress cannot control how many people are eligible for these programs once it defines eligibility (for example, for Social Security, to be age 62 and have paid Social Security taxes for a specified period). This spending is not completely uncontrollable, however, because Congress can change the eligibility standards and the amount that each eligible recipient can receive, although this is politically difficult.

About one-third of the military budget is comprised of uncontrollable costs of weapons development and deployment authorized in previous years (since it takes more than a year to build a major weapons system). The portion of the military budget that is uncontrollable rose during the 1980s.[29]

Controllable expenditures are those that Congress can increase or reduce as it sees fit—farm subsidies, the size of the military, road building, or education, for example.

In 1970, "only" 63% of the budget was uncontrollable; by 1990, 76% was.[30] Budget cuts must come from "controllable" expenditures, but as this part of the budget becomes smaller, Congress has less flexibility. When "quick fixes" to budget deficits are sought, the controllable parts of the budget are more vulnerable.

Budget Forecasting

Deciding how large the budget should be and how much should go to each government activity are part of the political process. Because the amount we can spend is largely a function of the revenue we collect, revenue projection is crucial to budget making.

To estimate accurately what revenues are likely to be, one has to estimate future rates of inflation, unemployment, and productivity. These economic indicators will in turn predict how much income tax and other revenue there may be. When business, industry, and farmers produce more goods and services, they normally make higher profits (which are taxed), or pay more to their shareholders (who pay taxes on that income), or hire more workers (who also pay more taxes).

Economic growth also affects how much spending will be needed. If factories are idle, workers are laid off and more money will be needed for unemployment insurance, welfare support, crime control, and even mental health care. A booming economy also requires spending to control its undesirable side effects, such as air and water pollution.

Small adjustments in predictions make an astoundingly large difference. For example, underestimating unemployment by 1% can mean a $17 billion difference in the budget: it reduces revenue by $12 billion and increases expenditures (for unemployment compensation and welfare) by $5 billion.[31]

Harry Truman once said that he was in search of a one-armed economist so that the guy could never make a statement and then say "On the other hand. . . ."[32] Years later it is just as difficult to get a firm prediction about economic conditions. In predicting economic conditions for 1989 on which the budget

What the President Could Say

In his inaugural address, President Bush noted, "We have more will than wallet." In his budget message, he wrote, "The president would like to embrace . . . the defense budget projections which are in the Reagan budget. Unfortunately, the current economic situation requires defense budget savings." And later, in an interview with high school students, President Bush told them that "we can't afford" to give a tuition tax credit for parents who send their children to private schools.

But, as Herbert Stein, chair of Nixon's Council of Economic Advisers, wrote, "What country [is he] talking about, and what does [he] mean by saying that we cannot 'afford' something? The answer, of course, is that we prefer to do other things. We cannot do more for defense, or education, or assistance to the poor or fighting drugs and crime because we prefer to use the national income for other things—essentially, for private consumption." Senator Robert Kerrey (D-Neb.), in referring to spending on education, commented that "the issue is not having more will than wallet. We have the wallet. What we need is the willingness to act."

Stein suggests that instead of saying "we cannot afford" whatever high priority the president happens to be discussing, he should say something like this:

"It is my judgment, after carefully considering the state of the nation, that the United States would be better-off if we spent somewhat more for defense, education, child care and assistance to poor people than I have recommended in my budget. I realize that this would involve some sacrifice for Americans. Primarily they would have to slow down the increase of their consumption in order to permit more of the national income to go to these pur-

poses. But I believe it would be worthwhile. We would become a stronger, better, kinder, and gentler nation. And the amount that I would propose to spend is not large, about $35 billion a year compared to $3,500 billion of private consumption. This would only slightly slow down the increase in a level of real consumption per capita that is already the highest in the history of the world.

"I have not included these added expenditures in my budget because there is much evidence that you, your parents, and your grandparents do not want me to do that. You may favor the expenditures, but you clearly do not want the tax increases or cuts in Social Security or Medicare that would be necessary to pay for them. . . . You and your families are unwilling to accept the slowdown in the increase in your consumption in order to have these expenditures.

"That is certainly your right. In a democracy the president cannot do what the people do not want him to do. . . . But in a democracy the people also have responsibilities as well as rights. They have a responsibility to behave in a way that will permit the society to survive and flourish. This is not a legal responsibility. . . . It is simply a matter of fact that if the people do not accept this responsibility the system will not work. . . . This responsibility extends to being willing to accept increases of taxes or reductions of government programs of particular benefit to oneself in order to pay for programs that are in the national interest."

Source: Stein quotations are from Herbert Stein, "Don't Say We Can't Afford It," *Washington Post National Weekly Edition,* April 17–23, 1989, p. 29. Kerrey quotation is from Robert Kerrey, "Education: Restructuring Isn't Enough," *Washington Post National Weekly Edition,* July 3–9, 1989, p. 29.

---

would be based, the Bush administration's estimate of gross national product was considerably above that of the Congressional Budget Office, which in turn was above that of several private corporate forecasts. Similarly, the administration thought that inflation, unemployment, and interest rates would be lower than did the others. This occurred because presidents usually rely on estimates of economic growth, inflation, and unemployment that are most favorable to their own economic program. President Reagan's projections were especially far off the mark. Since he cut taxes and raised military spending, in order to balance the budget, he had to count on a high level of growth in the national economy that did not materialize.

Since tax revenues depend upon economic activity, they were less than expected. Thus the Reagan administration projected $2 billion and $1 billion deficits in 1982 and 1983, but the country suffered $128 and $225 billion shortfalls instead.

David Stockman, Reagan's first budget director, described how such estimates were made for Reagan's first budget. The estimates were simply the result of a compromise. In order to justify a huge tax reduction, and show a balanced budget, tremendous economic growth and low inflation had to be projected. The administration's initial figures included a 2% projected inflation rate, a figure far below existing rates. The chair of the Council of Economic Advisers, Murray

What Is a Trillion Dollars Anyway?

It is nearly impossible for us to comprehend the magnitude of government spending when we hear that the budget is over $1 trillion. Just writing it out is astounding. One trillion is $1,000,000,000,000. What does that mean? Here are some ways to put it in perspective:

- A million seconds ago was only 11½ days ago. A trillion seconds ago was 31,700 years ago, about the time modern human beings evolved.
- If someone handed you a $100 bill every second, you would be a millionaire eight times over in one day. But, to be a trillionaire, you would have to be handed a $100 bill every second for 317 years.
- If you packed $1 bills into railroad boxcars, you could get $63.5 million in each boxcar. To get $1 trillion loaded in, you would have to have almost 16,000 boxcars. The train would be 167 miles long.
- If you laid $1 bills end to end, one million of them would only go about 100 miles. One billion would get you

around the earth four times. One trillion would allow you to go to the sun and several million miles beyond.

Source: Drawing by Mankoff; © 1979 The New Yorker Magazine, Inc.

"Did he say the budget was going to be a zillion billion krillion dollars or a killion billion zillion dollars?"

Source: Boyce Rensberger, "$1,000,000,000,000 — We're Talking Real Money," *Washington Post National Weekly Edition,* January 19, 1987, p. 32.

Weidenbaum, said "Nobody is going to predict 2% inflation on my watch. We'll be the laughingstock of the world."[33] So Stockman and Weidenbaum bargained over what the forecasts would be; Weidenbaum selected an inflation figure he could live with and Stockman raised the economic growth projections. Of course, both were horribly wrong, and that is why the real deficit was 100 times bigger than the projected one. Forecasts in later years also missed the mark because of unrealistic estimates of growth and unemployment.

The projections made by the Congressional Budget Office (CBO) are usually more reliable than those of the White House. The CBO, because it serves both parties, accepts neither the most nor the least rosy estimates of economic performance.

The American Political Economy

The American Quarter Century?

Before examining contemporary economic successes and problems, we should briefly look back at the U.S. economy since World War II. Such a look will reveal

some of the roots of our current problems and demonstrate that the health of the economy depends on many things, only some of which government can control.

In the late 1940s, following World War II, we were the undisputed economic power of the world. Optimistic (and perhaps jingoistic) Americans talked of the "American century," where America would dominate the world much as Britain had done in the nineteenth century and other powers had done in earlier eras. The economies of World War II allies and enemies alike (Britain, France, the Soviet Union, Germany, and Japan) were shattered by the expense and human loss of the war, the dislocation of populations in some nations, and the destruction of factories, businesses, and public facilities such as highways and railroads in others. In these circumstances our economy boomed, and we produced goods for the entire world.

The economic good times continued, fueled in part by our growing population, for 25 years. Slowdowns in economic growth and increases in unemployment were temporary, inflation was not serious, and productivity marched steadily upward. Our standard of living zoomed, as Americans bought cars, new homes, household appliances, and luxury items in quantities unheard of before. Most people could anticipate being better off in the future than in the present and felt sure that their children would be even better off. Economic improvement seemed inevitable, not for everyone, of course, but for most people.

The late 1960s brought the first obvious signs of trouble as inflation rose along with spending on the Vietnam War. Then in 1973 the bottom fell out of our economic machine. A group of oil-producing nations (called OPEC), which control most of the world's known reserves, forced a large price increase in oil. Dependent on foreign oil, Americans found prices skyrocketing, not only for gas for their cars but for almost everything else. Petroleum products ran our factories and our farm machinery and were essential ingredients in the manufacture of goods ranging from plastics to pesticides, essential chemicals to chapstick. The United States was not alone in its distress. All of the industrialized and much of the developing world also experienced rampant inflation. But the United States, used to being "on top of the world," may have been shaken more deeply.

The oil price shock was not the only blow to our economy. During the 1970s, the baby boom generation—those born in the late 1940s and early 1950s—entered the work force in record numbers. As a consequence, unemployment increased because the economy was unable to handle these millions of new workers. To add to our woes, other industrial nations of the world had long since recovered from the devastation of World War II and were giving us stiff competition in the international marketplace. Developing nations of Asia were also beginning to industrialize and, with low wage rates for their workers, were underselling us in international markets. Many of our heavy industries shriveled as U.S. and foreign manufacturers discovered they could buy steel and machinery cheaper in Japan, Korea, or Germany, and consumers at home and abroad decided they preferred energy-efficient foreign-made cars to those produced by the American auto industry. These developments increased unemployment as workers in declining industries were laid off.[34]

The economy of the middle and late 1970s, then, was characterized by higher than usual unemployment and by high inflation. Despite these woes, however, in the 1970s real income (that is, income adjusted for the fact that the dollar was worth less in 1979 than in 1970 due to inflation) increased by over one-fourth, and the distribution of income between the rich and poor changed little.[35] The average person was better off but felt worse off because of the specter of rising inflation, which reached "double digit" figures during

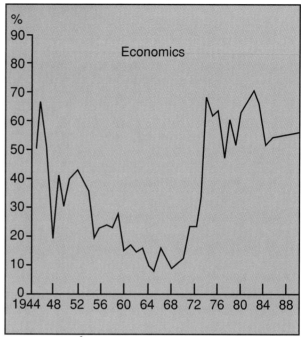

Figure 4 ■ Americans View Economic Concerns as Our Major Problem

The proportion of Americans who view economic concerns as our number-one problem jumped in 1973 and has stayed fairly high.

Note: Question: "What do you think is the most important problem facing this (the) country today? (Responses included are unemployment, budget deficit, taxes, trade deficit, economy, poverty.)

Source: Gallup polls as reported in Tom Smith, "The Polls: America's Most Important Problems," *Public Opinion Quarterly* 49 (Summer 1985): 268–74, updated from Gallup Report.

some months of the late 1970s (figure 4). During the decade, inflation totaled 112%, compared to only 31% in the 1960s and 20% in the 1950s. Economists could not agree on any solution to inflation that would not increase unemployment. Pessimists, looking at the shattered U.S. economy, noted that the "American century" had lasted only 25 years.

The Reagan Economic Program and Its Legacy

Ronald Reagan came to the White House with four economic goals: reduce inflation, lower taxes, increase military spending, and balance the budget. His 1980 election opponents, both Democrats and Republicans, had charged that these goals were incompatible, or, in the words of George Bush, "voodoo economics." Reagan and his advisers sought to accomplish these goals through **supply-side economics.**

The basic premise of this theory is that as government taxes less, more money is freed for private investment. Therefore, when the economy is sluggish, supply-siders advocate tax cuts to stimulate growth. They believe that people will save some of the money they would have paid in taxes, thus making more money available to lend to businesses for expansion and modernization. Taxpayers would also be left with more money to spend on consumption, and to satisfy the increased demand businesses would hire more workers. With increased employment fewer people collect unemployment compensation and more pay taxes. So, according to supply-side economics, even though the tax rate is lower, government revenue increases.

These ideas appealed to conservatives because they offered an economic rationale for smaller government. Thus, Reagan pushed a tax cut through Congress, resulting in the loss of billions of dollars of revenue. At the same time he proposed dramatic spending increases for the military. He also proposed cuts in social services, but these were not nearly as large as the lost revenue from the tax cuts or the increases in military spending. While Reagan cut deeply into some programs for the poor, he was not willing to cut substantially the much larger programs for the middle class, such as Medicare, Social Security, and veterans' benefits. These so-called **entitlement programs** are direct payments to individuals to which they are entitled by law simply by virtue of being in a particular classification. (For example, people are entitled to Medicare if they qualify by age and previous contributions to the Medicare fund.) Entitlement spending rose steeply in the Reagan years (see figure 5).

Successes.   As promised, Reagan did reduce taxes, increase military spending, and lower inflation. Inflation rates after 1982 were the lowest since the early 1970s. Part of this was due to a big drop in oil prices. However, most of the decrease in inflation was due to the Federal Reserve Board's policies of taking money out of the economy by raising prime interest rates and making it very expensive for businesses to borrow money. This tight money policy slowed growth, and with it inflation, but it also contributed to a severe recession in 1981 and 1982.

Reagan was committed to holding down wages as a means for cutting inflation; he had set an example with federal employees when he fired air traffic controllers who went on strike over salary and safety issues in 1981. But once the recession set in, high un-

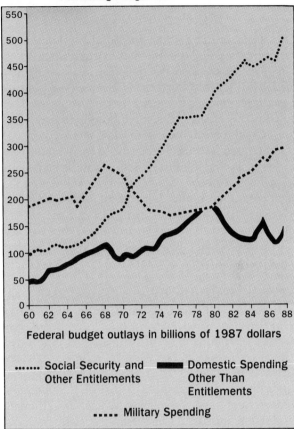

Figure 5 ■ Except for Entitlements, Domestic Spending Fell during Reagan Era

Federal budget outlays in billions of 1987 dollars

...... Social Security and Other Entitlements

■■■ Domestic Spending Other Than Entitlements

..... Military Spending

Over the past 30 years, spending on entitlements, such as Social Security, Medicare, and pensions, has risen dramatically. Military spending rose in the late 1960s, sank in the middle 1970s, and began to rise steeply in 1979. Domestic spending other than entitlements fell sharply during the first Reagan administration, then began to grow slowly. This includes spending for education, housing, social services, and other domestic needs.

Source: Budget of the U.S. Government, 1989.

employment itself drove down wages as workers threatened with layoffs agreed to forego pay increases and in some cases even to accept pay cuts and reduced fringe benefits.

The Fed's tight money made it difficult for everyone to borrow. For example, thousands of farmers who had purchased land at inflated prices with high-interest loans were driven into bankruptcy. Both bankers and farmers had counted on rising inflation and a "loose money" policy to make their loans and investments profitable. With the Fed's tight money policy and the sharp drop in inflation, farm land plummeted in value, deflating even more than wages. Having borrowed amounts far in excess of the new value of their land, farmers were unable to sell the land at prices equal to their debt when banks called in their loans. Thousands of farmers lost their land and homes and were thrown into an uncertain job market.

In 1982, unemployment reached 11%—its highest level since the Great Depression—but then began to fall as an economic recovery took hold. Higher levels of consumer spending, stimulated by the tax cut, and record levels of government spending increased the demand for goods, which in turn fueled more production and employment. Moreover, the economy had grown in response to the baby boom generation, but then in the latter part of the 1980s, the smaller number of children from the "baby bust" era (the middle and late 1960s) entered the work force leaving many parts of the country with labor shortages. By the time Reagan left office, the unemployment rate was around 5%.

Failures. With inflation at reasonable levels, tax rates lower, and unemployment below what it has been for many years, why do books about the economic situation of the post-Reagan years have titles such as *On Borrowed Time, Day of Reckoning,* and *Rendezvous with Reality?*[36] The reason is that the boom in our economy was built in large part on a foundation of debt. Supply-side economics did not work; though production increased somewhat, increased business activity did not generate enough tax revenue to make up for the lower rates. Instead, because of revenue loss from the tax cut, each year the Reagan administration spent $100 to $200 billion more than it received, creating a huge budget deficit. Like individuals, the government can, and usually does, spend more than it earns by borrowing money and paying interest. But it did so in unprecedented (at least for peacetime) amounts during the 1980s. Because of the ever-mounting deficit, we now pay about 14% of our national budget in interest to those from whom the government has borrowed.

Though in the 1980 election campaign Reagan was often quoted as saying that "balancing the budget is like protecting your virtue: you have to learn to say no,"[37] first-term Reagan deficits were nearly equal to the total of all deficits during the administrations of Franklin Roosevelt through Jimmy Carter. By the end of his second term, Reagan had nearly tripled our national debt.[38] At the beginning of the Reagan era, we were the world's largest creditor nation. Now we are the world's largest debtor nation. That is, we owe more to foreign creditors from whom we have borrowed than any other nation. We have had to borrow this money to finance our national debt.

A second negative legacy of the Reagan years is that we did not save or invest for the future. We consumed about as much as we earned. Indeed, if it were not for pension funds and the Social Security Trust Fund, collectively as consumers we would have spent all we earned.

Both government and private individuals borrow heavily. Buying on credit has become such a way of life for Americans that, while the number of corporate bankruptcies fell in the second half of the 1980s, individual bankruptcies doubled. In 1990, 90% of all bankruptcies were filed by individual consumers unable to pay their debts.[39]

Most public borrowing is to pay for consumption rather than to invest in our nation's future through spending for education, modernization of our nation's industries, or improvement of our rapidly deteriorating infrastructure of roads, bridges, and water treatment plants. Forty-two percent of America's highway bridges are closed or restricted to light traffic; a bridge fails every two days.[40]

Many economists believe that Japan's success in outpacing our economy is due to its much greater rate of saving and investment, even though, like the United States, it has quite a large budget deficit.[41] By the late 1980s, Japan's savings and investment levels were twice those of the United States. Recognizing what our "live for today" spending patterns will do to future generations, some have called our spending and savings patterns "fiscal child abuse," and others have likened it to "eating our seed corn."

Another consequence of the Reagan taxing and spending program is the trade and investment deficit. We buy much more from others than they buy from us. This makes us much more reliant on the international economy, decreases the number of jobs in American industries, and reduces our living standards because of money we pay to foreign industries and investors.

A final major consequence of the Reagan program is the growing gap between rich and poor. Poverty levels began to rise in the late 1970s and continued until 1986. At the same time, the Reagan budgets cut back social programs for the poor. The real income of the bottom half of the nation declined as that of the top half rose. This was due to unemployment, to the increase in Social Security taxes that hit lower-income earners harder than upper-income earners, and to the

Figure 6 ■ The Wealthiest Americans Increased their Income the Most during the Reagan Years

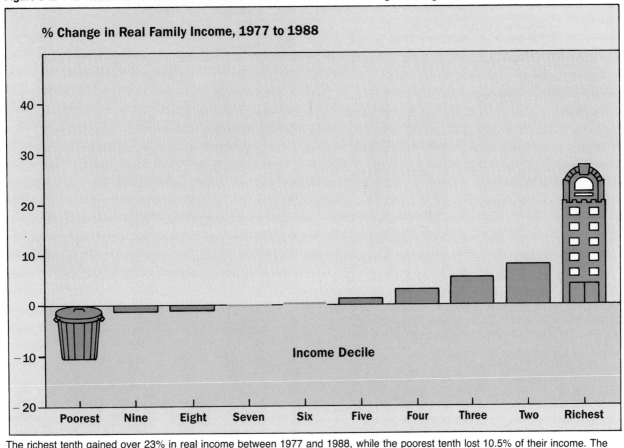

The richest tenth gained over 23% in real income between 1977 and 1988, while the poorest tenth lost 10.5% of their income. The four groups in the middle stayed about even with inflation. The richest 1% increased their income by 74%.

Note: All the figures are adjusted for inflation.

tax cuts that gave more tax breaks to the rich than to the poor (see figure 6).

Changes in the American Standard of Living

"America's families today find themselves on a treadmill. They must run as fast as possible—work harder than ever—to sustain a living standard no greater than that which prevailed in 1973."[42] This statement summarizes much about changes in our standard of living. In real dollars (that is, dollars adjusted for inflation), the average family today earns only about as much as it did in 1973, a high point in our recent economy, even though most families now have two wage earners, rather than one.

In the post-World War II decades through much of the 1970s, family income grew over 3% a year. Indeed, in 1966, a 50-year-old man could look back over a 10-year period in the work force and see that his income had risen over 30%. At the end of the 1980s he could look back over the same number of years and find his income had risen only 10%.[43] Today's workers earn less, in real terms, than their parents did at a comparable age (see figure 7).

The growth in living standards of the postwar era has nearly stopped, due to slowing productivity and decreasing average wages. Even in the high inflation days of the 1970s, wages kept ahead of inflation.[44] Surprisingly to those who remember the Carter era as a time of hardship, private wealth grew much faster between 1975 and 1980 than it did during the postrecession years of the Reagan administration.[45]

The overall stagnation of growth in family income conceals a growing split between those who are moving ahead and those who are falling behind. In the first group are those who are already well-off, middle-aged

Figure 7 ■ Younger Workers are Falling Behind

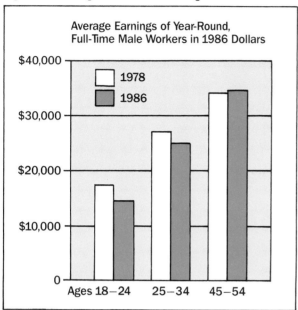

Source: Bureau of the Census; Spencer Rich, "The Twilight of the Big Paycheck, Blue Collar Era," *Washington Post National Weekly Edition*, June 13, 1988, p. 7.

The American postwar economy lifted millions of families into middle-class status and comfort. Above is a poverty-stricken family in 1936. Victims of the drought and depression, they had left Oklahoma, where they were homeless with little to eat, to find a better future in California. Below is the same family 43 years later in front of the daughter's home in Modesto.

and older Americans, and those with college educations. Falling behind are those who are poor or marginal to begin with, younger people, families headed by only one wage earner, and those whose education ended with high school.

Most middle-aged and older people established themselves in a job and bought a house (by far the biggest investment most families make) years ago, when economic times were good. These Americans have seen their homes increase in value and their wages rise steadily, at least until the 1980s. Most are pretty secure.

Younger Americans entered the work force when it was faltering. Opportunities have knocked for most college-educated young adults, but there are fewer well-paying jobs for blue-collar workers than there were 20 years ago. Heavy industries that traditionally paid high wages to unionized workers have fallen on hard times. The steel industry is an example.[46] We import an increasing share—now over 25%—of the steel we use. In 1989, there were only half as many jobs in the steel industry as there were a dozen years before, leaving thousands of former steel workers unemployed. Many others lost their highly paid jobs (sometimes upwards of $14 per hour) for jobs that barely pay minimum wage ($4.25 per hour in 1991).[47]

Most new jobs created in the 1980s were service jobs that pay low wages to unskilled workers.[48] Some service jobs pay good wages, but not as good as manufacturing jobs. The well-paying jobs are largely for people with college educations, but getting a college

FOCUS ON AN ISSUE

Should We Have a Balanced Budget Amendment?

The deficit has continued to grow despite the adoption of the 1985 Balanced Budget (**Gramm-Rudman**) Act. Although the act supposedly triggers automatic cuts in most programs, Congress and the president routinely violate the rules by putting large amounts "off-budget" and playing other games to avoid the automatic cuts. Since such limited progress has been made toward reducing the deficit despite Gramm-Rudman, some people argue that we need a balanced budget amendment to force Congress and the president to act.

A call for a constitutional convention to consider the amendment won support in 32 states by 1990; only 2 more are needed before Congress must act to call such a convention.

Should we have such an amendment? In order to decide, we need to consider the following questions.

Are Deficits Bad?

A 1990 Gallup Poll showed that most Americans thought the deficit was bad, but only a tiny fraction could come up with even one reason why. Are deficits really that bad? Liberal economists traditionally believed that moderate deficits were sometimes needed to stimulate the economy. A few find nothing wrong with even large deficits. Some of Reagan's economic advisers believed that deficits were temporary and would be eliminated with strong economic growth. Other defenders of the deficit point out that businesses and families regularly go into debt to finance new plants and new houses.

Most experts fear that the huge recent deficits will impair the long-term health of both the government and the economy. The economy suffers because government deficits, coupled with private debts, mean there is not enough money in the United States to finance this mass borrowing. We must borrow from foreigners. The fact that we are the world's largest debtor nation makes us increasingly vulnerable to the uncertainties of international markets.

The ever-larger portion of our national budget being consumed by interest on the national debt leaves less for other things. The huge deficits are a reason—or an excuse—to propose further massive cuts in domestic spending and to avoid dealing with real needs in our society. Many members of Congress from both parties fear that increasing deficits and

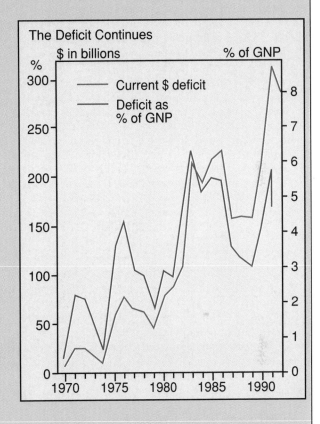

The Deficit Continues

$ in billions   % of GNP

- Current $ deficit
- Deficit as % of GNP

spiraling interest are seriously damaging our ability to meet these needs in areas such as health care and education.

Moreover, the huge deficits take away income from some and give to others in ways that most believe are not desirable. The interest paid on the massive public debt transfers wealth from the taxpayers to those from whom the government borrows. The average taxpayer, through tax dollars, is giving money to wealthier taxpayers and foreign investors.

The deficit also means we are borrowing from our children and grandchildren. Future generations will be stuck with paying our debt without much benefit to them. Our spending is largely for the military, entitlements, and interest on the national debt rather than for investments in research, education, or our infrastructure of roads and buildings that might benefit future generations.

(continued on next page)

Can a Balanced Budget Amendment Really Hold Down Spending?

Backers of the proposed amendment argue that it is only through a constitutional amendment that we can rein in big spenders in Congress and the White House. Since normal restraints do not work, this argument goes, we need to make an unbalanced budget unconstitutional. A more subtle analysis argues that the constitutional provision will give Congress backbone to do what members know they should do. They then will be able to tell their constituents that they could not support certain bills because of constitutional restrictions on spending.

Opponents argue that in the short run only a huge tax increase will allow us to balance the budget. A budget so far out of balance as those of 1981 through 1992 cannot be balanced simply by cutting "frills." Either domestic and military budgets would have to be cut dramatically or a tax increase would have to be implemented. Both seem politically infeasible. Recall that Newt Gingrich and his fellow budget negotiators in 1990 could not even agree on ways to cut $40 billion from the deficit, let alone nearly $300 billion, which is what the deficit in 1991 is likely to be.

Should We Deprive Our Lawmakers of Flexibility?

Proponents believe that lawmakers have proven incapable of balancing the budget, so a drastic step is needed. Opponents argue that a constitutional amendment removes necessary flexibility from budgetmakers; deficit spending might be necessary in a given year to avert or temper a recession or to respond to a defense emergency. In other words, sometimes there are good reasons to have an unbalanced budget. The Constitution could not be changed quickly enough to cope with a short-run emergency. An amendment with enough flexibility to take care of emergencies probably would not restrain lawmakers.

How Can We Know for Sure if the Budget Will Be Balanced?

Predicting revenue is not a science, as much as we would like to think otherwise. Moreover, officials base their predictions, in part, on political considerations. Presidents normally overestimate the income and underestimate the expenditures in their budgets. In his first two years, President Reagan's *proposed* budgets were not far out of balance. Only the end of the year actual budgets were. If a balanced budget means only that the *proposed* budget must be balanced, critics of the constitutional amendment fear that even more inaccuracies will enter into the estimation of revenues and expenditures so that the paper budget will

Source: TOLES, Copyright 1990 Buffalo News. Reprinted with permission of Universal Press Syndicate.

be a fiction. With a balanced budget amendment, flights of fancy may replace what hard thinking now exists.

The experience of Gramm-Rudman is in some ways rather frightening. It led to even more play acting about the budget than usual. The deficit was artificially reduced by selling off public land and public enterprises, a one-shot infusion of money that does nothing to solve any long-range spending problems (it is like selling your house to pay off a vacation or a gimmick like delaying military pay raises for a day). Spending items were put into an "off-budget category" and not counted in the estimate of the deficit. The off-budget deficit is twice the official national debt.

The huge surplus (almost $40 billion) in the Social Security Trust Fund is used to offset (on paper) part of the deficit in the rest of the budget. More dangerously, to make the budget look more balanced, trust fund balances in accounts designed to maintain and improve roads and air traffic are not spent even though the funds are desperately needed.

Thus, projections about income and expenses have become totally unrealistic. As one congressional staff member said, "Gramm-Rudman just about destroyed credible budgeting. Games have been played before, but I've never seen so many games as this time."[1] Even one of the co-sponsors of the Gramm-Rudman bill is so sick of these games, he has publicly chastised his colleagues for not facing up to the real deficit. In short, the budget-cutting bill is undermining the credibility of the government and the entire budget process.

If Gramm-Rudman distorts the process this much, the likely effect of a constitutional amendment would be even greater. Thus, opponents of the amendment argue that spending patterns will not be affected; what will be affected is the honesty in making budget projections.

(continued on next page)

A government worker trains to clean up hazardous waste.

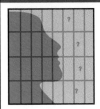
Fight or Flight?

In 1985, a 36-year-old foundry worker was splintered and crushed when a fellow employee accidentally turned on the power on a machine he was servicing.[1] Another man was pulverized in a meat grinder he was cleaning. In fact, about 100 to 150 workers meet grisly deaths in this way each year.

You are James Scully, a bureaucrat in the Occupational Safety and Health Administration (OSHA). OSHA was formed in 1970 with a broad and somewhat vague mandate "to ensure as far as possible every working man and woman . . . safe and healthful working conditions." The agency was to be restricted "only by technological and economic feasibility."

These horrible deaths are far removed from your office, yet very close to you. For years, you have worked to develop a regulation to reduce risks to workers who repair and clean dangerous machines. The regulation would include a simple lock on power switches to prevent them from being accidentally turned on while a worker was inside a piece of equipment. Your regulation was to take effect years ago. But when Ronald Reagan took office, you were told to forget about it. It was too "confrontational," your bosses said. The regulation might offend business by calling attention to worker deaths and injuries.

To the Reagan administration, reducing regulation is a high priority. Indeed, the president declared that slowing down the pace of regulation was "one of our administration's proudest achievements. . . . We have substantially reduced that burden, cutting red tape." But, in your opinion, cutting red tape really means unnecessary deaths for factory workers.

For the last several years, you have quietly fought to keep your proposed regulation alive. You and some of your OSHA colleagues have compiled scientific evidence on the problem. You have kept in touch with labor union leaders concerned about industrial safety. And you have sent information to the chair of the Senate Labor Committee, Edward Kennedy (D-Mass.), hoping that he or his committee will become an advocate for this regulation. You have also tried to deal with the Office of Management and Budget (OMB), which, during the Reagan administration, has worked to kill dozens of regulations. All regulations, except those from the independent regulatory commissions, must be approved by OMB. Officials there show no sign of wanting to approve yours. You have been keeping records documenting both the OMB and your bosses' attempts to kill the regulation.

Though you are a feisty person and have fought hard, you are discouraged. You are 65 and want to retire. You have little hope of ever getting your regulation through. The antiregulation sentiment still holds sway in both your agency and in the OMB. Though it is 1986, you have no guarantee that Ronald Reagan will be replaced by anyone more sympathetic to regulating to achieve safe workplaces.

Still, you hate to retire before you finish the job you set out to do. You have a strong commitment to protecting worker safety, and you do not like to admit defeat. You know that in politics, what is popular today is unpopular tomorrow, and you think that deregulatory zeal will be replaced by opinions more favorable to reasonable regulation. If you stay on in the agency and continue pressing the case for your regulation, you might eventually succeed.

So what do you do? Do you stay and fight? Or take flight and retire?

OUTLINE

If humans were angels, we would not need much government regulation. But in fact, regulation is needed because individuals do not always behave honestly, cautiously, and considerately. Some bankers and savings and loan officials make risky investments, so government regulates the amount of assets banks must have and insures savings. Some parents are not careful when they buy toys for their children, so government requires warnings on some toys and bans others. Some businesses ignore elementary safety considerations for their employees, so the government regulates many aspects of workplace safety. Some consumers believe everything they hear or have no basis for evaluating complicated information, so government regulates advertising and prosecutes those who lie. And some businesses risk the health and safety of their communities by spewing toxic chemicals into the air and water, so government limits the amount of such materials that can legally be emitted.

But government cannot protect us from all risks. How much risk should it protect us from? And how should government weigh the benefits of regulation in protecting us from risk against the costs of business and industry of those regulations?

The public gives no clear-cut answer to these questions. Americans often condemn regulation in the abstract but support specific kinds of regulations. For example, in a 1988 survey 64% of the public believed protecting the environment should be a top priority; only 3% believed it should not be a priority at all.[2] Though only 9% believe we have too much regulation to ensure product safety, 42% believe that there is too much regulation of business.[3] Moreover, regulation that is seen as beneficial by one group is regarded by another as wasteful and unnecessary red tape. This is why there is continuing controversy over what should be regulated, how much regulation is needed, and the regulatory mechanisms that should be used.

Benefits and Costs of Regulation

There have been many acknowledged successes of regulation.[4] For example, water pollution regulations have preserved a national heritage, changing the dying Great Lakes to lakes where fish and swimmers have returned. Lake Erie is no longer the cesspool that once caught on fire. The bald eagle, grizzly bear, and several other species are no longer in danger of extinction, thanks to federal regulation.[5] Because of government regulations mandating unleaded and lower leaded gasoline, the lead content of the air has dramatically decreased. Fewer children have brain damage and fewer adults have high blood pressure from airborne lead.[6]

Some consumer goods have been made safer too. Crib safety standards have reduced infant crib deaths by 44% since 1974, and standards for fire-resistant children's sleepwear have reduced serious burns and deaths by 20%. A regulation requiring collapsible steering columns on cars and trucks is estimated to have saved 26,000 lives over a 25-year period.[7]

Industrial accidents and deaths decreased because of OSHA's rules on workplace safety. In a two-year period, these rules prevented an estimated 350 deaths and saved $15 billion in lost time and employee compensation for accidents. Other successes could be listed.

The benefits of regulation are produced at a cost. Some are trivial, such as depriving hunters of the satisfaction of shooting eagles. The cost of regulation to industry has been estimated to be as high as $103 billion a year. This and every other estimate is controversial, however. Nevertheless, it is indisputable that, when complying with regulations, industry must increase its own costs to relieve the larger community of the burden of pollution, unsafe products, hazards to workers, or other negative aspects of business.[8]

Development of Regulation

Cycles of Regulation

Like other government activity, the push for government regulation comes in fits and starts. The first spurt came in the late 1800s, when a poor economy led to charges, especially by farmers, that the large corporations of the day were exploiting the public. In 1890 Congress passed a law prohibiting firms from conspiring to set prices or in other ways to restrain trade (the Sherman Anti-Trust Act). It also declared monopolies illegal. A **monopoly** is a company that controls a large share of the market for its goods and is therefore able to set prices. Congress also established the Interstate Commerce Commission for the purpose of regulating railroad charges.

The next burst of regulatory activity came after the turn of the century, in the progressive era. Demands for consumer protection arose largely because industrialization and railroad transportation created national markets for goods formerly produced and

consumed locally. In these new national markets, consumers had little recourse if the products they bought from distant companies were not safe or reliable. Consumer fraud became endemic. Business engaged in deceptive advertising, food products often contained harmful substances (Coca-cola contained cocaine; formaldehyde was used to preserve milk), and popular patent medicine usually contained alcohol or addictive drugs, such as opium.[9] Reformers also pointed to unsafe and unsanitary conditions in the meat-packing industry. After the media and so-called muckrakers highlighted these scandals, Congress banned certain food additives, prohibited false claims about products, and gave the Department of Agriculture power to inspect meat sold in interstate commerce.

The New Deal era spurred further regulatory activity. After 100 people died from an unsafe drug, Congress passed an act mandating that the Food and Drug Administration declare a drug safe before it could be marketed.

In the 1960s and 1970s reformers were again influential in pressuring Congress to undertake new regulatory activity. New agencies were established to regulate consumer product safety (Consumer Product Safety Commission), the environment (Environmental Protection Agency, EPA), and industrial safety (OSHA). The powers of older agencies, such as the Federal Trade Commission, were strengthened. In contrast, the 1980s were a period of little new regulatory activity at the national level. Reversing this trend the 1990s began with a flurry of new regulations.

The Electreat, a device first sold in 1918 could (so its manufacturers claimed) cure everything from headaches to tonsilitis and get rid of dandruff as a bonus. It was the first device outlawed by the FDA.

Kinds of Regulation

We can get a better sense of what regulation is by looking at different kinds of regulation:

1. *Requiring information.* Government may regulate by requiring that an employer, lender, or other entity provide certain kinds of information to employees or consumers. For example, credit card companies must provide cardholders with information about how to appeal charges that they think are not really theirs. Manufacturers of many food products must tell on the label how much salt, sugar, vitamins, and various ingredients their products contain. This allows consumers to see if their peppermint ice cream, for example, is colored with beet juice or red dye number 2, a potentially dangerous additive. This requirement is called **truth in labeling.**

At the turn of the century, many young children worked 12-hour days in unhealthy conditions. Shown here are children working in a vegetable cannery. New Deal era regulations outlawing most child labor were controversial when passed but now are widely accepted. Abuse of child labor laws is on the increase in some large urban areas.

Manufacturers sometimes oppose labeling the contents of their goods. The manufacturers of juice beverages resisted Food and Drug Administration (FDA) pressure to label the contents of their drinks more accurately.[10] Fruit punch, fruit blend, and fruit drink may in fact have no fruit; only for orange juice are there requirements for minimum amounts of juice to be in a "juice" product. The FDA and some public interest groups believe shoppers have a right to know if they are buying real juice or sugar water for their children.

The FDA also requires that when information *is* provided it be accurate. Many manufacturers have taken advantage of a new public awareness of the relationship between health and nutrition by labeling their products as "health" foods. The FDA is forcing manufacturers to remove words such as "fresh" from processed juices and "no cholesterol" from food products that are high in vegetable fats that could contribute to heart disease. It is also demanding that manufacturers remove from their packaging false claims that their products are "biodegradable" or in other ways "environmentally safe." Such consumer come-ons are called "green fraud."

2. *Licensing.* Government may regulate by requiring certain kinds of people to obtain licenses to practice their trade, take certain actions, or own certain goods. The federal government licenses radio and television

stations and nuclear power plants. States license people who practice trades or professions, such as doctors, beauticians, dentists, and many others. Licensing is economically valuable for those receiving a license because it allows them to practice their profession or trade and keeps others out.

3. *Setting standards.* Manufacturers must meet certain standards of environmental cleanliness, workplace safety, and employee wages and working conditions. Failure to maintain the standards results in legal penalties if convicted. A product called chicken soup must have a minimum of chicken in it, and hot dogs cannot include more than a certain proportion of bone, hair, insects, and other extraneous material. The FDA requires condoms to be tested for leaks. Manufacturers must destroy an entire batch of 1,000 if more than 4 are defective.[11]

4. *Economic incentives.* Higher taxes may be imposed on goods or activities viewed as less beneficial than on those deemed more beneficial. In this way, the less desirable action is penalized. An example is a tax on cars that use fuel inefficiently. Some people, particularly conservatives, believe that taxation is a better way to achieve regulatory goals than setting mandatory standards because it gives individuals or businesses an incentive to comply.

5. *Limitations of liability.* Some regulations are designed to discourage legal actions against individuals or firms. Congress has passed a law limiting the liability of nuclear power plants in case of a nuclear accident. Government, not the industry, picks up the cost of claims above a certain amount.

Reasons for Regulation

A basic principle of capitalism is that unrestricted competition among business firms gives us the best chance to obtain the economic goals we desire. Adam Smith believed, for example, that the "invisible hand" of the marketplace works to increase production and make individual firms more efficient.[12] Although each individual firm does not intend to work toward the greater good of society, the greater good is in fact achieved as each firm tries to maximize its own profit. If the economy did work this way, we would have little regulation. But unfortunately it goes awry in ways that threaten the public good, so government regulates to limit or correct these effects.

Damage to Common Property. One reason for regulation has been called the **tragedy of the com-**

Regulating Pizza

"Any way you slice it, it's a hot and gooey battle," reads a news report on how much cheese should be in a frozen pizza. The U.S. Department of Agriculture (USDA) proposed that a frozen meat pizza with less than 12% of its weight composed of real cheese products be labeled "imitation pizza." A seemingly minor issue, this proposal engendered serious debate between the makers of cheese and the makers of frozen pizza. Producers of dairy products want the government to require more real cheese in pizza. They claim that pizza buyers are being misled by phony cheese. In fact, USDA studies did show that more than one-half of frozen pizza manufacturers do not meet the minimal requirements of 12%. Proponents of the new regulations claim that pizza manufacturers use artificial cheese to cut the cost of making the product without passing the savings on to the consumers. The pizza manufacturers, who run a $1 billion a year industry, argue that the new regulation would raise prices for pizza buyers because real cheese costs more than artificial cheese. They believe that no one will want to buy something called "artificial pizza," so they will be forced to use real cheese in order to avoid the "artificial" label.

Consumer groups have mixed feelings. On the one hand, they do not want higher prices for pizza. On the other hand, they believe the public is deceived when pizza manufacturers are allowed to sell pizza without real cheese. Consumer groups usually favor truth in labeling so that customers can evaluate quality versus cost. Consumer groups point to the fact that over two-thirds of frozen pizza buyers believe their purchases contain real cheese, but in fact the top three brands contain at least one-half imitation cheese.

After four years, the USDA withdrew the proposal. Dairy producers and some farm groups were outraged.

Though not of much interest to these pizza eaters, the regulation of pizza ingredients is a sticky issue for several businesses and government agencies.

Influential members of Congress asked the General Accounting Office to investigate, and a House Agriculture subcommittee planned hearings. Thus, the sticky issue remains unresolved.

Why is the government involved in regulating cheese in pizza? First, some businesses favor this regulation and work hard to get it—in this case, the dairy industry. Second, consumer groups want consumers protected from what they consider misleading claims so they work for accurate labeling on products.

Source: News report in the *Lincoln Journal*, May 7, 1984, drawn from the syndication service of the *Baltimore Sun*. "The Mozzarella Wars," *Common Cause* (November/December 1986): 8; Ward Sinclair, "Say Cheese, and Watch Out," *Washington Post National Weekly Edition*, June 24, 1987, p. 34, "Pizza," *Washington Post National Weekly Edition*, August 24, 1987, p. 27.

---

mons.[13] The air we breathe and the water we drink are common to all of us. Yet individuals may seek to exploit them for their own uses to the detriment of the common good. To maximize their profits, farmers pump as much irrigation water as they need from rivers or aquifers, even in water-short areas, and industries spew toxic chemicals into the air or bury them in the soil. They are acting in accord with the profit motive. But misusing commonly held resources can have negative consequences for all of us.

Consider the case of Los Angeles and General Motors. Los Angeles once had a pollution-free electric

railway system. In the 1930s, General Motors bought the system and then destroyed it, because GM wanted to sell cars, trucks, and buses. The company replaced the electric system with noisy, polluting diesel buses, so uncomfortable and unreliable that Los Angelenos were given a great incentive to rely on private autos.

In 1949, after buying and destroying electric railway systems in over 100 cities, GM was fined a paltry $5,000 by the government for illegally conspiring to replace municipal services with its own. Meanwhile the company made millions of dollars. Now, due in large part to the reliance on cars, smog in Los Angeles is a major health hazard. Some studies claim that children who grow up in Los Angeles lose up to 50% of their lung capacity from breathing in the polluted air.[14] Obviously, it is absurd to charge GM with creating the entire automobile culture of Los Angeles, but clearly its drive for private profits did not contribute to the common good.

When market competition imposes a social cost on the community that is considered unacceptable, economists call it an **externality**. The actions of GM in Los Angeles created a major externality, as do the actions of chemical companies who dispose of their toxic wastes in unsafe ways. Students living in dorms who play their stereos very loudly create less serious externalities.

Although almost everything we do affects others, government does not regulate all externalities that impose costs. It cannot make you buy a new car, paint your house, or use deodorant. Appropriate levels of government must decide what externalities it wishes to eliminate and then how best to eliminate them, whether through setting standards, taxation, or other means of regulation.

Inefficient Competition.   Government intervention is also desired when competition is inefficient. Adam Smith believed that goods and labor would be used in a way to maximize profit and limit cost. Because of competition among firms desiring to sell their products to consumers, manufacturers would make goods as cheaply as possible. But sometimes competition is not efficient. For example, because it is not cost effective (due to large capital outlays) for each community to have more than one company laying gas pipelines or generating electric power, competition cannot work to drive down prices or increase efficiency. Thus utilities (such as gas and electric producers) are regulated by government in most countries; in the United States it is done largely by state governments. The government gives a utility a monopoly over service in a given geographic area (that is, allows only one power company to operate), but it regulates the prices charged by that monopoly because people do not have a choice of sellers of electricity or gas. Smith himself agreed that this form of government intervention was appropriate.

Lack of Necessary Coordination.   Another reason for regulation is that sometimes the free market pro-

duces an unacceptable lack of coordination. An obvious example is regulation of airline flights. The free market is not well suited to determine which planes shall have priority to take off at 2:00 P.M. on a certain runway at JFK Airport in New York. Competition could lead to disaster. Thus the Federal Aviation Administration has been empowered to coordinate air traffic patterns.

We could let the market make decisions about takeoff and landing priorities by selling takeoff rights for a fee. But regulation would still be needed to make sure that all the planes authorized to take off at a given time did so in a way to maximize safety.

Unacceptable Inequities.   Another reason for regulation is to promote equity. Equity in this context does not refer to equality in outcome but to ensuring fair conditions for participation in the marketplace. Sometimes individuals or groups are severely disadvantaged by the private marketplace. For example, legislation setting minimum wages, banning child labor, protecting workers' rights to organize, and defining minimum standards for workplace health and safety recognizes that there is an inequity in power between individual workers and employers.

Regulations forbidding race and gender discrimination are also designed to enhance equity. Consumer protection laws, such as those forbidding false advertising, and laws licensing pharmacists, physicians, lawyers, and public accountants are based on the assumption that consumers will often not have sufficient information to evaluate the competence of those selling the service or product. Government seeks to remedy an inequity in information between the buyer and the seller of a product or service.

Antitrust regulation reduces inequity by prohibiting monopolies. If one or a few firms control the supply of a product, they can act, and have acted, together to set the price at a high level or to sell products below cost to drive small businesses out of the market.

One firm may use antitrust laws to sue others, or the government itself may initiate antitrust activities. The enforcement of antitrust legislation has waxed and waned over the years. The breakup of AT&T, which formerly controlled all the long-distance telephone service in the United States, is the result of antitrust regulation. It opened the door for other firms to compete with AT&T to sell telephones and tele-

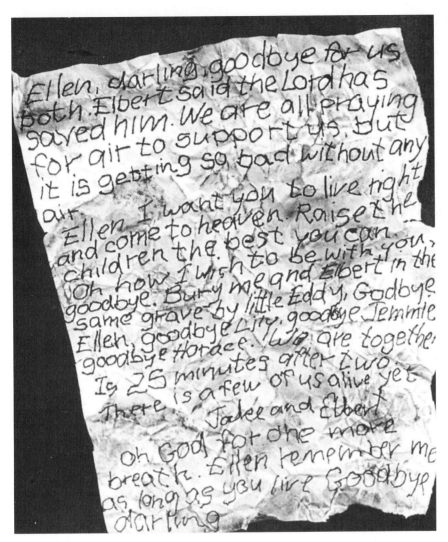

Jacob Vowell wrote this letter shortly before dying of suffocation in a mine disaster in Fraterville, Tennessee, in 1902. Such disasters eventually prompted government regulation of mining.

phone services. Whether this will result in a more efficient, less costly national telephone service is yet to be determined.[15]

Regulation to correct inequities is one of the most controversial types of regulation. Conservatives often argue that this type of regulation is inappropriate. They believe that the free market can solve problems: incompetent doctors and unsafe or ineffective products will sooner or later end up unwanted; pizza eaters can stop buying pizza with artificial cheese; unions can protect workers from unreasonable demands of corporations. (Some conservatives, however, oppose unions, believing they interfere with the free market for labor.)

Defenders of equity-based regulations point out that the workings of the market to provide vital information are too slow. People have been killed and injured before information about defective products or quack doctors became widely known. In the mid-1960s, many children were born with serious deformities because of the prescription drug thalidomide, which their mothers took during pregnancy. This incident caused Congress to set higher standards for drug safety and the Federal Drug Administration to tighten its drug-testing rules. And before 1972, 20 million consumers were injured each year by consumer products, and of those 30,000 were killed and over 100,000 permanently disabled. This prompted

Congress to establish the Consumer Product Safety Commission (CPSC), an independent regulatory agency mandated to establish safety standards for consumer products.

Some people have a good deal of faith in "educating" the public about risks. They believe that education campaigns, not regulation, are the best way to protect people. But education campaigns are not cost free, especially when maintained over a long period of time. Their effectiveness is not always high either. The government has waged a campaign to educate the public about the health hazards of smoking for 25 years. It has had a significant impact, but millions of Americans still smoke, and the campaign has cost tens of millions of dollars.

Congress does not regulate to remedy the effects of every inequity. Sometimes the costs of regulating are seen as higher than the gains to be achieved; in other cases, resistance to regulation by politically powerful groups is stronger than lobbying by potential beneficiaries of regulation.

National Regulation to Simplify Contradictory State Regulations. We have discussed conditions under which governments at all levels regulate. In a federal system, pressure specifically for national regulation arises when state governments have adopted different standards for regulating the same business activity. Businesses usually would rather have one federal regulation, especially if it is not too strong, than 10 or 30 or 50 separate state rules. After several years of lax federal regulatory activity during the 1980s, many states became quite active in enacting their own regulations. Some have become "regulatory Rambos."[16] Faced with new state regulations of their activities, pesticide manufacturers, credit card and insurance companies, auto manufacturers, used-car dealers, and other business and trade groups are appealing to the federal government for regulation. For example, President Reagan vetoed a federal law requiring energy savings standards for household appliances in 1986, but he found he had to backtrack in 1987 when industry as well as conservationists argued for it. Industry preferred a single federal statute to the hodgepodge of state regulations that had developed.[17] As one observer remarked, "Businesses may have miscalculated what federal deregulation would bring. . . . The paradoxical conclusion . . . is that [deregulation] eventually leads to more regulation."[18]

Regulatory Reform

As long as there has been regulation there have been demands for regulatory reform, and as regulation has increased, so has the sentiment for reform. Despite this, there is little consensus on what needs to be reformed and exactly how it should be done. As former EPA director Douglas Costle noted, "People are fed up with regulations, but that begins to fall apart the minute you start asking about specific regulations."[19]

Making Sure Regulations Are Beneficial

There are three general approaches to reforming regulation. One is to try to eliminate "unnecessary red tape" in the regulation process by making sure that every regulation has an overall benefit. Both Presidents Carter and Reagan were active in promoting this type of regulatory reform. During the Carter administration OSHA abolished over 1,100 of its 10,000 rules; many, such as the rule that required all toilet seats to be horseshoe-shaped, had been severely criticized as nitpicking. OSHA paperwork requirements, particularly for small businesses, were reduced, and safety inspections were concentrated on the industries with the worst safety records. The Reagan administration continued this pattern.

One of the major controversies in trying to reduce "bad" regulations is how to decide if a rule has more negative than positive effects, that is, if the risks the regulation is trying to prevent are great enough to justify the regulation. But how do we decide whether the risk involved in using a particular chemical, working in a hazardous environment, or using some sort of product is great enough to regulate? There is no agreement on this. In fact, in authorizing new regulations, Congress uses different standards of risk. Sometimes Congress applies a "no-risk" standard: if there are any risks at all, a substance is not to be used. Examples are regulations concerning safety in food or drugs: if a substance is found to cause cancer, it cannot be used.

Sometimes Congress uses a "margin of safety" criterion, telling the regulatory agency to find a reasonable standard and then allow an extra margin of safety. For example, standards for clean air mandate the Environmental Protection Agency to declare how much lead, sulfur, and other materials can be in the air before it is unsafe. Once the agency determines that, it is

The federal government is proposing an $11 million acre set aside program to protect the spotted owl's habitat in Washington, Oregon, and California. This would mean a 50% reduction in logging on national lands and a loss of up to 40,000 jobs. Any cost-benefit analysis depends on how one weighs the relative importance of jobs and environmental values.

supposed to make the standards a little stricter to allow the extra margin of safety.[20]

Sometimes Congress mandates a standard whereby cost of the regulation is to be weighed against the risk. The Office of Management and Budget has formalized this into a **cost-benefit analysis**. Many consumer product safety regulations have this risk standard. A product is not to be regulated unless the benefits outweigh the costs.

Generally, proregulation groups prefer the no-risk or extra margin standards, while antiregulation forces prefer a cost-benefit one. Critics of government regulation charge that agencies often do not take into account all the negative consequences of their rules. For example, pollution-control devices on autos raise the cost of the car for the consumer. Pollution and safety standards in industry raise the cost of the production process and may result in the product becoming uncompetitive on the world market. These critics argue for more use of cost-benefit analysis of each proposed rule.

However, critics of the Reagan and Carter administrations' reliance on cost-benefit analyses have charged that these analyses are not done fairly or competently.[21] They believe that costs are concrete and easily calculated, while benefits are often more difficult to put in dollar terms. How do you quantify saving human lives? If a particular rule is likely to save five lives per year at a cost of $5 million, does the regulation offer a net cost or a net benefit? It ultimately depends on a value judgment, which, critics charge, can be obscured by a cost-accountant mentality.

For example, in their cost analyses, OSHA figures a human life is worth $2 million, EPA and CPSC $1 million, and the Federal Aviation Administration $650,000.[22] Thus, using the $1 million estimate, the Consumer Product Safety Commission told manufacturers of reclining chairs they need not fix a problem with the chairs that had resulted in several children being strangled unless fixing it cost less than $.25 per chair. The CPSC's economists figured out that at more than $.25 for each of 40 million chairs manufactured, the cost of fixing the problem would be more than the lives of the children were worth.[23]

Making Regulators More Accountable

A second type of regulatory reform is to try to make regulators more accountable, that is, to ensure that they make the rules necessary to implement and enforce regulatory activity authorized by Congress. The legislative veto (see chapter 10) is one such mechanism that Congress has used in its oversight function. A second mechanism for monitoring the work of regulators is the review by the Office of Management and Budget (OMB) of rules proposed by executive branch agencies. This innovation by the Reagan administration was designed to give OMB the authority to identify and eliminate duplicate rules and to develop procedures for cost-benefit analyses.

Many strongly oppose this new power of OMB, arguing that it gives the president, through OMB, too much power over administrative rule making. The independence of regulatory agencies is being eroded. Regulations developed through the formal rules of agencies working according to due process have been killed by OMB without any public hearings or advance notification. This violates the spirit of the Administrative Procedure Act, which requires openness

Assessing Risk: How Much
Is It Worth to Get Rid of Acne?

Pimples, zits, acne—whatever you call them, skin blemishes are a curse to millions of teenagers and some of their elders. Acne "cures" are a multimillion-dollar business, but most are not very effective. But in the early 1980s, it appeared that a truly effective cure for serious acne had finally been discovered.

After a six-year investigation of its effectiveness and safety, the Food and Drug Administration (FDA) declared the drug, Accutane, effective. Approved in 1982, it was hailed as a wonder drug by thousands of patients and their doctors. But the FDA's studies had shown that the drug caused birth defects in animals. Did this pose a risk too great to justify letting the public buy it to cure acne? That was the question the FDA had to answer.

The FDA took a middle position. It stated that Accutane must not be given to patients "who are pregnant or intend to become pregnant." But shortly after the drug hit the market, its manufacturer, Hoffman-LaRoche, began receiving reports of miscarriages and birth defects in infants whose mothers took the drug. Though the manufacturer sent letters to doctors warning of these risks and produced new warning labels for the drug, the reports kept coming. In 1984, of 170 women who had taken Accutane during pregnancy, only 24 had normal births, 20 gave birth to infants with birth defects, and almost half had abortions, some of them because the women had been warned about the possibility of birth defects. Referring to a child born of a mother who had used Accutane, one lawyer reported, "She can't walk. She can't talk. She can't eat by herself. She can't do anything by herself."

Between 1984 and 1986, the manufacturer strengthened the warning on the label again and sent more mailings to doctors. But in 1985, a study published in a major medical journal showed that a pregnant woman taking Accutane was 26 times more likely than other women to have an infant with a major birth defect.

Based on this evidence, and studies by the FDA's own scientists, who estimated that around 1,000 birth defects

may have occurred because of the drug, the agency held a hearing to decide what to do. A panel of experts heard testimony from the manufacturer, doctors, and representatives of patients.

The agency considered three options. It could essentially use a "no-risk" standard and take the drug off the market because of the harm it had done. To do this suggested that no amount of warnings could adequately protect patients. On the other hand, the agency could do nothing at all. Perhaps birth defects were simply an unavoidable consequence of a powerful drug, and the warnings were adequate if a patient and her doctor were reasonably attentive. As one doctor said, the issue is "whether a drug of great benefit to many should be removed to reduce hurt to one. . . . It is an issue that we deal with on every drug (. . . even aspirin . . .). This one is a little more dramatic."

As an in-between step, the agency considered more regulation but not a total ban. Suggestions included allowing only certain doctors to dispense it or forcing women in the childbearing years to get a second opinion before being given a prescription.

Ultimately the agency decided the drug was not risky enough to ban, but too risky to handle the way it had been. In an unprecedented move, it ordered the manufacturer to warn customers of potential birth defects by using a picture of a deformed baby on the drug's packaging. As the agency spokesman said, "It . . . emphasize(s) to people that we're not talking about a remote risk of some minor birth defect but a very high risk of extremely severe birth defects that can . . . make the child unable to function." The agency also ordered that women users sign a consent form stating they understand the risks of the drug. Meanwhile, the manufacturer is being sued by patients whose babies were born deformed.

Sources: Philip J. Hilts and Susan Okie, "Balancing Risk vs. Benefits," *Washington Post National Weekly Edition*, May 2–8, 1988, p. 32; and "Acne Drug Maker Must Use Deformed Baby's Picture," *Lincoln Journal*, May 27, 1988.

in rule making, and diminishes governmental responsiveness. For example, EPA rules for limiting the amount of toxic chemicals that industries could dump in municipal sewage systems were killed three months after they were issued. This undoing of the rules followed an extensive lobbying campaign with OMB by chemical manufacturers and other producers of toxic wastes.[24] On another occasion, after following its

rule-making procedures, OSHA wrote a rule about limiting workers' exposure to a particular chemical. "OMB simply crossed it out."[25]

Deregulation

A third regulatory reform is **deregulation**, that is, ending regulation in a particular area. Proponents of deregulation argue that it is not enough to streamline paperwork and make regulators more accountable; in many cases regulators simply should not be regulating at all. Most of the major legislative deregulation occurred in the Carter administration when trucking, airlines, and banks were all deregulated.

Banking provides a good example of deregulation. Traditionally banks and savings and loan (S&L) institutions were heavily regulated and protected from competition. But during the 1970s and early 1980s interest rates were rising rapidly, and banks and S&Ls were competing fiercely to retain their depositors and attract new ones. They were also in competition with the federal government for investors' money as interest rates on treasury notes continued to rise. In the bipartisan deregulatory mood of the time Congress adopted a series of measures, beginning in 1980, to deregulate many aspects of the banking industry. To help S&Ls be more competitive, the cap was lifted on the interest they could pay depositors; at the same time Congress raised the maximum level of federal deposit insurance allowable on each account from $40,000 to $100,000. Both banks and S&Ls were given more freedom to decide what financial services to offer. Within days, interest was being paid on checking accounts; credit card companies raised their interest rates; brokerage, insurance firms, and even department stores got into the banking business; and S&L's offered a new range of services and made new types of investments formerly prohibited.

Reregulation

In politics as in physics, actions usually produce reactions. The actions to deregulate have brought about cries for some **reregulation,** a resumption of regulatory activity. While deregulation has brought about lower rates or fares in some industries, it has also brought new problems. The problems in the airline industry, illustrated in the Focus on an Issue box, are one example. Those in the financial industries are another.

Deregulation in the banking and savings and loan industries coupled with poor economic conditions contributed to record rates of bank and S&L failures in the late 1980s and early 1990s.[26] With the cap removed on interest rates some S&Ls attracted new depositors by paying interest rates that were more than double the interest rates their mortgage holders were paying. With these policies it was only a matter of time before the S&Ls would go broke, unless they

made windfall profits from their investments. As a result, many S&Ls, big and small, made increasingly risky investments in order to survive and profit in the now highly competitive atmosphere. Banks too made high-risk loans to foreign governments and domestic farmers, while some S&Ls made shaky real estate investments, then saw the bottom drop out of their investments when real estate prices plummeted.

During this period, federal scrutiny of bank and S&L activities fell off drastically, even though the government, through its federal deposit insurance program (FDIC), guaranteed each deposit (of up to $100,000) that the banks and S&Ls used for their risky investments. The Federal Home Loan Bank Board, which regulates S&Ls, was repeatedly denied its requests for more examiners and auditors. For example, in the first half of the 1980s the number of S&L examiners in Texas, the state hardest hit by S&L failures, dropped from 54 to 12.[27] In the last half of the 1980s, 1,000 banks failed, including the nation's eighth largest, Continental Illinois. Thanks to the federal deposit insurance program few individuals lost their savings, but it took an additional $4 billion loan from the government to restore Continental Illinois to solvency. At the beginning of the 1990s, 1,046 banks, holding over 12% of all banking industry assets, were

The bank failures of the 1930s, which wiped out the life savings of ordinary and wealthy citizens alike, led the government to provide insurance for depositors at banks and savings and loans. This program meant that the taxpayers in general, and not individual depositors, paid the bill when reckless and sometimes illegal actions of banks and savings and loans caused a new round of failures after deregulation in the 1970s.

FOCUS ON AN ISSUE

Should We
Reregulate the Airlines?

Before President Carter signed the airline deregulation bill in 1978, commercial airliners were heavily regulated. An airline had to gain the approval of the Civil Aeronautics Board (CAB) in order to fly any particular route and to set its fares. Originally this procedure was designed to help the struggling airline industry by protecting it from competition.

In the years since that 1938 law was passed, the airline industry grew in size and economic strength. Many felt that the regulations were hurting, not helping, the industry and its passengers. By the middle 1970s the time seemed right for deregulation. The oil crisis had caused airline rates to skyrocket and put many in economic difficulties.

The 1978 bill phased in deregulation. Airlines were allowed to enter new routes without CAB approval and were permitted flexibility in setting their rates. However, airlines serving certain routes between small communities were given subsidies in order to ensure that these communities would be served for at least 10 years.

The CAB itself was abolished, and regulation of airlines was left to the Federal Aviation Administration (FAA), which oversees safety matters.

Over a dozen years later, policymakers and the public differ over how successful airline deregulation has been. Some argue for reregulation, others believe that deregulation has worked well. In deciding how well deregulation has worked, consider these questions.

Has Deregulation Made the Airlines More Efficient and Competitive?

One of the reasons for deregulation was to make the industry more competitive. By opening up competition

Among federal regulations designed to insure the safety of airline passengers are regulation of the training and working conditions of pilots and air controllers.

among the airlines, it was hoped that they would seek ways to become more efficient and then lower fares.

At first it appeared that deregulation would increase competition. The number of airlines nearly tripled between 1978 and 1983. But since then many airlines have lost money and laid off workers, and some have folded or been bought out by larger carriers. By 1990, the eight largest airlines controlled about 90% of all commercial air travel in the United States. Some analysts believe that

on the FDIC's list of banks vulnerable to failure.[28] For the first time ever the FDIC, with a projected shortfall of more than $20 billion for the first half of the 1990s, considered borrowing money to keep the insurance fund solvent.[29]

The S&L crisis has proven much more costly. Nearly 1,000 S&Ls (out of 3,000) went hopelessly into debt in the deregulation era and 27% of all thrifts

failed. Covering the losses, the federal insurance company for S&Ls, the Federal Savings and Loan Insurance Corporation (FSLIC), went broke. As a consequence, the FDIC took control of over 200 of the institutions, trying to put them on a sounder financial base. In its hurried effort to get S&Ls back in private hands the FDIC has been accused of selling some of them well below their value to Wall Street speculators.

within a decade only three huge carriers—United, American, and Delta—and some of the small regional carriers will survive. If that happens, the big carriers may not compete as fiercely as they did in the decade after deregulation.

Competition has been further diminished because the airlines have divided up the nation into regional turfs. In 10 major cities, two-thirds of the air traffic is controlled by one airline, such as Trans World in St. Louis and Northwest in Minneapolis. Even in huge airports like Chicago and Atlanta, two airlines control three-fourths of the traffic. One GAO study showed that at concentrated hubs the fares of the dominant airlines were 27% higher than the fares at other airports.[1] The system is what economists call an oligopoly, a situation where a few firms dominate an industry. Thus, as critic Ralph Nader put it, deregulation has changed the air system from a regulated oligopoly to an unregulated oligopoly.

Source: © 1987, Boston Globe. Distributed by Los Angeles Times Syndicate. Reprinted by permission.

Has Deregulation Increased Passenger Traffic?

Between 1978 and 1988, the number of airline passengers increased by 65% and the number of flights by about 35%.[2] Some argue that this increase is largely a product of economic prosperity, but most believe that it was primarily due to greater competition over fares and routes brought by deregulation. Although fares increased for shorter, less-well-traveled routes, they dropped by as much as 17% overall (adjusted for inflation).[3] However, by the end of the 1980s, fares were going up, and during 1989–90 they rose faster than the cost of living.[4] Recession, higher fuel costs, and fear of terrorism affected the level of passenger traffic during this period and contributed to airline losses.

Are Airlines Less Safe Now?

Critics believe that, in the struggle to be competitive and profitable, airlines have increased their efficiency at the expense of passenger safety. Given the higher volume of air traffic, jets built in the 1960s have been kept in service beyond their planned life span. In addition there has been

a decline in the number of experienced mechanics available to service them. Pilots are being pushed harder by their airlines to fly more hours, sometimes in excess of the legal limits. Because of the increased stress, more pilots are quitting. Commuter airlines are having a difficult time finding experienced pilots at all.

Some of these safety problems are reflected in the increase in near midair crashes, from 311 in 1982 to 839 in 1986. Fortunately, this steady increase has not been accompanied by an equal increase in actual accidents. Although 1989 was an exceptionally bad year, far fewer people were killed in the 1980s than in the 1970s, and the overall accident rate for 1980–90 was half that for the previous 10 years.[5]

Supporters of deregulation point out that part of the safety problems has nothing to do with deregulation, per se, but rather with the loss, three years after deregulation, of thousands of air traffic controllers (whose job it is to monitor air traffic and communicate with pilots, telling them when it is safe to take off and land and what traffic

(continued on next page)

In short, deregulation in the financial industry has led to disaster. Proponents of deregulation argue that a truly free market would be more efficient because consistently bad business decisions would bring failure without benefit of a taxpayer rescue. But in the case of Continental Illinois and the hundreds of insolvent S&Ls, the government believed that the nation could not afford to let them go under. Huge banks defaulting and millions of people losing their savings would send shock waves throughout the nation, so the federal government stepped in to save them. Thus critics of banking deregulation argue that since banks have the luxury of Uncle Sam's pocketbook when things go wrong, they should be forced by Uncle Sam to conduct themselves in a prudent manner. The S&L bailout reflected this, by imposing tougher new regulations that S&Ls must now meet.

pattern they must follow). In 1981, in order to break their strike, President Reagan fired about two-thirds of the nation's 16,000 air controllers. Even though thousands of new controllers have been hired since then, there are fewer controllers than in 1978 even though air traffic has vastly increased. Further, only 62% of the air controllers now working are fully qualified compared to 80% before the strike. Experienced air controllers at major airports work many hours a week overtime and most believe their workloads are probably a danger to air safety, as are the outmoded computers still in many airports. After six years of denying a problem with the limited number of air controllers, in 1987 the administration began to hire more.

Has Airline Deregulation Limited Passenger Convenience?

Opponents of deregulation argue that it has made flying much less convenient. As one said, "Today's frequent flyers have become frequent whiners." Flights are frequently late. In order to be competitive, airlines overschedule flights at prime time. Every airline wants to fly to Chicago, for example, in the late afternoon. Thus, airlines schedule far more such flights than can be accommodated. In 1987, then Secretary of Transportation Elizabeth Dole, investigating this situation, found nearly 100 Delta and Eastern flights were more than 15 minutes late most of the time, due to deceptive scheduling.

Many delays are due to congestion at major airports; no new airports have been built since 1976. Airport expansions are often opposed by major carriers with special 20- to 30-year leasing arrangements with large airports where they control much of the traffic. At over half of the largest airports these long-term leases give a single airline a veto over airport expansion. Thus, the dominant airline can stop an expansion project that would provide new gates for potential competitors.[6] In addition to delays, pas-

sengers now have to contend with a byzantine system for setting fares. On one 1990 United Airlines domestic flight, five passengers with identical coach accommodations paid five different fares, ranging from $124 to $586. In order for passengers to take advantage of lower fares it is necessary to book and purchase tickets well in advance.

Complaints about lost baggage have also skyrocketed, and as one columnist wondered, "How can you trust an airline to get you there safely when they can't even keep track of your luggage?"[7]

Supporters of deregulation do not challenge the charges, but they point out that deregulation has allowed millions of people to fly who could not afford it before. Some of the problems of delays and baggage loss are due to the greater number of passengers the airlines are now carrying.

1. Kirk Victor, "Hub Cap," *National Journal*, May, 12, 1990, p. 1148.
2. Larry Eichel, "Flying the Unfriendly Skies," *Washington Monthly*, February 1990, pp. 12–13.
3. Steve Lohr, "War and Recession Speed Up the Airlines' Flights to Oblivion," *New York Times*, February 17, 1991, p. E5.
4. Eichel, "Flying the Unfriendly Skies," p. 11.
5. Ibid., p. 16.
6. Victor, "Hub Cap," p. 1145.
7. Dave Balderston, "A Judgment Call: Measuring the Safety of Airlines," *GAO Journal* (Spring 1988):39–45.
Other Sources: Margaret Kriz, "Winging It," *National Journal*, June 20, 1987 p. 1586; "How Late Are Those Planes," *Washington Post National Weekly Edition*, April 27, 1987, editorial; Paulette Thomas, "Bumpy Ride: Pilots Fear the Stress of Turmoil in the Airline Industry," *Wall Street Journal*, April 24, 1987, p. 33; Laura Parker, "They Make the Going Late," *Washington Post National Weekly Edition*, April 20, 1987, p. 11; "Be Careful Out There," *Time*, January 12, 1987, pp. 25–32; Herbert Rowen, "Deregulation Revisited," *Washington Post National Weekly Edition*," October 24–30, 1988, p. 5; Martha Hamilton, "Eastern Turns on the 'No-Flying' Sign," *Washington Post National Weekly Edition*, March 20–26, 1989; William Stockton, "When Eight Carriers Call the Shots," *New York Times*, November 20, 1988, Section 3, p. 1; Martha Hamilton, "From Here to There is Never a Straight Price," *Washington Post National Weekly Edition*, November 28-December 4, 1988, p. 20.

Regulatory Reform in the Reagan and Bush Administrations

Deregulation has had broad bipartisan support since the 1970s. However, there have been some partisan differences in the nature of this support. The Carter administration and Democrats in general tended to support deregulation to the extent that it made busi-

ness activity more efficient and less cumbersome and when it eliminated rules that were not beneficial to the public.

Many Republicans have gone further by opposing some kinds of regulation in principle as interference with market competition. This position was exemplified by the Reagan administration policy of stripping regulatory agencies of personnel and budgets. Agency

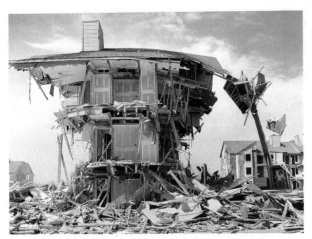

This unfinished condominium was razed when the S&L financing it went under.

budgets decreased 8% during Reagan's first term, with some agencies taking much larger cuts. The number of positions in the Interior Department's Office of Surface Mining, for example, was nearly halved, and its regional offices were abolished. In this way enforcement of strip-mining regulations was dramatically cut back. The Consumer Product Safety Commission lost 41% of its staff and 22% of its budget. On the whole, agencies regulating consumer and environmental interests were hardest hit; those regulating health and safety were cut less.[30] Not until 1988 did regulatory agencies reach the level of funding they had in 1980.

Critics point out that these attacks on regulation made some problems worse; understaffed agencies meant longer delays, larger backlogs, and inadequately researched decisions—the very problems that antiregulation forces complain about.

Another "deregulation" technique used by President Reagan was to appoint people to regulatory posts who favored either little regulation or self-regulation by industry. This meant that the number of regulations proposed and enacted decreased, and enforcement slowed too. Between 1980 and 1985, for example, OSHA cut its factory inspections by 40% and penalties for violators by 42%.[31] Only three new standards for toxic substances were issued in six years. Senator Edward Kennedy (D-Mass.) noted that the deregulation of OSHA is a "blueprint for how to effectively repeal a statute without changing the law."[32]

Work-related injuries began to increase in 1983, jumped by 12% (the largest increase since OSHA was created) the following year,[33] and continued to increase through 1988, the last year for which we have information. In 1987 and 1988, 21,000 people died in workplace accidents, not counting those who died of work-related illnesses such as black lung. This is far more people than have died in all of the earthquakes, fires, train wrecks, and plane crashes, plus the five worst floods, hurricanes, and tornadoes, since 1925.[34]

By Reagan's second term, a backlash against the effects of deregulation emerged.[35] The S&L crisis, the stock market crash, controversies over airline deregulation, scandals surrounding some top regulatory officials, and growing concern about the environment moved the public and Congress to call for more regulation. In a 1989 survey, workers listed safety as their highest job priority, above salary benefits and day care.[36] Regulatory activity increased and the president gave less attention to the goal of deregulation in his second term.[37]

President Bush chaired the Reagan task force that promoted deregulation. Although he called for more environmental protection in his election campaign, as a matter of policy he is opposed to new regulation and in favor of offering "incentives, choice and flexibility for industry to find the best solutions."[38] But because deregulation is not the priority for Bush that it was for Reagan, he made less of an effort to thwart the work of regulators. In fact, there was a surge in regulatory activity during the early 1990s. Bush appointed to head the Food and Drug Administration a man who has vowed to crack down on fraud, enforce truth-in-labeling, and revamp the procedures by which drugs are approved for public use. And more than 500 additional people were hired by the EPA just to write rules to implement the 1990 Clean Air Act.[39]

Although Bush did support the Clean Air Act of 1990, and appointed some supporters of regulation to his cabinet, in other areas his support for environmental regulation was extremely weak. His administration was slow to join international efforts to curb the effects of acid rain, and Chief of Staff John Sununu was an active opponent of regulation to slow the greenhouse effect. Bush's secretary of energy refused to request an increase in funding for cleanup of nuclear weapons plants, saying the money was not needed. Finally, Bush's energy policy deemphasized conservation and encouraged exploration and drilling in national refuge lands. It called for less stringent regulation of oil and gas pipelines and for making the

Figure 1 ■ Spending for Environmental Protection Fell During Reagan's First Term

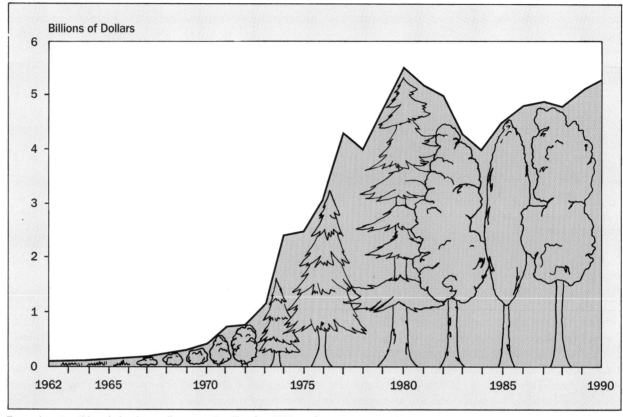

From almost nothing, federal spending rose steadily after 1973 as Congress passed legislation to control air, water, and hazardous waste pollution. Deregulation efforts caused a sharp drop in environmental spending between 1980 and 1984; afterward spending slowly rose again.

Source: Budget of the United States 1990. Historical Tables, Table 3.3.

licensing procedure for nuclear power plants more lenient by reducing public participation in the process.

Environmental Protection

An important goal of federal regulation is environmental protection. Such regulation is a fairly new mission of the federal government but an increasingly extensive one (see figure 1). The battles over environmental regulation parallel those over regulation in other areas. The crucial issue can be stated simply, but it cannot be answered simply. How can we define regulations and standards that protect society's interest in having a clean and healthy environment and at the same time not unreasonably handicap business and other producers of pollution? Historical and current

debates over environmental policy revolve around that issue.

Evolution of Government's Role

Eighteenth-century Americans did not worry about harming the environment. The continent, largely unsettled, was graced with resources that seemed almost infinite: "A fertile, widespreading country . . . blessed with a variety of soils . . . and watered . . . with innumerable streams, for the delight and accommodation of its inhabitants."[40]

The Constitution contains no hint of concern about preserving and protecting the environment. Indeed, the Founders' and our own orientation to the environment is rooted in the Western, Judeo-Christian tradition that the physical world exists to serve human needs.[41] This sentiment was reinforced during the

Picking Up the Pieces of Deregulation: The Savings and Loan Bailout

As member institutions in the savings and loan industry have continued to fail, the press has given increasing attention to the "villains" of this story: the bad managers (S&L owners and board members, including President Bush's son Jeb); members of Congress who failed to carry out their oversight function; and the dealmakers who put together high-risk or fraudulent real estate and development projects. But Charles E. Schumer (D-N.Y.) has said that the scandal is really about the "crisis of an idea." He was referring to deregulation and the way it was implemented in the banking and S&L industries. The government, he said, "behaved like a fire insurance company that said to its customers: 'Go ahead, play with matches. We'll cover you if anything goes wrong.'"[1]

The "we" Schumer refers to is of course American taxpayers. No one is yet certain exactly how much it will cost to rescue the S&L industry and to pay off insured depositors. Estimates run from $150 to $180 billion just for the Bush years and as high as $500 billion over the next 10 to 30 years. One plan for budgeting $50 billion annually to cover S&L losses would cost the average family with a $30,000 income $285 *annually* in taxes.[2]

Meanwhile Congress has created the Resolution Trust Corporation (RTC) and given it 5,000 employees to manage the $300 billion worth of assets that had been taken from failed S&Ls by the end of 1990. This property included not only bank buildings, junk bonds, and furniture but also ski resorts, marinas, 35% to 40% of the city of Colorado Springs, Colorado, and "fixtures from the South Fork Ranch featured in the television series 'Dallas.'"[3]

With the benefit of a "fire sale" in the summer of 1990 the RTC managed to reduce its holdings by half, but with every additional failed S&L it receives new inventory. The price of some of the real estate was being discounted up to 50%, and an estimated 2,000 to 3,000 houses were to be given away to nonprofit community groups.[4]

The revenue gained from RTC sales will not make a very big dent in the total bailout bill. Proposals to place the

tax burden for the S&L cleanup on those wealthy investors who profited most from the high interest rates of the 1980s (such as through a surtax on unearned income) have not made it out of congressional committee. Therefore, the burden of the bailout will probably fall on the average taxpayer. And, because our tax structure is now more regressive than it was a decade ago (see chapter 17), the burden will fall disproportionately on those in the middle- and lower-income brackets.

1. Quoted in Paul Taylor, "The Democrats Discover the Savings and Loan Scandal," *Washington Post National Weekly Edition*, June 4–10, 1990, p. 13.
2. "You—and S&L Bailout," *Lincoln Journal*, August, 20, 1990.
3. Stephen Labaton, "The Bailout Agency Becomes a Highly Motivated Seller," *New York Times*, March 31, 1991, p. E4.
4. Ibid.
Other Sources: James Bennet, "How the Cleaver Family Destroyed our S&Ls," *Washington Monthly*, September 1990, pp. 38–46; "60 Minutes," April 21, 1991.

eighteenth-century period known as the Enlightenment, which led people to believe that through science and learning, we could conquer almost any obstacle to human progress.[42] The possible negative consequences of science and technology for the environment were a long way away.

But in the nineteenth century, concern grew about the effect that the industrial revolution, coupled with rapid population growth, might have on the environment. Late in that century, a conservationist movement to preserve some of the natural environment from farmers and loggers who were clearing the land

In the 1870s, Congress appropriated money to survey, map, and photograph the previously uncharted West. The photographs, like this 1871 shot of Mammoth Hot Springs in Yellowstone, helped convince unbelievers that reports of glorious scenery in places like Yellowstone and the Tetons were true. In 1872, Yellowstone became the first national park.

resulted in the creation of the national forests and a national park system.[43]

Along with concern about saving some forests and other areas of scenic beauty came an awareness of pollution. The first effort to combat water pollution was an 1899 law requiring that individuals dumping waste into navigable waters get a permit from the Army Corps of Engineers. And in 1924, Congress banned oceangoing ships from dumping oil in coastal waters. Neither of these acts was enforced very well, but they did indicate an embryonic concern with pollution.

The modern environmental movement probably stems from a book, *Silent Spring,* published in 1962 by Rachel Carson. Carson showed that pesticides used in agriculture find their way into the air and water and harm crops, animals, and people. Moreover, she demonstrated that scientists and engineers did not know the extent of these harmful effects, nor did they seem particularly concerned. The chemical industry immediately attacked Carson, accusing her of hysteria and misstatement of facts. The industry's attacks drew widespread publicity to her views and raised the environmental consciousness of millions of Americans.

The decade and a half following the publicity over Carson's book was characterized by a burst of new regulatory activity. Beginning in 1964 and continuing through 1977, Congress passed a series of laws designed to protect the air and water from pollution and to deal with hazardous waste.

Public concern peaked too. Huge oil spills, rivers catching fire, and the growing impact of the automobile on air quality lent substance to these concerns. By 1970, opinion polls showed that the most frequently cited public problem was protecting the environment, surprising in light of the continuing protest against the Vietnam War.[44] The environmental movement had its protest too. In April 1970 Earth Day was inaugurated and hundreds of thousands of citizens across the nation demonstrated to show their concern about the environment. Every year since one day in April has been set aside to celebrate the planet's resources and to heighten environmental awareness.

In 1970, Congress gave citizens a more formal way to affect environmental policy. New legislation, the National Environmental Policy Act, mandated government agencies to prepare **environmental impact statements** for their projects or projects they fund. These analyses must detail the effect, including any negative consequences, a project or other activity will have on the environment. No new buildings, dams, sewers, pipelines or highways can be built nor any research or other government projects initiated until this statement has been filed.

Not only did the law give federal agencies the power to comment on each other's environmental impact statements, but it also gave citizens access. Added almost as an afterthought, this provision would become an important device for organizations interested in protecting the environment, giving them real opportunity to influence environmental policies. Within

An Earth Day celebrant illustrating a possible future scenario if air pollution is not curbed.

a few years, over 400 legal suits were filed to force the government to comply with the act's provisions, and by 1980, thousands had been filed.[45] Strictly enforced by the courts, the act affected the activities of dozens of federal agencies.

Another landmark move marking the growing federal involvement in environmental protection was the 1970 creation of the **Environmental Protection Agency (EPA)** by President Nixon.[46] Recognizing that responsibilities for pollution control were spread throughout the executive branch, Nixon, with congressional approval, brought together in the EPA staff from the departments of Interior; Health, Education, and Welfare; and Agriculture, as well as from the Food and Drug Administration and the Atomic Energy Commission. The EPA is an unusual regulatory agency. Unlike the independent regulatory commissions, which are headed by a several-member body and are independent of the president, the EPA has a single head who reports to the president.

In the early years the EPA's main responsibility was regulating air and water pollution. During the 1970s it received extensive new mandates to regulate hazardous waste, pesticides, and noise pollution. We will examine three major areas of EPA jurisdiction: air, water, and hazardous waste.

Protecting the Air

Three major sources account for about three-fourths of all air pollution: gas-burning vehicles (cars, trucks, buses), industry, and electric power.[47] In a society with growing population and wealth, pollution is likely to increase continually unless government acts to control it.

Federal Legislation. The growing Los Angeles smog in the 1940s first brought air pollution to public attention. But the federal government did not pass meaningful legislation to try to reduce air pollution until 1963, when it authorized the Department of Health, Education, and Welfare to help states fight air pollution. Four years later, federal legislation required states to set air quality standards.

The major federal clean air legislation was passed in 1970. In the Clean Air Act Amendments Congress acted boldly to establish federal leadership in cleaning up the air. Through a combination of requirements, Congress intended to reduce emissions by the major polluters.

The nation's foulest air is in Los Angeles. Ozone concentrations exceed EPA standards by 300%, though the air is better than it used to be. Local officials are now enacting tough new regulations to curb the use of gasoline-fueled cars and buses and reduce industrial emissions.

These complex amendments had several parts. First, they required auto manufacturers to reduce auto emissions by 90% within five years or face a fine of $10,000 on each auto that did not measure up. But no technology was available to meet these standards so automakers had to invent devices for reducing auto emissions. A second part of the act ordered the EPA to establish air quality standards for major pollutants. Other parts of the act required states to produce acceptable air pollution control plans and permitted citizens to sue to enforce the act.[48]

Passing a law is one thing, enforcing it another. Automakers immediately asked for more time to reduce emissions, claiming they could not meet the standards. At first the extension was refused, but after the price hike in oil in 1973 and the difficult financial situation of auto manufacturers in the mid-1970s, several extensions were granted. However, it became apparent that, counter to U.S. auto manufacturers' claims, the standards were technologically feasible since foreign manufacturers were able to meet them. Consequently, by the end of the 1970s, the standards had been restored, only to be partly rolled back by the Reagan administration.

Enforcing the standards for other companies in other industries has also been difficult. Though in theory, the EPA can have a noncomplying company closed down, this is simply not politically feasible or particularly wise. Generally, the agency is reluctant to enforce standards against large companies with political clout or small profit margins. The steel industry, for example, has a record of low compliance with EPA standards compared with other industries. It claims it cannot meet the standards without going broke. This may be true in some instances, but in other cases it is not, as demonstrated by the ability of at least one large steel company to muster the capital to take over other major companies. But to take action against a large industry requires significant political will all the way to the White House. That kind of commitment has not been evident.

Benefits from Clean Air Legislation.   Nearly two decades after the Clean Air Act Amendments, most people judge them at least a partial success. Auto emissions have been reduced significantly. Even with more miles being driven, even though trucks and diesel vehicles are exempt, and even though the standards affect only cars built after the regulations went into effect and not those already on the road, carbon monoxide concentrations decreased by one-third in the 1970s.[49]

Other aspects of air quality have improved significantly too. A 1990 EPA study estimated that sulfur dioxide emissions "into the air are less than 60% of what they would have been without pollution controls; that airborne particles are 30% of what they would have been otherwise; nitrogen oxides, 72%; carbon monoxide 43%, and lead 3%."[50] Yet EPA head William Reilly said that "112 million people are living in areas still exceeding the smog standards."[51] In 1990, Congress, with the support of the Bush administration, passed a new Clean Air Act aimed at reducing urban smog, airborne toxics, and the effects of acid rain (see You are There, chapter 1). One measure requires that the antipollution devices put in new cars be capable of reducing tail-pipe emissions by 98%.

Businesses and environmentalists differ wildly about what the net cost of these improvements has been. The estimates vary depending on what monetary value is put on intangibles such as human health, comfort, and appreciation of clean air. But the best estimates show that air pollution control has been a large net benefit to the nation. For example, although some people are laid off when factories choose to close rather than install pollution-control devices, even more people are employed making, distributing, and educating people about air pollution devices. Anne Burford, the antiregulation head of EPA, for example, estimated that 33,000 people were thrown out of work during the 1970s because of all forms of pollution control requirements; but

the air pollution control industry alone employs 300,000 people.[52] Although industries must pay employees to deal with federal regulations, and some pollution-control equipment costs millions, pollution devices improve health and ultimately mean fewer days lost from sickness, reduced cleaning costs, and longer life for materials less damaged by corrosion.[53] Cleaning up the air also increases agricultural output. For California crops alone, the damage from air pollution is estimated at $300 million a year.[54]

Problems in Improving Air Quality.   Despite these successes, serious problems remain. One is determining which methods of regulation are most effective. Recall there are many ways to regulate, and setting standards is only one of them. The Clean Air Act mandates the EPA to set standards indicating how much exposure to certain pollutants is acceptable. Industries must meet these standards for each pollutant for each of their smokestacks and other sources of emissions. Then the EPA seeks to enforce these standards.

The standards approach has flaws. It provides few incentives for industry to comply. Penalties are often not assessed, and when they are, the fines are usually less than the cost of complying with the standards. Secondly, the standards drawn for a national set of industries may not make sense in specific instances; a company might achieve compliance more cheaply using methods other than those the regulation specifies.

To deal with these objections the Carter administration adapted the policy of allowing some regulations to be based on the **bubble concept**. This policy allows companies to meet an overall standard based on emissions inside an imaginary bubble placed over a particular factory. For example, assume a factory has 10 smokestacks emitting pollutants. Under the old rules, each smokestack would have to meet EPA standards. Under the bubble concept one or more smokestacks might exceed the limits on emissions as long as the total emissions from the smokestacks met the standard. Thus, rather than reducing all 10 smokestacks to the required level, the company might find it cheaper to install equipment on 5 smokestacks to bring their emissions below the required amount and leave the other 5 above the required level. The bubble concept permits flexibility in determining how the standard will be met and saves business up to 80% of the cost of compliance with the standards.

An even more flexible system allows a multi-factory bubble. The standard is set for a small area

Needed: A Mega-Superfund

Even though the costs of cleaning up the nation's civilian toxic waste dumps will be immense, that cost is dwarfed by the estimated cost of cleaning up toxic waste and other pollution at the nation's military bases and nuclear weapons plants. Some estimate that around $200 billion will be needed (the Superfund was initially funded at less than $2 billion) to clean up what one person called "virtual museums of environmental misbehavior."[1]

Several of the plants began to build nuclear bombs over 40 years ago. After World War II, they maintained their wartime focus on building nuclear weapons to protect national security and gave little attention to their safety procedures or to the effects their actions might have on surrounding communities. Sometimes this was due to carelessness or ignorance, sometimes to greed and not wanting to spend the money to install proper pollution control equipment. Thus, leaking earthern pits are used as dumps for industrial chemicals and radioactive wastes. Sewage systems, some built when the plants opened, leak pollutants into the ground. Inadequate or nonexistent air pollution-control devices allow toxic and sometimes radioactive emissions into the air. Other radioactive waste is discharged into streams and rivers.

One of these plants is in Hanford, Washington. The community of Hanford is proud of its nuclear facilities. The high school team is called the "Bombers," and their emblem is a mushroom cloud. The local bowling alley, the Atomic Lanes, is not far from streets with names like Nuclear Lane. Despite this good neighborliness, over a period of 13 years in the 1940s and 1950s, the nuclear plant knowingly released into the air massive amounts of radioactive materials, including iodine, for test purposes. Downwind, near Mesa, Washington, in an area known as the "death mile," 14 of 108 residents have become ill with, or died of, cancer, and several children have died or were born handicapped.[2] Re-

Source: Reprinted by permission, Tribune Media Services.

searchers from the Centers for Disease Control believe that 20,000 children in eastern Washington may have been exposed to unhealthy levels of this iodine by drinking milk from cows grazing in contaminated pastures.[3]

In Fernald, Ohio, a red and white checkerboard design on a water tower and the name "Feed Materials Production Center" led some residents to believe a local firm produced animal feed. Instead it made uranium rods and components for warheads. Residents were stunned to find out that for 35 years, the plant had dumped radioactive refuse into pits in the ground that regularly overflowed when it rained. The plant also discharged 167,000 pounds of wastes into a local river and released about twice that much into the air. Though these actions were taken by the private company that ran the plant, they were approved and even encouraged by the supposed regulators, the Atomic Energy Commission. As Senator John Glenn (D-Ohio) commented ironically, "We are poisoning our people in the name of national security."[4]

(continued on next page)

---

people with little expertise in environmental issues, and dogged by a paranoia that has virtually brought it to a standstill."[69]

The magnitude of the efforts to dismantle the EPA mobilized grass-roots environmental supporters. Membership in environmental groups tripled between 1981 and 1983, and the common threat of the Reagan deregulatory efforts drew the various groups closer together.

Business too was uneasy. Though most business leaders wanted less regulation, few believed that environmental protection could be cut back as far as Burford seemed to be doing. During the 1970s, busi-

nesses had arrived at a working agreement with the EPA and spent billions of dollars cleaning up. Many corporate executives feared that the extreme cutbacks in environmental protection would create a backlash from Congress and environmentalists. They preferred consistency in regulation to a sharp change of direction. Moreover, business executives worried because business was being viewed as the "bad guy," putting private profit above public interest. This was not an image business wanted.

Many members of Congress were outraged by Burford's leadership. In a series of critical congressional hearings, EPA officials were called to testify 70

After the federal courts ruled that the EPA has the authority to regulate waste disposal at federal weapons plants, the agency fined the Department of Energy $300,000 for delays in implementing a cleanup plan for the Fernald plant. But it had no way to collect the fine, any more than it could force the Department of Energy to carry through on plans to clean up the Hanford Nuclear Reservation or the Rocky Flats plant near Denver. However, after receiving some bad press coverage, the Department of Energy agreed to pay a much smaller fine and to negotiate a new cleanup schedule.

In addition to the weapons plants, 871 domestic military installations produce more hazardous waste each year than the top U.S. chemical companies. Ninety-two of these sites are either on or about to be added to the Superfund list. The Department of Defense has identified 8,000 sites that may be in need of more than $20 billion of environmental restoration over the next 20 years.[5] This includes many bases now being closed to reduce military spending. None of these bases can be sold or converted to any civilian use until they are detoxified and made safe from such hazards as unexploded artillery and mortar shells. The *preliminary* cleanup costs of one ordinance testing site in Indiana is estimated at $550 million, while its closing will save taxpayers only $7 million a year.[6] In the 1990s, the bill for carelessness and neglect is coming due.

1. Cass Peterson, "A Monumental Cleanup Job," *Washington Post National Weekly Edition,* December 12–18, 1988, p. 11.
2. "Nuclear Danger and Deceit," *Newsweek,* October 31, 1988, pp. 20–30.
3. "They Lied to Us," *Time,* October 31, 1988, p. 64.
4. Ibid, p. 61.
5. Bill Turque and John McCormick, "The Military's Toxic Legacy," *Newsweek,* August 6, 1990, p. 20.
6. Ibid., p. 21.
Other Sources: John Hanrahan, "Testing Ground," *Common Cause,* January/February 1989; Mathew Wald, "When the Government Runs Afoul of Its Own Regulators," *New York Times,* March 10, 1991, p. E16.

Cheerleaders at Hanford, Washington, High School illustrate the civic pride in the nuclear weapons plant located nearby.

times.[70] Environmental groups used the hearings as a forum to criticize Burford's and the agency's scientific competence, enforcement, openness to the public, and a laundry list of other failings. One area of controversy was the Superfund. Evidence leaked by unhappy EPA staffers indicated that high-level EPA officials were dealing secretly with industry in dispersing the fund. When Congress asked for documents from the EPA, Burford refused to turn them over, citing executive privilege, and assigned two paper shredders to the hazardous waste office. Congress cited Burford for contempt. Burford, in turn, fired the Superfund ad-

ministrator (who was later convicted of lying to Congress) and four of her assistants.

With the presidential election campaign coming up, Burford was seen as too great a liability and was pressured to resign. The president then ordered the EPA to turn over to Congress the documents it had requested. The documents revealed that the Superfund was being used to advance ideological and partisan causes. Funding for cleanup of one California site was delayed to avoid helping a Democratic senatorial candidate; two sites in New Jersey were funded to help the campaign of a Republican senatorial candidate. Fines were reduced and loopholes found for friendly industries.

Burned by this experience, the president appointed William Ruckelshaus (EPA's first director) to head the agency again. Ruckelshaus, viewed as a moderate, was well respected by Congress, and the agency was given a significant budget boost. Within the next several months 20 top EPA officials from the Burford administration were dismissed. Ruckelshaus was credited with restoring morale and effectiveness to the agency by reaffirming its commitment to protecting the environment.

Thus, attempts to make the EPA a toothless tiger backfired. Burford and Reagan failed to sense the strong support by the public for environmental protection.

Though Ruckelshaus's and his successors' vision of the EPA's mission was much more in line with that of Congress than Burford's had been, the EPA has not regained its 1970s vigor. Moreover, the jobs Congress has asked it to do are huge compared to the resources the agency has. As one observer has said, "Congress has been prone to a pollutant-of-the-year mentality, a tendency to order the responsible executive agencies to attend to whatever environmental hazard may seem most publicly visible . . . at the moment."[71] This creates obstacles to the EPA's planning.

Attempts to control pollution are also frustrated by the public. We want clean air and water, but we do not want to give up gas-guzzling cars, plastic containers, energy-consuming conveniences, and other pollution-causing aspects of our life-styles. We use far more energy per person than any other nation, and with energy use comes pollution. Part of this heavy consumption is due to our wealth, but part is due to our wastefulness. High oil prices in the 1970s curbed energy use for awhile, but we have returned to our more wasteful ways. To ask the EPA to control pollution, then, is to ask it to protect us from ourselves.

Nevertheless, public opinion consistently gives environmental protection a high priority, although a recent poll indicated that while 84% of Americans thought pollution was a serious national problem, only 42% thought it was a problem in the area where they lived.[72] Yet very few want to spend less to clean up the environment than we do now; many want to spend more. Indeed, by 1989, 80% of the public agreed we should clean up the environment regardless of the cost.

The EPA's attempts to control pollution and hazardous substances are undermined by fast-changing technology, inconsistent goals of political leaders, and, of course, resistance by regulated groups. William Ruckelshaus once said that the EPA's mission is like trying to give someone an appendectomy while they are running the 100-yard dash.[73] By that he means that the agency is always shooting at a moving target; just when it has one pollutant under control, a dozen more emerge.

By 1990 the United States was spending 2% of its GNP just on pollution control and cleaning up the environment. Of this estimated $100 billion, private business paid about 63%; the federal government about 11%; local governments 22.5%; and state governments 3.5%. By the end of the century, environmental regulatory costs alone may surpass $150 billion. Add to this the costs of additional regulation for consumer protection and safety in the workplace, the hundreds of billions of dollars for the S&L bailout, and a possible bailout of the banking industry's FDIC. We can expect to see a continuing struggle over how the burden of these costs is divided among levels of government and between government and business.

Due to these staggering costs, there will probably be an increase in public involvement in regulatory politics and a broadening of concern from safety and conservation issues to those of taxpayer liability for bad management and deregulation. Environmental groups are calling for heavy new taxes (called "green taxes") to be imposed on "products and activities that pollute, deplete or otherwise degrade natural systems."[74] Such taxes would help to pay for mounting cleanup costs and at the same time encourage environmentally sound practices.

Conclusion: Is Regulation Responsive?

Government regulates economic activities largely to protect the health and safety of Americans, to maintain the purity of the natural environment, and to protect businesses. Regulation is often desired by business because it protects against competition from domestic or foreign competitors, but sometimes businesses complain that regulation hurts them by decreasing their autonomy and increasing their costs of operation. These complaints have been met with legislative attempts to deregulate and by budget cuts for, and lax enforcement by, regulatory agencies. But

Drilling and Spilling

The discovery of huge reserves of oil in Prudhoe Bay, Alaska, in 1968 set off an equally huge political controversy.[1] How was the United States going to get the oil from "up there" down here? Very quickly, a group of seven oil companies, including Exxon, Atlantic Richfield, Mobil, and Phillips Petroleum, joined together to propose constructing a huge pipeline from Prudhoe Bay in northern Alaska to Valdez on Alaska's southern coast. From there, the oil would be taken by tanker to West Coast ports for distribution across the United States.

The pipeline had many proponents. Oil producers saw huge profits from this rich new source. The Nixon administration wanted to increase the amount of oil produced in the United States. In 1973, when Middle Eastern and other foreign oil producers raised prices dramatically, government and the public nearly panicked. Immediately, our dependence on foreign oil became a major issue. The public, facing huge increases in the price of gas for their cars and oil to heat their homes, demanded more and cheaper oil. To government officials, and much of the public, the Alaska pipeline seemed like a good deal. Business and government officials in Alaska also backed the pipeline, believing the oil would make the state rich.

Most pipeline opponents were environmentalists. Environmental groups filed suit against the oil companies, charging that the pipeline and its construction would destroy much of the virgin timber and animal life in America's last frontier and, in places, destroy forever the fragile ecology of the tundra. Environmentalist were also concerned about the damage that might result from oil spills when oil from the pipeline was loaded and shipped from Valdez.

Despite these concerns the secretary of the interior approved the pipeline. The courts then blocked it, noting that some of the provisions of the plan violated federal law. Thus Congress had to make a decision.

After an extensive debate, Congress approved the pipeline. The majority believed that the concerns expressed by environmental groups were outweighed by the need for more domestic oil. Proponents argued that having the Alaska pipeline was a matter of national security. Moreover, by declaring that the pipeline was in accordance with provisions of the National Environmental Policy Act, a slim majority in Congress barred more suits by what some members called "environmental extremists" and further court review of the pipeline. In approving the pipeline, the

The Alaskan oil spill killed thousands of water fowl. Here scientists examine a bird killed by the oil. Months after the spill, workers in Prince William Sound had cleaned less than 13 miles of a 728-mile coastline.

majority of Congress apparently believed the assurances of the oil companies that they had contingency plans for spills and equipment for easy cleanup.

The pipeline opened in 1977, and for a dozen years no major castastrophe occurred. Nearly 300 billion gallons of oil were carried from the port of Valdez with relatively little spilling.[2]

There were problems, however. It was too expensive to ship the oil to the Midwest and eastern United States. Oil companies soon discovered it would be cheaper to sell the Alaskan oil to Japan, then buy foreign oil for the rest of the United States. However, since the rationale of the pipeline was to provide the United States with domestic oil, exporting Alaskan oil was not allowed, and it was shipped east.

Alaskan government officials, lured by the millions of dollars flowing into state businesses and tax coffers, relaxed their concern about possible accidents. Oil companies cut back on safety measures and standby emergency crews and blocked efforts to increase state inspections and safety regulations. Local communities that volunteered storage space for cleanup equipment were spurned by the companies.

In 1989, an Exxon tanker ran aground spilling 11 million gallons of crude oil into one of the most beautiful areas in North America, Prince William Sound. A few days after the spill, high winds dispersed the oil throughout the sound, so that the gooey slick covered 900 square miles and contaminated 1,200 miles of coastline. The spill killed thousands of birds, sea otters, and other marine animals, while closing the herring fishing industry for the year and threatening one of the world's largest salmon fishing grounds.

Though it had an 1,800-page contingency plan that assured the government it could take care of any spill in a few hours, Exxon was unable and unprepared to clean up such a massive spill. In addition to the millions spent by Exxon, Alaska and the federal government spent $135 million in the first year of the recovery effort.

Perhaps the disaster could have been avoided; certainly the magnitude of the disaster should have been avoidable. But the Prince William Sound scenario is repeated frequently on a smaller scale and with less severe consequences. Business and industry bent on making a profit with new technologies or new projects always assure government and the public that there will be "no problem." Critics are accused of being "antigrowth" or, as in the case of the pipeline, "environmental extremists." Often government is eager to accept these assurances because of the influence of business and sometimes because government policymakers believe the project is in the interests of national security (like the pipeline). Later, when an accident happens, government officials and business leaders appear to be shocked, though few others are.

Although recovery work was still incomplete, fishing catches returned to normal levels in the year after the spill. Escort vessels now guide loaded tankers out of the sound. The captain of the Exxon tanker, who was accused of drinking on the job, surrendered his pilot's license but was acquitted of criminal charges. In 1991, Exxon pleaded guilty to four misdemeanor violations of pollution laws and agreed to pay a $100 million fine, plus $1 billion in compensation (not counting money it had already spent on cleanup).

The settlement costs would have little financial impact on Exxon; all but the fine could be written off as business expenses. One estimate put the real cost of the settlement to Exxon at perhaps a half billion dollars. In addition, due in part to the price hikes adopted after the Valdez spill and again after Iraq's invasion of Kuwait, Exxon profits rose by more than 40% in 1990. However, shortly after the settlement was announced it was thrown out by a federal judge, who ruled that the $100 million fine, the largest ever assessed for criminal violation of federal pollution laws, was too lenient. Exxon withdrew its guilty pleas rather than negotiate a higher fine, leaving it to the state to decide whether to bring Exxon to trial on criminal charges.

1. David Heard Davis, *Energy Politics* (New York: St. Martin's Press, 1982), pp. 90–91; *Congressional Quarterly Almanac*, 1973, pp. 596–614.
2. Cass Peterson and Jay Mathews, "A Crude Awakening For Alaska," *Washington Post National Weekly Edition,* April 10–16, 1989, p. 7.
Other Sources: Jay Mathews, "The Sound and the Easing Fury," *Washington Post National Weekly Edition,* March 4–10, 1991, p. 33; *New York Times,* March 17, 1991, p. E5.

in an age when technology is racing ahead with unknown side effects, efforts to get government out of the business of protecting health, safety, and the environment were opposed by the public. Hence we are seeing "reregulation" to protect individuals, communities, and businesses from the free market. Though the public approves of cutting red tape, the deregulation efforts in the early 1980s went beyond what the public supported and stimulated a backlash. In undoing some of these excesses, Congress and the administration were being responsive.

In forming our opinions about government regulations and regulators, it is sometimes easy to forget that regulators are carrying out congressional acts. While bureaucrats may be overly zealous or overly lax in enforcing those laws they are mandated to enforce, ultimately it is Congress that decides what is to be regulated and calls the agency to heel when it is over-regulating or neglecting to regulate.

Regulation is a good example of fluctuations in government responsiveness to the public. At times, regulatory effort is directed primarily toward protect-ing business. At other times consumer and environ-mental groups have succeeded in getting government to regulate some business practices. In general, regu-lation exists because influential groups, sometimes representing a majority, other times not, desire gov-ernment action to protect their interests.

EPILOGUE

The Empire Strikes Back

James Scully decided to stay in OSHA and fight for his safety regulation. He was able to enlist some powerful allies on his side. Kennedy's committee, like many oth-ers in Congress, was upset with the increasing role of OMB in regulation. In 1988 they decided to hold hearings investigating that role. A few days before the hearings, OMB gave its approval to OSHA's machin-ery rule.

Scully's experience illustrates several important points about regulation and about presidential control of the bureaucracy. Though President Reagan put people in charge of the regulatory agencies that shared his own view that regulation was bad, the agencies were filled with civil servants who believed in the work of their agencies. Many of these people left in dismay and despair, but others, like Scully, stayed on to fight.[75] Reagan injured OSHA, FTC, EPA, and other regulatory agencies, but he did not kill them. To do that, he would have had to persuade Congress to pass legislation abolishing the agencies or their functions. He did not attempt this, and Congress would not have passed such legislation.

Indeed, bureaucrats unhappy with presidential leadership often find allies in members of Congress, as did many EPA staffers. Here Scully, labor union lead-ers, and congressional allies formed the sort of cozy triangle we have discussed before. Obviously, this tri-angle was far from completely successful in thwarting the president's will; the president had his way for seven years. But eventually, through persistence, they triumphed.

One conservative leader calls this the "empire strikes back" phenomenon, the victory of the perma-nent bureaucracy over presidential appointees moti-vated by ideology. Others point to additional reasons for the small resurgence of regulatory activity in Re-agan's last year. The public never really supported de-regulating worker safety or environmental cleanliness. Public unease was fed by the excesses of some earlier Reagan appointees, such as Anne Burford in the EPA. The pendulum had swung too far toward antiregula-tion and was bound to swing back.

Whatever the reasons for the change in climate, this hazardous machinery regulation was a personal victory for James Scully, who commented: "It was just a feeling something had to be done, saving a few hun-dred lives every year. I don't like to leave a job half done."[76] Two weeks after OMB gave its approval to the regulation, Scully's job was done and he retired.

KEY TERMS

monopoly

truth in labeling

tragedy of the
    commons

externality

antitrust regulation

cost-benefit analysis

deregulation

reregulation

environmental impact
    statement

Environmental
    Protection Agency
    (EPA)

bubble concept

greenhouse effect

from cradle to grave

Superfund

FURTHER READING

General

Kenneth Meier, *Regulation* (New York: St. Martin's Press, 1985). *A thorough and readable account of the politics of federal regulation.*

William Ophuls, *Ecology and the Politics of Scarcity* (San Francisco: Freeman, 1977). *An important and fascinating book about both ecology and politics.*

Michael D. Reagan, *Regulation* (Boston: Little, Brown, 1987). *A good introduction to the politics and economics of regulation. While the focus is on federal regulation, it also examines intergovernmental aspects of regulation.*

Walter Rosenbaum, *Environmental Politics and Policy* (Washington, D.C.: CQ Press, 1985). *Probably the best overview of environmental policy.*

Alan Stone, *Regulation and Its Alternatives* (Washington, D.C.: CQ Press, 1982). *A comprehensive analysis of the justifications and politics of regulation.*

Topical

David Bollier and Joan Claybrook, *Freedom from Harm* (Washington, D.C.: Public Citizen and Democracy project, 1986). *A review of the major achievements of and challenges to several major regulatory agencies from the perspective of Nader's Public Citizen movement.*

C. J. Bosso, *Pesticides and Politics* (Pittsburgh: University of Pittsburgh Press, 1987). *An analysis of how the government has regulated—and not regulated—pesticides over the past forty years.*

Rachael Carson, *Silent Spring* (New York: Fawcett, 1962). *This book, and industry's reaction to it, spurred the development of the modern environmental movement.*

Richard Harris and Sidney Milkis, *The Politics of Regulatory Change* (New York: Oxford University Press, 1989). *An evenhanded account of the rise and fall of deregulation during the Reagan administration.*

John Keeble, *Out of the Channel: the Exxon Valdez Oil Spill in Prince William Sound* (New York: Harper Collins, 1991). *A description of the spill, cleanup efforts and the continuing struggle between local residents, Exxon, and supporters of the pipeline.*

Ralph Nader, *Unsafe at Any Speed*, 2nd ed. (New York: Grossman, 1972). *This attack on General Motors' Corvair and GM's attack on Nader launched the Public Citizen movement.*

George Stigler, *The Citizen and the State* (Chicago: University of Chicago Press, 1975). *A defender of the free market system analyzes the effects of regulation.*

NOTES

1. Sources for this You Are There include Steven Waldman, "Regulation Comes Back," *Newsweek,* September 12, 1988, pp. 44–45; Frank Swoboda, "Examining the Reagan Administration's 'Proudest Achievements'," *Washington Post National Weekly Edition,* October 10–16, 1988, pp. 33–34; Richard Harris and Sidney Milkis, *The Politics of Regulatory Change* (New York: Oxford University Press, 1989).

2. 1988 Times Mirror Poll conducted by the Gallup Organization.

3. Cambridge Reports, survey of 1,424 Americans, April 1984, reported in *Washington Post National Weekly Edition,* September 10, 1984, p. 38.

4. Susan Tolchin and Martin Tolchin, *Dismantling America* (Boston: Houghton Mifflin, 1983), p. 135. This is based on research by Nicholas Ashford and reported in U.S. Senate Governmental Affairs Committee, 96th Congress, March 25, 1980, "Benefits of Environmental, Health, and Safety Regulation" (Washington, D.C.: U.S. Government Printing Office).

5. T. R. Reid, "Bald Eagle Soaring Up from Brink," *Washington Post* Syndicate, reprinted in *Lincoln Journal-Star,* March 21, 1989.

6. David Bollier and Joan Claybrook, *Freedom from Harm* (Washington, D.C.: Public Citizen and Democracy Project, 1986).

7. *Lincoln Journal,* April 19, 1987, p. 7.

8. George C. Eads and Michael Fix, *Relief or Reform?* (Washington, D.C.: Urban Institute Press, 1984).

9. Kenneth J. Meier, *Regulation* (New York: St. Martin's 1985), pp. 78–80.

10. Carole Sugarman, "If You Mix Apple and Orange Juices, Please Make It Clear," *Washington Post National Weekly Edition,* August 29–September 4, 1988, p. 33.

11. "Intelligence Report," *Parade,* November 27, 1988, p. 16.

12. Adam Smith, *An Inquiry into the Wealth of Nations* (1776; several editions; a recent one is Indianapolis, Ind.: Bobbs-Merrill, 1961).

13. See discussion in William Ophuls, *Ecology and the Politics of Scarcity* (San Francisco: Freeman, 1977).

14. NBC News Special Report on the 20th Anniversary of Earth Day, April 22, 1991.

15. Constantine Raymond Kraus and Alfred W. Duerig, *The Rape of Ma Bell: The Criminal Wrecking of the Best Telephone System in the World* (New York: Lyle Stuart, 1988). Kraus and Duerig, Bell engineers, argue, as the title of their book indicates, that this antitrust action has had negative effects.

16. Quotation from Neal R. Peirce, "Feds' Neglect Provokes Spate of State 'Regulatory Rambos,'" *Lincoln Journal-Star,* April 10, 1988.

17. *Congressional Quarterly Almanac, 1987* (Washington, D.C.: Congressional Quarterly, 1987), p. 289.

18. W. John Moore, "Dear Feds—Help," *National Journal,* July 9, 1988, pp. 1788–92.

19. Quoted in *National Journal,* December 22, 1981.

20. See discussion in Walter A. Rosenbaum, *Environmental Politics and Policy* (Washington, D.C.: CQ Press, 1985), pp. 90–95.

21. See Tolchin and Tolchin, *Dismantling America,* especially chapter 4. See Eads and Fix, *Relief or Reform?* pp. 241–45, for an assessment of cost savings under Reagan's regulatory policies.

22. *Fortune,* February 3, 1986; Michael Reagan, *Regulation* (Boston: Little, Brown, 1987), p. 126.

23. Bill McAllister, "If a Human Life Is Worth $1 Million, What's a Recliner Worth?" *Washington Post National Weekly Edition,* June 8, 1987, p. 33.

24. Tolchin and Tolchin, *Dismantling America.*

25. Judith Havemann, "How Do You Estimate Cancer Risk," *Washington Post National Weekly Edition,* July 28, 1986, pp. 31–32.

26. C. Todd Conover quoted in Hobart Rowen, "This Is Fundamentally Sound?" *Washington Post National Weekly Edition,* January 21, 1985, p. 5.

27. Paul Taylor, "The Democrats Discover the Savings and Loan Scandal," *Washington Post National Weekly Edition,* June 4–10, 1990, p. 13.

28. Michael Quint, with John C. Freed, "Bank Losses Worst in 50 Years, But No Danger to System Is Seen," *New York Times,* February 17, 1991, p. 12.

29. Champaign-Urbana *News-Gazette* (AP), February 26, 1991.

30. Eads and Fix, *Relief or Reform?* p. 153. See also Reagan, *Regulation,* pp. 105–6.

31. Peter Perl, "Corporate Expenses Can Be Hazardous to Your Health," *Washington Post National Weekly Edition,* September 8, 1986, p. 33.

32. Ibid.

33. Ibid.

34. "Danger on the Job," *Newsweek,* December 11, 1989, p. 42.

35. For an evaluation of the impact of Reagan's deregulation efforts, see Harris and Milkis, *The Politics of Regulatory Change.*

36. "Danger on the Job," p. 42.

37. William Niskanen in "Regulation Comes Back," *Newsweek,* September 12, 1988, p. 45.

38. Quoted in Robert Pear, "In Bush Presidency, the Regulators Ride Again," *New York Times,* April 28, 1991, p. E5.

39. Robert Pear, "U.S. Laws Delayed by Complex Rules and Partisanship," *New York Times,* March 31, 1991, p. 14.

40. John Jay, "The Federalist #2," in *The Federalist: A Commentary on the Constitution of the United States* (New York: Modern Library), pp. 8–9.

41. Lynn White, Jr., "The Historical Roots of Our Ecological Crisis," *Science* 155 (March 10, 1967).

42. See Robert Nisbet, *The History of the Idea of Progress* (New York: Basic Books, 1980), for an interesting examination of the idea of progress from antiquity to the present.

43. See Kenneth J. Meier, *Regulation* (New York: St. Martin's Press, 1985), chapter 6, for an overview of early attempts by the federal government to protect the environment.

44. James Anderson, David Brady, and Charles Bullock, *Public Policy and Politics in America* (North Scituate, Mass.: Duxbury Press, 1977), p. 74.

45. Meier, *Regulation,* p. 145; Norman Vig and Michael Kraft, "Environmental Policy from the Seventies to the Eighties," in Vig and Kraft, eds., *Environmental Policy in the 1980s* (Washington, D.C.: CQ Press, 1984), p. 16.

46. Information about the founding of the EPA is drawn from Steven A. Cohen, "EPA: A Qualified Success," in Sheldon Kamieniecki, Robert O'Brien, and Michael Clarke, eds., *Controversies in Environmental Policy,* (Albany, N.Y.: State University of New York Press, 1986), pp. 174–99; Meier, *Regulation,* pp. 142–46.

47. Rosenbaum, *Environmental Politics,* p. 108.

48. Meier, *Regulation,* p. 147.

49. L. J. White, *The Regulation of Air Pollutant Emissions for Motor Vehicles* (Washington, D.C.: American Enterprise Institute, 1982), p. 56.

50. William K. Stevens, "2% of G.N.P. Spent By U.S. on Cleanup," *New York Times,* December 23, 1990.

51. Quoted in *Time,* April 16, 1990, p. 21.

52. Rosenbaum, *Environmental Politics,* p. 127; Bollier and Claybrook, *Freedom from Harm,* p. 115. Michael Weisskopf, "A Qualified Failure," *Washington Post National Weekly Edition,* June 19–25, 1989, p. 10.

53. See Rosenbaum, *Environmental Politics,* p. 126–27; Bollier and Claybrook, *Freedom from Harm,* p. 116.

54. *Newsweek,* August 29, 1988, p. 49.

55. Robert Pear, "U.S. Laws Delayed by Complex Rules and partisanship," p. 14.

56. Tom Hamburger, "Toxic Emission Rate Rising: Called a Threat," *Minneapolis Star Tribune,* March 23, 1989, p. 1.

57. Meier, *Regulation,* p. 158.

58. Helen Ingram and Dean Mann, "Preserving the Clean Water Act," in Vig and Kraft, eds., *Environmental Policy in the 1980s,* p. 260.

59. Paul Hauge, quoted in *Newsweek,* August 1, 1988, p. 45.

60. See Lois Gibbs, *Love Canal* (Albany, N.Y.: State University of New York Press, 1983), for the Love Canal story from the perspective of the woman who organized the neighborhood to demand that government do something. Andrew Danzo, "The Big Sleazy," *Washington Monthly* (September 1988): 11–17, describes bureaucratic delay in helping the residents of Love Canal. See also Adeline Gordon Levine, *Love Canal: Science, Politics, and People* (Lexington, Mass.: D. C. Heath, 1982).

61. The Resource Conservation and Recovery Act of 1976 and the Toxic Substances Control Act of 1976.

62. Rosenbaum, *Environmental Politics,* p. 215.

63. *Time,* January 2, 1989, p. 47.

64. Rosenbaum, *Environmental Politics,* p. 208.

65. Meier, *Regulation,* p. 163.

66. Meier, *Regulation,* pp. 163–64; Dick Kirschten, "Ruckelshaus May Find EPA's Problems Are Budgetary as Much as Political," *National Journal,* March 26, 1983, pp. 659–60.

67. Richard Tobin, "Revising the Clean Air Act," in Vig and Kraft, eds., *Environmental Policy in the 1980s,* pp. 227–50.

68. Rosenbaum, *Environmental Politics,* p. 210.

69. Quoted in Meier, *Regulation,* p. 164 from Robert Crandall, "The Environment," *Regulation* 6 (January/February 1982): 29–32.

70. Meier, *Regulation,* p. 164.

71. Rosenbaum, *Environmental Politics,* p. 207.

72. Steven A. Holmes, "When Grass Looks Greener On This Side of the Fence," *New York Times,* April 21, 1991, p. E6.

73. Quoted in Bollier and Claybrook, *Freedom from Harm,* p. 95.

74. Philip Shabecoff, "Tax Proposed on Products and Activities

That Harm Environment," *New York Times,* February 10, 1991, p. 15.

75. See Harris and Milkis, *Politics of Regulatory Change,* for a close examination of the workings of the EPA and FTC under the direction of Reagan's antiregulatory appointees.

76. Waldman, "Regulation Comes Back," p. 44.

Foreign Policy

The Berlin Wall, separating East and West Berlin, came tumbling down in 1989 symbolizing the end of the Cold War.

implementing policy. The government officials best positioned to advise the president on foreign policy include the secretaries of defense and state, the national security advisor, and the head of the CIA. The Joint Chiefs of Staff, the U.S. ambassador to the United Nations, the secretary of the treasury, the director of the Arms Control Agency, and influential members of Congress are also frequently consulted.

These individuals represent a wide range of experience and bring different perspectives to the analysis of foreign policy issues. The secretary of state is usually concerned with the nation's diplomatic relations and the use of diplomatic channels to implement the president's policies. The secretary of defense (always a civilian) is primarily concerned with military and security issues and the use of the military to pursue foreign policy goals. Members of the Joint Chiefs of Staff are military professionals who give advice to the president on both the readiness of their service arms and the appropriateness of their use in specific situations. Members of Congress may be consulted because they are political allies of the president, because they are in leadership positions crucial for mobilizing support on an issue, or because they have developed expertise in military or foreign policy issues. through their committee assignments.

The president may also consult his wife, or friends and advisors outside of government, not because of their expertise in foreign or military policy but because he trusts in their good judgment and wants the perspective of people close to him who may have no organizational interests or policy agenda to further. Sometimes, however, roles overlap, as with Attorney General Robert Kennedy, who served as one of his brother's closest advisors in both domestic and foreign policy, or Secretary of State James Baker, who is a longtime friend and fishing partner of President Bush.

Who the president draws into his inner circle of advisors depends in large part on his experience and decision-making style. President Kennedy, who had almost no foreign policy experience, assembled a committee of cabinet heads and close advisors to help him construct his response to the Soviets during the Cuban missile crisis. But during the Persian Gulf crisis President Bush reportedly made the decision to send troops to Saudi Arabia relying almost exclusively on his own judgment and that of a few close advisors, including Brent Scowcroft, the national security advisor, and Richard Cheney, the secretary of defense.

President Bush has said that he finds foreign policy "more fun" than domestic policy and has allotted his attention and energies accordingly. To a lesser extent this was also true for Richard Nixon. If a president comes to office with a foreign policy agenda and expects to make his political reputation and leave his mark on history in this policy area, it is likely that he will surround himself with like-minded people and will replace or ignore the advice of those who disagree with him.

One might think that ex-governors like Carter and Reagan might compensate for their lack of foreign policy experience when they become president by surrounding themselves with experts, but both men chose foreign policy advisers with limited experience. When planning his response to the seizure of the American embassy in Iran in 1979, President Carter relied heavily on close political associates from Georgia and National Security Advisor Zbigniew Brzezinski, whose area of expertise was Eastern Europe, not the Middle East.

Most of President Reagan's foreign policy advisers had less experience than Carter's and were even more divided. It was said that "the Reagan administration certainly didn't invent internal battling over foreign policy, but it raised it to a new level."[2] The president's reluctance to get involved in resolving battles among his staff and foreign policy experts made it appear that no one was in charge of foreign policy. The secretaries of state and defense were frequently at odds over issues ranging from the Middle East to dealing with the Soviets, while the Iran-contra hearings revealed that the National Security Council was conducting independent policies without the knowledge or approval of either the secretary of state or the secretary of defense.

Specialists

The process of formulating long-term policy usually involves more people than the number involved in decision making in crisis situations. The State Department has experts on every region of the globe and on substantive policy issues such as economic assistance, trade, political affairs, and arms control.

Political officers in Washington and in our embassies and consulates abroad write daily summaries of important political and economic events in the countries to which they are assigned. This information is used to provide daily briefings for higher-level officials, but almost none of it ever reaches the president's desk and only a small portion of it can be read even by the secretary of state.

Important background work is also done by specialists in other cabinet departments and independent agencies, such as Defense, Treasury, Commerce, Agriculture, Justice, the Arms Control and Disarmament Agency, and the CIA. Their work can be crucial to the negotiation of arms control and law of the sea treaties, trade agreements, and immigration policy, for example.

We should not assume that these experts present neutral information that is somehow mechanically cranked out as public policy. Even if the experts do their best to provide the most accurate information and comprehensive policy alternatives possible, this information is used by top policymakers who see it through their own perceptual and ideological lenses. So, for example, information on human rights violations in Argentina received by President Reagan led to very different policy recommendations than the same information presented to President Carter. Nevertheless, issue and area specialists are crucially important in providing accurate information and the historical context for current policies.

Our Vietnam policies failed in part because many of our best Asian experts had been purged from the State Department during the McCarthy era. The Reagan administration ignored advisors who cautioned against his covert policies in Nicaragua and Iran and replaced State Department experts who disagreed with his Central America policies. More than most presidents, Reagan made appointments to key positions in the State Department based on political considerations rather than on career expertise.

Bush's appointments included both members of the foreign policy establishment who had held high positions in previous administrations and several associates from his CIA days, an organizational tie that makes many in Congress uncomfortable.

High turnover in specialist positions puts us at a disadvantage relative to our adversaries and allies. For example, the Soviet Union had much the same team of arms control negotiators for many years. Our negotiating teams change with each administration or more often. Since arms control is an extremely complex field, our negotiators were continually in the process of learning.

Also sometimes influential in foreign policymaking are experts outside government who are associated with various "think tanks." Primarily located in Washington, close to decision makers and the national media, these institutions—including the Institute for Policy Studies on the left of the political spectrum, the Heritage Foundation on the right, and the Brookings Institute, the American Enterprise Institute, the Center for Strategic and International Studies, and the Council on Foreign Relations in the middle—conduct and publish research on policy issues. These think tanks offer a home for foreign policy experts whose party is out of office and a place for academic foreign policy experts to get Washington experience and become more visible. By writing articles for national newspapers and journals and being interviewed on news and public affairs programs, experts in these institutions "wage perpetual war against each other" trying to determine the course of American foreign policy.[3]

Political Parties and Interest Groups

Party and interest group leaders have intermittent influence on foreign policy, depending on the issue and the president.

Presidents in the postwar era have usually proclaimed their desire to have a "bipartisan" foreign policy; that is, they want support from both parties so as not to make our foreign policy a subject of divisive squabbling. Presidents need that support when treaties are to be ratified, because it is rare for one party to have a two-thirds majority in the Senate or for members to be united in their ranks. Carter, for example, had to woo and win Republican support to secure ratification of the Panama Canal treaties.

Presidents like to say that in facing the rest of the world, Americans are all on the same side. But this is too simplistic. Policies shaping how we deal with the rest of the world are controversial and complex. Party positions do differ on this as on most other issues. For example, the roll-call votes of members of Congress on foreign policy differ according to party affiliation.[4] Democrats are more likely than Republicans to favor cuts in defense spending, to agree that the United States was partially responsible for the Cold War, and to believe in dismantling some U.S. alliances.[5]

Differences that do exist between the two major parties on foreign policy are usually apparent in the national platform each party issues in presidential election years. Why then does it often seem that the opposition party has no coherent alternative to the president's policy? This is probably because under normal circumstances members of Congress spend most of their time on the domestic issues that are so important to their constituents (especially at election time). In times of crises the opposition party will usually rally in support of administration policy so that the country can present a united front to the world. This is particularly true when U.S. troops are committed to combat or to areas where there is threat of war. Once these troops are in danger of attack or are actually engaged in battle, those who continue to oppose the president's actions can find themselves in the position of appearing to give higher priority to their policy preferences than to the safety of U.S. troops. At this point it is very difficult for the opposition party to oppose the president's policy effectively.

During the Persian Gulf War, President Bush won congressional support for the use of force by a fairly narrow margin, but once the air war began there was virtually no criticism of administration policies by members of Congress. There was substantial bipartisan criticism of Johnson's and Nixon's Vietnam policies, but this dissent came late in the course of the fighting, when public opinion was turning against the war and administration policies did not seem to be working. Even then Congress approved virtually all expenditures requested to wage the war.

Perhaps one of the reasons why our major parties do not present clear policy alternatives is because they do not have the tradition of forming shadow cabinets, as is done in Great Britain, for example. In a shadow cabinet leading members of an opposition party are given the responsibility of formulating policies that can serve as alternatives to those of the party in power.

In Congress, members of the opposition party are more likely to state policy alternatives on an ad hoc basis acting as individuals, not for the party. The public may be confused when it hears a half dozen or more policy alternatives presented by members of the same party, and it may even conclude that they are "lone rangers" trying to gain political advantage in a situation that seems to call for national unity.

A multiplicity of interest groups are concerned with foreign policy issues: international businesses; public interest groups, such as those who lobby on environmental issues; veterans' organizations; farmers who grow crops for export; labor unions; ethnic groups interested in their ancestral lands, for example, African-, Jewish-, Arab-, and Polish-Americans; and a myriad of specialized groups that focus on only one or two issues, such as the nuclear-freeze movement.

In general it is harder for interest groups to effect foreign policy than domestic policy. Part of the reason for this is the difference in the decision-making pro-

Asian Americans are increasingly active in politics. Here Korean Americans protest North Korean terrorism.

cess and the powerful role of the president in relation to Congress. However, there have been some very influential groups, such as the China Lobby, that worked to prevent United States recognition of the People's Republic of China during the early years of the cold war.

A more typical example of an effective interest group activity would be a farm or business organization lobbying on behalf of import quotas to protect their domestically produced goods. American business, farm, and labor groups sent 300 lobbyists to the international conference on trade and tariffs held in Geneva in 1990–91, far more than came from any other country represented in the negotiations.

Private citizens who are part of Washington's elite also play a role in foreign policy.[6] For example, until 1989, Henry Kissinger, former secretary of state, Brent Scowcroft, former national security adviser, and Lawrence Eagleburger, former under secretary of state, maintained a consulting business. They advised some of the world's largest corporations about foreign affairs and how international developments might affect the world economic climate in general and their corporations in particular. At the same time, Kissinger and his associates provided advice to government through their service on various advisory boards. Kissinger, for example, served on the president's Foreign Intelligence Advisory Board, where he had access to sensitive information. After Bush was elected, Scowcroft once again became national security adviser and Eagleburger returned to the State Department, thus providing an example of Washington's revolving door. During the Persian Gulf War Eagleburger served as President Bush's emissary to governments in the Middle East.

In the Nixon administration, foreign policymaking was tightly under the control of Nixon and Secretary of State Henry Kissinger. One of their first major achievements was to reestablish normal relationships with the People's Republic of China, governed by the Communist party and its leader, Mao Zedong, since 1949. Though Nixon had long argued against recognizing China, by 1968 he realized that normalization would help the United States in its diplomacy with the Soviet Union and the Third World.

Some former members of Congress and high-level political appointees have become registered agents (lobbyists) for foreign governments after leaving office. Those who are public officials one day are private citizens the next, and public officials again a few years later (rules about conflicts of interests are fairly fuzzy in this area).[7]

Public Opinion

Overall, the views of the public on foreign policy are not that different from those of foreign policymakers. When they do differ, public opinion has little direct effect on foreign policy most of the time. One reason is that only a minority of Americans know much about important foreign policy issues, and many have no opinion about them. Domestic issues impinge directly on our daily lives. But many citizens see foreign policy issues as remote and largely unimportant. In the late 1980s, 20% of the public had not heard of our involvement in Nicaragua, and 20% more did not know whom we supported there. Nicaragua received substantial press coverage, but much of our foreign policy is made incrementally over a long period of time and out of public view. Other policies, such as those on

trade and tariff issues, are very technical and receive limited coverage. Some of the most important decisions are made in "crisis" situations or in secrecy for national security reasons. On issues like the invasion of Grenada, for example, there was public opinion only after the fact; even Congress did not receive advance notice.

In general, in foreign matters the public is more likely to concede its ignorance on a wider range of issues than in domestic policy and accept the judgments of decision makers. Therefore, on most issues, it is easier for the president to influence public opinion through use of the media than it is for public opinion to change the president's opinion.

Sometimes, however, public opinion resists attempts to change it. It is more likely to remain firm when the public holds the administration in low repute or when the government is divided, as on Central America or, earlier, Vietnam. Deeply held opinions are also more resistant to administration pressure. For example, it would be difficult for a president to have a foreign policy that did not accept the nations of Western Europe as our primary allies.

The public can try to change the opinions of policymakers. It can vote out of office those who disagree with the majority views on foreign policy issues. However, it is difficult to mandate a president to do something (or not do it), since, as we saw in chapter 7, people vote on the basis of many different issues, personality traits, and party loyalties.[8]

Despite limitations on the public's influence in foreign policymaking, in some dramatic instances it does have an impact. For example, widespread opposition to direct U.S. involvement in Nicaragua to overthrow the Sandinista government restrained (or at least rechanneled) Reagan administration policies. Public opinion was quite sharply against Reagan in his Iran arms deals. Iran was about the least popular nation among Americans, and the public was not persuaded we should be sending weapons to it. This was a case of the public pressuring the president to enforce his own stated foreign policy, which was not to trade arms for hostages nor even to negotiate with hostage takers. This opinion then stimulated the press and Congress to continue their investigation of the sale of arms to Iran. The results of those investigations in turn fueled negative public opinion.

Ultimately, without some public support, foreign policy objectives that require substantial commitments of time and resources will prove unsuccessful. The necessity of public support for large-scale undertakings is evident in attempts to manipulate public access to information. This is most common during wartime, when the government can justify press censorship on national security grounds. Withholding negative information (for example, high casualty rates, slow progress, civilian losses) can help keep public support high. The Persian Gulf War was fought with keen attention to public opinion. The five-week air war preceding the ground attack was calculated not only to minimize military casualties and the length of the ground war but also to maintain public support for the president's policies. Moreover, the restricted press coverage, which did not allow casualties to be shown, enhanced that support.

Sometimes the withholding or manipulating of information can backfire, as it certainly did during the Vietnam War. And Reagan's use of covert action to skirt congressional and public opposition to his support for the contras eventually increased that opposition.

The Changing U.S. World Role

Isolationism

Historically, noninvolvement with other nations outside the Americas was the theme of our foreign policy. This policy is called **isolationism**. In the nineteenth and early twentieth century Americans generally stayed aloof from European conflicts and turned inward, busy with domestic expansion and development.

One important exception was our continuing military and political involvement in Latin America. The United States did not hesitate to use military force to impose its will on a variety of Caribbean and South American governments (see table 1). With little regard for national sovereignty, we sent troops to protect U.S. citizens or business interests and to replace existing governments with those more sympathetic to our wishes.

During this time, Americans did not think it appropriate to intervene in problems of Europe or to keep a large standing army at home. This attitude was an offshoot of the predominant mood in domestic affairs: preoccupation with economic growth and a

fear of strong central government. Isolationism was also a realistic position in the sense that the United States was not yet a world power. This isolationist sentiment lapsed briefly in 1917–19, when America entered World War I on the side of the British and French against Germany, but rapidly revived afterwards. Despite the wishes of President Woodrow Wilson, the United States refused to join the League of Nations, the ill-fated precursor to the United Nations. Although we have no public opinion polls from these early years, in 1937, 70% of Americans thought it was a mistake to have entered World War I.

In 1939 Britain declared war on Nazi Germany after that country invaded Poland. In 1940 Germany invaded the Netherlands, Norway, Denmark, and France and began bombing Britain. Led by President Franklin Roosevelt, the United States gave first covert, then open assistance to the British as they stood alone against Hitler's Germany. Germany's invasion of the Soviet Union in the summer of 1941 was the beginning of the end for the Nazis' aims of world conquest. However, it was not until the December 1941 Japanese attack on Pearl Harbor, Hawaii, that the public was willing to support U.S. entry into the war against Japan. When Germany and Italy then declared war on the United States, we fought in Europe alongside Britain, the Soviet Union, and remnant armies from the occupied nations of Europe.

The Cold War

The allied victory in 1945 brought a split between the Soviet Union and its Western allies. The Soviet Union lost 20 million people in the war (the United States lost 400,000). Given these losses in a German invasion that was only one of many invasions of Russian territory over the centuries, the Soviet government was determined, especially as a protection against Germany, to have friendly neighbors in Europe, just as we wanted them in Latin America. To ensure this, the Soviets were willing to use any means, including violence, to secure Communist governments in the ring of nations surrounding it—Poland, Czechoslovakia, Rumania, Hungary, and Bulgaria. Our wish for free elections in these nations was seen by the Soviet Union as an attempt to isolate it. The Soviets believed that we wanted to surround them with anti-Soviet governments, thus making their sacrifices in World War II futile. Many of our policymakers saw Soviet

Table 1 ■ U.S. Military Interventions Since 1900

Year(s)	Country	Year(s)	Country
1899–1901	Phillippines	1918–20	Soviet Russia
1900	China	1919	Honduras
1901	Colombia (Panama)	1920	China
1902	Colombia	1920	Guatemala
1902	Columbia	1921	Panama–Costa Rica
1903	Honduras	1922	Turkey
1903	Dominican Republic	1924	Honduras
1903	Syria	1924	China
1903–14	Panama	1925	China
1904	Dominican Republic	1925	Honduras
1904–05	Korea	1925	Panama
1904	Morocco	1926–33	Nicaragua
1904	Panama	1926	China
1904–05	Korea	1927	China
1906–09	Cuba	1933	Cuba
1907	Honduras	1940	Newfoundland, Bermuda, St. Lucia, Bahamas, Jamaica, Antigua, Trinidad, and British Guiana
1910	Nicaragua		
1911	Honduras		
1911	China		
1912	Honduras	1941	Greenland
1912	Panama	1941	Dutch Guiana
1912	Cuba	1941	Iceland
1912	China	1941–45	World War II (fully declared)
1912	Turkey		
1912–25	Nicaragua	1950–53	Korea
1912–41	China	1957	Lebanon
1913	Mexico	1961	Cuba
1914	Haiti	1964–73	Vietnam
1914	Dominican Republic	1965	Dominican Republic
1914–17	Mexico	1970	Laos
1915–34	Haiti	1970	Cambodia
1916–24	Dominican Republic	1975	Cambodia
1917–18	World War I (fully declared)	1980	Iran
		1982	Lebanon
1917–33	Cuba	1983	Grenada
1918–19	Mexico	1989	Panama
1918–20	Panama	1991	Iraq, Kuwait

Source: Data through the year 1965 are taken from *Congressional Record,* June 23, 1969, pp. 16840–43.

Figuring Out How U.S. Foreign Policy Is Made

One insight into U.S. foreign policymaking was offered by Nizar Hamdoon, Iraqi ambassador to the United States from 1983 to 1987, years when we supported Iraq in its war with Iran. Hamdoon lived through what he calls "every ambassador's nightmare" when, during his term, the Iraqi Air Force mistakenly attacked a U.S. ship. Dealing with this tragedy, he believed, confirmed several lessons he had learned about how Americans make foreign policy. Here are some of his insights:

1. Washington is driven by crises and expectations of crises. To influence policy, one needs to seize opportunities that arise during these crises.
2. Make contact with media and give them access. Don't be afraid of them. They shape public opinion, and public opinion is what matters, especially during a crisis. Be honest with the media, and when they call, be available.
3. Don't ignore the bureaucracy. A diplomat watches the internal debates of, and listens to gossip about, the middle-level bureaucracy. By the time policy pronouncements are made from the top, it may be too late to influence them.
4. Cultivate good relations with the "desk officer" at the State Department, that is, the official who is in charge of policymaking and information about your particular country. Also cultivate congressional staff. Hamdoon reported that the Iraqi Embassy held a lunch or dinner for congressional staff every few weeks.

5. Never feel secure about any issue. Things can happen quickly in Congress, the executive branch, or the media, and you had better be ready.
6. Take the long-range view of issues.
7. Reach out to all Americans, no matter what their position on issues. Be prepared to debate rationally and refute stereotypes of your country.
8. Get away from Washington. As Hamdoon said, "If you stick too long in the capital, you begin to think that America is a nation of opportunists, and that nobody cares about you unless you are a power broker in a business suit." But, he concluded, people outside Washington are not so influenced by the media and not so caught up in what's happening today.
9. Watch out for checks and balances. Washington is different from other capitals because in Paris, London, or Moscow there are central governments in charge of foreign policy. In the United States, you may deal with a State Department official today, only to find that the policy has been reversed by Congress tomorrow. The positive side of this, however, is that you can affect policy because it is so changeable. "Nothing is ever final in Washington. . . . Everything and everyone is workable."

Source: This box is summarized from Nizar Hamdoon, "The Washington Education of an Arab Diplomat," *Washington Post National Weekly Edition*, September 14, 1987, p. 24.

---

subversion of Eastern European governments as the beginning of a Soviet effort to conquer Europe.

As the only major power not decimated by the war, the United States responded vigorously to Soviet moves in Eastern Europe. The Marshall Plan provided economic relief to the nations of Western Europe in 1946 (aid was offered to some Eastern European governments but refused). In addition, the United States entered into military alliances with friendly nations in Europe and Asia to stop the spread of, or even to roll back, Soviet influence. The most important of these was NATO, the **North Atlantic Treaty Organization**, which in 1949 joined the United States, Canada, and their Western European allies in a mutual defense pact against Soviet aggression in Europe. Building these military alliances to compete with the Soviet Union and its Eastern European allies reflected the

cold war era that we had now entered. We were not in military battle with the Soviets, but the deep hostility between the two nations threatened to turn any conflict into a major armed confrontation.

The confrontation was not long in coming. The Soviet coup d'état in Czechoslovakia in 1948 and the rise to power of the Chinese Communist government of Mao Zedong in 1949 fueled U.S. fears that the Communists would dominate the world. Thus, when Communist North Korea attacked South Korea in 1950, U.S. leaders believed we had to stop the spread of communism in Korea before the Soviets undertook further expansion. This was the beginning of the **domino theory**; that is, the proposition that if one country fell to Communist rule, it would set off a chain reaction in neighboring countries, just like a long line of dominoes standing on end will fall in

FOCUS ON AN ISSUE

Is Military Intervention an Effective Foreign Policy Instrument?

From the late nineteenth century to the middle of this century the United States frequently used direct military intervention as a means to achieve its foreign policy objectives (see text table 1). During the cold war we were somewhat more reluctant to intervene with U.S. troops, preferring where possible to give military aid and training to indigenous forces in order to avoid confrontation with the Soviet Union. Even then, we maintained several hundred military installations and hundreds of thousands of troops abroad.

In the 1980s and 1990s the Reagan and Bush administrations demonstrated a renewed willingness to pursue U.S. objectives with military force, especially in situations where we had unrivaled military superiority. Some critics wonder whether, without the cold war to provide restraint, we will be involved in an increasing number of military interventions. Is military intervention an effective way to achieve our goals?

Do We Have the Necessary Level of Military Preparedness?

During the Carter and Reagan administrations there were strong indicators that the military was not prepared to carry out an interventionist role successfully: the aborted rescue of American hostages in Iran; the 246 Marines killed in an inadequately defended embassy compound in Lebanon; and the invasion of Grenada, during which we had to reinforce our initial invasion force to defeat a tiny, poorly armed force of Cuban construction workers.

Interventions in Panama (Operation Just Cause) and Iraq (Desert Storm) during the Bush administration suggested that a higher level of readiness had been achieved. The 7,000 troops Bush sent into Panama to remove President Manuel Noriega from power succeeded in defeating Noriega's defense forces and installing a new government. But the operation, waged in the residential area surrounding Noriega's headquarters, was not "surgical"; more Panamanian civilians than soldiers were killed.

The invasions of Panama and Grenada were regarded as military successes, even though clumsily executed. But the Persian Gulf War left the public with a different impression. It was short, fought largely from the air with high-tech weaponry, well-planned from the standpoint of minimizing American casualties, and the weapons, troops, and equipment functioned according to or above expectations.

The question, Is the military prepared to intervene? cannot be answered from the Gulf War experience alone any more than by looking only at the Grenada invasion. The circumstances under which each intervention is carried out have to be independently evaluated; what works in one situation might be totally inappropriate in another. But from the standpoint of personnel (training and morale) and equipment, the military appeared to be more battle ready in the early 1990s than it had been in the 1970s and early 1980s.

Can We Afford to Play an Interventionist Role?

No one doubts that if a crisis threatened our national security, we could find the necessary resources to respond.

sequence when the first one is toppled. If U.S. intervention could prevent the first country to come under attack from falling, others would stand firm. This rationale led us to intervene in Korea and later in Vietnam.

As the nucleus of a United Nations force, the United States drove the North Korean army out of South Korea in September 1950. But then the United States and its UN allies decided to "liberate" North Korea by invading it. The advance of U.N. troops to

the Chinese border with North Korea so threatened China that it sent massive armies into Korea and pushed the UN forces back into South Korea.

After UN forces regained control of South Korea, the commander of the UN troops, also the U.S. commander, General Douglas MacArthur, argued that we should drive the Communists completely out of Korea and launch an air strike against China. But President Truman feared MacArthur's proposals would bog the

However, our budgetary problems make it necessary for us to consider the economic consequences of our military activities. In committing troops to the Persian Gulf, President Bush made it clear that the United States would be unwilling to pay the costs of the war and to assume the major burden of the fighting. Because the Gulf War was fought under a United Nations mandate and because some of the world's richest countries—Kuwait, Saudi Arabia, and oil-dependent Germany and Japan—had most to gain from driving Iraq out of Kuwait, the United States was able to get substantial financial commitments to underwrite the costs of the war. Even then American taxpayers could end up paying half of the war's cost.

It is not likely that there will be a similar level of international backing for other U.S. objectives—certainly it would have been difficult to find other countries to underwrite the costs of the Panama or Grenada invasions. As we try to come to terms with our domestic economic problems, including the recession and the budget deficit, there is no mood in Congress to maintain our current level of military spending abroad. Public support for reduced spending has been growing steadily in response to the end of the cold war.

Do we want to become "guns for hire," a kind of world police force with wealthier nations paying the expenses for our armed forces? Even if we are working for goals approved by the United Nations, this role would likely be uncomfortable to most Americans.

Is the Use of Military Intervention Compatible with the Constitutional Division of War-making Powers?

What effect do military interventions have on our domestic goals? Paying the costs of intervention is one clear way our domestic goals can be affected. Another is the challenge to our constitutional system presented by presidential use of military force without congressional authorization.

As we discussed in chapter 11, politicians and scholars have been arguing for over 200 years about how Congress's constitutional authority to "declare war" limits the president's authority as commander in chief. During the debate in Congress over the War Powers Resolution Act in 1973, former Senator Jacob Javits (R-N.Y.) compiled a list of over 200 occasions when the president had sent troops into combat situations without congressional approval. In fact Congress has exercised its power to declare war only five times, and on only one of those occasions, the War of 1812, did it conduct a debate before issuing the declaration. Yet the two undeclared wars of Korea and Vietnam alone produced in excess of 100,000 American deaths, more than the combined losses of all of our declared wars, except for World War II.[1]

The War Powers Resolution Act was meant to curb what Congress believes is presidential usurpation of its authority, but no prior approval was sought for sending troops to Lebanon, Grenada, Panama, or the Persian Gulf. President Bush asked for a congressional resolution of support for use of force in the Persian Gulf only after 54 members of Congress sued him for breach of the War Powers Resolution Act. Even then Bush said he was not legally required to get such support.

The Founders, believing it too dangerous to give war powers to the president alone, were also unwilling to accept wording that would have given Congress the power to "make war." Instead they gave Congress the power to "declare war," leaving the president "the power to repel sudden attacks."[2] This leaves Congress and the president to struggle over who will decide what constitutes an attack on the United States and in which cases a military intervention is a war.

Have Military Interventions Been Successful?

To judge the success of a military intervention we have to be able to identify its objectives. In many cases this is not

(continued on next page)

United States and its allies in a prolonged war and perhaps even precipitate World War III. The Soviet Union had pledged to aid China if China were attacked. In the view of the Truman administration, our real enemy was the Soviet Union and our principal concern was Europe.

Thus the administration decided to pull back from its hope of unifying Korea and stick with its already achieved, original objective of freeing South Korea

from its invaders. Much of the American public reacted angrily to this; the magnitude of the resources necessary to fight a broad-scale war far from our shores was not appreciated.

One ugly outcome of this frustration was to fuel the already burning fires of McCarthyism (see chapter 14). Senator Joseph McCarthy of Wisconsin and his supporters believed that since the United States was so powerful, only traitors inside our government could made clear, or the real goals are hidden behind more palatable objectives. For example, in Central America and the Caribbean, we have usually intervened for the stated purpose of upholding the electoral process, encouraging democratic reform, or preventing Communist governments from coming to power. Often the underlying reason was to maintain in power governments supportive of U.S. interests and policies in the region. Intervention was effective in achieving this goal but far less successful in achieving the more overt aim of fostering democratic government in the region.

The Persian Gulf War was fought, according to the president, to make the world unsafe for dictators and to restore Kuwaiti independence. After the deaths of tens of thousands of Iraqis, the Gulf region had no fewer dictators than it had before the war, but Kuwait did regain its independence. The intervention was also successful in achieving the less openly stated goal of keeping a large part of the world's oil supply in the hands of governments sympathetic to wealthy, oil-dependent countries. In addition some would count the intervention a success from the standpoint of proving the military readiness of the United States and eliminating the Vietnam syndrome as a factor in foreign policymaking.

While military intervention can be effective in achieving an immediate or limited goal, it may be detrimental to long-range objectives. In Iraq our intervention led to a civil war against Saddam Hussein, which rebels believed we had encouraged and were obligated to support. But the aim of Desert Storm was to maintain stability in the region, not to create new kinds of instability. In Panama we ousted an unpopular government no longer serving U.S. interests but one we had helped put in place and whose president, Noriega, was on the CIA payroll. Hence a political intervention begat a military intervention, which may beget more political intervention.

Intervention can also give rise to new expectations and demands. Grenadians expected us to restore their economy, which we were unable to do. Panamanians were originally supportive of the U.S. invasion but then became distrustful of the U.S.-installed government (even though it had been popularly elected). Many became hostile to the United States itself over damage done to their economy and to private property. Some sued for compensation for damage to homes or businesses or for relatives killed in the fighting.

Direct intervention is a high-risk (and in some cases unlawful) tool of foreign policy; it requires great planning and skill, as well as luck and good timing, to be successful in its military aspects. It is even more difficult to make intervention work politically, in part because of its overt nature. With military interventions, unlike many covert actions, everyone knows for certain who is taking the action. Therefore, when intervention does not achieve what it was supposed to, either from the standpoint of U.S. policymakers or in the eyes of the populace of the target country, everyone knows whom to hold accountable. This may mean sacrificing long-term foreign policy goals for a short-term gain.

1. Ronald D. Elving, "America's Most Frequent Fight Has Been the Undeclared War," *Congressional Quarterly*, January 5, 1991, p. 37.
2. Joan Biskupic, "Constitution's Conflicting Clauses Underscored by Iraqi Crisis," *Congressional Quarterly*, January 5, 1991, p. 34. *Other Sources:* Edward Luttwak, *The Pentagon and the Art of War* (New York: Simon & Schuster, 1984), pp. 51–53; Carroll J. Doherty, "Bush Is Given Authorization To Use Force Against Iraq," *Congressional Quarterly*, January 12, 1991, pp. 65–70; Rochelle L. Stanfield, "Getting Panama Back on Its Feet," *National Journal*, December 30, 1989, p. 3113; Richard E. Cohen, "Marching Through the War Powers Act," *National Journal*, December 30, 1989, p. 3120; Frederick Kempe, "The Noriega Files," *Newsweek*, January 15, 1990, pp. 19–20; "Frontline" broadcast, April 9, 1991; "The U.S. As the World's Policeman? Ten Reasons to Find a Different Role," *The Defense Monitor* 20 (1991): 1–8.

have thwarted our will in China and Korea. This view substantially affected our foreign policymaking. Many of the State Department's most knowledgable and experienced area specialists were fired from their jobs on unfounded charges of subversion.

Containment in the Nuclear Age

Much of our relationship with the Soviet Union since the 1950s has been shaped by the nuclear age. The nuclear era began in 1945, when the United States dropped atomic bombs on the Japanese cities of Hiroshima and Nagasaki. Although the debate as to the wisdom and ethics of dropping these bombs still continues, it did bring the war in the Pacific to an end as Japan quickly surrendered.

At the close of the war, the United States was the only nuclear power. The Soviet Union exploded its first bomb in 1949, but it did not have an operational warhead until the mid-1950s and for awhile thereafter had no intercontinental bombers to deliver the bombs. Despite our nuclear superiority and capability,

Millions of Russian civilians as well as soldiers were killed in World War II. Grieving Soviets search for their friends and relatives after Nazi murder squads left a village in the Crimea in 1942.

we found our power limited. Nuclear weapons were of little use in the pursuit of most foreign policy objectives because the threat of inflicting mass destruction to achieve a nonvital objective was not credible to opponents. Thus during the period of nuclear superiority the United States saw its Nationalist allies lose to Communists in China, its French allies lose to Ho Chi Minh in Indochina, and an anti-Communist uprising in Hungary in 1956 crushed by Soviet tanks.

In 1955, the Soviet Union and its East European satellites formed the Warsaw Pact, a military alliance to counter NATO. People began to see international relations as a bipolar competition between a Western bloc of countries united under the U.S. nuclear umbrella and an Eastern bloc of nations operating under the protection of the Soviet nuclear umbrella.

American nuclear dominance began to erode in the late 1950s. Sputnik (the Soviet satellite that was the first to orbit the earth) showed that the Soviet Union had successfully built large rockets capable of delivering nuclear warheads. We were somewhat behind in this new technology, and the fear of Soviet advances led to a program to build and deploy missiles to supplement our bomber force.

Even with Soviet advances, American nuclear superiority was maintained for another decade. Yet everyone agreed that neither side could attack the other without the certain knowledge that the attacker as well

as the attacked would suffer enormous damage. Each side had the capability of destroying at least one-third of the other's population and nearly two-thirds of its industrial capacity in one strike.[9] No sane leader would risk so much damage by striking first.[10] This capability, with the appropriate acronym of MAD, is called **mutual assured destruction** (figure 1).

Despite public frustration with the cold war—being neither totally at war or at peace—successive administrations found that "rolling back" communism in the nuclear age was not possible without the kind of risk and commitment of resources most Americans were unwilling to assume. Thus, Eisenhower did not send in support for anti-Soviet rebels in Hungary in 1956, Kennedy denied U.S. air and ground support to Cuban rebels trying to overthrow Castro in 1961, and Johnson took no action when the Soviets invaded Czechoslovakia in 1968.

Meanwhile, changes were occurring in the Communist world. One of the basic premises of containment was that all Communist nations were controlled by the Soviet Union. As the 1950s progressed, it became clear that this was not true. Both Albania and Yugoslavia spurned Moscow's control. The Chinese became increasingly independent and in the early 1960s broke with the Soviet Union, declaring "there are many paths to socialism." Despite this, we continued to define most international events in terms of Communists versus anti-Communists no matter how

Figure 1 ■ The Rise and Decline of Isolationism (1964–85)

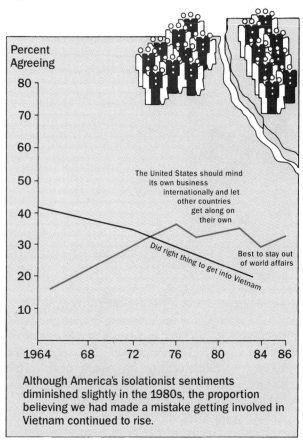

Percent Agreeing

80
70
60
50
40
30
20
10

The United States should mind its own business internationally and let other countries get along on their own

Did right thing to get into Vietnam

Best to stay out of world affairs

1964　68　72　76　80　84　86

Although America's isolationist sentiments diminished slightly in the 1980s, the proportion believing we had made a mistake getting involved in Vietnam continued to rise.

Source Polls by Civic Service, Inc., as reported in Lloyd Free and William Watts, "Internationalism Comes of Age . . . Again," *Public Opinion* 3 (April–May 1980): 46–50. Vietnam poll results from University of Michigan, Survey Research Center; 1983, *New York Times*, CBS Poll: General Social Survey, 1972–1986.

poorly such a characterization fit. Thus the stage was set for Vietnam, our longest war.

Vietnam

Early Period. Vietnam (Indochina) was a French colony from the 1860s until World War II, when it was occupied by Japan. Various nationalist movements, including the Indochinese Communist party led by Ho Chi Minh, gained popular support fighting against this occupation. When the Japanese were defeated, Ho Chi Minh's group and the other nationalists established a government in the North of Vietnam with its capital in Hanoi. They controlled only part of the South, however. The French, trying to regain con-

trol of Vietnam, established a competing Vietnamese government in the South. Although they spent hundreds of millions of dollars and lost many lives, the French were not able to defeat Ho Chi Minh's government in the North and could not even control large parts of the South. In 1954, the French troops were defeated by Ho's in a major battle.

During this time the United States became more and more involved. By 1954, it was underwriting 80% of the cost of the French effort in Vietnam. But after considerable deliberation, the Eisenhower administration refused to provide troops or air support to save the French because Eisenhower believed that this could bog us down in a long war requiring many troops.

The French wanted out, and at a conference in Geneva in 1954, an agreement was made mandating the forces of Ho Chi Minh to withdraw from the South. However, they were promised that elections would be held in 1956 to choose leaders for all of Vietnam. Until then, a temporary boundary separated the territory of Ho's government in the North from that of the French—and U.S.—backed government in the South.

The United States did not actively participate in the conference nor give its formal agreement to it, although it did issue a statement supporting the idea of free elections. In the years following Geneva the U.S. commitment to free elections disappeared. A new prime minister, Ngo Dinh Diem, was a staunch anti-Communist Catholic with influential friends in the U.S. Catholic community and Congress. With U.S. backing, Diem's government refused to participate in the elections scheduled for 1956. We believed the government of Ho would win the election. The temporary partition between the North and South continued and after the assassination of Diem in 1963, it soon became clear that the South Vietnamese government would collapse without more U.S. intervention.

Armed Intervention. In 1964, President Johnson presented the Tonkin Gulf resolution to Congress, followed by massive bombing of the North. In early 1965, he sent in U.S. troops with the belief that the war would be over "in a matter of months." After all, the United States had sophisticated equipment and training and complete air superiority.

But the **Vietnam War** dragged on for three more years before we saw the beginning of the "end" of our

The self-immolation by Buddhist monks in Saigon as political protests against Ngo Dinh Diem's government brought home to Americans the seriousness of Diem's opposition.

involvement, the **Tet offensive** of 1968. Only 10 days after President Johnson declared in his 1968 State of the Union address that most of South Vietnam was "secure," the Vietcong launched a massive attack to coincide with Tet, the Vietnamese New Year holiday. They struck against targets all over South Vietnam—the U.S. Embassy compound in Saigon, a major air base, 36 provincial capitals, and dozens of villages. No place seemed to be safe from the Vietcong.

Although the United States counterattacked with great military success, killing perhaps as many as 40,000 Vietcong, much of the U.S. public and many leaders grew increasingly distressed by the war. All our military efforts had seemingly not made one square foot of Vietnam truly secure. Every night the public saw the United States bombing and rocketing cities and villages on their television screens. They heard that one-eighth of the Vietnamese population were

refugees due to the destruction of their towns and cities. The president and top military leaders declared the Tet attacks failures, but others echoed Senator Symington who asked: "What do we win, if we win?"[11]

After Tet, the Joint Chiefs of Staff requested over 200,000 more troops to add to the 500,000 currently in Vietnam. Stunned by this request, President Johnson decided to undertake a review of Vietnam policy. The Tet offensive gave more credibility to those in the administration who had been against the war and shook the faith of those who were only marginally committed to it. Even the Joint Chiefs were unsure how many years and troops it might take to win. Johnson refused to authorize the troop increase for Vietnam and, instead, in a national television broadcast, appealed to North Vietnam for peace talks and announced that he would not run for

President Johnson listens in anguish to a tape sent by his son-in-law (Charles Robb, then an officer in Vietnam, now a U.S. senator from Virginia), talking about the men lost in battle in Vietnam.

reelection. The peace talks began in May 1968 and dragged on through the administration of Johnson's successor, Richard Nixon.

Nixon's Vietnam Strategies. President Nixon wanted to leave Vietnam without appearing to have lost the war. To accomplish this, he tried "Vietnamizing" the war by forcing the South Vietnamese government to give more responsibility to the South Vietnamese army, and he authorized what was termed the "mad dog" strategy of massive bombing of Hanoi. All the while, he was withdrawing U.S. troops.

One of Nixon's most controversial war policies was his decision to expand the war into Cambodia. The United States supported a coup against Cambodia's neutralist leader who, the Nixon administration believed, did not do enough to prevent North Vietnamese troops from using Cambodia as a sanctuary and staging ground for attacks on the South. Shortly afterward, the president ordered an invasion of Cam-

bodia, supposedly to destroy a huge underground headquarters of the North Vietnamese army near the Vietnamese border.

In addition to igniting the largest campus protests of the war, the invasion finally led to congressional protest, including a resolution that no funds were authorized for continued ground action there. Nixon had planned to withdraw the troops anyway and did so quickly. But bombing in Cambodia continued until 1973, when Congress forbade the use of funds for this purpose. This was the only time Congress actually blocked presidential policies in the war.

Despite the president's belief that the invasion (or "incursion," as he preferred to call it) was a success, it widened the war further, failed to find evidence of any headquarters, increased support for North Vietnam among Cambodians, and, through the continued massive bombing, led to support for the murderous, domestic Communist forces in Cambodia who eventually took power in 1975. It did, of course, allow the administration to present an aggressive posture while withdrawing tens of thousands of U.S. troops from Vietnam.[12]

In 1973 an agreement was signed with North Vietnam. The same agreement might have been reached in 1969, but President Nixon believed that this would jeopardize his reelection chances in 1972 and perhaps other foreign policy goals, too.[13] The victory of the Vietcong and North Vietnamese finally occurred in 1975 as the South Vietnamese army disintegrated in the face of a Communist attack. Most high South Vietnamese officials escaped, but thousands of ordinary people who had cooperated with the United States over the years of our involvement there did not. In a final irony, Saigon, the capital of the South, was renamed Ho Chi Minh City by the victorious North Vietnamese and Vietcong.

Lessons from Vietnam. Much of our thinking about foreign policy today is an attempt to understand policy failures in Vietnam and to apply these lessons to current situations. Despite the fact that at its peak in 1968–69 our military force in Vietnam exceeded one-half million, had sophisticated equipment and training, and had complete air superiority, we were eventually defeated. Why did we fail?

■ *We did not have clear goals.* Policymakers never agreed on whether we were fighting China, the Soviet Union, North Vietnam, or rebels (the Vietcong)

AMERICAN DIVERSITY

The War Against the War

Even though it was at first a minority position, dissent over the war became immense. In 1965, "teach-ins" began on college campuses. Growing numbers of intellectuals, public officials, clergy, and others called for withdrawal. George Kennan, the former State Department official who authored the "containment doctrine," argued that the doctrine did not apply to places where stable democracies with popular support did not exist. Thousands of men refused the draft and went to Canada or to jail. Some anti–Vietnam War demonstrations numbered in the tens of thousands; 50,000 marched on the Pentagon in 1967 and 750,000 marched on Washington in 1969. Demonstrations on college campuses seemed to be everyday occurrences. Administration officials began to avoid appearances in all but the most conservative settings, fearing abuse, disruption, and shouts of "Hey, hey, LBJ, how many kids did you kill today?" Although even among young people support for the war exceeded opposition, the tumult and opposition were the greatest for any U.S. war.

President Nixon was almost paranoid about protesters. He traveled only to the most conservative campuses. During some of the largest anti-Vietnam demonstrations in Washington, with tens of thousands of protesters outside the White House, he made a point of the fact that he was watching television and ignoring the protest.

The 1970 invasion of Cambodia precipitated the largest protest demonstrations of the war and the deaths of student demonstrators at Kent State and Jackson State universities. Over 500 campuses canceled classes, and 51 of them stayed closed the rest of the semester. Estimates are that over half the campuses had some sort of protest, involving four million students. Many college campuses resembled areas under martial law, as police and the National Guard moved in to quell the disruptions. ROTC buildings were destroyed on 30 campuses.[1] CBS news anchor Walter Cronkite began his newscasts during this period by stating: "Today's student demonstrations occurred at . . ." and a map flashed on the screen indicating all the campuses that were up in arms or closed down in protest.

Dissent also infected the military itself. By 1971, desertion in Vietnam reached the highest rate in any era of

In a march on Washington, antiwar protestors put flowers in guns of military police to symbolize peace.

our history. Refusals by soldiers to go into combat were common. American troops sabotaged helicopters and hundreds "fragged" (threw grenades at) their officers.[2]

Dissent on the war constrained both administrations in considering possible escalation of the war. The president could be sure that announcements of additional troops would be met by protests on campuses and in the streets. And, while both presidents claimed not to be affected by such demonstrations, neither wanted to preside over a nation that was an armed camp. President Johnson was especially troubled, as he believed his domestic policies had opened a new era of abundance and equality for all. To see himself reviled by so many was profoundly depressing. He told friends, "The only difference between the Kennedy assassination and mine is that I am alive and it has been more torturous."[3]

1. Nancy Zaroulis and Gerald Sullivan, *Who Spoke Up? American Protest against the War in Vietnam 1963–1975* (New York: Doubleday, 1984).
2. Richard Gabriel and Paul Savage, *Crisis in Command* (New York: Hill and Wang, 1978), p.45.
3. David H. Halberstam, *The Best and the Brightest* (Greenwich, Conn.: Fawcett, 1969), p. 778.

in the South. It was not clear what or whom we were trying to defend or what Vietnam was supposed to look like after the North was defeated.

■ *We did not understand the political aspects of the war.* Supporting a series of unpopular South Vietnamese governments, we were at first oblivious to the vast indigenous opposition to the South Vietnamese government from Communists, other nationalists, and Buddhists. Our inability to construct an effective policy for "winning the hearts and minds" of the domestic opposition to the South Vietnamese government appears to have been a fatal weakness of policymakers from Eisenhower through Nixon.

■ *We did not understand the nature of guerrilla warfare.* Our opponents, the Vietcong and North Vietnamese forces who infiltrated the South, were not militarily strong, but they did not have to be. Although we inflicted heavy casualties on them, they were able to demonstrate to the people of the South that their government and its ally, the United States, could not protect them or their villages. And, in fact, the Vietcong were able to dominate much of the rural South. Our policies—to "destroy villages in order to save them" and to remove people from their own villages to be taken to "strategic hamlets," where

presumably they were safe from the Vietcong—were bitterly resented by many South Vietnamese.

■ *We were impatient with the war and we were unwilling to devote unending resources to winning it.* We knew from the British experience in defeating Communist guerrillas in Malaysia that we would need at least 10 soldiers to the guerrillas' 1, and that we might need 10 years to win the war, but no leader dared tell the public that we must commit ourselves for that long. We wanted to fight the war on the cheap and were unwilling to invest the human resources or time needed to defeat a guerrilla enemy. Although this stance was rational, it did not seem to lead to the obvious question of whether our objectives were worth the effort we were making.

■ *We did not have public support.* Although public opinion was generally supportive during the first years of the war, support eroded as it appeared we were bogged down in an interminable and indecisive conflict. Only about 20% of the public favored an immediate withdrawal in 1965, but by mid-1969, support for withdrawal began to increase and by 1970 reached 50%. By 1971 public support for an immediate withdrawal grew to overwhelming proportions.[14]

This photo of a naked South Vietnamese girl screaming from a napalm attack by "friendly" forces was one of the most famous photographs of the war and one that fueled antiwar protest. The girl, Kim Phuc, survived although she is still in pain and under treatment for her wounds. Now 27 years old, she studies pharmacology in Havana, Cuba.

The United States persisted in Vietnam for nearly 11 years because most policymakers believed in standing firm against what they saw as Communist aggression in Vietnam. Supporters of the war believed that if Vietnam "fell" to the Communists, other nations in the area would fall like dominos. Once involved, Presidents Johnson and Nixon believed that the United States could not show weakness by withdrawing without victory. They felt our "credibility" as a great power was at stake.

Detente

One of the many paradoxes of the Vietnam War era is that while the war was at its peak intensity, the Nixon administration was quietly making diplomatic overtures to the very powers whose influence we were trying to contain by fighting the war: the Soviet Union and China.

Richard Nixon had come to office after public opinion had begun to turn against the war. Perhaps partly for this reason and partly because his central interest was in foreign and not domestic policy, he immediately began looking for ways to shape international relations in the post–Vietnam War era. A man whose career was built on making political hay out of his staunch anti-Communism, President Nixon was well placed to make overtures to the Soviet Union without fear of being attacked by any but the most diehard conservatives. Thus Nixon and his national security adviser and later Secretary of State Henry Kissinger developed a policy called **detente**, which was designed to deescalate cold war rhetoric and to promote the notion that relations with the Soviet Union could be conducted in ways other than confrontation. We could reward the Soviet Union for "good behavior" on the international scene and at the same time reduce our own military expenditures, slow the arms race, and perhaps step back from the brink of war. The detente doctrine recognized that although the Soviet Union would remain our adversary, it too had legitimate interests in the world. It also recognized the growing military strength of the Soviet Union and that it was in our interests to pursue bilateral agreements such as on arms control, that would try to limit this strength.

The first notable achievement of the policy of detente was the Strategic Arms Limitation talks which produced a treaty **(SALT I)**, signed by President Nixon and Soviet leader Leonid Brezhnev in 1972. SALT I limited the number of ABM (antiballistic missile—a defensive missile) launchers that each side could possess and included a five-year freeze (later extended to 1980) on the number of offensive missiles each side possessed. At the time the Soviets had *more* missile launchers than we did but we had better ones.

Detente was not so successful in other areas. The United States continued its Vietnam struggle. The Soviets backed the Egyptians in the 1973 Middle East war, while the United States supported Israel. The Soviets actively supported a Marxist, anti-U.S. faction in Angola, while we supported two pro-U.S. factions. Each side accused the other of violating the spirit of detente.

During this era of new diplomacy with the Soviet Union, President Nixon also sent out feelers through third parties to see if China was interested in reestablishing diplomatic ties. After two years of negotiations through third parties, the first cultural exchange (a visit by the U.S. Ping Pong team) was arranged in 1971. Henry Kissinger visited the same year and by the time of President Nixon's visit in 1972, many nations had resumed diplomatic relations with China and it had been restored to its seat in the UN Security Council. (Full diplomatic recognition by the United States did not come until the Carter administration.)

The resumption of diplomatic relations between China and the United States was one of the most remarkable achievements of the Nixon-Kissinger attempts to make a break through in the cold war stalemate. Nonetheless, it was consistent with their balance-of-power approach to foreign policy. By making this effort during a period of hostility in relations between the Soviet Union and China, Nixon was probably hoping to gain leverage in dealings with the Soviet Union (what some referred to as "playing the China card").

The Nixon-Kissinger visits to China were all the more remarkable because they occurred while U.S. troops were still fighting in Vietnam. It had been the specter of a Sino-Soviet led Communist bloc and a near paranoid fear of "yellow hordes" advancing throughout Asia that led us to fight in Korea and Vietnam. Within a few short years China's image was recast from dreaded enemy to friendly ally, and cold war fears of world Communist domination were greatly diminished.

Cold War Revival

The doctrine of detente complemented the mood of isolationism and weariness that grew in the wake of the Vietnam War. Vietnam shattered the belief in containment and U.S. illusions that it could serve as the world's police force. Many Americans believed that both our aims and tactics in Vietnam were immoral. Others believed our aims were just but unachievable. Still others believed we should have stayed until we won. All these sentiments led to a good deal of public self-examination about the war, although there was no witchhunt for scapegoats as there had been after Korea.

Public and elite opinion after the war was divided. Isolationist, go-it-alone sentiment peaked immediately after the war but then declined (see figure 1).

Early in the Carter administration, attitudes of **cooperative internationalism** seemed to flower.[15] Cooperative internationalists believe that the world is far more complex than cold war rhetoric suggests. They believe problems of global poverty, inequitable distribution of wealth, and regional competitiveness are substantial threats to world order and that the United States should work with other nations to solve these problems.

With the Soviet invasion of Afghanistan in 1979, public and elite opinion shifted back. Cold war views, never completely dead, became much more respectable again.

Adherents of **cold war internationalism** continued to view the world largely in light of U.S.-Soviet competition. World problems were seen as focal points for this competition rather than as discrete problems. Cold warriors gave priority to strengthening the U.S. military capability.[16] Many of them believed we should have stayed in Vietnam until we won and that only the weakness of our political leaders and media caused our defeat. They saw the Soviet Union as the epitome of aggressiveness and recklessness and the United States as peace loving and virtuous. Our military spending and international involvements were seen as efforts for peace, while the Soviets' involvements were viewed as far more malevolent.

The revival of old fears made it difficult for the Carter administration to build on agreements reached with the Soviets during the era of detente. Carter continued the negotiations begun during the Ford Administration on a follow-up treaty to SALT I, and in 1979 he and President Brezhnev signed **SALT II**, which placed limitations on offensive missiles. But the treaty immediately came under fire by opponents in Congress and the public who charged that we did not have the means to verify Soviet compliance with the treaty. They also claimed that by focusing on numerical parity and ignoring size and qualitative differences in missiles, the agreement conceded superiority to the Soviets.

Supporters argued that it was in our interest to try to limit the numbers of nuclear weapons, especially at a time when we *were* still ahead in the overall missile race. Furthermore any agreement capable of winning approval from both the United States and the Soviets would have to be one that placed constraints on both sides. But the stunning invasion of Afghanistan by the Soviets in 1979 ended the chance of gaining Senate approval.

The Reagan administration took office in 1981 determined to challenge the Soviet Union in every way possible. During his first term, Reagan totally renounced the Nixon-Kissinger principles of detente, and his rhetoric labeled the Soviets as an "evil empire." He increased military spending to record peacetime levels. Despite the rhetoric, however, the administration did not risk confrontation. Anti-Soviet action took the form of providing aid to groups fighting forces in places like Angola, Afghanistan, Ethiopia and Nicaragua.

Though the election of Reagan put a cold warrior in the White House, the public was not willing to buy cold war arguments wholeheartedly. Vietnam had increased public fears of U.S. involvement in long wars with fuzzy objectives. Congressional and public support was decidedly tepid for military involvement in Central America to topple the leftist government of Nicaragua. Support for our 1983 Grenada invasion was high, but it was a brief episode against a tiny country. Reagan's dispatch of "peacekeeping" troops to Lebanon, where over 200 were killed, brought about public and congressional outrage, which led to troop withdrawal. Memories of Vietnam were rekindled in discussions about each of these issues.

By Reagan's second term, a dramatic drop in public support for increased military spending and growing public pressure for progress on arms control helped push the administration toward a less belligerent stance. Violent rhetoric was toned down and conciliatory gestures multiplied.[17] Washingtonians believed that President Reagan wanted to reach some agreement with the Soviets in order to be remembered as a peacemaking president. When Mikhail Gorbachev assumed power in 1985, opportunities for serious negotiations arose.

Glasnost: The Gorbachev Era

In 1985, Mikhail Gorbachev's election as general secretary of the Communist party of the Soviet Union was not much of a surprise. But since then, he has done nothing *but* surprise. Calling for "new thinking," he began to shake up Soviet society as it had not been shaken since the Russian Revolution in 1917.[18] Faced with a stagnating economy and a conservative, often corrupt Soviet leadership, Gorbachev encouraged competition in the economy, criticism of corruption and inefficiencies by government agencies, and free elections of some government legislative bodies. In these elections, complete with exit polling by Western news media, several Communist party leaders were defeated by reformers. Gorbachev's slogan for these internal reforms was *perestroika,* or restructuring. Even the KGB, the long-feared Soviet secret police, tried to appear more open and agreed to be featured in stories for Soviet television. Like a major threat to the status quo in any society, these reforms are a risky gamble.

In addition to shaking up domestic Soviet society, Gorbachev challenged the status quo in the international community with his policy of *glasnost,* or opening to the outside world. He encouraged foreign investment and requested foreign aid to help rebuild the Soviet economy; he made it easier for Soviet citizens to emigrate, pulled Soviet troops out of Afghanistan, and reduced aid to Soviet-backed governments in Nicaragua and Cuba. In 1988 Gorbachev announced to the United Nations that the Communist party has no monopoly on the truth and backed up this statement by accepting multi-party elections in Eastern Europe.

Gorbachev also took the initiative in resuming arms control negotiations, and he agreed to direct talks with President Reagan on the reduction of medium-range missiles deployed in Europe. These missiles can reach the Soviet Union from Western Eu-

Source: Dana Summers, © 1989, Washington Post Writers Group, Reprinted with permission.

rope, and vice versa, but do not have the range to travel between continents (that is, from the United States to the Soviet Union or vice versa). Reagan and Gorbachev reached an agreement on intermediate nuclear forces (INF) in 1987. Under this agreement, the United States and the Soviet Union would remove from Europe all missiles with a range of from 300 to 3,100 miles. To ensure compliance the United States sent inspectors or monitors to the Soviet Union and the Soviets sent them to Western Europe and the United States to observe production facilities and the dismantling and removal of the missiles.

These bold moves challenged our most dearly held stereotypes about the Soviet Union. If it was the "evil empire," as Reagan claimed, why was Gorbachev doing these things? But even President Reagan became convinced that Gorbachev sincerely wanted peace, and by the end of his second term Reagan was discussing with the Soviet leader the possibility of the "zero option," or the total elimination of United States and Soviet nuclear weapons in Europe.

During the first two years of the Bush administration the Soviet empire in Eastern Europe disintegrated with such rapidity that all policymakers were caught off guard. The Soviet-dominated governments of Eastern Europe were dismantled, Communist parties changed their names, opposition parties formed, and free multi-party elections were held. In Czechoslovakia a dissident writer newly released from prison was elected president. In Poland the Communist martial law regime was replaced by civilian government headed by a prominent figure in Solidarity, the labor union that symbolized mass resistance to Communist rule in the 1980s. In Rumania the president and his wife were arrested, summarily tried by a military court, and executed the same day.

In late 1989, demonstrators assaulted the most visible symbol of the cold war, the Berlin Wall (built

Americans destroy a Pershing missile in compliance with the INF Treaty with the Soviets.

by the Russians in 1961 to divide Russian-occupied East Berlin from NATO-occupied West Berlin), and began tearing it down. A year later the reunification of Germany marked the end of the post–World War II power alliance in Europe. By 1991, as the new unified German government was selling pieces of the Berlin War as souvenirs of the cold war, every nation in Eastern Europe was in the process of political and economic restructuring. Newspaper and magazine headlines were asking "Is the Cold War Over?" and suggesting that a new era had dawned.

The second half of the 1980s was dominated by Gorbachev's policies of *glasnot* and *perestroika*. The Soviet president's role in ending the cold war received an international seal of approval when he was awarded the Nobel Peace Prize in 1990.

As the United States prepared for the transition from the Reagan to the Bush administration, Gorbachev continued his diplomatic offensive. At the United Nations, in late 1988, for example, he announced that the Soviet Union would unilaterally remove 10,000 tanks, 800 planes, and half a million soldiers from Eastern Europe. He called on the Western powers to reciprocate. A few months later he proposed large cutbacks in short-range nuclear forces in Europe.

These proposals seemed to perplex and confuse U.S. policymakers. Some conservatives seemed to believe that if they stonewalled the proposals, Gorbachev would eventually give the United States whatever it wanted. Other experts pointed out that the administration was throwing away important opportunities to reach real agreements with the Soviets on moving toward a less militarized Europe and world. Indeed, one journalist called Bush "recklessly timid" for his waver-

Moscow residents have a "Beeg Mahk attack."

ing response. Bush, for his part, was said to fear making the same mistake Kennedy did when he authorized an ill-fated invasion of Cuba too soon after taking office. Though Bush did make some proposals for reductions in conventional forces in Europe, the United States was being cast in the eyes of the world as the foot-dragging party in the effort to reduce world tensions.

Critics in the Bush administration complained that Gorbachev's initiatives were public relations gimmicks. Certainly, every world leader tries to shape international public opinion, and Gorbachev is no exception. Indeed he has been quite skillful in wooing Western Europeans. But we too try to influence world opinion, and our early complaints about Gorbachev may have reflected our impression that his efforts were more effective than ours were.

Another criticism is that Gorbachev does not want genuine reform but is simply taking steps to avoid economic collapse. The Soviet economy is in horrible shape. Its agricultural output cannot feed its people, its industry stagnates because of overcentralized planning, its government red tape creates rampant petty (and not so petty) corruption. Consumers cannot get the goods they need. Military spending is a huge drain on the economy. With a much smaller total economic output, the Soviets spent a higher proportion of that output on their military (perhaps as high as 20% compared to our peak of 7%). All the negative effects that high military spending has on our economic productivity and innovation (see chapter 20) are greatly magnified in the Soviet economy. One way to relieve the burden on the economy was to reduce troop commitments around the world. But, to say that Gorbachev's initiatives will help the Soviet economy is not to say that he *had* to take any or all of these particular initiatives.

Some observers went to the other extreme and imagine that Gorbachev's leadership would make the Soviet Union into an American-style democracy. This is unlikely. As George Kennan has said about Russia becoming like us, "This it is not doing, could not do, and should not be expected to do."[19] The Soviets have had no experience with democracy. In 1917, with only a few months intervening, they moved from the authoritarianism of the czars to the authoritarianism of the Communists, who held power until 1991. However their system evolves, it will be quite different from ours.

Gorbachev's critics felt vindicated in their views when the Soviet president appeared to backtrack on internal reforms during 1990–91. He also took a hard line toward independence movements in the Baltic republics of Latvia, Estonia, and Lithuania, which were forcibly annexed by the Soviet Union at the end of World War II. Pushing the intent of *perestroika* to its limits, these republics tried to reclaim their status as independent nations. Many people were killed when Gorbachev sent Soviet troops into Lithuania and Latvia to quash demonstrators and local militia.

Critics believed that this was strong evidence that Gorbachev did not want profound change but would tolerate only that change necessary to keep the country afloat. Others believed that Gorbachev was sincere but did not have the political strength to carry out the full measure of reform he would like to see enacted. In this view, the Soviet military, in alliance with "hard-liners" from the party's old guard who feared the breakup of the Soviet Union, forced a get-tough policy on Gorbachev. In essence they believed that Gorbachev was not fully in charge of the national government or of the party apparatus.

In August, 1991 while Gorbachev vacationed in the Crimea, a handful of party hard-liners and key people in the KGB and Defense Ministry joined forces to take over the Soviet government. Poorly planned and without organizational depth or popular support, the coup lasted only three days. Its leaders underestimated the ability of Russian Republic President Boris Yeltsin to use his popularity to mobilize Moscovites in mass demonstrations against the coup. Nor did they anticipate the military's refusal to fire on demonstrators or force them off the streets.

Held indirectly responsible for the coup by many for having put in power those who led it, Gorbachev resumed the Presidency in a weakened position. Radical reformers like Yeltsin, who heads the Soviet Union's most populous republic, forced Gorbachev into more rapid enactment of perestroika and glasnost policies. Under this pressure, Gorbachev resigned as head of the Communist Party and stripped the party of its role in government. With no strong center left in Moscow, the Baltic states immediately declared their independence. Soon other republics followed suit or announced their intent to redefine their relationship with the national government inside a reformulated federal structure.

Faced with massive restructuring problems and the possibility of food shortages, Gorbachev made major foreign policy concessions to western governments in order to obtain economic aid. Among them was an agreement to remove Soviet military forces from Cuba, the last vestige of cold war competition in the western hemisphere.

Table 2 ■ Americans' changing views of the Soviet Union and China

	Percentage of Americans Having a Favorable Opinion of	
Year	Soviet Union	China
1976	21%	20%
1989	62%	72%

Source: Gallup Report No. 284, May, 1989, cover page.

In challenging our stereotypes about the Soviet Union and its role in the world (see Table 2), Gorbachev's actions, and consequent changes in the Communist world, have also challenged the assumptions we hold about ourselves. Since World War II, we have defined ourselves as the leader of the democratic world. Given our tremendous resources and military strength, Western Europe, Japan, and other democracies (and some nations that are not democracies) looked to us for protection against the Soviet threat. But if the Soviets are not a threat, our protection and leadership may not be needed and we may have less influence in a new international order.

In this new era, the nations of Europe and elsewhere are groping to figure out what the new alignment of the world order will be and whether the United States is just another major power or will remain *the* major democratic power. A former secretary of state once remarked about postwar Britain that it had "lost an empire and not yet found a role." In the post–cold war era, like Britain, we have lost an enemy and are searching for a role.

A New World Order?

During the past 40 years we have thought that military strength was our most important asset in our effort to keep the world "free." But now, as one expert on the Soviet Union said, "It is the end of the postwar world. We're not going to invade them and they're not going to invade us. The challenge now is that economic strength is the more important chip."[20]

By 1990 both Presidents Bush and Gorbachev were referring to a "new world order," although no one seems quite certain yet what this means in terms of concrete foreign policies. What is "new" about the new world order is the absence of the old pattern of East-West military competition in international relations. In the new order foreign policies presumably will be less dependent on military capabilities and more reliant on diplomatic and economic strategies. With the breakup of the power blocs there will be more independently formulated defense and foreign policies, and if new blocs or alliances are formed it is likely to be for the purpose of economic competition.

As a new world order takes shape, how will our goals be affected? Will our relationships with old allies remain the same in the absence of a common enemy? In this section we will review U.S. policies toward Europe, East Asia, the Middle East, and the less developed countries of Africa, Latin America, and Asia, and look at some of the issues facing U.S. policymakers as they try to reformulate goals and strategies for the post–cold war era.

The New Europe

For decades we gave highest policy priority to our relationships with Great Britain and the western part of the European continent. This was due in large part to our shared heritage, to our commitment to democratic government, and, in the postwar years, to our common membership in NATO.

Today, as the Soviet empire disintegrates, the extent of our military commitment to the defense of Europe is being reassessed, just as Europeans are questioning the need for such a strong U.S. presence on their soil. From its beginnings in 1949 problems have existed within NATO over leadership and strategic policy; these differences intensified over the years as the alliance grew to encompass 16 members (see figure 2 for a complete list of members).

In the early years of the alliance, the United States was by far the strongest power in the West. Britain, France, Germany, and the others were shattered by World War II, but as the years passed these nations regained their economic power. As they became stronger they wished to assume a more powerful role in the alliance. They feared that the United States, with its Asian interests and adventures, could drag them into wars they did not wish to fight. They also worried that they might be vulnerable to Soviet military power because the United States would not think it worthwhile to risk all-out war. France, which never accepted U.S. domination of NATO, withdrew from some military aspects of the alliance.

One focus of their discontent was nuclear weapons. Of the European powers, only Britain and France

possessed them. Because their forces were small, even they would have to rely on the U.S. "nuclear umbrella" in case of a nuclear war. So Europe felt increasingly dependent on an ally that might not view its interests in the same way.

At the same time, our European allies have worried about the hard-line stance of the United States against the Soviets. Throughout most of the previous 20 years, they have perceived the Soviets as less threatening than we have. They resented the Senate's rejection of SALT II and the Reagan administration's military buildup and slowness to engage in arms control negotiations.

The NATO allies also resented U.S. requests that they assume a bigger share of the costs of defending Europe. They believed they were being forced to pay for the budget difficulties of the United States.

Gorbachev's proposals to further reduce nuclear and conventional forces in Europe created a new strain within the alliance. The Germans, in particular, worry about the thousands of short-range nuclear weapons that remain in their country even though the medium-range missiles are being removed. The Germans fear that if nuclear missiles are fired, they will land in Germany. Hence, their statement, "The shorter the range, the deader the German."[21] They are therefore eager to rid their territory of nuclear weapons.

The United States and Britain, however, have been less enthusiastic about negotiations over short-range forces. They have wanted to make reductions in missiles contingent upon reductions in conventional

Figure 2 ■ Military and Economic Alliances in Europe

Former Warsaw Pact members

NATO and EEC members

NATO member only

Non-members

Our primary military allies in NATO are also (along with Japan) our chief economic competitors, through their membership in the European Economic Community, or the Common Market. Turkey is the only European member of NATO which does not belong to the EEC, but it has applied for membership. Some former Warsaw Pact members have also expressed an interest in joining the EEC. NATO members not shown: The United States, Canada, and Iceland. Warsaw Pact member not shown: the formerly independent East Germany.

Before anti-coup demonstrators in Moscow, a Soviet soldier displays the flag with a large hole where the hammer and sickle had been, while in Red Square more coup opponents unfurl the pre-revolutionary flag of Russia. This flag now flies over the Russian White House and the headquarters of the Communist Party.

forces (troops, tanks, and other nonnuclear weapons), because the Soviets outnumbered NATO in these forces.

The numbers on which this argument was based have become obsolete in the new Europe. With the election of independent governments in Eastern Europe there will no longer be coordination of security policy within a Soviet-dominated common alliance. The Warsaw Pact ceased to exist in 1991. Therefore, it seems unlikely that NATO countries will continue to accept U.S. domination of their alliance or perhaps even the necessity of a NATO. The United States has already agreed to reduce by half the number of its troops stationed in Europe. With no irony, one French legislator commented, "The Atlantic Alliance has never been as threatened as by the crumbling of one of its main strengths—the threat of Soviet military power."[22]

The absorption of Warsaw Pact member East Germany into NATO's West Germany may be a portent of a new military configuration in Europe.

In addition to reevaluating relationships with NATO, U.S. policymakers must also formulate new policies toward former Warsaw Pact countries. As independent actors their behavior in the international arena will be harder to predict, and it will be particularly difficult to plan long-range policy because no one can be certain what kind of governments and economic systems will emerge in these countries.

Indeed President Bush has said that the new enemy in Europe is "instability and unpredictability."[23] This uncertainty helps to explain the perplexity of U.S. policymakers as to what our role should be in Europe. Sam Nunn (D-Ga.), chair of the Senate Armed Services Committee, has said that the administration and our

European allies have not even reached a consensus on what we would like Europe to look like in a few years. Therefore, we have not had specific ideas about the agreement we would like to reach with the Soviets. As Nunn said, "Of course we'd like for them to get out [of Eastern Europe] completely. But if that requires the United States to get out [of Western Europe] completely too, have we thought through that?"[24] And indeed Bush has said he could not tolerate a nuclear-free Europe. However NATO is firmly committed to further reductions in its reliance on nuclear weapons.

The use of force by the Soviets to crush independence movements in the Baltic states in 1990–91, and announcements that Soviet troops would not be withdrawn from Eastern Europe until 1995, gave support to Bush's go-slow policy. But after the 1991 coup and the breakup of the Soviet Union, further reductions in troops and armaments in Europe are increasingly attractive to many U.S. policymakers. So too are prospects for a nuclear test ban treaty and limits on longer-range nuclear weapons. Supporting thousands of troops in Germany and elsewhere in Western Europe and developing and testing nuclear weapons are a huge drain on our resources and contribute to the budget deficit. Reducing military spending might also help us revive our economy and reorient it back to producing innovative goods for a civilian market. If the cold war is over, then the United States will need all its economic strength to compete.

There is no doubt that the new Europe is gearing itself up for economic competition with the rest of the world, not for a military confrontation within Europe. In 1992 the **European Economic Community (EEC),** an organization formed in 1957 to foster political and economic integration in Europe, will remove all internal economic barriers and customs posts for member nations and work toward creating a common currency and monetary system. The membership of EEC, or the Common Market as it is often called, has expanded from its original six members to encompass all of NATO except the United States, Iceland, Turkey, and Canada.

The very countries that have served as our staunchest military allies are at the same time among our strongest economic competitors. And they are about to become even stronger. This will be one of the major policy challenges facing the United States in the 1990s because it threatens to make worse our already record-setting trade deficits. Of particular concern is

Common Market competition in the export of agricultural goods. Although much is made about farm subsidies in the United States, European farmers are among the most highly subsidized in the world. The removal of import quotas and fees within the EEC and a unified policy on price supports for European farmers will make it even harder for us to export our agricultural products to Europe.

Another leading economic issue in the coming years will be the economic reconstruction of Eastern Europe. At the beginning of the 1990s, most of these countries are in desperate need of foreign investment, loans and credits, and technical assistance. The United States, already the world's largest debtor nation, will probably not be in as strong a position to help these countries as Germany will be (although West Germany has already taken on East Germany's huge foreign debt). But certainly we will be in competition with the Common Market to develop export markets and investment opportunities for private capital in Eastern Europe's newly privatized economies.

With the breakup of the Warsaw Pact, the countries of Eastern Europe might eventually try to join the Common Market since they will surely be too weak to compete with it as exporters. This raises the possibility for the twenty-first century of an even broader European integration, with U.S. influence drastically reduced from its level in postwar years.

East Asia

United States relationships with the countries of Asia will almost certainly be affected by the end of the Cold War because they have had a strong military component. We have defense treaties with both Japan and South Korea and a military agreement with China that allows us to operate jointly with the Chinese army a number of electronic listening posts along the Chinese-Soviet border. We have military bases in Japan, a large military contingent (remnants of the Korean War) in South Korea, and in the Philippines some of our largest military installations outside U.S. territory. We also operate the Seventh Fleet off the coast of China, although one of its functions, protecting Taiwan from invasion by the Chinese mainland, does not have the priority it once did. Most of these agreements were aimed at protecting allies in Asia, and ultimately ourselves, against

Soviet expansionism, so it seems likely that they will be of declining significance.

An area of continuing friction in our dealings with Japan has been the division of economic responsibility for Japan's defense. Since the end of the allied occupation of Japan, we have assumed a large part of the responsibility for Japan's defense by including Japan under our "nuclear umbrella." Under Japan's constitution, which was authored by U.S. occupation forces after World War II, Japan is prohibited from using war as an instrument of national policy and forbidden from creating an "offensive" military establishment. Japan does in fact have armed forces, including the world's third largest navy, but they are small in comparison to those of countries of comparable economic strength.

Despite the fact that it was the United States that encouraged Japan to adopt its present defense posture, Americans have increasingly resented that Japan has continued to spend only 1–2% of its gross national product on defense (compared to our present 5–6%), while its economy consistently surpasses ours in growth and productivity. With Japan now on very good terms with the Soviets, the Chinese, and the South Koreans, it will probably have little use for continued inclusion under the U.S. nuclear umbrella.

Trade problems in East Asia will continue to loom large in our foreign policy. This area has some of the fastest growing economies in the world, particularly Taiwan, South Korea, Hong Kong, and Singapore, which are often referred to as the four little dragons. Developing export and investment opportunities in the potentially massive Chinese market will continue to receive priority in our relations with the People's Republic, as is evidenced by the token actions taken against that government for its brutal repression of the prodemocracy movement in 1989. However, the major foreign policy issue in Asia will undoubtedly be our trade relations with Japan.

According to a popular 1989 joke:

> George Bush gets bonked on the head and lapses into a coma. He wakes up in 1992 to find Budget Director Richard Darman at his bedside. "Golly, Dick," says Bush, "how are things?" Replies Darman: "In the three years you've been asleep we've got inflation down to 1%, the GNP is growing at 4% clip, and we're actually running a budget surplus." Bush: "Wow. Only 1% inflation. What does a cup of coffee cost now?" Darman: "Only a hundred yen."

The joke reveals American fears that we are losing the economic war to Japan. Indeed, over half (54%) of the American public thinks the Japanese economy is stronger than ours. Only 29% thinks ours is stronger.[25]

The majority is only partly right. We are still the biggest economy in the world, and our per capita income is higher than Japan's. But the Japanese economy is not only growing much faster than ours, it exports more goods to us than we export to Japan, it has a lower unemployment rate, and the Japanese save about three times more than we do, thus freeing more funds for business investment. In terms of trends, therefore, their economy is on a sharper upward curve than ours.

Reflecting this reality, Americans perceive the Japanese economy in a largely positive light. Most Americans believe that Japanese companies are better managed than U.S. firms, that Japanese workers work harder, and that Japanese technology is better.

Americans are almost evenly split on the question of whether the United States or Japan makes better products.[26] On the other hand, a slight majority believe that Japanese trade practices are unfair, and 14% think it is "very likely" that Japan will become our enemy.[27]

As our overall economic performance continues to suffer in comparison to Japan's, a gap has developed in American and Japanese perceptions of one another. While polls show that the United States is the most popular nation in Japan (chosen by 30% of all respondents), Japan is only the third most popular nation in the United States (chosen by a mere 2% of all respondents), finishing well behind Canada and Great Britain.[28] This poor showing was exacerbated by American perceptions of Japan's role in the Persian Gulf War. Many believed that American lives were being risked to protect Japan's oil supply, while Japan sent no troops and tried to reduce its share of war costs.

Japan's image has suffered so badly in the United States that the Japanese government budgeted $375 million in 1991 to promote scholarly, political, and cultural exchanges between our two countries. Some American scholars denounced this effort as a government public relations gimmick, while others who were enthusiastic about the program thought it could work only if it had no government involvement. This prompted one Japanese official to complain that "the Japanese government has become a kind of leper, with everything it approaches being seen as smeared. Why can't the government of Japan be seen as sincerely wanting to do good deeds?"[29]

The Middle East

A major concern of U.S. policy in the 1990s will be finding a settlement to Arab-Israeli disputes and to the Palestinian problem in particular. The United States would like to have good relations with the Arab world because of its large population and immense oil wealth. However, this is a region of the world to which the United States had weak ties until the creation of the state of Israel.

Israel is our staunchest ally in the Middle East. A Jewish island in an Islamic sea, Israel became a nation in 1948 after British control over the area called Palestine came to an end. Israel has had to fight for survival ever since, because most of the Arab governments in the region do not recognize its right to exist.

The crux of the problem is that Israel was created from territory to which both Arabs and Jews laid claim. All the pages in this textbook could not document the claims and counterclaims of which group was there first in the largest numbers, but both Arabs and Jews have a special identity with the land. It is the birthplace of the Jewish religion and the location of many sacred Muslim shrines.

In 1948, neighboring Arab states attacked Israel when it declared itself a state, but in the first Arab-Israeli war the Israelis inflicted the first of a series of defeats on the Arab nations largely because the Arabs were divided. Jordan, Egypt, Syria, and Lebanon all had expansionist ideas and were almost as opposed to other Arab nations gaining territory as they were to Israel's existence.

This first defeat left hundreds of thousands of Palestinians homeless. They fled from Israel in fear or in panic when the war started, and would not return. Thousands of Jews also fled or were driven from the Arab nations when the war began, but they were welcomed to Israel. The Arab nations did not wish to resettle the Palestinians, however, believing that they would constitute useful and continuing evidence of the rightfulness of Arab claims to Israeli territory.

The fate of these Palestinians and their descendants, some of whom still live in refugee camps while others have settled elsewhere in the Middle East and around the world, is at the heart of the Arab-Israeli problem. Since 1948, more Palestinians have been brought under Israeli control, especially in 1967, when in the third Arab-Israeli war, the Israelis captured the Golan Heights from Syria, the Gaza Strip and the Sinai Peninsula from Egypt, the West Bank from Jordan, and the eastern part of Jerusalem.

The United States has recognized the state of Israel since its creation and since the 1967 war has given substantial economic and military aid. It has regarded Israel as a loyal and democratic outpost in a part of the world where our ties historically have been weak. In turn, Israel served as an ally for U.S. military and intelligence activities against the growing Soviet presence in the Mediterranean.

Although some believed that our policy was lopsidedly pro-Israel, we did try to maintain good relations with the Arab and Muslim countries that were not directly allied with the Soviet Union, and, through the 1970s, gave Egypt and Iran more aid than Israel. In fact we were major contributors to the military buildup in Iran and the Arab countries of Egypt, Jordan, Saudi Arabia, and Iraq.

After the 1973 Yom Kippur War, the United States took an increasingly active role in trying to promote a peace accord between Israel and its Arab neighbors. The Carter administration was instrumental in negotiating a peace settlement between Egypt and Israel, with President Carter personally serving as a go-between for Egyptian president Anwar Sadat and Israeli prime minister Menachim Begin. In these **Camp David accords,** Israel agreed to evacuate the Sinai Peninsula and return control to the Egyptians in return for Egypt's diplomatic recognition of Israel. This was very important to Israel because until then no Arab state had recognized Israel's right to exist.

The Camp David agreements left the Palestinian question unsettled, and that question has continued to fester. Since 1967, Israel has built Jewish settlements on the West Bank territory and in many ways has incorporated the area into its economic and political life. Many Israelis are adamantly opposed to giving it up. But Arabs believe the West Bank must be returned to Arab control in order to have any peace in the area. Some favor complete independence for the area—an independent Palestinian state. Others would rather see the West Bank become part of Jordan. Some Israelis suggest that it could be a semiautonomous state under the protection of Israel.

This issue is a continuing source of unrest. Palestinians have formed a variety of political organizations, some of them terrorist, to work for the liberation of Palestine. But the Palestinian leadership has

Figure 3 ■ Israel and Its Neighbors

The West Bank and the Golan Heights, parts of Jordan and Syria, respectively, were captured by Israel in 1967 and have been partially settled by Jewish Israelis who live in villages separate from the Arab population. The West Bank was the site of the *intifada*.

been deeply divided over strategy and tactics, including the role of terrorism.

The conflict developed some new twists in 1988, when the militance of Palestinians in the West Bank increased. In a movement called the *intifada,* meaning uprising, Palestinians, often children, stoned Israeli soldiers. In retaliation, the Israelis bulldozed the houses of Palestinians engaged in anti-Israeli activity. These actions, in turn, created Palestinian martyrs, intensified Palestinian hatred of the Israelis, undermined Israel's image abroad, and fostered the Peace Now movement in Israel that advocates negotiations with the Palestinians (figure 3).

In hopes of moving toward a settlement, Yasser Arafat, the leader of the largest Palestinian group, the Palestine Liberation Organization (PLO), announced that the group recognized Israel's right to exist and would be willing to participate in an international peace conference. Despite these encouraging signs, no specific movements toward the negotiating table were made.

In the United States, support for Israel weakened during the *intifada,* partly in response to televised coverage of Israel's occupation policies. The pro-Israel lobby, spearheaded by groups of Jewish-Americans with a special concern for Israel, remains a strong force in Congress, though many do not approve of the Israeli government's intransigence in dealing with the Palestinian liberation movement. They believe such intransigence as well as Israeli actions on the West Bank are weakening Israel's commitment to democracy and tolerance.

During the Persian Gulf War Saddam Hussein tried to link his invasion of Kuwait to the Palestinian question. This won strong support for him from the PLO and from Jordan, but few others in the international community believed that Hussein's takeover of Kuwait was motivated by a desire to see the Palestinian question resolved. Nevertheless, at the war's end the United States tried to use its strengthened position in the Middle East to force negotiations between Arabs and Israelis. This dismayed many Israelis who, after absorbing Scud missile attacks and staying out of the war at the request of the United States, felt the United States was accepting Iraqi linkage of the war with the Palestinian cause.

Israeli soldiers patrol an Arab village in the West Bank.

Even if a resolution is found to the Palestinian-Israeli territorial dispute, it will not necessarily bring an end to Middle East tensions. Long before Israel was a state there were territorial and leadership disputes among Arab nations in the region: objections to the leadership claims of the Saudi and Kuwaiti ruling families are long-standing, as are Syria's territorial claims on Lebanon, which it now occupies. There are differences between Shite and Sunni Muslims over whether Muslim states should have religious or secular leadership. This was an important issue in the eight-year war between Iraq and Iran and will probably continue to be a source of conflict throughout the Muslim world in the 1990s. Because much of this world lies within or near the oil-rich and strategically important Persian Gulf area, outsiders, especially energy-dependent countries like the United States, Japan, France, and Germany, care very much how these disputes are resolved. The United States has established a massive military presence in the Persian Gulf. Although the Gulf War was short, withdrawal of troops from the area may occur very slowly if U.S. policymakers decide to try to use these forces to shape power relations within the region.

Relations with Developing Nations

Some believe that the most perplexing foreign policy issues of the next decade will concern the **Third World**—those developing nations of Africa, Asia, and Latin America whose economies are generally poor and rural and whose populations are often inadequately fed and housed and sometimes even starving.

Before discussing the Third World, we might ask why it is called that. The term, as used by Westerners, does show a definite parochialism. The First World refers to the industrialized Western democracies of North America, Europe, and Japan. The Second World denotes the Soviet Union and the industrialized countries of Eastern Europe. The Third World then refers to the other nations of the world, which are striving for political and economic development. Sometimes analysts also refer to a Fourth World—those nations at the very bottom of the world income scale that seem to lack any prospect of improvement in their economic conditions, such as Bangladesh and Chad. With the end of the cold war, the terms First and Second World may fall into disuse, and we may stop referring to countries as if they were all part of political blocs. The "Third World" is useful for suggesting a relationship to industrialized countries, but it obscures the vastly different levels of development among countries of Asia, Africa, and Latin America.

Economic Challenges. In the 1950s and 1960s, there was a good deal of optimism that African and Asian nations, newly freed from their colonial masters in Western Europe (Britain, Portugal, France, the Netherlands, Belgium), were ready to pursue an independent course. Three decades later, most of the optimism is gone. Except for some oil-producing nations and the "four little dragons," most Third World nations are as mired in poverty as ever.

The reasons for the lagging progress in education, income, and development of stable political institutions are complex. Western leaders blame the Third World nations themselves. They claim these nations have neglected their own agricultural base; unable to feed their people they must spend scarce money on food imports. Western leaders also charge that many Third World governments have been corrupt and that few have made an effort to improve the lot of the average person. Millions have been spent on arms purchases from the Soviet Union, the United States, Great Britain, France, and Brazil. Other criticisms focus on the high birth rate of these developing nations, a situation that causes improvements in economic output and food production to be more than counterbalanced by increased population. Still others blame the poor economic performance on the low levels of private enterprise in many Third World economies.

Third World leaders do not accept these charges. They believe that they are as exploited now as they were in colonial days, partly because they are dependent upon the markets of the West to sell their raw materials and to buy finished goods. They argue that Western powers "stack the deck," buying raw materials cheap and selling finished products dear, leaving the Third World in perpetual poverty.

Despite relief assistance in times of crisis, such as the Ethiopian famine, the West has not done much to aid the Third World. U.S. foreign aid, for example, is less than .25% of our gross national product, with only a sixth of that going to the poorest nations.[30] Yet most Americans think we spend too much for foreign aid even though we give proportionally less than other Western nations.

Third World leaders want more foreign aid from the West, higher and more stable prices for the raw materials they sell, and a different tariff structure so that they can sell their finished products in Western markets. In other words, they want the West to give them preferential economic treatment to redress what they see as past and present exploitation.

Some U.S. administrations have been more sympathetic to the plight of the Third World than others. The Carter administration at times tried to focus on cooperation with the Third World, but the Reagan administration rejected categorically any of the Third World claims of exploitation by Western powers.

In the past decade, the economic growth and standard of living of many Third World nations have declined. This is especially true for Africa, which has 28 of the world's 42 poorest countries and where per capita incomes have fallen for 12 consecutive years.[31] One reason is the ever-mounting interest on debt owed by these nations. During the recessions and hard times of the 1970s and early 1980s, many oil-importing countries went deeply into debt. Other oil- and gas-producing countries such as Brazil and Mexico borrowed large amounts during boom periods, often encouraged to do so by Western banks looking for places to invest. Unlike the United States, which is also heavily in debt, the economies of most Third World nations are not growing fast enough to provide the means to repay the debt or even keep up with the interest payments. Many countries of Latin America have debts that far exceed the value of the goods they export annually.[32] Paying the interest on the debt leaves no money for investment in the economy; the money flows to banks and lenders outside the country, many of them in the United States.

To cope with the debt, governments of these nations have had to launch austerity programs, limiting public services and levying higher taxes. In some cases, these austerity programs have been forced on them by the World Bank and International Monetary Fund as a condition of renegotiating loans so they can be repaid more slowly. As a result, food prices have risen, causing standards of living to decline and political unrest to increase. For example, in 1988, rioting in Venezuela took as many as 500 lives. In Argentina, the economic chaos created by a $2 billion debt is strengthening radical parties. In Mexico, paying interest on the debt has threatened the stability of the government and the livelihood of the middle and working classes, who saw their real wages fall by 40% at the end of the 1980s.

The Bush administration has proposed to lend more money to the debtor nations, who then could pay it back to the banks. If that plan is implemented, the lender banks will not suffer, though the taxpayers will. Other observers favor a plan whereby the banks, which made loans carelessly, would have to reduce their interest rates and share in the pain of this international crisis. As a president of one Latin American country declared, we must have "a new approach to the debt or [witness] the destruction of democracy in the region."[33]

Political Challenges. A major challenge to U.S. policy in the Third World is to define what our interests are and what we can reasonably do to advance them. In the past developing nations often became centers of conflict between the United States and the Soviet Union. The logic at work was described by Arthur Schlesinger in his report on the priorities of the Kennedy administration (although he refers to the Dominican Republic, this could apply anywhere):

> There are three probabilities in descending order of preference: a decent democratic regime, a continuation of the Trujillo regime [a brutal right-wing dictatorship], or a Castro regime [a Communist government]. We ought to aim at the first, but we really can't renounce the second until we are sure we can avoid the third.[34]

This logic has led us to support abusive right-wing dictatorships because we have seen them as preferable, and more subject to our influence, than those of the left.

When leftist or Marxist regimes have come to power, we have often tried to overthrow them. Sometimes we have used economic sanctions or covert means to try to end these regimes, such as in Chile in 1970–73. At other times, we have used military force, as in Lebanon in 1958, Cuba in 1961, the Dominican Republic in 1965, and Grenada in 1983. In still other instances, we have provided military and economic aid to rebels, as in Angola in the 1970s and 1980s and in Nicaragua in the 1980s.

President Reagan's policy was to support almost any force fighting against Third World leftist or Communist governments. His administration gave support to anti-Communist forces in places like Nicaragua, where there were no Soviet troops, as well as in Afghanistan, where there were.

Critics of U.S. policy toward the developing nations suggest that one solution to our dilemma is to define our interests more clearly. Their point is that our security is not always threatened when leftist governments take over. For too long we defined Third World conflict in terms of a global struggle, when we should have been taking seriously internal conditions that long preceded the cold war. Even when a government or movement did have ties to the Soviets, it did not always mean it was automatically opposed to all U.S. interests. An example can be found in Angola, where a Marxist government used Cuban troops to defend American-owned Gulf Oil fields from American-backed rebel troops.[35]

In sum, our relations with the Third World are important, yet in most cases neither military aid, military intervention, nor economic aid has worked well in promoting economic progress, democratic govern-

ment, or positive attitudes toward the United States. Some may ask why we should come to the aid of leftist governments with poor human rights records who are militantly anti-American in their foreign policy rhetoric. Putting aside the humanitarian issues and looking at Third World problems in terms of our national interests, can it be argued that it is in our interest that three-quarters of the world's population cannot afford to buy the agricultural and industrial goods we hope to export? For many years the world's largest economies have been one another's principal trading partners. With the populations of these countries stabilizing, can their economies continue to grow without parallel growth in Third World economies?

Where Do We Go from Here?

With all of our relationships—those with opponents and allies alike—in flux, the 1990s will be both an exciting and unsettling time. When the dust settles, if there is a new world order in which international competition is much less dependent upon military capabilities, we will have an opportunity to rethink some of our basic foreign policy goals. If the Soviet Union continues on its present path of turning inward to cope with the problems of political and economic restructuring, then we will need to be far less concerned with nuclear deterrence and containment. There is also little imminent danger of any new major power

Source: Reprinted with special permission of North America Syndicate, Inc.

Can Economic Sanctions Work?

When the United Nations voted to place economic sanctions on Iraq for its invasion of Kuwait in August 1990, it set off another round in an old debate on the usefulness of such measures. There is a widespread belief that economic sanctions are not effective in getting governments to change their behavior. The argument against sanctions is that they require unrealistic amounts of time and international cooperation to bring about the desired results. The longer the sanctions are in effect, the argument continues, the greater the temptation for nations to pursue their own economic interests by trading or selling prohibited goods to the targeted nation.

Those who believe that under the right circumstances economic sanctions can work point to their use against the government of South Africa. South Africa, one of the largest countries in Africa, is governed by a white minority of 5 million in a nation of about 30 million. Due to the system of **apartheid,** the huge black majority had no say in government and lacked basic civil rights, including the right to vote, the right to marry a person of another race, equal opportunities for good jobs and pay, and the right to live in most areas of the country. Blacks assigned to live in rural areas, for example, needed special permission to stay in an urban area more than three days. Often black men who got jobs in the city had to leave their families behind because they could not get passes for them. All black adults had to carry identification cards, and thousands were arrested each year for not having proper identification. Most public facilities were segregated. Both black and white critics of the regime were subject to arbitrary arrest and indefinite imprisonment.

The Reagan administration, a supporter of the white government of South Africa, developed a policy called "constructive engagement." The idea of constructive engagement was to keep good relations with South Africa and try to persuade its government slowly to adopt more humane race relations laws. The administration was impervious to attempts to persuade it to join a United Nations effort to take stronger actions against the white government, such as economic boycotts, in order to bring about change at a faster rate.

In 1985, however, increased black protest and demonstrations in South Africa focused world attention on apartheid. As police moved to suppress demonstrations, many demonstrators were killed. In the United States, demonstrators also began to protest South African policies. In Washington, D.C., protesters gathered daily outside the South African embassy to shout "Apartheid No, Freedom Yes." College students and others around the nation also staged demonstrations in cities and on campuses.

---

establishing a military presence in Latin America, so we might concentrate less on keeping Communist governments out of these countries and more on how to help with the enormous development problems facing them.

Containment may take on a new meaning in the 1990s, as we try to limit the economic reach of Japan, Germany, and the Common Market. This will not be easy as we enter the decade in a recession, with rising unemployment and inflation, and as the world's largest debtor country: we have spent much of the last two decades building up our nuclear and conventional arms capabilities and running up huge budget and trade deficits. We import far more goods from other countries than they import from us. Although we lead the world in exporting some goods, such as agricultural products and jet planes, we import increasing amounts of other goods, such as automobiles, steel, clothing, shoes, and electronics.

Increasingly American business and labor leaders are seeing competition and lost jobs as problems in foreign policy. They want government help and as a result, political support for protectionist policies is growing. **Protectionism** means banning goods from abroad, putting quotas on imports, or levying tariffs (taxes) on imports to make them more expensive and therefore less competitive in the United States. We have used protectionist policies to help American farmers and the manufacturers of automobiles, textiles, clothing, computer chips, and other goods. For example, President Carter negotiated a quota on Japanese autos in the late 1970s. The Japanese agreed to it because they feared we would put a high tariff on their cars if they did not. In 1983, President Reagan put a four-year tariff on large Japanese motorcycles to make them so expensive that Americans would buy American-made Harley-Davidsons. And in 1987, Rea-

Corporations were pressured to remove their businesses from South Africa, and colleges, churches, cities, and foundations were pressured to "divest," sell stocks of companies that had investments in South Africa, and to refuse to do business with companies that operated in South Africa.

These protests gained widespread public attention. The presence of celebrities and a number of members of Congress among those arrested for their protest activities put the South African issue on the nightly news. Both conservatives and liberals demanded more action by South Africa to humanize its policies or against South Africa if it did not.

In 1985, in the face of public opinion and a Congress threatening to impose severe restrictions on U.S. economic involvement with South Africa, the president dropped the policy of constructive engagement and imposed some mild economic sanctions. He banned the sale of computers to South African police agencies and the export of advanced computer technology to any South African organization, and he also forbade loans to South African businesses or government.

The change in policy toward South Africa is a good example of how under the right circumstances public opinion and interest group activity can affect foreign policy. In this case it might be said that government policy was coopted by the private sector. The actions taken by corporations, under shareholder and public pressure, to divest their holdings in the South African economy had a greater impact than the limited action taken by the U.S. government. Divestiture occurred on an international scale, with corporations from all parts of the world pulling out of South Africa. These actions, coupled with sanctions placed on South Africa by the United Nations, have undoubtedly played a role in the changes that have occurred since the late 1980s.

The white-controlled government stopped requiring blacks to carry internal passports or identity cards, desegregated public facilities, and lifted bans on the African National Congress (ANC) and other antiapartheid organizations. In 1991, in an event given live international television coverage, Nelson Mandela, a leading official of the ANC, was released from prison after serving nearly 30 years. The present government of President F. W. de Klerk has called for the elimination of all remaining apartheid laws, including those on mandatory racial classifications, housing segregation, and restrictions on property ownership. De Klerk also proposes a new constitution in which blacks would finally receive the right to vote. In response Bush lifted U.S. economic sanctions in 1991.

South Africa has a long way to go before apartheid is fully erased and blacks are restored to full citizenship, but most of the progress that has been made came after international economic sanctions were placed on the white-controlled government. Change has not come quickly or without violence, but there is a possibility that the apartheid system can be abolished without full-scale civil war.

gan approved a large tariff on Japanese microchips and Japanese products using them.

Protectionism is also an issue with our European allies. After steel imports from Europe increased rapidly, in 1982 the Reagan administration forced the European community to accept a "voluntary" export agreement limiting steel imports to a small proportion of the market. European exports of low-cost agricultural products including beef and poultry threatened some of the U.S. world markets. A mini–trade war developed, with the United States restricting imports of European pasta, and the Europeans answering with tariffs on American walnuts.

Protecting American industries sounds patriotic. Supporters of protectionism argue that protectionist policies help make domestic industries more efficient and competitive and save American jobs. They point to Harley-Davidson, which, with tariff protection, raised the quality of its products, its productivity, and its profits.

Protectionist policies usually mean higher consumer prices, however. Auto quotas added about $1,300 to the price of each new Japanese car and $650 to each new American car sold here. Each job saved by the import quotas on Japanese cars cost American consumers $160,000.[36] It would have been much cheaper to have compensated the auto workers thrown out of work and retrained them for other jobs. Quotas imposed on some clothing raised prices by an estimated 20%.[37] And the tariffs on computer chips doubled the price of chips within a year, thus increasing computer prices. The tariff also diminished the competitiveness of U.S. computer firms, such as Apple, Hewlett-Packard, and Compaq, which bought chips from Japan. Thus the tariff ended up helping the Japanese computer industry more than our own.

This raises a second concern about protectionist policies: they may not work. Despite Harley-Davidson's success, domestic producers protected by tariffs may not have an incentive to buy and use new equipment, become more efficient, and lower the price of their goods. We now have policies protecting the steel and textile industries, for example. For the most part, both are so inefficient and decrepit that they cannot compete at home *or* abroad. This sad state of affairs was the justification for protectionist policies, but is has become the consequence of them too.

Finally, critics of protectionism say that it invites other nations to aim their own protectionist policies at goods we want to export to them.

Protectionism in the form of quotas and tariffs is gradually increasing among major industrial powers. Forms of protectionism now apply to 30% to 40% of all trade, and as these examples have shown, we too are guilty of throwing up trade barriers.[38]

President Bush is a free trade supporter and has in fact proposed a free trade zone for all of the Americas (similar to what will exist in the Common Market after 1992). But this is an area of foreign policy in which Congress has legislative authority, and under a 1988 trade law, the president is required to retaliate against unfair trade practices.

Demands for protectionist legislation will undoubtedly grow in the 1990s. Members of Congress are much more responsive to the economic needs of their constituents than the president is, and they can force the White House to accept new tariffs, quotas, and other protectionist measures. Their adoption may force countries like Japan to open their doors to more U.S. imports, as Chrysler chairman Lee Iacocca argues,[39] or it could lead, as others fear, to a trade war. Trade wars have the potential to expand into military competition to protect market access, so this is a policy area that requires great skill and finesse from decision makers.

The 1990s may be a period during which we can concentrate on strengthening our economy and developing the diplomatic and economic rather than the military instruments of foreign policy. The end of the cold war, however, could lead to an increased use of our conventional military capabilities. For the three decades that the logic of MAD governed our foreign policies, the United States and the Soviet Union had to behave in a way that avoided conflicts that might end in a nuclear holocaust. The Soviet Union's nuclear capabilities remain the same, but its willingness to use

Antiforeign sentiment at work in Japan and the United States. The Japanese are smashing a U.S.-made car, while Americans smash goods made by the Japanese firm Toshiba.

military force outside its borders changed drastically during the period of internal reform and secessionist struggles. This gives the United States greater latitude to use the enormous conventional capability built up during the Carter and Reagan administrations to shape a new world order.

Conclusion: Is Our Foreign Policy Responsive?

Our foreign policies reflect our conflicting values and goals. Because we value freedom we sometimes support groups and nations trying to overthrow brutal dictatorships. But because we fear communism we support many undemocratic and even terroristic governments.

We desire a strong alliance system and have entered into treaties with many nations around the world. Yet when our allies are strong and independent, they often disagree with us over our short-run goals and policies. We pride ourselves on our strength and power and have spent billions of dollars to build a strong military, yet after Vietnam we were uncertain how to use that power.

The post-cold war era is providing even more challenges to our definition of our role in the world. It seems clear from the Soviets' cooperation with the United States in the Gulf War that, whatever difficulties exist between our two countries, relations will not return to their cold war pattern. In 1991, nine years after the Strategic Arms Limitations Talks began, Bush and Gorbachev reached agreement on reducing long-range nuclear weapons by 30%. It is the first agreement ever on *reduction* of numbers of ICBMs, bombers, and submarines.

It is too early to tell how the U.S.-led allied victory in the Persian Gulf War will affect the direction of our foreign policy. The war clearly boosted American morale and caused a rush of patriotic fervor, so much so that some claim it has laid to rest the so-called Vietnam syndrome. Will this renewed belief in America's ability "to get the job done" lead us to look for new jobs for our armed forces to take on?

Is the direction of our foreign policy responsive to the public? Public attitudes do not provide much of a constraint in most specific foreign policy decisions. Much of the public is not aware of what is going on in most places most of the time. Ordinarily they are more concerned about domestic issues, particularly those affecting their pocketbooks. When presidents want to pursue a particular foreign policy, the public will usually go along, at least in the short run, especially if the president can convince them that our national security is threatened.

At most, then, public attitudes constrain the general policy directions of the president and Congress, although presidents can do a lot to shape these attitudes. Over the long term, as in Vietnam, the administration must be somewhat responsive to public sentiment that intensely opposes administration policy.

In the mid-1980s, the administration tried to escape the constraints of responsiveness by engaging in private activities in pursuit of its own foreign policy objectives. We saw "a shadowy new world," where "retired military men lead supposedly private organizations to intervene in foreign military operations."[40] Some observers fear this is a serious breach of the American tradition of civilian control over the military. Others believe that such operations are necessary and justifiable in protecting our security. In the long run, however, such operations weaken democratic government and responsibility to the people.

In 1989 President Bush committed troops to combat in Panama without congressional approval, and in 1990 he sent hundreds of thousands to a potential combat zone in the gulf before seeking congressional support. Does this amount to a usurpation of Congress's right to declare war? Although the public generally gives the president wide discretion in carrying out foreign policy, the president cannot be above the law in this or in any other aspect of governing.

EPILOGUE

Fulbright Votes Yes . . . But Soon Regrets It

Senator Fulbright and all but two of his Senate colleagues and all the members of the House of Representatives voted in favor of the Tonkin Gulf resolution, which gave the president power to "take all necessary steps, including the use of armed force, to assist any member of the . . . Southeast Asia Collective Defense treaty requesting assistance." To the president, the resolution was "like Grandma's nightshirt—it covered everything." Presidents Johnson and Nixon used the resolution to justify each act of escalation in Vietnam. After President Nixon sent U.S. troops to invade Cambodia in 1970, the Senate repealed the Tonkin Gulf resolution, but by then it was too late.

Although he urged his Senate colleagues to support the resolution, J. William Fulbright had doubts about it and about U.S. involvement from the beginning. When the president used the resolution to justify sending tens of thousands of American troops to Vietnam in 1965, Fulbright felt betrayed. In 1966, he and his committee held widely publicized hearings on the war, giving an opportunity not only for the administration to defend its policy but for distinguished opponents of the war to voice their doubts. From then on, Senator Fulbright became the leading congressional critic of administration Vietnam policy.

Later evidence from Senate hearings in 1968 and from the Pentagon Papers revealed there had been a good deal of deceit in the president's report about the events in Tonkin Gulf. The president had been preparing plans for escalation of the war throughout 1964 and was waiting for an appropriate event to allow him to unleash them. Our destroyers were not on "routine patrol" as the president had indicated but rather were on an espionage mission in North Vietnamese waters. The captain of the *Maddox* indicated that no North Vietnamese ships were ever sighted and the reported "radar contact" may have been an "overeager sonarman's" imagination. A White House official reported that the president had been carrying the resolution in his pocket long before the "incidents" occurred and was simply waiting for the right opportunity to present it to Congress.[41]

This incident reveals the importance of the president in foreign policy making, particularly in crisis decisions. Without an alternative source of reliable information, members of Congress and the public must rely on the president for information and guidance. Congress is reluctant to challenge him when confrontation with an enemy is at hand.

KEY TERMS

Tonkin Gulf resolution
containment
Monroe Doctrine
isolationism
cold war
domino theory
mutual assured
  destruction
Vietnam War
Tet offensive
detente
SALT I
cooperative
  internationalism

cold war
  internationalism
perestroika
glasnost
Hiroshima and
  Nagasaki
SALT II
NATO
European Economic
  Community (EEC)
Camp David accords
Third World
apartheid
protectionism

FURTHER READING

General

J. William Fulbright with Seth Tillman, *The Price of Empire* (New York: Pantheon, 1989). *Fulbright, still active, discusses where American foreign policy should be headed in the 1990s.*

Charles W. Kegley and Eugene R. Wittkopf, *American Foreign Policy,* 3rd ed. (New York: St. Martins Press, 1987). *A comprehensive text on the making of American foreign policy.*

James Nathan and James Oliver, *United States Foreign Policy and World Order,* 4th ed. (Boston: Little, Brown, 1989). *An introduction to U.S. foreign policy after World War II.*

Topical

James G. Blight and David A. Welch, *On the Brink* (New York: Hill and Wang, 1989); Graham Allison and William Ury, eds. *Windows of Opportunity: From Cold War to Peaceful*

Competition in U.S.-Soviet Relations (Cambridge, Mass.: Ball-inger Publishing Company, 1989). *These books are interesting in that both contain analyses by U.S. and Soviet scholars. The first is an outgrowth of a conference sponsored in 1987 to examine what really went on in the Cuban missile crisis of 1962. The second is a more general examination of issues facing the United States and the Soviet Union in the 1990s.*

Kevin Buckley, *Panama: The Whole Story* (New York: Simon and Schuster, 1991). *An account of how the United States got Noriega on its payroll, of how he fell out of favor, and of the U.S. invasion to overthrow him.*

James Chace, *Endless War: How We Got Involved In Central America and What Can Be Done* (New York: Random House, 1984). *An analysis of U.S. involvement in Central America from a rather critical perspective. A book that continues the saga of U.S. foreign policy in the region is* Roy Gutman, *Banana Diplomacy* (New York: Simon & Schuster, 1988). *Gutman describes this policy as "incoherent."*

David Forsythe, *Human Rights and American Foreign Policy*, 2nd ed. (Lincoln, Neb.: University of Nebraska Press, 1989). *How human rights issues affect the making of foreign policy.*

Mikhail Gorbachev, *Perestroika: New Thinking for Our Country and the World.* (New York: Harper & Row, 1987). *Gorbachev outlines his plans and hopes for Perestroika. In Russia and the West,* Jerry Hough *examines Gorbachev's policies and their impact on U.S. foreign policy.* (New York: Simon & Schuster, 1988). *Gorbachev's rise to power, his reform program, and precarious position in the Communist Party are described in Why Gorbachev Happened by* Robert G. Kaiser (New York: Simon and Schuster, 1991).

Michael Herr, *Dispatches* (New York: Avon, 1984). *A young reporter's view on the tragedy and comedy of the war from the perspective of those in Vietnam.*

Walter Isaacson and Evan Thomas, *The Wise Men: Six Friends and the World They Made* (New York: Simon & Schuster, 1986). *An insight into the foreign policy making establishment that dominated the postwar era into the early 1960s.*

Stanley Karnow, *Vietnam* (New York: Penguin, 1984). *A comprehensive and middle-of-the-road analysis of our Vietnam involvement from beginning to end.*

Barry Rubin, *Secrets of State: The State Department and the Struggle over U.S. Foreign Policy* (New York: Oxford University Press, 1985). *After learning about conflicts among those charged with making foreign policy, readers will finish the book surprised we have a foreign policy at all.*

Hedrick Smith. *The New Russians* (New York: Random House, 1990). *An engrossing account of the workings of Soviet society, many of which Gorbachev is trying to change.*

Strobe Talbott, *Deadly Gambits* (New York: Knopf, 1984). *An illuminating but depressing account of how the Reagan administration approached arms control negotiations in its first term. Talbott also described Carter's arms control policymaking in* Endgame (New York: Harper & Row, 1979).

Richard H. Ullman, *Securing Europe* (Princeton, N.J.: Princeton University Press, 1991). *Describes the breakup of military alliances in Europe, possibilities for restructuring, and the future of NATO.*

Bob Woodward. *The Commanders* (New York: Simon and Schuster, 1991). *An examination of military policy-making in the Bush Administration, with a special focus on the invasion of Panama and Operation Desert Storm.*

NOTES

1. Walter LaFeber, *New York Times*, July 3, 1983.
2. Elizabeth Drew, "Letter from Washington," *New Yorker*, July 28, 1986, p. 68.
3. Quotation by Leslie Gelb and Anthony Lake, cited in "The New Establishment," *National Journal*, January 21, 1989, p. 135.
4. Barry B. Hughes, *The Domestic Context of American Foreign Policy* (San Francisco: W. H. Freeman, 1978), chapter 5.
5. Robert Weissberg, *Public Opinion and Popular Government* (New York: Prentice-Hall, 1976).
6. Information in this paragraph is based on Jeff Gerth with Sarah Bartlett, "Kissinger and Friends and Revolving Doors," *New York Times*, April 30, 1989, p. 1ff.
7. For a discussion of the foreign policy establishment, see Walter Isaacson and Evan Thomas, *The Wise Men: Six Friends and the World They Made* (New York: Simon & Schuster, 1986).
8. For example, only 15% of voters in 1984 saw foreign policy as an important issue. See *Los Angeles Times* exit polls, November 6, 1984, reported in the *National Journal*, November 10, 1984, p. 2131.
9. Bruce Russett, *The Prisoners of Insecurity* (San Francisco: W. H. Freeman, 1983).
10. Ibid.
11. Quoted in Thomas G. Patterson, J. Garry Clifford, and K. Hagan, *American Foreign Policy* (Lexington, Mass.: D. C. Heath, 1983), p. 522.
12. William Shawcross, *Sideshow: Kissinger, Nixon and the Destruction of Cambodia* (New York: Pocket Books, 1979), p. 99. The Nixon-Kissinger Cambodian policies are defended in Henry Kissinger, *White House Years* (Boston: Little Brown, 1979).
13. See James Nathan and James Oliver, *United States Foreign Policy and World Order*, 2nd ed. (Boston: Little Brown, 1981), pp. 359-61.
14. Robert Weissberg, *Public Opinion and Popular Government*, pp. 144-48.
15. Ole Holsti, "The Three-Headed Eagle," *International Studies Quarterly* 23 (September 1979): 339-59; Michael Mandelbaum and William Schneider, "The New Internationalisms," in Kenneth Oye, Donald Rothchild, and Robert J. Lieber, eds., *The Eagle Entangled: U.S. Foreign Policy in a Complex World* (New York: Longman, 1979), pp. 34-88.
16. Thomas L. Hughes, "The Twilight of Internationalism," *Foreign Policy* 61 (Winter 1985-86): 25-48.
17. For an analysis of U.S.-Soviet relations in the Reagan era, see Alexander Dallin and Gail Lapidus, "Reagan and the Russians," in Kenneth Oye, Robert Lieber, and Donald Rothchild, eds., *Eagle Insurgent?* (Boston: Little Brown, 1987); Kenneth Oye, "Constrained Confidence and the Evolution of Reagan Foreign Policy,"

in Oye, Lieber, and Rothchild, eds., *Eagle Resurgent?;* John Newhouse, "The Abolitionist," Parts 1 and 2, *New Yorker,* January 2 and 9, 1989.

18. See George F. Kennan, "After the Cold War," *New York Times Magazine,* February 5, 1989, pp. 32ff.

19. Ibid.

20. Jerry Hough, quoted in Daniel Patrick Moynihan, *The New Leader,* January 23, 1989, p. 11.

21. Strobe Talbott, "Why Kohl Is Right," *Time,* May 15, 1989, p. 26.

22. Quoted in David Morrison, "Brooding about 'Burden Sharing,'" *National Journal,* November 26, 1988, p. 3010.

23. Quoted in Strobe Talbott, "Sorry to See the Cold War Go," *Time,* August 20, 1990, p. 56.

24. Kennan, "After the Cold War."

25. Richard Morin, "Guess Who Americans Think Is Number One?" *Washington Post National Weekly Edition,* February 27–March 5, 1989.

26. Ibid.

27. "Looking East: A Newsweek Poll," *Newsweek,* February 22, 1988, p. 48.

28. December 1989 poll conducted by the Japanese newspaper *Mainichi Shimbun, Lincoln Journal* (AP), January 2, 1990.

29. Quoted in Steven R. Weisman, "Furor in Japan Over U.S. Funding Program," *New York Times,* March 3, 1991, p. 14.

30. Steven Greenhouse, "Poor Nations Get Unspecified Pledge of More Aid," *New York Times,* September 16, 1990, p. 4.

31. Ibid.

32. See Pedro-Pablo Kuczynski, "Latin American Debt," *Foreign Affairs* 61 (Winter 1982–83): 344–64.

33. Quoted in Jim Fain (Cox News Service), "Latin Debt Solution Eludes Bush," *Lincoln Star,* March 8, 1989, p. 7; see also Bruce Stokes, "A Long Uphill Climb," *National Journal,* April 15, 1989, pp. 926–30.

34. Arthur Schlesinger, Jr., *A Thousand Days* (Boston: Houghton Mifflin, 1985), p. 769.

35. Oye, "Constrained Confidence."

36. Alan Binder, *Hard Heads, Soft Hearts* (New York: Addison-Wesley, 1988).

37. "What Am I Bid for This Fine Quota?" *Times,* March 16, 1987, p. 59; "The Battle Over Barriers," *Time,* October 7, 1985, pp. 22–35.

38. James Nathan and James Oliver, *United States Foreign Policy and World Order,* 4th ed. (Glenview, Ill.: Scott-Foresman, 1989), p. 480.

39. Lee Iacocca, "Call Me A Protectionist," *New York Times,* February 10, 1991.

40. Anthony Lewis, "Reagan Doctrine is Corrupting Institutions," *Lincoln Star,* April 27, 1987.

41. Nathan and Oliver, *United States Foreign Policy,* p. 271.

20 Military Spending

A Tomahawk cruise missile streaks toward a target in Iraq.

defense system for surface-to-air missile sites, which are usually located in isolated, sparsely populated areas. The Patriot destroys an enemy missile in a spray of shrapnel that comes when its 200-pound warhead explodes on approaching or hitting the incoming missile. If the debris falls in an isolated area no damage is done, but in the gulf the Patriot was used to defend urban areas such as Tel Aviv. Falling debris and/or active warheads destroyed more than 1,000 structures in Israel alone.[1]

Other experts pointed out that the Patriot was not put to a real test in the gulf because the Scuds used by the Iraqis were inaccurate and crude compared to the more sophisticated kind of missile the Patriot was designed to intercept. Similar observations were made about much of the high-tech equipment deployed in the gulf. Retired Admiral Gene LaRocque, for example, said the gulf campaign never saw "the full chaos that comes with war" and therefore did not provide a real test of many of the weapons systems or equipment.[2] There was no ground war of sufficient duration to test such controversial equipment as the M-1 Abrams and M-2 Bradley tanks, for example. In addition the war was very one-sided: the Iraqis had virtually no air defense system for stealth to evade, their pilots did not come out to challenge allied pilots, and their soldiers put up almost no fight on the ground. American flyers said that carrying out their missions against Iraqi troops on the Kuwaiti border was like "shooting fish in a barrel."

After the war was over and damage assessment began, the media began to suggest that our bombing had not been as accurate as first reported.[3] Most of the explosives dropped on Iraq were carried by old B-52s, although military spokesmen claimed that almost half of the direct hits were made by "smart bombs" carried on the newer and

more advanced F-117As.[4] Other stealth planes, such as the B-1 and B-2 bombers, were not used because they are designed for long-range missions, not brush wars.

Military briefings and videotapes of bombing missions emphasized the "surgical precision" of the air strikes inside Iraq. Because Iraq was all but closed off to reporters little additional photographic evidence was available to the public. However, military reports of sorties flown and tons of explosives dropped indicate that the air war may be better characterized by the term "carpet bombing" than by "surgical precision." More than 2,000 sorties were flown in the first *day* of the war (compared to 850 a *week* at the height of the Vietnam War) and more explosives dropped in the first 12 hours than were dropped on Hiroshima and Nagasaki. Military briefings showed tapes of direct hits on defense and communications facilities, but only 7% of all bombs dropped were "smart" bombs and a reported 70% of bombs dropped missed their targets.[5] Most of the civilian infrastructure of the country was also destroyed and civilian deaths were estimated in the thousands.

1. John Kifner, "Deadly Debris Shows Limits of Patriot Missile Defenses," *New York Times,* January 27, 1991, p. 8.
2. Quoted in "The War in the Gulf: A Reference Guide," *Champaign-Urbana News Gazette (Charlotte Observer),* February 26, 1991, p. T-27.
3. David Sarasohn, "Not So Smart," *Lincoln Journal* (Newhouse News), April 2, 1991.
4. Eric Schmitt with Michael Gordon, "Unforeseen Problems in Air War Forced Allies to Improvise Tactics," *New York Times,* March 10, 1991, p. 11.
5. "Bill Moyers: After The War," PBS *Frontline* broadcast, June 18, 1991. *Other Sources:* Jeffrey Denny, "Problem Weapons in the Persian Gulf," *Common Cause Magazine,* January/February 1991, pp. 34–36; William J. Broad, "The Patriots Success: Because of 'Star Wars' or in Spite of It?" *New York Times,* February 10, 1991, p. E5; "High Tech Weapons Getting Ultimate Test in Gulf Conflict," and "Tapes Show High-Tech Weaponry Doing Its Job," *Champaign News-Gazette,* January 20, 1991.

Most experts agree that the buildup had positive effects on military preparedness. In the 1970s, during and after Vietnam, the morale of the armed forces was low, reflecting public hostility to the war and the military. The quality of troops was going downhill, especially after the draft was ended in 1972. In the 1980s, the quality of personnel improved. The increase in spending allowed the military to increase pay. This in turn has enabled it to recruit from a broader cross section of the population and to attract more people with high school diplomas. Most now are high school graduates, compared to 1980 when barely half were.[22] Drug use and discipline problems have declined. Perhaps in part due to higher pay, morale has also improved. In 1986, about 30% of enlisted people were

satisfied with military life, almost twice as many as in 1978. Officers also reported substantially increased satisfaction.[23]

Stockpiles of ammunition and spare parts grew somewhat, as did the size of the navy (some of the ships were ordered in the Carter administration). The number of nuclear weapons, fighters, and tanks increased. The Gulf War was fought almost entirely from these inventories.

But there is another side to the story. Funds for operation and maintenance were slighted. Much needed training, such as miles driven per tank, steaming days per ship, and training days per battalion, did not increase at all, with a few exceptions.[24] Despite the vast procurement of new weapons, the average age of

An MX silo in Wyoming.

In order to cope with these budget pressures at a time when the public and Congress want to rein in the military budget, the Pentagon is faced with a number of unpleasant choices: cut personnel or training, cancel some new weapons systems that billions have been invested in, retire old weapons faster than scheduled, or cut back on spare parts and ammunition. The Bush administration has indicated it favors cutting personnel as the best means of reducing military spending.

Who Makes Decisions on Military Spending?

Decisions about how much is spent on the military, and how that money is spent, are made by the president and Congress. Their decisions are shaped by the Department of Defense, by interest groups and military contractors, and sometimes by the public. Therefore, many more people are involved in determining spending levels and deciding what weapons systems and equipment to develop and purchase than are involved in the setting of actual defense policy. The same factors that produce inconsistencies and incoherence in our foreign policy lead to waste, inefficiency, and redundancies in our military expenditures. Some of this is a function of the intragovernmental rivalries and interest group competition that are natural by-products of our type of democracy, and some is the result of the sheer size of the military budget.

The President and Congress

Budget requests by the Department of Defense (DOD), like other agencies, are forwarded to the president through the Office of Management and Budget (OMB). The OMB and the president scrutinize these requests, and then the president sends his own recommendation to Congress.

Annual spending on the military approached $300 billion as we began the 1990s, or about 5.5% of the GNP. Congress and the president must decide not only on the total spending level but also on how to allocate this amount to different defense needs. In 1990, for example, weapons procurement accounted for 28% of the budget, military pay and fringe benefits for 26%, operation and maintenance of military bases and equipment for 30%, and research, development and testing for 13%. The remaining 3% was divided

our weapons, airplanes, and ships increased. In fact, much of the increased spending bought more expensive weapons rather than more weapons.

Since 1986, the rate of increase in military spending has slowed dramatically and when adjusted for inflation has actually been falling by a few percent each year. But the military has been caught in a spiral of expenditures it has difficulty controlling. On the one hand are the operating and supply costs for all the new weapons purchased in the 1980s, and on the other hand there are the bills coming due for the weapons ordered for delivery in the 1990s. These purchases were apparently made with the idea that the increase in the Pentagon budget would continue at the same rate. As a high-ranking Reagan Pentagon official said, "We assumed the defense budget would go up ad infinitum [forever]."[25] Now the military is faced with too many superweapons and not enough money to support them.

among all other needs (military construction and family housing, for example). In the 1992 budget the itemization of these various costs required 88 pages of small print. Intelligence costs are buried in other categories; exact spending levels are not made public. Neither are amounts spent on classified or "black" programs such as space satellite systems. These are estimated to cost an additional $22 to $36 billion annually.[26]

Legislation details such trivia as the authorization of the sale of recordings of U.S. Air Force band concerts, but, as it does with any other complicated budget, Congress focuses on only a few issues in its review of the Department of Defense budget—new programs, military pay, and weapons procurement. Little attention is paid to the most important problems of global strategies and the proper role for the military. Congressional military experts of both parties have decried this emphasis.[27]

Although weapons systems are scrutinized closely it is difficult for Congress to vote against new systems proposed and backed by the president and the Pentagon. Congress rarely, if ever, denies a major weapons system to a president who is persistent enough to keep going after it.[28] The MX missile, for example, was opposed by Congress for many years but eventually approved. Sometimes Congress keeps weapons systems alive even when the president (and occasionally the Department of Defense) does not want them (see the box on the B-1 bomber).

There are a number of reasons why Congress rarely votes against a weapons system. One is that members want to appear to be improving national security. They believe their political futures will be enhanced if they are on the record supporting a "strong defense"—typically thought to mean more dollars for the military.

A second reason why Congress goes along is that most members are not experts in military issues. Few members have military experience. Although military service does not make one an expert, it can provide a more realistic basis for comparing the claims of military brass with those of their critics.[29]

A few members, especially those who have spent time on the Armed Services committees, have become extremely knowledgeable in the highly complex fields of weaponry and military strategy. Traditionally, these members have been more inclined than the rest of Congress to vote for military requests. This is because the party leadership in Congress has tended to nominate supporters of military spending for positions on the committees while members who do not start out

as supporters tend to be converted to a promilitary spending posture after serving on the committees. In recent years, however, more liberals and moderates have joined these committees. The House Armed Services Committee has a dynamic chair, Les Aspin (D-Wis.), who is anything but a Pentagon rubber stamp. The Appropriations Subcommittee on Defense has also been shaken up by new leadership.

Nevertheless, members often vote for new weapons projects because they see them as a way to bring jobs and businesses to their districts. Military spending is, as one member puts it, "the last really big barrel of pork that's out there."[30] The Pentagon has become sophisticated at developing political support for weapons by giving many regions around the country part of the contracts and subcontracts; this practice is called **contract spreading.** The B-1 bomber had subcontracts in more than 400 of the 435 House districts.

Both business and labor see immediate profits and jobs in military procurement, and members will fight hard to keep military installations and weapons programs that affect their own districts. In votes on the MX missile, supporters made it a point to inform their colleagues about how many jobs might be lost in their districts if the MX was killed.[31] Indeed, the guidance system alone in the MX was produced by 553 suppliers located in 26 states.[32] Individual members cannot resist trying to help their districts, but cumulatively these instincts are detrimental to an efficient military force.[33]

Members on committees that review military budgets are in a particularly good position to win bases and weapons contracts for their districts and states. Ninety percent of the contracts for the Strategic Defense Initiative went to states with senators on committees that reviewed the program.[34]

"AT LAST! A WEAPONS SYSTEM ABSOLUTELY IMPERVIOUS TO ATTACK: IT HAS COMPONENTS MANUFACTURED IN ALL 435 CONGRESSIONAL DISTRICTS!"

FOCUS ON AN ISSUE

Femmes Fatales: Should Women Serve in Combat Units?

Twenty years ago, women were only 1% of the armed forces; now they are over 11%. The change is due to the removal of the congressionally imposed 2% limit on women in the military and the switch in 1972 to an all-volunteer army. Women are represented in almost all the military's occupational categories, but the largest proportions of them are in administration, communications and intelligence, mechanical, supply and support, and medical specialties.

Women have been reasonably well integrated into most aspects of military life. However, at least one barrier remains: women are barred from battlefield combat positions and may also not serve on ships likely to come under fire.

Is this a good policy? Let us look at some of the issues involved.

Can We Distinguish between Combat and Noncombat Positions?

To enforce the policy of no women in combat positions, we have to be able to distinguish between combat and noncombat positions. In many cases, the categorizations seem arbitrary. The Reagan administration closed several military occupations to women because of their combat probability. Yet later most of these occupations were re-opened to women because there were not enough qualified men to fill the specialties.

Trying to decide what is combat and what is not leads to anomalies. Several women flew in crews responsible for refueling the attack planes in the 1986 raid on Libya. Nearly 200 women took part in the invasion of Grenada. Women officers fly over guerrillas fighting in Honduras; they command air force operating crews in West Germany, designated a combat zone and they serve as pilots and crew in the Military Airlift Command. Women repair warplanes, drive trucks full of ammunition, and work with nuclear warheads. They train pilots in attack skills that they cannot use themselves. All these are considered noncombat positions.

Women are stationed in missile silos, ready to launch nuclear weapons. In case of a nuclear war, they would be early targets. Women serve on destroyer tenders, but not on destroyers, even though the tenders are in the same carrier group. There were no women on the U.S.S. *Stark* when it was hit by an Iraqi missile in 1987, but they were one-fourth of the crew on the destroyer tender in the Per-

Women members of a military police unit on a U.S. base in Saudi Arabia.

sian Gulf that helped fix it. Women can command units of the army's combat electronic warfare battalions but cannot serve as platoon leaders within those units. Women are not allowed on navy warships, but they can serve in Coast Guard ships of all kinds, which, if war broke out, would be under the command of the navy secretary. The fuzziness of these categories is reflected in the words of an army spokesperson: "We have a combat exclusion rule but that doesn't mean women are excluded from combat. They are going to face hostile fire, and they are prepared for it."[1]

Are Women Capable of Combat?

Social biologists argue endlessly about whether male aggressiveness is inborn or nurtured in an environment that encourages men, but not women, to be aggressive. Clearly, not all women would be psychologically able to fight in combat, but then neither would all men.

Some combat jobs require physical strength; marching with an 80-pound pack on her back would be difficult for a small woman. On average, men do have greater physical size, endurance, and strength than women. However, allowing women to volunteer for combat duty and accepting only those who could pass physical tests required of all infantry members is different from arguing that all women are physically unsuitable for combat. Moreover, not all combat jobs (pilots, for example) require great physical strength. In the Gulf War brute strength counted far less than the skill to operate and maintain high-tech weaponry.

(continued on next page)

Although armies are, of course, traditionally male, we have many instances of women fighting in combat. In modern times, Israeli and Soviet women have fought; in earlier American history, a few women fought in the revolutionary and Civil wars. In the invasion of Panama, a captain in the army's military police led her platoon (which included other women) in a skirmish against the Panamanian defense forces. It was the first recorded incident of an American woman leading troops in battle.

Do Women in Combat Make Men Less Willing to Fight?

Some opponents of women in combat argue that men in combat would try to protect their women comrades and thus be impeded in their own fighting effectiveness. Others argue that "civilianizing" the armed forces, including having women in fighting positions, makes men less willing to risk their lives.

There is little evidence with which to evaluate this argument. Women who believe they should be allowed to fight do not take the argument seriously. Said one woman Navy officer, "So what if I get my guts blown all over the ship and it freaks the guys out? They would freak out if another guy had his guts blown all over, too."[2]

Do Women Have a Right to Serve in Combat?

Hardly anyone argues that women should be forced to do combat duty. But some argue that women who want it have a right to it. After all, it is difficult to rise to the top in the military unless a person has had experience in combat units. No chief of staff has gotten there by being an expert in supply or maintenance duties. Denying women the right to combat experience also deprives them of the right to aim at the highest levels of military command. Depriving women of the right to be in combat units may also deny women other experiences necessary to do their job. For example, one expert in silencing nuclear submarines filed complaints against the Navy for not allowing her to go to sea to see the results of her efforts. In response to these complaints Congresswoman Patricia Schroeder (D.-Colo.) has drafted legislation that would authorize the creation of an experimental unit in the army in which women would assume combat roles. In recognition of the role of women pilots in the Gulf War, Congress repealed a 1948 law barring Airforce and Navy women from flying in combat. Now it is up to their commanding officers to decide whether they will be given such assignments.

Is the No-Combat Rule Enforceable?

Some people believe that women are too well integrated into the services to be withdrawn from danger in wartime.

We have already had experience with this in Grenada, Panama, and the Persian Gulf. When their battalions were summoned for deployment to Grenada, several female military police officers were stopped at the loading ramp and sent back to their barracks three times before being allowed to go. When they arrived in Grenada, they were ordered back to the States. Later they were sent back to Grenada. "I felt like a yo-yo," said one. In the invasion of Panama women in the army's military police were told they would be pulled out if their units saw combat. But once there these women stayed with their platoons, even with those engaged in combat. Removing women from potential combat zones in time of war would create confusion and hamper military operations. As the Coast Guard commandant declared, "If I have a woman commanding a ship in the Bering Sea, I am not about to bring that ship home nor am I about to fly a helicopter out there to pick up its commanding officer just because she happens to wear a skirt once in a while. Forget it."

In any large-scale military operation it would be virtually impossible to replace women with suitably trained male personnel on short notice. In the Gulf War, there were 35,000 women among the 540,000 American troops. Replacing them would have been difficult; as it was, the Pentagon had to call up tens of thousands of reservists.

Based on their indispensable role in Operation Desert Storm women may find more job categories opening to them in the military. Is the public ready for this? One army spokesman has said that the central "question is whether America is ready for their daughters to come back home in a body bag the way their sons do." Little notice was ever taken of army nurses who were killed in Vietnam, perhaps because they were regarded as deaths of noncombatants. In the Gulf War five female soldiers were killed, including one helicopter pilot, and two were captured. The deaths received far less public attention than did the posting to the Gulf of women with infants and young children. Even on this issue the public seemed more concerned with cases in which the only parent or both parents were sent than with the women-in-combat issue. But whether the public is ready for it or not, if war should break out again, it is unlikely that women will be very far removed from the fighting.

1. "Female MPS on the Firing Line in Panama," *Lincoln Journal* (Newsday), December 29, 1989, p. 2.

2. This and following quotations are from "Women in Combat?" *Newsweek*, November 11, 1985, pp. 36–38. *Other sources:* James Fallows, *National Defense* (New York: Vintage, 1981); "Women in the Military: Operation Equality," *National Journal*, November 1, 1986, p. 2648; Richard Halloran, "Military Women," *New York Times*, March 13, 1988; Molly Moore, "Rethinking a Woman's Place," *Washington Post National Weekly Report*, January 29–February 4, 1990, p. 32; Michael R. Gordon, "U.S. Tells Calmer Story of Woman's Invasion Role, *New York Times*, January 9, 1990; "Our Women in the Desert," *Newsweek*, September 10, 1990, pp. 22–25.

Because military spending is concentrated in several large states, political pressure is more concentrated and intense. Seventy-five percent of the military contract dollars go to the 14 states with the majority of Electoral College votes.[35] California, for example, receives 17% of all defense contracts, Texas 8%, and New York 7%. Many states are quite dependent on military spending. It accounts for over 9% of the business generated in Virginia, Hawaii, Connecticut, and Washington. Iowa is the only state where less than 4% of the state's business comes from military spending.[36] Realizing their dependence on Pentagon business, many states and cities lobby hard for defense contracts. Michigan spends over $1 million a year to teach Michigan businesses how to capture defense contracts; New York offered new roads, housing, sewage treatment plants, and more to win a new army base.

Although most U.S. businesses are not dependent on military contracts, some of the nation's largest corporations are, and they lobby heavily. The late Senator Henry Jackson of Washington was often called, only half facetiously, the "Senator from Boeing." This reflects the reality that Boeing Aircraft, the largest corporation in Washington, is an important part of the state's economy and has a vital interest in military spending for planes.

Members of Congress feel intense pressure to keep the military dollars flowing. However, there seems to be little relationship between voting on defense policy issues and the amount of defense spending in a member's district or state (or the member's own investments in military contractors).[37] Exceptions are the most senior members of Congress, especially those on the Armed Services Committee who have greater than average amounts of military spending in their districts.

Members are also persuaded to vote for many weapons systems because the initial outlay seems so modest. In fact, only 3% of the ultimate cost of a weapons system is spent in the early research and development stage. But then, after more is sunk into the weapon, it is argued that we should not waste the money by abandoning the project, regardless of its effectiveness.[38]

Like an alcoholic in moments of sobriety, Congress sometimes realizes it has a problem dealing with weapons procurement and military spending generally. Pressures to help home districts lead to budget deficits and inefficient use of resources, and interfere with the Pentagon's ability to set priorities One such

pressure is for keeping open military bases around the nation. We have far more military bases than we need, but since they provide jobs and help local businesses, members of Congress are very protective of bases in their districts. Even when the Pentagon proposes closing some, members of Congress whose district or state bases are threatened combine forces to kill the proposal. Former Senator Barry Goldwater (R-Ariz.), a strong supporter of the military but a fiscal conservative in other ways, once sent around a list of military bases that the Pentagon thought should be closed. He asked all senators to volunteer one base for closing in their own states in order to share the losses. Not a single senator volunteered.[39] President Carter was successful in getting over 200 bases closed, but the major ones he wanted axed were saved by congressional pressure.

In 1988, in an attempt to curb spending and at the same time avoid having to vote to close bases bringing business and jobs to their constituencies, Congress passed a law giving base-closing authority to a bipartisan civilian commission. The commission, appointed by the secretary of defense in consultation with congressional leaders, draws up the plan for closing specific bases. If Congress fails to overturn it, the base-closing plan goes into effect.[40] The law specifies that Congress must accept or reject the whole package. In late 1988, the commission came up with an initial package to close 86 bases, partially close a few others, and reduce the missions at several dozen more. Most, though not all, of the affected bases were small. Despite complaints from members where the bases to be closed were located, Congress accepted the package. In 1991, when a new list of base closings was prepared, members rushed to protect installations in their districts by pointing to some "crucial" role they had played in the Gulf War.

Turning over decisions to a commission may work for base closing, but it does not seem to be an appropriate way to proceed when decisions are needed on which new weapons systems to choose.

The Department of Defense

Recommendations for military spending made to the president and then to Congress come from the Department of Defense. The department, often referred to as the Pentagon because of the shape of its huge building, has a budget equal to the entire gross national product of Canada and larger than the total economic output of all but 9 or 10 nations in the world. It employs over 30% of all civilian federal employees.[41]

Headed by the secretary of defense, who is appointed by the president, the department was created by a post–World War II merger of separate departments of the army, navy, and air force in order to reduce interservice rivalries and provide the president with coherent advice on military strategy.

The Joint Chiefs of Staff.   In theory, military strategy and spending levels are recommended to the secretary of defense by the **Joint Chiefs of Staff (JCS).** The Joint Chiefs, with their staff of nearly 2,000, are comprised of the chiefs of the four services—air force, army, marines, and navy—and a JCS chair who can be from any of the services. They are supposed to coordinate policy and decide the role of each service, which weapons systems to buy, what global military strategy to employ, and, if necessary, how to fight a war. However, because they all wear "two hats"—one as head of their own service and another as a member of this coordinating group—they ultimately engage in logrolling. Instead of choosing the best fighter aircraft, for example, they choose one that the navy wants and one that the air force wants. In Vietnam, the JCS permitted five air commands to operate, resulting in confusion and loss of lives. None of the service chiefs wished to relinquish control to another service.

The desire of each service branch to maintain its independence from the others has meant that the chiefs spend much of their time protecting their service turfs. Their unwillingness to coordinate important decisions on the design and acquisition of equipment and weaponry has led to serious inefficiencies. For example, when U.S. forces landed at Inchon during the biggest battle of the Korean War, the Joint Chiefs were arguing about the number of parking spaces to be given to the marines at the Pentagon.[42]

John Lehman, who as Reagan's secretary of the navy was very successful in outdoing other services in getting funds for his branch, argues that "the Defense Department is incapable of allocating priorities and rationalizing decisions."[43] The air force developed

The Pentagon is by far the largest agency in the federal government.

plans for the MX missiles without consulting the army, which is charged with defending missile sites.[44] In our invasion of Grenada, soldiers and pilots had difficulty communicating because their radios were incompatible.[45] In one instance American planes were bombing American ground troops (not an unusual occurrence in war). Problems with communication were so bad that after several unsuccessful attempts by the ground troops to contact the air force using sophisticated military radio equipment, one soldier finally made a credit card pay phone call to Washington to alert them to the bombing errors.

Interservice rivalries have also kept the Joint Chiefs from designing an effective command structure. This led to terrible coordination problems in Korea and Vietnam.[46] Despite the fighting skills of the American troops invading Grenada, the operation was botched by poor planning and coordination. The invasion was run by naval officers, even though it was a land conflict. There was no single command for the ground forces because the army and navy could not agree on who was to lead.[47]

Debate over the role of the JCS has been going on for almost 40 years.[48] Some changes have been made. In 1986, Congress gave the chair of the JCS somewhat more authority, a seat on the National Security Council, and a vice chair to help cope with interservice rivalry. But little has changed, and real change seems remote without a radical organizational reform. Some have suggested a single military chief of staff as one possibility of increasing the effectiveness of our military leadership.

Other Pentagon Officials.   Because of the weakness of the JCS, decisions pass into the hands of the secretary of defense and the secretary's aides and staff. For example, by refusing to comment on whether they thought the United States would be advantaged militarily by renouncing SALT II the JCS left it to Secretary of Defense Caspar Weinberger and the president to decide whether to retract our agreement to abide by the terms of the unratified treaty.

Defense Department heads, as political appointees, come and go fairly rapidly, so most never fully grasp the complexities of military strategy, the Pentagon or its budget. In practice, much real power is held by professional career civilian employees of the department who have detailed knowledge of the budget and programs.

The Pentagon is filled with officers whose functions seem redundant and unclear. After assignment to the Pentagon staff, officers trained to lead troops into battle become lobbyists, speech writers, and public relations specialists. A navy lieutenant, who at sea might supervise 100 men, in the Pentagon manages the dining room of the chairman for the Joint Chiefs, while a lieutenant commander, who might command a small ship or oversee the weapons of a destroyer in wartime, runs the Pentagon Officers Athletic Club.[49] The Air Force Systems Command (in charge of weapons acquisition) has 34 generals, over 10,000 other officers, and 16,000 enlisted people. Its only function is to supervise purchasing; it does not design, test, or operate weapons systems.[50]

The air force has 248 lieutenant colonels commanding squadrons of fighter bombers, missiles, and support aircraft and 12,500 lieutenant colonels "supporting" them. Other services are similar.[51] This bloated officer corps may add to the waste and cost overruns in defense contracts because officers are moved so swiftly from one Pentagon assignment to another (in order to make room for all officers needing training) that no one has the opportunity to learn a job well enough to do it efficiently.[52]

The Defense Industry

Before World War II, there was no private defense industry because government arsenals built almost all our weapons. Along with sophisticated military airplanes came the defense industry, with the specialized capability to build them. Contracting to private industry quickly became the normal way to build weapons. By 1958, only 10% of our weapons were still built in government arsenals, and our defense industry was huge.[53]

Today over 30,000 companies engage in military production. If it were a separate national economy, the U.S. military industry would be the thirteenth largest in the world. Military contractors employ over three million workers in a very profitable enterprise.[54] Military spending touches almost every locality; of the nation's 3,000 counties, only 9 do not receive some Department of Defense money. Universities too have come to depend on military funds for their scientific research as the rate of spending for education has declined. There is little doubt that overall the military has more influence on our lives and our economy than it had 20 or 30 years ago. Experts differ on the importance of the defense industry and its allies in shaping military spending, although all agree that it is important.

It was President Dwight Eisenhower, a professional soldier, who first warned Americans about the growing power of the **military-industrial complex.** He was referring to the military and its allies in defense industries who push us toward ever greater military spending to further their own interests. As he noted in a 1961 speech:

> This conjunction of an immense military establishment and a large arms industry is new in the American experience. The total influence—economic, political, even spiritual—is felt in every city, every statehouse, every office of the federal government. We recognize the imperative need for this development. Yet we must not fail to comprehend its grave implications. . . .
>
> In the councils of government, we must guard against the acquisition of unwarranted influence, whether sought or unsought, by the military-industrial complex. The potential for the disastrous rise of misplaced power exists and will persist.
>
> We must never let the weight of this combination endanger our liberties or democratic processes.

Since Eisenhower's speech, the influence of this establishment has grown much stronger. Along with members of Congress who use their seats on armed services committees to support Pentagon and defense contractors' demands, this group provides an excellent example of an iron triangle.

President Dwight D. Eisenhower was one of the first to alert Americans to the danger of the growing military-industrial complex.

When promoting the development and purchase of new weapons, there is a common outlook and economic interest between the military and their contractors. The strength of this alliance led one conservative senator to write in the equally conservative *Wall Street Journal* that defense had become "the nation's largest entitlement program and has reared a new generation of welfare queens—the defense industry."[55]

Profits from military contracts are far higher than in civilian work. Not only are the overall totals higher, but within corporations making both military and civilian goods, profits are much higher in military production. A 1986 General Accounting Office (GAO) report showed that during the Carter administration, profits of military contracts were 35% higher than commercial manufacturing, while during the Reagan administration they were 120% higher. The GAO estimated that the Pentagon could save about $6 billion annually if it paid its contractors the same profit as commercial manufacturers got.[56]

Executive salaries are much higher in corporations that do military contracting than they are in other large corporations. Some workers are paid better too.[57]

To keep the supply of public money coming, military contractors spend millions of dollars on congressional campaigns, advertising, and lobbying.[58]

Of course, there are people who work to make military spending more accountable. Sometimes this group is called the "dissident triangle," in contrast to the iron triangle of military contractors, members of the armed forces committees, and Pentagon officials.[59] The dissident triangle is composed of Pentagon whistle blowers such as Ernest Fitzgerald (see chapter 12), some congressional allies (most of whom do not have large bases or military contractors in their districts and are therefore free to be critical), and some members of the press. Members of the press get leaks about Pentagon misdeeds from the whistle blowers and members of Congress. Stories written about the Pentagon reach high-ranking eyes quickly thereafter through the "Early Bird," a 16-page compendium of stories from newspapers and wire services, put together by the Pentagon and distributed to high-ranking military and civilian officials. During the Reagan administration, critics believed that the best way to get the attention of the secretary of defense was to have a critical article appear in the "Early Bird." Criticism of the Pentagon sometimes brings about reform efforts in Congress or within the Pentagon itself by creating the possibility for negative public opinion. Still, the dissident triangle is more skilled at publicizing Pentagon misdeeds than getting policies to prevent them.

The Public

Public opinion on military spending usually responds to the appeals of political leaders and to the domestic and international environment. But public opinion on spending can constrain the administration. Support for increased military spending rose rapidly in the late 1970s and pressured President Carter to increase the defense budget (figure 4). During the bitter debate over the SALT II treaty, the sentiment of both the public and the administration was fueled by charges that we were behind the Russians, then by the invasion of Afghanistan, anti-Communist labor unrest in Poland, and the Iranian hostage crisis. The proportion of the public supporting increases in defense spending grew rapidly until 1981. Dramatic increases in military spending during the last Carter year and first Reagan years caused public support for further increases in military spending to tumble as fast as it had risen. Whereas 60% supported increases in 1980, only 15% did so in 1988, returning to post-Vietnam low points. Indeed, by 1983, public cynicism about waste in the military budget and the belief that military spending is eroding other federal programs prompted Congress to start putting the brakes on military spending.

By the end of Reagan's second term, most Americans remained skeptical. One poll taken in Reagan's last month showed that although most Americans thought he was right to try to build up the military, only 36% said they now felt more secure, and about half believed that Reagan had kept the security of the United States about the same as before.[60] Most thought a significant amount had been wasted; only 8% of the public thought the Pentagon wasted less than 10% of what it received.

Can the Decision-Making Process Be Reformed?

It is clear that interservice rivalries, constituent-oriented political decision making in Congress, poorly trained civilian and military personnel in the Pentagon, and the military-industrial complex in its cozy, iron triangle relationship with key members of Congress all contribute to the waste, fraud, and inefficiency in our military budget. Before discussing some

Figure 4 ■ Public Support for Increased Military Spending Weakened Substantially in the Mid-1980s

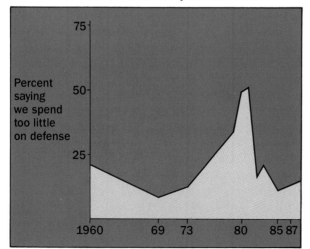

Source: Gallup Poll Data, January 25–28, 1985; April 1986; May 1987.

Not only does the armaments industry lobby Congress and the Pentagon, it also seeks to influence the opinion of those in the public who read national newspapers and elite journals. Here Lockheed advertises the virtues of their military airlift planes in an attempt to win congressional approval to buy from them.

Two Sides of a Very Cozy Triangle

Numerous major corporations have been the subject of allegations of fraud in their dealings with the Pentagon. One was General Dynamics, a firm that does most of its business with the government. It was the corporation that received the most from the military spending in the first Reagan administration. Among other weapons, General Dynamics builds the Trident nuclear missile submarine, the F-16 fighter plane, and the M-1 tank. In 1988, it had government contracts of over $6 billion.

Investigations of the corporation illustrate well the lack of control and accountability in the military procurement process. The Pentagon's Defense Contract Audit agency challenged $244 million in costs that the corporation charged to the government. For example, as overhead, the corporation charged the government for a $14,000 party at a Washington country club. Other allegations range from mischarging the government $.5 million for personal trips in the president's private jets, to $155 for the kenneling of a dog. General Dynamic's president admitted some mischarging and agreed to withdraw $23 million in charges.[1]

General Dynamics was also accused of negotiating a contract with a Pentagon official while offering him a job at General Dynamics. The company denied that the sequence of events was a conflict of interest.

An $800 million cost overrun for submarines led investigators to accuse General Dynamics of engaging in the common practice of deliberately bidding lower than cost, then renegotiating the price upward. Under this practice, if the Pentagon refuses to pick up the tab for an overrun, the corporation threatens to stop production. After some negotiation, the Pentagon did pay over half the funds. The navy official with whom General Dynamics negotiated later was hired as a consultant by General Dynamics.

The company discovered that its workers had made faulty welds and faked their welding reports. This meant repairs costing $100 million. The company asked the Pentagon for the funds, claiming it was liable under a standard clause in the procurement contracts calling for the government to be liable in case of worker negligence. Although the secretary of the navy first thought this claim was "pre-

posterous," in fact General Dynamics had a strong legal case. While the company denies there was any quid pro quo, General Dynamics was awarded another contract to build more submarines after dropping its $100 million claim. There are also charges that the navy agreed to let the corporation increase its profit on some ships in return for dropping the claim.

Each of these problems seems endemic to the current process: lack of control over charges, cost overruns, conflicts of interest, and government paying the tab for corporate mistakes. A former executive vice president of General Dynamics commented, "I was part of a team convinced that the way we did business was just fine . . . we were out to make money and to hell with the national interest." (This man fled the United States after being charged for taking over $1 million in kickbacks from a subcontractor.) An unnamed "former top Pentagon official" noted that "whenever you have so much money, you are going to have people doing a lot of reprehensible things to get the money. The sums are so huge now they pretty much defy control."[2]

Yet the government is as dependent on General Dynamics—it is the only supplier of the Trident submarine—as General Dynamics is on the Pentagon. For this reason, and because of the other ties between the Pentagon and its large military contractors, General Dynamics received only mild punishment for its infractions.

The current relationship of the Pentagon to military contractors is perhaps best summarized by Lee Iococca, the well-known chair of Chrysler Corporation. When he asks his suppliers who also do business with the military whether it is easy money, they laugh, look around to see if they are overheard, and then say, "It's like shooting fish in a barrel."[3]

1. "General Dynamics Under Fire," *Time,* April 8, 1985, p. 24. See also Winston Williams, "Bungling the Military Buildup," *New York Times,* January 27, 1985, section 3, pp. 1 and 8.
2. Ibid., p. 26.
3. Rick Atkinson and Fred Hiatt, "Oh, That Golden Safety Net," *Washington Post National Weekly Edition,* April 22, 1985, p. 7.

must know it will be. Then they pretend to be surprised when the projects have cost overruns (if they are not pretending, they are slow learners).

The other reason that the system bears little resemblance to a free market is that there are only a limited number of contractors to bid on each major system. One defense analyst claimed that there are re-

ally only five companies that can make fighter planes, three that can make bombers, three that can construct torpedoes, and two that can make nuclear submarines.[68] The government must make sure each of the companies stays in business to be available for future work. Thus, contracts are awarded, not just with an eye toward efficiency and low cost but with regard to

Red, White, and Blue Fruitcake

The Pentagon keeps thousands of its middle-level officers busy writing specifications. These are necessary to prevent contractors from cutting corners. However, overly detailed specifications mean that even when off-the-shelf products exist, they do not meet requirements and that relatively few companies will bid for the business. Those who do must hire people to figure out the regulations, while the Pentagon is filled with people who inspect the products—even fruitcakes—to the nth degree.

Military Specification MIL-F-1499F, written by the Army's Research, Development and Engineering Command, is 18 pages long and includes charts, amendments, and cross-references to other publications. The specification provides detailed standards for every ingredient and pan to be used. It indicates that the fruitcake shall contain candied orange peel "thoroughly deragged and processed with sugar and corn syrup to not less than 72% soluble solids." The raisins must be soaked "as necessary to prevent clumping," and the shortening is to have stability of "not less than 100 hours." The flavoring "shall be pure or artificial vanilla in such quantities that its presence shall be organoleptically detected" (that means you can taste it).

The batter should "consist of equal parts by weight of cake batter specified in Table I, and fruit and nut blend specified in Table II blended in such a manner as to meet the requirements of (specification number) 3.5." The batter is to be placed in cans with liners and tops "clinched on loosely to allow for the escape of moisture and gasses evolved during processing." The baked cake must "conform to inside contour of the can or can liner with no point on the top lid greater than ¾ inch from the side of the can where the cake did not touch the lid during baking."

To test the cake, one should "bisect it horizontally or vertically with a sharp knife." The cake "shall not crumble nor show any compression streaks, gummy centers, soggy areas, be excessively dry or over processed."

No directions were provided as to how to lick the bowl.

---

the economic health of all major suppliers. The current system, said a former navy undersecretary, contains "most of the negative features of both highly regulated utilities and perfectly competitive markets, with few of the advantages of either. It produces almost none of the stability enjoyed by most regulated utilities and very few of the positive incentives to lower cost and increase creativity that are the hallmarks of competition.[69]

Can waste and fraud in the procurement system be brought under control through tighter regulation by Congress? There are dozens of committees and subcommittees that oversee the Pentagon and make continual demands for information and accountability. In one year, Pentagon officials spent over 1,400 hours testifying before 91 congressional committees and subcommittees and responded to 85,000 written and 592,000 phone inquiries from Congress.[70] Its procurement regulations now take up 1,152 feet of shelf space.[71] With each new weapons acquisition scandal, Congress creates more rules and regulations requiring ever more paperwork and creating the need (or perceived need) for more bureaucrats in the Pentagon to oversee the work.

Regulations are of little use unless they are enforced, and the heightened public concern that came with the Pentagon scandals of the mid-1980s did lead to more aggressive enforcement. Under the category of white-collar crimes the Justice Department now gives highest priority to fraud in defense procurement, ranking it above insider stock trading and bank fraud. In the last half of the 1980s there were 30 felony convictions among the nation's largest defense contractors. Charges included "phony testing of nuclear weapons, trafficking in secret documents and creative accounting that bilked taxpayers."[72] In one two-year period there were more than 500 criminal convictions for offenses committed by small suppliers involved in defense procurement or individuals who worked in these companies (including 11 presidents or owners). In 1990, 60 of the nation's top 100 defense contractors were involved in 450 different cases under investigation by the Justice Department. About $500 million in fines and damages was collected from small suppliers, and judgments as large as $17 million were levied against large contractors.[73]

One development that may have the greatest reforming effect on the procurement system is declining military budgets. In response to the end of the cold war and to the overall fiscal problems presented by huge budget deficits, the defense budget has been falling at an annual after-inflation rate of 2.6% after a half decade (1980–1985) in which it nearly doubled in size.[74] This has led the Pentagon to cancel some weapons systems with large cost overruns.

With decreases in real spending projected through the end of the decade, the Pentagon is worried that some of its large and small contractors may find it unprofitable to stay in business. This has slowed the pace of reform as the Pentagon tries to protect the contractors most vital to weapons production. It has reduced the use of competitive bidding and accepted the fact that most big weapons systems cannot be produced at a predetermined cost. However, it is unlikely that we will see the kind of profit margins in these industries that marked the Reagan era of high spending.[75]

A blue-ribbon committee appointed by President Reagan proposed that the Pentagon buy more parts and supplies off the shelf instead of having them custom-designed to specifications. The committee also suggested that Congress meddle less in the day-to-day management of the Pentagon, and that it budget 2 years at a time. These recommendations are, however, nothing new. Five other presidential commissions over the past 20 years have made similar recommendations without much impact.

More critical observers call for a more dramatic set of reforms, including firing those at the top of the Defense Department who cannot get the process under control, putting top corporate executives in jail when they are convicted of fraud instead of just assessing fines, barring even the biggest firms that cheat the government from bidding for future weapons contracts, and building incentives for Pentagon purchasing departments to save money by letting them keep part of it for their own projects.[76]

Perhaps the most useful reform would be to drop the pretense that our major weapons manufacturers are private enterprises, in any real sense of the term. They are not; they are public in the sense that government must guarantee their survival, and for many of them, government is the major source of their business. Perhaps an acknowledgment of that might lead to some rethinking of the total relationship between the government and weapons contractors rather than just more regulations, a bigger Pentagon bureaucracy to enforce them, and more bribery and overruns to weaken public confidence in the whole system. Public ownership of some types of weapons production systems should not be ruled out. This idea might seem farfetched, but until 50 years ago, most armaments in

"Cost Underruns"

After reading the millions of words written about military spending and military performance in the 1980s, one might think that no weapon ever worked or was manufactured within its budget. But, in fact, some do work and a few prove to be cheaper than planned. For example, in 1987, the price of an air-to-surface missile system, the Maverick, actually fell! As a result, the air force was able to buy 60% more missiles than it had planned.

One reason this occurred is that the air force made the manufacture of the missile more competitive. After paying $122,000 for each missile manufactured by Hughes Aircraft, the air force decided to let Raytheon Corporation produce them too, instead of the usual procedure of giving one company an exclusive contract. Within two years, Hughes's price fell to $89,000 per missile, and Raytheon's was even lower.

This success is not unique; several other systems have also experienced reduced costs when some competition was allowed. Indeed, the price of one missile dropped from $1 million to $400,000 apiece when the Pentagon simply threatened to allow competition.

This kind of limited competition in which two contractors make the same item, like the Maverick, is called **split-sourcing.** The contractors bid against each other for each new contract. The winner gets most of the contract, the loser the rest. Split-sourcing is not truly competitive bidding but allows some competition. The idea is that the loser gets enough to stay in business, and keeping two companies in business keeps the price down and reduces the Pentagon's dependence on a single company for a weapon. Indeed, whereas the price of most weapons goes up over time, split-source weapons decrease in cost. As one journalist remarked, "Most contractors object bitterly to split-sourcing—a sure sign it is a good idea."[1]

Unfortunately, split-sourcing is under continual attack, not only from manufacturers but from Congress too. It costs a little more in the initial stages of production to have two production lines instead of one. And split-sourcing is not really appropriate for extremely complicated systems or for those where only a few planes, missiles, or other units will be built.

Sources: Sandra Sugawara, "Putting Adam Smith to Work in the Pentagon," *Washington Post National Weekly Edition,* March 13–19, 1989, p. 31; Greg Easterbrook, "Sack Weinberger, Bankrupt General Dynamics, and Other Procurement Reforms," *Washington Monthly* (January 1987): 33–43.

1. Quoted in Easterbrook, "Sack Weinberger."

the United States were built by government enter-prises. In many other Western democracies, weapons are currently built by quasi-public firms.

The Effect of Military Spending on the Economy

The amount of money we spend on the military has important effects, not only on our military prepared-ness but also on the state of the entire economy: un-employment, inflation, deficits, investment in industry and in housing, consumer spending, and what gov-ernment spends on other things such as health, edu-cation, welfare and highways. Funds for military spending must come from somewhere. The govern-ment must either raise the funds through taxes, cut back on other programs, or borrow the money.

Although common wisdom suggests that military spending is good for our economy, careful investiga-tions have reached more pessimistic conclusions. As Dwight Eisenhower once commented, "The world in arms is not spending money alone. It is spending the sweat of its laborers, the genius of its scientists, the hopes of its children."

Employment

It seems obvious that military spending increases em-ployment. After all, an estimated seven million people either manufacture or use military goods as employees of the Department of Defense or in industries making armaments and other military equipment.[77] Thus, when major weapons systems are considered by Con-gress, organized labor as well as business almost al-ways argues that they will increase employment.

However, some studies have shown that spending on the military creates *fewer* jobs than other kinds of spending. If all the money spent on the military be-tween 1950 and 1975 had been targeted for civilian purposes, an estimated 100 million jobs would have been created rather than the 7 million that actually were.[78] Our role as a world power would not let us deflect all, or even most, of our military spending to other purposes. And clearly there is some margin of error in this kind of estimate. But the figures do indicate (even if they are wrong by 100%) that as an employ-ment mechanism, military spending is not very efficient compared to other kinds of spending. California is one

of the biggest winners in military contracting, yet one state agency estimated that military spending cost Cal-ifornia about 300,000 jobs compared to equivalent spending in the civilian sector.[79]

Part of the reason that domestic spending (either public or private) produces more jobs than military spending is that the latter supports a higher-income work force. Scientists and engineers are paid more than teachers or hospital aides, for example. Second, military spending is highly capital-intensive; far less of it goes into salaries and more goes into equipment, buildings, and land, compared to other spending.

Some argue that military spending is useful for employment training; those serving in the armed forces receive education and job-related skills that can later help them obtain better jobs in the civilian econ-omy. However, it is more efficient to provide direct funding for education for youth than to rely on in-creased education as a spinoff from military training.

Investment

One of the most dramatic effects of military spending is to reduce investment in business and industry. One study showed that for every $1 billion spent on the military in the United States, investment declined by $290 million.[80] Funds that might otherwise go to in-dustrial investment (such as individuals buying stock in corporations) are taken by the government through taxes or borrowing (when individuals buy govern-ment bonds). Thus, because of military spending, the funds available to invest in expanded production of housing, machinery, and equipment for the domestic economy declined.

This hinders the U.S. economy in its competition with other nations. For example, for every $100 of new capital investments in 1980, the United States put $38 into the military; Japan put only $4. The arms race drained most industries and benefited only a few.[81] A study by the Council on Economic Priorities showed that in 13 major industrial nations since World War II, the share of money spent on the mili-tary was inversely related to economic performance, both employment and growth. Those who spend more, like the United States, have higher unemploy-ment and lower growth than those who spend less.[82]

Individuals across the ideological spectrum are concerned about our flagging economy and loss of worldwide economic leadership. One suggested solu-tion is to increase our investment in our businesses and industries so that they might expand and modernize and thus provide more jobs and meet foreign competition.

Technological Innovation

The United States appears to be falling behind other countries, especially Japan, in technological innovations in industry. Our world domination of markets in automobiles, steel, machine tools, televisions, and other areas has ended, largely because our nation's industries have lagged behind others in adopting innovative production processes, allowing them to make more reliable goods more cheaply. A 1991 study issued by the Council on Competitiveness found that of the 94 technologies, from aerospace to telecommunications, considered crucial to our economic prosperity we are so far behind in 15 that we "are not likely to figure in the world market through the mid-1990s." In 18 other critical technologies U.S. industries were found to be behind or likely to fall behind by the mid-1990s.[83]

One reason for this failure is the increasing size of military spending. Of course there have been many innovative by-products of investments in military spending. But the high-cost, low-volume production manufacturing techniques used in military industries are not suited to civilian markets.

A presidential commission on industrial competitiveness pointed out that most military research is of little commercial use. It is too exotic and too slow in development. For example, weapons systems use electronic parts five or more years behind commercial systems.[84] In fact, now the military borrows more civilian technology than the reverse.

Because technological lags have forced them out of the civilian market, several industries are now becoming completely dominated by the military market. In 1979, for example, 45% of our radio and television manufacturing output was sold to the Department of Defense. By 1985, that proportion had risen to 63%.[85] Many would argue that this is healthy neither for the industries nor for the possibilities of innovations for the consumer market.

Research for military production uses much of our nation's scientific and engineering brainpower. Today, between one-third and one-half of our engineers work on defense projects.[86] The detrimental effect of this on our civilian economy has been noticed since the 1950s. As one expert put it, "It would be

absurd to believe that a majority or even a substantial minority of the nation's technological talent could be long devoted to weaponry without any sacrifice of progress in the civilian sectors of the economy."[87] Since we have been on a "wartime" footing in our military spending almost continually since World War II, it is now becoming clear that these long-term negative consequences are here.

One Pentagon whistle blower who notes that Westinghouse engineers took 63 hours to design a three-inch piece of straight wire (and charged over $14,000) remarked that "engineers who devote many hours to designing a three-inch piece of wire are not using their time to design products that could compete with Sony or Toyota. Worse, engineers long employed in such boondoggles soon lose their skills."[88]

Almost 70% of the federal research and development (R&D) budget goes for military research, compared to 50% in 1980. Our laser R&D, for example, focused on high-energy X-ray lasers for the Strategic Defense Initiative, while Japan was doing laser research for industrial welding and compact disk players.[89]

Effects on Other Government Spending

Money channeled to military purposes results in less being available for domestic needs. For example, on the average, $1 billion spent for defense reduces spending on education by almost $80 million and also depresses spending on health and hospitals.[90] While we are spending more on the military than on education our major economic competitors do the reverse.

Distributional Effects

Military spending disproportionately occurs in the Sunbelt states. The five large industrial states of New

A Peace Dividend?

When President Bush took office in 1989 there was great optimism that our changing relations with the Soviet Union and the breakup of the Warsaw Pact would translate into reductions in our defense budget. The potential reductions and the amount of money freed up from defense spending for domestic needs has been referred to as the **peace dividend.**

Initially the Bush administration, Congress, defense experts, and former government officials had vastly different conceptions of the size of the peace dividend. The president was willing only to lower the rate of increase in defense spending, while many members of Congress were calling for an annual decline between 1991 and 1995, and some outside experts advocated cutting the defense budget in half by the year 2000.

Defense's share of the GNP has already dropped from 11.1% in 1955 to about 5.5% in 1990, and it is projected to fall to 3.6% of GNP by 1996.[1] In order to protect the largest contractors on whom the Pentagon is most dependent, defense budget cuts will probably come in the area of personnel. Army divisions, air wings, and navy ships will all be cut to achieve a personnel reduction of 25% by 1995. As one analyst said, "Cheney wants to circle the wagons around the hardware," because if big-ticket procurement programs are protected, "then industry is kept pretty well humming."[2]

Some wasteful, unreliable, or oversubscribed weapons systems, such as the Bradley Fighting Vehicle and movable MX missiles, have been marked for termination or phaseout. However production of the B-2 continues, a new advanced tactical fighter plane has been ordered, and increases are projected for SDI.

With only incremental annual reductions in military spending experts do not predict the kind of recessionary impact that post-Vietnam spending cuts had. California and Massachusetts have been losing defense-related jobs ever since the builddown began in 1987.

Some see the 1990s as offering an opportunity for Congress to develop what defense analyst Seymour Melman calls a "policy of national economic conversion."[3] This would be a comprehensive plan for reallocating human and material resources from military to civilian employment.

The gradual shift in our spending priorities will not free up any dramatically large sums of money, however. In fact, the peace dividend is not really cash money but a decrease in the spending of money the U.S. Treasury does not have. President Bush has called the dividend a "mirage" that "leads to false expectations."[4] And under current budget regulations, funding reductions in one functional area of the budget (such as defense) cannot be transferred to fund spending increases in another (such as health and human services).

Nevertheless, both Congress and the public are considering possible uses for these "savings." Some would like to see the peace dividend used to cut the budget deficit; others want to use it to cut taxes. However, 62% of those responding to a 1990 poll said they would spend the money "to fight problems such as drugs and homelessness."[5]

The peace dividend may take somewhat longer to materialize than originally projected due to the Persian Gulf War. Early estimates put the war's cost at $56 billion, with $54.5 billion underwritten by allied contributions. Revised estimates project costs in excess of $100 billion; if these prove true, the first several years of "savings" would evaporate.

1. Kirk Victor, "Worries for Workers," *National Journal,* January 13, 1990, p. 59. And, *New York Times,* August 4, 1991, p. 18.
2. Quoted in David C. Morrison, "Cushions for Contractors," *National Journal,* January 13, 1990, p. 65.
3. Kirk Victor, "Worries for Workers," p. 57.
4. David E. Rosenbaum, "Peace Dividend: A Dream for Every Dollar," *New York Times,* February 2, 1990, p. E1.
5. *New York Times*/CBS poll taken in January 1990, reported in *New York Times,* February 18, 1990, p. E5.
Other Sources: Robert Guskind, "Risks by Region," *National Journal,* January 13, 1990, pp. 62–64.

York, Illinois, Michigan, Ohio, and Pennsylvania lose an estimated one million jobs compared to what they would have if military spending were directed toward civilian use. Southern states are the greatest beneficiaries of military spending.[91]

Despite the apparent gain for congressional districts from military spending and military installations, in fact only one-quarter of the nation's congressional districts, in only 15 states, collects more from defense spending than their residents contribute to it in taxes.

Inflation

Military spending need not contribute to inflation (rising prices) if taxes are raised, other spending is lowered, or the nation is in a recession. But government is often reluctant to raise taxes to pay for this spending, so inflation occurs. This was certainly true of Johnson's 1965–1968 Vietnam expenditures. However, relatively little inflation has occurred in the 1980s because some domestic spending has been curbed and because of the recession in the early 1980s.

Military spending can contribute to inflation because it has no effect on "demand" in our economy. Money spent on building new housing or opening a new college means that people with money can buy a new home or send their children to college. But there is no demand for tanks or missiles in the civilian economy. Thus, people have money (unless taxes are raised to pay for the military spending) but fewer goods to buy because increased military spending reduces the amount of money available for investment in the civilian sector. And if supply is low relative to demand, prices usually go up.

The Rise and Fall of the United States?

In 1987, historian Paul Kennedy published a book, *The Rise and Fall of the Great Powers,* which created considerably more controversy than most academic books do.[92] Kennedy argued that over the past five centuries, nations have become the leading powers in the world because of their strong economic growth brought about by innovation and investment. With the economic growth came expanded international commitments, which in turn required substantial spending on military forces designed to protect growing worldwide interests. Then, the resources of money and talent diverted from industrial innovation and growth to the military caused a decline in economic growth. At that point, a nation recedes in importance, and a new number-one power emerges. Kennedy shows how this happened to several major powers, including Imperial Spain, nineteenth-century Britain, and Hitler's Germany.

Kennedy argued that the United States is going through this cycle now. We had tremendous economic growth after World War II. Our role as military protector of weakened Western Europe and parts of Asia after that war caused us to make military commitments in practically every part of the world. Now, as our industrial base shrinks and our trade deficit mounts, the burdens and costs of this worldwide role are becoming more apparent. Like other great powers before us, we are devoting an increasingly large portion of our national human resources, especially scientific ones, to the military. We are lagging behind our competitor nations in spending on education, and we are increasingly investing our scientific resources in military research. We may have fallen prone to what Kennedy calls **imperial overstretch.** Powerful though we still are, we have made more defense commitments than we can afford within the limits of our resources. And we have not adjusted our strategic policy to deal with that overstretch.

Kennedy claims that the Soviet Union has gone through the same process, but declined even faster because its economy is poorer relative to its commitments than ours is.

Kennedy's book touched a sensitive chord among many Americans, insecure and concerned about the rising power of Japan and the European community. Critics attacked Kennedy for unrealistically portraying the United States as on its way to becoming a third-rate power. But Kennedy does not argue that we are destined to become a weak nation. On the contrary, we still have a significant proportion of the world's population and resources. But he argues that we inevitably will shrink in relative power as the economies of other nations, especially Japan and China, will propel them to the front ranks of nations.

Americans like to think that we can have everything, and our political leaders usually encourage us in these beliefs. Thus we think we can have guns *and* butter, record-breaking military budgets *and* technological leadership. In the short run perhaps we can, but it appears that in the long run we cannot. In fact, one critic of our military spending argues that "a choice is being made, not simply between guns and butter, but between guns and competence in the means of production themselves."[93] We are hurting our major source of national security, our economy.

Conclusion: To Whom Is Military Spending Responsive?

In some ways high levels of military spending are responsive to the public. Spending to combat the perceived Communist military threat reflected public opinion about the dangers of communism. Spending to put new bases and military projects in localities around the nation is responsive to the public's desires for hometown economic benefits. Spending to keep our military forces well equipped and up to date is responsive to public sentiments favoring a strong America.

But in other ways, military spending is not responsive to the pubic. A substantial majority of the public believes that the military is wasteful. Much of the public believes that the government is being cheated by military contractors. And, although the public sees short-run economic benefits in military spending in their localities, economists worry that too much military spending may be seriously damaging the long-term health of our economy.

On the whole, military spending is usually responsive to powerful economic interests. Yet it was the widespread beliefs about the dangers of communism and the Soviet Union that allowed these groups to push military spending ever upward. Changes in the Soviet Union may affect public opinion and further reduce support for military spending. However, until members of Congress weigh the short-term gain to their districts against long-term economic and strategic considerations, military spending is likely to continue at a high level.

EPILOGUE

Nunn Supports Star Wars

Sam Nunn decided to support the president on this key SDI vote. By a vote of 50 to 49, the Senate tabled the proposal to cut SDI to $3.2 billion. Nunn was one of only nine Democrats supporting the President. Although he thought SDI plans unrealistic, he believed they had some value at the bargaining table with the Soviets, who might be willing to give up something to get the United States to drop SDI. Eventually, Congress funded SDI more than its opponents wanted but less than the $5 billion the president wanted.[94]

The story of Nunn and the SDI illustrates some important points about military spending. SDI is an exaggerated example of some of the problems discussed in the chapter. Billions are being spent on technology that is widely thought to be unworkable in actual combat. Despite this, the program has a ready-made constituency of businesses (and universities) eager to obtain Star Wars contracts and members of Congress eager to have jobs in their districts. The weapon was introduced without any attention to overall strategic planning. In this case, the idea of a nuclear defense was totally at odds with our existing nuclear capabilities and plans, which had relied on offensive nuclear strength. Moreover, the serious impact on our existing arms agreement with the Soviets was not widely discussed until two years after the program was funded.

Even when members of Congress do not approve of what the president and the Pentagon have proposed, it is easier to vote for than against major weapons systems. Voting for another year of research and development always leaves future options open. Moreover, the president usually has the upper hand in a weapons debate because he can claim a project is essential to national security or important as a "bargaining chip" in negotiations.

Still, growing opposition and budget cutbacks have pushed the SDI plans farther into the future. Originally, Congress was to make a firm decision in 1992 or 1993 whether to allow SDI to go to the development stage. Now that decision time appears to be much later. Although billions of dollars of Star Wars research poured into many congressional districts, supporters of the program still fear that it will never reach fruition. President Bush supports SDI, but he does not have the same fervor Reagan did. Still, after the Gulf war he requested major spending increases and, based on the performance of the Patriot missile, Senator Nunn proposed a crash program to build a tactical anti-ballistic missile system. If the past is any indication of the future, the economic interests benefiting from Star Wars contracts will combine with other advocates of more military spending to ensure that some sort of Star Wars program will survive.

KEY TERMS

Strategic Defense
  Initiative (SDI or
  Star Wars)
window of
  vulnerability
first strike
second strike
strategic triad
bean counting
contract spreading

Joint Chiefs of Staff
  (JCS)
military-industrial
  complex
cost overruns
split-sourcing
peace dividend
imperial overstretch

FURTHER READING

General

A whole library of books analyzing our military emerged in the 1980s. Following are some of the best.

James Fallows, *National Defense* (New York: Vintage, 1981). *Argues that more spending on the military may create a weaker defense.*

Arthur Hadley, *The Straw Giant* (New York: Random House, 1986). *Hadley explains why we should not be surprised at the disasters that befall our military and suggests several reforms beginning with the Joint Chiefs.*

Richard Halloran, *To Arm a Nation* (New York: Macmillan, 1986). *Halloran suggests that to rebuild our military forces, we first need to decide what their mission should be. Halloran also believes the current leadership structure of the military is completely inadequate.*

Edward Luttwak, *The Pentagon and the Art of War* (New York: Simon & Schuster, 1984). *Although Luttwak favors high military spending, he is a severe critic of the defense establishment. He argues that the military has produced nothing but failure since Vietnam, largely because of a conservative, top-heavy military leadership.*

Richard Stubbing, *The Defense Game* (New York: Harper & Row, 1986). *A readable though detailed examination of what goes wrong in the Pentagon's budgeting and weapons acquisitions processes. Stubbing also examines the successes and failures of our secretaries of defense from McNamara to Weinberger.*

Topical

A. Ernest Fitzgerald, *The Pentagonists* (New York: Houghton Mifflin, 1989). *The premier Pentagon whistle blower argues that the current state of the Pentagon is corrupting industry, public officials, universities, and the military and is robbing us of our industrial base.*

Paul Kennedy, *The Rise and Fall of the Great Powers* (New York: Random House, 1987). *Kennedy argues that powerful nations of the past declined in large part because they overextended themselves militarily, thus causing economic decline.*

John Lehman, *Command of the Seas* (New York: Scribners, 1989). *Reagan's brash and successful secretary of the navy presents a provocative inside analysis of what's wrong with our military establishment.*

Mark Perry, *Four Stars* (Boston: Houghton Mifflin, 1989). *An analysis of the role of the Joint Chiefs of Staff from its creation to the present.*

Harry G. Summers, Jr., *On Strategy: A Critical Analysis of the Vietnam War* (New York: Dell, 1984). *A colonel of infantry and instructor at the Army War College argues that society failed the military but also that the army forgot some of the basics of warfare.*

NOTES

1. Center for Defense Information, "Star Wars: Vision and Reality," *The Defense Monitor* 15 (1986): 2.
2. Ibid.
3. Michael Isikoff, "In Washington, SDI Isn't a Dream, It's Big Business," *Washington Post National Weekly Edition*, October 27, 1986, p. 7.
4. Quoted in William Leuchtenburg, "Meet the People Who Get Paid to Think the Unthinkable," *Washington Post National Weekly Edition*, May 6, 1985, p. 35.
5. Philip W. Dyer, "American Security Policy: Increasing Ambiguities," in David P. Forsythe, *American Foreign Policy in an Uncertain World* (Lincoln: University of Nebraska Press, 1984), pp. 105–28.
6. Harry G. Summers, Jr., "A Bankrupt Military Strategy." *The Atlantic*, June 1989, pp. 34–40. Richard Stubbing, *The Defense Game* (New York: Harper & Row, 1986), p. 60.
7. *The Defense Monitor* 18 (1989): 1.
8. Barry Gewen, "Mr. Smith's Washington," *The New Leader*, May 2, 1988, p. 18.
9. Richard Stubbing, quoted in *Newsweek*, January 23, 1989, p. 16.
10. See Robert Kaufman, "The Causes of the Slowdown in Soviet Defense," *Survival* 27 (1985): 179–92; and Charles W. Ostrom, Jr. and Robin F. Marra, "U.S. Defense Spending and the Soviet Estimate," *American Political Science Review* 80 (September 1986): 819–42.
11. Based on actual outlays for 1990 as shown in the 1992 U.S. budget.
12. James Fallows, *National Defense* (New York: Vintage, 1981).
13. *The Defense Monitor* 19 (1990).
14. Michael Gordon, "Why Things Go Wrong," *National Journal*, March 12, 1983, p. 567.
15. *The Defense Monitor* 19 (1990): 6.
16. Scott Shuger, "Why Did the Navy Shoot Down 290 Civilians?" *Washington Monthly*, October 1988, pp. 20–25; "A Case of Human Error," *Newsweek*, August 15, 1988, pp. 18–24.
17. Norman Augustine, *Augustine's Laws* (New York: American Institute of Aeronautics and Astronautics, 1982); Franklin Spinney, *Defense Facts of Life* (Boulder, Colo.: Westview Press, 1985).

18. Edward Luttwak, "Why We Need More Waste, Fraud and Mismanagement in the Pentagon," *Commentary* 73 (February 1982): 17–30.

19. The other services are considering such guidelines.

20. David Evans, "Why Designer Jeeps Can't Win the War," *Washington Post National Weekly Edition,* August 18, 1986, p. 23–24.

21. A good evaluation of the impact of the major part of the increased military spending, with perspectives from many points of view, is found in a series in the *New York Times* beginning May 14, 1985, and running through that week.

22. James Fallows, "The Spend Up," *Harpers,* July 1986, pp. 27–30.

23. "They're in the Army Now—and They're Liking It," *Washington Post National Weekly Edition,* October 13, 1986, p. 38.

24. Franklin Spinney, "Look What $2 Trillion Didn't Buy for Defense," *Washington Post National Weekly Edition,* November 14–20, 1988, p. 23. One exception is that flying hours of Air Force fighter pilots increased.

25. Lawrence Korb, cited in George Wilson "At the Pentagon Bracing for the Deluge," *Washington Post National Weekly Edition,* November 21–28, 1988, pp. 31–32.

26. The higher figure is from Tim Weiner, *Blank Check: The Pentagon's Black Budget* (Warner Books, 1990). Lower estimates are given in *The Defense Monitor* 16 (1987): 6. The breakdown of defense costs provided in the budget prepared by OMB includes a category for the National Foreign Intelligence Program, but the exact amounts are classified.

27. Center for Defense Information, *The Common Defense* 15 (1986): 2–3.

28. The MX Survives, Just Like Every Other Weapons System," *Washington Post National Weekly Edition,* April 8, 1985, p. 14.

29. Fallows, *National Defense,* pp. 136–37.

30. Jerry Hagstrom and Robert Guskind, "Lobbying the Pentagon," *National Journal,* May 31, 1986, p. 1316.

31. Bruce Ray, "The Responsiveness of the U.S. Congressional Armed Services Committees to Their Parent Bodies," *Legislative Studies Quarterly* 5 (November 1980): 501–16; Center for Defense Information, "No Business Like War Business," *The Defense Monitor* 16 (1987).

32. Spinney, "Look What $2 Trillion Didn't Buy for Defense."

33. Hagstrom and Guskind, "Lobbying the Pentagon."

34. "Star Wars Contracts Called 'Pork Barrel'," *Lincoln Journal,* October 27, 1986, p. 8.

35. Spinney, "Look What $2 Trillion Didn't Buy for Defense."

36. Hagstrom and Guskind, "Lobbying the Pentagon."

37. Stephen Cobb, "Defense Spending and Defense Voting in the House," *American Journal of Sociology* 82 (July 1976): 163–82; Charles Gray and Glen Gregory, "Military Spending and Senate Voting, *Journal of Peace Research* 1 (1968): 44–54; Bruce Russett, *What Price Vigilance?* (New Haven: Yale University Press, 1970); Susan Welch and John Peters, "The Impact of Defense Holdings on Voting for the Military Budget," paper presented at the International Political Science Association, Research Roundtable on Political Corruption and Political Finance, Oxford, March 1984.

38. Cited in Boston Study Group, *The Price of Defense* (New York: Time Books, 1974), p. 234. Les Aspin, "The Defense Budget and Foreign Policy: The Role of Congress," *Daedalus* (Summer 1975): 155–74.

39. Nick Kotz, *Wild Blue Yonder* (New York: Pantheon, 1988).

40. David Morrison, "Caught Off Base," *National Journal,* April 1, 1989, pp. 801–5.

41. *Statistical Abstract, 1989* (Washington, D.C.: U.S. Bureau of the Census, 1989), p. 319, table 514.

42. Arthur Hadley, *The Straw Giant* (New York: Random House, 1986).

43. John Lehman, *Command of the Seas* (New York: Scribners, 1989). Quoted in David Morrison, "Defense Focus," *National Journal,* March 12, 1988, p. 707.

44. Fallows, *National Defense,* pp. 21, 211.

45. Fred Hiatt, "The Pentagon's Good News Crowd: Masking Military Mistakes," *Washington Post National Weekly Edition,* November 12, 1984, pp. 23ff.

46. Fred Hiatt, "The War Within the Pentagon," *Washington Post National Weekly Edition,* August 6, 1984, p. 6.

47. Edward Luttwak, *The Pentagon and the Art of War* (New York: Simon & Schuster, 1984), pp. 51–53.

48. Theodore Bauer and Eston T. White, "The Joint Chiefs of Staff," in John E. Endicott and Roy Stafford, eds., *American Defense Policy,* 4th ed. (Baltimore: Johns Hopkins, 1977), pp. 297–305; Morton Halperin, "The President and the Military," in ibid., pp. 306–13; Hadley, *The Straw Giant;* Richard Halloran, *To Arm a Nation* (New York:Macmillan, 1986).

49. James Bennet, "So Many Officers, So Little to Do," *Washington Monthly,* February 1990, p. 23.

50. Greg Easterbrook, "Sack Weinberger, Bankrupt General Dynamics, and Other Procurement Reforms," *Washington Monthly,* January 1987, pp. 33–43; Luttwak, *The Pentagon,* chapter 6.

51. Lars-Erik Nelson, "Challenging Military State's High Cost," *Lincoln Journal,* March 2, 1989, New York News wire service.

52. James Bennet, "So Many Officers," p. 23.

53. Rick Atkinson and Fred Hiatt, "Oh That Golden Safety Net," *Washington Post National Weekly Edition,* April 22, 1985.

54. Center for Defense Information, "No Business Like War Business," *The Defense Monitor* 16 (1987): 2. See also Charles Tiebout, "The Regional Impact of Defense Expenditures: Its Measurement and Problems of Adjustment," in Roger Bolton, *Defense and Disarmament* (Englewood Cliffs, N.J.: Prentice-Hall, 1966); Jacques Gansler, *The Defense Industry* (Cambridge, Mass.: MIT Press, 1980); Ronald Fox, *Arming America* (Boston: Harvard University School of Business, 1974).

55. Charles Grassley, quoted in the *Washington Post National Weekly Edition,* April 8, 1985, p. 11.

56. "Defense Contractor Profits Soar," *Chicago Tribune,* December 26, 1986, p. 36; see also Fallows, "The Spend Up"; Center for Defense Information, "No Business Like War Business."

57. William Weida and Frank L. Gertcher, *The Political Economy of National Defense* (Boulder, Colo.: Westview Press, 1987); Fred Hiatt and Rick Atkinson, "The Defense Boom," *Washington Post National Weekly Edition,* April 29, 1985, p. 19.

58. Center for Defense Information, "No Business Like War Business."

59. Hedrick Smith, *The Power Game* (New York: Random House, 1988), pp. 161–63.

60. George C. Wilson, "Not Enough Bang for the Buck," *Washington Post National Weekly Edition,* December 5–11, 1988.

61. See reports from *Newsweek,* July 25, 1983, p. 69; *Time,* July 25, 1983; and other news reports in October 1984 of the "coffeepot caper" and in May and June 1985 of the ashtray mess. See also, Center for Defense Information, "Waste in Military Procurement:

The Prospects for Reform," *The Defense Monitor* 15 (1986). The quotation from the Pentagon official is from Richard Stubbing and Richard Mendel, "How to Save $50 Billion a Year" *The Atlantic,* June 1989), p. 53.

62. *Common Cause,* July/August 1983.

63. Center for Defense Information, *The Defense Monitor* 13 (1984): 7.

64. Luttwak, *The Pentagon,* especially chapter 6.

65. Ibid, p. 184.

66. Gordon Adams, *The Iron Triangle* (New York: Council on Economic Priorities, 1981).

67. *Washington Monthly,* March 1985, p. 55; Easterbrook, "Sack Weinberger."

68. Edward Luttwak, "The Pentagon's Procurement Problem: It's the System," *Washington Post National Weekly Edition,* July 4–10, 1988, pp. 23–24.

69. James Woolsey, quoted in Malcolm Gladwell, "The Latest Defense Scandal Is Deja Vu All Over Again," *Washington Post National Weekly Edition,* August 15–21, 1988, p. 33.

70. David Ignatius, "Is This Any Way for a Country to Buy Weapons?" *Washington Post National Weekly Edition,* July 4–10, 1988, p. 23.

71. Lehman, *Command of the Seas,* quoted in Clay Blair, "When Lehman Ruled the Ocean Blue," *Washington Post National Weekly Edition,* February 6–12, 1989, p. 36.

72. *Lincoln Journal (Los Angeles Times),* May 10, 1990, p. 1.

73. Ibid.

74. David C. Morrison, "Cushions for Contractors," *National Journal,* January 13, 1990, p. 65.

75. Richard W. Stevenson, "Military Contractors Struggle As Rules of the Game Change," *New York Times,* January 6, 1991.

76. Easterbrook, "Sack Weinberger," pp. 33–43.

77. Boston Study Group, *The Price of Defense.* The preceding quote from Eisenhower is found in "Indefensible," *The Atlantic,* June 1989, p. 33.

78. Ibid.

79. William Boly, "The 130 Billion Dud," *California Magazine,* February 1983, pp. 62ff.

80. Russett, *What Price Vigilance?* p. 135. See also Bruce Russett, "Defense Expenditures and National Well Being," *American Political Science Review* 76 (December 1982): 767–77.

81. Fred Hiatt and Rick Atkinson, "The Hidden Costs of the Defense Buildup," *Washington Post National Weekly Edition,* December 16, 1985, pp. 10–11.

82. Boly, "The 130 Billion Dud," p. 64. See also Center for Defense Information, *The Defense Monitor* 14 (1985): 4.

83. Champaign-Urbana *News-Gazette* (AP), March 20, 1991, p. 1.

84. Bruce Stokes, "Fighting Separate Wars," *National Journal,* March 14, 1987, p. 606; see also Hiatt and Atkinson, "The Hidden Costs."

85. Bennett Harrison, "Do We Need an Industrial Policy?" *Harpers,* February 1985), p. 42.

86. Lester Thurow, "How to Wreck the Economy," *New York Review of Books,* May 14, 1981; Boly, "The 130 Billion Dud."

87. Thurow, "How to Wreck the Economy."

88. A. Ernest Fitzgerald, *The Pentagonists* (New York: Houghton Mifflin, 1989). Quoted in Nick Kotz, "The Need for More Military Morality," *Washington Post National Weekly Edition,* February 27–March 5, 1989, p. 35.

89. Center for Defense Information, "Militarism in America," *The Defense Monitor* 15 (1986).

90. Russett, "Defense Expenditures."

91. Marion Anderson, *The Empty Pork Barrel: Unemployment and the Pentagon Budget* (Lansing, Mich.: Employment Research Associates, 1982), cited in Seymour Melman, *Profits Without Production* (New York: Knopf, 1983), appendix V, Consumer Spending.

92. New York: Random House, 1987.

93. Seymour Melman, quoted in Hiatt and Atkinson, "The Hidden Costs."

94. For background on Congress and Star Wars during this period, see *Congressional Quarterly,* November 1, 1986, Key votes; Pat Towell, "Sam Nunn, The Careful Exercise of Power," *Congressional Quarterly Weekly Report,* June 14, 1986, pp. 1329–33; Pat Towell, "Dispute over ABM Treaty Stalls Defense Bill in Senate," *Congressional Quarterly Weekly Report,* May 23, 1987, p. 1064–65; Pat Towell, "Nunn Blasts Administration on ABM Treaty," *Congressional Quarterly Weekly Report,* March 14, 1987, pp. 457–58; Center for Defense Information, "Star Wars: Vision and Reality," *The Defense Monitor* 15 (1986); David C. Morrison, "Shooting Down Star Wars," *National Journal,* October 25, 1986, pp. 2544–49.

APPENDIX A

The Declaration of Independence*

In Congress, July 4, 1776.

A Declaration by the Representatives of the United States of America, in General Congress assembled.

When in the Course of human Events, it becomes necessary for one People to dissolve the Political Bonds which have connected them with another, and to assume among the Powers of the Earth, the separate and equal Station to which the Laws of Nature and of Nature's God entitle them, a decent Respect to the Opinions of Mankind requires that they should declare the causes which impel them to the Separation.

We hold these Truths to be self-evident, that all Men are created equal, that they are endowed by their Creator with certain unalienable Rights, that among these are Life, Liberty, and the Pursuit of Happiness— That to secure these Rights, Governments are instituted among Men, deriving their just Powers from the Consent of the Governed, that whenever any Form of Government becomes destructive of these Ends, it is the Right of the People to alter or to abolish it, and to institute new Government, laying its Foundation on such Principles, and organizing its Powers in such Forms, as to them shall seem most likely to effect their Safety and Happiness. Prudence, indeed, will dictate that Governments long established should not be changed for light and transient Causes; and accordingly all Experience hath shewn, that Mankind are more disposed to suffer, while Evils are sufferable, than to right themselves by abolishing the Forms to which they are accustomed. But when a long Train of Abuses and Usurpations, pursuing invariably the same Object, evinces a Design to reduce them under absolute Despotism, it is their Right, it is their Duty, to throw off such Government, and to provide new Guards for their future Security. Such has been the patient Sufferance of these Colonies; and such is now the Necessity which constrains them to alter their former Systems of Government. The History of the present King of Great Britain is a History of repeated Injuries and Usurpations, all having in direct Object the Establishment of an absolute Tyranny over these States. To prove this, let facts be submitted to a candid World.

He has refused his Assent to Laws, the most wholesome and necessary for the public Good.

He has forbidden his Governors to pass Laws of immediate and pressing Importance, unless suspended in their Operation till his Assent should be obtained; and when so suspended, he has utterly neglected to attend to them.

He has refused to pass other Laws for the Accommodation of large Districts of People, unless those People would relinquish the Right of Representation in the Legislature, a Right inestimable to them, and formidable to Tyrants only.

He has called together Legislative Bodies at Places unusual, uncomfortable, and distant from the Depository of their Public Records, for the sole Purpose of fatiguing them into Compliance with his Measures.

He has dissolved Representative Houses repeatedly, for opposing with manly Firmness his Invasions on the Rights of the People.

He has refused for a long Time, after such Dissolutions, to cause others to be elected; whereby the Legislative Powers, incapable of Annihilation, have returned to the People at large for their exercise; the State remaining in the mean time exposed to all the Dangers of Invasion from without, and Convulsions within.

He has endeavoured to prevent the Population of these States; for that Purpose obstructing the Laws for Naturalization of Foreigners; refusing to pass others to encourage their Migration hither, and raising the Conditions of new Appropriations of Lands.

He has obstructed the Administration of Justice, by refusing his Assent to Laws for establishing Judiciary Powers.

He has made Judges dependent on his Will alone, for the Tenure of their offices, and the Amount and payments of their Salaries.

*The spelling, capitalization, and punctuation of the original have been retained here.

He has erected a Multitude of new Offices, and sent hither Swarms of Officers to harass our People, and eat out their Substance.

He has kept among us, in times of Peace, Standing Armies, without the consent of our Legislatures.

He has affected to render the Military independent of, and superior to the Civil Power.

He has combined with others to subject us to a Jurisdiction foreign to our Constitution, and unacknowledged by our Laws; giving his Assent to their Acts of pretended Legislation:

For quartering large Bodies of Armed Troops among us:

For protecting them, by a mock Trial, from Punishment for any Murders which they should commit on the Inhabitants of these States:

For cutting off our Trade with all Parts of the World:

For imposing Taxes on us without our Consent:

For depriving us, in many cases, of the Benefits of Trial by Jury:

For transporting us beyond Seas to be tried for pretended Offences:

For abolishing the free System of English Laws in a neighbouring Province, establishing therein an arbitrary Government, and enlarging its Boundaries, so as to render it at once an Example and fit Instrument for introducing the same absolute Rule into these Colonies:

For taking away our Charters, abolishing our most valuable Laws, and altering fundamentally the Forms of our Governments:

For suspending our own Legislatures, and declaring themselves invested with Power to legislate for us in all Cases whatsoever.

He has abdicated Government here, by declaring us out of his Protection and waging War against us.

He has plundered our Seas, ravaged our Coasts, burnt our towns, and destroyed the Lives of our People.

He is, at this Time, transporting large Armies of foreign Mercenaries to compleat the works of Death, Desolation, and Tyranny, already begun with circumstances of Cruelty and Perfidy, scarcely paralleled in the most barbarous Ages, and totally unworthy the Head of a civilized Nation.

He has constrained our fellow Citizens taken Captive on the high Seas to bear Arms against their Country, to become the Executioners of their Friends and Brethren, or to fall themselves by their Hands.

He has excited domestic Insurrections amongst us, and has endeavoured to bring on the Inhabitants of our Frontiers, the merciless Indian Savages, whose known Rule of Warfare, is an undistinguished Destruction, of all Ages, Sexes and Conditions.

In every state of these Oppressions we have Petitioned for Redress in the most humble Terms: Our repeated Petitions have been answered only by repeated Injury. A Prince, whose Character is thus marked by every act which may define a Tyrant, is unfit to be the Ruler of a free People.

Nor have we been wanting in Attentions to our British Brethren. We have warned them from Time to Time of Attempts by their Legislature to extend an unwarrantable Jurisdiction over us. We have reminded them of the Circumstances of our Emigration and Settlement here. We have appealed to their native Justice and Magnanimity, and we have conjured them by the Ties of our common Kindred to disavow these Usurpations, which, would inevitably interrupt our Connections and Correspondence. They too have been deaf to the Voice of Justice and of Consanguinity. We must, therefore, acquiesce in the Necessity, which denounces our Separation, and hold them, as we hold the rest of Mankind, Enemies in War, in Peace, Friends.

We, therefore, the Representatives of the UNITED STATES OF AMERICA, in General Congress Assembled, appealing to the Supreme Judge of the World for the Rectitude of our Intentions, do, in the Name, and by Authority of the good People of these Colonies, solemnly Publish and Declare, That these United Colonies are, and of Right ought to be, Free and Independent States; that they are absolved from all Allegiance to the British Crown, and that all political Connection between them and the State of Great Britain, is and ought to be totally dissolved; and that as Free and Independent States, they have full Power to levy War, conclude Peace, contract Alliances, establish Commerce, and to do all other Acts and Things which Independent States may of right do. And for the support of this declaration, with a firm Reliance on the Protection of divine Providence, we mutually pledge to each other our Lives, our Fortunes, and our sacred Honor.

Constitution of the United States of America*

We the people of the United States, in Order to form a more perfect Union, establish Justice, insure domestic Tranquility, provide for the common defence, promote the general Welfare, and secure the Blessings of Liberty to ourselves and our posterity, do ordain and establish this Constitution for the United States of America.

Article I.

Section 1.

All legislative Powers herein granted shall be vested in a Congress of the United States, which shall consist of a Senate and House of Representatives.

Section 2.

The House of Representatives shall be composed of Members chosen every second Year by the People of the several States, and the Electors in each State shall have the Qualifications requisite for Electors of the most numerous Branch of the State Legislature.

No person shall be a Representative who shall not have attained to the Age of twenty-five Years, and been seven Years a Citizen of the United States, and who shall not, when elected, be an Inhabitant of that State in which he shall be chosen.

Representatives and direct [Taxes][1] shall be apportioned among the several States which may be included within this Union, according to their respective Numbers [which shall be determined by adding to the whole Number of free Persons, including those bound to Service for a Term of Years, and excluding Indians not taxed, three fifths of all other Persons].[2] The actual Enumeration shall be made within three Years after the first Meeting of the Congress of the United States, and within every subsequent Term of ten Years, in such Manner as they shall by Law direct. The Number of Representatives shall not exceed one for every thirty Thousand, but each State shall have at Least one Representative; and until such enumeration shall be made, the State of New Hampshire shall be entitled to chuse three, Massachusetts eight, Rhode Island and Providence Plantations one, Connecticut five, New-York six, New Jersy four, Pennsylvania eight, Delaware one, Maryland six, Virginia ten, North Carolina five, South Carolina five, and Georgia three.

When vacancies happen in the Representation from any State, the Executive Authority thereof shall issue Writs of Election to fill such Vacancies.

The House of Representatives shall chuse their Speaker and other Officers; and shall have the sole Power of Impeachment.

Section 3.

The Senate of the United States shall be composed of two Senators from each State [chosen by the Legislature thereof],[3] for six Years; and each Senator shall have one Vote.

Immediately after they shall be assembled in Consequence of the first Election, they shall be divided as equally as may be into three Classes. The Seats of the Senators of the first Class shall be vacated at the Expiration of the second year, of the second Class at the Expiration of the fourth Year, and of the third Class at the Expiration of the sixth Year, so that one third may be chosen every second Year [and if Vacancies happen by Resignation, or otherwise, during the Recess of the Legislature of any State, the Executive thereof may make temporary Appointments until the next Meeting of the Legislature, which shall then fill such Vacancies.][4]

---

*The spelling, capitalization, and punctuation of the original have been retained here. Brackets indicate passages that have been altered by amendments to the Constitution.
1. Modified by the Sixteenth Amendment.
2. Modified by the Fourteenth Amendment.
3. Repealed by the Seventeenth Amendment.
4. Modified by the Seventeenth Amendment.

No Person shall be a Senator who shall not have attained to the Age of thirty Years, and been nine Years a Citizen of the United States, and who shall not, when elected, be an Inhabitant of that State for which he shall be chosen.

The Vice President of the United States shall be President of the Senate, but shall have no Vote, unless they be equally divided.

The Senate shall chuse their other Officers, and also a President pro tempore, in the Absence of the Vice President, or when he shall exercise the Office of President of the United States.

The Senate shall have the sole Power to try all Impeachments. When sitting for that Purpose, they shall be on Oath or Affirmation. When the President of the United States is tried, the Chief Justice shall preside: And no Person shall be convicted without the Concurrence of two thirds of the Members present.

Judgment in Cases of Impeachment shall not extend further than to removal from Office, and disqualification to hold and enjoy any Office of honor, Trust or Profit under the United States; but the Party convicted shall nevertheless be liable and subject to Indictment, Trial, Judgment and Punishment, according to Law.

Section 4.

The Times, Places and Manner of holding Elections for Senators and Representatives, shall be prescribed in each State by the Legislature thereof; but the Congress may at any time by Law make or alter such Regulations, except as to the Places of chusing Senators.

[The Congress shall assemble at least once in every Year, and such Meeting shall be on the first Monday in December, unless they shall by Law appoint a different Day.][5]

Section 5.

Each House shall be the Judge of the Elections, Returns and Qualifications of its own Members, and a Majority of each shall constitute a Quorum to do Business; but a smaller Number may adjourn from day to day, and may be authorized to compel the Attendance of absent Members, in such Manner, and under such Penalties as each House may provide.

Each House may determine the Rules of its Proceedings, punish its Members for disorderly Behav-

5. Changed by the Twentieth Amendment.

iour, and, with the Concurrence of two thirds, expel a Member.

Each House shall keep a Journal of its Proceedings, and from time to time publish the same, excepting such Parts as may in their Judgment require Secrecy; and the Yeas and Nays of the Members of either House on any question shall, at the Desire of one fifth of those present, be entered on the Journal.

Neither House, during the Session of Congress, shall, without the Consent of the other, adjourn for more than three days, nor to any other Place than that in which the two Houses shall be sitting.

Section 6.

The Senators and Representatives shall receive a Compensation for their Services, to be ascertained by Law, and paid out of the Treasury of the United States. They shall in all Cases, except Treason, Felony and Breach of the Peace, be privileged from Arrest during their Attendance at the Session of their respective Houses, and in going to and returning from the same; and for any Speech or Debate in either House, they shall not be questioned in any other Place.

No Senator or Representative shall, during the Time for which he was elected, be appointed to any civil Office under the Authority of the United States, which shall have been created, or the Emoluments whereof shall have been encreased during such time; and no Person holding any Office under the United States, shall be a Member of either House during his Continuance in Office.

Section 7.

All Bills for raising Revenue shall originate in the House of Representatives; but the Senate may propose or concur with Amendments as on other Bills.

Every Bill which shall have passed the House of Representatives and the Senate, shall, before it become a Law, be presented to the President of the United States; If he approves he shall sign it, but if not he shall return it, with his objections to that House in which it shall have originated, who shall enter the Objections at large on their Journal, and proceed to reconsider it. If after such Reconsideration two thirds of that House shall agree to pass the Bill, it shall be sent, together with the Objections, to the other House, by which it shall likewise be reconsidered, and if approved by two thirds of that House, it shall become a Law. But in all such Cases the Votes of both Houses shall be determined by yeas and Nays, and the Names of the Persons voting for and against the Bill shall be entered on the Journal of each House respectively. If any Bill shall not be returned by the President within ten Days (Sundays excepted) after it shall have been presented to him, the Same shall be a Law, in like Manner as if he had signed it, unless the Congress by their Adjournment prevent its Return, in which Case it shall not be a Law.

Every Order, Resolution, or Vote to which the Concurrence of the Senate and House of Representatives may be necessary (except on a question of Adjournment) shall be presented to the President of the United States; and before the Same shall take Effect, shall be approved by him, or being disapproved by him, shall be repassed by two thirds of the Senate and House of Representatives, according to the Rules and Limitations prescribed in the Case of a Bill.

Section 8.

The Congress shall have Power To lay and collect Taxes, Duties, Imposts and Excises, to pay the Debts and provide for the common Defence and general Welfare of the United States; but all Duties, Imposts and Excises shall be uniform throughout the United States;

To borrow Money on the credit of the United States;

To regulate Commerce with foreign Nations, and among the several States, and with the Indian Tribes;

To establish a uniform Rule of Naturalization, and uniform Laws on the subject of Bankruptcies throughout the United States;

To coin Money, regulate the Value thereof, and of foreign Coin, and fix the Standard of Weights and Measures;

To provide for the Punishment of counterfeiting the Securities and current Coin of the United States.

To establish Post Offices and post Roads;

To promote the Progress of Science and useful Arts, by securing for limited Times to Authors and Inventors the exclusive Right to their respective Writings and Discoveries;

To constitute Tribunals inferior to the supreme Court;

To define and punish Piracies and Felonies committed on the high Seas, and Offences against the Law of Nations;

To declare War, grant Letters of Marque and Reprisal, and make Rules concerning Captures on Land and Water;

To raise and support Armies, but no Appropriation of Money to that Use shall be for a longer Term than two Years;

To provide and maintain a Navy;

To make Rules for the Government and Regulation of the land and naval Forces;

To provide for calling forth the Militia to execute the Laws of the Union, suppress Insurrections and repel Invasions;

To provide for organizing, arming, and disciplining the Militia, and for governing such Part of them as may be employed in the Service of the United States, reserving to the States respectively, the Appointment of the Officers, and the Authority of training the Militia according to the discipline prescribed by Congress;

To exercise exclusive Legislation in all Cases whatsoever, over such District (not exceeding ten Miles square) as may, by Cession of particular States, and the Acceptance of Congress, become the Seat of the Government of the United States, and to exercise like Authority over all Places purchased by the Consent of the Legislature of the State in which the Same shall be, for the Erection of forts, Magazines, Arsenals, dockYards, and other needful Buildings;—And

To make all Laws which shall be necessary and proper for carrying into Execution the foregoing Powers, and all other Powers vested by this Constitution in the Government of the United States, or in any Department or Officer thereof.

Section 9.

The Migration or Importation of such Persons as any of the States now existing shall think proper to admit, shall not be prohibited by the Congress prior to the Year one thousand eight hundred and eight, but a Tax or duty may be imposed on such Importation, not exceeding ten dollars for each Person.

The Privilege of the Writ of Habeas Corpus shall not be suspended, unless when in Cases of Rebellion or Invasion the public Safety may require it.

No Bill of Attainder or ex post facto Law shall be passed.

[No Capitation, or other direct, Tax shall be laid, unless in Proportion to the Census or Enumeration herein before directed to be taken.][6]

No Tax or Duty shall be laid on Articles exported from any State.

6. Modified by the Sixteenth Amendment.

No Preference shall be given by any Regulation of Commerce or Revenue to the Ports of one State over those of another; nor shall Vessels bound to, or from, one State, be obliged to enter, clear, or pay Duties in another.

No Money shall be drawn from the Treasury, but in Consequence of Appropriations made by Law; and a regular Statement and Account of the Receipts and Expenditures of all public Money shall be published from time to time.

No Title of Nobility shall be granted by the United States; and no Person holding any Office or Profit or Trust under them, shall, without the Consent of the Congress, accept of any present, Emolument, Office, or Title, of any kind whatever, from any King, Prince, or foreign State.

Section 10.

No state shall enter into any Treaty, Alliance, or Confederation; grant Letters of Marque and Reprisal; coin Money; emit Bills of Credit; make any Thing but gold and silver Coin a Tender in Payment of Debts; pass any Bill of Attainder, ex post facto Law, or Law impairing the Obligation of Contracts, or grant any Title of Nobility.

No State shall, without the Consent of the Congress, lay any Imposts or Duties on Imports or Exports, except what may be absolutely necessary for executing its inspection Laws; and the net Produce of all Duties and Imposts, laid by any State on Imports or Exports, shall be for the Use of the Treasury of the United States; and all such Laws shall be subject to the Revision and Controul of the Congress.

No State shall, without the Consent of Congress, lay any duty of Tonnage, keep Troops, or Ships of War in time of Peace, enter into any Agreement or Compact with another State, or with a foreign Power or engage in War, unless actually invaded, or in such imminent Danger as will not admit of delay.

Article II.

Section 1.

The executive Power shall be vested in a President of the United States of America. He shall hold his Office during the Term of four Years, and, together with the Vice President, chosen for the Same Term, be elected, as follows.

Each State shall appoint, in such Manner as the Legislature thereof may direct, a Number of Electors, equal to the whole Number of Senators and Representatives to which the State may be entitled in the Congress; but no Senator or Representative, or Person holding an Office of Trust or Profit under the United States, shall be appointed an Elector.

[The Electors shall meet in their respective States, and vote by Ballot for two Persons of whom one at least shall not be an Inhabitant of the same State with themselves. And they shall make a List of all the Persons voted for, and of the Number of Votes for each; which List they shall sign and certify, and transmit sealed to the Seat of the Government of the United States, directed to the President of the Senate. The President of the Senate shall, in the Presence of the Senate and House of Representatives, open all the Certificates, and the Votes shall then be counted. The Person having the greatest Number of Votes shall be the President, if such Number be a Majority of the whole Number of Electors appointed; and if there be more than one who have such Majority, and have an equal Number of Votes, then the House of Representatives shall immediately chuse by Ballot one of them for President; and if no Person have a Majority, then from the five highest on the List the said House shall in like Manner chuse the President. But in chusing the President, the Votes shall be taken by States, the Representation from each State having one Vote; A quorum for this Purpose shall consist of a Member or Members from two thirds of the States, and a Majority of all the states shall be necessary to a Choice. In every Case, after the Choice of the President, the Person having the greatest Number of Votes of the Electors shall be the Vice President. But if there should remain two or more who have equal Votes, the Senate shall chuse from them by Ballot the Vice President.][7]

The Congress may determine the Time of chusing the Electors, and the Day on which they shall give their Votes; which Day shall be the same throughout the United States.

No person except a natural born Citizen, or a Citizen of the United States, at the time of the Adoption of this Constitution, shall be eligible to the Office of President; neither shall any Person be eligible to that Office who shall not have attained to the Age of thirty five Years, and been fourteen Years a Resident within the United States.

7. Changed by the Twelfth Amendment.

[In Case of the Removal of the President from Office, or of his Death, Resignation, or Inability to discharge the Powers and Duties of the said Office, the same shall devolve on the Vice President, and the Congress may by Law provide for the Case of Removal, Death, Resignation or Inability, both of the President and Vice President, declaring what Officer shall then act as President, and such Officer shall act accordingly, until the Disability be removed, or a President shall be elected.][8]

The President shall, at stated Times, receive for his Services, a Compensation, which shall neither be encreased nor diminished during the Period for which he shall have been elected, and he shall not receive within that Period any other Emolument from the United States, or any of them.

Before he enter on the Execution of his Office, he shall take the following Oath or Affirmation:—"I do solemnly swear (or affirm) that I will faithfully execute the Office of President of the United States, and will to the best of my Ability, preserve, protect and defend the constitution of the United States."

Section 2.

The President shall be Commander in Chief of the Army and Navy of the United States, and of the Militia of the several States, when called into the actual Service of the United States; he may require the Opinion, in writing, of the principal Officer in each of the executive Departments, upon any Subject relating to the Duties of their respective Offices, and he shall have Power to grant Reprieves and Pardons for Offences against the United States, except in Cases of Impeachment.

He shall have Power, by and with the Advice and Consent of the Senate, to make Treaties, provided two thirds of the Senators present concur; and he shall nominate, and by and with the Advice and Consent of the Senate, shall appoint Ambassadors, other public Ministers and Consuls, Judges of the supreme Court, and all other Officers of the United States, whose Appointments are not herein otherwise provided for, and which shall be established by Law; but the Congress may by Law vest the Appointment of such inferior Officers, as they think proper, in the President alone, in the Courts of Law, or in the Heads of Departments.

The President shall have Power to fill up all Vacancies that may happen during the Recess of the Senate, by granting Commissions which shall expire at the end of their next Session.

Section 3.

He shall from time to time give to the Congress Information of the State of the Union, and recommend to their Consideration such Measures as he shall judge necessary and expedient; he may, on extraordinary Occasions, convene both Houses, or either of them, and in Case of Disagreement between them, with Respect to the Time of Adjournment, he may adjourn them to such Time as he shall think proper; he shall receive Ambassadors and other public Ministers; he shall take Care that the Laws be faithfully executed, and shall Commission all the Officers of the United States.

Section 4.

The President, Vice President and all civil Officers of the United States, shall be removed from Office on Impeachment for, and Conviction of, Treason, Bribery, or other high Crimes and Misdemeanors.

Article III. _____

Section 1.

The judicial Power of the United States, shall be vested in one supreme Court, and in such inferior Courts as the Congress may from time to time ordain and establish. The Judges, both of the supreme and inferior Courts, shall hold their Offices during good Behaviour, and shall, at stated Times, receive for their Services, a Compensation, which shall not be diminished during their Continuance in Office.

Section 2.

The judicial Power shall extend to all Cases, in Law and Equity, arising under this Constitution, the Laws of the United States, and Treaties made, or which shall be made, under their Authority;—to all Cases affecting Ambassadors, other public Ministers and Consuls;—to all Cases of admiralty and maritime Jurisdiction;—to Controversies to which the United States shall be a Party;—to Controversies between two or more States;[—between a State and Citizens of

8. Modified by the Twenty-fifth Amendment.

another State;]⁹—between Citizens of different States,—between Citizens of the same State claiming Lands under Grants of different States, [and between a state, or the Citizens thereof, and foreign States, Citizens or Subjects.]¹⁰

In all cases affecting Ambassadors, other public Ministers and Consuls, and those in which a State shall be Party, the supreme Court shall have original Jurisdiction. In all the other Cases before mentioned, the supreme Court shall have appellate Jurisdiction, both as to Law and Fact, with such Exceptions, and under such Regulations as the Congress shall make.

The Trial of all Crimes, except in Cases of Impeachment, shall be by Jury; and such Trial shall be held in the State where the said Crimes shall have been committed; but when not committed within any State, the Trial shall be at such Place or Places as the Congress may by Law have directed.

Section 3.

Treason against the United States, shall consist only in levying War against them, or in adhering to their Enemies, giving them Aid and Comfort. No Person shall be convicted of Treason unless on the Testimony of two Witnesses to the same overt Act, or on Confession in open Court.

The Congress shall have Power to declare the Punishment of Treason, but no Attainder of Treason shall work Corruption of Blood, or Forfeiture except during the Life of the Person attainted.

Article IV. _____

Section 1.

Full Faith and Credit shall be given in each State to the public Acts, Records, and judicial Proceedings of every other State. And the Congress may by general Laws prescribe the Manner in which such Acts, Records and Proceedings shall be proved, and the Effect thereof.

Section 2.

The Citizens of each State shall be entitled to all Privileges and Immunities of Citizens in the several States.

A Person charged in any State with Treason, Felony, or other Crime, who shall flee from Justice, and be found in another State, shall on Demand of the executive Authority of the State from which he fled, be delivered up, to be removed to the State having Jurisdiction of the Crime.

[No Person held to Service or Labour in one State under the Laws thereof, escaping into another, shall, in Consequence of any Law or Regulation therein, be discharged from such Service or Labour, but shall be delivered up on Claim of the Party to whom such Service or Labour may be due.]¹¹

Section 3.

New States may be admitted by the Congress into this Union; but no new State shall be formed or erected within the Jurisdiction of any other State; nor any State be formed by the Junction of two or more States, or Parts of States, without the Consent of the Legislatures of the States concerned as well as of the Congress.

The Congress shall have Power to dispose of and make all needful Rules and Regulations respecting the Territory or other Property belonging to the United States; and nothing in this Constitution shall be so construed as to Prejudice any Claimes of the United States, or of any particular State.

Section 4.

The United States shall guarantee to every State in this Union a Republican Form of Government, and shall protect each of them against Invasion, and on Application of the Legislature, or of the Executive (when the Legislature cannot be convened) against domestic Violence.

Article V. _____

The Congress, whenever two thirds of both Houses shall deem it necessary, shall propose Amendments to this Constitution, or on the Application of the Legislatures of two thirds of the several States, shall call a Convention for proposing Amendments, which, in either Case, shall be valid to all Intents and Purposes, as Part of this Constitution, when ratified by the Legislatures of three fourths of the several States, or by

---

9. Modified by the Eleventh Amendment.
10. Modified by the Eleventh Amendment.

11. Repealed by the Thirteenth Amendment.

Conventions in three fourths thereof, as the one or the other Mode of Ratification may be proposed by the Congress; Provided that no Amendment which may be made prior to the Year One thousand eight hundred and eight shall in any Manner affect the first and fourth Clauses in the Ninth Section of the first Article; and that no State, without its Consent, shall be deprived of its equal Suffrage in the Senate.

Article VI.

All Debts contracted and Engagements entered into, before the Adoption of this Constitution, shall be as valid against the United States under this Constitution, as under the Confederation.

This Constitution, and the laws of the United States which shall be made in Pursuance thereof; and all Treaties made, or which shall be made, under the Authority of the United States, shall be the supreme Law of the Land; and the Judges in every State shall be bound thereby, any Thing in the Constitution or Laws of any State to the Contrary notwithstanding.

The Senators and Representatives before mentioned, and the Members of the several State Legislatures, and all executive and judicial Officers, both of the United States and of the several States, shall be bound by Oath or Affirmation, to support this Constitution; but no religious Text shall ever be required as a Qualification to any Office or public Trust under the United States.

Article VII.

The Ratification of the Conventions of nine States, shall be sufficient for the Establishment of this constitution between the States so ratifying the Same.

Done in Convention by the Unanimous Consent of the States present the Seventeenth Day of September in the Year of our Lord one thousand seven hundred and Eighty seven and of the Independence of the United States of America the Twelfth. IN WITNESS whereof we have hereunto subscribed our Names.

Go. WASHINGTON
Presid't. and deputy from Virginia

Attest
William Jackson
Secretary

Delaware
Geo. Read
Gunning Bedford jun
John Dickinson
Richard Basset
Jaco. Broon

Massachusetts
Nathaniel Gorham
Rufus King

Connecticut
Wm. Saml. Johnson
Roger Sherman

New York
Alexander Hamilton

New Jersey
Wh. Livingston
David Brearley.
Wm. Paterson.
Jona. Dayton

Pennsylvania
B. Franklin
Thomas Mifflin
Robt. Morris
Geo. Clymer
Thos. FitzSimons
Jared Ingersoll
James Wilson
Gouv. Morris

Viriginia
John Blair
James Madison Jr.

North Carolina
Wm. Blount
Richd. Dobbs Spaight.
Hu. Williamson

South Carolina
J. Rutledge
Charles Cotesworth Pinckney
Charles Pinckney
Pierce Butler.

Georgia
William Few
Abr. Baldwin

New Hampshire
John Langdon
Nicholas Gilman

Maryland
James McHenry
Dan of St. Thos. Jenifer
Danl. Carroll.

Amendment I[12]

Congress shall make no law respecting an establishment of religion, or prohibiting the free exercise thereof; or abridging the freedom of speech, or of the press; or the right of the people peaceably to assemble, and to petition the Government for a redress of grievances.

Amendment II

A well regulated militia, being necessary to the security of a free State, the right of the people to keep and bear arms, shall not be infringed.

12. The first ten amendments were passed by Congress on September 25, 1789, and were ratified on December 15, 1791.

Amendment III

No Soldier shall, in time of peace be quartered in any house, without the consent of the owner, nor in time of war, but in a manner to be prescribed by law.

Amendment IV

The right of the people to be secure in their persons, houses, papers, and effects, against unreasonable searches and seizures, shall not be violated, and no warrants shall issue, but upon probable cause, supported by oath or affirmation, and particularly describing the place to be searched, and the persons or things to be seized.

Amendment V

No person shall be held to answer for a capital, or otherwise infamous crime, unless on a presentment or indictment of a Grand Jury, except in cases arising in the land or naval forces, or in the militia, when in actual service in time of war or public danger; nor shall any person be subject for the same offence to be twice put in jeopardy of life or limb; nor shall be compelled in any criminal case to be a witness against himself, nor be deprived of life, liberty, or property, without due process of law; nor shall private property be taken for public use, without just compensation.

Amendment VI

In all criminal prosecutions, the accused shall enjoy the right to a speedy and public trial, by an impartial jury of the State and district wherein the crime shall have been committed, which district shall have been previously ascertained by law, and to be informed of the nature and cause of the accusation; to be confronted with the witnesses against him; to have compulsory process for obtaining witnesses in his favor, and to have the assistance of counsel for his defence.

Amendment VII

In Suits at common law, where the value in controversy shall exceed twenty dollars, the right of trial by jury shall be preserved, and no fact tried by a jury, shall be otherwise reexamined in any Court of the United States, than according to the rules of the common law.

Amendment VIII

Excessive bail shall not be required, nor excessive fines imposed, nor cruel and unusual punishments inflicted.

Amendment IX

The enumeration in the Constitution, of certain rights, shall not be construed to deny or disparage others retained by the people.

Amendment X

The powers not delegated to the United States by the Constitution, nor prohibited by it to the States, are reserved to the States respectively, or to the people.

Amendment XI
(Ratified February 7, 1795)

The Judicial power of the United States shall not be construed to extend to any suit in law or equity, commenced or prosecuted against one of the United States by Citizens of another State, or by Citizens or Subjects of any Foreign State.

Amendment XII
(Ratified June 15, 1804)

The Electors shall meet in their respective states, and vote by ballot for President and Vice-President, one of whom, at least, shall not be an inhabitant of the same state with themselves; they shall name in their ballots the person voted for as President, and in distinct ballots the person voted for as Vice President, and they shall make distinct lists of all persons voted for as President, and of all persons voted for as Vice-President, and of the number of votes for each, which lists they shall sign and certify, and transmit sealed to the seat of the government of the United States, directed to the President of the Senate;—The President of the Senate shall, in the presence of the Senate and House of Representatives, open all the certificates and the votes shall then be counted;—The person having the greatest number of votes for President, shall be the President, if such number be a majority of the whole number of Electors appointed; and if no person have such majority, then from the persons having the highest numbers not exceeding three on the list of those voted for as President, the House of Representatives shall choose immediately, by ballot, the President. But in choosing the President, the votes shall be taken by states, the representation from each state having one vote; a quorum for this purpose shall consist of a member or members from two-thirds of the states, and a majority of all the states shall be necessary to a choice. [And if the House of Representatives shall not choose a President whenever the right of choice shall devolve upon them, before the fourth day of March next following, then the Vice-President shall act as President, as in the case of the death or other constitutional disability of the President.][13]—The person having the greatest number of votes as Vice-President, shall be the Vice-President, if such number be a majority of the whole number of Electors appointed, and if no person have a majority, then from the two highest numbers on the list, the Senate shall choose the Vice-President; a quorum for the purpose shall consist of two-thirds of the whole number of Senators, and a majority of the whole number shall be necessary to a choice. But no person constitutionally ineligible to the office of President shall be eligible to that of Vice-President of the United States.

Amendment XIII
(Ratified on December 6, 1865)

Section 1.

Neither slavery nor involuntary servitude, except as a punishment for crime whereof the party shall have been duly convicted, shall exist within the United States, or any place subject to their jurisdiction.

Section 2.

Congress shall have power to enforce this article by appropriate legislation.

Amendment XIV
(Ratified on July 9, 1868)

All persons born or naturalized in the United States, and subject to the jurisdiction thereof, are citizens of the United States and of the State wherein they reside.

No State shall make or enforce any law which shall abridge the privileges or immunities of citizens of the United States; nor shall any State deprive any person of life, liberty, or property, without due process of law; nor deny to any person within its jurisdiction the equal protection of the laws.

Section 2.

Representatives shall be apportioned among the several States according to their respective numbers, counting the whole number of persons in each State, excluding Indians not taxed. But when the right to vote at any election for the choice of electors for President and Vice President of the United States, Representatives in Congress, the Executive and Judicial officers of a State, or the members of the Legislature thereof, is denied to any of the male inhabitants of such State, being [twenty-one][14] years of age, and citizens of the United States, or in any way abridged, except for participation in rebellion, or other crime, the basis of representation therein shall be reduced in the proportion which the number of such male citizens shall bear to the whole number of male citizens twenty-one years of age in such State.

Section 3.

No person shall be a Senator or Representative in Congress, or elector of President and Vice President, or hold any office, civil or military, under the United States, or under any State, who having previously taken an oath, as a member of Congress, or as an officer of the United States, or as a member of any State legislature, or as an executive or judicial officer of any State, to support the Constitution of the United States, shall have engaged in insurrection or rebellion against the same, or given aid or comfort to the enemies thereof. But Congress may by a vote of two-thirds of each House, remove such disability.

Section 4.

The validity of the public debt of the United States, authorized by law, including debts incurred for payment of pensions and bounties for services in suppressing insurrection or rebellion, shall not be questioned. But neither the United States nor any State shall assume or pay any debt or obligation incurred in

---

13. Changed by the Twentieth Amendment.

14. Changed by the Twenty-sixth Amendment.

aid of insurrection or rebellion against the United States, or any claim for the loss or emancipation of any slave, but all such debts, obligations and claims shall be held illegal and void.

Section 5.

The Congress shall have power to enforce, by appropriate legislation, the provisions of this article.

Amendment XV
(Ratified on February 3, 1870)

Section 1.

The right of citizens of the United States to vote shall not be denied or abridged by the United States or by any State on account of race, color, or previous condition of servitude.

Section 2.

The Congress shall have power to enforce this article by appropriate legislation.

Amendment XVI
(Ratified on February 3, 1913)

The Congress shall have power to lay and collect taxes on incomes, from whatever source derived, without apportionment among the several States, and without regard to any census or enumeration.

Amendment XVII
(Ratified on April 8, 1913)

The Senate of the United States shall be composed of two Senators from each State, elected by the people thereof, for six years; and each Senator shall have one vote. The electors in each State shall have the qualifications requisite for electors of the most numerous branch of the State legislatures.

When vacancies happen in the representation of any State in the Senate, the executive authority of such State shall issue writs of election to fill such vacancies: *Provided,* That the legislature of any State may empower the executive thereof to make temporary appointments until the people fill the vacancies by election as the legislature may direct.

This amendment shall not be so construed as to affect the election or term of any Senator chosen before it becomes valid as part of the Constitution.

Amendment XVIII
(Ratified on January 16, 1919)

Section 1.

After one year from the ratification of this article the manufacture, sale, or transportation of intoxicating liquors within, the importation thereof into, or the exportation thereof from the United States and all territory subject to the jurisdiction thereof for beverage purposes is hereby prohibited.

Section 2.

The Congress and the several States shall have concurrent power to enforce this article by appropriate legislation.

Section 3.

This article shall be inoperative unless it shall have been ratified as an amendment to the Constitution by the legislatures of the several States, as provided in the Constitution, within seven years from the date of the submission hereof to the States by the Congress.[15]

Amendment XIX
(Ratified on August 18, 1920)

The right of citizens of the United States to vote shall not be denied or abridged by the United States or by any State on account of sex.

Congress shall have power to enforce this article by appropriate legislation.

Amendment XX
(Ratified on January 23, 1933)

Section 1.

The terms of the President and Vice President shall end at noon on the 20th day of January, and the terms of Senators and Representatives at noon on the 3rd

15. The Eighteenth Amendment was repealed by the Twenty-first Amendment.

day of January, of the years in which such terms would have ended if this article had not been ratified, and the terms of their successors shall then begin.

Section 2.

The Congress shall assemble at least once in every year, and such meeting shall begin at noon on the 3rd day of January, unless they shall by law appoint a different day.

Section 3.

If, at the time fixed for the beginning of the term of the President, the President elect shall have died, the Vice President elect shall become President. If a President shall not have been chosen before the time fixed for the beginning of his term, or if the President elect shall have failed to qualify, then the Vice President elect shall act as President until a President shall have qualified; and the Congress may by law provide for the case wherein neither a President elect nor a Vice President elect shall have qualified, declaring who shall then act as President, or the manner in which one who is to act shall be selected, and such person shall act accordingly until a President or Vice President shall have qualified.

Section 4.

The Congress may by law provide for the case of the death of any of the persons from whom the House of Representatives may choose a President whenever the rights of choice shall have devolved upon them, and for the case of the death of any of the persons from whom the Senate may choose a Vice President whenever the right of choice shall have devolved upon them.

Section 5.

Sections 1 and 2 shall take effect on the 15th day of October following the ratification of this article.

Section 6.

This article shall be inoperative unless it shall have been ratified as an amendment to the Constitution by the legislatures of three-fourths of the several States within seven years from the date of its submission.

Amendment XXI _____
(Ratified on December 5, 1933)

Section 1.

The eighteenth article of amendment to the Constitution of the United States is hereby repealed.

Section 2.

The transportation or importation into any State, Territory, or possession of the United States for delivery or use therein of intoxicating liquors, in violation of the laws thereof, is hereby prohibited.

Section 3.

This article shall be inoperative unless it shall have been ratified as an amendment to the Constitution by conventions in the several States, as provided in the Constitution, within seven years from the date of the submission hereof to the States by the Congress.

Amendment XXII _____
(Ratified on February 27, 1951)

No person shall be elected to the office of the President more than twice, and no person who has held the office of President, or acted as President, for more than two years of a term to which some other person was elected President shall be elected to the office of the President more than once. But this Article shall not apply to any person holding the office of President when this Article was proposed by the Congress, and shall not prevent any person who may be holding the office of President, or acting as President, during the term within which this Article becomes operative from holding the office of President or acting as President during the remainder of such term.

Amendment XXIII _____
(Ratified on March 29, 1961)

Section 1.

The District constituting the seat of Government of the United States shall appoint in such manner as the Congress may direct:

A number of electors of President and Vice President equal to the whole number of Senators and Representatives in Congress to which the District would be entitled if it were a State, but in no event more than the least populous State; they shall be in addition to those appointed by the States, but they shall be considered, for the purposes of the election of President and Vice President, to be electors appointed by a State; and they shall meet in the District and perform such duties as provided by the twelfth article of amendment.

Section 2.

The Congress shall have power to enforce this article by appropriate legislation.

Amendment XXIV
(Ratified on January 23, 1964)

Section 1.

The right of citizens of the United States to vote in any primary or other election for President or Vice President, for electors for President or Vice President, or for Senator or Representative in Congress, shall not be denied or abridged by the United States or any State by reason of failure to pay any poll tax or other tax.

Section 2.

The Congress shall have power to enforce this article by appropriate legislation.

Amendment XXV
(Ratified on February 10, 1967)

Section 1.

In case of the removal of the President from office or of his death or resignation, the Vice President shall become President.

Section 2.

Whenever there is a vacancy in the office of the Vice President, the President shall nominate a Vice President who shall take office upon confirmation by a majority vote of both Houses of Congress.

Section 3.

Whenever the President transmits to the President pro tempore of the Senate and the Speaker of the House of Representatives his written declaration that he is unable to discharge the powers and duties of his office, and until he transmits to them a written declaration to the contrary, such powers and duties shall be discharged by the Vice President as Acting President.

Section 4.

Whenever the Vice President and a majority of either the principal officers of the executive departments or of such other body as Congress may by law provide, transmit to the President pro tempore of the Senate and the Speaker of the House of Representatives their written declaration that the President is unable to discharge the powers and duties of his office, the Vice President shall immediately assume the powers and duties of the offices as Acting President.

Thereafter, when the President transmits to the President pro tempore of the Senate and the Speaker of the House of Representatives his written declaration that no inability exists, he shall resume the powers and duties of his office unless the Vice President and a majority of either the principal officers of the executive department or of such other body as Congress may by law provide, transmit within four days to the President pro tempore of the Senate and the Speaker of the House of Representatives their written declaration that the President is unable to discharge the powers and duties of his office. Thereupon Congress shall decide the issue, assembling within forty-eight hours for that purpose if not in session. If the Congress, within twenty-one days after receipt of the latter written declaration, or, if Congress is not in session, within twenty-one days after Congress is required to assemble, determines by two-thirds vote of both Houses that the President is unable to discharge the powers and duties of his office, the Vice President shall continue to discharge the same as Acting President; otherwise; the President shall resume the powers and duties of his office.

Amendment XXVI

(Ratified on July 1, 1971)

Section 1.

The right of citizens of the United States, who are eighteen years of age or older, to vote shall not be denied or abridged by the United States or by any State on account of age.

Section 2.

The Congress shall have the power to enforce this article by appropriate legislation.

Federalist Paper #10

Among the numerous advantages promised by a well-constructed Union, none deserves to be more accurately developed than its tendency to break and control the violence of faction. The friend of popular governments never finds himself so much alarmed for their character and fate as when he contemplates their propensity to this dangerous vice. He will not fail, therefore, to set a due value on any plan which, without violating the principles to which he is attached, provides a proper cure for it. The instability, injustice, and confusion introduced into the public councils have, in truth, been the mortal diseases under which popular governments have everywhere perished, as they continue to be the favorite and fruitful topics from which the adversaries to liberty derive their most specious declamations. The valuable improvements made by the American constitutions on the popular models, both ancient and modern, cannot certainly be too much admired; but it would be an unwarrantable partiality to contend that they have as effectually obviated the danger on this side, as was wished and expected. Complaints are everywhere heard from our most considerate and virtuous citizens, equally the friends of public and private faith and of public and personal liberty, that our governments are too unstable, that the public good is disregarded in the conflicts of rival parties, and that measures are too often decided, not according to the rules of justice and the rights of the minor party, but by the superior force of an interested and overbearing majority. However anxiously we may wish that these complaints had no foundation, the evidence of known facts will not permit us to deny that they are in some degree true. It will be found, indeed, on a candid review of our situation, that some of the distresses under which we labor have been erroneously charged on the operation of our governments; but it will be found, at the same time, that other causes will not alone account for many of our heaviest misfortunes; and, particularly, for that prevailing and increasing distrust of public engagements and alarm for private rights which are echoed from one end of the continent to the other. These must be chiefly, if not wholly, effects of the unsteadiness and injustice with which a factious spirit has tainted our public administration.

By a faction I understand a number of citizens, whether amounting to a majority or minority of the whole, who are united and actuated by some common impulse of passion, or of interest, adverse to the rights of other citizens, or the permanent and aggregate interests of the community.

There are two methods of curing the mischiefs of faction: the one, by removing its causes; the other, by controlling its effects.

There are again two methods of removing the causes of faction: the one, by destroying the liberty which is essential to its existence; the other, by giving to every citizen the same opinions, the same passions, and the same interests.

It could never be more truly said than of the first remedy that it was worse than the disease. Liberty is to faction what air is to fire, an aliment without which it instantly expires. But it could not be a less folly to abolish liberty, which is essential to political life, because it nourishes faction than it would be to wish the annihilation of air, which is essential to animal life, because it imparts to fire its destructive agency.

The second expedient is as impracticable as the first would be unwise. As long as the reason of man continues fallible, and his is at liberty to exercise it, different opinions will be formed. As long as the connection subsists between his reason and his self-love, his opinions and his passions will have a reciprocal influence on each other; and the former will be objects to which the latter will attach themselves. The diversity in the faculties of men, from which the rights of property originate, is not less an insuperable obstacle to a uniformity of interests. The protection of these faculties is the first object of government. From the protection of different and unequal faculties of acquiring property, the possession of different degrees and kinds of property immediately results; and from the influence of these on the sentiments and views of the respective proprietors ensues a division of the society into different interests and parties.

The latent causes of faction are thus sown in the nature of man; and we see them everywhere brought into different degrees of activity, according to the different circumstances of civil society. A zeal for different opinions concerning religion, concerning government, and many other points, as well of speculation as of practice; an attachment to different leaders ambitiously contending for pre-eminence and power; or to persons of other descriptions whose fortunes have been interesting to the human passions, have, in turn, divided mankind into parties, inflamed them with mutual animosity, and rendered them much more disposed to vex and oppress each other than to cooperate for their common good. So strong is this propensity of mankind to fall into mutual animosities that where no substantial occasion presents itself the most frivolous and fanciful distinctions have been sufficient to kindle their unfriendly passions and excite their most violent conflicts. But the most common and durable source of factions has been the verious and unequal distribution of property. Those who hold and those who are without property have ever formed distinct interests in society. Those who are creditors, and those who are debtors, fall under a like discrimination. A landed interest, a manufacturing interest, a mercantile interest, a moneyed interest, with many lesser interests, grow up of necessity in civilized nations, and divide them into different classes, actuated by different sentiments and views. The regulation of these various and interfering interests forms the principal task of modern legislation and involves the spirit of party and faction in the necessary and ordinary operations of government.

No man is allowed to be a judge in his own cause, because his interest would certainly bias his judgment, and, not improbably, corrupt his integrity. With equal, nay with greater reason, a body of men are unfit to be both judges and parties at the same time; yet what are many of the most important acts of legislation but so many judicial determinations, not indeed concerning the rights of single persons, but concerning the rights of large bodies of citizens? And what are the different classes of legislators but advocates and parties to the causes which they determine? Is a law proposed concerning private debts? It is a question to which the creditors are parties on one side and the debtors on the other. Justice ought to hold the balance between them. Yet the parties are, and must be, themselves the judges; and the most numerous party, or in other words, the most powerful faction must be expected to prevail. Shall domestic manufacturers be encouraged, and in what degree, by restrictions on foreign manufacturers? are questions which would be differently decided by the landed and the manufacturing classes, and probably by neither with a sole regard to justice and the public good. The apportionment of taxes on the various descriptions of property is an act which seems to require the most exact impartiality; yet there is, perhaps, no legislative act in which greater opportunity and temptation are given to a predominant party to trample on the rules of justice. Every shilling with which they overburden the inferior number is a shilling saved to their own pockets.

It is in vain to say that enlightened statesmen will be able to adjust these clashing interests and render them all subservient to the public good. Enlightened statesmen will not always be at the helm. Nor, in many cases, can such an adjustment be made at all without taking into view indirect and remote considerations, which will rarely prevail over the immediate interest which one party may find in disregarding the rights of another or the good of the whole.

The inference to which we are brought is that the *causes* of faction cannot be removed and that relief is only to be sought in the means of controlling its *effects*.

If a faction consists of less than a majority, relief is supplied by the republican principle, which enables the majority to defeat its sinister views by regular vote. It may clog the administration, it may convulse the society; but it will be unable to execute and mask its violence under the forms of the Constitution. When a majority is included in a faction, the form of popular government, on the other hand, enables it to sacrifice to its ruling passion or interest both the public good and the rights of other citizens. To secure the public good and private rights against the danger of such a faction, and at the same time to preserve the spirit and the form of popular government, is then the great object to which our inquiries are directed. Let me add that it is the great desideratum by which alone this form of government can be rescued from the opprobrium under which it has so long labored and be recommended to the esteem and adoption of mankind.

By what means is this object attainable? Evidently by one of two only. Either the existence of the same passion or interest in a majority at the same time must be prevented, or the majority, having such coexistent passion or interest, must be rendered, by their number and local situation, unable to concert and carry into effect schemes of oppression. If the impulse and the opportunity be suffered to coincide, we well know that neither moral nor religious motives can be relied on as an adequate control. They are not found to be such on the injustice and violence of individuals, and lose their efficacy in proportion to the number combined together, that is, in proportion as their efficacy becomes needful.

From this view of the subject it may be concluded that a pure democracy, by which I mean a society consisting of a small number of citizens, who assemble and administer the government in person, can admit of no cure for the mischiefs of faction. A common passion or interest will, in almost every case, be felt by a majority of the whole; a communication and concert results from the form of government itself; and there is nothing to check the inducements to sacrifice the weaker party or an obnoxious individual. Hence it is that such democracies have ever been spectacles of turbulence and contention; have ever been found incompatible with personal security or the rights of property; and have in general been as short in their lives as they have been violent in their deaths. Theoretic politicians, who have patronized this species of government, have erroneously supposed that by reducing mankind to a perfect equality in their political rights, they would at the same time be perfectly equalized and assimilated in their possessions, their opinions, and their passions.

A republic, by which I mean a government in which the scheme of representation takes place, opens a different prospect and promises the cure for which we are seeking. Let us examine the points in which it varies from pure democracy, and we shall comprehend both the nature of the cure and the efficacy which it must derive from the Union.

The two great points of difference between a democracy and a republic are: first, the delegation of the government, in the latter, to a small number of citizens elected by the rest; secondly, the greater number of citizens and greater sphere of country over which the latter may be extended.

The effect of the first difference is, on the one hand, to refine and enlarge the public views by passing them through the medium of a chosen body of citizens, whose wisdom may best discern the true interest of their country and whose patriotism and love of justice will be least likely to sacrifice it to temporary or partial considerations. Under such a regulation it may well happen that the public voice, pronounced by the representatives of the people, will be more consonant to the public good than if pronounced by the people themselves, convened for the purpose. On the other hand, the effect may be inverted. Men of factious tempers, of local prejudices, or of sinister designs, may, by intrigue, by corruption, or by other means, first obtain the suffrages, and then betray the interests of the people. The question resulting is, whether small or extensive republics are most favorable to the election of proper guardians of the public weal; and it is clearly decided in favor of the latter by two obvious considerations.

In the first place it is to be remarked that however small the republic may be the representatives must be raised to a certain number in order to guard against the cabals of a few; and that however large it may be they must be limited to a certain number in order to guard against the confusion of a multitude. Hence, the number of representatives in the two cases not being in proportion to that of the constituents, and being proportionally greatest in the small republic, it follows that if the proportion of fit characters be not less in the large than in the small republic, the former will present a greater option, and consequently a greater probability of a fit choice.

In the next place, as each representative will be chosen by a greater number of citizens in the large than in the small republic, it will be more difficult for unworthy candidates to practice with success the vicious arts by which elections are too often carried; and the suffrages of the people being more free, will be more likely to center on men who possess the most attractive merit and the most diffusive and established characters.

It must be confessed that in this, as in most other cases, there is a mean, on both sides of which inconveniencies will be found to lie. By enlarging too much the number of electors, you render the representative too little acquainted with all their local circumstances and lesser interests; as by reducing it too much, you render him unduly attached to these, and too little fit to comprehend and pursue great and national objects. The federal Constitution forms a happy combination in this respect; the great and aggregate interests being referred to the national, the local and particular to the State legislatures.

GLOSSARY

Key terms are defined in the text where first mentioned.

Abscam   A 1981 FBI undercover operation in which six House members and one senator were convicted of taking bribes.

American Civil Liberties Union (ACLU)   A nonpartisan organization that seeks to protect the civil liberties of all Americans.

Amicus curiae   In Latin, "friend of the court." A third party that gives advice in a legal case to which it is not a party.

Anti-trust legislation   Laws that prohibit monopolies.

Baker vs. Carr   A 1962 Supreme Court decision giving voters the right to use the courts to rectify the malapportionment of legislative districts.

Balanced budget amendment   A proposed constitutional amendment that would require balancing the federal budget.

Balanced government   Refers to the idea that the different branches of government all represent different interests, forcing the various factions to work out compromises acceptable to all.

Bandwagon effect   The tendency of voters to follow the lead of the media, which declare some candidates winners and others losers, and vote for the perceived winner. The extent of this effect is unknown.

Bay of Pigs Invasion   The disastrous **CIA**-backed invasion of Cuba in 1961, mounted by Cuban exiles and intended to overthrow the government of Fidel Castro.

Behavioral approach   The study of politics by looking at the behavior of public officials, voters and other participants in politics, rather than by focusing on institutions or law.

Bible Belt   A term used to describe portions of the South and Midwest that were strongly influenced by Protestant fundamentalists.

Black Codes   Laws passed by Southern states following the **Civil War** that denied most legal rights to the newly freed slaves.

Boll Weevils   Conservative Democratic members of Congress, mainly from the South, who vote more often with the Republicans than with their own party.

Brownlow Committee   Appointed by Franklin Roosevelt in 1935, the committee recommended ways of improving the management of the federal bureaucracy and increasing the president's influence over it.

Budget and Accounting Act of 1921   This act gives the president the power to propose a budget and led to presidential dominance in the budget process. It also created the **Bureau of the Budget,** changed to the **Office of Management and Budget** in 1970.

Bureaucratic continuity   The stability provided by career-oriented civil servants, who remain in government for many years while presidents, legislators and political appointees come and go.

Bureau of the Budget   Established in 1921 and later changed to the **Office of Management and Budget,** the BOB was designed as the president's primary means of developing federal budget policy.

Captured agencies   Refers to the theory that regulatory agencies often end up working on behalf of the interests they are supposed to regulate.

Central Intelligence Agency (CIA)   Created after World War II, the CIA is a federal agency charged with coordinating overseas intelligence activities for the United States.

City-state   In ancient Greece, a self-governing state such as Athens or Sparta, consisting of an independent city and its surrounding territory.

Civil War   The war between the Union and the Confederacy (1861–1865), fought mainly over the question of whether the national or state governments were to exercise ultimate political power. Slavery was the issue that precipitated this great conflict.

Coalition building   The union of **pressure groups** that share similar concerns.

Committee of the Whole   Refers to the informal entity the House of Representatives makes itself into to debate a bill.

Commodity groups   **Pressure groups** that represent producers of specific products, such as cattle, tobacco or milk producers.

Concurrent resolutions   Special resolutions expressing the sentiment of Congress, passed by one house with the other concurring, but not requiring the president's signature.

Conscientious objectors   Persons who oppose all wars and refuse military service on the basis of religious or moral principles.

Constitution   The body of basic rules and principles that establish the functions, limits and nature of a government.

Contras   Rebels who have fought to overthrow the Sandinista government of Nicaragua.

Cost overruns   The amount by which the cost of a certain project exceeds the expected cost.

Cost-plus project   A project for which the contractor is reimbursed for all of its costs in addition to a set, agreed-upon profit rate.

Credentials committee   A body responsible for examining the credentials of political convention delegates.

Cuban Missile Crisis   The 1962 stand-off between the United States and the Soviet Union over an offensive missile build-up in Cuba. The Soviets finally agreed to remove all the missiles from Cuban soil.

Deficit   A condition in which expenditures exceed revenues.

Demagogue   A leader who obtains political power by appealing to the emotions and biases of the populace.

Departments   Executive divisions of the federal government, such as the Departments of Defense and Labor, each headed by a cabinet officer.

Direct lobbying   Direct personal encounters between lobbyists and the public officials they are attempting to influence.

Dixiecrat   A member of a group of southern segregationist Democrats who formed the States' Rights Party in 1948.

Education Amendments of 1972   These forbid discrimination on the basis of sex in schools and colleges that receive federal aid.

Empirical approach   In political science, the attempt to describe politics and government as they are, rather than how they should be. Compare **normative approach.**

Equal Credit Opportunity Act   This act forbids discrimination on the basis of sex or marital status in credit transactions.

Equal Employment Opportunity Commission (EEOC)   The EEOC enforces the Civil Rights Act of 1964, which forbids discrimination on the basis of sex or race in hiring, promotion and firing.

Exit polls   Election-day poll of voters leaving the polling places, conducted mainly by television networks and major newspapers.

Federal Communication Commission (FCC)   A regulatory agency that controls interstate and foreign communication via radio, television, telegraph, telephone, and cable. The FCC licenses radio and television stations.

Federal Election Commission   Created in 1975, the commission enforces federal laws on campaign financing.

Federal Register   A government publication describing bureaucratic actions and detailing regulations proposed by government agencies.

Federal Reserve Board   Created by Congress in 1913, the board regulates the lending practices of banks and plays a major role in determining monetary policy.

Felonies   Crimes considered more serious than misdemeanors, and carrying more stringent punishment.

Fifteenth Amendment   An amendment to the Constitution, ratified in 1870, which prohibits denying voting rights on the basis of race, color or previous condition of servitude.

Fixed-cost project   A project that a contractor has agreed to undertake for a specified sum.

Frontrunners   Candidates whom political pros and the media have portrayed as likely winners.

Fundraiser   An event, such as a luncheon or cocktail party, hosted by a legislator or candidate for which participants pay an entrance fee.

Gender gap   An observable pattern of modest but consistent differences in opinion between men and women on various public policy issues.

GOP   Grand Old Party or Republican Party, which formed in 1856 after the Whig Party split. The GOP was abolitionist and a supporter of the Union.

Grace Commission   A special commission established by President Reagan to recommend ways of cutting government waste.

Grand jury   A jury of citizens who meet in private session to evaluate accusations in a given criminal case and to determine if there is enough evidence to warrant a trial.

Grass roots lobbying   The mass mobilization of members of an interest group to apply pressure to public officials, usually in the form of a mass mailing.

Honoraria   Legal payments made to legislators who speak before special interest groups or other groups of citizens.

ICBM   Intercontinental ballistic missiles, or land-based missiles.

Impeachment and removal   A two-step process by which Congress may remove presidents, judges, and other civil officers accused of malfeasance. The House decides questions of impeachment; if a majority favors impeachment, the Senate decides whether to remove the accused from office.

Imperial presidency   A term that came into use at the end of the 1960s to describe the growing power of the presidency.

Impoundment   A refusal by the president to spend money appropriated by Congress for a specific program.

Incrementalism   A congressional spending pattern in which budgets usually increase slightly from year to year.

Independent   A voter who is not aligned with any political party.

Independent expenditures   Campaign contributions made on behalf of issues or candidates, but not made directly to candidates or political parties.

Indirect lobbying   Attempts to influence legislators through such non-traditional means as letter-writing campaigns.

Individualistic political culture   One of three primary political cultures in the United States. One in which politics is seen as a way of getting ahead, of obtaining benefits for oneself or one's group, and in which corruption is tolerated. See **moralistic** and **traditionalistic** political cultures.

Industrial policy   A strategy that calls for an active government role in improving a nation's economy and its competitiveness in world markets.

Injunction   A court order demanding that a person or group perform a specific act or refrain from performing a specific act.

Inquisition   A medieval institution of the Roman Catholic Church used to identify and punish heretics.

Institutional approach   An investigation of government that focuses on institutions, such as Congress or the civil service, and their rules and procedures.

Investigative reporting   In-depth news reporting, particularly that which exposes corruption and wrongdoing on the part of government officials and big institutions.

Issue consistency   The extent to which individuals who identify themselves as "liberal" or "conservative" take issue positions that reflect their professed leanings.

Issue voting   Refers to citizens who vote for candidates whose stands on specific issues are consistent with their own.

Jeffersonian Republicans (Jeffersonians)   Opponents of a strong national government. They challenged the **Federalists** in the early years of the Republic.

Joint resolutions   Measures that have the force of law and must be approved by both houses of Congress and signed by the president.

Justices of the peace   Magistrates at the lowest level of some state court systems, responsible mainly for acting on minor offenses and committing cases to higher courts for trial.

Kitchen cabinet   A group of informal advisers, usually longtime associates, who assist the president on public policy questions.

Know-Nothing Party   An extreme right-wing party in mid-nineteenth-century America that opposed Catholics and immigrants.

Lame duck   An officeholder, legislature or administration that has lost an election but holds power until the inauguration of a successor.

Landslide   An election won by a candidate who receives an overwhelming majority of the votes, such as more than a ten-point gap.

Legislative calendar   An agenda or calendar containing the names of all bills or resolutions of a particular type to be considered by committees or either legislative chamber.

Line-item veto   A proposal that would give a president the power to veto one or more provisions of a bill while allowing the remainder of the bill to become law.

Litigation   Legal action.

Mandamus, writ of   A court order demanding government officials or a lower court to perform a specified duty.

Marble cake federalism   The idea that different levels of government work together in carrying out policies; governments are intermixed, as in a marble cake.

McGovern-Fraser Commission   A commission formed after 1968 by the Democratic Party to consider changes making convention delegates more representative of all Democratic voters.

Minimum tax   A proposed tax that would require corporations and individuals with high incomes to pay a certain minimum amount in federal taxes.

MIRV   Stands for multiple independently targeted reentry vehicles; an offensive missile system that uses a single rocket to launch a number of warheads, each of which could be aimed at a different target.

Misdemeanors   Crimes of less seriousness than felonies, ordinarily punishable by fine or imprisonment in a local rather than a state institution.

Missouri Compromise of 1820   A set of laws by which Congress attempted to control slavery in the territories, maintaining the balance between slave and nonslave states.

Mixed economies   Countries that incorporate elements of both capitalist and socialist practices in the workings of their economies.

Moralistic political culture   One of three political cultures in the United States. One in which people feel obligated to take part in politics to bring about change for the better, and in which corruption is not tolerated. See **individualistic** and **traditionalistic** political cultures.

Nader's Raiders   The name given to people who work in any of the "public interest" organizations founded by consumer advocate and regulatory watchdog Ralph Nader.

National chair   The head of a political party organization, appointed by the national committee of that party, usually at the direction of the party's presidential nominee.

National Organization for Women (NOW)   A group formed in 1966 to fight primarily for political and economic rights for women.

New Deal Coalition   The broadly based coalition of southern conservatives, northern liberals and ethnic and religious minorities that sustained the Democratic Party for some 40 years.

News release A printed handout given by public relations workers to members of the media, offering ideas or information for new stories.

Nineteenth Amendment An amendment to the Constitution, ratified in 1920, guaranteeing women the vote.

Normative approach An approach by which political scientists consider how people *should* behave with regard to political matters, as opposed to an **empirical approach.**

Nullification A doctrine advocated by supporters of state-centered federalism, holding that a state could nullify laws of Congress.

Obstruction of justice A deliberate attempt to impede the progress of a criminal investigation or trial.

Occupational Safety and Health Administration (OSHA) An agency formed in 1970 and charged with ensuring safe and healthful working conditions for all American workers.

Office of Management and Budget (OMB) A White House agency with primary responsibility for preparing the federal budget.

Overlapping membership The term refers to the tendency of individuals to join more than one group. This tends to moderate a group's appeals, since its members also belong to other groups with different interests.

Parliamentary democracy A system in which voters elect only their representatives in parliament; the chief executive is chosen by parliament, as in Britain.

Party boss The head of a political "machine," a highly disciplined state or local party organization that controls power in its area.

Party convention A gathering of party delegates, on the local, state or national level, to set policy and strategy and to select candidates for elective office.

Pendleton Act of 1883 This act created the Civil Service Commission, designed to protect civil servants from arbitrary dismissal for political reasons and to staff bureaucracies with people who have proven their competence by taking competitive examinations.

Pentagon Papers A top-secret study, eventually made public, of how and why the United States became embroiled in the **Vietnam War;** the study was commissioned by Secretary of Defense Robert McNamara during the Johnson administration.

Platform committee The group that drafts the policy statement of a political party's convention.

Plebiscite A direct vote by all the people on a certain public measure. Theodore Lowi has spoken of the "Plebiscitary" presidency, whereby the president makes himself the focus of national government through use of the mass media.

Pocket veto A legislative bill dies by pocket veto if a president refuses to sign it and Congress adjourns within ten working days.

Political equality The principle that every citizen of a democracy has an equal opportunity to try to influence government.

Political trust The extent to which citizens place trust in their government, its institutions and its officials.

Precedents In law, judicial decisions that may be used subsequently as standards in similar cases.

Precinct The basic unit of the American electoral process—in a large city perhaps only a few blocks—designed for the administration of elections. Citizens vote in precinct polling places.

Pressure group An organization representing specific interests that seeks some sort of government assistance or attempts to influence public policy. Also known as an "interest group."

Pretrial hearings Preliminary examinations of the cases of persons accused of a crime.

Probable cause In law, reasonable grounds for belief that a particular person has committed a particular crime.

Professional association A **pressure group** that promotes the interests of a professional occupation, such as medicine, law or teaching.

Prohibition Party A political party founded in 1869 that seeks to ban the sale of liquor in the United States.

Public interest A term generally denoting a policy goal, designed to serve the interests of society as a whole, or the largest number of people. Defining the public interest is the subject of intense debate on most issues.

Quorum calls Often used as a delaying tactic, quorum calls are demands that all members of a legislative body be counted to determine if a quorum exists.

"Red Scare" Prompted by the Russian Revolution in 1917, this was a large-scale crackdown on so-called seditious activities in the United States.

Reelection constituency Those individuals a member of Congress believes will vote for him or her. Differs from a geographical, loyalist or personal constituency.

Religious tests Tests once used in some states to limit the right to vote or hold office to members of the "established church."

Responsiveness The extent to which government conforms to the wishes of individuals, groups or institutions.

Right against self-incrimination A right granted by the Fifth Amendment, providing that persons accused of a crime shall not be compelled to be witnesses against themselves.

Sandinistas The name of the group that overthrew Nicaraguan dictator Anastasio Somoza in 1978 and which now governs Nicaragua.

Scientific polls Systematic, probability-based sampling techniques that attempt to gauge public sentiment based on the responses of a small, selected group of individuals.

Senior Executive Service The SES was created in 1978 to attract high-ranking civil servants by offering them challenging jobs and monetary rewards for exceptional achievement.

Sharecroppers Tenant farmers who lease land and equipment from landowners, turning over a share of their crops in lieu of rent.

Shield laws Laws that protect news reporters from having to identify their sources of information.

Social choice An approach to political science based on the assumption that political behavior is determined by costs and benefits.

Social issue An important, non-economic issue affecting significant numbers of the populace, such as crime, racial conflict or changing values.

Special prosecutor A prosecutor charged with investigating and prosecuting alleged violations of federal criminal laws by the president, vice president, senior government officials, members of Congress or the judiciary.

"Star Wars" The popular name for former President Reagan's proposed space-based nuclear defense system, known officially as the Strategic Defense Initiative.

States' rights The belief that the power of the federal government should not be increased at the expense of the states' power.

Statutes Laws passed by the legislative body of a representative government.

Structural unemployment Joblessness that results from the rapidly changing nature of the economy, which displaces, for example, auto and steel industry workers.

Subgovernment A mutually supportive group comprising a **pressure group,** an executive agency and a congressional committee or subcommittee with common policy interests that makes public policy decisions with little interference from the president or Congress as a whole and little awareness by the public. Also known as an iron triangle.

Subpoena A court order requiring someone to appear in court to give testimony under penalty of punishment.

Super-delegates Democratic delegates, one-fifth of the total sent to the national convention who are appointed by Democratic Party organizations, in order to retain some party control over the convention. Most are public officials, such as members of Congress.

Tariff A special tax or "duty" imposed on imported or exported goods.

Tax deductions Certain expenses or payments that may be deducted from one's taxable income.

Tax exemptions Certain amount deductible from one's annual income in calculating income tax.

Third party A political party made up of independents or dissidents from the major parties, often advocating radical change or pushing single issues.

Trade association An interest or **pressure group** that represents a single industry, such as builders.

Traditionalistic political culture One of three political cultures in the United States. One in which politics is left to a small elite and is viewed as a way to maintain the status quo. See **individualistic** and **moralistic** political cultures.

Treason The betrayal of one's country by knowingly aiding its enemies.

Turnout The proportion of eligible citizens who vote in an election.

Unanimous consent agreements Procedures by which a legislative body may dispense with standard rules and limit debate and amendments.

Underdogs Candidates for public office who are thought to have little chance of being elected.

United Nations An international organization formed in 1945 for the purpose of promoting peace and world-wide cooperation. It is headquartered in New York.

Unscientific polls Also known as "straw polls," these are unsystematic samplings of popular sentiments.

Weber, Max German social scientist, author of pioneering studies on the nature of bureaucracies.

Whigs Members of the Whig Party, founded in 1834 by National Republicans and several other factions who opposed Jacksonian Democrats.

Wire services News-gathering organizations such as the Associated Press and United Press International that provide news stories and other editorial features to the media organizations that are their members.

Yuppies Young upwardly mobile professionals.

NAME INDEX

SUBJECT INDEX

ABC bill, 491

ABC/Washington Post Poll, 98n

Abington School District v. Schempp, 434n

Able-bodied poor, and poverty programs, 503

Abolition of slavery, 40

Abortion, 442–446
conservative support for, 147
opinions on, 81, 417–418
and party representation, 148
reasons for, 444t
right to, 121–122
statistics on, 442f, 445f

Abortion Rights Action League, 122

Abrams v. United States, 421n

Abscam, 236f, 270

Access
to the courts, 401–402
to government, buying, 266–268

Accountability
of government, 105
presidential, and a parliamentary system, 344
in a two-party system, 152

Accutane, safety of, 562

Acid rain, 567

Acquired immune deficiency syndrome. *See* AIDS

Act for Better Child Care Services, 491

Adair v. United States, 391n

Adderley v. Florida, 424n

Adkins v. Children's Hospital, 391n

Administrative Procedure Act (1946), 370, 561–562

Administrative reform, as a control measure, 378

Administrators, use of opinion surveys, 89

Adopt-a-Picket program, 105

Adversarial relationship, between politicians and the media, 221, 225–229

Advertising, deceptive, 555

AFBF. *See* Farm Bureau Federation

Affirmative action, 477–482

Afghanistan, Soviet invasion of, 654

AFL-CIO, 115
as an interest group, 113

Africa
economic change in, 622
immigration from, 5

African-Americans
discrimination against, 455–456
See also Blacks

African National Congress (ANC), 625

Age
and newscasting, 233–234
and political participation, 14
and poverty status, 503
and voter participation, 177f, 178
and voter preferences (1988), 195

Agency registration, 180–181

Agenda
media impact on public, 238
setting by politicians, 236–237

Agriculture
farm subsidy, 516–517
interest groups representing, 116–117

Agriculture, Department of, 364, 372, 515

Aid programs, domestic, consensus on paying for, 525

AIDS, 359–360, 383
and health care costs, 496, 498

Aid to Families with Dependent Children (AFDC), 60, 65, 501, 506–507
consensus on changes in, 513
percentage female-headed families, 502
and poverty, 504

Air Force Systems Command, 650, 653

Air quality
distribution of toxic pollutants, 573
protection of, 571–574

Air traffic controllers, 565–566
and drug use, 376

Akron v. Akron Center for Reproductive Health, 443n

Alabama, Republican vote in, 147

Albania
non-Soviet socialism in, 603
and Yugoslavia, 53–54

Allegheny County v. ACLU, 436n

Alliances in Europe, 615f

"All Things Considered", 245

All-volunteer army, women in, 646

Amalgamated Food Employees v. Logan Valley Plaza, 424n

Amendments
balanced budget, proposed, 543
Constitutional, 41–42
Eighth, 40, 440
Fifteenth, 40, 170, 453, 456, 472
Fifth, 40, 388, 403, 437
First, 40, 111, 403, 420, 423, 424, 426, 429, 430
Fourteenth, 40, 392, 393, 403, 404, 420, 456, 457, 472
Fourth, 40, 376, 403, 437
Nineteenth, 40, 173, 472
Ninth, 40
procedures for, 39, 39f
Second, 40
Seventeenth, 33, 40
Seventh, 40
Sixth, 40, 428, 439
Tenth, 40, 54, 58
Thirteenth, 40, 456
Twenty-fifth, 329
Twenty-fourth, 40, 171–172
Twenty-second, 328
Twenty-sixth, 40, 174
Twenty-third, 40
See also Bill of Rights; Constitution

American Agriculture Movement (AAM), 117–118

American Association of Retired Persons (AARP), 118, 264
services of, 112–113

American Bankers Association, 236

American Bar Association (ABA), 109, 118

American century, 537

American Civil Liberties Union (ACLU), 109, 401, 432

American College of Obstetrics and Gynecology, 110